This Is the Perfect Book for You If:

You've walked a city street with other people on their way to work. Many of them look resigned, stressed, or a little blank. These people are obviously not looking forward to their workday. Suddenly you realize that you are not just an observer. You are one of them.

Or

Like a leaf in the wind, you have been blown into a career by the winds of circumstance and by decisions that seemed like the right thing to do at the time.

Or

You entered the job market with high hopes that you would be starting a terrific career. By now it is painfully apparent that you made some sort of misjudgment: Somehow you have found yourself in the job from hell—or, even worse, you are bored most of the time with the daily grind of tasks that don't even begin to make use of your intelligence and abilities.

Or

You used to really enjoy your work. It used to be full of challenges. When friends sang the career blues, it never crossed your mind that anything like that could ever happen to you. But now your gum has lost its flavor on the bedpost.

Or

You have visited career counselors and read numerous books on career and personal growth. You have done everything you can think of to find your true vocation. You know much more about yourself. Yet dark clouds still obscure your future direction.

Or

You are a mindful young person. You and your friends are trying to figure out what to do with your lives. You want to have a career that really sings and soars, that gives you a real life. Your friends are deciding their fates the same way their parents did—and you know how *that* turned out.

Or

You had a job. You knew it wasn't the right one, but at least it paid the bills. Now it is gone or about to slip away. You could follow the crowd and repeat your last mistake or take this opportunity to carve out a new and better future.

Or

You are good at your job. You just don't seem to have a sense of purpose. You want to do something that means more to you personally. You may close your eyes and imagine pounding through stormy seas at the helm of a Greenpeace rubber boat just inches ahead of a Japanese whaling ship. But then the vision fades. When you open your eyes, you are back in your day-to-day life. Sure, it would be exciting on that boat, but it doesn't seem very realistic. Nevertheless, you definitely want to do something with your life that matters.

Also by Nicholas Lore

Now What?

The

PATHFINDER

HOW TO CHOOSE OR CHANGE

YOUR CAREER FOR A LIFETIME OF

SATISFACTION AND SUCCESS

NICHOLAS LORE

A TOUCHSTONE BOOK

PUBLISHED BY SIMON & SCHUSTER

NEW YORK LONDON TORONTO SYDNEY NEW DELHI

Touchstone
A Division of Simon & Schuster, Inc.
1230 Avenue of the Americas
New York, NY 10020

First Touchstone trade paperback edition January 2012

TOUCHSTONE and colophon are registered trademarks of Simon & Schuster Inc.

For information about special discounts for bulk purchases, please contact Simon & Schuster Special Sales at 1-866-506-1949 or business@simonandschuster.com.

The Simon & Schuster Speakers Bureau can bring authors to your live event. For more information or to book an event, contact the Simon & Schuster Speakers Bureau at 1-866-248-3049 or visit our website at www.simonspeakers.com.

Manufactured in the United States of America

10   9   8   7   6   5   4   3

Library of Congress Cataloging-in-Publication Data

Lore, Nicholas.
  The pathfinder : how to choose or change your career for a lifetime of satisfaction and success / by Nicholas Lore.—1st Touchstone trade pbk. ed.
    p. cm.
  Rev. ed. of: The Pathfinder : how to choose or change your career for a lifetime of satisfaction and success. c1998.
  1. Career changes. 2. Job satisfaction. I. Title.
  HF5384.L67   2011
  650.14—dc23

                                                        2011043709

ISBN 978-1-4516-0832-8
ISBN 978-1-4391-8866-8 (ebook)

For Mitra

My Wife, Twin Flame, and Inspiration

....

CONTENTS

Whatever you can do, or dream you can, begin it.
Boldness has genius, power, and magic in it.

—Johann Wolfgang von Goethe

The PATHFINDER

Section 1

LIVING A LIFE
YOU LOVE

You have never used a book like this before. It is designed to take you through the process of choosing your future career rather than just reading about doing so. As you continue through *The Pathfinder*, it will become your personal career coach and guide. Many people say that this book seems to be speaking directly to them alone. Of course this is not true, but you will find that you have an opportunity to develop a very personal coaching relationship with *The Pathfinder*. This relationship will help you deal successfully with everything you need to consider, as well as learn practical new ways to move forward from your present uncertainty and design a career that will fit you elegantly, perfectly, like custom-tailored clothes. I hope you will choose to be a participant, and not just a reader. If you want to change your career, or if you are a younger person making a first-time career choice, you've found a book that was written just for you.

CHAPTER 1

•

THIS CAN BE YOUR GUIDE

Once, I was in the same situation you are facing today. It was time to decide what to do with my life. I committed myself to doing whatever was necessary to make a truly excellent career choice because I passionately wanted to wake up in the morning looking forward to going to work each day. This is the book I searched for then but did not find.

I remember an extraordinary, imaginary book that first framed my boyhood vision of what I hope *The Pathfinder* will be for you. Each month, Donald Duck's nephews, Huey, Dewey, and Louie, would find themselves in the middle of a full-tilt comic-book adventure. When things got completely hopeless, when the forces of chaos seemed sure to win, they always pulled off a miracle. Out of their knapsack came their infallible guide and problem solver, *The Junior Woodchuck Guidebook*. It had an absolutely perfect, creative solution for every situation they stumbled into, no matter how obscure or difficult. It was the complete guide to life.

Since then, I have passionately sought those rare volumes of chuckery that surface in the real world. Every once in a while, one appears—the seminal guidebook to some aspect of life. Inspired by these wonderful books, *The Pathfinder* is intended to be one small chapter of *The Junior Woodchuck Guidebook*: how to decide what to do with your life. Whether you are in midcareer change or are making career decisions for the first time, it is designed to get you successfully through the process of planning your future.

How can an intelligent person, committed to choosing a new career path, decide exactly which direction to pursue? That is a question I began asking many years ago. At the time, I was restless and bored with my job. I ran a conservation and solar energy company on the coast of Maine. I had written and been responsible for passing legislation that saved thousands of beautiful historic houses from destruction and had recently been commended for excellence by the White House. My office looked out on a beautiful harbor where lobster boats and foghorns greeted the new day. Yet I had trouble getting through the workday. Even with an extensive background in psychology and Eastern philosophy, I had difficulty understanding why my workday left so much to be desired. How could it be that working on interesting projects in an idyllic setting and making a positive difference in the world and getting recognition could get boring? It was an absolute mystery to me.

I then searched all over New England to find someone to help me solve my problem. I called nearly every counselor in the region. I told them I was seeking to choose a new career where I would be able to wake up in the morning and look forward to work. I said I wanted to find a vocation that was challenging, creative, and that I would passionately enjoy, where I could use my talents to their fullest, doing something that mattered to me. None of them seemed to know what it took to have a really phenomenal career. In fact, I could tell from their voices that many of them didn't seem to love what they did, either.

Finally, I took my problem to a wise old man who was a fellow member of my boat club. As it turned out, I was lucky enough to pick the ideal supporter, R. Buckminster Fuller. Many people have heard of Bucky because he invented the geodesic dome. The building at Epcot Center that looks like a huge silvery ball is one of his many revolutionary designs. Bucky was much more than an architect. If you can imagine Obi-Wan Kenobi and Yoda combined in a real person who was at the same time a master futurist, scientist, engineer, architect, inventor, mathematician, philosopher, and mystic, you get a little hint as to who he was. I struggled with my dilemma for what seemed like eons. Ultimately, with his encouragement, I decided to dedicate my life to tackling the very problem I had so much trouble solving myself. I founded an organization dedicated to developing more effective ways to help people make career and education choices.

Since 1981, that organization, Rockport Institute (www.rockportinstitute.com), has been a pioneer in developing career coaching programs that successfully guide clients through the process of career decision making. These programs consist of clear-cut steps that help clients choose a specific career that will be highly satisfying, give them the opportunity to reach their goals, use their talents at the highest possible level, and be practical and achievable. From the beginning, we have been committed to developing the best tools to help people make the best decisions. Rockport Institute has helped many thousands of clients from all walks of life: young and old, rich and poor, scientists, professionals, executives in career change, artists, professional athletes, students, and people reentering the workforce. Our clients include people who have been fabulously successful and others who never reached their goals because of an ill-fitting career. We have had the opportunity to serve as personal career consultants to several national and global leaders, C-level executives of Fortune 500 companies, senior policy makers of four presidential administrations, and people in nearly every field of endeavor. Our clients have one thing in common: a strong desire for a very fulfilling career.

For the last thirty years, as director of Rockport Institute, my single-minded passion has been to help intelligent, complex people like you live remarkable lives that are self-expressed and satisfying by stretching themselves beyond their everyday circumstances and the perceived limitations that hold them back. I have written this book to duplicate, as closely as possible, the experience you would have if we were to sit together in the same room and work step-by-step until you reach your goal:

knowing for sure what you will do with your life—or, at least, this part of it. In these pages, you will find a pathway through the process of deciding what to do with your life that can actually get you to (or closer to) the goal line. For the first time, you will have access to most of what you need to reach your goal of picking an outrageously excellent new direction, choosing your first career, or tuning up your present path. By looking from new perspectives at the questions you have previously been unable to answer, you will finally have a chance to sort them out.

You will also have an opportunity to look into areas of your life you may have never considered before. You will find some of these components absolutely critical to making the best possible career decision. *The Pathfinder* will help you break everything important down into small, bite-size pieces and deal with them one by one. Far from offering a generic, cookie-cutter approach, this book will enable you to customize your journey through the morass of questions and uncertainties to fit your own particular needs.

I will completely respect and appreciate you and your unique nature. At the same time, I won't pull punches or be too polite to give it to you straight. I don't mind at all if you jump up and down and curse me when you get frustrated. After all, I'm just a book.

The Pathfinder will help you examine every aspect of your life that relates to career. Designed to be a universal guide, it should work for you regardless of your age, background, education, point of view, and experience. If you are a recently deposed emperor, you won't be treated like a teenager. And if you are a teenager, don't worry, you won't be treated like a deposed emperor. Rather than just discussing theoretical ideals about career fulfillment, *The Pathfinder* is designed to actually take you toward your goal of deciding exactly what you will do with your life.

Using this book as your guide may take you all the way to your goal of designing a career that is both perfect for you and practical. It has guided many thousands of intelligent, committed people all the way to having 100 percent certainty about what they will do with their lives. Others make it most of the way or partway to that goal, but need time, experience, professional coaching, or something else to cross the finish line. The Rockport Career Design Method you will use throughout this book helps you answer the question "What am I sure will be the important components of my work?" The most powerful way to design your career is to become sure about the answers to questions such as "How will I make best use of my natural talents and personality?" "What workplace environment will support my best effort?" "How important is it to do something that personally matters to me, and what specifically will that be?" Asking and answering those big questions about your future build islands of certainty that move your career design project forward. Becoming absolutely sure about one piece of the puzzle makes it easier to sort out the other pieces.

You Can Do It!

The difficulties you may have faced, the times you have gotten stuck, and the less than perfect decisions you may have made previously do not signify that there is something wrong with you or that the world of work must be a hard, dark, cold, dreary place. If you want to do something with your life that really sings and soars, all you need to do is to start your journey here. No matter what your situation, you can do it if you go for it wholeheartedly and keep going until you arrive at your destination. But remember, this book can't do it for you. Only you can make the choices that build your future work, piece by piece.

Decide How You Are Going to Keep Track of Everything

Before you start this career design process, please decide what format you will use to keep notes and do inquiries. If you are 100 percent digital, create a folder or whatever works for you to organize this project. If not, get a good notebook. An old-fashioned three-ring binder would be perfect. In any event, don't use your head to store your clues, insights, decisions, and questions. Write them down.

CHAPTER 2

•

YOU ARE WHAT YOU DO

The Pathfinder contains inquiries as a way to generate clues about what is important to you. These inquiries are tools that provide a useful way to ask good questions and choose definite components and elements of your future work. Here's the first.

INQUIRY 1

Back to the Beginning

Remember back to your childhood, back to the beginning of the journey. Remember your childhood visions of the future.

What were those dreams? What were those wild fantasies of yours? What seemingly perfect careers did you imagine as you were growing up?

How did you feel when you imagined yourself in the midst of one of these fantasies? Feel now what it felt like then.

If you were like most of us, you dreamed of an exciting future where you were passionately engaged in life. Perhaps you dreamed of being a rock star or a professional athlete, a detective, or the first empress of the galaxy. You might have envisioned yourself as a brilliant surgeon, as an artist, or swinging from a vine over a bottomless chasm. Wiser now, you might smile at the naïveté of childhood dreams. Your vision may not have been reasonable or practical, but it was certainly passionate. It put you in the midst of a life that was fully lived.

How well does the word "work" fit with your childhood dream job? Doesn't it seem strangely out of place? The way these fantasies usually occur seems to fit better into the category of "adventurous vacation" or "getting paid to play." Our dream jobs are more play than work. When people dream of being a lawyer, they aren't thinking about being buried under endless piles of deadly dull paperwork or having to defend an unscrupulous client. In our dreams of being a fireman, we are fighting the fire, not repacking the hoses or passing long nights in the firehouse playing endless games of pinochle with two cards missing from the deck.

When you get down to the very skinny truth, under all the sophisticated conversation and pretense, no one really wants to work if that includes a life of suffering. One definition of the word "work" that is not in the dictionary, but nevertheless is a part of our internal dictionary, goes something like "Work—something I would rather do less of" or "something I have to do when I would rather do something else." Underneath all the serious reasons people give to explain why they want to change careers, lead a company, write a book, or drive an eighteen-wheeler, there is an essential, powerful motivation that's not discussed in polite, sophisticated company. They want to do something they are passionate about. They want satisfaction, an adventure. And they want to have fun.

I don't mean idle, frivolous fun. In our visions, we savor life, we are brilliant at what we do, and people appreciate our contribution. Our dreams are shaped by our own individual inner templates of what matters the most to each of us: self-expression, adventure, power, a certain picture we have of success, enjoyment, making a difference, being a member of a team that's going for it 100 percent, making beautiful things, personal growth, solving problems, healing, teaching, machismo, raising a family.

> *The secret of success is making your vocation your vacation.*
>
> —MARK TWAIN

If you were to look around, there do seem to be some people involved in careers that include all the elements we value. There is a satisfied minority that actually looks forward to going to work. Sure, they call it "work" in front of other people. They are being polite.

Reality 101—What's Really Going On out There?

> *Most men would feel insulted if it were proposed to employ them in throwing stones over a wall, and then throwing them back again, merely that they might earn their wages. But many are no more worthily employed now.*
>
> —HENRY DAVID THOREAU

When I was a boy, my friends and I would watch the men in dark suits walk to the train station for the ride into Philadelphia. We were, in our blessed state, Tarzans of the jungle pretending to see the "civilized" world for the first time from our hidden vantage point at the edge of the bamboo grove. The men seemed to drag enormous, invisible weights along with them, as if they were sucked toward the city by some mysterious, invisible magnet. We imagined that they were zombies answering the call

LIFE IN
HELL

© 1990
BY MATT
GROENING

YOUR WORKING-DAY EMOTION CHECKLIST

9:00 AM	9:05 AM	9:29 AM	9:45 AM	10:04 AM	10:31 AM	10:37 AM	10:42 AM
☐ PURE GRUMPINESS	☐ CAFFEINE JOLT-O-RAMA	☐ EARLY-MORNING STUPEFACTION	☐ SPLITTING HEADACHE #1	☐ MOMENTARY PANIC ATTACK	☐ CAFFEINE OVERDOSE	☐ PERVERTED DAYDREAMS	☐ MID-MORNING NUMBNESS

10:52 AM	11:03 AM	11:09 AM	11:33 AM	11:35 AM	11:57 AM	12:00 PM	12:09 PM
☐ SUDDEN FIT OF HOSTILITY	☐ LINGERING SULKINESS	☐ PRETENDING TO WORK	☐ REBUFFED FLIRTATION WITH CO-WORKER	☐ TEMPORARY DEMENTIA	☐ "HEAD IN A VISE" FEELING	☐ JOYLESS LUNCH-EATING	☐ MIRTHLESS JOKE-TELLING

12:23 PM	12:35 PM	12:47 PM	1:00 PM	1:19 PM	1:25 PM	1:42 PM	1:52 PM
☐ BELCHING DISCONTENT	☐ SUDDEN AWARENESS OF ONE'S SHALLOWNESS	☐ WAVES OF NAUSEA	☐ RESENTMENT OF OTHERS	☐ EARLY AFTERNOON CATATONIA	☐ SPLITTING HEADACHE #2	☐ GNAWING OF THE BOWELS	☐ THAT "NO WAY OUT" FEELING

2:06 PM	2:30 PM	2:44 PM	2:55 PM	2:59 PM	3:09 PM	3:14 PM	3:36 PM
☐ STRANGE TRANCE-LIKE STATE	☐ URGE TO MURDER BOSS	☐ FOOLING AROUND AT THE COPY MACHINE	☐ WHINING TO THE PERSON NEXT TO YOU	☐ UNREALISTIC PLANS TO QUIT THIS LOUSY JOB	☐ MID-AFTERNOON TORPOR	☐ EVEN MORE PERVERTED DAYDREAMS	☐ EMOTIONAL DEADNESS

3:47 PM	3:59 PM	4:01 PM	4:09 PM	4:25 PM	4:33 PM	4:59 PM	5:00 PM
☐ WATCHING THE CLOCK	☐ WORRYING ABOUT SENILITY	☐ SPLITTING HEADACHE #3	☐ FEAR OF GETTING FIRED	☐ LOTTERY FANTASIES	☐ CONTEMPLATING TV TONIGHT	☐ UNCONTROLLABLE JUMPINESS	☐ TEMPORARY PERKINESS

of the voodoo master. We did not have to stretch our imaginations very far. They did look a little like zombies. They had lost the joy of living.

Every once in a while, I take a ride on the subway during the morning rush hour. Even though I no longer watch from the edge of the jungle, I still observe people on their way to work. At first glance, they seem fine, concentrating on their newspapers or lost in thought. But look again, with the eyes of a child. What's really happening here? Perhaps "resignation" is the best word to describe the general mood. Many of these folks are enduring, submitting. My friends and I were being theatrical in imagining zombie magnets pulling people to dark fates, but, hey, let's face it: These people are definitely not looking forward to going to work. Maybe they are still half asleep? Might they awaken by the end of the day? Take the same subway when people are on the way home from work. Any improvement? Actually, if anything, it has gotten worse. Now there is fatigue mixed with the resignation. Some of them look like they've just done fifteen rounds in the ring.

The trouble with the rat race is that even if you win, you're still a rat.

—LILY TOMLIN

To make these observations a little more scientific, I have also ridden the subway when people were on their way to see their beloved football team play. The train is filled with a spirit of excitement, enthusiasm. People talk and joke with others they have never met before. The mood is playful, with the channels of communication open, the passion for life obvious. It's irresistibly delicious. So now we know, after careful scientific inquiry, that it is not the subway ride that darkens the riders' lives. It must be something about their work.

Not everyone on the subway is dreading work. As a matter of fact, some people are more satisfied than they look. They are hiding it. Try stepping onto the subway one morning filled with enthusiasm, doing a little soft-shoe routine, whistling, radiant, alive. People will shoot you looks that suggest that you must be on the way to the Mad Hatter's tea party. You are a threat to their resignation. If there were more people like you around, they might have to wake up and get a life. They want to make sure that you do not disturb their somnambulism, so they glower in your direction to stop that infernal dance that's intruding on their dark daze. So the people who love their work play it cool. They camouflage their enthusiasm in order to look "normal."

If you divided the subway riders into categories, based on overall career satisfaction, you would discover a wide range of levels of fulfillment. Many surveys have looked into this question over the years. Some of them paint an overly rosy picture because people tend to respond to casual "How's it going?" questions with "all's well." In-depth surveys suggest that most people are not satisfied with their work. At Rockport Institute, we surveyed 1,500 college grads from ages twenty-one to sixty in an attempt to get at the unvarnished truth. Here's what we found. (We did round off the numbers a little.)

The Career Satisfaction Scale on the next pages contains some good news as well as some very bad news. First the bad: 40 percent of American workers are at least somewhat unhappy with their jobs. Ten percent are in a condition I call "career hell," a condition very dangerous to their well-being, their health, and to everyone around them. If you include the Neutrals, fully 70 percent of us go to work without much enthusiasm or passion.

> *Death is not the greatest loss in life. The greatest loss*
> *is what dies inside us while we live.*
>
> —NORMAN COUSINS

The good news is that about 30 percent of us experience career satisfaction, either liking or loving our work. To me, the most exciting news is that about 10 percent report that they love their work. This significant minority has somehow managed to pull together all the important elements to have its dreams come true. So often we imagine things going well for a distant and mysterious group of people, such as the ones we see on TV: the movie stars, writers, and Nobel Prize winners. To have fully 10 percent of people operating at the highest levels of career satisfaction gives hope that you can do it too. After all, how difficult can it be to be in the top 10 percent if you dedicate your energy to achieving that end?

The American Way of Career Selection

Before we delve into how you can make a career choice that fits you perfectly, let's take a look at how people usually decide. The American way of career selection goes something like this: During your junior year of high school, the tribal elders, consisting of your parents and your guidance counselor, initiate you into ancient secrets learned empirically over many generations. They whisper the secret in your ear: "Start to think about what you may want to do."

You, as green as the jolly giant, don't notice that this meager advice might be insufficient to plan a brilliant future. You begin your quest. That night you pry your attention away from teenage angst and raging hormones long enough to follow their sage advice. You "think about what you may want to do." Perhaps some ideas for potential careers appear out of the mist, like distant, mysterious mountains. Perhaps they don't. You get no really useful guidance from school guidance counselors or your parents, none of whom realizes that such an important and personal decision must be based on knowing much more about yourself and the world than you do at this tender age.

Career Satisfaction Scale

0 to 10 Scale	Estimated Percentage of Population	General Description	Effect on Personal Life	Contribution to Workplace
10	10 percent	*Work occurs as passionate play.* Looks forward to going to work; work seen as vehicle for full self-expression; difficulties interpreted as positive challenges; personal growth and contribution to self-esteem linked to work; little distinction between work and rest of life; sense of purpose and making a difference; uses talents fully; work fits personality; usually exhibits eagerness and alacrity.	Self-actualized lifestyle; generous—often participates in "service" to others; loves life; active participant in all aspects of life; goes for the gusto, playful; high level of personal integrity; self-esteem not a major issue; significant increase in longevity and disease resistance.	Work is an expression of a clear personal sense of purpose or mission; self-generating, does not need supervision; trustworthy—will persist until objective is reached; almost always contributes and is appropriate to the situation; takes correction as an opportunity; the presence of a person living at this level raises others with whom he or she works.
8	20 percent	*Positive.* Enjoys work much of the time; feels useful; has a sense of mission or that work is meaningful, career meets perceived needs, contributes to positive self-esteem; good fit between work, talents, and personality; high level of competence; value appreciated by others; would say work is "pretty good. I like my job."	Satisfying career enhances other areas of life such as self-esteem, quality of family life and other relationships; increased resistance to disease and longevity; overall sense of well-being, enjoys life much of the time.	Usually makes a positive contribution to the organization and other people; effective worker; fairly flexible; needs a minimum of supervision but may not be fully self-generating; handles responsibility well; decision making usually based on what's needed rather than personal agenda.
6	30 percent	*Neutral.* Accepts work situation without struggle; can appear to be a valued worker in a procedure-driven organization. Common in government agencies and large, stable corporations. Some may say they like their work, others may grouse. If so, complaining is often simple socializing in an environment where complaining is a preferred mode of communication.	Leads a life that has little positive effect on the community but usually has no significant negative effect, either. Relationships and other aspects of life outside work may be "normal" but narrow.	May produce quality results in repetitive tasks; contributions are mechanical; little potential for real leadership, initiative, or creativity; resists change; conservatism affects judgment—at best, furthers own ends; would hire the person with the best résumé rather than the best candidate; destructive when placed in a position beyond grasp.

4	30 percent	*Negative.* Goes to work because forced by circumstances to do so; actively dislikes significant parts of job; daily routine marked by struggle, suffering, clock watching, resentment, resignation; areas of life other than work may be satisfying; work either doesn't use abilities fully or requires talents not possessed; may be a clash between personality or values and environment; complains about job.	Even though other areas of life may be healthy, career stress usually has negative effect on relationships, health, and longevity. May spend considerable portion of spare time recovering from work. Some erosion of self-esteem contributes to resignation or feelings of powerlessness in other areas.	Destructive to the workplace. Even if lack of satisfaction is hidden, it spreads to other employees; often ineffective because usually wants to be somewhere else; motivated by need rather than by choice. May need supervision to produce consistent high-quality results.
2	10 percent	*Career hell.* Work is a constant struggle, takes an act of will to go to work each day; strong sense of resentment, deep suffering; major clash between talents or personality or values and requirements of the job; symptoms similar to people between 2 and 4 on this scale except that here the dissatisfaction is more intense and the person feels completely trapped; each day at work erodes self-esteem; profound negative effect on other areas of life.	Because work is so enervating, little psychological room to do more than survive; reduced capacity to support others; difficulty in maintaining healthy relationships; marked hostility or resignation toward workplace; life may be shortened by several years; diminished immune system.	Dangerous and very destructive to environment; liability to self, others, and workplace; resistance (may be passive) to supervision; poor concentration; agenda is at odds with organization's mission; may feel vindicated by failures of others; needs constant watching.

Much later you find yourself queued up to pick your college major. You remember the mantra "Start to think about what you may want to do." By the time you reach the head of the line, you have decided. Years later you will tell friends that your major in Polynesian philosophy "seemed like a good idea at the time." Years pass. Like the majority of college graduates, you will have embarked on a career that has nothing at all to do with your college major. How did you make that final choice? "Well," you say, "it seemed like a good idea at the time."

If you are a younger reader, you may think that I am exaggerating. I wish I were. Ask some of my older, midcareer readers who are hit-and-run victims of this process. Look closely. You will know them by the tire tracks across their souls.

Here are the results of two studies for all of you statistics lovers: In a Gallup survey of 1.7 million workers, only about 20 percent said they used their best strengths every day at work. In a Rockport Institute survey, more than 70 percent of successful professionals surveyed thought that they could have done a much better job of making decisions about their lives. They said that they had not known how to go about making choices in a competent way. In another survey, 64 percent of college seniors said they had serious doubts that they had picked the right major.

Many people put more energy, creativity, and commitment into deciding which house to buy or where to go on vacation than into deciding what to do with their lives. More often than not, they drift into a career that doesn't really fit their talents or live up to their dreams. Others get stuck along the way and spend their lives making unnecessary compromises. Some blindly follow or resist the family career template. If they come from a family of cannibals, they'll either dine at McFingers or become a strict vegan.

Since the do-it-yourself method, without professional assistance, often fails, what about career counselors? Some colleges provide extremely competent job-hunting assistance, but very few do an excellent job of helping students decide on a career direction. In fact, I have met just a few people who said that their college career center was useful as a source of decision-making tools and coaching, and most of them went to schools that use the philosophy, methods, and tools found in this book. The vast majority agree that college career counselors are well meaning but just do not have the necessary tools at their disposal to be really effective.

It's not really their fault. Always look to the top to see who is asleep at the wheel. It is the college presidents who don't seem to care. If they were anything other than totally complacent, it might occur to them to take a survey of alums and ask questions like, "Did you make use of the career center to design a fitting career? If so, how effective was it in helping you sort out your life direction?" What they would find is that nearly all college graduates agree that college career centers are totally ineffective when it comes to helping students design a career they will flourish in and love. Have you ever known anyone who decided what to do with his or her life as a result of visiting career services? Shouldn't one important goal of every college or university be to graduate students who at least know generally where they are going and what they will do with their lives—based not on fantasy but on a powerful, in-depth investigation of the many facets of life that bear on career success and satisfaction? Of what real value is a career center that is good at helping graduates find jobs they don't really want?

Most professional career counseling and coaching is not much better. Several years ago, I conducted a survey of people who had used professional career assistance in New England. Some said that the counseling or coaching was helpful, but the great majority had not been able to decide what to do with their lives. Being certain about your future career is like pregnancy: Either you is or you ain't. You can't be 68 percent pregnant. If working with a career coach or counselor doesn't use a methodology that gets you to the goal of certainty about your future, you will still be where you started out: unsure, questioning, uncertain. Isn't that the same situation you are facing now? Even though most career counselors are well intentioned, their methods were developed more than fifty years ago to help an unsophisticated public deal with simpler decisions. You may have been exposed to outdated counseling in school or in subsequent attempts to make career decisions. Most people who call themselves career coaches have little training. How effective were these methods in helping you? In these complex times, it becomes more obvious every year that the usual methods of choosing life direction and career path are pitifully inadequate.

If you have worked hard trying to pick a satisfying career and it hasn't worked out, please let the following sentence seep into the very core of your being: *It's not your fault!* Nor is it the fault of a psychological shortcoming or some fatal flaw in your character. It is simply that the tools you have been using aren't adequate to the task. If you have felt frustrated or depressed that you have been unable to choose well, that is completely normal. It's got to get to you after a while if you try to pound in nails with a sponge instead of a hammer.

Every aspect of your life is directly related to how well your career fits you. People who are engaged in satisfying, challenging careers that match their talents, personalities, and goals usually achieve a higher degree of success than people who do not care passionately for what they do. They are healthier, live longer, and tend to be more satisfied with other aspects of their lives. They feel their lives are meaningful and a source of joy. An ill-fitting career contributes significantly to stress and depression, and has a profoundly negative effect on self-esteem.

We are what we repeatedly do.

—ARISTOTLE

Whether you are midcareer and contemplating a change or at the beginning of your work life and making a first choice, it is extremely important to make the best possible decisions. If you choose well, your life will be enriched in many ways by your work. If you make a mistake now, you place an unnecessary burden on your shoulders that may be difficult to carry and equally hard to put down.

You spend more time working than doing anything else. Since making the best possible career choice has an enormous impact on the overall quality of your life, attempting this adventure without expert guidance can end in disaster. Left to their own devices, people often find themselves in careers that don't match their talents and desires. To someone who has never worn shoes, there would not seem to be much difference between size 10 and size 9. However, if you have size 10 feet and spend your life wearing size 9 shoes, you are constantly aware that a small miscalculation makes the difference between comfort and pain. Some people wind up bored or burned out. Some are successful yet remain unfulfilled. Midcareer people who take the risk to improve their lives by making a career change often find their new careers are not much of an improvement. Others pick something impractical or unrealistic, without considering how they could go about making the shift to a new field. These people have done their best, but their best wasn't good enough.

> *If you do not feel yourself growing in your work and your life*
> *broadening and deepening, if your task is not a perpetual*
> *tonic to you, you have not found your place.*

> —ORISON SWETT MARDEN

The Benefits of a Career That Fits

You enjoy better health, a longer life, more vitality. Read the obituary notices of very successful people. Notice how many celebrated (and notorious) people live into their eighties and nineties. Other than inheriting good genes and taking care of your body, leading a satisfied, purposeful life is the most effective thing you can do to live a long, long life. Most of the people whose deaths are reported in the national media dedicated their energy to the wholehearted pursuit of something that mattered to them. That's why they became so successful that their death was deemed worthy of mention. You may also infer that they must have found an elegant fit for their talents to have become so accomplished in their fields. Even the gangsters and dictators must have excelled at their evildoings to generate such worldwide notoriety. People whose work is fulfilling are more resistant to disease and heal more quickly when they do get sick. Why not turn your sick days into vacation days? People die in disproportionate numbers within three years of their retirement because they have nothing exciting for which to live.

You have enhanced personal and professional relationships. If you want great relationships, live your life fully. Others want to be around people who lift their spirits out of the petty pace of day-to-day routine. Your enthusiasm will spark those around you, who then become better company themselves. Having your working life be a major source of satisfaction and self-esteem has a powerful positive effect on the other areas of life, including your relationships. You're more fun to be around.

You're more successful and more productive. There is a close relationship between career satisfaction and material success. People who enjoy their work put their heart and soul into their careers. How much do you accomplish when you are completely immersed in a task that you really enjoy? Compare this with your productivity when you are forced to do something you don't want to do.

You have heightened self-esteem. We have managed to turn self-esteem into something mysterious and complex. Simply said, self-esteem is the reputation you have with yourself. How much do you admire people who grumble about their lives, blame their circumstances, and resign themselves to a life of mediocrity? If your career is not satisfying and your self-esteem is low, you're probably not neurotic. You're just being honest with yourself! Create a future you will be proud of. Spend your days doing something you love.

You become a better role model for children. How can you teach your children, or any young person who looks up to you, to live their lives fully if you don't live yours fully? They watch your actions. When your words don't match your actions, they know instantly that you are full of *caca del toro*. Your children will model themselves after who you are and what you do. If you want to be proud of them, live so that you are proud of yourself.

> *Nothing has a stronger influence psychologically on . . .*
> *children than the unlived lives of their parents.*
>
> —Carl Jung

You lead a life that counts. Your career is your best opportunity to make a contribution. Somehow, it's not the same thing spending your life in a job that is meaningless and then trying to make a difference in your spare time.

You look forward to life. Just as laughter is infectious, so are listlessness, dissatisfaction, and boredom. This ennui will follow you home from work and infect the other parts of your life. Having a career that fits perfectly restores the enthusiasm that came so naturally early in your life.

*I think that what we are seeking is an experience of being alive,
so that our life experiences on the purely physical plane will
have resonances within our own innermost being and reality,
so that we actually feel the rapture of being alive.*

—JOSEPH CAMPBELL

You have a deeper, richer, more authentic sense of humor. Humor that wells up from a core of well-being and satisfaction is very different from the cynical jokes of those trapped in a life of resignation. Wouldn't you rather have your wit generated by happiness instead of resignation? You might even find yourself smiling and snapping your fingers when you're stuck on the thruway during rush hour, happy with thoughts of work well done and the joy of living.

INQUIRY 2

What Would It Be Like to Have a Career That Fits Perfectly?

Imagine waking up in the morning with excitement and enthusiasm for the coming workday. Imagine spending your life doing something that you care about deeply, with most of your time engaged in activities that use your talents fully.

What would it be like to attain a high degree of mastery and success while engaged in activities you enjoy? Take a minute now and actually imagine what it would be like. Close your eyes and visualize yourself in a career you love. Make it as real as possible. Play a scene in your mind's eye from beginning to end. Try to actually see, feel, and hear yourself in the midst of working happily at this new job. What would it be like to have a career that fits you perfectly? What would it feel like?

The Costs of Having a Career That Fits

- **You will have to control your impulse** to constantly remind your friends how much you enjoy your career.

- **You might have to get new friends.** When you begin to live from a commitment to have your life work brilliantly, you might discover that you have outgrown some of the people who will champion their lack of fulfillment until their dying day.

> *Keep away from people who try to belittle your ambitions.*
> *Small people always do that, but the really great make*
> *you feel that you, too, can become great.*
>
> —MARK TWAIN

- **You will lose some of your best reasons to complain.** Most of us have a certain investment in complaining. If you think this doesn't apply to you, try to refrain completely from complaining for the next month. An unfulfilling career is ideal raw material for this hobby. You would have to find other things to grumble about.

- **People will talk behind your back.** When you are just one of the herd of moderately dissatisfied people, you don't attract much attention. When your career really takes off, there will be plenty of jealous gossiping.

- **You will not be a member of the biggest, most popular club.** You will be in a minority and perhaps feel slightly out of the mainstream, like a monk in a bordello.

- **It takes more heart, more energy, and more commitment to have a career that really sings.** You would have to ask more of yourself, inquire more deeply, put more time and energy into choosing your direction.

- **You would have to exchange comfort for vitality.** This is by far the biggest reason people pay the terrible price that having an ill-fitting career exacts. If you want a full life, you have to give up whatever addiction you might have to comfort, to not rocking your boat, and to avoiding the feelings of fear and uncertainty that are always one's companion on journeys outside the safety of the daily routine. A passionately lived life is not always comfortable. Going for it involves being open to all of life: the joys, the sorrows, the mundane, as well as the magic, the splendid victories, the most abject defeats. You might even stop closing your eyes during the scary parts of the movie.

CHAPTER 3

•

HOW TO DECIDE

You're at the amusement park, about to bash around in bumper cars for the first time. They tell you how to do it: "Climb in, clip on the safety harness, get moving in the general direction of the other cars, then put the pedal to the metal and try to crash into the other cars." That's all you need to know to have a smashing good time.

When you are old enough to learn to drive a real car, you discover that there is a lot more to it than bumper cars. Our culture has its own completely automatic, habitual way of instructing us in the art of career design that is just about as useful as bumper car instructions would be for driving a real car. It takes more than all the conventional wisdom one picks up along the way to choose a career that will satisfy and fulfill you.

This chapter lays out some basic principles about how to move from wherever you are, through figuring out where you want to get to, and then narrowing down the possibilities until you are sure exactly and specifically what you will do with your life.

Creating Your Future, Step-by-Step

Choosing a vocation that is not a compromise need not be a terribly daunting task, if you go about it in a way that is effective. Basically, it is simply a process of posing questions and then answering them. It is a little like buying your first house. You start the house-buying process by making a commitment to yourself that you are going to own your own home. Then you start to explore. You are not really starting from square one, because your mind is already filled to the brim with wishes, dreams, feelings, preferences, prejudices, and everything you already know and believe about houses. As you go through the decision-making process, you may alter some of your dreams and hopes. You may discover that some of what you think you know about houses is not necessarily so. The more you dig into the subject, the more you learn. The more energy you give to the project, the more likely it will be that you will buy a house that you'll love.

At some point, you will probably realize that doing a great job of picking a house is a lot more complex and demanding than you thought. You discover that there are many important questions to consider that you hadn't even thought of before. After lots of careful consideration, you begin to make some smaller decisions. You may decide that the house absolutely must have four bedrooms, or a large country kitchen, or that it must be located on a quiet side street. As your explorations continue, you make more and more of these smaller decisions. As you make them, other pieces of the puzzle come together naturally. While all this was going on, you are out there in the real world, looking at houses, checking out the realities such as how much of a mortgage you can manage, and other practical matters. Each of the pieces contributes to the others. The research helps you make decisions. Each decision helps you explore the areas you have not yet made decisions about. And continuing to explore helps you make more decisions. The house you eventually decide to buy may be quite different from your original idea because its features are the result of in-depth exploration and an ongoing process of decision making.

One thing that is very important to notice is that deciding on definite components of your future work has a much more powerful effect on putting together the pieces of the puzzle than your preferences do. For example, if you have decided that the house absolutely must have four bedrooms, then you would not even bother to look at houses with fewer bedrooms. Your preferences do not have the same power. In fact, they often make things more confusing. Let's suppose you have lots of strong preferences but no clear commitments. You might dream of a house with five bedrooms, two fireplaces, a huge backyard with a stream, nice, friendly, quiet neighbors, a big party room, and a large Dutch windmill coming out of the roof. That's a wonderful dream. But since you are living in the ephemeral world of dreams, you are highly susceptible to becoming lost in the twilight zone. When the real estate agent shows you a house with a large Dutch windmill coming out of the roof, you jump for it. After all, if you don't grab it today, someone else will. Only later do you discover that the neighbors file their teeth to a point and raise cobras. When you return to reality, you discover that the house has only two bedrooms, the fireplace doesn't work, and the stream is actually sewage outflow from your neighbor's house.

You could easily make the same mistake in choosing your new career. To make sure this does not happen, please take the time to get completely clear about how *The Pathfinder* will guide you through this process. If you spend the time now to completely understand these steps, burn them into your memory, and keep them in the forefront of your mind as you go through this journey, you will not lose your way. First a few general principles. Then in the next chapter, we will get more specific.

Take a look at the igloo illustration on page 23. To the right of the letter *A* are eight boxes. Each represents an important area to consider as part of deciding what you will do. They will each be described in the next chapter. The many inquiries in this book are designed to help you explore each of these areas in depth. They are different from the usual career explorations you may have done in the past. Most traditional career exercises just help you sort out what you already know about yourself. You wind up with more information but no closer to deciding what to do. Why does that happen?

Our minds are continually running in a nonstop stream of impressions, memories,

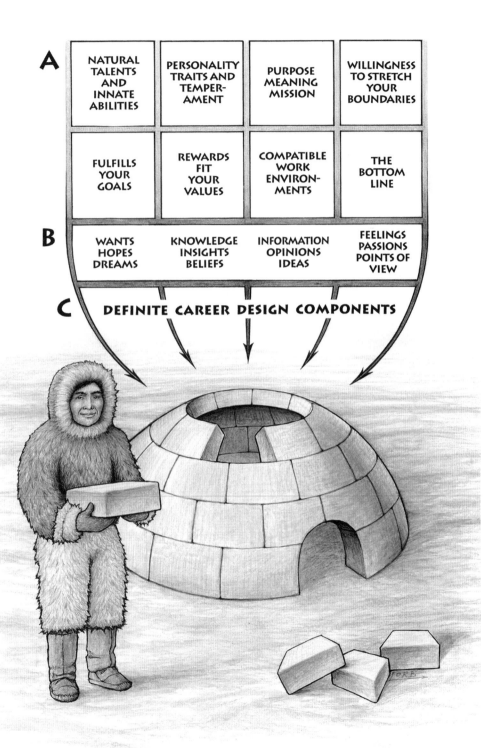

A

NATURAL TALENTS AND INNATE ABILITIES	PERSONALITY TRAITS AND TEMPER-AMENT	PURPOSE MEANING MISSION	WILLINGNESS TO STRETCH YOUR BOUNDARIES
FULFILLS YOUR GOALS	REWARDS FIT YOUR VALUES	COMPATIBLE WORK ENVIRON-MENTS	THE BOTTOM LINE

B

WANTS HOPES DREAMS	KNOWLEDGE INSIGHTS BELIEFS	INFORMATION OPINIONS IDEAS	FEELINGS PASSIONS POINTS OF VIEW

C DEFINITE CAREER DESIGN COMPONENTS

information, hopes, dreams, opinions, feelings, passions, and ideas. You could think of it as your own personal soap opera, the never-ending parade of thoughts flowing by. When you dump more information about yourself or about potential careers into this cauldron of random, quicksilver thoughts and impressions, the information becomes more flotsam and jetsam—just more stuff swirling around in your head. Have you noticed that thoughts about your future career (and everything else) seem to pop up in your mind as concerns, worries, and uncertainties that flow by and then disappear without getting anything important decided? This is shown at *B* on the illustration. This is the part of your brain that is perfectly designed for writing romantic poetry, conversing at parties, and living the everyday parts of your life. Without it, life wouldn't be much fun. But it doesn't work very well as the place to conduct your career choice process.

The inquiries in this book give you an opportunity to go much further, to make a leap to the domain of certainty, a domain where the big question is not "What do I want?" but "What am I sure will *definitely* be an important component of my future career?" This is shown at *C* in the illustration. The inquiries in *The Pathfinder* are designed to allow you to break down all the important questions into small pieces and then make smaller decisions, choosing definite components that add up, one at a time, into the final big career decision, like the blocks the Inuit (Eskimo) is building into a nice, solid igloo.*

The Pathfinder will guide you through a series of steps that lead toward the final goal of deciding exactly what you will do with your life, or at least as much of your life as you want to decide about now. Each of these steps builds toward that final goal. Let's take a look at each of them now. I've broken down the career choice process into several steps for the sake of clarity. In reality, deciding what you will do is not quite as neat and linear as that. You will be engaged in several of these steps: research, making some smaller decisions, investigating, asking new questions, all at the same time. But as time goes on, you will find that you are more and more clear and the final goal will become closer as you fit the pieces of the puzzle together. And then, one day soon, you will have put together enough of the pieces that you will see the light at the end of the tunnel. Later on you will get to know chapter 14, "The Rockport Career Design Method," which is a short, practical guide to the method we'll use. Right now let's get a basic sense of how you will design your future work so you can start looking from this perspective:

1. **Make a commitment to decide on your future vocation.** The first step is to decide to decide. Wanting to decide will not get your plane off the ground.

---

* A component can be anything that defines a part of your career design: a talent or trait that must be used often, a value that must be fulfilled by your work, or any other definite piece of the puzzle you select as a "must-have."

What do you suppose the glazed-over, office-bound people you see taking the subway to work are thinking about? Probably they are thinking the same sort of things we all think: "I wish my life was ___." "Wouldn't it be great if I could ___?" "What I want is ___." People can entertain themselves forever this way. But no matter how much they wish and hope and dream, they keep getting on the same subway each morning and going off to the same old job. You need to get clear enough about your commitment to the quality of your life that you can take potent and resourceful action to make your commitments become your reality. The way to do that is to step out and make definite promises that you are willing to keep, even when it looks scary.

2. **Make designing your future career your number one priority.** Don't just fit it into the cracks of your life. You will get what you give.

3. **Begin by looking in.** The idea is to design a career that fits you rather than trying to squeeze into something the wrong shape or a few sizes too small. To do that, you must turn your attention inward. Get to know yourself thoroughly. Inquire into every aspect of your nature and personality. Even if you know yourself well, find ways to observe your past and present from new viewpoints, especially those that provide tangible, realistic, and practical clues about the best fit between you and the working world.

4. **Seek full self-expression.** You would be wise to honor every aspect and each domain of your life. Many poor-fitting careers result from considering only external rewards like money and status. Consider each thoroughly if you want your work to be balanced and harmonious. Full self-expression doesn't necessarily mean swinging from the chandeliers. It means including all the important parts of your nature and your intentions. A career that fits perfectly demands that you be who you are fully and do what you do naturally.

   All other creatures on the planet, from the lowest amoeba to the great blue whale, express all their component elements in a perfect dance with the world around them. Only human beings have unfulfilled lives. Only humans suffer from career discontent. But, then again, we may be the only inhabitants of the earth who get to decide what we will do with our lives. Since we have the option to be the authors of our destinies, why not do it well? The reward for taking on the adventure of choosing and creating a career is a life of fulfillment. There is nothing magical about this. It is simply a function of learning to have all aspects of your nature play together in harmony, like the instruments of an orchestra.

So without any intentional, fancy way of adjusting yourself, to express yourself freely as you are is the most important thing to make yourself happy, and to make others happy.

—SUZUKI ROSHI

5. **Break down the big question—"What am I going to do with my life?"**—into smaller, more manageable chunks. If you are like most of us, when you attempt to make career decisions, you imagine careers that might be interesting (doctor, lawyer, Indian chief). Your mind hops from one potentially interesting career to another. Your romantic imagination kicks in. You think of all the positive aspects of the job: "Let's see, I really like the idea of becoming an Indian chief. It seems like an exciting job, working outside, nature all around, not a boring desk job, great clothes, etcetera." Then, after a while, you have an attack of negative considerations, an attack of the "Yeahbut" thoughts: "I'm allergic to feathers, those cold winter nights in the teepee, and what about cavalry attacks?" You are left with a veritable blizzard of mental images and opinions about potential careers yet are no nearer to making a definite decision about which one to pursue. What's worse, using this method, you tend to get foggier rather than clearer.

The more you think about a career, the more your opinions—both positive and negative—get stuck onto the original picture. After a while, whenever the thought of that particular career surfaces in your mind, all you see is all the stuff stuck to it. When you think "Indian chief," up pops a picture of a cavalry attack. When you break down the "What shall I do with my life?" question into small chunks, thinking about it all gets easier.

Natural talents and innate abilities. Everyone is born with a unique group of talents that are as individual as a fingerprint or snowflake. These talents give each person a special ability to do certain kinds of tasks easily and happily, yet also make other tasks seem like pure torture. Can you imagine your favorite improvisational comedian as an accountant? Talents are completely different from acquired knowledge, skills, and interests. Your interests can change. You can gain new skills and knowledge. Your natural, inherited talents remain with you for your entire life. They are the hand you have been dealt by Mother Nature. You can't change them. You can, however, learn to play the hand you have been dealt brilliantly and to your best advantage.

Personality traits and temperament. Many people are engaged in careers that make it necessary to suppress themselves at the job. An elegant fit between you and your work includes and supports the full self-expression of your personality. Telltale signs of a career that doesn't fit your personality include: the necessity to assume a different personality at work, restricted self-expression, activities that conflict with your values.

Passion, meaning, mission, purpose. People who are enthusiastic about their work are usually engaged in something they care about and are proud of what they do. They feel they are making a contribution. They may need to go to work to pay the bills, but that is not what gets them out of bed in the morning.

Willingness to stretch your boundaries. One of our clients was a forty-year-old woman who decided to pursue a career in medicine. Her previous college record was insufficient for entry into medical school. She had no money to finance a medical education. Her willingness to stretch beyond what seemed possible was so strong that she went back to college and completed prerequisite courses. She gained admission to a fine medical school and managed to creatively finance her education. Other clients are unwilling or unable to make more than a modest stretch in a new direction. I encourage you to stretch as far as possible toward a career choice that will not be a compromise. At the same time, be completely realistic. It makes no sense to make plans you are unwilling or unable to achieve.

Fulfills your goals. To have something to shoot for is an important part of the joy of working. A custom-designed career supports you to fulfill your personal and family goals and gives you a sense of challenge on the job.

Rewards fit your values. Like a biscuit you give a dog, rewards are the motivators that help keep you happily performing your tricks at work. Some rewards mean more to you than others. That is because they are linked with your values. If recognition for doing something well is a value important to you, then it may also be a necessary reward to motivate you to keep performing well. Doing without adequate recognition will slowly erode your well-being on the job.

Compatible work environments. Each person flourishes in some work environments and finds others stressful or otherwise inappropriate. Several different aspects of the environment that surrounds you play a vital role in the quality of your work life. You live in a certain geographical environment.

The company you work for has a particular organizational environment, style, and corporate personality that affect you every minute you are there. On a smaller scale, your immediate work environment includes the physical work setting, the tone or mood of your office, and your relationships with others, including your supervisor, fellow employees, and clients or customers.

The bottom line. Are the careers you are considering really suitable, doable, and available? Do they really fit you? The decisions you make about your career direction are no more than pipe dreams unless they are achievable and actually turn out as you hope they will. Research is the key to understanding the reality of potential future careers.

6. **Ask resourceful questions.** The quality of your life depends on the choices you make. Your choices stem from how well you answer fundamental questions about yourself and your future. The quality of your answers directly depends on how focused, how succinct, and how clear you are willing to be when posing important questions.

Questions are the creative acts of intelligence.

—FRANK KINGDOMY

Like most intelligent people, you may have already learned a great deal about yourself. Many people who know themselves well still have difficulty making the best decisions. Getting a PhD in psychology has never made anyone well adjusted or happy. However, *the way* that you understand yourself and *how you use* this knowledge are often more important than *how much* you know about yourself. The art of inquiry is an essential skill in designing your life. The better the job you do of framing the question, the better the answers will serve you. In fact, when you frame a question perfectly, the answer often seems to fall from the question naturally and easily, like rain from a thundercloud.

One secret to successfully asking and answering important questions is to break them down into small chunks. Answering the question "What shall I do with the rest of my life?" is a mammoth endeavor. The only possible way to tackle it is to break it down into small, manageable questions. As our ancient ancestors knew, you eat a mammoth one bite at a time.

7. **Delve into all important questions using inquiry tools and self-tests that help you become absolutely sure what the elements of your future work will be.** As you continue on through these pages, you will come upon many guided

assignments and exercises called inquiries. Some of them are like telescopes or microscopes. They allow you to look farther or deeper. Some are a bit like the transporter room on the starship *Enterprise*. They give you access to new possibilities and new worlds. Others serve the function of a crowbar, prying you off the rock you are clinging to for dear life. Each is designed to delve into one important area in a way that allows you to get clear enough to make some decisions. You must remember that these tools are only little black squiggles on white paper. They will not do it for you or to you. Only your wholehearted engagement with the inquiries can make it happen.

You may find that some chapters and inquiries focus on things you do not need to investigate. If you are sure about some parts of your career design, skip the chapters that cover those areas. Just use what you need.

8. **Design your career one piece at a time.** Build with definite components. Tentative decisions engender fuzzy commitments, which in turn give rise to irresolute actions. Often people attempt to hold back on making decisions until they have done all the research and answered all the important questions. They have mounds of information but nothing definite nailed down. They try to manage the wild herd of mustang dreams, needs, wants, insights, and goals stampeding through their minds. As attractive as this method seems, there is one small problem with it: It just doesn't work! At Rockport, we see a steady stream of clients who have spent years trying to do it this way. They know themselves as well as the canary knows its cage. But they still haven't decided what to do with their lives. The only way I know that works consistently is to build a piece at a time, to make a series of smaller choices that fit together like the blocks of snow in an igloo. It doesn't matter if you make big decisions or small ones. Each is a worthy piece of the puzzle. Build your future career one block at a time. Build it from solid chunks, made from components that you have chosen as definite parts of your future work. The best question you can ask is "What am I sure will be some of the definite components of my work?"

9. **Fit together everything you are sure of like pieces of a puzzle.** Construct your future block by block, piece by piece. The building blocks are made of the one and only element you have to work with that is as solid as the blocks of snow in an igloo: certainty. You build with whatever you are certain of as you go through this career design process. There are really only two ways to be sure of anything. You can look inside yourself and uncover preexisting requirements, elements about which you are already sure. For example, you might already be sure that you will work in the world of

business—or perhaps you're sure that you definitely *won't* work in the business world. The other way to be sure is to declare some element you want to be a definite requirement: You make a commitment, a promise to yourself. If you decide that you will work outdoors most of the time, future components you add to the "Definite" column have to be consistent with that choice. That commitment will also bring up new questions and guide you in adding other components to your design.

- Passions, insights, and dreams live in the realm of inquiry, where they serve as guides. But they become as evanescent as clouds when you take them out to the career construction site. If you build your future on a foundation of solid rock, using as building blocks the career components you have become sure of and the definite decisions you have made, you will be more able to stand firm when doubts and difficulties arise.

- Taking things one step at a time and building from solid chunks is like putting together the pieces of a jigsaw puzzle. When you start assembling a large, complex puzzle, you have a tabletop covered with a seemingly endless number of unconnected pieces. It's difficult to fit the first few pieces together. Once you have fit some together, it becomes much easier to add new pieces. It is also a bit like doing a crossword puzzle. First you fill in whatever you can. When there is a piece of the puzzle you cannot find, instead of getting frantic, you simply work on answering other parts of the puzzle. Then, later on, you return to the part you could not figure out before. Because you have filled in some other, related pieces, it is now much easier to answer the previously unanswerable question. So we will concentrate on what you can answer.

10. **Go for vitality, not comfort.** Be unreasonable. At every moment, you have one essential choice: to let the programming steer the boat or to take the helm yourself. Your present circumstances, your mood, the thoughts that pass by all have a life of their own, independent of your will. You can, at any moment, take flight on new wings into an unprecedented life by making a choice for vitality, for living fully, for *life* spelled in capital letters. It is, however, an expensive journey. You pay by giving up the familiar, comfortable, everyday ways of living and thinking that are the wages and rewards of going with the flow of your programming. The willingness to feel fear and keep going forward distinguishes the living from the merely breathing. In fact, it is not just the so-called negative emotions that are uncomfortable. When you choose to live fully, your palette of experiences, thoughts,

emotions, and possibilities expands. This leads you onto new ground in other areas of your life as well. And, folks, all that newness swirling around just ain't comfortable.

The question is not whether to take risks but which ones to take. The peril of being reasonable is that you miss all the fun. It's not enough to edge your way cautiously toward the cliff. Learn to revel in taking risks for the sake of your soul. Every choice you make gives birth instantly to certain risks as surely as your shadow follows you.

There are really only two ways to approach life—as a victim or as a gallant fighter—and you must decide if you want to act or react, deal your own cards or play with a stacked deck. And if you don't decide which way to play with life, it will always play with you.

—MERLE SHAIN

11. **Go out into the world and do research to discover what sort of work matches the pieces of the puzzle you have assembled so far.** Your definite components become the specifications you use to come up with specific careers that may fit. Now it is time to look out into the world and see what sort of work these specifications fit. Do some research. You want to list a few possible careers and then find out more about them.

12. **Persist in spite of obstacles and setbacks.** Don't stop until you know what you are going to do with your life. If you quit before you reach your goal, you won't reach it. That last statement seems almost idiotically obvious, doesn't it? Yet it is the number one reason people do not get what they want.

Let me tell you the secret that has led me to my goal. My strength lies solely in my tenacity.

—LOUIS PASTEUR

Throughout history, men and women who have made extraordinary contributions have been asked the secret of their genius. The one thing that most of them agree on is the power of persistence. No matter how brilliant your idea or how large your dream, without exceptional tenacity it is likely to remain unrealized. The quirk of human nature that makes it difficult to persist when the going gets rough is that most people are more committed to experiencing their habitual, comfortable range of inner sensations than they are to accomplishing what they have said they will do. If you are willing to experience fear, disappointment, humiliation, and embarrassment, and keep going anyway, you become an unstoppable force of nature. As we shall see in later chapters, the secret to perseverance is a simple one: have a commitment to getting the job done that's bigger than a desire for comfort and ease.

As you travel through *The Pathfinder*, you will discover that your biggest difficulty in persisting, as well as in making the final decision, is something I call "Yeahbuts." These are thoughts generated inside you by a device that seeks to keep you safe by keeping everything in your life the same. You will meet up with it often on this journey. For the time being, begin to notice that you have attacks of thoughts that try to persuade you to give up on making any substantial changes to your life.

> *Never give in, never give in, never, never, never, never.*
>
> —WINSTON CHURCHILL

13. **Keep whittling down your list of possible careers until you know enough to make the final decision.** Then make the leap and make the choice! Once you put together many pieces of the puzzle, there comes a moment of existential choice. It's time to leap; to decide on your future career. For most people, the final answer will not appear out of the fog on its own. You have to make your own final choice. A few weeks or months ago, it may have seemed like an impossibly large leap. Now you are ready. Because you have worked so diligently making some of the smaller decisions, it is easier to decide. In the movies, the hero often has to make impossibly long, death-defying leaps from the roof of one building to another. Making the final decision may feel a little like this. But all the work you have done has paid off. It has brought the buildings sufficiently close together so that making the leap is now within the range of what you know you can do.

14. **Celebrate!** When you have decided what to do with your life, celebrate! You owe it to yourself. Or, even better, why not celebrate that you started this process today? Tomorrow celebrate that you are moving toward your goal. When you get stuck, celebrate that you are stuck. Celebrate when the sun shines and when the cold winds blow. Make this process one of joyful creation rather than a job that you have to do.

More Words to the Wise

Please do not believe anything I say or jump to conclusions too easily. Trust yourself. Don't blindly accept the word of experts. As you read along, look into your own life to see whether what I say seems valid to you.

Wherever you are now on the journey toward a fulfilling career is the perfect place to begin. There couldn't be a more advantageous place for you to start from, because, for you, there is no other possible starting point. Your life has taken you to where you are today. It didn't take you somewhere else. You wound up here! This is it! This is what you have to work with. If you are young and shiny and naïve, use your enthusiasm to propel you. But look carefully before you leap. If you are crusty and jaded, use your experience to separate wheat from chaff. You just have to manage cynicism. If all has not gone well so far in your search for the perfect career, use your experience to guide you away from making the same mistakes. Watch out that you are not seduced by the inner voices that speak from resignation. And, wherever you are, remember these great words of wisdom:

No matter where you go, there you are.

—BUCKAROO BANZAI

To have a great career, have a great life. To have work that really sings and soars takes expanding your commitment to excellence to include other aspects of your life. At any moment, each important area of your life is either expanding, contracting, or hovering. If other areas are contracting, this may sabotage your journey along the path to having a very satisfying career. To get moving in this career choice process, you would be wise to up the ante in the rest of your life. As you wend your way through *The Pathfinder*, you will find that sometimes you will focus directly on career issues. Other times the view will expand to include your entire life. When that happens, please expand your inquiry so that it is broad enough to consider your life as a whole.

You may need resources in addition to this book. I have done my best to include everything you could possibly need to go through the process of choosing your future career. This new edition of *The Pathfinder* contains many new, cutting-edge inquiries and methods we use with clients at Rockport Institute, as well as many changes and improvements. For some readers, the combination of their energy plus time plus this book will be sufficient to get them to their goal. For others, it may not.

The final choice you make about your future work will affect all the areas of your life: your sense of personal fulfillment, the level of success and security you reach, your health and longevity, your sense of self-worth, as well as the quality of your relationships. This may turn out to be one of the most important decisions you ever make. This book has worked for many of the hundreds of thousands of people who have used it to coach themselves through designing their perfect career. I suggest that you dig in, use this book as your coach and guide, participate 100 percent, and, at some point, evaluate whether using this book, or any book, is likely to get you to your goal. I suggest that you ask yourself, "Should I undertake this journey on my own or get some professional assistance?"

Most people do not seek help in choosing their work because of ancient cultural habits. Career choice has been a do-it-yourself project since the dawn of time. But, then again, most people aren't very fulfilled or maximally successful in their work. Throughout human history, most simply chose the obvious: If you were a man, you did what your father did; if you were a woman, you raised children. In the late 1800s, there were only about one hundred different careers to choose from, and very few of those were available to women. Now there are more than ten thousand different jobs from which to choose. Before the 1960s, people didn't expect to like their work. They just wanted to make a living, get ahead, and keep the wolf away from their door. Now that we want more—satisfaction, success, self-expression, and time for a life outside of work—making the best choice takes more than a good guess.

If you broke your arm, you wouldn't set it yourself; you would find a doctor. If you were sued, you wouldn't defend yourself. During my more than thirty years as director of Rockport Institute, we have coached more than fourteen thousand clients through designing their careers. I have talked with many readers of this book about their experiences. From all of this involvement, I have gotten a pretty good idea of what it takes. Given the low percentage of people who believe their work is a good fit, the do-it-yourself method, even with a good book, is not always sufficient to make the best career choice. In the future, I think our culture will learn to make career design an important part of one's education, and that career design coaches and courses will play an increasing role in helping midcareer changers through these important decisions.

In my experience, the best way to design work that is both a great fit and attainable is to participate in a career design process like the Rockport Institute Career Choice Program, or a similar program from another source, instead of going it alone. The most effective programs include natural-talent testing and a complete career design process that coaches you through the complex process of making the best choice. If one-on-one coaching is not feasible for you, the next-best strategy is to use a natural talent assessment program, and use *The Pathfinder* to coach yourself.

Each of us is born with a unique and complex profile of natural gifts and personality traits. Mother Nature deals each of us a very specific hand of talents. The source of what we do best and enjoy most is various combinations of these individual components. The things we do well are, for the most part, natural talents working together in various combinations. Most of us are not aware of the individual pieces that make up our strengths. If you have a clear understanding of your unique profile of natural abilities and how they fit together with your personality, you can combine them in new ways and design your future career to include everything important. Testing also helps you understand what tasks to minimize or stay away from; why some tasks are enjoyable while others seem like torture. People who report both success and fulfillment in their work almost always have an elegant and excellent fit between their natural abilities and what they do all day.

Chapter 17, "Natural Talents," is designed to help you get a useful, though rough, assessment of your natural talents. I would be less than honest, however, to say that this can replace high-quality, objective, scientific testing. This is one area where self-assessment just does not work very well. Good abilities testing can give you a definite edge in making an excellent career decision. This kind of testing is available from several sources, including Rockport Institute. It is something that I believe every young person should do and something I recommend to all career changers.

I would also get a book that covers personality type in more depth than is possible here. One excellent book is *Do What You Are* by Paul Tieger and Barbara Barron-Tieger. As I said, *The Pathfinder* alone works just fine for many people. It may be all you need. Try it. See what works for you. If you think you need some professional assistance, check out the programs at www.rockportinstitute.com.

Another strategy I recommend is to form a small group of like-minded people to work together and support one another through the career choice process. Career design works least well in monologue because we are all imprisoned within our own points of view and by a lifetime of interpretations we take for truth. Expert career coaching or a group of committed companions provides perspectives impossible to discover with the do-it-alone method. Just this week, I heard from a group of women, all Smith College grads of different ages, who found one another through alumnae services, and formed a *Pathfinder* group that was very effective in assisting them through choosing a career.

Two mistakes to avoid. There are two mistakes you might make in going through *The Pathfinder*. The most common is to remain in the role of observer; a reader instead of a participant. At a championship tennis match, the players are participating totally, giving all they have to the game. Everyone else is just an observer. Their minds are commenting on the game, critiquing, as a journalist would. They are not playing the game. They are just watching as the game unfolds. If you remain in the role of observer, *The Pathfinder*'s process will not work. What will make this process turn out as well as you hope is full participation, unreserved, with as much energy and commitment as you can muster.

The other mistake folks make is to get too compulsive. You do not need to examine every leaf on every tree along the path of your journey. Don't make this more complicated than it already is. Concentrate on the central issues, the important stuff. Don't sweat the details.

How long will it take? Most people take months to go through this process. I suggest that you allow it to take exactly as long as it takes. Mark your calendar for three to six months from now. If you still haven't chosen your career by then, it is time to start wondering what is taking so long. No matter what the difficulty, you should be able to diagnose the problem and figure out what to do about it within the pages of this book. Some people move very slowly. They need a great deal of time to let things bubble up. It takes them ten years to decide to marry their lover and all week to decide what to do Friday night. If this describes you, give yourself one year at the most. Note to students: This project may take longer. Get to know yourself and the world intimately.

I have difficulty making big decisions. Why should I think that suddenly anything will change? It can and will change, if you are willing. Most of the difficulties people experience stem from using commitment problems as a shield to hold off the new and the unknown. What people perceive as a problem is often a solution they subconsciously concocted to deal with other problems. When you were a child, did you usually have trouble deciding what to do when other kids asked you to come out and play? If not, you are in good shape. Don't worry. It will all work out. *The Pathfinder* is, in a sense, a course on how to create and follow through on commitments. So you are in the right place at the right time.

How will I know that I made the right decisions? You won't know for sure until time passes and you have reached your objective. You can't know for sure how anything in the future will turn out until you get there. If you give the career choice process your best effort, and you are willing to do whatever it takes to arrive at your destination, you can be fairly sure that you will make the best choice. If you diligently work your way through *The Pathfinder*, you will have the best possible chance of choosing a career that will be deeply rewarding in many ways, for the rest of your life.

What if I'm not completely ready to decide now? That's fine. I suggest you stick your toe in and try the water in a place you think you will like. If you have issues you want to work on, go right to the chapters that deal with them. If you like the water, dive in headfirst.

Why are some concepts repeated in different parts of this book? Learning anything, especially ways of thinking that go beyond ingrained habits, requires repetition. Sometimes an important idea that could make a huge change in the quality of my life has to hit me over the head many times before I get it in my bones instead of as an intellectual concept. I often read something and think, "I already know that." If I look a little more closely, I will notice that even though I know it, I'm not living it. I may not have made it into a daily practice. Living a life you love requires reviewing the habitual ways you live your life and sometimes making changes.

To Choose or Not to Choose

Sometimes people put off choosing a career because they feel they have some growing or changing to do. That's fine if you are nineteen and need to get to know yourself and the world a little better. It also makes sense if you are recovering from a catastrophe or from some sort of deep-seated psychological problem that would seriously subvert this project. But often people put it off because it is confronting and brings up all sorts of feelings such as doubts and fears. All sorts of Yeahbut thoughts arise: "Am I ready?" "Do I have time?" "What if it doesn't work?" The best way to tell if you are ready is to ask, "Do I have the intention to choose a new direction? Am I willing to do what it takes?" That's all you need: the commitment to move it forward. If your favorite hobby is exploring your own inner mysteries, through personal growth or therapy, don't put off deciding what to do with your life until you explore the back passage of your internal labyrinth. Who knows how long it will take or if you will ever do it to your satisfaction.

An Apology

Throughout this book, I will point out the many ways you could go astray. It may seem that sometimes I am treating you like a wild and intractable barbarian. Often people do not reach the outcome they most want because they do not recognize and master those parts of their nature that are willful, opposed to change, and operate invisibly, completely on autopilot. It is not enough to be hopeful. When you are truly committed to making something difficult happen, you naturally take stock of the forces that oppose you so that you can deal with them resourcefully. If human evolution were compressed into twenty-four hours, then just two seconds ago our ancestors were hunter-gatherers, using stone tools and eating one another's brains. Most of us, me included, are hard cases, either rebellious ("independent thinkers," as we would characterize it) or too quick to succumb to beliefs we have not really investigated ("good team players"). Most of us need to be reminded occasionally to stay on the narrow road to excellence. I am committed to your being spectacularly successful in designing your future career. I will point out many times how you could get sidetracked by the idiosyncrasies of human nature. Please forgive me if I do that when it is unnecessary. There is no way I can be sensitive to you as an individual when we are not working within a close, personal coaching relationship.

•

CHAPTER 4

USE *THE PATHFINDER* AS YOUR GUIDE

The Pathfinder consists of four sections. This first, "Living a Life You Love," is like the first part of a roller-coaster ride, where you chug up the incline before the fast ride downhill. You have already read most of it, so I need not explain what it is about except to say that near the end you will do several inquiries that begin your career design project.

The second section is "How to Get from Here to There (The Library)." This is like a library, with chapters on many areas vital to designing your work such as dealing with "Yeahbut" thoughts, making the best decisions, choosing goals, and doing research.

The third is "Design Your Career." This section is the step-by-step career design process that is the heart of this book. You'll work through three big questions: *"Who am I?"* includes areas like your talents and personality. *"Why work?"* covers meaning, mission, purpose, values, and rewards. *"Work where?"* is about the workplace environment. Then the last part of this section covers *Making the Choice.*

The fourth is "Marketing and Job Search."

Your Own Customized Career Design Project

Use *The Pathfinder* as a guide to design a career that fits you as well as custom-tailored clothes, and, as you move through your life, to make choices and overcome new situations and obstacles. You may want to use it now to design a career from the ground up, to help solve a specific problem, or get clarity on an issue. As a result, there are different approaches you could take to use it in a way appropriate to your situation.

One approach is to use it the same way that Donald Duck's nephews Huey, Dewey, and Louie use *The Junior Woodchuck Guidebook* to pull a triumphant victory from the jaws of defeat just before the razor-sharp teeth snap shut. When you have a problem, look up the specific solution. Or, if you have made definite decisions about your future work except that one nagging area, just dig into that. *The Pathfinder* contains chapters that stand on their own to cover specific topics in depth.

If you are planning to use *The Pathfinder* as your guidebook to choosing your future career, it is always best to look from a beginner's mind, to assume that you don't know exactly what it will take to make the best choices. In that case, start at the beginning and let the book coach you all the way through your career design process, step-by-step. If you want to skip section 2 and go directly from this first section to the third, "Design Your Career," where you work through this project step-by-step, fine. This may be the best method for you if you would describe yourself as some combination of practical, down-to-earth, goal oriented, direct, quick to get to the point, and impatient, or if you learn best by doing or don't particularly enjoy reading. Spend a few minutes familiarizing yourself with the chapters in the middle section so you know what they contain and can turn to them when you need them. If some seem relevant to your present situation, go ahead and use them now.

Many of you will find the second section extremely useful. For example, who does not have difficulties dealing with Yeahbuts? Who could not learn to ask better questions or develop more skill in making decisions, setting goals, and completing projects (especially this one)? If that describes you, I recommend that you read some or all of section 2 before going on to the in-depth career design section. Or, if you read more than one book at a time, you could read and use the second and third sections at the same time, considering them to be two different books.

If a particular chapter or inquiry covers something that you have already mastered or handled fully, don't feel you necessarily need to slavishly go through it again. Be creative. This is a dynamic, living process, not one to be done mechanically. Do it as a passionate dance rather than as dishes that must be washed.

I hope this process will be a great deal of fun for you. Some chapters will be smooth sailing. Others may challenge every fiber of your being, especially if you are playing for high stakes: a truly exceptional and highly satisfying future. You may feel like you are stuck or wasting your time at least once. Expect that you may want to quit, that you will feel afraid, that you will try to talk yourself into unnecessary compromises, or that you will decide that this method doesn't work. All of this is just good old crazy human nature hard at work, trying to reduce the risks and make you feel as comfortable as a couch potato watching a good soap opera with a big bag of chips.

Get Started with Inquiries

Even though you'll do most of your career design in the third section, let's do a few basic inquiries now, partly to move toward your goal and also to gain some familiarity with the Rockport Career Design Method. We developed this methodology over more than thirty years of research and practical experimentation working with more than fourteen thousand private clients who, like you, were passionately committed to living successful, fulfilled lives. These tools, methods, and strategies were designed to get you from here to there—"there" being your goal of choosing a specific career. What we will do now is a basic introduction, similar to taking a first flying lesson. In that first lesson, the instructor lets you take control of the plane and fly in a straight line for a few minutes. Later on, in chapter 14, "The Rockport Career Design Method," you will get more familiar with this methodology so you'll be able to take off, land, and even do career aerial acrobatics. Here's how it works:

INVESTIGATE →		DECIDE →	DESIGN
Gather Clues	Work the Clues	Definite Career Design Components	Careers to Explore

Decision Point ↗

You begin in *detective/investigator mode*, searching out the clues that might be useful in understanding the fit between yourself and the working world. A clue is any observation or information that might provide insight about the fit between you and the world of work. Then you "work" the clues by investigating, researching, and considering them. The goal of working clues is to move them to the *decision point*, and then to choose some of them as *definite career design components*. Building definite components is one of the central strategies of the Rockport Career Design Method. From a designer's point of view, these components are specifications. While you are finding and working *clues*, you'll also keep a list of *career ideas*, writing down any careers or jobs that might be worth investigating. When you have sufficient definite career components, it is time to switch to *designer mode* and check out how well your career possibilities fit your specifications—comparing, contrasting, researching, adding new careers, and crossing off ones you've realized are not a good fit, until you can finally narrow it down to a definite choice. The goal is to reach the point where you can say with certainty, "I know exactly what work I will do. It is a great fit and within range of what I can accomplish."

Why does this method work? Consider for a minute how people usually decide on their careers. They think about different kinds of work they might be interested in without building definite specifications. That may be a good way to pick a new pair of shoes or decide which movie to see but not to design what to do with your life. Most career methodologies consist almost entirely of clue discovery, so you take off and fly around a little. They then leave you in the middle of the air with no way to land on solid ground. With this method, you start with clues, investigate, choose some clues as definite components, check out what careers fit your specifications, and then narrow down the possibilities to a definite choice.

INQUIRY 3

What I Want

Let's take a look at what is important to you. Checkmark all the statements that describe what you want to have as part of your future work, including those statements that describe the positive points of your present work. This inquiry is just about wants, dreams, and hopes, not what you think you can achieve.

_____ I enjoy going to work. I don't have trouble getting up in the morning because what I do is interesting and challenging.

_____ My work is a natural expression of my talents and personality.

_____ Success comes easily to me because I am extremely good at what I do.

_____ I am proud of what I do and enjoy telling other people about it.

_____ I am highly respected at work because I'm so good at what I do.

_____ Work is often so enjoyable it feels more like play.

_____ My job provides a flow of interesting problems to solve, ones I find exciting and challenging.

_____ I don't have to pretend to be someone else at work because my personality suits my work.

_____ I'm paid to make use of my own best and most natural forms of creative expression.

_____ My work environment brings out my best efforts.

_____ My job fits my most important values and allows me to fulfill my goals in terms of personal growth and achievement goals, income, stability, and so on.

___ The result of my efforts makes a contribution that personally matters to me. I feel I am doing something that makes a difference.

___ My job does not take over my entire life. I have plenty of time for friends, family, and fun outside of work.

___ I like the people I work with.

___ I am on a winning team that is having a great time getting the job done.

___ A day on the job leaves me feeling energized, not burned out.

1. Now go back over these statements and place an *X* before those statements that are not now sufficiently fulfilled in your present or recent work. Identifying what you want is a very useful source of clues about what sort of work will fit. I recommend that you start writing down important clues. If you're not sure you need to do this, ask any detective if he writes down his clues or just tries to keep them organized in his head.

2. As you go through designing your future career using *The Pathfinder*, there are three categories of information that you will add to and work with throughout this process:

   Clues
   Definite Career Design Components
   Career Ideas

   All three are essential to your success in this project. You will be working with these three documents throughout designing your new career. In a later chapter, we will dig in deeper and work with all three lists. But for now, let's just get started without a lot of explanation.
   Start three documents now, one for each category. You could do this by creating a separate digital document for each, start an actual physical notebook, or have your personal robotic assistant do it for you. Or you could download a template from www.rockportinstitute.com. Name the first document "Clues"; the second, "Definite Career Design Components"; and the third, "Career Ideas." You will use these three documents throughout designing your future work.

3. Clues. Write down anything you think might turn out to be an important clue from the exercise you just completed. For example, if you noticed

that you want your work to involve solving more interesting, challenging problems, write down that clue. Make it as specific as possible. If you made lots of *X* marks above, you may have several clues to write down.

Look a little deeper at other career-related wants and write them down as clues. What do you most want? Consider all the passionate desires, hopes, and dreams that surface in your mind from time to time. What would have you hop out of bed in the morning with some enthusiasm? These aren't necessarily definite components or commitments. The whole point of writing down clues is to work them, consider and research them, doing whatever is necessary to move them in the direction of turning some of them into definite components. Keep adding to this list, refining, getting more specific as you work your way through designing your future work.

4. Definite components. One big goal of this process is to turn clues into definite components. Sometimes it takes considerable thought and/or research to turn a clue into a definite component. Other times it falls into your lap with no effort, and you just know that you must include it in your design. Look over the exercise you just finished. Do any definite components come to mind? Are you willing to commit to anything as a definite component? For example, if you noticed that one thing missing from your current work is the sense that you're making a contribution that personally matters to you, and if you know this must be an important component of your future work, put it down on this new Definite Components document. And if nothing seems definite now, don't worry. That is what you will work on throughout this book.

5. Career ideas. There may be some careers you are already considering or dreaming about. You may have thought of some new career/job ideas from doing this exercise. If so, put them down on your Career Ideas document. Right now this is a loose list of career ideas and possibilities. Add new possible career/job ideas that occur to you as this project moves forward.

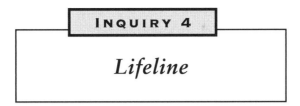

INQUIRY 4

Lifeline

Let's take a look into your future.

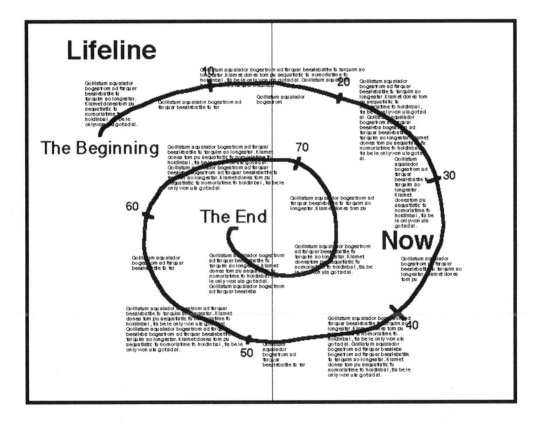

One way to do this inquiry is to use a large sheet of real paper, legal size or even bigger. If your world is paperless, use software that will let you draw curvy lines and add words so it looks like this illustration. Write "Lifeline" in big letters at the top of the page.

Next you will draw your "lifeline." One end will represent your birth; the other, the end of your life. With a heavy pen or marker, draw a long line across your document. The line can curve, curl, spiral, zigzag, or do anything else that pleases you. Try to leave room for writing on both sides of the line.

At one end, write "The Beginning." At the other, write "The End." Draw short lines to mark each decade of your life—past, present, and future—as shown in the illustration. Write "Now" in bigger letters at the place that represents your present age.

Start at the beginning of your life. Write in significant events, from the time of your birth to the present time. Focus on events where you experienced significant growth, a personal transformation, a major life event, went after or accomplished an important goal, and times when your life was profoundly altered in other ways.

Imagine your life continuing along this lifeline into the future. What significant milestones do you want to reach at various times in the future? Write them in, along your lifeline, at the appropriate place. You might find it helpful to frame your inquiries like this: "What would I most like to accomplish between the years of X and Y?" "What would I want to have done?" "Who would I like to be by then?" "What would I like to have by then?" Don't let yourself be bound by overly reasonable, practical thinking. This inquiry is about what you would really like to have. At this point, it is not about definite commitments. At the same time, don't write in entries that you know are just grandiose pipe dreams. Your favorite movie star will not fall for you and become your love slave. If you are fifty and out of shape, you will not be a world-famous ballerina. (You might have a chance in opera, though.)

Continue to let your imagination fly, where it will, into the future. Keep asking questions that encourage you to visualize what you would like your life to be like. You need not confine yourself to career-related entries. Look in all the other areas of your life as well. Consider relationships, personal goals, financial issues, and so on.

Your imagination is your preview of life's coming attractions.

—A L B E R T   E I N S T E I N

When you are finished, go over your entries. Many people notice that the past has many entries, but the future is almost completely empty. That alone can be a very powerful clue. People who get what they want know what they want. If you have not written much in your future, it may be time to do so now. On the other hand, it may be enough to simply notice that your future is kind of blank and work on this as you design your future career. Look at what you have accomplished in this inquiry. It may be that, by answering some of these questions, you have come up with some important clues about who you intend to be, what you want to do and have in the future. If so, add them to your Clues document.

More useful than clues are definite choices, building sure and certain elements of your future work. Is there anything you discovered in this inquiry that you are willing to declare as a definite component of your future work? If so, add it to your Definite Career Design Components.

Being Coachable

Even the Lone Ranger had the support and devotion of Tonto. The coaching, mentoring, and encouragement of trusty companions make a big difference in designing the perfect career for you. Why? Because commitments are as ephemeral as breath exhaled onto a cold window in midwinter. When you are having difficulties, a single attack of "Yeahbut maybe I should compromise a little for the sake of practicality" can bring an inglorious end to the fulfillment of your dream.

When I was in high school, the coach came straight from central casting: a big rough lout with a whistle and all the subtlety of a bulldog. I'm not sure he had any name other than Coach. My entire relationship with him was one of nonstop passive resistance to his demands that we take a few more laps around the track. Times have changed, and the concept of coaching has expanded into every area of life where people want to be more effective. People striving to be their best have discovered that they can go farther faster with a dedicated, skilled person by their side to guide them, advise them, and keep them on the track of fulfilling their goals. Now there are professional coaches for financial affairs, voice, relationships, sexual skills, executive development, wardrobe, and spirit as well as your personal and physical development.

If I had been more committed to athletics as a teen, I might have welcomed Coach's input. I even might have learned a great deal from him. I will never know what could have been. Whatever he told me to do, I either avoided, resisted, refused, or converted to my own interpretation. Professional coaches say that their clients pay them for their expert assistance and then do exactly as I did in high school. Studies indicate that, most of the time, people don't even follow their doctor's advice. How about you? When the prescription bottle says to take one every six hours, do you follow the instructions rigorously or take one when you remember? Authors of self-help books say that they are happily surprised when they meet readers who have actually participated wholeheartedly from cover to cover. No wonder most readers don't get the results they'd hoped for.

If you were a master of the art of making career choices, you would not be reading this now. Yet you are stuck with having to do it yourself. You also, most likely, want to do a really excellent job of designing your future. It all adds up to one inescapable conclusion: If you are going to get the most from this book, you are going to have to play 100 percent! My first suggestion is that you allow me the privilege of being your coach throughout this process. Second, I ask you to suspend whatever degree of uncoachability you suffer from while you go through this process. Surrendering your uncoachability does not mean giving up your independence. During the American Revolution, independence and resistance went hand in hand; in coaching relationships, they make strange bedfellows. True independence means being free from the domination of your own internal automatic behaviors, not doing what you feel like when the urge strikes.

To be truly coachable, you need to master one of the more obnoxious traits of the human mind. We humans believe that the constant opining of the little voice in our heads is the truth. Whatever opinion our mind offers, we accept it as the one and only reality, even in regard to subjects about which we know nothing. Everyone knows that the music he likes is really the best music, the people he thinks are cool are really the cool people, and that the world would run perfectly if all the leaders would just listen to him. Each of our minds is the omniscient god of a teeny, tiny universe. If you were a master of whatever you seek coaching for, you wouldn't need a coach in the first place. A good coach tells you things you don't want to hear and asks you to do things you don't want to do so that you can have the life you most want to have. Your usual way of evaluating other people may not work, since coaches worth their salt will constantly ask you for more than you want to give. The only way you will know if the coach knows anything is to act fully on his or her coaching rather than constantly judging and evaluating everything asked of you. Given the fact that we human beings are usually either resistant or compliant, this alone is going to take some commitment and practice!

Train yourself to do everything your coach advises, and do it as closely as you possibly can to the way your coach suggests that you do it. To understand this aspect of coaching, watch the film *The Karate Kid*. Whenever you don't understand exactly what your coach is up to, think, "Wax on, wax off." If you don't know what this means, see *The Karate Kid* right away. Promise yourself that you will follow the coaching fully for some fixed period of time. At the end of that time period, see if you achieved or are moving toward the objectives you targeted. Give your coach a break. You may have achieved enormous benefits even if you haven't yet reached the final goal. The big question is "Is this working? Will this get me to my goal if I keep at it?" Then, if it isn't working, fire the coach and get a better one.

The secret to success in choosing your career or in any endeavor is to put out a 100 percent effort and to be 100 percent accountable for the results you get. In doing the exercises in *The Pathfinder*, get perfectly clear what is asked of you, then throw yourself into the assignment. Give it everything you've got. Be aware of the very human tendency to resist participating fully. Don't let that tendency run the show. Then, when you are finished doing what the book asks, make up your own ways to move the process forward. Never *just* follow instructions. Follow the instructions and then unleash your creativity. After all, no one knows you as well as you do. Trust yourself to make up appropriate inquiries into the most important questions you are facing. Ask yourself over and over again, "What else can I do?" If you are just doing the assignments in this book, without pushing the envelope to break your own sound barrier, you are not participating fully. If you do all of that and it still doesn't work, fire me as your coach. Dump the book in the trash can. Then go find another coach and give it 100 percent again. Please don't ever give up on living an extraordinary life.

HOW TO GET FROM HERE TO THERE (THE LIBRARY)

This second section of *The Pathfinder* is a library with chapters containing useful perspectives, approaches, and techniques. Like a set of specialized tools, you can pull one out when you need it, or read some or all of them now. Some chapters are the equivalent of an entire book but condensed into fewer words. They will help you become more effective in making the best choices, deal successfully with indecision, confusion, uncertainty, and fear, push through procrastination, get unstuck, turn your dreams into reality, and more. Here is an expanded table of contents of these chapters:

"Why You Don't Get What You Want"—Gets to the source of how and why we make unnecessary career compromises. This is the first of a three-chapter minicourse to bring about a permanent shift in your ability to make the best choices and achieve your career goals.

"The Power of Commitment"—The second part of the three-chapter inquiry into how to get what you want without settling for less.

"Making Decisions—A Short Course"—The final part of the three-part course. We make decisions using habitual methods that may not lead to the quality of life we want.

"Goals and Projects"—Goal setting and project management. The more skill you have in these two areas, the more likely that you will reach your goals.

"Questions"—How to ask and answer all the important questions in your career design project. Improve your skill in using powerful questions to move you forward.

"When You Get Stuck"—How to get moving when you are stopped.

"The Bottom Line—Research"—Learn what you need to know to make the best choices.

"Right Livelihood"—Giving as much as you get.

"Seven Keys"—Some basic principles of designing a career (and life) you love.

"The Rockport Career Design Method"—You should definitely read this chapter before starting on the inquiries in section 3. It is the owner's manual for this career design process—the systematic methodology we use at Rockport.

    If you don't think you need to read these chapters, you could move directly to the inquiries in section 3, "Design Your Career." However, unless you are in a big hurry or are a "just the basics, please" person, I recommend that you not only read them but spend the time to master whichever of these chapters you find useful. Many readers and clients say they keep coming back to them over and over. The more skill you have in these areas, the more likely you will make the best choices and find your way to a career you love.

•

CHAPTER 5

WHY YOU DON'T GET
WHAT YOU WANT

*Our doubts are traitors and make us lose the good
we oft might win, by fearing to attempt.*

—WILLIAM SHAKESPEARE

Nearly everyone has difficulty turning his or her most passionate dreams into reality. Many of us can imagine ourselves doing work that fulfills everything important to us. Yet when we attempt to bring that imagined world into existence, we fall prey to doubts and difficulties, blaming the circumstances or ourselves. In this chapter we look at the culprit that keeps parts of our lives going around and around in the same old groove. The next few pages present a model of how our brains work when we seek to expand into new territory. This is a useful perspective from which to look as you take a giant step forward into the future. You do not need to suspend your beliefs about how your mind works. If you think your ego keeps your id from going further than baying at the full moon, fine. Since this is simply a useful model, it doesn't matter if it is the truth or not. What does matter is whether this model helps you be more resourceful in actually living a life you love.

An Anatomy of the Human Mind

Take a look at the illustration on the next page. It is a record of someone's satisfaction as he goes through life. It could be a chart of satisfaction at work, love life, or any other aspect of life. At the bottom of the scale, below 20 percent, life holds no real satisfaction. You are in the pits. Things seem about as bad as they could be. At the top, above 80 percent, you are completely in love with life. No matter what happens, you see the bright side. When you discover that your wonderful new lover is an ax murderer, you think, "Yes, but he's so good at it."

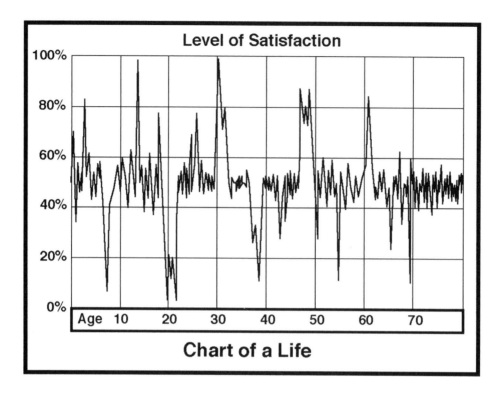

Chart of a Life

Consider your satisfaction with any part of your life in relation to this scale. Let's say your satisfaction in love relationships usually hovers around 50 percent on the scale. Your love life is okay but not great. Then something happens that drives your level of satisfaction down to a 10 percent or a 20 percent. Unlike Humpty Dumpty, it does not take all the king's horses and all the king's men to put you back together again. It just takes time. Sooner or later, you will find yourself back at good old 50 percent again. Rarely do people stay deep in the pits for long. Somehow they find their way back to their usual level of satisfaction. They may change partners to get back to 50 percent or they may work things out in their existing relationship. They will do *anything* to return to their usual, customary level of satisfaction. It is not 100 percent, it's not 90 percent, but it is what they are used to. Like a thermostat, we seem to be set for a certain "temperature" of satisfaction.

What happens when a miracle occurs, and your love life really takes off? Your relationship flourishes, or you fall in love. Suddenly you find yourself on cloud nine. In this state of bliss, even washing the dishes can feel like dancing through fields of flowers. Life has become perfectly satisfying. You have soared to 90 to 100 percent on our chart. Will it last? Will you live happily forever after? Of course not. Either you will slowly drift back to 50 percent, or you will somehow screw it up so that you land with a thud back at 50 percent. You may sincerely want to have a very satisfying love life. It could be something you strive for, work for, and care about deeply. But you keep winding up at good old, same old, predictable 50 percent. Why?

Right now you may be asking, "What does all this have to do with choosing a career?" Nothing at all if your life and your work are as deeply fulfilling as you'd like them to be. Nothing at all if you are willing to leave your life to the ebb and flow of circumstance. If you plan to have a deeply satisfying career—one that goes beyond the ordinary level of satisfaction and success most people accept—then it may be worth noticing that there seems to be a mechanism at work that tends to keep people stuck to the same spot on the flypaper of life. The better you are at unsticking the stuck, the more power you have over how your life will be.

Look at the illustration below. It looks like a seesaw that is balanced in the middle, because no one is sitting on either end. Let's use it to demonstrate how minds work. Don't worry about the objects under the ends of the seesaw. We'll get to them in a minute.

EQUILIBRIUM

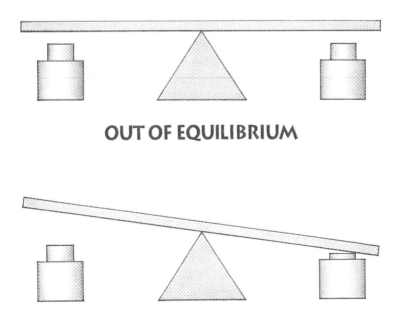

OUT OF EQUILIBRIUM

Living things naturally return to a state of balance. When we are disturbed by forces acting on us, our inner machinery kicks in and returns us to a balanced state of equilibrium, just like this seesaw. *Homeostasis* is the word we use to describe the ability of an organism to maintain equilibrium. Most of the systems in animal and human physiology are controlled by homeostasis. We don't like to be off balance. We tend to keep things at an even keel. This system operates at all levels. Our blood stays the same temperature. We say, "I'm in a rut," or "I'm stuck in the same old groove."

Every time something in our lives gets out of balance, our internal machinery sets off behaviors designed to return us to equilibrium. In the illustration on page 55, the objects under the ends of the seesaw are switches. You can see that when balance is disturbed, the seesaw tips a little bit one way or the other, and it pushes one of the switches. Pushing one of the switches sets off a behavior designed to return you to equilibrium. Notice that no matter which way the seesaw moves, it sets off one of the switches. So, whether your life has hit the skids or is on cloud nine, powerful forces of homeostasis are at work to return you to equilibrium.

Reptile Brains, Mammal Brains

To understand how this tendency toward equilibrium controls our lives, let's look back to an earlier time, when reptiles and amphibians were number one on the evolutionary hit parade. Imagine a frog sitting by a pond. It's a wonderful, sunny day with some nice, juicy flies buzzing around. Suddenly the frog sees a large shadow moving nearby. It leaps for the pond. It does not think, "Something is heading my way. I wonder if it's a friend with frog food or a Frenchman with a copper pot." It doesn't think at all. It reacts instantly. The perceived threat knocks it out of equilibrium, and it reacts automatically to get the seesaw back into balance. Frogs that jump at shadows are frogs that survive to make more frogs.

Even with the development of the higher-tech mammal brain, the old software remained in place: Jump first, ask questions later. And the software that was passed down from reptiles to early mammals and then to us carried a big lesson: "The same" is good; "different" means danger.

The Formation of Habits

If you were one of Mother Nature's engineers, charged with improving the design of mammal survival devices, you would try to find some way that the animal could come face-to-face with recurring threats and deal with them successfully without getting so upset that it was incapacitated. That's exactly what nature did. After the mammal has repeated something a few times, it becomes a habit. A habit is an automated reaction designed to keep you at equilibrium while at the same time successfully deal-ing with a threat. Habits get the job done without all the upset. Horses take the same path up the hill time after time. They are creatures of habit, predictable.

Much of what you and I do comes from this mammal part of our brains. We, too, are creatures of habit. The first time I drove a car on a narrow two-lane road, the cars whizzing by in the other direction seemed like a huge threat to my survival. Every ounce of my attention was concentrated on them. After a few days' experience, I paid no conscious attention to them. Once anything has become a habit, we don't have to pay attention to it anymore. The rub with this elegant piece of survival machinery is that, generally speaking, our lives are governed by our habits. When we are aware that our lives are controlled by preprogrammed software, it becomes possible to cap-tain our own ship and steer it to a destination we choose.

The Human Brain

The development of our human brain was another major transformation in the evo-lution of intelligence. One of the new features that nature gave us is our ability to project ourselves into situations that haven't happened yet. You and I can stand on a hilltop, look out across the landscape, and think, "You know, it looks to me like that could be a field where lions might hang out." When we imagine walking through the field and being attacked by lions, we feel fear, experience a surge of adrenaline, and decide to go another way. This design feature gives us an enormous survival advan-tage. We can imagine potential threats without actually having to experience them.

Consider this: You come out of a movie theater and discover that it is pouring rain. A dark alley runs back alongside the theater. You realize that you could save two blocks getting to your car if you cut through the alley. As you consider taking the shortcut, you imagine muggers hiding in its shadowy recesses. You feel a thrill of fear just thinking about it. You decide to stick to the safer, well-lit main street. What is happening here is that you got yanked out of equilibrium just thinking about walking through the alley. Unlike the horse, you don't have to get mugged to learn.

So we possess an extraordinary survival advantage. But along with the benefits comes the biggest problem faced by people who wish to create anything new in their lives. The big problem is that the most advanced human parts of our survival systems operate exactly the same ways that the reptile and mammal parts do. If something throws you out of equilibrium, your homeostasis machinery reacts automatically. The design function of these systems on all levels—from the human part of your brain down to the ancient, primordial parts of it—is survival. All the parts of your survival system defend your physical body from harm as they do for the horse and the frog.

We humans have a lot more than our bodies to defend. And therein lies the source of the difficulties we have in making our most passionate dreams come true.

We have an identity. We see ourselves as separate from the rest of the world. Way back in prehistoric times, when you were hairier and your forehead was a half inch high, your abilities to create concepts and to distinguish yourself from your environment led to having an identity independent from your body. This is what we commonly refer to as the ego. Your ego, or identity, is flexible. It changes from moment to moment, from situation to situation. It is not as simple as "Me Tarzan. You Jane." To Tarzan, there is more than one Tarzan to identify with. There is Tarzan the king of the jungle, Tarzan the wonder-filled, naïve English lord. There is Tarzan the lonely, horny guy, Tarzan the clever, hairless ape, and so forth.

The human part of our survival system is designed to defend our identity as well as our body. Anytime there is even a hint of a threat to the survival of our identity, we are instantly thrown out of equilibrium into an automatic survival reaction. Since we have multiple identities, the system defends whomever or whatever we consider ourselves to be at that moment. Sometimes this works in our best interests. Sometimes it doesn't. If your survival system protects your identity at all costs, it will react if something seems to threaten your identity. *It will do almost anything to keep everything the same.*

Your survival system will defend who you have been in the past, in regard to your career. If your work experience has been a fully successful, profoundly satisfying experience so far, the survival system will go balls to the wall to make sure it stays that way. If you have been doing work that isn't highly satisfying, guess what? It will work just as hard to defend the status quo, no matter how much you wish it weren't so. If you are a young person without much work experience, you are not exempt from the system. It also defends how you look at life: your personal philosophy, opinions, point of view, and beliefs. No matter what you believe or what rules you accept about work or anything else, your system will make sure that your life continually validates your rules.

Meet Jiminy Lizard

Jiminy Cricket sits on Pinocchio's shoulder and tells him what to do in the children's tale of the wooden puppet who wants to be a real boy. Pinocchio's conscience is always with him, telling him to be good. The voice of the survival-centric software that's always with us tells us to stay safe. I call the voice Jiminy Lizard. Jiminy whispers in our ear, directing our thoughts and behaviors to survive as hunter-gatherers in a world that no longer exists. Whenever we even think about going after something that stretches us outside of our everyday comfort zone, Jiminy warns us off with all the reasons it won't work out.

The Yeahbuts

The frog and the horse react physically to threats. The human part of our brain has another less direct but equally effective way to run from a perceived danger: the "Yeahbut." When you think about taking the shortcut through the dark alley, your mind thinks, "Yeahbut, I might get mugged." Whenever you consider stepping into unknown territory in any area of your life, you will develop a case of the Yeahbuts. The simple act of seriously entertaining the thought of expanding your life drives the system out of equilibrium, which triggers a survival reaction: a massive attack of the Yeahbuts.

Don't turn the Yeahbuts into a new enemy. Ninety percent of the time, they, like the other parts of your survival systems, are your ally. If you are dancing at the edge of the Grand Canyon, the Yeahbuts warn you of the danger. Remember, without the Yeahbuts, you would have taken the shortcut through the alley. We are designed to be at equilibrium most of the time. People who are usually out of equilibrium are stressed and more prone to disease.

Yeahbuts are a problem only when you seek to add new dimensions to your life; to take a giant step. When you intend to create something new in your life, the survival system interprets movement toward that goal—or even serious speculation about going after such a goal—as a threat to the survival of your good old, same old identity and launches a Yeahbut campaign to get you back to good old, same old equilibrium. Since it is just a machine, it doesn't know the difference between survival and personal growth. As soon as you consider committing yourself to improving the quality of your life, your system gets thrown off balance, and the Yeahbuts begin. Most of us have very limited skills in successfully intervening in the automatic, mechanical functioning of this system.

Different people have various degrees of hair trigger. Some people can dream endlessly about possible futures and stay in a state of equilibrium. It is only when they start making commitments or plans that they get attacked. Other people have only to vaguely entertain wisps of thought of something new to trigger a massive attack of the Yeahbuts.

The Yeahbuts are effective in getting you back to equilibrium because they are very persistent. They are not intelligent. They just don't give up until you are back at even keel again. Like a persistent fisherman, the system tries out different lures until it finds one that snags you. Anyone who has ever quit smoking or given up any long-standing habit knows exactly what I mean. At the most vulnerable moment, the little voice says, "Hey, have a puff to remember what it tastes like. It won't hurt. I'm in control. I can stop when I want. After all, I'm out with my buddies. I'm having a beer. I always used to have a cigarette when I had a beer. They go together perfectly. It would taste so good right now. I'll smoke only one." It's a very, very powerful force.

There are endless Yeahbuts that get in the way of choosing and creating the perfect career. Here are a few of my own personal favorites:

- I'm too young, too old, too stupid, too smart.

- I'm the wrong sex, the wrong color.

- I didn't/don't/won't have the right opportunities.

- I have lots of energy and stick to it once I decide. It's just so difficult to sort out what to do. If only I could decide.

- I'm constrained by my circumstances, my mortgage, my bad back, no time. The circumstances are like a vise around me, holding me here. I can't do anything about it.

- I don't have enough willpower. I'm not a risk taker.

- I'm not committed enough. I have this habit of quitting.

- I can't do anything I would really want to do.

- I'm really trying. It's not my fault. Really!

- I don't have enough money. I don't have enough talent.

- I can't do what I want because the fun careers pay less.

- I'm sensitive, an artist. I couldn't possibly have a regular job because I see through the banalities of crass materialism.

- I want to help people, but this is a cruel, heartless world where only the lawyers win.

- It takes putting my nose to the grindstone, year after year, and that's not my style.

- It's hopeless. I have this fatal flaw. It's my karma.

- I'm an immigrant. My English isn't good enough.

- I should have been born in an earlier time.

- I don't have the courage to go out and push and make cold calls and do the things that I need to do to get that kind of job I want.

- I'm over-/under-educated, over-/under-qualified, have too much/too little experience, and all the experience I have is really a detriment because it's in the wrong field.

- I just got out of college. They didn't teach me what Shinola is anyway.

- I went to the wrong college, didn't have enough college, didn't go to college, got a degree in an area that is completely useless in today's marketplace.

- My skills are antiquated, outdated, underrated.

- What makes me think I can decide now, when I have failed to for all these years?

Like all of us, you probably have some others besides these little gems. They are the lyrics to the song the townspeople's chorus sings in the old opera *It's Not Fair*. What kind of an opera is it? Hint: It's something you use in the shower.

Thoughts aren't the only Yeahbuts. Nearly every aspect of our lives involves built-in survival systems seeking equilibrium. Sometimes your emotions are Yeahbuts. The most powerful is fear. Whenever I think of doing something that would stretch me into really unfamiliar territory, something brand new and somehow threatening, up comes fear. At fifteen I sat by the phone (yes, they were connected to the wall back then) trying to get up the courage to ask out a girl who was way above my status in the tribe. I was completely terrified. What if she said no? What if she said something that revealed my lowly status? What if she laughed? Fear is one of the most powerful Yeahbuts. Until recently, life was all about survival. When faced with a saber-toothed tiger, those who tried to pet the nice kitty didn't survive to reproduce. The ones who ran for their life did. As a result, our brains snap into a fear-based mode at the slightest provocation.

> *And in the night imagining some fear,*
> *how easy is a bush supposed a bear.*

> —WILLIAM SHAKESPEARE

The groups we identify with also have a profound effect on what we consider possible. Anything outside the range of "normal" may occur as a Yeahbut. Just like our hunter-gatherer ancestors, we are what zoologists call "tribal primates." In ancient times, each of us belonged to one tribe. Now we belong to and are influenced by the wisdom, values, and rules of multiple tribes. The tribes each of us belongs to include our families, our peer groups, people we consider "like us" in background, our racial and cultural identity, people with similar viewpoints such as political beliefs, the region we identify with, and our national identity. All of these influence how life occurs for us: what we think and believe and how we behave. Each tribe has its own ideas of which careers are acceptable and which aren't, what goals are worthy, and a specific set of tribal taboos: the limits of reasonable behavior, and what the members should and shouldn't do. All tribes have their own fixed beliefs about nearly everything. Think of all the women who had to choose from a limited range of careers—nursing, teaching, or secretarial work—because the culture, and often their families, communicated nothing more than limiting Yeahbuts. Then remember the many pioneering women who did not succumb to their own or the cultural Yeahbuts and created breakthrough lives that brought our culture forward into new territory. As you will see as you read on, there are effective methods for dealing with Yeahbuts, but first, let's take a look at the Yeahbuts that seek to limit you.

INQUIRY 5

Yeahbuts

1. Make a list of the Yeahbuts that have power over you. Get some hints from the list of common Yeahbuts you just read, but do not depend entirely on the list to find your own examples. Look back to times when you had a big decision to make or were considering doing something that was a stretch. What objections did your mind come up with? What did you worry about? Which Yeahbuts hooked you and succeeded in shutting down your dreams and plans?

2. Prioritize this list based on which of these Yeahbuts usually work best to kill off your dreams and plans. Number one on the list should be the one that gets you nearly every time.

3. Now that you have a list of your top Yeahbuts, here's your assignment: Whenever one or more of them arises, separate it out from the herd of thoughts, and brand it as what it really is, a Yeahbut. Whenever you are considering taking a giant step, it is useful to assume that every thought that opposes taking this step is a Yeahbut thrown at you by your internal survival mechanism. Just because it is a Yeahbut doesn't mean it isn't valid. But when you recognize a Yeahbut as a Yeahbut, you can consider it to be a problem to solve rather than getting hooked. Whenever you have an attack of Yeahbuts, now you can choose to see it for what it is instead of getting swept away again and again. By focusing your attention on your thoughts and recognizing when they are automatic survival reactions, your Yeahbuts will have less power over you. Go over this list regularly. Noticing and staying present to your Yeahbuts is like working out: The more you do it, the more strength you build.

After reading these pages, you might be feeling a little uncomfortable. We all want to feel in control of our fate. Now that you understand what we human beings are up against when we seek to grow and expand, you know why you do not get what you want. It is important to recognize that most of the worthwhile accomplishments of our species have occurred in spite of the powerful grip of this survival system. If this system were as omnipotent as it seems, we would all be back in the cave, wishing there was some way to warm up the place. How can you successfully intercede so that you can make your dreams come true? Turn the page. Read the next chapter, "The Power of Commitment." For more on how this survival system works, read the article "Why You Do What You Do" on the Rockport Institute website.

CHAPTER 6

•

THE POWER OF COMMITMENT

Until one is committed, there is hesitancy, the chance to draw back, always ineffectiveness. Concerning all acts of initiative (and creation), there is one elementary truth, the ignorance of which kills countless ideas and splendid plans: that the moment one definitely commits oneself, then Providence moves too. All sorts of things occur to help one that would never otherwise have occurred. A whole stream of events issues from the decision, raising in one's favor all manner of unforeseen incidents and meetings and material assistance, which no man could have dreamt would have come his way. I have learned a deep respect for one of Goethe's couplets:

> *Whatever you can do, or dream you can, begin it.*
> *Boldness has genius, power, and magic in it.*

—W. H. MURRAY

If you really thought about the human dilemma—your human dilemma—as you read the last chapter, it should not now be a mystery why so many good intentions go nowhere and why New Year's resolutions often vanish like dew in the desert. To slip back to the same old behaviors is not a personal problem; it is a universal phenomenon. There is not one single human being walking the earth who does not suffer from a serious case of the Yeahbuts when he or she seeks to expand personal horizons into unknown territory. Most of us carry around the mental baggage of those times when the Yeahbuts frustrated our desire to invent a new future for ourselves and turn it into reality. Some of us have even gone so far as to demonize this aspect of our humanity. Ancient spiritual guidebooks are filled with tales of being tempted by the Yeahbut from hell. It's not a devil whispering in your ear when you hear words like "Maybe I will just have one more piece of chocolate." It's just the ancient voice of your flesh and bones speaking to you, trying to fill you up with sugar so that you will be a little more comfortable and return to equilibrium.

WANTING

COMMITTING

Imagine what it would be like if you could simply choose to pursue a substantial personal goal and were able to go after it without having to do battle with doubts and fears. I'd be willing to bet that the people you most admire throughout the course of human history attained something extraordinary in their lives because they found a way to keep their ambitions on course. They were so dedicated to their intentions that they became essentially an unstoppable force of nature. These folks had the same Yeahbuts you do. If their projects required much bigger steps, they likely had much bigger attacks of Yeahbuts. Countless people never become known for their gifts because a bad case of the Yeahbuts got the best of them. The world is filled with disappointed dreamers.

Yeahbuts are a problem only because they disguise their true identity. They speak in your voice, inside your head, so you think they are thoughts that "you" are actively thinking. If Yeahbuts spoke in the voice of Bugs Bunny, you would know them for what they are rather than accept them as the truth. You would recognize the Bugs voice as a mechanical device playing a prerecorded tape in your head. Similarly, you never think, "I'm doing a really excellent job of keeping my heart beating today." Yet Yeahbuts are just as automatic as your heartbeat, completely beyond your control. They are the output from a stimulus-response mechanism, the voice of Jiminy Lizard.

So if these automatic internal voices run the show when you otherwise might reach for the stars, what can you do to expose their true nature in order to have some say in where and how far your life goes? The first step is learning to distinguish your voice from the voice of the Yeahbuts. To do that, you have to get your own voice speaking loudly, clearly, and in words distinctly your own. One way to do that is to say what you want most and what is most important to you. Put some words out onto the playing field of your mind that are definitely not Yeahbuts. Put your heart into it. This gives you clues to what you're committed to. An example might be "I want to do work that leaves me satisfied at the end of the day." Or, "What's important to me is my family." One thing we know with absolute certainty is that Jiminy L. won't be speaking persuasively for making big commitments or creating new behaviors. That's not his nature. You can also be sure that at some point soon after you declare your intention, Jiminy will chime in, using your voice to engage in some good old back-porch worrying, bitching, and doubting. This is a clue: Very rarely does he say anything supportive. Once you begin to separate your thoughts from the Yeahbuts, you instantly create the possibility of becoming the unstoppable agent of your intentions. Then you can begin a continually expanding practice of steering your own vessel.

Let's look at a case of managing the power of your patterns from the past. Say you're a smoker who would like to give up the noxious weed. You throw away your pack. The next day, while you're sitting around the Long Branch with your buddies, having a few shots of red-eye and a game of Texas Hold 'em, everyone else is smoking. A voice in your head says, "Why not have a smoke? Just one." And down comes the curtain on your attempt to quit.

Now let's take a look at how creating a clear commitment separates your voice from that of Jiminy Lizard. This time you do it differently. When you decide that you want to quit, you know the Yeahbuts will have a field day adding seductive words to the powerful sensations of withdrawal, and your good intentions won't be enough defense. So this time you make a promise to yourself: "I am now and forever a nonsmoker." You establish a connection between that commitment and what is most important to you: "I want my children to be nonsmokers, and I want to live long enough to see them grow up." You do what you need to do to keep this commitment no matter what. You know that when you are most vulnerable, the Yeahbuts will rise up and try to seduce you back to equilibrium. In the heat of an attack, the volume of the Yeahbuts can get so loud that you may not even remember your commitment to quit. You gather your forces and take actions that support your commitment: You notice when the Yeahbuts are strongest and move to counteract them. Since the urge seems strongest during poker games, you start hanging out in places not associated with cigarettes, poker, or booze. You look for other ways to turn down the volume of the Yeahbuts. You even find creative forms of counterattack. For example: You think of the political figure you despise most. You make out a check to his or her reelection committee in an amount that would really hurt (if you are of average means, perhaps several hundred bucks; if you're rich, make it several thousand), and stamp, seal, and address the envelope. Then give it to a friend who is so strong and streetwise that you will not be able to bullshit him or her. Have that person check in with you every day or two for the first month, then once a week, in person if possible, and ask if you have smoked. If there is even a flicker of concealment in your eyes, or if your assistant senses that you are covering guilty tracks, into the mail goes the envelope.

Then if you find yourself in the saloon at the poker table, a few sloshes of red-eye into the wind, and a deluge of Yeahbuts overtakes you ("Yeahbut a cigarette would taste *so* good right now." "Yeahbut I'm not really addicted anymore."), you have backup. As you reach for a light, you have a vision of your envelope with little wings on it, flying away toward your worst political nightmare. In a flash, you awake from the spell and recall your commitment. You remember that Yeahbuts are not your own true voice. You are going to keep your solemn vow. The storm subsides. With nothing but a commitment and a little smart planning, you have reduced it to a tempest in a teapot. A sweet sonata with harpsichords and pedal steel guitars fills the air. You did it! You did it!

Notice that in the stop-smoking story, a trustworthy supporter was enlisted to help keep the promise. Never underestimate the power of a network of support, people who will help you stay in touch with what you are committed to and keep you from starting down the slippery slope of listening too attentively to your Yeahbuts. Alcoholics Anonymous works in part because recovering alcoholics are surrounded by a community of support. When you put your shoulder to the wheel and begin to design a new custom-fit career, you would be wise to, at the very least, surround yourself with people who will encourage you to go for it. The last thing you need is everyone else's Yeahbuts joining yours in a galactic strike force totally dedicated to having your life stay exactly the same forever.

The C-Word

Over the course of our lives, we have added so much baggage to our personal concept of commitment that it has become a rat's nest of unexamined impressions and illusions. If you are anything like me, your own definition of the word includes the notion that making a commitment involves saying you are going to do something you don't really want to do.

What the word actually means is less complicated. It comes from Middle English meaning "to bring together." Its effect is to bind the present and the future. Simply said, a commitment is *a pledge to do something*. In effect, when you make a promise to yourself and perhaps to others, you speak something new into existence. Wanting to be a rock star, go to medical school, or triple the income of your company exists only as wishful thinking. With a definite commitment, however, you put yourself in action on a journey from your speaking it in the present to fulfillment of what you spoke in the future. If you master the art of creating and living from commitments, they can be the most powerful tools in your toolbox. They are the tools to make things happen in your life that would not happen otherwise.

Let's say that you want a large lily pond in your backyard. You know how big you want it and where you want it. It is hot and humid outside, and you must dig it today because this is your only free day for the next six months. You also know yourself all too well. You know that if the soil is rocky or filled with roots, you are likely to get discouraged. You know that as you get tired and sweaty, your mind tends to come up with an increasingly compelling barrage of reasons (Yeahbuts) why the pond should be smaller, shallower, maybe even abandoned altogether. But you truly want a big, glorious pond. To make it happen, you pull out the right tool for the job: the C-word. Remember, a commitment is a pledge to produce a specific result. So, knowing that the pond is likely to shrink the hotter the day gets, you make a commitment in the form of a promise and tie it to something important to you. The more specific the promise you make, the better. You might say something like this: "I will dig the pond and finish it today no matter what difficulties arise. It will be X long by Y wide and Z deep. Having my home be a sanctuary is important to me, and a lily pond will definitely enhance my experience of that." With a stated commitment like that, when you start having thoughts of quitting, you are more likely to be able to contextualize those thoughts as an attack of Yeahbuts rather than the voice of a reasonable, universal truth coming down from on high. (It's also not a bad idea to tell everyone in the neighborhood about your plans so that you're threatened with looking like a jerk if you come up with a pond the size of a pothole.)

With a clear commitment and action consistent with that commitment, something amazing happens: Your commitment transforms your Yeahbuts from an undermining element to a useful one—from Jiminy Lizard whispering in your ear to a to-do list. Let's say that you and I go on a trek. For the sake of adventure, we decide to walk in a perfectly straight line from one side of the country to the other. We meet plenty of obstacles that take ingenuity to surmount but nothing that stirs up serious Yeahbuts. Then we find ourselves in Wyoming looking up at Grand Teton, all 13,766 awesome feet of it. Immediately we each have a massive air raid of Yeahbuts: "I don't know how to do this. I'm not in condition. We don't know what route to follow. We don't have any equipment. We don't have a guide." Without a definite commitment, the Yeahbuts would suck us back to good old, safe old equilibrium. We would think of something we had to do that was much more important than climbing a mountain. Two weeks later we would hardly recall that we had been thinking of making such a heroic climb.

On the other hand, let's say that we are absolutely, definitely committed to our promise to walk the straight line across the country. We are aware that Yeahbuts will arise, and we are prepared for them. As the Yeahbuts arise, we then hear them differently. We hear them rattling off a list of everything we need to do to get over the mountain successfully: "We need to take climbing lessons, work on getting into condition, get a map, buy some equipment, and find a guide."

When the subject of commitment comes up, one or more variations of a very popular Yeahbut often arises for us: "If only I were more committed. Commitment has always been a problem for me. If only I had the self-discipline to follow through on my commitments." Let's take a closer look at this.

What if every moment of our lives expresses one commitment or another? When your car breaks down, you don't just get out, walk away, and buy a new one. You are committed to keeping your car. The fact that many people wear a wristwatch points to a commitment to know the time. You could teach your dog to read the hands of a clock, but it wouldn't mean anything to him, because dogs are not creatures of commitment. When the car breaks down on the way to the veterinarian, your dog does not worry about being late. As far as he is concerned, all that has happened is the parade of wonderful smells has slowed down.

We do not suffer from a shortage of commitments, but what we are committed to does not live up to our dreams. You can easily tell what you are committed to. Just look at your life as it is now. That's exactly what you are committed to. If you are committed to something other than the way it is now, you will be in action consistent with that commitment. You get no points for thinking about it. While this may seem like very bad news, it actually is the best news you could have. There is no mystery, nothing to figure out. You have to know where you are now before you can get somewhere else.

It takes courage to tell the truth about what you are committed to. Most of us are not completely, unshakably committed to having a truly marvelous career or marriage or anything else. For the most part, we are committed to comfort, low risk, and equilibrium. Remember, wanting/wishing and commitment are two completely different domains. Since you are on the path to having a truly excellent career, let's take a closer look at how you can best manage your life so that you wind up getting what you truly want.

Holding to the New Course

Once you set a new course by creating a commitment, the challenge becomes sticking with it. Your homeostasis system has a memory, and it will keep trying to return you to the old setting. The latest studies of habit formation say that you need to hold to the new course for at least three months before the new setting becomes equilibrium—a new habit. Even then, you can't relax completely. You will still have attacks of Yeahbuts from time to time, but they will be of reduced intensity. For example, someone who has stopped smoking will have established a whole new set of habits after three months. Cravings may still occur, but the intensity of the battle with the Yeahbuts will have subsided.

Dancing around what you want to change over a long period of time simply empowers the old pattern. It's hard for the human brain to change an old pattern but relatively easy to create a new one. If you want to create something new in your life, commit yourself to the new behavior you most want, not some halfway measure that has strings of the old behavior attached. Gather your forces and allies to face the onslaught of the Yeahbuts, and go for it. You must be willing to go through whatever arises for the first few months, until the new habit gets established. The Yeahbuts will fire all of their big guns. You may be battered by storms of emotions. Powerful desires to return to your old setting will arise. Jiminy L. will offer extremely persuasive sales pitches, spoken convincingly in your own voice. The world around you will continue to argue for the old setting. Eventually the universe will turn in your favor and completely support your intentions. If you are not practiced in dancing a jig with the physical universe, it might be slow to respond. Sometimes it turns slowly, like a supertanker, but if you keep holding the wheel firmly, it will eventually come around.

The secret of creating anything new in your life consists of creating new commitments, getting support, and then holding the tiller to your new course until it becomes established as a behavior. This works equally well whether you want to create a new career that truly fits and expresses you or be more effective in some other area of life.

How to Win the Battle of the Yeahbuts

The Yeahbuts are a normal part of your survival system. They are merely doing their job keeping you on the path to continued survival. They have a long and successful track record of running people's lives over many thousands of years. If you want to make your own choices and have more say over how and where your life goes, you will have to deal with your Yeahbuts.

The first step is being willing to notice and then declare that the voices telling you to avoid stretching into the unknown are Yeahbuts and not thoughts that you have created intentionally. The next step is to practice listening to the Yeahbuts rattle on without being compelled to obey them. When you can reliably distinguish them from other thoughts, they lose much of their power over you.

Even when you have learned to reinterpret some of your thoughts as Yeahbuts, you will still forget when the going gets rough. These Yeahbuts are so compelling, so convincing, that you will get lost in them again and again. You need to have something that whacks you upside the head and reminds you to wake up and have more of a say in your life. Once again, that tool is the C-word. By making your commitments clear, writing them down, choosing appropriate action, and having a network of people you can trust to remind you, you can learn to go your own way.

Friends

When you transform your life from "I am my psychology, feelings, and interpretations" to "I am my commitments," you may discover that some of your closest friends speak with the voice of your Yeahbuts. Relationships, established groups, and organizations have survival systems that are just as entrenched as those of individuals. Almost everything is tuned to keeping the status quo shuffling along. When your life really takes off, some of your friends are very likely to perceive this as a threat because you, not they, are stepping out into a new future. They will cajole you to keep within conventional bounds, to be reasonable, to do the "right" thing.

To me, real friends are those people who will stand for you expressing yourself fully, who will go out of their way to support you to keep your word, to go the extra mile, to get out of the box, to make your dreams come true. The only people who will do that are those who are doing it themselves. Everyone else will be dancing to the tune of his or her Yeahbuts. Keep them as buddies, but do not ask them to do for you what they will not do for themselves. Nothing is more powerful than a great network of support. In fact, you will not be able to break out of the grip of automatic living without the help of other people. Find new friends who are also willing to stand out in the wild winds with you. Create a group of friends dedicated to supporting one another to make the entire group's dreams come true. Train yourselves to speak for your friends' commitments rather than from some reheated conventional wisdom.

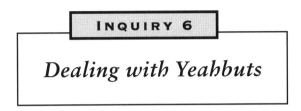

INQUIRY 6

Dealing with Yeahbuts

The two main techniques for dealing with Yeahbuts are ones we have already spoken about: creating commitments and developing a network of people who support you to follow through. Here are some other methods.

You can add strength to your commitments by visualizing yourself in the midst of whatever outcome the commitment is intended to produce. If your goal is to begin a circumnavigation of the globe in your sailboat in two years, actually picture yourself doing it. Make it as real and as satisfying as you can. Hear the sounds, feel the rocking of the waves. Taste the salt spray. See what you would see: the sails, your hands stretched out in front of you on the wheel, bright light leaking in around the outside of your sunglasses. Feel how you would feel. Have a conversation with your first mate. See if you can make it almost as real as actually doing it. Revisit this visualization often, particularly if you are having kamikaze Yeahbut raids. If your goal is merely an abstraction or some words on a page, it becomes easy prey for the Yeahbuts. The more real you make your goal, the more insubstantial the Yeahbuts will seem.

The following methods focus on disarming the power the Yeahbuts have over you. They lose power when you know them for what they are: tapes being played by an automatic system. Everything you can do to reveal them as something other than your own proactively generated thoughts helps to break their spell. Whatever you do to deal with them, make it enjoyable. Have fun. Lighten up. When you can laugh at ghosts, they disappear. Pick methods that fit your personality. Here are some things you can do:

- Make a list of them. Don't bother with the little ones. Concentrate on the big guns, the ones that could shoot your dreams out of the sky. Carry the list around with you like you would carry the bird-identification field book with you on a birding excursion. Give them numbers or short names. When you have an attack, identify them by number. "Here comes old number 9." "Just as I expected, a Willie and a Pete arriving together."

- Allow them to come into your mind unopposed. Do not fight or resist Yeahbuts. Let them be there, but don't dress them up and take them to the show. Fighting them or entertaining them makes them important.

- Learn mindfulness meditation, the most direct way of noticing that your thoughts just happen on their own, and that you have very little to do with what you think most of the time. When someone has actually experienced this, it is much easier to recognize that your Yeahbuts are completely automatic.

- Make displays that keep you present. A display is a sign or other graphic that reminds you of what you said you were going to do. I always have a large sign on the ceiling right above the office sofa where I relax. Every time I lean back, there is a reminder of that challenging project I said I was going to do. Put displays where you can't avoid seeing them: your medicine cabinet, your screen saver, above your bed. Once you stop noticing it, move it. Collages make great reminders. So does a friend's call to ask how it's going.

- Study them from a distance. Become a Yeahbut scholar. Treat them like bugs stuck on a pin.

- Pretend they are a voice coming over the radio rather than from inside your head. Think them in the voice of a cartoon character instead of your own voice. Imagine what it would be like if your most persistent Yeahbuts occurred in SpongeBob's or Bugs Bunny's voice.

- Convert them to allies. Turn them into a to-do list. When you have an attack of Yeahbuts, write them down on a page of your notebook titled "Yeahbuts Converted to To-Dos." Then speculate on strategies to resolve them. Thank them for their good advice.

If none of the above works, you need to find a coach who is a master at dealing with Yeahbuts—or at least enlist someone you can trust completely to stand with you, to keep you awake to your commitments.

Questions About Commitments

How do I get rid of the Yeahbuts? Perhaps a lobotomy might work.
What if I have trouble keeping the commitments I make? No problem. We all

do. Once you accept that you are dealing with a universal phenomenon, you can quit feeling like there is something wrong with you and get to work learning to master the art of making big promises and fulfilling them. Learning to keep your word when you make outrageous promises requires making a regular practice of doing this, like brushing your teeth or working out. Start small with little promises that stretch you. Avoid taking on massive stretches at first. As you would when working out, start small and build capacity through practice. You can do it. Sure, you will fail sometimes. Your mind will fall asleep now and then to what you are committed to. That's okay. Stopping is the only way to fail permanently. So keep picking yourself up and putting yourself back on the path.

How do I deal with the discomfort, uncertainty, and fear I experience when I am out of my comfort zone? When you create and live from big, outrageous commitments, these experiences are natural and inevitable. They are part of the survival system's warning siren to let you know that you are out of equilibrium. They sound for both real and imagined threats to your survival. The system doesn't know the difference, just like the warning buzzer in your car that tells you to put on your seat belt: It doesn't know whether you're about to drive or are just turning on the engine to listen to the radio. All you can do is recognize that Yeahbuts are inevitable and stop trying to make them go away. Feel the fear and go forward.

CHAPTER 7

•

MAKING DECISIONS—
A SHORT COURSE

We are educated in a system where we are taught the importance of memorizing the date of the Battle of Hastings but nothing about many things that really matter, like: how to think for yourself, how to make decisions, how to change a tire. In the course of this book, you examine all the domains of your life. You may gain new skills and discover potent untapped resources. More than anything else, you make choices—choices that alter the course of your life. One decision can give you a life that sings. Another may turn out to be a mistake that haunts you to the end of your days. Since the quality of your life depends on the choices you make, it follows that one of the most potent skills a person can possess is masterful decision making.

Each person comes up with his or her own homegrown style of reaching resolution. We absorb various methods that seem to work for us during our youth. Then, unconsciously, we entrust the big decisions we make throughout the rest of our lives to these methods and never think about them again. It never occurs to most of us to question the effectiveness of our way of reaching decisions. And rarely do people consciously decide how they will go about making decisions. You might ask yourself, "How well do my techniques work? Am I sure that the ways I arrive at conclusions are the most resourceful? Are they completely trustworthy to ensure that I create the quality of life I want?"

Everyone makes thousands of decisions each day: whether to get out of bed, whether to make the bed, shower, wear the blue shirt or the white shirt, finish the work you brought home or not, give the cat liver or chicken, and so forth. Mostly decisions are made by our internal decision-making software, without any conscious process. The first decision of the day, to get out of bed or not, is probably made by habitual compliance with the circumstances of your life. If you roll over and go back to the Land of Nod, there will be consequences. If you do it too often, you won't have a bed to roll over in. So it seems there is no choice. To make the bed or not is the next challenge. This decision may come from a deep wellspring of personal philosophy, such as "I'll just mess it up again tonight, so why bother?" Or "All good people make their beds." Again, we don't have to puzzle over this one. Our standard modus operandi for dealing with bed making takes over and does the deciding. We never have to stand naked in the face of existential choice. To make or not to make is rarely a matter of free choice.

There's nothing wrong with this. The more we can consign routine decisions to automatic processes, the more time we have to deal with other things. But, in fact, ancient habit-forming software turns everything routine into a habit, and that includes how we make decisions. Habits are 100 percent automatic machinery at work. They are the perfect solution for dealing with routine, but you don't want a machine choosing your career.

Let's take a look at how people decide and how you decide. Let's see if your traditional methods are the best tools for the job, and, if not, you can switch to something that works better.

Some people always favor one method. Others go through a process that combines methods. For example, some folks may rigorously plot out and analyze every aspect of the available options and then give over the final decision to their feelings. Other people use different methods for different situations. Here are some of the most common methods we trust to do the decision making for us.

Logic, analysis, common sense. The thinking man's approach. People who use this method describe this approach as rational, sensible, prudent, moderate, and balanced. They list the pros and cons of the careers they are considering, assign numerical values to them, add up the scores, and—presto!—the career with the best pro-to-con ratio wins. We can't really say that they made the decision, however. They gave over the authority to decide to a set of rules. Nothing wrong with that except that you are reading this book because *you* want to decide what to do with your life.

Feelings, inclinations, passions. Feelings are the spice in the dance of life, the soul of the arts, and one of the most delightful things about living in this corner of the universe. People who use feelings to decide say they rely on intuition or "go with the gut." Nothing wrong with that, but, again, *we* aren't deciding; our feelings are. Feelings are like weather. They come and go. You may not always cry at the funeral or laugh at the punch line.

We may control how much we reveal our feelings to others, but the feelings themselves have lives of their own. We don't control them any more than we control the rain. Let them be the spice, not the recipe.

Romantic yearnings. People imagine themselves in careers and then fall in love with the image they created. (We sometimes do this with that seemingly magic someone as well.) We float on a cloud of sweet dreams, envisioning ourselves in the midst of a glorious future. We think people who try to talk some sense into us are trying to burst our bubble. (They are.) One of the reasons the divorce rate is so high is that people marry a fantasy rather than a real person. The person or the career they imagine exists only in their head. They forget that working at the job, on the other hand, takes place on the ground.

Resonance. "I know it's right if it resonates with me" used to be called "going with your gut feeling," instinct, or intuition in pre–New Age times. I have asked many people exactly what they mean by "resonance." The first person I asked was a physicist. He said resonance is the increase in amplitude of oscillation of a system exposed to a periodic force whose frequency is very close to the natural frequency of the system. That's when I swore off going to physicists for advice. Everyone has an individual interpretation. Sometimes people say that resonance is a warm glow that spreads out from their left gazorch; sometimes a feeling like a soft wind blowing through their head; sometimes a voice that says, "This is right." Nearly everyone reports that when he experiences resonance, he is mindful and aware, peaceful and relaxed. If you are on the verge of choosing a career that calls you out into new and unknown territory, that asks you for all you have to give, you are more likely to feel like you are standing by the door of the plane about to make your first parachute jump.

External sources. The media, experts, parents, spouses, friends, magazines, career counselors, common sense, and horoscopes. It's amazing how many people follow the recommendations of others to make the most important decisions of their lives. Whatever you do, don't become a doctor because it would make your mom happy. She will not have to get up every morning and go to work with you. No one can possibly know you as well as you can. No one will ever care as much as you do how well your life works.

External sources are fabulous research tools, but please don't abandon the helm of your ship to them. Magazines often publish articles with titles like "The Fifteen Super-Growth Careers of the Coming Decade." That would be great information if the magazines were always right and if you're committed to being in a super-growth area. Nevertheless, the fact that a certain career is favorably mentioned in the media gives it a special, glossy appeal. So does the word of an expert. As Zen master Suzuki Roshi said, "In the beginner's mind, there are many possibilities, but in the expert's mind, there are few." Or, as they used to say back in Maine, "An expert? Why, that's just a damn fool far from home." So, figure out what is most important to you first. Then use the media, your mother, and the experts to research which careers match your commitments.

Reaction, rebellion, compliance. Doing the opposite of what you don't like about what you are doing now, doing the opposite of what you are told or expected to do, or going along with what "they" want you to do all turn you into a puppet. For many career changers, doing the opposite of what is wrong with the current job becomes the most important criterion for something new. Rebellion and compliance are two sides of the same coin. These are all reactions to the external. You as the decision maker are nowhere in sight.

Random. Just let it unfold, go with the flow, take the promotion you are offered, roll the dice, choose the major with the shortest registration line, look in the want ads, and select a career because you think they might offer you the job. If this method had a sound, it would be "Oh, well." This method implies that it doesn't matter, and maybe you don't matter either. If it looks like you are "letting the universe choose," take another look: You may see deep resignation.

Shoulds and Yeahbuts. People are often propelled into doing all sorts of things they don't really want to do because of the little voice in their head that tells them what they should do and shouldn't do. One of the noisiest in the chorus of voices that natter and chatter away inside each person's head is the one that constantly compares you (and everyone else) to a fixed set of standards and ideals. This voice rates the people we meet (and ourselves) by attractiveness, intelligence, class, erotic potential, ability, degree of fit into our social order, and a long list of other criteria. If it were played aloud over the intercom at work, this voice would probably get you fired. When you are thinking about possible careers, it babbles and gabbles away, letting you know, in no uncertain terms, exactly what's wrong with you or whatever you are considering. Since it is mechanistic (you know that because you can't stop it), it has no creative imagination or enthusiasm for possibilities outside the data it has gleaned from your past. The Shoulds operate very much like Yeahbuts, and they both cloud the decision-making process.

There is absolutely nothing wrong with using all or any of the above methods to make decisions. Humans have used them successfully for many thousands of years. Our civilization is the result. There are, however, two flies in the soup. When we allow any of these methods to run the show, we abdicate the captain's chair to the rule of the technique. The counselor becomes king. If we allow the method to do the choosing, we become its slave: a slave to feelings. A slave to other people's opinions. A slave to practicality. And so forth.

The second problem with relying on these methods is that you may have trouble reaching a final decision. Many people never quite get to the finish line. They reach the point where they know what their usual method says they should do, but they are not 100 percent sold on the idea. Life creeps on at its petty pace, but somehow they never quite get to the point of committing themselves and moving forward. Other people may just give themselves up to the decision the method made for them ("Well, I guess this must be the best thing to do"), but they move ahead with reluctance.

They're right to feel that they haven't really quite decided: They haven't. Their ambivalence leads to an uncertain commitment, which then results in restrained or unfocused action. There is an old story of a samurai leader who was taking one hundred warriors into battle. He lined them up. He asked all the men ready to die for him to step forward. Sixty of them stepped forward. He then had them behead the forty who hesitated. He knew that he was better off going into battle with sixty totally committed samurai than with a larger but flakier force. Personally, I think he may have overreacted slightly. I would have had the forty flakies go buy the pizza. But, other than the beheading part, this story contains some very good advice for all of us. To have your dreams come true, make sure that you are 100 percent behind the decisions you make. The best way to get 100 percent behind your decisions is to make them yourself by exercising free choice.

Free Choice

Recently we visited a couple, former neighbors who had taken the leap and moved to the beautiful but remote eastern shore of the Chesapeake Bay. Every window of their new home commanded smashing views of the bay. The place was absolutely magical. They had given up many conveniences to make this move. Now the trip to work was a very long commute. Their kids could no longer attend their former excellent high school. Looking through a scrapbook of their move, I came across a long pros-and-cons list. I laughed to myself because this was so like them. These people are logical and analytical with a capital *L* and *A*. Looking more closely, I noticed that the pros list for making the move was short and the cons list almost endless. At dinner, I asked how they had decided to make their adventurous move. They said that after making their pros-and-cons list, they both had felt disappointed with the outcome. They realized that logic pointed one way, feelings another. But for this very important decision, they wanted to do the pointing themselves rather than leave it to either automatic process. They began to inquire into one of the more profound questions a person can ask: Is it possible to make a free choice, and, if so, how?

They wondered if free choice could be as simple as just pointing to one of the options and saying, "I'll have that one." After some discussion, they recognized that doing it that way would be more like pin the tail on the donkey than free choice. As they looked deeper into the puzzle, they discovered a secret that I'll reveal in the following inquiry. At first, you might not like it very much. It is too simple.

Let's start by taking a look at what we mean by free choice. One possible definition of free choice is "to select freely without being ruled by conditioned thinking." Another is "to select freely, after thoughtful deliberation."

The first definition, "to select freely without being ruled by conditioned thinking," expresses the intention to find a pathway through all the opinions, rules, apparent limitations, and considerations that usually blind people to seeing beyond their own noses. If we want to make our own selections from the menu of life, without being ruled by the preexisting programming, we must learn some new skills.

INQUIRY 7

Practicing Free Choice

1. Pay attention to how you make decisions now. The first step in learning
    to exercise free choice is to become acutely aware of exactly how you
    make decisions now. You need to witness yourself in action, sitting right
    on the handlebars of reality as it hits the curves at a hundred miles an
    hour. A little bit of direct observation of how you make decisions now
    is a prerequisite for free choice because, otherwise, the way you usually
    make decisions will continue to operate automatically, like a monkey on
    your back. With a little observation, you can get the monkey around to
    the front, where you can keep your eye on the little rascal. It has then lost
    some of its power to control you. You will notice when it grabs the steer-
    ing wheel.

    Begin to pay attention to what actually happens when you make a
    decision. Write down three important decisions you have made over the
    last few years.

    Now write down three less important decisions you have made in the
    last few months. Start with the first of the six decisions you have written
    down. Close your eyes and go through the process of making the decision
    as if you are watching a movie from beginning to end. What did you do
    first? Then what came next? What occurred after that? What part did
    the following common decision-making methods play: logic, analysis,
    common sense, feelings, romantic yearnings, external sources, reaction,
    rebellion, compliance, random, Shoulds, and Yeahbuts? Did you start
    out with one or more methods and then switch to another one later? Did
    you trust one method above all others? Did you use some combination of
    methods? Actually follow the process through to the end.

    Ask yourself how the process worked for that first decision: "I started
    by having romantic yearnings, then did research, analysis, and talked
    with other people, and then made the final decision by going with my
    strong desire for one of the options."

    Go through the same process for each of the other decisions. When
    you finish, you should have a clear idea of how you make decisions.

    The next question is How well does this method or methods work
    for you? Do you get what you want? How well do the decisions hold up

over time? Do you feel that you made the right decision every time? If not, where did your methods fail you? Do you experience having made the decision yourself, or does it seem as if the methods made it for you? If you switched to another method, could the outcomes be improved? If you think it might be useful to expand your decision-making skills, please consider the following method. If not, go on to another chapter.

2. Learn all you can about the matter in question. The secret of free choice is revealed in the second definition: "to select freely, after thoughtful deliberation." Let's take these steps one at a time. First, let's deal with the "thoughtful deliberation" part. Later we'll get to selecting freely.

It would be sheer insanity to attempt to make important decisions without knowing everything you can about the matter in question. The more you know, the better off you will be. Thoughtful deliberation involves rigorous research, discussion, study, reflection, meditation, speculation, calculation, and education. This may seem obvious, but, since some people spend more time and effort in researching what car to buy than in choosing what to do with their lives, it seems a point worth repeating.

What do you look into and thoughtfully deliberate? Everything that might be important! Fortunately, you already have a full set of powerful research tools at your disposal. The conventional decision-making methods we discussed a few paragraphs ago make the ideal set of research tools. Using them as telescopes and microscopes is completely different from relying on them to make the decision for you. As research tools, they provide you with everything you need to know: access to all the diverse aspects of your personality as well as practical information about the external world. You don't need to be told to use your habitual methods and techniques. That will happen all by itself. Intentionally use the ones you usually do not use. If you normally lay out reasons on a spreadsheet, delve more deeply into your feelings. If you tend to go with your feelings, take an in-depth look at the practical and analytical side. If you usually look to the outside world for answers, make sure to listen for the soft internal voices that say "What if . . . ?" and "I wonder . . ." Explore all of it thoroughly. Look at your potential choices from as many perspectives and directions as you can. Here's how you can use as allies some of the methods that usually dominate the decision-making process, to ensure that you make the best choices.

• Logic, analysis, common sense. Read everything appropriate. Find out all you can. Become an expert on the subject. Read a year or two of recent issues of the trade magazines in whatever fields you are considering. Read books. Make a list of all the important questions you need to answer in order to know enough to decide. Make pros-and-cons lists. Do some in-depth career testing to evaluate your talents and personality.

- Feelings, inclinations, preferences, "the gut." Your internal resources provide some of the most important clues. If you know these methods well, you have your own rituals to process them. If they are less familiar to you, use the inquiries in *The Pathfinder* to dig deeply into these areas.

- Resonance. Look within to check out whether you and your potential choices are on the same or a complementary wavelength. What "vibes" do you pick up? Are you called toward a future that is compelling? Sometimes resonance is misleading. If you are thinking of something that is a huge stretch for you, you may simply feel terrified. This is often a good sign that you are on the right track. Check beneath emotions for resonance. Feelings and resonance are two separate domains.

- Romantic yearnings. An overwhelming passion for something can distort your view of it. If you are the sort of person who regularly falls in love with exciting new possibilities, put on your mental sunglasses to avoid being blinded by the sparkle. If, on the other hand, you harbor a consistent, long-term passion for something, you may want to consider it a powerful clue. But remember, just because you have a passionate interest in snakes doesn't mean that you have to be a charmer. Also, it might be very different to do something all day, every day, than to dream about it or have it as a hobby. In Maine, there are few lobstermen who enjoy eating lobster. And those of you who rarely have romantic yearnings? Don't worry about it.

- External sources. Ask everybody who knows anything about the careers you are considering—especially practitioners of those careers. Read and listen to what the experts have to say. Talk with some of them to form your own opinion. Ask your friends and family. Don't rely solely on computer or print sources. Talk to real people.

- Reaction, rebellion, compliance. Strong negative feelings and reactions are powerful resources. It's a lot easier to find out how people really feel about things by asking what they don't like than it is to ask them what they do like. People are always crystal clear about what they don't like. Career counselors constantly hear new clients say, "I don't know what I want, but I know what I don't want." If you have a rebellious streak, turn it into an ally. Many of the great leaps in human evolution, art, and business were created by rebels with a cause. If you have a compliant streak, make sure to notice whether it pulls you in a particular direction. Is it fine with you if it makes your choices for you?

- Random. There can be a certain magic to randomness. Don't consider it to be worthless as a resource. Sometimes what appears to be random may not be quite as it seems. How can you use randomness in your quest? Sorry, there are no rules for it; that's why it's called random. Just remember to consider the events and happenings that *seem* random as important parts of the puzzle. Don't dismiss anything too fast because you can't explain it or because it looks like coincidence.

- Shoulds and Yeahbuts. The voices in your head that constantly throw up opposition to new possibilities and compare everything in your corner of the universe with your standards and ideals are great sources of raw data. If you are clear that you do not *have* to do what the Shoulds and Yeahbuts say, then you can enlist these noisy voices as allies. They will, at the very least, come up with everything that might be wrong with whatever you are considering. Sometimes they offer practical, down-to-earth viewpoints that are invaluable. To make choices free from the domination of Shoulds and Yeahbuts, you need to be very clear about what they are: one way of looking at something, not the whole picture.

3. Make a choice. After you have looked from every possible viewpoint at what you are trying to decide, you arrive at a cliff, the moment of choice. You can leap courageously into the unknown or turn around, go back home, put your feet up, and take a nap. Okay, here's the part where you discover the secret to choosing freely. A dramatic drum roll please, maestro! You lay all the possible choices out before you. If you are deciding whether to buy the tie with the big pink palm tree or the one with hundreds of mating rabbits on 3-D velvet, you can do this physically. For choices with less physical substance, such as which career to pick, it helps to write down the different choices on a piece of paper. This is the part you have been waiting for, so get ready.

   Now point to one of them and say, "I pick that one." That's all there is to it. I've done this with enough people that I can hear the long, stunned silence. Then the muttering begins. Remember, back there a few pages ago, I told you that you might not like this part at first? But, you say, what is this choice based on? Nothing, absolutely nothing, zilch, nada. That's why it is free choice. If it were based on something, it wouldn't be free choice; it would be based on whatever is making the decision for you. It's true that we are a bit attached to having our choice based on something. After all, we want to be able to justify it to someone, as if our being The Ones Who Get to Say is not enough. You don't have to justify anything. After all that work, you know your free choice is not at all random. You have done extensive research. You have become intimately familiar with everything that relates, in any way, to the matter. You have explored your internal universe. You have talked with other people. You have become fully aware of your talents, tendencies, and leanings. You know what is important to you. Now that you have accomplished all that, you are in a perfect position to actually make the choice yourself—a free choice illuminated by your thoughtful deliberation into everything important, but not weighed down by it.

Please don't jump to conclusions about this. Think about it for a while. Give it a chance to sink in. This whole concept seems so radical that many people can't get their minds around it right away. And please remember that we humans are generally much more suspicious of things that seem too simple than of things that seem too complicated.

Remember the definition of free choice: to select freely, after thoughtful deliberation. How else are you going to select freely other than to simply say, "I choose that one," after complete and thoughtful deliberation? If you figure out some better way, please let me know.

I didn't say that exercising free choice should necessarily be the way to decide everything from now on. You may, like me, prefer to decide which movie to go to based on sheer, primitive, drum-pounding emotion, unclouded by rational thought. For really important decisions, though, like what to do with your life, or whom to marry, free choice after extensive research is a methodology that puts you in the driver's seat.

4. Make some small choices to practice and get the hang of it. Start off with something really small. Use free choice to decide what you will do next Friday night. First of all, notice how you usually decide what to do on Friday nights. Do you have something you do out of habit? Do you use some method to pick among a range of only three or four habitual options? Do you wait for a friend to call and suggest something? Do you decide based on horniness or guilt or practicality? Notice if you get

railroaded into the decision by habits, desires, or other people. You want to build your deciding muscles with practice on this small scale so that you're ready for a big decision such as what to do with the rest of your life. This process may make Friday night more exciting than usual. Really dig into it and use your conventional decision-making methods as tools to look into every corner of the issue at hand. Write down the possible choices on a piece of paper. Then pick one of them. Yes, just pick one. Then go and do it. It may feel strange at first, like appearing onstage at Carnegie Hall dressed as the tooth fairy. But you will get over it. Before long, you will relish having the ability and the skill to make your own decisions. Mastering the art of free choice turns you into a dangerous character. You will find that you are not wimping out in situations you might have previously. You may surprise your friends. In medieval Japan, the samurai who were Zen adepts were the most dangerous foes. They were completely unpredictable because they chose freely, in the moment, rather than relying on habitual patterns of behavior that their enemies could anticipate and exploit.

Keep practicing. Keep raising the stakes by using the method in bigger and bigger decisions.

5. Look back over this inquiry for clues. Add whatever you find to your Clues list. If there is anything you are willing to choose as a definite career component, add it to your Definite Career Design Components. If any new career or job comes to mind, add it to your Career Ideas. Ask yourself why that career appeals to you, and see if that suggests more clues. If you now know that a career on your Career Ideas list does not fit, remove it. See if that suggests any clues. Remember to keep recording and working with your clues, moving them toward definite career components.

•

CHAPTER 8

GOALS AND PROJECTS

In the long run, you only hit what you aim at. Therefore, though you should fail immediately, you had better aim at something high.

—HENRY DAVID THOREAU

A Future of Limitless Possibilities

When you ask the question "What are my options?" you automatically limit your-self to existing choices, choices that *are part of what conventional wisdom says is likely.* (You can think of conventional wisdom as what people have said so often that it seems true; it is so accepted that no one even has to say it anymore.) Options are what come immediately to mind as an automatic part of our thinking. Ask what options kids in bad neighborhoods have, and we think: "They can join a gang, hide indoors, or maybe learn to box."

At Rockport, we are less interested in options, however, than in possibilities, looking beyond the limitations of the obvious. As soon as you ask, "What is pos-sible?" you open up a world that never existed before. Goals provide keys to that world.

Many years ago, a fifteen-year-old boy named John Goddard sat down at his kitchen table and wrote out a list of 127 life goals he called "My Life List." Since then, he expanded his list to 600 goals, with more than 500 of them accomplished, including a recent rounding of Cape Horn. I consider my friend John to be the world's premier goal setter. The list gives only a surface glimpse of John's life, how-ever.

All goals checked off on John's list represented powerful learning experiences for him, many of them extraordinary adventures. For example, goal number one was to explore the Nile. And when John said explore the Nile, he didn't mean cruise a cou-ple of miles along the bank. He organized the first expedition to explore every inch of the Nile from source to mouth, all by kayak.

When I asked him recently to reveal the secret of his ability to create and fulfill so many amazing goals, he said to tell you first that he is in no way an extraordinary person. He says he is just like you and me. What he does is very simple. He writes down what he most wants to do. Then he commits to doing it. It becomes a goal, then a project to plan, with actions to take. Then it becomes an adventure to live. The point is not to become a goal setter but to live an extraordinary life. Clear goals are the path to that kind of life.

Making big, unreasonable promises to yourself, as John Goddard did, stretches you out into new territory and becomes a force for extraordinary results.

I once saw a TV news feature story about two professional golfers. They were the same age, looked alike, had gone to PGA school together, were best friends, and each had 2.2 children, cute blond wives, and the same stroke average. Two people could not be more alike unless they were twins. One of them had won several major tournaments that year and was raking in huge sums of money. The other was working as a golf pro at a country club and had never won anything, even though he had participated in tournaments. The point of the story was supposed to be something about the fickle finger of fate. But as they were interviewed, it became evident that there was one big difference between the two golfers. The winning golfer, when asked about his future goals, said his goal was to be the best and most successful golfer in the world. The other fellow said that his goal was to keep making a living playing golf. One had created an extraordinary vision for the future and was going for it 200 percent. The other was happy to putt around in the comfort zone.

Having bigger goals does not make you a better person. You may be happy in your comfort zone. You may want to have a pleasant career, kids, retire to Florida, and watch TV until one day you don't wake up. If so, I suggest that you really swing out and set some goals about the kind of parent you will be, when you will move to Florida, and so forth. Whatever you want, your having clarity and certainty about your goals makes it much more likely that you will achieve them. Here is John Goddard's original list, with check marks showing which goals he has accomplished so far. (As I'm writing this, John is in his eighties.)

Explore:

√ 1. Nile River
√ 2. Amazon River
√ 3. Congo River
√ 4 Colorado River
   5. Yangtze River, China
   6. Niger River
   7. Orinoco River, Venezuela
√ 8. Rio Coco, Nicaragua

Study Primitive Culture In:

√   9. The Congo
√ 10. New Guinea
√ 11. Brazil
√ 12. Borneo
√ 13. The Sudan
√ 14. Australia
√ 15. Kenya
√ 16. The Philippines
√ 17. Tanganyika
√ 18. Ethiopia
√ 19. Nigeria
√ 20. Alaska

Climb:

   21. Mount Everest
   22. Mount Aconcagua
   23. Mount McKinley
√ 24. Mount Huascaran
√ 25. Mount Kilimanjaro
√ 26. Mount Ararat
√ 27. Mount Kenya
   28. Mount Cook
√ 29. Mount Popocatepetl
√ 30. The Matterhorn
√ 31. Mount Rainier
√ 32. Mount Fuji
√ 33. Mount Vesuvius
√ 34. Mount Bromo
√ 35. Grand Tetons
√ 36. Mount Baldy
√ 37. Carry out careers in medicine and exploration
   38. Visit every country in the world (30 to go)
√ 39. Study Navajo and Hopi Indians
√ 40. Learn to fly a plane
√ 41. Ride horse in Rose Parade

Photograph:

      42. Iguaçú Falls, Brazil
√ 43. Victoria Falls, Rhodesia
√ 44. Sutherland Falls, New Zealand
√ 45. Yosemite Falls
√ 46. Niagara Falls
√ 47. Retrace travels of Marco Polo and Alexander the Great

Explore Underwater:

√ 48. Coral reefs of Florida
√ 49. Great Barrier Reef, Australia
√ 50. Red Sea
√ 51. Fiji Islands
√ 52. The Bahamas
√ 53. Explore Okefenokee Swamp and the Everglades

Visit:

      54. North and South Poles
√ 55. Great Wall of China
√ 56. Panama and Suez Canals
√ 57. Easter Island
√ 58. The Galápagos Islands
√ 59. Vatican City
√ 60. The Taj Mahal
√ 61. The Eiffel Tower
√ 62. The Blue Grotto
√ 63. The Tower of London
√ 64. The Leaning Tower of Pisa
√ 65. The Sacred Well of Chichén Itzá, Mexico
√ 66. Climb Ayers Rock in Australia
      67. Follow River Jordan from Sea of Galilee to Dead Sea

Swim In:

√ 68. Lake Victoria
√ 69. Lake Superior
√ 70. Lake Tanganyika
√ 71. Lake Titicaca, South America
√ 72. Lake Nicaragua

Accomplish:

√   73. Become an Eagle Scout
√   74. Dive in a submarine
√   75. Land on and take off from an aircraft carrier
√   76. Fly in a blimp, a hot air balloon, and a glider
√   77. Ride an elephant, camel, ostrich, and bronco
√   78. Skin-dive to forty feet and hold breath for two and a half minutes
√   79. Catch a ten-pound lobster and ten-inch abalone
√   80. Play flute and violin
√   81. Type fifty words a minute
√   82. Take a parachute jump
√   83. Learn water and snow skiing
√   84. Go on a church mission
√   85. Follow the John Muir Trail
√   86. Study native medicines and bring back useful ones
√   87. Bag camera trophies of elephant, lion, rhino, cheetah, cape buffalo, and whale
√   88. Learn to fence
√   89. Learn jujitsu
√   90. Teach a college course
√   91. Watch a cremation ceremony in Bali
√   92. Explore depths of the sea
     93. Appear in a Tarzan movie
     94. Own a horse, chimpanzee, cheetah, ocelot, and coyote (has owned a horse, ocelot, and coyote so far)
     95. Become a ham radio operator
√   96. Build own telescope
√   97. Write a book
√   98. Publish an article in *National Geographic* magazine
√   99. High-jump five feet
√ 100. Broad jump fifteen feet
√ 101. Run a mile in five minutes
√ 102. Weigh 175 pounds stripped
√ 103. Perform two hundred sit-ups and twenty pull-ups
√ 104. Learn French, Spanish, and Arabic
    105. Study dragon lizards on Komodo Island
√ 106. Visit birthplace of Grandfather Sorenson in Denmark
√ 107. Visit birthplace of Grandfather Goddard in England
√ 108. Ship aboard a freighter as a seaman
    109. Read the entire *Encyclopaedia Britannica*
√ 110. Read the Bible from cover to cover

√ 111. Read the works of Shakespeare, Plato, Aristotle, Dickens, Thoreau, Poe, Rousseau, Bacon, Hemingway, Twain, Burroughs, Conrad, Talmage, Tolstoi, Longfellow, Keats, Whittier, and Emerson

√ 112. Become familiar with the compositions of Bach, Beethoven, Debussy, Ibert, Mendelssohn, Lalo, Rimski-Korsakov, Respighi, Liszt, Rachmaninoff, Stravinsky, Toch, Tchaikovsky, and Verdi

√ 113. Become proficient in the use of a plane, motorcycle, tractor, surfboard, rifle, pistol, canoe, microscope, football, basketball, bow and arrow, lariat, and boomerang

√ 114. Compose music

√ 115. Play "Clair de Lune" on the piano

√ 116. Watch fire-walking ceremony

√ 117. Milk a poisonous snake

√ 118. Light a match with a .22 rifle

√ 119. Visit a movie studio

√ 120. Climb Cheops Pyramid

√ 121. Become a member of the Explorers Club and the Adventurers' Club

√ 122. Learn to play polo

√ 123. Travel through the Grand Canyon on foot and by boat

√ 124. Circumnavigate the globe (has done it four times)

   125. Visit the moon

√ 126. Marry and have children

√ 127. Live to see the twenty-first century

Mastering the Art of Accomplishment

Nearly all of the people who accomplish a great deal during their lives have mastered the art of accomplishment cycles. They have a great idea. They commit to it. They do whatever it takes to make it happen, with velocity. Then they complete it and go on to another project. You will become a dangerous enemy of mediocrity when you master the whole cycle: creation, action, and completion.

Nearly everyone is better at some parts of the cycle than at others. Some folks are terrific at the first part of the creation phase. They have great ideas but stop when it comes time to commit. Other people may be quite skilled at taking action but have trouble completing anything powerfully. If you want to make your dreams come true, become skilled in working through all three phases of the cycle.

To get any important project moving with velocity, accelerate your accomplishment cycles in those domains of your life where you have stopped. Clean up your desk, forgive your boss for being a jerk, throw away all the junk you have saved for a rainy day but haven't used for years, call up your mom and apologize for being so weird when you went home last Thanksgiving. Keeping things incomplete is a drag on your ability to move through accomplishment cycles with velocity.

Creation. In this first phase of accomplishment, you turn ideas into goals. Having an idea does not automatically start a new accomplishment cycle. Without a commitment, an idea is just a dream. A wish. This is why New Year's resolutions usually don't get off the ground. When you commit to the idea and put that commitment into words, you start a new accomplishment cycle rolling. Let's suppose that you come up with the wild idea of taking a spur-of-the-moment trip to Bali. You play with the idea for a while and then say you are going for it. Out of that commitment, you write down the end state and end date of what you will accomplish: "I'll be in Bali for two weeks starting___."

Action. Usually this phase takes 90 percent of the time and energy you put into any project. The action phase begins with planning, designing, and researching, moves on to implementing and monitoring, and ends when you reach your destination. For your Bali trip, this phase consists of everything from planning how to convince your boss to give you time off, to buying guidebooks and packing your bags, to snoozing on the plane as you wing your way across the sea. As the plane touches down on the tarmac in Bali, you end the action phase of your get-to-Bali project.

Completion. Sitting on the beach, looking out over the sparkling water, you know it's time to declare your project complete. Yes! You did it. This final phase is not so much a matter of doing anything as it is of acknowledging what you have done and declaring your project complete.

Completion closes the circle of the cycle. When you are complete, you experience increased energy, personal power, satisfaction, and pleasure. You are free to create something else new.

Managing the Creation Phase

You'll want your goal to specify when and how you'll know you have achieved it. If your career goal is not measurable, how will you know when you get there? Framing the goal as "enjoy my new job more than my present one" is vague. With a little thought, it might be sharpened up: "At least three days each week, my work will be pleasurable and enjoyable. The other two days, I may not be completely turned on, but I won't be bored or highly stressed." People often wind up with vague, nonspecific goals because they say, "I don't know when it will be finished, so how can I write down a date?" Goals are an active intention, not a prediction. They focus your energy and direct your attention toward things you desire to accomplish. That way you can plan, execute, monitor, and adjust as necessary.

To keep yourself inspired throughout the project, also state your goal in terms of exactly what really lights you up—your metagoal. An inspiring statement for the career designer might be, "I'm like a kid in a sandbox, having the time of my life." At the heart of our fondest dreams are our metagoals. The prefix *meta-* means "transcending" or "more comprehensive." Most people who want to have millions of dollars don't want all that money because their dream is to have a big pile of dirty pieces of green paper. They have a larger, more comprehensive, abstract goal in mind: perhaps prosperity or security, or to win the game of monkey on the mountain. These metalevel goals are the real goals behind the surface goals we set and work on consciously. If you want to get to the metagoal behind "I want a house," you might ask, "Why? What will I get by having a house? What do I really want?" You might really want to feel safe, or to attract a mate, or to own a place where you can do whatever you please.

Most of the goals you set have a metagoal behind them. When you buy a puppy, get married, or wash the dishes, you are fulfilling one or more of them, usually without realizing it. The first step in goal setting is to get clear about these metagoals. Without being clear, you're more likely to get what you don't really want.

Frequently people want to jump right into action. If you focus on your to-do list or on specific goals, you will have much more difficulty sticking with the plan than if you work on all levels of goals. The specific goal of physical fitness lacks any appeal when it's time to go running on a cold, gray winter morning. Being aware that this item on your to-do list goes beyond the specific goal to the metagoal of having a hot and sexy body makes it much easier to pull those sneakers on. What you really want is the metagoal, not the icy wind in your face or even enhanced lung capacity. Begin goal setting at the highest level. Go from the general to the specific. It will not work the other way around. You cannot figure out your life goals by working on a to-do list.

Creating your inspiring vision statement may help you get to the heart of what you truly want, your metagoal. If you say, "I want a house," that seems a fairly straightforward goal. Looking more deeply, however, you could ask, "What will a house give me? What do I really want?" The real answer might be something fairly conventional, like feeling safe, or it might be having total freedom to do whatever you want, including painting the place purple with pink sparkles.

Without being clear, you're more likely to get what you don't really want. When you are clear that your metagoal in buying a house is to feel safe (and *safe* means a neighborhood where people know one another), you have a better chance of buying the right house. You can stand up against the pressure of a "good deal" or a friend's recommendation. You might even see that you don't need to own a house at all. Being unclear about metagoals constitutes the slippery slope to buyer's remorse.

If your goals represent what you think you *should* want—what might please your parents or spouse, your cultural identity, or your boss but are not authentically your own—you will have difficulty achieving them. Align your goals with your deepest principles and values and with your most genuine dreams and desires. Let your dad set his own goals. If you can't authentically take on your company's goals as your own, get a job in a company where you can. Life is short. Don't waste time and energy going after stuff you don't really want.

A good way to figure out how far you are willing to stretch to have your dreams come true is to draw a line horizontally across a piece of paper. At the left end of the line, write down what would be a reasonable goal to pursue. On the right end of the line, write down what you really want and would go after if you had no barriers to achieving it. This may even be a goal that seems completely over-the-top and into the realm of impossibility. Then fill in the space between the two extremes with intermediate goals that represent a progression from your more reasonable, safer goal to your outrageous goal.

The only way to discover the limits of the possible
is to go beyond them into the impossible.

—ARTHUR C. CLARKE

Then consider how far you are willing to stretch toward the goal on the right side of the page. Don't make assumptions. There may be, with creativity and dedication, a way you could make the impossible happen. Brainstorm. Talk with people who take on and fulfill outrageous goals. Use their experience to come up with possible solutions that shift your perception of your goal from impossible to possible but challenging. Then again, you may not be willing to stretch far from the reasonable goal on the left side of the page.

You have to be completely honest with yourself. Don't set goals based on wishes and hopes but on what you are ready and willing to make happen, even if difficulties and problems arise. Keep your feet on the ground and your eyes on the stars.

Managing the Action Phase

The skill you bring to bear on managing the action phase of your project makes all the difference in the results. Even people with a massive commitment often do not reach their goals, because they have charged into random action with bugles blowing, as if force and enthusiasm would save the day. Now that you understand the cyclical nature of projects, we can get down to fulfilling them.

Planning. After the creation phase, you have your goal stated clearly. Now write down the major steps to get from here to there in chronological order, based on start date. You can think of the major steps as milestones or markers along the road that tell you how far you have traveled. You can estimate when you should complete each milestone so that you arrive at your goal by the time you want. For example, the illustration in the goals inquiry in this chapter shows a few milestones with some of the actions to reach them. You know some milestones have to be completed before you get to others. In the example in the illustration, the milestone *Fully understand my natural talents* obviously has to come before *Learn about careers that fit my natural talents.* The whole point of having milestones is to keep your project on track and on time.

If you have a tendency to limit planning to what seems reasonably within your comfort range rather than planning what will be most effective, stretch yourself. Even if you don't quite make an ambitious milestone by the desired date, you will have gone further than if you had planned on playing it safe. If you are committed to a plan that seems more challenging than what you think you can handle alone, hire a coach.

Now, under each milestone, write down the individual actions you need to take to reach that milestone (numbered in the illustration on page 102). Again, you will find that some actions naturally have to come before others. Others can be completed within the same time frame. Do not skimp on this process. You are building your road map to success.

Incidentally, do not take the instruction about writing things down as merely a suggestion. Your brain is a bad place to keep your plans, and time is a great pickpocket.

Create displays. In small-town America, a common display used to be a giant vertical thermometer set up in front of the fire station when volunteers raised money for a new fire engine. As money came in, the mercury was painted ever higher, until the goal was reached. Devise your own cheerful, visual way of tracking your project. This just might be your chance to award yourself those gold stars you've always deserved. Make it big, if possible: bigger than a file folder, smaller than the firehouse thermometer. A display can also remind you of your goal. If you want a career that allows you free time to garden, for example, you might create a collage of magnificent gardens with some sort of project-tracking chart in the middle. A display helps you track progress visually and keeps your vision for your project in front of you.

Execute, monitor, and adjust. Having a plan makes the next step simple: Follow the plan. Along the way, check regularly to make sure that you are on the right track, but there's no need to worry. Going off course will not doom your project; stopping or going back and forth over the same ground will. A tendency to research everything in greater and greater detail, for instance, can undermine the whole project. There is some truth to the proverb "You make the path by walking." When you get hampered by roadblocks or swerve off course, make corrections. Results from earlier actions may indicate that you need to adjust later actions. You may discover facts you hadn't considered that call for an alteration in the plan. Be flexible—not to procrastinate, but to make the plan more true to your goal.

When you get well and truly stuck, turn to the "When You Get Stuck" chapter. It is a guide to diagnosing and dealing with the difficulties that arise in the course of any project.

Managing the Completion Phase

Declaring your project complete is an existential act: "This is finished because I said so." The result may not necessarily look at all like you thought it would—or hoped it would. If you think about it, how often does anything turn out exactly like your original idea? If you can't dance with chaos, you can't dance at all. Nearly all of us could enhance our capacity to deal with this last phase of the cycle.

Without declaring the project complete, people can get stuck in the past, which hampers their being alive in the present. A common way to get stuck is to leave a project in a state that does not meet your level of satisfaction. You spend your evenings designing and making a beautiful coffee table. You had planned to put a beautiful multicoat French polish finish on the whole thing, top and bottom. But after six months, you're tired of it and skip the underside. Forever after, whenever you look at your beautiful table, you don't see the intricate inlay work, because you're thinking about the unfinished underside. A more obvious way to get stuck is by abandoning a project midstream: the half-knit sweater, the tuba collecting dust in the attic, the PhD program you put on hold when you had a child, and so forth.

You can be complete with the past by acknowledging what's so in the present: "The underside of that table is unfinished, but I'm a different person from who I was six months ago, I have other things I want to do, and I say I'm done. By any measure, it's a fabulous table."

"I never liked the color of that sweater; I'm rolling the yarn back into a ball the cat can play with."

"I'm never going to play the tuba again; I'm giving it to the high school."

"I stopped the PhD program for a good reason, and that's the past. This is now, and I'm creating a new project to explore finishing the PhD."

Natural cycles tend to move naturally toward completion. The moon doesn't ever get stuck in the sky. Human accomplishment cycles take some human attention to be complete, but it's worth it. We pay a psychological price for resisting the flow of creation, action, and completion.

Avoiding common pitfalls

Follow the plan, not your feelings. If you keep completing the actions in your plan, step-by-step, you will probably reach your goal. If you do only what you feel like doing, you definitely won't.

Don't give short shrift to the creation phase. Your rushing through the creation phase and settling for a vague or uninspiring goal will lead to suffering in the action phase. Planning will be impossible. Frequently people want to jump right into action. But that's a short sprint that doesn't win races.

Don't stay in creation forever. If you love to speculate endlessly on what is possible, or if you want the statement of your goal to blind you with its brilliance before you move forward, knock it off. State a goal that you can commit to in terms that inspire you, and move on. A better expression of the goal may occur to you later.

Don't plan or research forever. If you suspect that you're the exact opposite of the person who jumps into action without planning—in fact, you usually collect truckloads of information before you move a step—let go and give yourself permission to swing out. If you need help moving on, get a coach.

Don't ignore the completion phase. Your ignoring the completion phase will leave you unsatisfied and wondering why. Intentionally completing something is like walking a friend to your front door when he's leaving and saying good-bye. Not completing is like having him walk out without saying anything.

Everything Is Connected

Decisions about life goals, such as buying a house, are intimately connected with goals regarding other things: your family, children, work, recreation, finances, geography, self-expression, lifestyle, community, and much more. So it is with your career goals. We often make the mistake of separating life into modules instead of thinking of it as a whole, a complex network of domains that all interrelate and depend on one another. Compartmentalizing everything works beautifully for organizing your kitchen shelves, but not so well for designing your life.

Remember that each part of your life is interwoven with everything else. Don't stop with career goals. Create goals for your marriage, your hobby, your community involvement. Make up some health and fitness goals, satisfaction and well-being goals, and so forth. Make up parenting goals, but don't make up goals for your children, and don't make your goals their goals. They are not employees. They are perfectly capable of making up their own goals without your help. Encourage them to become masterful at setting their own goals. If you concentrate on your goal of continually pushing the envelope to be a truly great parent, they might even learn something from your example.

Nothing is ever accomplished by a reasonable man.

—GEORGE BERNARD SHAW

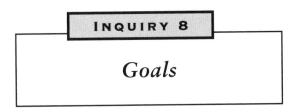

INQUIRY 8

Goals

In this inquiry, you will have an opportunity to look into every area of your life, decide what you most want, and set goals to turn your dreams into reality. This inquiry is a complete goal-setting workshop boiled down to a few pages. Give your goals the dignity of your time and attention to plan them out as fully as you can. That is the purpose of this inquiry. Since you are in the process of making career decisions, you will not be able to map out your career goals completely until you have decided on your future career. You can, however, begin the process. How do you eat an elephant? One bite at a time.

1. Start a "Goals and Projects" document. Set up a goal planner like the sample in this chapter, with several template pages to set goals in various areas of your life, or download a template from www.rockportinstitute .com. Keep this close to your Clues document because your goals may be some of the strongest clues about what careers will fit best.

2. Write down major areas of your life as headings at the top of a new page or document, one category to a page. You can choose as many areas as you want, although it is easier to work with just a few that are most important to you. If you are likely to get bogged down in too much detail, just work with categories that relate to choosing your career. For example, if you are a woman considering having children, goals in that category might have a major impact on your career decisions. Here is a list of possible categories. You may think of others that apply to you.

Adventures	Health and Fitness	Relationships
Awards	Help Others	Research
Career	Hobbies	Retirement
Clubs	Home	Service
Communication	Inventions	Sex
Community	Love Life	Skill Development
Contribution	Marriage	Spiritual
Education	Music	Sports
Family	Parties	Study
Finances	Personal Growth	Travel
Friends	Philanthropy	Wardrobe
Fun	Politics	
Garden/Grounds	Reading	

NEW CAREER

Target Date: 3/1

Choose a new career that is practical, that I will enjoy and fits me perfectly

Vision/metagoal: Play like a kid in a sandbox, having the time of my life

Milestone →		Fully understand my natural talents	10/15
✓	1	Go through chapter 17 of The Pathfinder again	9/25
Completed action "✓" → ✓	2	Do the career testing program to learn about my natural abilities	10/1 ← Action target date
	3	Ask friends and mentors (listed below) their opinions of my best talents ← Action	10/1
		Decide what subject matter will be central to my work	10/30 ← Milestone date
	1	Do chapter 21 in The Pathfinder	10/15
	2	Read appropriate books, articles, find themes	10/20
	3	Make a list of what matters to me and narrow down	10/20
		Learn about careers that fit my natural talents	12/15

3. Create measurable goals for every area of your life that affects your work. Set a date by which you want to complete that goal. To identify your metagoal and make sure your goal statement is what you really mean, ask, "What do I want that goal to give me? What would that make possible?" From identifying your metagoal, create a vision of the goal that inspires you.

4. For each goal, decide what milestones will be needed to reach the goal. For each milestone, list the individual actions you need to take to reach that milestone. Make sure that your stated actions are not clumps of actions. "Research careers in robotics" is a clump of actions—more like a milestone. An action would be "Talk to Ed, the robot expert."

5. When you are finished, go over your entries. If you have created goals that are important to you, you almost certainly have some things to enter in your Definite Career Design Components list.

6. Visit your Goals list often. Some of your goals may require daily attention; others may be on a weekly, monthly, or yearly timeline. You can make adjustments to your list on a daily basis, move goals forward or backward in time or importance, change or abandon others, and so forth. A powerful way to manage your goals is to pick a date every year to reevaluate your goals and accomplishments, set new goals for the coming year, and establish monthly milestones, weekly goals, and daily action steps.

7. Look back over this inquiry for clues. Add whatever you find to your Clues list. If there is anything you are willing to choose as a definite career component, add it to your Definite Career Design Components. If any new career or job comes to mind, add it to your Career Ideas. Ask yourself why that career appeals to you and see if that suggests more clues. If you now know that a career on your Career Ideas list does not fit, remove it. See if that suggests any clues. Remember to keep recording and working with your clues, moving them toward definite career components.

CHAPTER 9

·

QUESTIONS

If you could think of every important question that has some bearing on the quality of your future and then answer each one fully, career decision making would be a simple job. In this chapter, you are going to have an opportunity to do just that.

Asking Resourceful Questions

As you know, answering life's important questions means wrestling with the unknown. You can, however, make the process as painless as possible by enhancing your skill in the art of questioning. The people around you who are making significant contributions are masters at answering difficult questions. It helps that they know how to ask the questions. They are not necessarily more brilliant than the rest of us. If you are experiencing difficulties in resolving uncertainties, the problem may lie in the questions you are asking. Most of us give little thought to crafting our questions; we go with whatever pops into our minds. The quality of any answer, however, depends heavily on the quality of the question.

Take the question "Do I need more education?" Even if you don't care about that particular question, it makes a good example because many people making career decisions, both young and old, struggle with it. You could print this question in huge letters on your bedroom ceiling and think about it every morning and evening, day after day, month after month, and never move an inch toward resolution. It may not address your real concern, which makes it impossible to answer. Your real question may be "Am I willing to go back to school?" or "Is there any realistic way I could go back to school, given my finances and crazy schedule?" Sometimes the real question is just an attack of insecurity, such as "Wouldn't I feel completely out of place in a classroom full of twenty-year-old undergraduates?"

As you work through this chapter—and, for that matter, the rest of this book—see if you can discover what essential questions are hiding under the ones on the surface. You probably don't need therapy to uncover your real life-planning questions. You simply need to poke around a little to uncover them.

Sometimes there is more than one real question. There may be several distinct questions collapsed into one overly general, fuzzy question. "Do I need more education?" may be covering several other questions: "Am I certain enough that X is my ideal career that I should risk pouring more time and money into school? How much suffering am I willing to endure? Is there any way possible to go back to school full-time? How long would it take if I went at night? Am I willing to work all day and study every other waking moment? Could I get into the local school that has the courses I need? Would I be willing to move away from Froghollow to get more education?" By brainstorming, you will discover whether the general question leads to more specific questions. If you find more than one specific question lurking beneath the surface, see if one of them is the primary question: the deal maker or the deal breaker.

How to Answer Questions

If half of finding the right answer is asking the right question, the other half is answering it skillfully. Even for the big questions, there are only three places you can possibly look to find the answers: inside yourself, in the outside world, or, if the answer does not exist inside or outside, you can always make up the answer. After asking the right question, the first step in finding the answer is looking in the right place. You would be amazed how often people get stuck in the midst of an inquiry because they don't know where to look—or because they keep looking for something that doesn't exist.

Looking inside is what you do to find answers to questions about your preferences, personality, wants, needs, hopes, dreams, ideals, requirements, experiences, and so forth. Answers to many of your questions, from the profound to the mundane to the ridiculous, can be found inside yourself: "What matters to me most?" "What would I like to do this weekend?" "How do I feel about squid?" are all questions that can possibly be answered by looking inside yourself. You may discover that you already have some specific, definite requirements for your future career that you can access by simply asking yourself the right questions.

Looking out to the external world is what you do to find many other answers. The answer to "Is there a growing job market for acrobats?" does not exist within. Research (looking outside) is the key.

Make up the answer is what you must do if you need answers that do not exist anywhere else. We have worked with hundreds of people who have spent years in a futile search to discover their calling in life. They believe that they are here on earth for some preordained purpose, yet the answer eludes them.

One of the great myths is that you can find all the answers within yourself, if only you know how and where to look. Fortunately, the third source of answers, inventing them, magically releases you from the bondage of forever seeking. This should be very good news indeed. Inventing answers offers a way out of being permanently stuck in neutral when you cannot find the answer to an important question within you or in the world around you. To invent an answer is to make a choice, a declaration, to get out in front of the train and lay your own tracks instead of remaining merely a passenger in your life. You make an existential leap, point to what you most want, and claim it as your own.

Knowing Where to Look for Answers

How do you know which of the three doors has the answer hidden behind it? First of all, decide if the answer can be found inside or outside. This is usually easy to decide. If the question is "How do I feel about moving to a colder climate?" the answer is obviously found internally. If the question is "How much do charter boat captains make in the Virgin Islands?" you will need to ask someone with experience. Where people run into difficulty is in determining if the answer is to be found internally or if they have to invent the answer themselves. This is unbelievably easy to determine. Here's how you do it. First, look inside. Poke around and see if the answer is in there. If it is, it will appear. You may have to give it some serious thought, meditate on the subject, and give it a few days to bubble up, or wait for circumstances to develop.

If you cannot come up with the answer within a few days, most likely you never will. You do not have some secret cave of answers hidden deep within yourself. (That is just a myth perpetrated on all of us by Freudian analysts fulfilling their subconscious need to keep their clients coming back for years so they can continue to make a living.) Most of what is inside you is readily accessible. If you cannot find the answer inside yourself, it is probably hopeless to continue to look there. You will have to make up the answer and decide for yourself.

When you make up answers, you can pick anything you want. You can pick an answer that makes you feel as safe and secure as a bug in a rug. Or you can go for it and make up an answer that would make you stretch but give you everything you want. Making up the answers is quite simple. Here's my favorite method: First, figure out what you would most like the answer to be. For example, if the question you have been unable to resolve by looking in or out is "Am I willing to start my own company?" look to see what answer you would prefer if you had a choice. Which answer would move your life forward the most? Which answer brings out your passion? The next step is simply to decide that the answer you lean toward is the one and only answer for you. Then commit to doing whatever it takes to make it happen. That's all there is to it, folks. Inventing an answer can be nothing more than selecting the most desired possibility, hanging your star on it, and being responsible for making it happen.

Sometimes the answer may involve looking in more than one place. For example, if you are trying to decide what sort of organization you want to be associated with, you may want to look for answers both inside and outside. Unless you are intimately familiar with a wide range of organizations, you need to do some research. Then you check out how you feel and what you think about what you uncover in your external research.

Each of us is more comfortable in one of the three places where answers can be found. "Innies" introspect. "Outies" extrospect. Hardly anyone is adept at making up the answers himself. Identify your preferred source for answers, then practice leaving home base to visit the two less familiar areas. You will find the answers to your thorniest questions in the places you visit least often.

INQUIRY 9

Questions

The process of career choice consists of asking and answering questions. This is your chance to clarify your important questions, get them all out on the table, and get them answered.

In this inquiry, you ask all the questions you need to answer to decide what to do with your life. You figure out where to find the answers and, finally, what you need to do to get your questions answered. These questions are your career choice "to-do" list. You may wonder what in the world I'm talking about. Well, if making this big decision is a matter of asking the right questions and answering them, then your questions will be, in essence, a list of everything you need to delve into and answer in order to make your final choice. If you do whatever you need to do to answer *all* of your important questions, you will reach your goal (or discover more questions you hadn't thought of).

1. Create a "Questions" document or download a template from www .rockportinstitute.com. Organize it like this "Important Questions" table.

Important Questions		
The Question	Where to find the answer	How can I answer it?

2. Write down everything you might need to choose your future career. Keep adding to this list until you have every important question written down. Focus on the big, weighty, important ones—the ones you absolutely must resolve in order to make your career decisions. Don't get bogged down in every little question, or you will drown in your own thinking.

3. See if any of your questions are too broad or unclear to answer. If so, figure out how to word them more succinctly or more specifically. Look beneath the surface to see what the real questions might be.

4. When you have written down all your questions, decide where you need to look to answer each of them (outside, inside, or make up the answer), and mark or write that in the middle column. Remember that sometimes you have to look in more than one place to find the answer. For example, you might have to do some research and then see how you feel about it or then make up the final answer. This step is critical. Knowing where to look gives you some power.

5. After completing the steps above, review your important questions again, this time to fill in the right-hand column, "How Can I Answer It?" For each question, ask yourself, "What would I do to answer this question?" *Be very specific.* Remember, the question is "How can I answer it?" not "Am I willing?" Don't let your perceived limitations dictate what it will take to answer a question. You're writing what it would take to find the answers without regard for whether you want to do it. Write down the best answer to the question rather than what would be easy, reasonable, or comfortable. Don't fool yourself. Some answers may be more complicated than others are or involve several steps.

6. Decide if you are willing to do what it takes to answer the question. If you are, put a star on the form by the question to symbolize your commitment to do what it takes to get it answered. If you aren't willing, perhaps you can face up to your unwillingness, find a way around it, or come up with another equally effective way to get to the answer.

7. I recommend working on your important questions every couple of days. Go over everything you have written. Look at it anew. Spend more time on the items you rushed through or held at arm's length. Do your other inquiries—but *do not stop working on this list.* Keep working to answer the questions. If you don't concentrate your energy on answering these questions, you will not move ahead.

8. *Do not read the list of questions at the end of this inquiry* until you have come up with your own Important Questions list and completed at least steps 1 through 4. *This may be difficult. Nobody wants to get bossed around by a book. But please formulate your own questions before reading the list.* Only then consider the list of questions below to fill in any gaps. Why? Your engaging in an inquiry to clarify what questions are most important to you will prove infinitely more useful than just browsing through someone else's list. In this case, the easy way is not the best way.

9. When you have listed every important question you can think of by yourself, only then consider the list below. Transfer the ones that are important to you to your Important Questions list and go through steps 1 through 6 with them. You don't need to answer them all. Some may already be on your list, and some won't matter to you.

    For the time being, handle the questions you think are of primary importance. Answer all of them that you can. Begin to wrestle with the ones you cannot answer fully. (If you did this inquiry with regard to your entire life, I guarantee that within a year or two, your life would be functioning at a level you could not even imagine now.)

The Questions List

Geographical Environment

- Would you prefer to work or live in a specific geographic area, locality, or a certain type of physical environment? If so, based on what?—availability of suitable work, a certain-size city or town, demographics, feels like home to you, recreational opportunities, natural beauty, peace, excitement, another family member's needs, the weather suits your clothes?

- How important is this?

- Do you prefer an urban, suburban, or rural environment?

Physical Environment

- Indoors or outdoors: how much of each?

- How much travel required: extended trips, occasionally, rarely, or never away from home?

- Your physical location: sit at a desk, visit several locations each day, in front of a group of people, traveling constantly, work on top of a phone pole?

- Do you prefer an office-oriented environment, workshop, medical facility, classroom, and so on?

- Private office or cubicle? A desk in a large office with lots of other people around you?

- How large an office?

- Status of your office space important?

- Are there factors such as lighting, noise, pollutants that affect you or the quality of your work?

Organizational Environment

- Employee or self-employed?

- Profit, nonprofit, government?

- Service organization or producer of goods?

- Mammoth organization, big, medium, small, tiny, or just you and the dog?

- Organizational purpose, philosophy, style?

- Every organization has a life span. Each stage of its life creates a different organizational environment with different advantages and disadvantages. Is this important to you? If so, what stage fits you?

1. *Start-up phase*—Being in at the very beginning, maximum opportunity to influence the basic structure of the organization, fewest rules, long hours, pioneering spirit, biggest opportunity to carve out a big chunk of personal territory and/or significant ownership, most risky, prone to an early death.

2. *Entrepreneurial phase*—The excitement and rewards of quick growth, risky, unstable, filled with the unexpected, environment tinged with adventure and uncertainty, creative problem solving is highly valued and rewarded, pioneering spirit, opportunity to create the perfect niche for yourself, usually requires long hours, good chance for quick promotion.

3. *Leveling-off phase*—Safer, less need for battlefield problem-solving skills but still room for creativity and new thinking, perfect for those seeking to build a well-oiled and stable system and for those who want stability and security as well as growth and creativity, may require long hours.

4. *Stability phase*—Everything is worked out, organization run by a fixed set of policies and procedures, even keel, everything stays the same, safest nest for the security minded, lower level of appreciation for creativity and individualism, usually has conservative values, likes the steady step-by-step approach, you feel like a cog in the wheel because that's exactly what you are.

5. *Decline phase*—Like the stability phase in character, except has more pathological tendencies than other phases. Not a healthy place to be for anyone except those who love to save sinking ships. Innovative people are often brought in to try to save the ship, but their ideas are not implemented because the organization is still run by stability-phase management people who would rather sink than change.

- Opportunities for advancement based on performance or political maneuvering or seniority?

Human Environment

- How will you relate with other people at work?

- What combination of extroversion and introversion?

- Describe how often you will be in direct contact with other people.

- What percentage of your workday will consist mainly of face-to-face conversations with a constant stream of people?

- What percentage will be a mix of extroverted and introverted activities? How much introverted time?

- Is your introverted time to be spent alone with the door closed or working by yourself with others around?

- With whom will you relate or be in contact: fellow workers, customers, clients, adults, children?

  - What are the reasons for meeting with them?

  - What do you get from being with them? What do they get?

  - What population do you work with or serve: young, old, professionals; people with problems or in need; people seeking to purchase something, to learn something, or solve a problem; people from other countries and cultures; people from a particular profession or from a particular background or socioeconomic group?

- If more than one kind of relationship, what percentage of each?

- In what kind of relationship with others?

  - If there is a teamwork approach, what sort of a team? How big? How varied the members' jobs?

  - Degree of collaboration toward a common goal?

  - Degree of independence and interdependence?

  - What sort of people are your fellow employees? What special qualities or characteristics? Professionals, technical, support, blue-collar, traditional, liberal, conservative, creative, supportive, cooperative, highly motivated, not dysfunctional, young, and so on?

  - Are you supervised? How much? How often? What style?

- Type of supervision structure: traditional top-down approach or something else?

- How much structure to your supervision? Clear lines of authority necessary?

- Will the people you work with be the people with whom you spend your leisure time?

- How connected or isolated will your work environment be from the rest of your life?

Work Definition

- Not defined at all.

- Big-picture objectives are defined.

- Not only are objectives defined but methodology and procedures concerning how to reach objectives are also laid out clearly.

- How is it defined for you?

Pace

- Furious, fast, moderate, slow?

- Steady, varied?

- Busy all day, or lots of time to relax?

Decision Making

- How much? All day? Occasionally?

- What kind of problems/issues?

- What kind of decisions?

- What decision-making rhythm? Steady and flowing?

- One decision-making scale has at one end a constant flow of spontaneous decisions. At the other end of the scale is meticulous, deliberative, carefully planned decision making. What point along the scale fits you?

Predictability

- When you show up at work, will you have a pretty good idea of what you will be facing? Possibilities range from arriving at work without the slightest clue about the day's work to total predictability.

Variety

- How much variety is built into the average day?

- How much must work differ from year to year, month to month, day to day, within the day?

- Continual new projects, assignments?

- New problems to face? How often? Consistently, daily, occasionally, one new big problem every month or year?

- Degree of routine?

- Emergency firefighting: how much, how often?

Time Management

- How much of your life will be spent working? To arrive at a useful estimate of how much of your life will be spent working, add time spent directly at work to the time spent in support of work, including commuting, buying and caring for work clothes or equipment, entertaining, networking, homework, outside time thinking or worrying about work, and time needed to recover from work.

- What is the ideal expenditure of your total time on work and work-related activities? How close to your ideal are you willing to come?

- How many hours per week are you willing to work?

- How often are you willing to rise to the call of emergencies and special situations that require you to give every waking hour and ounce of energy to your work?

- How important is it to you to have time for family, hobbies, and so forth? How much is ideal? How much is necessary?

Security

- There are several potentially important aspects to the question of security. The very word means different things, sometimes radically different things, to different people. To some folks, it means a secure nest in a stable organization. To others, carving out their own slice of the pie on their own terms as an entrepreneur is the only real security.

- There has been a radical shift in the degree of job security available to workers in the last few years. If you want a safe, lifetime nest, there are still places that can offer one. These days, the prevalent philosophy of job security is to be so skilled, so needed, that you will have headhunters lined up outside your door bidding for you. What does security mean to you? What does job security mean to you?

- What kind of security is important to you?

- How important is it?

- What degree of security is necessary?

- Are you looking for a long-term nest, a work family, a place to hang your hat for a few years, a step toward some future goal?

Preparation for Retirement

- Do you intend to retire or work until you fall off the face of the earth?

- How long will you work? Some people plan to retire at fifty-five, forty-five, or even thirty-five, and make it happen.

- How do you intend to be secure in your years of retirement?

- What part will your employer play in saving for your retirement?

- Do you intend to stay with an organization that will provide you with a pension?

Portability

Some careers, like nursing and physical therapy, are so portable that you can find a job on short notice anywhere in the world. Many high-tech careers are also portable. If you decide to move to another city, you can easily find a suitable new job. In fact, in some careers, you move up the ladder by moving from company to company.

- Is it important for your career to be portable?

- If so, how important? How portable?

Degree of Continuing Challenge

- What do you mean by challenge?

- How much challenge do you need?

- What would provide enough challenge?

Other Factors to Consider

- What plans/commitments do you (or other people in your life) have that may affect your career?

- Personal plans?

- Are you planning a marriage? A divorce?

- Whose career comes first, yours or your spouse's? Is there some way that both of you can win and have what you want? (There usually is, if you both abandon "me first" attitudes and commit to a win-win outcome. You might look for a book or two on the subject of win-win problem solving.)

- Are there children involved?

- What about your parents?

- Do you hope to move to your dream location?

- Do you want to retire early?

Competition and Cooperation

In a tribe of chimpanzees, each ape's position within the tribe is a result of some mix of competitive spirit, talent, and managing its network of connections, not unlike another species we know. There is no way to avoid competition and politics unless you become a hermit. There are people in every workplace who continually stir the competition and politics pot. Other folks experience profound stress when these issues arise. It is business as usual in the animal kingdom for individuals to keep testing those just above them on the totem pole. You would do well to be clear about what supports your success and well-being, what generates sufficient spice in your work life, and what is too stressful.

- How naturally competitive are you?

- Does success involve competing with others?

- Do you thrive in a competitive environment or prefer a cooperative environment?

- How much of each?

- If you seek competition, do you prefer that it exists between you and fellow employees or between your organization and others?

- If you seek a cooperative environment, what do you mean? How much?

- Is it a problem for you if there is significant competition in moving up to the level you seek?

Future Demand

- Do you need to be in a career field that is expanding rapidly? Steadily? Maintaining the same number of people employed?

- If you go into a field that is not expanding or is shrinking, how can you position yourself so that you will be one of the people who gets to keep playing the game?

Difficulty in Getting into the Field in the First Place

Range: from easy (fast-food restaurant burger flipper) to fierce (movie star or senator).

- How much difficulty are you willing to face?

- How much of a problem is it for you to go after a particular career if there is uncertainty about whether you will be able to get into the field?

- Only a small number of philosophy PhD candidates have faced the fact that just one in ten will find a job in their field. How carefully have you considered this question in regard to fields that you are considering?

- If you are considering a very competitive field, what would it take to make sure that you are one of the people who succeed?

Rewards

To some degree, your identity consists of your relationship with yourself and your relationship with the world around you. Any quality you include as an important part of your identity can be fortified or undercut by the realities of your career. People who think of themselves as caring may not thrive in a job where they constantly have to get tough with others. A job that allows them to manage in their naturally supportive style offers more rewards, primary among them that they can be themselves on the job.

- How important to you is the freedom to be yourself on the job?

- What are some of the dimensions of your identity that you would be unwilling to have undermined by a workplace that devalues that dimension?

- What careers would you be most proud to pursue? Are these on your Career Ideas list?

- How would you like to be perceived by yourself and others with regard to your work? Being perceived by others in a particular way is always an important ingredient of the constant two-way conversation between you and the world around you. One of the important rewards your career bestows is the way that the other people in your life perceive you. How you are reflected in the eyes of the people around you will either nourish or deplete your self-esteem. We all have an ego that needs to be fed by the world around us.

- Do you care how you appear in the eyes of others? What careers would be a blow to your self-esteem if your friends found out? What careers would you be most proud of if others knew?

- How important is it to make full use of your gifts—talents, personality, and so forth? (Consider this one carefully, since it has a huge impact on your long-term satisfaction and success and is often overlooked.)

- Is it important to solve problems in a particular way, relating with people in the way you relate best, being creative in some specific way?

- What about your income and income potential—now, in five years, later on?

- Other financial rewards?

- Stock plans?

- Partial ownership or partnership?

- Positioning yourself for the future?

- How important is it that you receive acknowledgment, praise, or recognition for your work by the organization, a supervisor, others, the world, and so forth? How much is enough?

Power and Status

Even if you have not rated power and status as important values, as a primate, status is always part of the game. Your personal definition, however, may be nothing much like the commonly agreed-upon definition. You may seek the power and status associated with having "higher values" than power and status.

- What do power and status mean to you?

- How important are they to you?

- Do you seek public recognition or fame?

- Is it important to have your work known beyond your immediate circle?

- How much do you value the respect or admiration of others?

- How important is your status (at work, in your field, in the community, or more widely)?

What Else Is Important?

- Comfort versus adventure?

- Natural, easy fit with your work?

- Designing your life so that you are at equilibrium—your work supports you in being who you are naturally?

- Performing functions that you find satisfying?

- Having fun at work?

Social Impact: Altruism

Some people care that the product or service their employer produces not be harmful or make a negative impact on society. Others don't really care.

- To some folks, it's important to contribute to society or to the well-being of others. What is true for you?

- If it is important for you to make a contribution, what specific areas do you care about most?

- On which specific group do you want to make an impact?

- What kind of impact?

- How much of an impact?

- Must your specific work make a direct contribution?

- Is it all right if you do not make a direct contribution but work for an organization that does something you care about or believe in?

10. Look back over this inquiry for clues. Add whatever you find to your Clues list. If there is anything you are willing to choose as a definite career component, add it to your Definite Career Design Components. If any new career or job comes to mind, add it to your Career Ideas. Ask yourself why that career appeals to you, and see if that suggests more clues. Remove from your Career Ideas list any career that you now know doesn't fit. See if that suggests any clues. Remember to keep recording and working with your clues, moving them toward definite career components.

CHAPTER 10

•

WHEN YOU GET STUCK

We will either find a way or make one.

—HANNIBAL

In the midst of trying to decide what to do with your life, you may reach a point where you don't know what to do next. Any of the following might be true:

- You are confused, uncertain, stuck.

- The careers you were considering evaporated when you found out more about them.

- The pieces do not seem to fit together.

- All careers that seem attractive to you seem impossible to achieve.

- Your life has been very busy for the last two months. You just noticed that you haven't really done much to move your career decision making forward.

- You try to work on choosing your future career, but you find yourself just staring at your notebook.

- You can't even imagine what you could do to get moving.

You are stuck, right? Well, maybe not. You are stuck when you fall into a pit of quicksand, sink up to your neck, and there's no one around and no branches to grab. You are stuck when the traffic stops completely and it is thirty miles to the next exit. You are stuck when the forces of evil coat your body with superglue and stick you to the front of a missile that is now hurtling through space. Ninety percent of the time, though, when we say "stuck," it may be more accurate to say we are "stopped."

From time to time, we all blame our lack of progress on confusion, not knowing what to do, our impossibly busy lives, a flaw in our psychological makeup, other people, lack of data, writer's block, parents, race, gender, and a world that treats us unfairly, or we blame some other insurmountable circumstance. We attribute the cause of our difficulty to the circumstances; to what seems like the one and only reality.

It is possible to consider "stuck" in a new light, as our own personal interpretation of what's occurring. When you say "stuck," you unconsciously and unknowingly make another statement: that the circumstances are the cause of our situation, and you lose power. The circumstances run the show. If you create a new interpretation, "I am stopped," you instantly put yourself in the driver's seat. The ability to create a new interpretation is a powerful ally. Once you begin to look at your situation from this perspective, you can start to diagnose the problem and figure out how to deal with it.

What to Do When You Are Stopped

What saves a man is to take a step.

—ANTOINE DE SAINT-EXUPÉRY

I knew a couple who ran a very effective workshop for writers with writer's block. They didn't sit around and analyze the problem or have people share their doubts and fears. They created all sorts of smoke and mirrors in the form of writing exercises so that the class wouldn't notice that the real strategy was to get them moving. Once they started writing, writer's block disappeared. Likewise, when you stop and think you are stuck, here is what I suggest: *When stopped, start!*

Yes, gentle reader, this is the only choice you have, other than to stay where you are. Here's how to do it.

- Reinterpret your situation. Look from the "I'm stopped, not stuck" point of view. You do not have to resolve your family relationships, develop more willpower, or change in any way. You want to abandon the interpretation of yourself as a helpless victim of the mysterious forces of stuckness.

- Find ways to remind yourself of your new interpretation. Put a big sign on your refrigerator, on the mirror, on the ceiling above your bed, train a flock of mynah birds to repeat it again and again as they fly around your house, get a friend or a coach to remind you, write it in big letters: When Stopped, Start!

Here are some of the things you can do once you have created that new, more resourceful interpretation:

- Go on to something else. Come back later to the part that isn't moving. Do something different. It need not be the perfect thing. Since you don't know what the perfect thing is, do *anything* different.

- Do something new in other areas of your life to loosen up your brain. If you never go dancing, go out and dance till dawn.

- Break down the stuck part into manageable bites. What twenty-minute activity would clarify or move this project forward in any way?

> *Insanity is doing the same thing over and over and expecting a different result.*
>
> —RITA MAE BROWN

- Reframe your questions. Read or review chapter 9, "Questions."

- Look at your situation from new points of view. Get friends to brainstorm with you. Don't invite those friends who share your perspective. For example, if you are an African American who feels held back because of your race, you might invite friends of other races over to brainstorm.

- Find the most qualified experts in whatever has you stopped and ask them how to get moving.

- Get professional assistance. Hire a coach. If you want coaching to assist you through choosing your career, this person should be a highly trained career coach, preferably using Rockport Institute methodology or another set of effective tools. Most life coaches, career coaches, and counselors have not had sufficient training in the art and science of career design to help you reach your goal effectively. You might check out the Rockport Institute Career Choice Program at www.rockportinstitute.com or participate in a similar career design coaching program.

- Take a vacation in paradise.

- Take a course or workshop that opens a new dimension in your life:

    Do an Outward Bound course.

Take the Landmark Forum weekend workshop, a brilliant course for people who want to create a future of their own design.

Study NLP (Neuro-Linguistic Programming), a set of techniques to change the programming of your mind.

Look into Positive Psychology, a powerful reinterpretation of the field.

Get Rolfed! Every year your body becomes older, more solid, frozen, inflexible. This will set your body free. Rolfing (named after founder Ida Rolf) is very popular with professional dancers and others who prize physical freedom.

- Take up the daily practice of mindfulness meditation and/or yoga.

- Lighten up! Play. Do something you have always wanted to do. (Ignore Yeah-buts.)

- If these don't appeal to you, find another way to achieve breakthroughs, a fresh view of life, and more power to create new interpretations.

Diagnose Your Difficulty and Get Moving Again

Only a few kinds of difficulty can stop you. Once you identify the specific difficulty, you can deal with it.

Look at the figure on the next page, the illustration of a journey to a specific destination, in this case choosing your career. The problems and breakdowns that might occur on the journey to the distant city are the same as those that can get in the way of any journey or project. If you are stopped, it is always one of these:

1. **A commitment problem.** If you find yourself just sitting in the car reading brochures about the wonders of your destination and not actually putting the pedal to the metal, you have a commitment problem. The way you can tell if you are having a commitment problem is whether you are actively moving your career choice process forward. If someone says he is going to go down to the store to get a bottle of orange juice, and hours later you find him still reading about the relative merits of different kinds of oranges or stirring orange food coloring into a glass of water, it is fairly safe to say he is committed to something other than what he said. When it comes to commitments, actions speak much louder than words. Deal with it by

re-creating your commitment. Read the chapter called "Why You Don't Get What You Want," the one called "The Power of Commitment," and whichever other chapters you think may be appropriate to help you focus on declaring what you are committed to and getting into action.

2. **A lack of necessary skills and tools.** Sometimes people get stopped because they simply do not know how to do something that is vital to moving forward. For example, they may not be adept at researching on the Internet or they may not know how to type. The bottleneck may be a missing tool, such as a computer, a car, or a good suit. Other times the problem might be more intangible, like reluctance to cold-call people you do not know. Don't let anything stop you or reduce the effectiveness of your career choice process. Learn what you need to know. Buy or borrow the tools you need.

3. **A direction problem.** If you are headed in a direction that is not bearing fruit, reassess. Find a more effective direction or route. If you cannot figure out which way to go, go any other way than the way you are going now.

4. **A velocity or momentum problem.** If you have been driving for a week and you have gone only twenty miles on your thousand-mile journey, you have a velocity problem. At this rate, it will take you a year to get to your destination and two lifetimes to choose your career. When you are engaged in an important project such as deciding what to do with your life, a velocity problem is almost always a symptom of resistance to disturbing the equilibrium of your life. The way you deal with it is to speed up. I know this sounds simplistic, but can you think of any other way to solve a velocity problem? The way to speed up is to put some urgency into your project. What are the consequences of puttering along? What does it cost you? Are you willing to pay the cost? Make sure you have milestones with dates. Then manage yourself in a way that gets you to your milestones on time.

When in doubt, gallop.

—FRENCH FOREIGN LEGION PROVERB

Sometimes other events in your life can absorb your attention. If you are falling in love, moving, changing to another job in your field, or mourning the death of a close relative, you may want to put *The Pathfinder* away for a month or two until you have the freedom to get moving again.

5. **Error correction.** Sometimes it is difficult to know when you are off course. You may be exploring blind alleys or doing what is comfortable instead of what moves your project along most powerfully. Focus on your goal and keep asking yourself: "How is this action specifically related to my goal? Is this working? What would work better?" When you discover that you are off course, get back on!

> *I am not discouraged, because every wrong attempt*
> *discarded is another step forward.*
>
> —THOMAS EDISON

6. **Overcome obstacles.** Many things can get in your way and bring your project to a screeching halt. Roadblocks and difficulties are just problems to solve. The real culprits in killing off projects are our old friends the Yeahbuts. People abandon their project because "I didn't have the grades to get into the program," "I'm too tired after work to deal with this," "My husband doesn't like the idea," "It just seems impossible," and so forth. It is usually not the circumstances that stop us, no matter how sure we are that they are the cause of our difficulties. What stops people is nearly always one of two things: Your goal got shot down by Yeahbuts, or your commitment snuck off in the dark when your back was turned. When you face a roadblock, renew your commitment, get out your chain saw and shovel, and get the barrier out of the road. No matter what the roadblock is, there is some way through it or around it. If you find you are unwilling to do what it takes, that's okay. Go back to the drawing board and consider other directions and destinations. Sometimes when I point out to a client that there is always a way through or around, they argue for the roadblock. You are not the roadblock's lawyer. Don't do that. Whose side are you on anyway?

Living in a State of Consonance

There is one other obstacle besides the Yeahbuts that is often a major culprit in stopping the voyager dead in his or her tracks: inner conflict. Even though it may seem difficult to resolve these inevitable conflicts, it is actually much easier than it appears to be. Instead of continuing to support a state of inner warfare, create a state of consonance. Consonance means being in agreement or accord, harmonious, compatible, congruous. To achieve harmonious living, all you have to do is create a state, a ground of being, where your outside agrees with your inside, and the various parts of your personality work together to achieve the same goals and you are not at war with yourself. Your work is in harmony with what matters. Your journey is in accord with your map. You are aligned.

When there is a lack of harmony between your inner and outer life or between important parts of your personality, it is difficult to move forward. Your personal power erodes. You have less trust in yourself. Other people pick up this dissonance and tend not to trust you either. One of the best examples of dissonance, the opposite of consonance, is the famous photograph from 1974 in which a disgraced Richard Nixon is smiling and waving as he boards a helicopter on the White House lawn after having been forced to resign the presidency. Most people are highly sensitive to dissonance. Don't you pick it up instantly when people say they're doing great when obviously they aren't? If you are that sensitive to other people's dissonance, imagine how a lack of harmony in your own life affects you.

If someone passionately wants to do work she cares about and doesn't act on her desire, she lives in a state of jangling discord. This is a most uncomfortable place to be. She finds herself compelled to do something—anything—to make that terrible feeling go away.

All of us experience a lack of congruence sometimes. When we tell our children they must live up to a standard of perfection that we don't follow ourselves, that is hardly congruent behavior. Sure, we are just doing our best to be good parents. But kids pick up the lack of congruence instantly, just like we pick it up in other people. They know that Long Wind speaks with forked tongue. Don't expect to live happily ever after in a state of perfect harmony. What we can do is notice when we aren't in a state of consonance and begin to correct ourselves to get back in synch. Just deal with the big stuff, and the small stuff will take care of itself.

There are two different kinds of dissonance. Sometimes the dissonance is a conflict, or lack of communication, between different parts of your personality. For example, one part wants to go to the beach, while another part thinks you should stay home and finish the work you have to get done by Monday. Or one part wants to have an exciting, satisfying career, while another part wants to play it safe. The other kind of dissonance is a conflict between your inner vision and your real day-to-day life, between inside and outside. You may be a burglar who hates to steal or the head of a large federal agency with total disdain for bureaucratic environments.

If you get shut down by dissonance, here's an effective tool to resolve inner conflicts. The following inquiry, created at the Esalen Institute, an alternative educational research center in Big Sur, California, in the 1970s, is the best method I know for resolving both kinds of dissonance. It coaches you to find creative ways to have your cake and eat it too—to satisfy internal factions that have not found common ground before. It works just as effectively as a tool to resolve dissonance between your dreams and your real life. When you do not follow through in turning your dreams into reality, it is often because internal voices have spoken convincingly for another agenda. Most dissonance is internal, a conflict between different parts of your personality. Using this inquiry, you can negotiate between those parts that look from very different points of view. You can find a way to have all of your internal cast of characters get what they want.

INQUIRY 10

A Parts Party

We grew up in a culture that promotes the belief that each of us has one personality, one identity. In reality, it seems more like each of us is inhabited by a whole cast of characters, each with a singular point of view and agenda. It isn't just mentally ill people who have multiple personalities. We all do. There may be a character who wants to do what feels good now, a hedonist. Another one may be cautious and security minded. Yet another has the soul of an adventurer. Perhaps you are inhabited by some rebellious characters and other more compliant ones. If you think of yourself as a single identity, you are sure to be conflicted. If you realize that you are an ensemble production, it makes it easier to reach a state of consonance. The problem is not that you are inhabited by all these different characters, but that they don't communicate. They don't party together. They are like people who live in the same apartment building but never speak to one another, let alone really get to know one another. Your life works best when they all work together to produce aligned outcomes that benefit the entire building and everyone in it. A parts party is a great way to introduce them and get them playing together. You might even start to have regular parties every time internal conflicts arise. Or you might just like hanging out with your internal menagerie. Here's how to give a parts party.

1. Identify your important internal characters, or subpersonalities. Write down their identifying characteristics on a page in your notebook. Then give each of them an apt name such as: Ms. or Mr. Responsible, the Kid, the Rebel, the Saboteur, the Saint, the Whore, the Star, the Beast, Dr. Know-It-All, the Guru, the Mother, the Problem Solver, the Cynic, the Lover, the Creative One, the Philosopher, the Fool, the Hedonist, the Comedian, the Radical, the Conservative, the Good Neighbor, the Basket Case, the Friend, and so forth. Chapter 18, "Natural Roles," is a good place to look to identify some of these characters. They can have different

genders, even be of different species, as appropriate. You may even want to imagine what they look like, or find other ways to distinguish them clearly. You could give them distinctive clothes or physical characteristics. Do what it takes to make them distinct from one another.

2. Pick something that has you conflicted. Perhaps you want a career that is adventurous and provides security, or one that is both meaningful and practical. Create a definite agenda for your party. (As you may have noticed, this party is actually an awful lot like a meeting. Don't tell your more fun-loving characters, or they may not show up.) The agenda may be to give everyone a chance to talk about the situation you face, to speak from their point of view, and then to discover a way that all of these characters can get what they want: a plan that generates internal consonance.

3. Schedule a time for the party. You will need an hour or so in a quiet location where nothing will disturb you. Decide which of your subpersonalities should attend the party. Invite the ones most invested in the matter at hand.

4. Select a host/conflict manager to lead the discussions and negotiations. This can be you or one of the characters. If you pick an internal character, pick one who is strong, fair, and diplomatic.

5. Get the party started by sitting in a comfortable, open position and closing your eyes. Imagine all the invited internal characters sitting around a big round table wearing clothes that would fit their personalities.

6. Turn over the party to the host. Give all interested characters a chance to speak their minds. What are their points of view, their agendas? What do they want you to do? Let them argue for their own interests. Let them get clear exactly what the most important conflicts are.

7. Negotiate. The host/conflict manager needs to be especially creative in supporting all parties to come up with win-win solutions. Get each character to brainstorm what would allow him to get what he wants, and make sure other characters get what they want too. It may be possible to have a life of both adventure and security. Most other differing agendas can find common ground as well. Get them to negotiate a solution that respects and fulfills all the characters. Remember that they are all on your side. They are you. They just have different points of view about what will keep you safe and happy.

8. Agree on a unified plan that allows all players to get their agendas fulfilled.

One parts party may not be enough. You may want to hold one regularly. Who knows, some of your internal characters who don't communicate now may get along so well that they become wanton weasels of love, going wild in your brain.

How to Keep Going Once You Have Started Moving Again

The way to stay in the driver's seat is to see clearly which aspects of a project you flow through like a cork in a mountain stream, and at which points you get stopped. You can be sure that you will tend to get stopped in the same place or places time after time. People who have a commitment problem on one important part of their life will very likely have the same problem arise elsewhere. Put a great deal of creativity and energy into getting through the rough spots; the places where you are less than naturally proficient. When you are stopped, it's a matter of recognizing that your wheels are spinning and getting out to push yourself out of the mud. The way to train yourself to up the ante and get your project moving is to pay attention to where you fall short. Forget about trying to make sure that you are getting positively stroked all the time. Concentrate your energy on filling in what is missing. Nothing gives better strokes than a life lived fully. And nothing contributes more to having a fully lived life than keeping your projects in motion all the way through to completion.

CHAPTER 11

•

THE BOTTOM LINE—RESEARCH

During the first stages of choosing your future direction, you spend most of your time and energy looking into yourself. Once you have created enough definite components to be able to identify careers that might fit you, it's time to do extensive research out in the real world. Remember, you can answer any question by looking in one of three places: inside yourself, outside in the wide world, and, if there is no answer in either of those places, you can always make up the answer. This chapter is about the questions you can answer only by looking outside of yourself. You need to:

- Find the best clues.

- Work your clues with the goal of turning some into definite components.

- See if reality matches your vision and beliefs.

- Learn about fields and career areas you are considering—separate fact from fantasy through reading and getting the opinions of people in the field.

- Figure out what fields, careers, and jobs fit your specifications.

- Find people, especially industry leaders, to add to your network of support.

- Find out what you need to do to get into a new field.

- Identify and learn about potential employers.

Do What Works

The best research tool is broad-based curiosity. There is no single best research tool. Do everything you can think of to learn what you need to know.

Do everything you don't want to do. Nearly everyone does the opposite. Driven by comfort-seeking machinery, we tend to avoid the parts that are a little scary or outside our everyday experience. Introverts may resist talking with people they don't know and asking tough questions. Extroverts may not read enough about the subject of their interest. People who are sensitive to rejection (and who isn't?) may avoid situations where they might hear the dreaded word *no*.

Ask powerful questions. Figure out exactly what you want to know ahead of time. Read chapter 9, "Questions," and use that methodology to sharpen your questions. Practice asking your questions with a friend (or in the bathroom mirror) until you are as clear and pointed as a laser beam. Avoid asking a busy person questions you could find out by reading or other research.

Don't lump research and job search together. Separate these two activities. They have different goals, even if they sometimes use the same methods, such as talking with people. When your goal is learning about careers you are considering, seek out people who can answer your most important questions, and let them know that information is *all* you are seeking. When you are looking for a job, your intention is completely different: to get in front of decision makers; to talk with people who could actually hire you. If you mix the two, you may pollute the mind of an important decision maker with a first impression: "This person is trying to figure out what to do with his life." You want the impression you leave with a decision maker to be something more like: "Wow! This person would be a valuable asset to us."

Talk with lots of people. Even if you are a hermit living in a cave, you have to talk with people. Lots of people. Your future depends on it. The more points of view you access, the more accurate a picture you will get. Suppose you are considering the field of physical therapy. You speak to two PTs who don't like their jobs; a third tells you that you'll never get accepted at a good school. If you stop there, you kill off this field as a possibility. If you speak with *ten* physical therapists, however, you might find that most of them love their work, and a couple even have tips on getting into PT school. That can at least keep physical therapy in the running, and it doesn't doom what you might find to be the perfect new career for you. "Talking," incidentally, includes talking with your fingers. Use the Internet to identify many potential information sources. Focus on finding and communicating with experts, master practitioners, and people with deep experience. Don't get lost in the endless, mindless digital chatter of people with lots of opinions and little experience.

Resist trying to prove what you want to believe. Give your hopes, dreams, and pre-existing beliefs a rigorous examination, if not a rest. Watch for a tendency to seek evidence that stacks the deck in favor of what you want to believe. It may not match reality. This is not easy, but avoiding that trap will pay off. Law schools pour out an endless stream of graduates who would have made other choices if they had done more research and critical thinking before signing up. Be especially wary when you think you have found the answer. Maybe you have, but check it out broadly and deeply, and make sure you haven't overlooked something important.

Information Sources

There are endless research sources. The more you use, the better able you will be to make the best possible decisions. Here are a few:

The Internet is the way to find almost anything. You can find people who are deeply knowledgeable about everything under the sun. Even left-handed bagpipe repair people probably have some sort of online group. And people on the Internet are generally very friendly and willing to share what they know. Every group seems to have a range of participants, from the newly curious to a few real old masters. The problem is always sorting out who are the masters and who just want to appear to be experts and love to offer an opinion. Seek wisdom before opinion and learn to separate the two. I used to participate in an active community of people interested in a particular model of sailboat. At first, I soaked up every bit of information indiscriminately, but it didn't take long to figure out who really knew their stuff. After you follow a group for a while, the pecking order can be discerned. Create friendships with those in the know.

You can use online resources to reach industry leaders more directly and easily than any other way except going to conferences. If you show up at their offices or call on the phone, you will not likely get past the guardians who shield them from interruptions. With energetic research, you can often find a direct path to the movers and shakers. You may have to learn some new skills to do this well. I know a fellow who can find out almost anything about almost anyone in less than an hour. You can build that capacity too. You just have to give up thinking it should happen instantly.

Your network of friends, relatives, and others should be a primary research vehicle. It is not just a matter of talking to people you know. Get out there and create a wider and deeper pool of people who can inform you and otherwise be of assistance. In chapter 28, "The Job Search," the inquiry called "The Networking Game" provides tools to enlarge and deepen your network of supporters. As you read the rest of this list of research resources, note that many of them are really opportunities to get to know people who can help you.

Books are the source for in-depth research. Your library will not stock the best and latest books on most subjects. To learn about a field, buy and read a wide range of books that look at the subject in question from different perspectives: books written by people in the field, books about leaders in the field, books about the field by journalists, and textbooks teaching the subject matter you would need to learn. If you aren't interested in the textbooks, you may not be interested in the field. Become an expert. This is not the time to save a few dollars. Reading a wide range of books provides multiple viewpoints, just like talking with many people to learn what you need to know and form your own enlightened viewpoint.

The library is the resource everyone has forgotten, now that the online world is so much more convenient. However, your library can be a useful source for a wide range of research tools unavailable online. Try to find the library in your area with the largest specialty collection of career information. This may be in the career resources office of a local university, a college, or a public library. There you will (hopefully) find a vast array of books on various occupations, the growth outlook for different careers, employer directories, and much more. They may also have job-market studies, local employer listings, and access to other information you are seeking. The business section of your library can provide information about specific organizations: their growth, products, competition, philosophy, and future outlook. Use the library to do periodical searches. You can glean a great deal from reading every magazine article written about a career area over the last few years. Many libraries now have extensive computer resources such as links to other library databases and the Internet. They often subscribe to paid databases that would not be available on your computer. Your best resource at the library is the information resources professional, otherwise known as the reference librarian.

Trade publications are the best way to learn the real inside lowdown about any field of interest. When you read commercial and association trade journals, you find out what is really happening in the field, what insiders think, what concerns and worries they have, what problems you might like to help solve. There is no better way to transport yourself into the pulsing heart and soul of a field. This is the field itself, not something written about it by outsiders or academics. Here you learn who is who and what topics are hot. Here you read profiles on organizations and industry leaders, and collect invaluable contact information for insiders. Read at least the last year of the most popular trade magazines in fields you are considering, from cover to cover. Don't neglect the ads, the help-wanted pages, and the news bulletins; they sometimes hold more information than the articles. Use trade journals to find editors of newsletters about the field. Make them a part of your network. Most of them are used to getting several calls per day from subscribers looking for answers to their questions. If you are friendly and respectful, there is no reason they wouldn't be willing to talk to you.

Conferences, conventions, trade shows, seminars, and industry-specific organizations are the best place to meet people who work in an industry you are researching. This is the best way to meet decision makers—the people who might eventually hire you. You have an opportunity to meet people at all levels, from CEOs on down, speak with experts, and visit booths offering a wide range of related products. You can usually find a way into industry events, even if you might have to join an organization or apply some *Mission: Impossible* techniques to get into some. If you cannot gain admission to an industry event, you can still hang around the hotel where it is taking place, visiting hospitality suites hosted by participating organizations, meeting people in the lobby, and so forth. Participating in professional development seminars in a field of interest and joining industry-specific groups are other great methods for meeting people and learning at the same time.

Trade associations are an excellent source of information on the careers within the industry they serve. They often have materials developed specifically for people interested in pursuing these careers. Their more senior employees usually have a stethoscope on the pulse of the industry. You might even be able to talk them into letting you use their libraries, which often contain voluminous collections of materials in their specialty.

Your professional career coach, if you have one, is your partner in research. Most likely, he or she won't actually go out and do the research for you but will help you design an effective research strategy, suggest resources, point you in the right direction, and help you make sense of what you uncover.

Volunteering and internships take you into the very heart of a field, so you can find out what it is like from the inside. No matter how many people you speak with or how many books you read, there is no substitute for actually working in a field that is of interest. One caution, though: Volunteers and interns are usually given the lowliest of work to do. If you are thinking of becoming the captain of a Greenpeace ship intercepting whalers on the high seas, licking envelopes in the local office may not give you the authentic experience you seek.

How to Find Out What You Need to Know

Here are three tips to make sure that your career research gets to the goal line:

1. **Do twenty times as much research as you feel like doing.** I sometimes have clients come back from doing research as a homework assignment and discover that they have just scratched the surface. It is not enough to talk with one or two people or read a book or two. After all, you are deciding what to do with your life. The career you choose will be how you spend your

days, year after year. I recommend speaking with an absolute minimum of ten people in each field of interest; the more the better. Read everything you can find on the subject.

2. **Seek to discover new questions as well as answers.** The more you learn, the more new and important questions you will uncover. As research progresses, your questions will improve. As the quality of your questions improves, so will the clarity and usefulness of the answers.

3. **Think like a detective or a spy.** You are not writing a college paper here. Pretend that you are a detective and that people's lives depend on the focus, depth, and accuracy of your research. (The quality of at least one life *does* depend on it.) My personal research guru is James Garner's character Jim Rockford in the ancient TV series *The Rockford Files*. Rockford can always come up with a creative way to get access to anyone and anything. He even carries a printing press in the trunk of his car to print up business cards to fit the need.

Most research is not very difficult. For example, identifying potential employers is a straightforward task once you have narrowed your search down to a specific job title and geographic area. A systems analyst looking for a job in Portland, Oregon, should have no difficulty in uncovering every company in town that might hire him or her. Once you identify the potential employers, you can employ a combination of library research, sleuthing, and networking to find the kinds of projects they work on, corporate personality and culture, and so on. It is much more difficult to find out what a potential career is really like. That's why it is so important to think like a detective and do much more research than you may feel like doing.

Informational Interviews

In a sense, all the conversations you have with other people about potential careers are informational interviews. Here are a few basic principles:

Hold off on informational interviewing until you are ready. Save this for later in your project, after you have learned everything you can from other resources, and after you have narrowed down your Career Ideas list. Use these valuable human resources in the most effective way, as the source to get the answers to the questions you cannot find elsewhere.

Don't pretend you want information when you really want a job. Use informational interviewing for only that: getting your questions answered. Hidden agendas insult people's generosity in speaking with you. And you end up looking bad.

Write down and memorize your questions ahead of time. This is one way you can dramatically increase the quality of these interviews. The more clarity you have about what you need to know, the better the answers you will get. To get you started, below is a list of generic questions, only some of which you may want to ask. Make up your own list. Keep it reasonably short. Refine your questions until you are sure they are to the point. Ask your most important questions first in case you run out of time. Do not ask how much money someone makes.

Take notes. Jot down enough of the answer that you can remember it later. Taking notes will also slow down any tendency to sound like a machine gun—and will show the interviewee you are serious.

Say thank you. Thank the interviewee. He or she took the time to help you. The next day, send a note (by mail, not email) thanking him/her again.

- What do you find most satisfying and most frustrating about your job?

- What changes are occurring in your field and company?

- Are you expected to take work home at night or fulfill social obligations that eat into time away from the job?

- How often and how much do you work odd hours, overtime, and so on?

- How much of your day do you spend working with . . . (people, speedboats, bats, computers, and so on)?

- What functional skills do you use most?

- What personality traits, talents, and skills fit your job best?

- What kind of person does best in this work?

- How often and how do you . . . (use creative problem solving, travel overseas, and so forth) on the job?

- How much of your time do you spend working with things or information, as distinguished from working with people?

- What kind of interactions do you have with peers, colleagues, supervisors, managers, clients, and so on?

- Who do you go to when you need advice or support? Is there enough available?

- How much and what kind of variety and routine does your work include?

- Do you feel you are able to express yourself at work?

- What kind of challenges does your work provide?

- What is it like to work at this organization? (There are many questions you could ask about working in a particular organization.)

- Do you find your work competitive? Cooperative? How so?

- Is it a secure job/field, in terms of income-earning potential, opportunities, future demand, and so forth?

- What kind of relationship do you have with your clients, colleagues, supervisor, staff?

- How much do you work one-on-one with people?

- How much deadline pressure comes with the job?

- Is it important to have a detail orientation?

- How much reading and researching are involved?

- How much decision making is involved?

- How much persuading or selling is involved?

- What are the sources of satisfaction for you in this career?

- What's a starting salary for this field?

- What is the potential for growth?

- Where do various growth tracks lead?

- Is your job portable?

- What's a typical day like?

- What do you find stressful, annoying, or unpleasant about your work?

- Why do you feel your work is meaningful, important, valued?

- How much of a typical workday consists of administrative work?

- How predictable is a given day, week?

- What education and certification and other requirements are required for this type of work?

- What would I need to do to become an attractive candidate for a job in this field? What alternatives require less education?

- How long were you in school, training to learn your profession?

- What is your work environment like?

- What is the best way to gain entrance to your field or company?

- Do you belong to a professional association? How do I contact it?

- What books and trade publications do you recommend I read to learn more?

- If you were in my position, how would you go about getting into this field?

- What employers would be most likely to offer what I am seeking?

- May I contact you if other questions arise?

- Can you refer me to other people in your field who could answer further questions, give a different perspective?

Is It Possible? Realistic? How Far Will I Stretch?

These questions need to be answered if your new career is to turn out to be more than a pipe dream. Make sure. Check out the relationship between potential careers and reality.

"**Is it possible?**" is a common question when considering career direction. If you are five foot two, clumsy, and thinking of being a professional football player, the answer is probably no. There are always some things that just aren't possible. However, many things that seem doubtful could be possible with a stretch. The history of human life is an ever-swelling stream of breakthroughs into new possibilities that then become new realities, available to all of us. Fifty thousand years ago, breakthroughs came at a slow pace. Every once in a while, someone would have a flash of insight and invent a slightly more efficient stone tool. Now the breaking waves of new possibility pour over us endlessly. Asking "Is it possible?" in this day and age is like asking "Could I get wet?" while standing at the edge of an ocean. Nevertheless, you need to ask yourself this question. If it doesn't seem possible to you, then you need to either abandon it or see if you are willing to turn it into a genuine possibility.

"Is it realistic?" and **"How far am I willing to stretch?"** When you ask, "Is it realistic?" there is often a more relevant question lurking just under the surface. Let's suppose that you are forty and have been working for all of your adult life for a big company. Now you are thinking of starting your own business. Very likely you will be peppered with a barrage of inner voices asking "Is it realistic?" over and over. The answer depends on what you mean by realistic. If you mean "Is it safe?" the answer is always no. Nothing is safe. Is it safe to stay where you are? What do you mean by safe?

Sometimes when people ask, "Is it realistic?" what they really mean is "Am I willing to do what it takes to accomplish that goal? Am I willing to pay the price? How far am I willing to stretch?" Only you can answer that question. But remember, there are three places you can find answers to questions: inside, outside, and invent the answer. Most people would look inside themselves for the answer to this question. What is sure to happen when you do that? You guessed it: a huge attack of Yeahbuts. When you ask good old, same old you this question, you have about the same chance of getting a yes as a teenaged you asking to borrow the family car the day after running over your dad's golf clubs. Then again, I'm not advocating blind optimism, either. You don't want to make up some hopeful, fanciful, positive answer that you are not willing to live up to. I suggest that you reread chapter 7, titled "Making Decisions—A Short Course." Perhaps you would be willing to raise the stakes and make a truly free choice about how far you are willing to stretch.

"Is it realistic?" can also mean "Does it fit with my commitments?" You may need more information to make a choice.

CHAPTER 12

•

RIGHT LIVELIHOOD

When the sun rises, I go to work.
When the sun goes down, I take my rest,
I dig the well from which I drink,
I farm the soil which yields my food,
I share creation. Kings can do no more.

—ANONYMOUS, FROM CHINA, 2,500 BC

Right livelihood is an ancient Asian philosophical concept that proposes a perfect working relationship and flow between you and the world around you. Like the farmer who wrote the poem above, when you achieve right livelihood, you are in perfect harmony with creation. You have become ecologically appropriate.

The figure illustrates the flow of energy in any part of the natural world that is ecologically in tune. In and out! In and out! On we go! There is a perfect, harmonious balance between you and the rest of the universe. There is nothing abstract, unrealistic, or mystical about living a life of right livelihood. All living creatures do it, from gorilla to mosquito. Right livelihood does not require green leaves above, soft New Age music playing, or a passion for saving the world. For some, working as a lawyer may be a perfect expression of right livelihood. The thousands of different jobs available do not exist by accident. They are all an integral part of the complex web that we humans have spun. On close examination, right livelihood is really a very practical set of guidelines for living. Here's one interpretation of the components:

1. **Your work fully expresses all aspects of your nature.** It fits your innate talents perfectly. It expresses your temperament and personality fully, even those parts that you do not see as positive. It provides the rewards that matter to you. It fulfills your goals. It occurs in an environment that is suitable and appropriate to who you are.

2. **The subject of your work is something in which you have a passionate and abiding interest.** It is deeply meaningful to you. It continues to appeal to you as the years roll by.

3. **Your work continually nourishes you.** It provides a natural route for your evolution. It challenges you to continue to learn and grow.

4. **It does no harm to anyone.** It is ecologically sound. It does not oppose appropriate stewardship of the earth.

5. **It serves humanity in some way.** You and I cannot judge what is appropriate service for another person. In the larger scheme of things, an IRS agent is just as important a part of the fabric of humanity as is a teacher, a mother, or an entrepreneur. Perhaps without IRS agents, nobody would pay taxes, everything would crumble, and Mad Max would take over.

6. **It is freely accepted.** You work because you choose to, not because you are compelled to.

7. **You are "being" yourself.**

Freedom and Surrender

A happy life is one which is in accord with its own nature.

— S e n e c a

We live in a time in which one of the most prized cultural ideals is "doing what I want." Many of us wish we were more like the movie stars, the novelists, and other creative types who seem to do exactly what they want. We pity our neighbor who never does. The very thought of being dominated and controlled by the circumstances of our lives conjures up images of dictatorships, slavery, subjugation. There is a big difference between being free to do what you want and having the talent and personality to make it happen. Full self-expression is attainable only when you mix elements of creativity and boundless possibility with the wisdom to pick something that fits who you are and the special gifts you have to offer the world. Let's inquire further by taking a brief look at one of the big questions humankind has puzzled over since the beginning of time: What is the nature of human nature? Why are we the way we are?

Nurture and Nature

For years, a debate has raged between the advocates of two different theories of human ability. One group asserts that the personality traits and abilities that distinguish each of us are the result of parenting, environment, and certain events that shape our lives. According to this "nurture" theory, each of us starts life as an empty vessel of potential, a blank slate to be written on by life. The opposing point of view is the "nature" theory. It asserts that we are shaped by our genetic heritage into complicated machines whose behavior is programmed from beginning to end. According to this theory, we are trapped within a life predetermined by our DNA, unable to alter our fixed destiny. Each of the two camps continues to insist it is right.

Now that the results of many years of scientific study are in, it seems neither side got it quite right. The truth is somewhere in the middle. It turns out that human behavior is a mixture of nature and nurture. As the studies continue to pile up, however, what has surprised much of the scientific community is the enormous weight of evidence proving that we are much more the product of genetics than was previously considered possible. Like it or not, the simple fact is that much of who you are today is innate, fixed, hardwired. No one knows exactly how much of your character is hardwired, or the result of genetics. No one knows exactly how much was learned or how much of what you learned was shaped over the anvil of your inborn nature.

Whether your most prized qualities are attributable to nature or nurture is not really all that important. It's just water over the dam now anyway. What is important is that you are the way you are: a wonderfully unique collection of talents and traits, points of view, habits, and behaviors. They are now all mixed together to make up the spicy little bit of heaven and hell called you.

If you can let go of the notion that you should be or could be somehow different or better than you are, the whole perspective on education, personal growth, and career choice changes dramatically. Instead of trying to shape yourself or your children into a mold, the task shifts to encouraging growth toward a fully realized expression of one's natural potential. We then transform from small-time tinhorn god to gardener. This is not necessarily bad news. You may find that you enjoy gardening more than godding. Instead of trying to change into something you aren't—a more extroverted person, a more analytical person, or whatever—learn to recognize, appreciate, and express what you have been given.

When your work combines your natural strengths and requires only minimum time spent doing things that you are not naturally gifted at, it is like swimming downstream in a swift river. To ignore your temperament and natural talents in designing your career will very likely result in a life spent in a never-ending battle swimming upstream against the river of life. Swimming upstream is hard work and slow going. When you turn around and go with the flow, you get farther faster, and your journey is a lot more fun.

When you begin to design your future career around the way you actually are, you will discover that many of the inborn qualities you considered to be negatives turn out to be some of your biggest strengths. Here's an example: I have always been talkative. At the age when most kids can barely speak a few words, I was holding long conversations with everyone, including the mailman. In the early years of elementary school, I had a great time participating fully in class in my own talkative, enthusiastic style. As the years rolled by, education became a matter of sitting quietly and politely while the teachers transferred their big buckets of facts into our little empty ones. I began to suspect that something was wrong with me. The message being sent was: Noisy, playful, and enthusiastic were appropriate only in social settings, not in the serious settings of school and work.

When I made early career decisions, I never thought to design lots of talking into the mix. Naturally, I found myself in work where I had to sit quietly and politely much too often. When I committed myself to choosing a career I would love and began to design it from the ground up, I began to see all of my various characteristics as the building blocks I had to work with, rather than from a judgmental perspective of good or bad, right or wrong. I got down to the truth: Rocks are hard, water is wet, and I make a lot of noise. So, instead of squishing myself into the same old mold, I designed lots of talking into my career. One of the most powerful things you can do for yourself and your future is to accept and appreciate the whole range of your characteristics, talents, and quirks. They are what you have to offer the world. Then dig in and design yourself a future that is a perfect custom fit with you as you are. Even the characteristics you consider to be your liabilities or psychological shortcomings are worthy of your respect. If you resist authority, maybe you should work for yourself. If you like to blow up buildings, how about becoming a demolition contractor?

> *The question "Who ought to be boss?" is like asking, "Who ought to be the tenor in the quartet?" Obviously, the man who can sing tenor.*
>
> —HENRY FORD

I am not advocating becoming complacent about personal growth and self-improvement. Quite the opposite. Remember that joyfully surrendering to life as it is is only one half of the paradox. There may be times when you want to expand your range of possibilities or take on something that stretches you further than you have ever gone before. That impulse or intention is just as much an element of your makeup—and therefore just as important an element of your expression of right livelihood—as your talents. It's terrific when introverted people join Toastmasters International and learn to be comfortable and capable in front of a room filled with people. They may have great personal breakthroughs as they extend their range of possibilities. They may even discover a previously concealed talent this way. But if they are truly introverted, they are probably not going to enjoy being onstage for several hours every day, in which case it would be foolish indeed for them to choose a public speaking career.

Rather than try to change yourself, joyfully accept the genetic cards you have been dealt. Then get to work creating new possibilities if you so desire. Learn new skills. Join Toastmasters if you want to be more comfortable or improve your skills in front of a group. If you are not very good at detail work, get creative and find a way to become competent dealing with the details you have to face. But choose a career with a bare minimum of detail work. If you are afraid of heights, you may want to learn to climb mountains to master your fear. But think twice before you become a riveter building skyscrapers.

Another aspect of right livelihood is serving humanity in some way, big or small. Each person is either part of the solution, part of the problem, or a neutral factor. Some things are obviously part of the problem: anything that would make the earth less livable for your great-grandchildren, corporate officials whose greed dehumanizes both employees and customers, politicians whose actions are most concerned with reelection. We have had lawyer clients comment that their work is parasitic, yet I know criminal defense attorneys who feel they are making an important contribution. Sanitation workers obviously contribute; what about investment bankers? Since there is no list, you will have to use your own sense of ethics and understanding of what you believe makes a positive contribution. Perhaps a good teacher is part of the solution and a bad one part of the problem. But how does one really know? Perhaps it is the intention behind your choices and actions that makes the difference. If it matters to you to contribute, you most likely will. In chapter 21, "Passions, Meaning, Mission, Purpose," you will have a chance to look at what matters to you and, if you choose, include it in your work.

•

CHAPTER 13

SEVEN KEYS

These seven keys unlock doors to transforming your ability to generate a future that goes beyond the limits of what has previously seemed possible. This chapter presents some ways to explore beyond your normal boundaries. Boundaries may seem to provide safety, but they also confine you. Don't discount the keys if they look unfamiliar. You're probably reading this book anyway because you ran out of ideas. Give the keys a fair trial. You don't need special equipment. Just dive in.

1. **Create your future from the present, not the past.** Designing the perfect career is like creating a painting that expresses you fully and completely. Rather than add dabs of paint to something you painted years ago, start at the beginning with a blank canvas. Take your time. Consider everything very carefully before including it in the final picture. This is your opportunity to have your life be exactly the way you want it to be.

   Most of the time, we are so busy thinking, categorizing, and comparing that we don't even notice that automatic internal software runs habitual patterns throughout our days, our lives, while we live under the illusion that we are making the decisions and directing our activities and thoughts.

   A computer doesn't make choices. It just runs a program—the automated processing of data through a set of built-in rules. If you truly want to have a great career, you might find it useful to confront how much of your thoughts, points of view, behaviors, and decision making are rooted in habits—that is, the past. If you want to learn to think for yourself, you have to face up to the fact that sometimes (or, perhaps, even more often) we don't. Just because we humans have a marvelous capacity for intelligence doesn't mean we use it. Just because we can think doesn't mean we do.

   Few people think more than two or three times a year. I have made an international reputation for myself by thinking once or twice a week.

   —GEORGE BERNARD SHAW

   Promise yourself that you will determine your future as free as possible from all the voices of your past: the Yeahbuts and fears, your memories, parents, friends, tribes, successes, failures, and the media. That declaration to yourself is the key to creating new possibilities and extraordinary results that take you beyond the world you have known. The bottom-line question is, Are you going to design your future, or is your past going to keep doing it for you? Declare your future, make an audacious promise that takes you into a new future, make it specific, then get to work doing what you said you were going to do, all the while recognizing that your brain's defensive system will do anything to get you back to the same old life you are used to living.

2. **Throw away your assumptions.** We all tend to hold on to our pet notions about life the way that some people save twenty-year-old *National Geographic*s in the attic. Each of us has an unexamined collection of beliefs, opinions, and points of view about how life works that we trust blindly and completely. We live by a rule book we wrote (or inherited) but never read. We think we know our limits, how far we can travel from the safety of the world we know, and what would happen if we jumped off the edge of the known world. For routine issues, automatically following this internal rule book works just fine, but with regard to choosing one's life's work, it pays to rewrite a few of the rules.

    Yes, you might have to make some compromises along the way. But don't start off assuming you have to make them. Just because you didn't have a stellar history at college doesn't mean that you can't become a doctor. Just because you are a middle manager with a wife, kids, two cars, and a mortgage doesn't mean that you cannot own your own successful beach bar in Negril. As you go through this process, you have plenty of chances to decide what compromises you are willing to make, if any. You can choose them consciously rather than assuming there is no other possibility. In any event, the one way to avoid making unnecessary compromises is to challenge your assumptions and throw away the ones that aren't useful.

3. **Embrace "not knowing."** Imagine sitting on a rural hilltop at night. In the sky, you notice a blinking light that slowly circles overhead. It makes no sound and offers no clues to its origin. If you are like me, your mind immediately and automatically comes up with explanations about the source of the light: It's a helicopter. It's a saucer. I'm hallucinating. It's something the government isn't telling us about. It's not easy to allow the light to remain a total mystery. Our nature is to explain, to justify. We like quick answers because we are uncomfortable with uncertainty. Think about it. Wouldn't you rather be thought of as someone who knows than someone who doesn't?

There is a story in Japan about a learned professor who visits the local Zen master to receive enlightenment. As they sit face-to-face, the professor explains at great length all that he has learned during his life-long scholarly study of Buddhism. As he rattles on and on, the master pours him a cup of tea. The professor is startled when the master continues to pour until the tea overflows the cup onto the tabletop. The professor cries, "Stop! Can't you see there's no room?" The Zen master bows to him, and the professor sees himself for the first time as an overfull cup. The difference between a master and a know-it-all is that the master, in any field, brings a beginner's mind, fresh and open to unlimited possibilities, to each new day.

4. **Since you may never discover the truth, invent it.** Most of us are very fixated on what everything around us signifies. We want to understand the "real meaning" of events, concepts, and our lives. What did it really mean when he didn't call? What did it really mean when Napoléon put his hand in his coat? We habitually jump to conclusions and instantly assign meaning to everything.

The best way to predict the future is to invent it.

—ALAN KAY

Once we know what something "really means," history repeatedly tells us that we will gladly die defending that point of view. It never occurs to us that, to someone else, it could mean something entirely different. Or it might mean absolutely nothing. If something can mean completely different things to different people who may be even smarter or more experienced than you, then meaning might be flexible. That opens up the possibility that you could actually create what various things mean to you. When your spouse leaves hairs on the bathroom sink, it may be impossible to let them be nothing more than hairs on the sink, devoid of meaning. But the hairs don't have to mean "The guy/woman is a slob" or "He/she doesn't care that the hairs upset me." You could instead have the hairs mean "My beloved is near. All is well."

In any endeavor that takes you, the explorer, into new territory, it is enormously useful to keep reminding yourself that all your definitions and judgments are only one point of view. Remember that almost all human beings think that their opinions and beliefs are the "real" truth. Even the belief that there is "real" truth may be nothing more than your opinion; your own personal—or not so personal—interpretation. (The more people around you who believe the same thing, the more real it seems.) Once you can notice that interpretation is pretty much all there is, you are free to keep your inherited points of view or invent others that most powerfully support you to be all that you can be.

Physical concepts are the creation of the human mind, and are not, however it may seem, determined by our external world. In our endeavor to understand reality, we are somewhat like a man trying to understand the mechanism of a closed watch.

—ALBERT EINSTEIN

5. **Get to know the realm of possibility.** There is a big difference between "options" and "possibilities." Everyone has options. Your options consist of a fixed set of predetermined scenarios, points of view, and perceived limitations that already reside in your inner data bank. When you ask "What are my options?" you are taking inventory of your internal stockroom. If you depend on your options to formulate your future, that future will be no more than a rearrangement of your past.

Possibilities are completely different. When you ask "What is possible?" you must stretch your imagination out of the confines of the familiar. You have to stretch your wings, get out of the box, and look around.

If I were to wish for anything, I would not wish for wealth and power but for the passionate sense of what might be, for the eye which, ever young and ardent, sees the possible. Pleasure disappoints, possibility never. And what wine is so sparkling, what so fraught, what so intoxicating as possibility!

—SØREN KIERKEGAARD

Possibility is the great motivator. A prevailing condition of few options and no possibilities is, I believe, more directly the cause of the persistence of our inner-city social problems than is lack of opportunity. To have a life beyond the mediocre, ask not "What are my options?" but "What is possible?"

6. **Learn to separate Yeahbuts from original thoughts.** For anyone committed to having his dreams come true, this is, by far, the one critical skill to master. The natural law that operates and controls the lives of all biological organisms is the law of homeostasis. Your body and mind contain millions of little switches, like thermostats, that control your perceptions and actions. When you exercise, your body heats up above 98.6 degrees. That throws a switch that produces a whole range of actions designed to get you cooled back down to the temperature you are set for, 98.6 degrees. When your temperature returns to equilibrium, all the machinery working to cool you down stops.

What most people do not usually realize is that the same kind of mechanism makes decisions for them. Your "comfort zone" is the range of thoughts and actions you can get away with without triggering one of these mechanisms. The internal survival machinery compares what you are doing or thinking of doing with its database of what you have done before. It assumes that whatever you have done, day after day, is "safe."

Anything outside the comfort zone is perceived as a threat to your survival. It can't distinguish real dangers from personal growth. When you learn to distinguish Yeahbuts from other thoughts, they lose their power over you. You recognize that what your Yeahbuts consider dangerous and react to so strongly is actually a great opportunity to step into new territory wearing new shoes.

Security is mostly a superstition. It does not exist in nature, nor do the children of men as a whole experience it. Avoiding danger is no safer in the long run than outright exposure. Life is a daring adventure, or nothing.

—HELEN KELLER

7. **Dance on the edge of the sword.** To live fully, one needs to master two completely different realms. On the one hand, you must learn to live in the realm of possibility and invention, or your life will be nothing more than clockwork gears turning predictably and automatically. On the other hand, having your feet firmly planted on terra firma is necessary to realize your dreams. If you live mainly in the realm of possibility, you will become a dreamer who accomplishes little. Dancing on the edge of the sword is the art of living in both realms at once, perfectly balanced. When you lean too far to one side, get your balance back as soon as possible. With practice, you will find that you can be present to both at the same moment. Which side do you usually lean toward?

CHAPTER 14

•

THE ROCKPORT CAREER
DESIGN METHOD

The Rockport Career Design Method is a specific methodology; a set of tools and inquiries to design a career that will fit you like custom-tailored clothing. At Rockport Institute, we have been experimenting, changing, improving, and creating new methods for more than thirty years, continually incorporating new wisdom from a wide range of fields—all based on a commitment to you—so that you have the tools you need to design a career you will love.

If you read it like a novel, it won't do much for you. Your success depends on your active participation. You can't master the art of making love or choosing a career by reading a book. Mastery takes dedicated effort and practice. It takes committed, high-energy, full-tilt-boogie participation to have the kind of life you want. I suggest that you become intimately familiar with this method by reading this chapter more than once.

How It Works

The Rockport Career Design Method employs three main tools. As a carpenter uses a hammer and a saw in building a house, so you will use the career design tools many times during your career design project. Each tool is a document that you create and then use as you discover more about yourself and careers, adding to the document, deleting, refining, and researching as appropriate. Later in this chapter, we will get to know them well:

- **Clues:** a list of anything you consider potentially useful in choosing career design components.

- **Definite career design components:** a list of the elements that you have decided are the specifications your future work must match, phrased so that your components are specific and as focused as a laser beam.

- **Career ideas:** the place to write down every career that might fit you.

157

The one big question you ask during your work with these documents is "What am I sure will definitely be some of the components of my future career?" This question is the heart of the Rockport method. It is different from questions such as "What do I like?" or "What are some good careers out there?" Every time you answer this "What am I sure of" question, you add a new component to your Definite Career Design Components list, building the design of your future work step-by-step, based on certainty, not wishes, hopes, or maybes. Adding new components to your design often suggests new clues and career ideas as well.

The documents support you in moving through the stages of the career design process: *investigate, decide,* and *design.* A series of exercises in the third section of this book will guide you through the process. We call these exercises inquiries because they are about asking, questioning, exploring. You've already done a few in earlier parts of *The Pathfinder.* The inquiries are all designed to help create some definite components of your future career, little islands of certainty in the midst of the raging storm of thoughts, emotions, opinions, and hopes. To make it easier, we have broken the process down into small, manageable steps. You will have a chance to look into every area of your life that may be related to your future career.

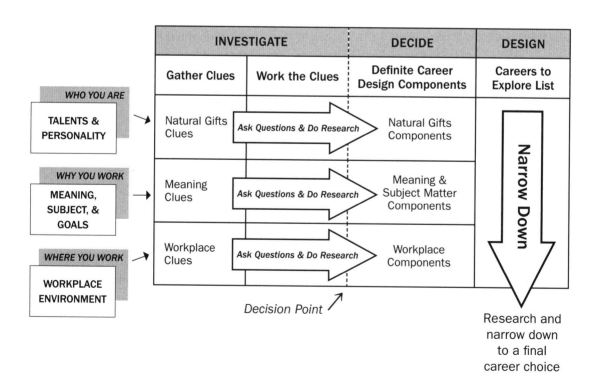

You start the career choice process by putting on your invisible detective hat. As an investigator, you search for and gather clues, then work those clues by observing, considering, and researching them from various viewpoints. The goal is to see if any clue or combination of clues suggests a definite component that you would like to claim as part of your future career.

For example, a friend tells you that you never seem to get enough of talking with and doing things with people, face-to-face. This one hits you right between the ears as an accurate observation. Now you have a good clue. You do some investigating, paying more attention to what you do naturally in your day-to-day life, and you notice that what your friend said is completely accurate.

You become more convinced that spending most of your time working with people may turn out to be an important career design component. You also look back at your past and realize that you are always happy dealing directly with people. This is so clear to you that you can now move to decision mode and add one item to your Definite Career Design Components document: In your future career, you will definitely spend most of your time working directly with people face-to-face.

Once you have investigated and decided on enough pieces of the puzzle (definite career design components), you move into the third mode: design. In design mode, you combine the components that you have decided are essential to you and speculate on careers that might fit that combination. As you research specific careers on your Career Ideas list, learning more about them, you toss out careers that don't fit and perhaps add more careers to explore that you hadn't thought of before, coming ever closer to being able to choose your final and definite career.

Let's say you come up with the following definite career design components, although in real life you will come up with a lot more than two:

- I will spend most of my time working directly with people, face-to-face.

- My work will combine teaching and problem solving as major daily elements.

After some head scratching, research, and talking with other people, you come up with the following list of careers to explore: college professor, teacher of advanced-placement courses in high school, corporate trainer, golf pro at a country club, organizational development consultant-trainer, developer of online educational presentations, seminar leader, and public speaker. They all fit the specifications. After doing a lot of research, you choose to become a corporate trainer.

When you are in the midst of the design process, you work in all three modes at once. For example, once you start exploring specific careers and seeing why some don't fit you, that provides more clues, which puts you back in investigator mode. Once this project gets rolling, you do detective work, make decisions, and, after a while, explore specific careers all at once. Let's look at how you do it.

Investigate

In this mode, you come up with and work clues that will help you find the best fit between you and the working world. You don't want to be like the dumb cop in the movies who jumps to erroneous conclusions based on too few clues and an over-abundance of self-righteous opinions. Instead you model your participation on the hero who keeps searching and working the clues until he can point a finger with confidence at the one who did the dastardly deed.

You take multiple steps in solving your career questions, just as a good detective does in solving a crime. As a first step, you collect as many clues as you can. At this stage, you don't know what will ultimately be useful and what won't. Some clues, such as your natural talents and personality traits, will be as obvious as a fingerprint-covered dagger sticking out of the victim's back. Some will be more subtle. These might prove to be strong clues or they might not. Still, you make note of them. Any of them might turn out to be important. Some clues may take a lot of work to uncover, mull over, or research. You need to be open-minded and thorough, leaving no stone unturned. You need to poke around anywhere you might find a good, strong, juicy clue.

Clues

A clue is *anything you consider potentially useful in choosing career design components.* You may be able to explain why you think it is useful, or you may just have a hunch. Don't dismiss any clue too quickly in the early stages. It could be an observation, an insight, or a piece of information. In the personal realm, a clue can be about who you are, what you do well, how you behave, what matters to you, and so on. Clues can be information, observations, hunches, or insights. A friend said that at age twenty he didn't know how to reconcile his great loves: women, drawing, and tying trout flies. He ultimately became a well-known plastic surgeon. If you're not sure about a clue, you can do some work on it with questions and research to see if it has lasting value. Early in your career design project, the best clues will be about you.

- How you think

- How you behave in various situations

- What you do well or not so well

- What you learn about yourself from exercises in this book

- Subjects you enjoy or master easily

- Passions and interests

- Your positive or negative reaction to something you learn about a particular career

- Wants

- Goals

- Insights

- Dreams

- Fantasies

- The things you care about

- Your outlook on life

- What attracts or repels you

- Your quirks and idiosyncrasies

- What other people say about you

- Your natural talents

- Tasks you enjoy

- Limitations

Notice that you are not yet looking for clues about careers themselves. In the early stages of the career design process, looking for clues means paying attention to *you* and how you function. Until you have fully taken your own measure, it's premature to try to squeeze yourself into ideas about careers. Your investigation ultimately will focus on clues related to externals such as the workplace, the economy, and other practical pieces of the puzzle. But first you need to investigate the *you* that you want a career to fit.

Some clues include the external world: "I love the idea of building Conestoga wagons, but there are only two small shops that make them now, and employment opportunities look dim." A clue can also be an idea that pops up: "Maybe I could make all sorts of wagons and carriages for the movie industry."

The inquiries in the following section are divided into the three big questions you need to ask and answer to choose a career that gives you both success and satisfaction:

- Part 1, "Who am I?" Your innate talents and gifts, temperament, personality traits, roles you play on the stage of life, and best workplace functions.

- Part 2, "Why work?" Meaning, mission, purpose, values, rewards, and goals.

- Part 3, "Work where?" The workplace environment.

- Part 4, "Making the choice." Exploring careers that may fit and narrowing them down to the final choice.

The book provides a lot of assistance in both finding and working these clues. But don't depend on the inquiries in this book as your sole source of clues. In addition to working through these inquiries, start paying attention to your everyday life. What do you enjoy so much that you lose track of time? What do you enjoy that others think is difficult or a chore? What do you read? What do you talk about with your friends? What are you passionate about? Make your everyday life an important part of your investigation. Keep a sharp eye peeled. Because we do not always see ourselves with perfect clarity, you can use some outside sources, such as friends, family, coworkers, teachers, bosses, and others who may be able to supply some useful observations. Some clues will turn out to be central and important; others may not turn out to be important at all.

An example: When I was designing my career many years ago, I noticed that what I liked about the Super Bowl wasn't the football game. It was the TV commercials—not just watching them for enjoyment but also critiquing them and noticing which were effective. For some reason I found this compelling, even though I had no interest in marketing or advertising. This provided a very strong clue. When I began to investigate this clue, paying more attention to my daily life, I discovered that I walked around all day critiquing everything. In restaurants, I critiqued the food and the service; in movies, I noticed every flaw; in talking with people, I always listened for what was going on below the surface. This talent got me into trouble when I offered unsolicited advice or coaching, or tried to improve things that nobody else wanted changed. Then I went through a testing program that measured natural talents, similar to the Pathfinder Career Testing Program we do at Rockport Institute. I tested extremely high in this ability, one we call Diagnostic Reasoning, and realized that I needed to include it as a part of my daily work.

I ended up designing my career so I could enjoy using my "positive critic" talent every day: coaching people, training professionals in my field, inventing new methods, even writing the words you are reading now. What started as something I noticed watching the Super Bowl became a powerful clue that turned into a huge design element of my career and became one of the big reasons I love my work.

How to Work a Clue

Pick the strongest clues and then work them. For a detective, this means choosing the clues that narrow the field of suspects. "Woman" cuts the list of possible suspects in half, but "six-foot woman" is a better clue. The detective asks questions the clue suggests and investigates where that leads, what it signifies, and how it fits together with other clues, then finally figures out what conclusions it supports. That's exactly what you do as a career detective. When you're in investigative mode, you have a particular relationship with everything in your life: Instead of just living life, you are at the same time observing yourself and what's going on with you as if you're a detective working on the biggest case of your life.

The illustration shows how to work a clue:

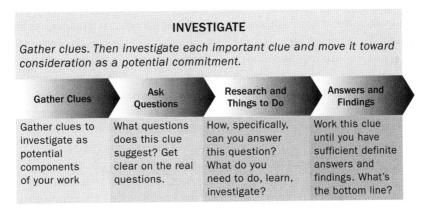

INVESTIGATE

Gather clues. Then investigate each important clue and move it toward consideration as a potential commitment.

Gather Clues	Ask Questions	Research and Things to Do	Answers and Findings
Gather clues to investigate as potential components of your work	What questions does this clue suggest? Get clear on the real questions.	How, specifically, can you answer this question? What do you need to do, learn, investigate?	Work this clue until you have sufficient definite answers and findings. What's the bottom line?

Out of all the clues you have collected, pick the most important and useful ones, and do what any detective would do: Ask questions about those clues. These questions are all subsets of the big question you are working on answering: *"What am I sure will definitely be some of the components of my future career?"* The strategy is to move each clue in the direction of making a choice about whether it becomes a definite design element of your future career.

I thought my Super Bowl clue was worth investigating, so I started observing and asking questions such as:

- What exactly is going on when I'm critiquing ads during the Super Bowl?

- What natural talents am I using?

- Where else do I do the same thing?

- How often do I do it?

- Is it fun whenever I do it?

- Where is it useful? Where does it get me in trouble?

- How can I find out more?

When you have some good questions about a particular clue, you go on to the next step, asking:

- How specifically can I answer this question?

- What do I need to do, learn, investigate?

- How can I move this clue forward so that I can decide if it will be a definite career design element?

Once you have worked the clue sufficiently and have some definite answers and findings, you can then switch from investigating to deciding—making a choice about the clue you have been working on. Will it be a definite career design element or not? More about this later.

How Do I Know Which Are the Best Clues?

There are two ways of looking at which clues are the best. One way is personal: Which clues do you care about most? Which are you most sure you want as a definite component of your future work? The other way of assessing clues is even more useful: Which clues will help in pointing toward specific jobs? The best clues lead to the most useful definite components. Gather clues with an eye to what matters most to you and give extra weight to clues that point toward specific types of careers.

Asking Razor-Sharp Questions

Your most useful investigative tool is asking and answering questions. People whose job is to get high-quality answers—such as scientists, real-life detectives, and journalists—know that half the battle in getting the best answers is asking good questions. Usually we just ask whatever questions pop into our minds. Nevertheless, the quality of the answers we get is directly related to the quality of the questions we ask. Spend some time honing your questions to a sharp point. You want them focused and specific to help you move the clue toward making a definite decision about it. Use chapter 9, "Questions," to improve your skill at asking and answering questions.

Choosing Definite Career Design Components

I suppose it might be possible to make a sculpture out of smoke or fog, like skywriting. But as soon as the wind blows (or you sneeze), the whole creation disappears. So instead of trying to design your career from wishes, hopes, and maybes, you want to use solid elements that you have decided must definitely be a part of your design.

Once you have investigated a clue, asked good questions, and answered them, you may reach the point where you know enough about a specific clue to be able to ask the big career design question: *"What am I sure will definitely be some of the components of my future career?"* When you make a definite decision about a clue, think of it as a specification; a design element of your future career. When you decide a certain element will not be a part of your career, you are also adding to your design. For example: "I won't work behind a desk more than a couple of hours a day." You may not be sure what you will do, but you know that most of the time it won't be done behind a desk.

Let's say that you are passionate about talking in front of groups of people and writing. Fine. You also like ice cream, dark eyes, salsa dancing, and Jamaica. So what? Your passions and other clues don't get really juicy until you claim them as definite career design components. You can't design with maybes.

If you decide that writing and making presentations to groups will definitely be major components of your work, you have some major specifications to add to your Career Design Components list. Stepping into the decision mode is one of the most powerful parts of creating a new future. You are not just the engineer driving the train, you are also the guy out in front laying new track. Not only do you get to drive, but you also decide where the train is going. Don't let anyone (spouse, parents, friends, fellow tribe members) tell you where the train is going. No one cares as much about your life as you do. No one else will walk to work in your shoes.

Deciding isn't mysterious. We all work in decision mode all the time: "I'm going to see this movie, not that one." "I will work out today." Most of us don't notice when we're deciding. We tend to give credit to our desires or circumstances. If someone asks why we are working out today, we say things like "I want to have giant biceps" or "I need to lose ten pounds." But lots of people want the biceps or weight loss and don't do anything about it. The real reason you are working out today is that you decided to—and then did it. You created a future that wasn't going to happen automatically by making a choice and then taking action to fulfill that commitment.

All around you, in the wider culture we live in, are many who live this way. If you listen closely to interviews with some of the people you most admire and respect, you will find that they are out in front of their own train, laying new track. They may describe it differently, but that is what they are doing. They are declaring how it will be and then doing what is necessary to make it happen. And that is what you can do to create your future career.

It doesn't take an extraordinary person to live this way. But it does take willingness, commitment, and persistence; the willingness to stand out and be a little different from the crowd, a commitment to a fully lived life, and the persistence to keep working on your design until it is fully shaped and becomes the life you are living every day.

What is it that makes the U.S. Declaration of Independence so extraordinary? A bunch of guys got together and wrote a letter to King George that said, basically, "Dear George, this is how it's going to be from now on, because we said so. Signed, The Guys." That's it, and that's what is so amazing about this document. The signers had no evidence to stand on. In fact, the most likely outcome was that they would hang as traitors. They stepped out in front of the train and laid new track.

So why doesn't everyone do this? How come most people seem to be just barely hanging on to the caboose? Because thinking for yourself and acting consistently with that take more effort than going with the flow. Jumping on the train and hoping for a great destination leave you stuck going wherever the train was headed. Equally ineffective is expecting that announcing your intentions will make anything happen. You have to be willing to do what it takes to forge your declaration into reality. After the Declaration of Independence, the rest of the world, particularly England, didn't just say, "What a jolly good idea. Let's get behind those Americans and support their big dream." The Americans had to fight to make their declaration real.

Fortunately, no universal law says that you have to struggle every inch of the way. You just have to be willing. You have to be more committed to having the kind of life you want than you are to the easier road of compromise. You have to be willing to drop the stops, no matter what they are. Here's a little secret. I have no idea how or why this works, but it does. Sometimes when people totally commit to creating something new in their lives and live that commitment without excuses, their word, their promise, becomes an almost unstoppable force of nature. In time, the path smooths out and obstacles disappear. It seems as if the entire universe turns in their favor. It may challenge them for a while, but as they persist, circumstances shift and dance in harmony with them. Now, forget I told you that, so you won't slack off and just expect it to happen. To gain more skill in creating and fulfilling declarations, promises, and commitments, and in dealing with the obstacles and Yeahbuts that arise to kill them off, I suggest you read and master chapters 5 and 6, "Why You Don't Get What You Want" and "The Power of Commitment."

Making the Best Choices

One of the tools to design your future career is decision making. It's a tool like any other: Just as a hammer pounds nails into hard materials, decision making moves you from unsure to certain, from wanting to committing, from thinking about something to declaring how it will be. Every carpenter knows that having high-quality tools makes a big difference in the final result. The same is true with decision making. Take a look at how you make decisions. Are they up to the job of designing your future? If not, I suggest that you read and master chapter 7, "Making Decisions—A Short Course."

Building Your Definite Components

Your answers to the question "What am I sure will definitely be components of my future career?" are the building blocks; the specifications of your future career. Make them clear and strong and what you really mean. Here are some examples. If you find something that rings your bell, steal it.

- I will move around on a typical day, not chained to a desk or computer.

- I will do work that changes the way people think about themselves.

- I will do work that focuses on physical objects in the real world.

- I will be on the leading edge of innovation.

- I will do work that involves finding and using ideas and information from different fields and sources.

- My work will have some structure yet still allow plenty of room for invention, imagination, and innovation.

- I will not work for a dysfunctional company that cares only for the bottom line and not for its employees' quality of life.

- I will do work that involves explaining complex concepts in simple ways.

- I will manage a group of people.

- I will work in sales and/or marketing.

- I will be an artist, a sensualist, a creator of beauty.

- My work will let me live in a rural area somewhere in the Rocky Mountains.

- I will diagnose and fix organizational problems.

- I will do work that involves successfully solving problems every day.

- I will primarily design solutions rather than implement solutions.

- My career will fit in with my goal to have children.

- No boss will look over my shoulder.

- My career will make a big, positive difference in many people's lives.

- I will use my diagnostic problem-solving talent at least several times a day.

- I will build or repair physical systems, buildings, machines, or something similar.

- I will gather, compile, and analyze data 20 to 30 percent of the time.

- I will apply my favorite processes (researching problems by reading, finding underlying patterns, brainstorming solutions, discovering, designing, teaching, organizing, counseling) to a variety of content (whether it be different people, companies, or subject matters).

- My work will mainly involve short-term projects.

- Communicating with other people will be my central job function.

- My work will not involve drumming up business.

- I will work alone 50 percent of the time. Unless I work with a partner I really like—then it could drop down to about 25 percent of the time.

- I will not study for any more degrees. But I would take a few courses if necessary.

- I will do work that I am proud of and enjoy telling other people about.

- I will do work that I have a large degree of control over.

- I will do work that is good for the world.

- I will earn $250,000 a year or more.

- I will do work that does not require formal clothing more than one day a week. I will wear casual yet hip/fun clothes.

- My work environment will be casual, relaxed, friendly, fun.

Career Ideas

Your Career Ideas list is one of the three tools you continue to work with throughout designing your future work. It starts out as a place to jot down careers that might be a good fit or that appeal to you in some way. You may consider some career ideas as serious contenders; others may be less realistic but still worth writing down because they contain a germ of an idea that might turn into a good clue. As your career design process moves forward, you add to this list and delete careers that you've decided are not a good fit. Both adding and deleting provide a powerful opportunity to generate clues: "Why do I think this career fits?" "Why is it appealing?" "What doesn't fit about this one?"

Design

In designing your future career, you take the elements you declared as definite pieces of the puzzle and fit them together into a final masterpiece—or, at first, into multiple careers that fit your specifications. Your role as designer includes all of these synonyms: architect, artist, author, creator, director, engineer, inventor, master builder, planner, and prime mover. Everything around you—the building you are in, the art on your wall, this book, your computer, the clothes you are wearing, the ring on your finger—was created by someone who worked in designer/artist/inventor/author mode. And that is exactly what you are going to do: craft your life, create your future.

For the American founding fathers, the Declaration of Independence began the creation of a new nation. The next step was designing the future United States, which included, among many other steps, drafting the Constitution. From that design flowed all the freedoms and opportunities that made it a unique and extraordinary place and provided a model for other countries around the world. From now on in *The Pathfinder*, you will be doing the same thing with your own life.

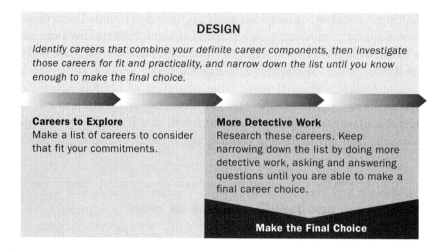

DESIGN

Identify careers that combine your definite career components, then investigate those careers for fit and practicality, and narrow down the list until you know enough to make the final choice.

Careers to Explore
Make a list of careers to consider that fit your commitments.

More Detective Work
Research these careers. Keep narrowing down the list by doing more detective work, asking and answering questions until you are able to make a final career choice.

Make the Final Choice

In design mode, you work with your Definite Career Design Components and your Career Ideas lists, researching, adding, deleting, and coming up with the final careers to explore that fit your definite career components. Then you will research and consider them with the aim of whittling down to the final choice. Some components are more useful in pointing toward specific careers. Designating your components as gold, silver, or bronze is a useful way of focusing on the components that are most likely to help you uncover careers that might fit. These ratings are approximations. You will have to decide which is which. Here are some guidelines:

- *Gold* points directly to a very specific range of careers, such as work with animals, market new products, teach as my main function, buy a business, senior management, coaching and training as my main function, or expert in a social science field.

- *Silver* points less specifically than gold to a broader range of careers. For example: writing 25 percent of the day, in a growing technology business, science, portable, or mainly interacting with people. Sometimes combining silver components creates an alchemical reaction, and, melded together, they turn to gold. Example: work outdoors, plus never wear shoes to work. With that combination, most careers vanish, and all that's left are lifeguard, surfing instructor, and very few other possibilities. This also suggests that, to avoid frostbite, you might need to move to a warmer climate.

- *Bronze* is vitally important to you, since you consider it a definite career design component, but it does not point to an identifiable job: dress casually, live in the city, not micromanaged, or office with a door. "Make a positive difference" is a bronze component even though it may be your most passionate choice. Once you have identified how you will do that (make a positive difference *with children*, for instance), it becomes a gold or silver component, because you can now name a finite number of careers that could fulfill this specification.

Deciding which are gold, silver, and bronze focuses your attention. Work with the gold first and then the silver. If you discover that most of your components are bronze, you have more work to do. It is impossible to move forward without gold and silver components.

Once you have a list of careers that seem to fit your specifications, you go back into detective mode, investigating and researching each of these careers. Most of the work you have done previously has been speculative and centered on you, the way that a custom tailor takes measurements as the first step in producing custom-made clothing. Now you look outside yourself at real careers in the real world. Part 4 of section 3, "Putting It All Together," has inquiries and resources to help you think of careers that may fit.

As you learn more about possible careers that match your specifications, you will probably find useful new clues you had not considered before. These may lead to new commitments and new definite career design components. Nothing is more useful than the real world to help separate reality from fantasy. The first steps you took, to understand the *you* your career is supposed to fit, are essential. Because that part of the process is internally focused, however, it is almost impossible to avoid making naïve and false assumptions about the real world. Now you have a chance to compare and align the internal and external worlds. Researching actual careers provides practical data that may require you to change some of your career design specifications or recognize that to fulfill your commitments will ask more of you than you previously thought.

Some careers will sink to the bottom and get crossed off your list. Others will rise to the top. As you learn more about a particular career, you will learn more about yourself and what you need and want. As you narrow the list, you get closer and closer to making a final choice. If you continue with this career design method— finding good clues, asking and answering questions, choosing definite components, researching careers that fit your components—you should be able to reach a final choice and say, "I know exactly what I am going to do. It is a great fit for me, and I know I can make it happen. I'm certain of my goal."

INQUIRY 11

Shorter Career Design Guide

This is a short guide to the Rockport Career Design Method—like the quick start-up guide that might come with a camera or computer. As you work your way through the inquiries in section 3, designing your career piece by piece, refer back to this guide to keep track of where you are at any time in the process.

This graphic illustrates the entire Rockport Career Design Method.

INVESTIGATE		DECIDE	DESIGN
Gather Clues	Work the Clues	Definite Career Design Components	Explore Specific Careers and Decide
Find clues about possible career design components	Investigate the clues with the goal of deciding which will become definite components	Choose definite career design components (specifications)	Select careers that fit your specifications. Research and narrow down to the final choice.

The next section of *The Pathfinder* consists of inquiries and tools to investigate and answer the following questions:

- **"Who am I?"**—innate talents and gifts, temperament, personality traits, roles you play on the stage of life, and best workplace functions.

- **"Why work?"**—meaning, mission, purpose, values, rewards, and goals.

- **"Work where?"**—the workplace environment.

At the top of the illustration, you see the three stages of career design: "Investigate," "Decide," and "Design."

How to Design Your Career

Create a notebook, either in a digital format or on paper. You could also download a preformatted notebook from www.rockportinstitute.com. Don't try to do this in your head. Start separate documents and name them:

- Clues—anything worth exploring that might turn into a definite career design component.

- Definite Career Design Components—answers to the question "What am I sure will definitely be important components of my future work?"

- Career Ideas—As you work through designing your career, write down any career or job possibilities that might be worth exploring. At first, this is a list of possibilities, not a serious, final list. Cross off careers that you find do not fit. Use this list to generate clues. When you add a career, consider why you added it. What makes it appealing? When you cross off a career, ask what about it made it unappealing.

Step 1: Gather Clues

Divide the Clues part of your notebook into three parts, to which you'll be adding regularly: "Who Am I?," "Why Work?," and "Work Where?" Then work your way through the chapters in section 3, which consist of inquiries and investigations into various aspects of your nature and intentions. Investigate these areas, finding and gathering clues. If there are parts of the puzzle that you have already answered to your satisfaction, just skip the chapters that cover those areas. Follow your own creative path through this book.

Step 2: Career Ideas

Whenever you think of a career or job you believe may be a good fit, add it to your Career Ideas list. Then, to discover more clues, ask yourself, "Why? What makes this attractive to me?"

Whenever one of your career ideas gets shot down because you realize it is not a good fit, delete it from your Career Ideas list, then ask, "Why is this career no longer a possibility? What specifically makes it not a good fit?" This is a great source of clues throughout the career design process.

Research the careers on this list as you move forward in designing your career so that you can cross off ones that are not a match for you. The main activities with this list are adding careers that might fit, deleting those that definitely do not fit, and using the list as part of your investigative work—for example, asking and answering questions such as "What do these careers have in common?" and "Does this career really fit?"

Step 3: Work the Strong Clues

Pick the best clues and work them by asking questions and doing research until you know enough to choose some as definite career design components.

- Observe. Pay attention to your everyday life; at work and in the rest of your life. Look for behaviors, traits, talents. Look back over your past for clues about where you and the working world would best fit together. Observe yourself as if you were a scientist studying some rare and unique creature.

- Notice connections between clues. When you consider strong clues all together, do any themes stand out? Are there any patterns among your clues?

Extra care now may save you from years of agony later. Stay loose and open-minded; some clues will pan out and become large components of your career, and some will fall by the wayside.

Step 4: Add to Your Definite Career Design Components

Everything you add to this document answers the big question: "What am I sure will definitely be some of the important components of my future career?" Concentrate on gold and silver components as much as possible.

Gold—most valuable because they point directly to a fairly narrow range of specific careers.
Silver—helpful but point to a broader range of careers than gold components.
Bronze—important to you but do not point to specific careers.

Step 5: Explore and Research

By this point, you will have refined the careers on your Career Ideas list to a very few contenders that meet your specifications well enough for you to research them in depth. Add to and subtract from the list as appropriate.

Do everything necessary to find out how well these potential careers fit your specifications and to learn what it would take to land the job or start the business. This includes talking with several people who do or did the exact same careers you are researching.

Step 6: Narrow Down the List to Your Final Career Choice

Research, compare, and contrast until you make a final choice. Use part 4, "Putting It All Together," to do this.

Step 7: Once You Have Made Your Choice, Don't Forget to Celebrate!

....

DESIGN YOUR CAREER

....

Section 3 is *The Pathfinder* workbook. It will take you through everything you need to consider in order to pick work you will love. By the time you have finished this section, hopefully you will be ready to make the choice, or at least you should be a lot closer than you are now. Each chapter delves into an important piece of the puzzle. For example: your personality, natural talents, what's meaningful to you.

At the beginning of any project, you want to get very sure of your goal and destination. Let's do that now.

Diving into the Mist

It takes courage to stand up for the possibility of a life lived fully. Making a definite decision to have a career that is highly satisfying and in which you will be very successful may seem like nothing more than a remote possibility or naïve optimism. So the question on the table is: Are you up for it? Please don't be glib in answering. The reason people have so much trouble changing or choosing careers, losing weight, or quitting smoking is that they are unwilling to take a stand for what they want, to venture into new territory, to be a little uncomfortable and uncertain, but that's what it takes to get out of the same old groove. So take your pick. Each choice has its advantages.

____ **I'm going to go for it!**

____ I want to go for it, but I'm not sure I'm ready. I'll read more of the book and then decide.

____ Not now. I'm exploring and gathering information. Maybe later.

Okay. If you have decided definitely not now, you might consider putting this book away for the time being. You can't ride if you won't take up the reins. Put it somewhere on display in your library where you will see it often. If you like, you could even surround it with flashing lights and large neon arrows. Each time you notice it, it will remind you to ask yourself, "Is it time yet?"

Looking through *The Pathfinder*, you may be concerned by the amount of inquiry and research this career design project asks of you. It asks you to dig into all aspects you need to handle to make the best choice because the usual methods of picking a career, the lite version, don't work, and as a result only about 20 to 45 percent of your friends like their work, if the surveys are to be believed.

When you learn to fly an airplane, you spend time on the ground covering the basics. The real learning begins once you take off and get your plane up into the wild blue yonder. Up until now, what you have been reading could be mistaken for ground school. It is time to climb into the cockpit, fire up your engines, and take off. We are going to go to work on designing your future, piece by piece.

Starting off on a journey together, the first thing to do is get clear exactly what you want to accomplish by going through this career design project. What sort of results would you most want, if you could have it all, without reservations.

Your degree of clarity about your final goal has a huge influence on whether you actually get there and on the degree of difficulty you will face along the way. Let's suppose that you were going to take a vacation. You decide you are going to Europe. You call the airline and try to book a flight. "Where to?" the agent asks. "Europe," you answer. "Where in Europe?" the agent asks. "Just Europe," you say. They won't sell you a trip to Europe. You have to be more specific. You have to be committed to your destination. It makes no sense to work on designing your future without a clear, definite, and powerful declaration of what you are up to, and what is your goal.

INQUIRY 12

Declare My Commitment to Design My Future Work

Close your eyes, take a big breath, and say what you intend to create for yourself. It could be something like one of these following statements, or something completely different. Whatever you promise, make it your own, and don't say it if you don't mean it.

- I promise I will choose a long-term career for myself within the next four months, a career that will be highly satisfying, fulfills my values, fits elegantly with my natural talents, is something I care about deeply, and allows me to reach my most important life goals.

- I promise to choose a form of enjoyable, purposeful self-expression that, to other people, looks like work (and pays like work).

- I promise to decide what I will do with myself in regard to my work within the next month. I will decide whether to quit my present job and seek another job in my field or change to a new field. If I decide to stay in my present field, I will get completely clear what the specifications of the new job will be. I will train myself not to make the mistakes in evaluating potential jobs that I have made in the past. If I decide to change, I will give myself another two months to decide exactly what I will do.

- I promise to try to figure it out.

- I promise to do my best.

Write down what you promised. Keep it where it won't disappear.

Courage

It takes courage to be the author of your life. When you are struggling through one of the difficult parts of turning your dreams into reality, you may wonder why you always get stuck with having to put up with so much fear and uncertainty. Why, you wonder, couldn't I feel more courageous, like those other people do?

You don't feel courageous because courage is not an emotion. There is no such thing as feeling "courageous." It is an imaginary emotion. Courage consists of doing what you said you would do even when you don't want to.

In the face of danger, you have a choice to be the delegate of either your commitments or your feelings. It's as simple and as difficult as that.

Courage is not the absence of fear, but rather the judgment that something else is more important than fear.

—AMBROSE REDMOON

Part 1

WHO AM I?—PERSONALITY, TALENTS, ROLES, FUNCTIONS

CHAPTER 15

•

TEMPERAMENT AND PERSONALITY

Making sure that your personality matches your work is one of the most important things you can do to guarantee that your career will be highly satisfying and stay that way for years to come. Imagine what it would be like if you took a slow and steady plow horse and switched it with a high-strung Thoroughbred racehorse. Both of them would fail miserably at their new jobs. The racehorse would feel restrained and come to hate the farmer and the plow. The plow horse would come in last every time. You might say that the plow horse would finish last because it has different talents, a different physical build. True. However, it also has a plow horse personality. Even if it had the racehorse's body, it would still be out of place on the racetrack. It is the combination of talents and personality that makes up the most basic factors of "fit."

It doesn't take this extreme degree of misfit between personality and work to drag down your effectiveness and satisfaction. Even a seemingly small mismatch can make going to work much less pleasant. It's like ingesting lead or radioactive substances: There is no safe level. Every little bit adds up. Conversely, the more perfect the match between your work and your personality, the more happy and successful you will be.

Many people believe that personality is flexible, flowing, ever changing. They think their temperament is like soft clay, readily moldable to a new shape by growth experiences or therapy. They may have observed friends who have changed radically, become more caring, more effective, or less constrained by inner demons. Their friends may behave differently, but they have not really changed into new people. What they've done is to learn new, more effective ways of living. Or they've mastered habitual patterns—mislearnings that used to hold them back from full self-expression. They have learned to step out into a fuller life in which they can more authentically express themselves. But they are still the same person, with the same basic temperament.

No one knows what percentage of our personalities is bequeathed to us by our genes and how much is learned. Even though the majority of our mental software is learned as we develop throughout childhood, the basic structure of our personalities, our temperament, is inherent. Scientists can now accurately predict whether a newborn baby will grow up to be extroverted or introverted by observing a few telltale clues in the hospital shortly after birth. If your degree of extroversion and introversion is the gift of your genes, why would someone who is born introverted want to be extroverted? For the same reason that people start to smoke cigarettes: to be cool. But there is nothing cool about rejecting one's authentic self. Changing from one thing to another is, at best, extremely difficult. Try changing a table into a chair. It is one thing for an introverted person to learn to become more effective or more comfortable in social situations. That is certainly a worthwhile project. It is yet another to try to change into someone else. Although the plow horse may dream of racing, and may enjoy a hobby of racing with the other plow horses on weekends, it would not have much fun if it actually had to compete with the Thoroughbreds.

Does it sound like I am saying that you should not reach for the stars, that some people are predestined to drag a plow behind them like a ball and chain? Not at all. I used the horse example to demonstrate how deeply our thinking is embedded in cultural ideals, and how much this subverts our ability to choose a career that fits our own personalities. Even those of us whose natures are slow and steady are going to be more attracted to being a racehorse than a plow horse. We have ideals and standards about personality, just as we do about everything else. Often people pick the wrong career because they are paying attention to their standards rather than getting in touch with who they are.

There seems to be something defeatist and elitist in saying that a plow horse should plow and a racehorse should race. Raised in a revolutionary culture, we were taught to resist going with the flow and to fight to the top of the mountain. It seems counterintuitive to suggest that wholehearted acceptance of one's own individual nature is a more profound form of personal growth than change. But most of the people we most admire reached their level of achievement not by changing into someone else but by embracing their natures fully and using their personalities as instruments of self-expression. They added on to what was already a part of them. They not only chose work that fit their temperaments but also learned to use their personalities proactively to further their intentions. You do not get very far if you spend your energy resisting or doing battle with your nature. If you have patterns you need to change, points of view or behaviors that do not serve you, then master them. But, please, choose a career that perfectly fits your personality as it is now.

In this chapter, you will have an opportunity to look at the basic structure of your personality and what career may fit. First, though, you will have a chance to assess your basic temperament. Then you will look at some other important aspects of your personality.

The ancient Greeks recognized that each individual is born with a distinct personality. They categorized people's temperaments into four types. In modern times, psychologist Carl Jung expanded the concept. More recently, a test called the Myers-Briggs Type Indicator expanded the concept of personality type even further. The test divides human temperament into sixteen basic personality types by asking you which of four pairs of opposites is most like you. Each of these sixteen types is described by four letters. Here are the pairs of opposites and the letters that represent them:

E	Extroversion	Introversion	**I**
N	Intuition	Sensing	**S**
F	Feeling	Thinking	**T**
P	Perceiving	Judging	**J**

For example, if your answers to questions about extroversion and introversion leaned toward extroversion, the first letter of your four-letter type would be *E*, for extroversion.

To decide which of the sixteen types represents your personality, work your way through the four lists of opposite traits that follow. This simple personality-type sorter is no substitute for the most recent, in-depth version of the Myers-Briggs Type Indicator, called the MBTI Step II, which I highly recommend. The temperament sorter that follows should give you a reasonably accurate reading of your personality type. Read one pair of opposites—left column, then right column—and put a mark next to the statement that best describes you. Don't burn out your wiring trying to decide which is the real you. Use your intuition. Take the first answer that pops into your head. If neither alternative fits, or both describe you equally, don't mark either side. As you finish each of the four sets, add up how many marks you made in each column. Write the numbers in the spaces at the end of each column.

E **Extrovert**	**I** **Introvert**
Outgoing, gregarious, expansive	Attention on rich inner life
Many social relationships	A few deep, personal relationships
Expressive, congenial	Reflective, quiet observer
Public	Private
Mixer, mingler at parties	One-on-one conversations
When studying at the library, finds a place near other people	When studying at the library, finds a private place where others will not intrude
Lonely when often alone	Savors and seeks time alone
Easily begins new relationships	Gets to know people more slowly
Discusses everything with everyone	Shares personal life with intimates
Speaks first	Thinks first
Loves to be in midst of things	Loves to close his or her office door
Action	Reflection, quiet times
Works out ideas with others' input	Works ideas out internally
Talks	Listens
Enjoys being the center of attention	Resists being the center of attention
The outer world	The world of ideas
Acts	Ponders
Objective	Subjective
Reality = immediate environment	Reality = ideas and understanding
Easy to read	More difficult to read
___ **Number of E responses**	___ **Number of I responses**

N **Intuitives**	**S** **Sensors**
Energy focused on what could be	Energy focused on what is
Possibility, potential	Actuality, reality
Lives in the future	Lives in the present
Conceptual	Realistic, straightforward
General	Specific
Insights, ideas, inferences, hunches	Facts, examples, evidence
Figurative	Literal
Analogies, metaphors	Detailed information
A love for new ideas	Likes new ideas with practical applications
Anticipation of future events	Deals with events when they happen
Seeks inspiration	Seeks enjoyment
In the clouds	Down-to-earth
Especially aware of sense impressions that relate to inspirations and ideas	Very aware of all sorts of sense impressions
Inventors, initiators	Pleasure lovers, consumers
Often restless	Often contented
Original	Imitative
Seeks future expansion	Seeks to possess
Willing to sacrifice present pleasure to bring future possibilities into existence	Dislikes sacrificing present pleasure for future goals
Turns achieving goals and building for the future into an art	Turns living in the moment into an art
Strong appreciation of initiative, inspired leadership, entrepreneurship	Strong appreciation of comfort, luxury, beauty, recreation, pleasure
Learns new skills	Refines existing skills
___ **Number of N responses**	___ **Number of S responses**

T **Thinking**	**F** **Feeling**
Objective	Subjective
Principles	Personal values
Analytical	Caring, compassionate, tender
Logical, cool	Passionate, warm
Dissect	Care
Clarify	Forgive
Compare, emphasize	Appreciate
Explaining	Understanding
Divide	Include
Explore	Caress
Laws, rules, policy	Extenuating circumstances
Impersonal	Personal
Thoughtful	Sentimental
Mainly interested in things other than human relationships	Very strong interest in human relationships
Truthful	Tactful
Brief and businesslike	Friendly; has difficulty remaining businesslike
Justice	Harmony, mercy
Achievement	Appreciation
Cultivate	Cherish, adore, nourish, sympathize
Contrast, separate	Include, relate
___ **Number of T responses**	___ **Number of F responses**

J Judging	P Perceiving
Comfortable after decisions made	Comfortable leaving options open
Sets fixed goals and concentrates on achieving them on schedule	Goals are more open-ended, subject to change
Decided	Flexible, curious
Enjoys having projects framed by definite deadlines	Feels that deadlines should be adjustable
Work now; enjoy if there is time	Enjoy now
Planned	Spontaneous
Structured	Vague, indeterminate, amorphous
Loves to reach completion, finish projects	Loves to begin new projects
Product oriented; wants to get the job done	Process oriented; more interested in how the task will be accomplished
Prefers knowing what he or she is getting into ahead of time	Very adaptable to changing situations
Steady, sustained effort	On-and-off effort
Decisive	Puts off decisions
Present situation must be made to conform to the rules, customs, plans, specifications	Rules, customs, plans, and specifications flex to be appropriate to the changing situation
Avoid unplanned or undesirable experiences	Depend on an ability to handle unplanned or undesirable experiences resourcefully
Exacting	Tolerant
Make the right decision, do the right thing	Have as many experiences as possible, miss nothing
As student, may carry out an orderly and systematic study plan	As student, may put off studying until the last minute
Sometimes accused of being too rigid	Sometimes accused of being too indecisive

Should be, must be, definitely, absolutely	Could be, might be, perhaps, maybe
Definite, clear-cut, final	Tentative, experimental, exploratory provisional, contingent

___ **Number of J responses**   ___ **Number of P responses**

Now that you are finished, transfer your scores here.

___ Number of E responses   ___ Number of I responses

___ Number of N responses   ___ Number of S responses

___ Number of T responses   ___ Number of F responses

___ Number of J responses   ___ Number of P responses

If you have a higher score on one side of a pair, that letter becomes part of your four-letter type. For example:

<u>10</u> Number of E responses   <u>5</u> Number of I responses

<u>6</u> Number of N responses   <u>2</u> Number of S responses

<u>5</u> Number of T responses   <u>12</u> Number of F responses

<u>3</u> Number of J responses   <u>9</u> Number of P responses

Notice that, in this example, the numbers do not add up to the total number of questions. That's because the test taker, as requested, did not answer questions where he or she was not sure that either answer fit. Since the scores were higher for E, N, F, and P, the test taker's type would be ENFP. In the pages that follow, there are encapsulated descriptions of all sixteen types. If you get the same score, or nearly the same score on both sides of a pair of opposites, read the descriptions of both types. For example, if E, N, and F were all definite, but the scores for P and J were almost the same, read both ENFP and ENFJ. You will probably find that you have characteristics of both types. Remember, the point of doing this inquiry is not to pigeon-hole yourself with a four-letter type but to get clear on important aspects of your makeup—your personal blueprint. Use this inquiry as a mirror to see yourself more clearly. Don't accept the results as truth. Use them to find clues. That's the main value of all career tests. If you are in the middle in more than one pair of opposites, don't worry. This is perfectly natural. Many other people have scores in the middle. It doesn't mean you are wishy-washy or undecided. It just means that you are balanced in regard to these traits. That's fine. The only downside is that it makes it harder to come up with a definite four-letter type. The point of this inquiry is clue acquisition, not necessarily defining a specific personality type. Your personality might be a combination of more than one type. If you highlight the traits that best describe you in each of the temperament types that seem to fit you partially, you will wind up with a list of your temperament traits, even if you do not exactly match one type or another.

The careers suggested for each type *are only examples*, not a list from which to choose your future career. Use the recommended careers list for your type to understand better how your various personality traits might be expressed in your work. These careers are suggested as possible matches for your temperament—not your talents, your interests, or what matters to you. Often an in-depth look at these other areas suggests careers that are very different from the ones listed here. Some people feel the need to have a career that is a direct expression of their temperament. They would usually be most attracted to careers that were similar to ones listed for their type. Others are perfectly satisfied if they can do whatever they do in a style that allows them to be themselves freely at work, without having to manufacture a politically correct persona.

For example, for someone whose temperament includes a built-in tendency toward helping people to be their best, that tendency could be expressed most directly by choosing a career where that quality would be of profound importance, such as teaching, coaching, or counseling. That trait could also be expressed less directly in many other careers. But in some careers, this trait might be socially unacceptable. As you read through the key words that describe your type, ask yourself which ones are most important to express in your career. If most of the key words for your type describe you accurately, and you are committed to finding work you love, wouldn't you think it necessary to choose a career that would fit elegantly with those descriptive words?

Read the traits for your personality type, looking for clues. Most likely, some traits will fit you and others won't. Add whatever you find to your Clues. Ask, "Is there anything I am willing to choose as a definite component?" Add anything you choose to your Definite Career Design Components. Do any new careers or jobs come to mind? If so, add them to your Career Ideas. Remember to keep working with your clues, moving them toward selecting new definite components.

ENFP

Enthusiastic, expressive, emotional, warm, evocative, imaginative, original, artistic, perceptive, affirming, supportive, cooperative, positive, open, responsive, sensitive, playful, fun loving, multifaceted, gregarious, zestful, spontaneous, idealistic, improvisers, enthusiastic initiators of new projects, possibilities, and relationships, agents of change. Their focus is on self-expression and possibilities: "what could be" rather than "what is." Life is a celebration and a creative adventure. Masters of the start-up phase. Lose interest when the project or relationship becomes routine or when the primary goal is well on the way to accomplishment. Often eloquent in expressing their vision of a world where ideals are actualized. They might say the glass is full rather than half full or half empty. They are quick to see the potential in people and situations. Frequently have a positive attitude in situations others would consider to be negative. May enjoy a rainy day as much as a sunny one. Management style is focused on the people rather than task oriented. They encourage and serve as mentors rather than command. Work in bursts of enthusiasm mixed with times when little gets done. Need careers that are personally meaningful, creative, and allow for full self-expression and that contribute to other people in some way. Extremely versatile. They may have friends from many walks of life, a wide range of interests and hobbies, and they gain a professional level of mastery without formal training.

activist: social causes
actor
agent for actors, artists, writers
buyer
clergy in low-dogma faiths
coach: personal growth
  and effectiveness
counselor: relationship,
  spiritual, career
consultant: communications,
  education, human resources,
  presentation, personal
  effectiveness
director/producer: films
entrepreneur
fund-raiser

healer: alternative disciplines
human resources specialist
journalist
midwife
ombudsman
passenger service representative
physician: family, holistic
psychologist
public relations
recreation leader
religious activities director
social scientist
teacher
therapist in active, participatory,
  growth-oriented discipline
trainer

INFP

Idealistic, warm, caring, creative, imaginative, original, artistic, perceptive, supportive, empathetic, cooperative, compassionate, responsive, sensitive, gentle, tenderhearted, devoted, loyal, virtuous, self-critical, perfectionistic, self-sacrificing, deep, multifaceted, daydreamers, persistent, determined, hardworking, improvisers, initiators of new projects and possibilities, agents of change. Drawn to possibilities: "what could be" rather than "what is." Values oriented with high level of personal integrity. Their focus is on understanding themselves, personal growth, and contributing to society in a meaningful way. Under surface appearances, they are complex and driven to seek perfection and improvement: in themselves, their relationships, and their self-expression. If their careers do not express their idealism and drive for improvement, they usually become bored and restless. Dislike conflict, dealing with trivialities, and engaging in meaningless social chatter. Thrive on acknowledgment and recognition so long as they are not the center of attention. Need a private work space, autonomy, and a minimum of bureaucratic rules.

activist
administrator: education or
    social service nonprofit
architect
artist
attorney devoted to righting
    wrongs
clergy in low-dogma faiths
coach: personal growth and
    effectiveness
consultant: education, human
    resources
counselor: relationship,
    spiritual, career
developer of training programs
director of social service agency
editor
entrepreneur

healer: alternative disciplines
health care worker
human resources specialist
librarian
midwife
nurse
physician: psychiatrist,
    family, holistic
psychologist
researcher
social scientist
social worker
songwriter/musician
speech pathologist
teacher
therapist
writer, poet, or journalist

ENFJ

Enthusiastic, caring, concerned, cooperative, congenial, diplomatic, interactive, facilitating, diligent, emotional, sincere, interpersonally sensitive, warm, supportive, tolerant, creative, imaginative, articulate, extraordinary social skills, smooth, persuasive motivator, teachers/preachers, verbal, natural leaders, active, lively, humorous, entertaining, witty, values oriented. Uncannily perceptive about others' needs and what motivates them. Often rise to leadership positions. Concerned with the betterment of humanity and work to effect positive change. They have such a gift for persuasively using language that others may consider them to be glib and insincere when actually they are forthright and openhearted. Do not deal well with resistance and conflict. Easily hurt and offended if their well-meaning crusades meet with criticism and rejection. Take everything personally. Put people before rules. Strong desire to give and receive affirmation. Manage by encouragement.

actor	*mediator*
advertising account executive	*newscaster*
camp director	*outplacement counselor*
clergy	*politician*
consultant	*producer: films, television*
counselor: career, relationship,	*promotions*
personal growth	*public relations*
dean	*public speaker*
director of communications	*recruiter*
director of social service	*sales*
nonprofit	*sales manager*
entrepreneur	*supervisor*
fund-raiser	*teacher*
health practitioner: holistic	*trainer*

INFJ

Gentle, introspective, insightful, idealistic, intellectual, inquisitive, sincere, quiet strength, steady, dependable, conscientious, orderly, deliberate, diligent, compassionate, caring, concerned, peace loving, accepting, intense, sometimes stubborn. Dreamers, catalysts, many interests, seek and promote harmony. Many feel at home in academia, studying complex concepts, enjoying theory-oriented courses. They are quietly aware of the dynamics between people.

Because they are gentle and quiet, their gifts and rich inner life may go untapped. Their caring, nurturing nature can remain unnoticed, since they may not feel comfortable expressing these feelings openly. Consequently, they may feel isolated. Need a great deal of solitude and private personal space. Dislike tension and conflict. Give a great deal of focused energy and commitment to their projects, at work and at home. Although usually compliant, they can become extremely stubborn in pursuit of important goals. Seek careers that further their humanistic ideals and engage their values.

accountant
administrator: health care,
    social work
analyst
architect
artist
clergy
composer
consultant: organizational
    development
coordinator
editor
entrepreneur
human resources planner
judge

librarian
management analyst
novelist
photographer: portrait
physician
physical therapist
poet
psychologist
researcher
scientist
social scientist
social worker
technician: health care
writer

ENTP

Enthusiastic, puzzle masters, objective, inventive, independent, conceptual thinkers, creative problem solvers, entrepreneurial risk takers, improvisers, competitive, questioning, rebellious, rule breakers, gregarious, witty, involved, strategic, versatile, clever, adaptable, energetic, action-oriented agents of change. Improve systems, processes, and organizations. Relentlessly test and challenge the status quo with new, well-thought-out ideas, and argue vehemently in favor of possibilities and opportunities others have not noticed. Can wear out their colleagues with their drive and challenging nature. See the big picture and how the details fit together. The most naturally entrepreneurial of all types. Usually not motivated by security. Their lives are often punctuated with extreme ups and downs as they energetically pursue new ideas. They have only one direction: ahead at full speed, leaving a trail of incomplete projects, tools, and plans in their wake. Their idea of fun and best creative self-expression involves devising new conceptual modeling and dreaming up imaginative and exciting ventures. Need lots of room to maneuver. When forced to dwell on details and routine operating procedures, they become bored and restless. Respect competence, not authority. Seek work that allows them to solve complex problems and develop real-world solutions. Often surrounded with the latest technology.

advertising: creative director
agent: literary
CEO: high-tech
computer repair
consultant: management
designer
engineer: high-tech
entrepreneur
industrial designer
inventor
investment broker
journalist
lawyer

manager: leading-edge company
marketer
political analyst
politician
public relations
publicity
sales
software designer
special projects developer
systems analyst
strategic planner
technician: high-tech
venture capitalist

INTP

Logical, original, speculative quick thinkers, ingenious, inventive, cerebral, deep, ruminative, critical, skeptical, questioning, reflective problem solvers, flaw finders, architects and builders of systems, lifelong learners, precise, reserved, detached, absentminded professors. Seekers of logical purity. They love to analyze, critique, and develop new ideas rather than get involved in the implementation phase. Continually engage in mental challenges that involve building complex conceptual models leading to logically flawless solutions. Because they are open-ended and possibility oriented, an endless stream of new data pours in, making it difficult for them to finish developing whatever idea they are working on. Everything is open to revision. Consequently, they are at their best as architects of new ideas where there are endless hypothetical possibilities to be explored, and no need for one final, concrete answer. Their holy grail is conceptual perfection. May consider the project complete and lose interest when they have it figured out. To them, reality consists of thought processes, not the physical universe. Often seem lost in the complex tunnels of their own inner processes. Seek work that allows them to develop intellectual mastery, provides a continual flow of new challenges, and offers privacy, a quiet environment, and independence. Thrive in organizations where their self-reliance is valued and colleagues meet their high standards for competency.

archaeologist
architect
artist
biologist
chemist
computer programmer
computer software designer
computer systems analyst
economist
electronic technician
engineer
financial analyst

historian
judge
lawyer
mathematician
musician
philosopher
physicist
researcher
social scientist
sociologist
strategic planner
writer

ENTJ

Born to lead, outgoing, involved, fully engaged, ambitious, take-charge, impersonal, hearty, robust, type A+, impatient, bossy, controlling, confrontational, argumentative, critical, sharp-tongued, intimidating, arrogant, direct, demanding, strategic, tough-minded, organized, orderly, efficient, long-range planners, objective problem solvers. Self-determined and independent. Skilled verbal communicators. Firmly believe that their way is best. Hold on to their point of view without compromise until some brave soul is able to convince them, through extensive argument and definitive proof, that another way is better. They consider all aspects of life to be the playing field for their favorite game: monkey on the mountain. Their energy is focused on winning, getting to the top, beating the competition, reaching the goal. See life and evaluate other people as part of this game. Assess others hierarchically, above them or below them on the mountain. Tend to look down on people who will not engage them in competition. Often generate hostility and rebellion from their employees and children. Show affection for others by helping them improve. Seek power. Learn by fully engaged discussion (also known as arguing). At their best planning and organizing challenging projects, providing the leadership, straight-ahead energy, and drive to keep up the momentum, and efficiently managing people and forces to reach the objective.

administrator
athlete
computer systems analyst
consultant: management
corporate executive
credit investigator
economic analyst
engineer: project manager
entrepreneur
financial planner
lawyer

manager: senior level
military officer
mortgage banker
office manager
president, CEO
program designer
sales
sales or marketing manager
stockbroker
supervisor
team leader

INTJ

Innovative, independent, individualist, self-sufficient, serious, determined, diligent, resourceful, impersonal, reserved, quick minded, insightful, demanding, critical, argumentative debaters, may seem aloof to others, strategic, tough-minded, organized, orderly, efficient, global, long-range visionaries, planners, objective problem solvers. Self-determined and independent. Use resources efficiently. Do not waste their time on trivialities. True to their own visions. Can become stubborn when they are supposed to do things in a way that differs from their own opinions of the best methodology. Oriented toward new ideas, possibilities, and improving systems. Their motto is "everything could use improvement." This includes processes, systems, information, technology, organizations, other people, and themselves. Many use education as a path to success and earn advanced degrees. Usually one of the first to buy the latest computer and upgrade to new, improved software and other technology. Show affection for others by helping them improve. Learn by in-depth study of the subject and by discussing and arguing. May not realize that other, more thin-skinned individuals do not interpret arguing in the positive way that INTJs do. Attain personal growth by confronting anything within themselves that could be ameliorated. Constantly stretch themselves in new directions. Highly competent. Read and understand both conceptual and practical materials. Excellent at planning, execution, and follow-through. They see the big picture, thinking and ably organizing the details into a coherent plan. Often rise to the top in organizations. At their best where they can conceptualize a new project and then push it through to completion; then do it all over again with a new project.

administrator
analyst: business or financial
architect
CEO: high-tech
computer programmer
computer systems analyst
design engineer
consultant
curriculum designer
designer
engineer

entrepreneur
inventor
judge
lawyer
pharmacologist
physician: cardiologist, neurologist
psychologist
researcher
scientist
teacher: college
technician

ESFP

"Live for today. Face the consequences tomorrow." Warm, positive, friendly, popular, vivacious, helpful, generous, inclusive, tolerant, enthusiastic, gregarious, action oriented, robust, zestful, spontaneous, flexible, energetic, alert, fun loving, playful, impulsive, thrill seekers. Realistic, practical. A great deal of common sense. The focus is on people. Accepting, live-and-let-live attitude, go with the flow. Sunny disposition, love life. Laugh easily, even at themselves. Adventurous, fearless, willing to try anything that involves sensation and risk. Tuned in to and relish the world around them. Smell the roses without stopping. Plunge in headfirst. Live in the present, spurred into action to meet today's needs. Seek immediate gratification, harmony, positive experiences. Avoid or repress unpleasant or negative experiences. Do not naturally plan ahead. Dislike routines, procedures, limits, conflict, and slow-moving, long-range projects. Learn by interactive, hands-on participation. Do best in careers that allow them to generate immediate, tangible results while having fun harmoniously relating with other people in the center of the action.

bus driver
carpenter
child care provider
coach
comedian
events coordinator
fund-raiser
lifeguard
mechanic
mediator

merchandiser
musician: rock & roll
nurse: emergency room
performer
physical therapist
physician: emergency room
police officer
producer: film
promoter
public relations

receptionist
sales
sales manager
small business, retail store
supervisor

teacher: preschool
tour operator
travel agent
veterinarian
waiter or waitress

ISFP

Gentle, sensitive, quiet, modest, self-effacing, giving, warm, genuine, service oriented, helpful, generous, inclusive, tolerant, people pleasing, considerate, respectful, loyal, trusting, devoted, compassionate, caring, supportive, nurturing, encouraging, serene, easygoing, fun loving, open, flexible, realistic, practical, independent. Extremely observant and in touch, especially with the sensual world, both externally and within themselves. Savor the sweetness of life. A great deal of common sense. Accepting, live-and-let-live attitude, go with the flow. No need to lead, compete, influence, or control. Seek harmony. Do not impose their values on others. Find their own practical and creative way to do things. Often seek self-expression through crafts or hands-on arts. At their best in work that expresses their personal values and helps or provides a service to others. May forgo college for a practical education in the trades, crafts, or service professions.

administrator
artisan, craftsperson
beautician
bookkeeper
botanist
carpenter
chef
computer operator
cosmetologist
dancer
electrician
forester
gardener
household worker
interior designer
jeweler
landscape designer

luthier
massage therapist
mechanic
medical: office personnel
medical technician
nurse
physical therapist
plant nursery: herbs, other
    specialties
painter
potter
secretary
shopkeeper
surveyor
teacher: elementary or adult,
    nature, science, art
weaver

ESFJ

Gracious, amiable, affirming, gentle, giving, warm, genuine, cordial, kindly, caring, concerned, dutiful, reliable, punctual, polite, tactful, socially appropriate, thoughtful, self-sacrificing, nurturer, people pleasing, efficient managers, event planners, goal oriented, helpful, cooperative, consistent, extremely loyal, traditional, rule bound, uncomplicated. Perfectly in tune with others' needs and sensitive to nuances, they are natural hosts and hostesses. Their presence contributes graciousness, harmony, fraternity, and fellowship to whatever they are engaged in. Both female and male ESFJs relate to people in a way that combines warmhearted "mothering" and caring, considerate "innkeeping." So eager are they to please that they put others' needs before their own, ignoring their personal well-being as they care for the people most important to them. They seek harmony, avoid conflict, follow the rules, keep their commitments, and ignore problems by pretending they do not exist. Sensitive to criticism. Need appreciation and praise. Particularly concerned with etiquette, "shoulds" and "should nots." Family and home are often their central passion. Value stability, harmony, relationships, and practical, hands-on experience. The day-to-day events in their lives are carefully planned and meticulously managed. At their best in professions that provide helpful, caring, practical service to others and do not require them to learn theories. They are particularly good at planning events, organizing people, and managing the day-to-day aspects of projects that deal with producing tangible results. When they learn an effective new method, it becomes standard operating procedure. Their extraordinary effectiveness comes from picking the perfect, tried-and-true procedure from their internal database at exactly the right time.

bartender
caterer
chef
child care provider
customer service representative
event planner/coordinator
fitness coach
flight attendant
hairdresser
host or hostess
innkeeper
maître d'

manager: office, restaurant, hotel
optometrist
personal banker
real estate agent
receptionist
sales: tangibles
secretary
small business, retail store
social worker
teacher: elementary school, special
education, home economics

ISFJ

Warm, conscientious, loyal, considerate, helpful, calm, quiet, devoted, gentle, open, nurturing, practical, patient, responsible, dependable, very observant, sensitive, holistic, inclusive, spontaneous, pragmatic, tactile, respectful, non-competitive, sympathetic, painstaking and thorough, efficient, traditional. The most service oriented of all the types. Very much in touch with their inner processes as well as the world around them. Seek harmony for themselves and all others. Serene, appreciative, in tune. Do not impose themselves or their opinions on others. Do not need to control. Find their own creative way to get the job done. Learn by doing. Uninterested in abstractions and theories. Use standard operating procedures only when they are the best method for reaching the goal. Often creative and highly skilled but so averse to imposing that they are easily overlooked and their contributions go unnoticed.

administrator: social services
counselor
curator
customer service representative
dietitian
dentist/dental hygienist
educational administrator
entrepreneur
guidance counselor
hairdresser, cosmetologist
health service worker
household worker
innkeeper
librarian
manager: restaurant
massage therapist

media specialist
medical technologist
nurse
occupational therapist
personal assistant
personnel administrator
physical therapist
physician: family practice or
    receptionist
priest/minister/rabbi/monk/nun
religious educator
sales: retail
secretary
speech pathologist
teacher: preschool, elementary,
    adult, ESL

ESTP

Outgoing, realistic, pragmatic problem solvers, action oriented, robust, zestful, spontaneous, energetic, alert, laid-back, direct, fearless, resourceful, expedient, competitive, spontaneous, flexible, gregarious, objective. Adventurous, willing to try anything that involves sensation and risk. Plunge in headfirst;

then analyze. "Live for today. Face the consequences tomorrow." No tolerance for theories and abstractions. Short attention span. Usually have a laidback attitude, value individual rights and personal freedom. Do not naturally plan ahead. Prefer to deal with what life throws at them. Adapt to the present situation. React to emergencies instantly and appropriately. A passion for tackling tough jobs and winning in impossible situations. Football hero mentality. Break the rules more often than any other type. Often find themselves in trouble in strict bureaucracies. Dislike being tied down. Learn by doing; rarely read the manual. Want a big return for their investment of time, energy, money. Lively, entertaining centers of attention. The ultimate party-hearty souls. Always willing to put off mundane tasks for the thrill of something new and exciting. Often attracted to motorcycles, fast cars, powerboats, skydiving, and similar quick thrills, the new and the unexplored, tactile pleasures, high-risk sports. May enjoy working with their hands.

athlete
athletic coach
auctioneer
carpenter
contractor
entrepreneur
explorer
field technician
firefighter
fitness instructor
heavy-equipment operator
lifeguard
manager: hands-on, day-to-day
    operations
marketer

mechanic
military
negotiator
news reporter
paramedic
photographer: combat or adventure
pilot
police officer or detective
promoter
real estate agent
sales
stunt person
troubleshooter, problem solver
truck driver
waiter or waitress

ISTP

Independent, reserved, cool, curious, expedient, flexible, logical, analytical, realistic, spontaneous, action oriented. Adventurous, willing to try anything that involves sensation and risk. Usually have a relaxed, laid-back attitude, value individual rights and personal freedom. Enthusiastic about and absorbed in their immediate interests. Constantly scanning and observing the world around them. Do not naturally plan ahead. Prefer to deal with what life throws at them. Adapt to the present situation. Follow the path of least resistance. React to emergencies instantly and appropriately. Live-and-let-live philosophy, laissez-faire approach to life. Dislike rules, being tied down, or imposing themselves on others. Often attracted to motorcycles, fast cars, powerboats, skydiving, and similar quick thrills, the new and the unexplored, tactile pleasures, high-risk sports. May enjoy working with their hands. Things or objective information are the focus, rather than people.

ambulance driver	*mechanic*
athletic coach	*military*
bus driver	*optometrist*
carpenter	*pharmacist*
chef	*photographer: news*
construction worker	*physician: pathology*
dental assistant	*pilot*
diver	*recreational attendant*
engineer	*secretary*
entrepreneur	*service worker*
farmer	*stunt person*
field technician	*surveyor*
laborer	*technician*
lifeguard	*troubleshooter, problem solver*
manager: hands-on,	*truck driver*
day-to-day operations	*video-camera operator*

ESTJ

Systematic, serious, thorough, down-to-earth, efficient, decisive, hardworking, dutiful, loyal, sincere, conservative, aggressive, in charge. Focused, controlled, and controlling. A strong sense of responsibility. Gregarious, active, socially gifted, partygoers. Make their points of view known. "Macho" or "macha." Often rise to positions of responsibility, such as senior-level management. Want their work to be practical, pragmatic, immediate, objective, have clear and unambiguous objectives, require follow-through and perseverance, involve facts, and produce tangible, measurable results. Natural managers and administrators. Type A personalities. Keep their commitments at any cost. Think from the viewpoint of "should" and "should not." Have difficulty appreciating and learning from other points of view. Work first, play later. Drawn to work in stable, structured, hierarchical organizations using standard operating procedures. Follow the rules. Seekers of security. They safeguard and maintain traditions and traditional values. A tendency to trample other people (usually unknowingly) as they plow straight ahead to accomplish their goals. A high percentage of military people have this personality type.

athletic coach
bank employee
cashier
chef
computer systems analyst
contractor
corporate executive: all levels
dietitian
electrician
engineer
entrepreneur
funeral director
insurance agent, broker,
    or underwriter
judge
manager: retail store, operations,
    projects, restaurant, bank,
    government

mechanic
military
nurse
optometrist
pharmacist
physician
police officer
purchasing agent
sales
school principal
stockbroker
supervisor
teacher of practical material:
    math, gym, shop, technical

ISTJ

Systematic, serious, thorough, down-to-earth, efficient, decisive, hardworking, dutiful, loyal, reserved, sincere, conservative. A strong sense of responsibility. Very private but learn extroverted social behaviors for the sake of practicality. Want their work to be practical, pragmatic, immediate, objective, have clear and unambiguous objectives, require follow-through and perseverance, involve facts, and produce tangible, measurable results. Often have type A personalities. Keep their commitments at any cost. Think from the point of view of "should" and "should not." Work first, play later. Drawn to work in stable, structured, hierarchical organizations using standard operating procedures. Seekers of security. They safeguard and maintain traditions and traditional values. A high percentage of military people have this personality type.

accountant
administrator
analyst

auditor
bank employee
bus driver

chef
chemist
computer systems analyst,
  operator, programmer
corporate executive: all levels
dentist
dietitian
electrician
engineer
entrepreneur
farmer
field technician
government employee
guard
IRS agent

manager: retail store, operations,
  projects
mechanic
military
operator: machinery
pharmacist
police officer
school principal
speech pathologist
surgeon
teacher of practical material: math,
  gym, shop, technical
technical writer
technician: lab, science, engineering,
  health

INQUIRY 13B

Other Personality Traits

Here are some other personality traits to consider as part of your self-assessment.

1. Please draw a mark on the line at the appropriate place on each scale.

2. Write a description of yourself that contains your traits that stand out most in the previous temperament and personality self-assessments. For example, you might write:
    "I am imaginative, enthusiastic, cheerful, flexible, optimistic, warm, intimate, confident, persevering, independent, bold. I am a leader, unconventional and adventurous." Or: "I am a restrained, conventional, shrewd, pessimistic loner." Be honest. Seek the truth rather than stroke your ego.

> Cautious _____|_____Impulsive
> Realistic_____|_____Imaginative
> Quiet, subdued_____|_____Enthusiastic, cheerful

Rigid_____|_____Flexible
Pessimistic_____|_____Optimistic
Reasonable_____|_____Compassionate, sympathetic
Self-indulgent_____|_____Disciplined
Low need to influence others____|___Persuasive
Suspicious_____|_____Trusting
Warm_____|_____Cool
Strict_____|_____Tolerant, permissive
Expedient_____|_____Moralistic
Forthright, genuine_____|_____Sophisticated, polished, shrewd
Chaotic_____|_____Organized
Traditional_____|_____Original
Tough-minded_____|_____Emotionally sensitive
Reserved, private_____|_____Sharing, open
Expressive_____|_____Contained
Dependable_____|_____Inconsistent
Content_____|_____Ambitious
Self-confident_____|_____Worrying
Uncomplicated_____|_____Complicated
Yielding_____|_____Tenacious, persevering
Concern for others_____|_____Self-centered
Scheduled_____|_____Spontaneous
Loner_____|_____Sociable
Laid-back, easygoing_____|_____Assertive, aggressive, driven
Relaxed_____|_____Tense
Dependent_____|_____Self-reliant
Joiner_____|_____Socially independent
Shy_____|_____Bold
Follows urges_____|_____Controlled
Leader_____|_____Follower
Conventional, conforming____|____Unconventional, rebellious
Restrained_____|_____Adventurous

3. Look back over this inquiry for clues. Add whatever you find to your Clues list. Ask, "Is there anything I am willing to choose as a definite component?" Add anything you choose to your Definite Career Design Components. Do any new careers or jobs come to mind? If so, add them to your Career Ideas.

CHAPTER 16

•

YOUR CORE PERSONALITY

The next few pages delve into aspects of your nature that often provide excellent clues.

INQUIRY 14

Tribal/Maestro Orientation

1. Rate yourself. Read each pair of opposites (left to right) and place a check mark next to the sentence that describes you best. Pick statements that describe how you really are rather than how you would like to be. Do this quickly; don't think about it or quibble with the wording. Just mark the one that rings most true for you. If you can't decide which side describes you better, go on to the next item. If both options describe you equally, mark both of them. If you find that you are marking both options on more than a very few pairs, go back and try to pick one side or the other when possible.

I am on somewhat the same wavelength as others.	*I am on my own wavelength.*
I prefer to be a part of a team.	*I prefer to do my own thing in my own way.*
I am one of the gang.	*I float among different groups as needed.*
I listen to music that is similar to what my peers listen to.	*My taste in music is different than that of most of my peers.*

I tend not to go too deep in my reading matter.	*I read in-depth subject matter.*
I am, in many ways, like other people.	*I consider myself unique and different from others.*
I know just enough in my interest areas.	*I tend to go deeper into my interests than others.*
I'm attracted to team sports or activities.	*I'm attracted to solo sports or activities.*
I prefer to collaborate on ideas with others.	*I prefer my own, individual ideas.*
I see myself as a general businessperson.	*I see myself as an expert in a specialized field.*
I tend toward popular TV shows and movies.	*My taste in TV and movies is different than most.*
I dress somewhat like most people I know.	*I have a unique, personal style of dressing.*
I fit in naturally.	*I can fit in if I work at it.*
I am good at managing people.	*I'd rather not manage people.*
I'm comfortable with all kinds of people.	*I'm comfortable with people who are like me.*
Life is about friends and family.	*Life is about being really good at something.*
I prefer to follow someone else's lead.	*I prefer to come up with my own ideas.*
I can take or give orders easily.	*I don't like to be told what to do.*
I'm pretty much like most people.	*I'm different from most people.*

I cooperate.	*I challenge.*
Sometimes I wish I stood out more from the crowd.	*Sometimes I wish I were a bit more "normal."*
My dreams of the future are similar to my friends'.	*I dream of a different and highly personal lifestyle.*
___*Total check marks for Tribal*	___*Total check marks for Maestro*

Note: The self-assessment you just completed is not an accurate scientific assessment of these traits. It is a rough approximation. Accurate Tribal-Maestro testing is part of natural talent testing programs and places you at a specific point on a continuum: a scale that at one end is highly Tribal and at the other, highly Maestro. You could be right in the middle, mostly one with a dash of the other, or anywhere along this scale. It may be enough for you to know that you lean one way or the other. Some readers may be able to recognize that they are completely Tribal or completely Maestro.

The Maestro Personality

Maestros make up about 25 percent of the total population. They are individual workers, preferring to be valued for their mastery of a particular discipline or subject. Their success depends directly on special training or a talent for a chosen field. At work, they like to have people seek them out for their mastery, expertise, or knowledge. They most enjoy being appreciated and valued for the unique contribution they make. Maestros usually gravitate to careers that put them on a raised platform of expertise, like a college professor. They tend to understand the world through a unique, personal, and subjective way of thinking. They are on their own wavelength.

As children, they often delve deeply into interests and hobbies. They often recognize at an early age that their perspectives are different from the group's. This tendency continues throughout life. Maestros who have made the mistake of selecting a Tribal career often report that their job "seems like something that anyone could do."

Extroverted Maestros are performers. They may not necessarily perform in front of a large audience, but even with an audience of one, they communicate their expertise to others. As extroverts, they are usually in direct communication with other people. Examples: college professor who loves the classroom, seminar leader, spokesperson for a technical subject, courtroom lawyer, politician, actor, comedian, performance artist, dancer, consultant, trainer. Introverted Maestros internally process information related to their special area of expertise. Many of the career areas usually thought of as "professional" are filled with introverted Maestros. Examples: scientist, artist, college professor who most enjoys the research and writing, technician, medical specialist, accountant, poet, analyst, lawyer, economist, novelist, inventor.

The Tribal Personality

About 75 percent of people have a personality type that we describe as Tribal. They are group workers, usually most successful and satisfied working with and through other people as members of an organization, group, or "tribe." They have a broad, generalist frame of reference for life, usually getting bored with work that is highly specialized and narrow in scope. They are at their best contributing to the goals of an organization. They are on the same wavelength as the group. Like a member of a flock of birds or a herd of gazelles, they move with the flow of the group. This does not necessarily mean (though it often does) that they have a special understanding of human nature and motivation. However, because they are attuned to the tribe, they derive many of their values, goals, and points of view from their tribe. Most of the kids who are members of the "in crowd" in high school are extroverted Tribals.

Because they are on the same wavelength as others, many Tribals are more naturally gifted than Maestros at understanding human nature. For example, exceptional sales managers and supervisors are Tribals who have an inborn understanding of human psychology, demonstrated by an ability to motivate employees effectively. Their success often depends on their interpersonal abilities or their gift for fitting easily into the culture of an organization. Tribals choose careers in business, management, personnel, high school teaching, training, supervision, sales, advertising, public relations, administration, banking, homemaking, and so forth.

Extroverted Tribals are outgoing, people-oriented individuals who are found where the action is. They like to spend their workday in the part of the beehive where there are plenty of others bees to interact with. Examples: salesperson, receptionist, lobbyist, supervisor, office manager, foreperson, waiter, flight attendant, contractor, restaurant manager, and "networker" style of CEO. Introverted Tribals work in a quieter part of the beehive, where they can close their doors and get some privacy. They work internally for the goals of the organization. Examples: manager of projects that involve more planning than direct supervision, administrator, clerical worker, corporate accountant, patent examiner, underwriter, corporate lawyer.

Which Are You?

Having a clear understanding of where you are on the Tribal-Maestro scale tells you a great deal about the nature of your ideal career, what kinds of relationships with other people fit you best, and why your present work situation may fall short. Of course, most people are some combination of the two. Knowing exactly where you are on the scale—what percentage Tribal and what percentage Maestro—is very useful in picking a career that fits perfectly.

Tribals and Maestros answer the question "What do you do for a living?" differently. A Tribal answers by stating what it is he or she does: "I am a manager at Galactic Communications." Even though they may use the same words, Maestros answer from a different place. Their answers are more statements of their identity: "I am a scientist." "I am an artist." If they have chosen their career well, a large part of their identity is wrapped around what they do for a living. Of course, a part of everyone's identity, for better or worse, is derived from what they do for a living. But for Maestros, their career takes up a much bigger chunk of their identity than for Tribals. Ideally, Maestros should choose a subject area they are passionate about and spend their lives becoming more and more masterful. A Maestro without a specialty is like a cat without claws, a bird without wings. The good news is that it is never too late to get started. If you are a Maestro and are not doing something that you are passionate about, you had better get to it. You will probably never be satisfied until you do.

For Tribals, things are a little more flexible. Change is easier. Even though the workplace has become so highly specialized, Tribals move from job to job within an organization based on factors other than specialized knowledge. They learn as they go. Their ability to manage, administer, market, or supervise is more important than technical knowledge.

It is less important for Tribals to choose a specific career during their first years of college. Although they often go to college with specific educational objectives, when they look back on their college years later in life, they usually say that what was most valuable was something other than the specific subject matter learned in the classroom. Ideally, Maestros go to college to get an early start learning a specialty. A young person with a Maestro personality should select a career direction early and obtain the specialized training to become a professional or expert. For them, the selection of subject matter is critically important. If they are not passionate about the subject matter, they will not be able to say proudly, "I am a . . ." Tribals often give more weight to other pieces of the puzzle.

Many careers do not line up neatly on one side of the line or the other, fitting either Tribals or Maestros. The great majority of retail store owners are Tribals, but a Maestro with a raging passion for radio-controlled model airplanes, sewing, mountaineering equipment, or some other specialty where the customers would constantly seek their expertise might love owning such a specialty store. College professors who fall in the middle of the scale, partly Tribal and partly Maestro, say that they would like to pull the chairs into a circle and be more of a facilitator rather than lecture from the front of the room. Most high school teachers are Tribals. They do not have the need or desire to be on the raised platform of mastery that most college professors attain. As far as the kids are concerned, a high school teacher is just another person, an older member of the group with the job of teaching. In fact, these days, to be a high school teacher is sometimes much more like being a supervisor than a professor. Those schoolteachers who are Maestros behave and teach like professors. Think back to your high school days. Which of your teachers were Maestros and which were Tribals?

Like many people in jobs that do not fit them in regard to this scale, you can always try to bend the job to fit you. Sometimes this works. In many cases, it doesn't. Secretaries with Maestro personalities often adapt their jobs to their personalities by mastering some specialized aspect of the job, perhaps becoming the office expert on the word-processing software. By doing so, other employees come to them for problem solving and instruction, a role that suits their personalities better than the usual work that secretaries perform. In choosing your future career, you want to make as few compromises as possible. Generally speaking, picking something that does not fit your combination of Tribal and Maestro elements increases your risk of winding up in an unsatisfying career.

Extroversion and Introversion

While it may be useful shorthand to think of yourself as an extrovert or introvert, in truth, almost everyone is a mixture of both traits. People who think of themselves as either an extrovert or an introvert become confused when they find themselves desiring to spend more time on the opposite side of what seems to be their dominant trait. The trick is to figure out what percentage you are of each and design your career so that you have a harmonious balance between both. If you are right in the middle, 50 percent extrovert, and 50 percent introvert, and in your job you spend most of your time alone, you will, in time, develop a powerful desire for more people contact. Most likely, you will spend a great deal of your time outside of work in the company of others. If your job has you in face-to-face conversation all day, you will, most likely, want to spend your free time at home, curled up on the couch reading or watching TV, recovering from your overly extroverted job. When either side is not getting enough of what it needs, powerful inner forces influence you to seek the proper balance.

In my never-ending quest to do inexpensive research studies, I once asked a male friend who was recently divorced and spending time in singles bars to approach as many single women as possible and go through a questionnaire on extroversion and introversion with them. He thought this volunteer job as a psychological researcher was a heaven-sent opportunity and applied himself with enormous enthusiasm. What we discovered was that more than 70 percent of the women he met at singles bars on weeknights said that their jobs were considerably less extroverted than they would prefer. After work, they felt the insistent beat of powerful inner drums to get out of the house and mingle with others. The reverse happens with people whose jobs are too extroverted for them.

One of the common misconceptions about this subject is that extroverts get their energy from being with other people, and that introverts get theirs from being alone. Nobody gets their energy from external sources. It always comes from within. In fact, it could be said that what you are is energy. But you will definitely feel a loss of energy and fulfillment if your life does not allow you the proper balance between these two forces. It does not work very well to spend your time outside of work recovering from an imbalance on the job. You don't want your after-work activities driven by compulsion rather than free choice. That's one more reason why it is important to choose a career that provides the balance you need.

Another myth is that extroversion involves dancing on tabletops and that introversion means sitting quietly in the corner. A more useful way of thinking of these two traits is that the extroverted part of a person lives externally, with attention focused on and interacting with the outer world, while the introverted side looks within. This does not necessarily mean being alone. Many illustrators who work for graphic arts companies are introverts. They often work in the same room as several other illustrators. Even though they have lots of company, most find a good match for their dominant introverted side because their work is internally focused.

The way to discover the perfect balance is to look back through your life and assess the percentage of each trait by reliving various jobs, schools, and what you did in your spare time. What combination of activities gives you the perfect balance? Do your best to turn your insights into percentages. For example, "I am sixty percent introverted and forty percent extroverted." Then consider how you could achieve this balance at work.

Combining Tribal/Maestro and Extroversion/Introversion

Combining both of these scales can provide you with a general sense of what careers might fit you. The examples here may not include careers that interest you. The descriptions may not seem to describe you perfectly. But from these simplified guidelines, you should be able to fit these concepts together with your sense of yourself.

Introverted Tribals like working as a part of the human beehive, often as a part of an organization, but they are happiest in a quieter part of the beehive where they can mainly work internally rather than spend most of the day interacting with other people. Because they are more introverted, they do their best work either alone or with a small group of people they know well. Modern office-cubicle settings may be suited to some introverted Tribals: They excel at project-based work that allows them to contribute to the whole by working in a semiprivate space. They can sense the hum of other Tribals rubbing their wings together. Even though they may not interact with others as much as their extroverted Tribal office mates, they know that at any moment they can grab a cup of coffee and collaborate with a buddy around the corner. They are the true unsung heroes. Tribals serve as the backbone of organizations. Professionally, they fit with many different jobs in organizations, wherever they can contribute to the goals of the organization in a way that allows them to spend a considerable portion of their day working internally. If you score as an Introverted Tribal, particularly if you are very introverted, you may feel that our description of Tribals doesn't apply to you. You may not feel that you are on the same wavelength with other people. You may not want to be part of a group. Still, your score suggests that even if you wind up practicing in a specialized area, you will most likely be happiest working for an organization rather than being out on your own. There are, for instance, plenty of perfectly happy introverted computer programmers who score as Tribals. Examples: managers of projects that involve more planning than direct supervision, administrators, underwriters, lawyers working within a corporation, orchestral musicians, and business owners who prefer to work behind the scenes.

Extroverted Tribals are happiest spending their workdays interacting, talking, and socializing in a part of the beehive where there are plenty of other bees to rub wings with. They are at their best in work that provides a double dose of people. Their Tribal side drives them to be a member of a community; their extroverted side has them interacting much of the day within that community. They are the nonstop, people-oriented, shiny, happy party people in all those beer and cola ads. Getting things done with and through other people most of the day is how they prefer to work and play.

They may ask themselves, "Why write when I can talk to someone?" Examples: marketing-oriented CEOs, sales representatives, hosts, greeters, people managers, executives, spokespersons, promoters, supervisors, day care providers, recreation therapists, nurses, advertising account managers, marketing presenters, K–12 teachers, and personal trainers.

Introverted Maestros make up a large percentage of the people we think of as "professionals." They are experts who work internally in their chosen discipline, thinking and problem solving in their area of specialty. Introverted Maestros prefer to do a whole project or job with their attention mostly on their inner world. Some are inclined to be scholarly, scientific, or professional, and occasionally eccentric. They perceive and do things their own way. Many introverted Maestro physicians work with patients all day but direct much of their attention internally, figuring out what is broken and how to fix it. Even though we call their extroverted Maestro cousins "performers," in fact, many fine performers, including some of the greatest actors and singer-songwriters, are introverted Maestros. Examples: scientists, engineers, college professors who most enjoy the research and writing, artists, specialist physicians, attorneys, dentists, inventors, technicians, analysts, accountants, consultants, master craftspeople, writers, and many computer industry professionals.

Extroverted Maestros are performers. They are experts or masters in a particular area, at their best performing their mastery in front of others. Not only do they see the world in a highly personal way, but they are compelled to use their talent, knowledge, and wisdom in an extroverted manner. When geared to take a lead role as an expert, they direct, advise, and guide others in their field of mastery. As entrepreneurs, they are often visionary leaders with special technical competence who develop a loyal following. Examples: college professors who love the classroom, seminar leaders, spokespersons for technical subjects, politicians, actors, comedians, performance artists, physicians in high-contact specialties, charismatic leaders, consultants, trainers, orchestral conductors.

Look back over this inquiry for clues. Add whatever you find to your Clues list. Ask, "Is there anything I am willing to choose as a definite component?" Add anything you choose to your Definite Career Design Components. Do any new careers or jobs come to mind? If so, add them to your Career Ideas. Remember to keep working with your clues, moving them toward selecting new definite components.

CHAPTER 17

•

NATURAL TALENTS

The important thing in life is to have a great aim and to possess the aptitude and the perseverance to attain it.

—JOHANN WOLFGANG VON GOETHE

Take a duck. Put it in a pond. Even if it was raised in the desert and has no swimming experience, it will be instantly at home in its new environment. In a matter of minutes, it will happily be doing what ducks do to make a living, exhibiting perfect natural mastery. It would be hard to find a more suitable candidate for pond life than a duck, even one with no previous experience. That's because ducks are designed for the environment they inhabit. They have an ideal set of talents for their job. They have webbed feet, bills shaped for obtaining the special foods available pond side, and hollow feathers that act as a raft to keep them floating high in the water. They have a waterproofing system that keeps them dry and a layer of down to keep them warm in near-freezing water. All the beasts of the field and the birds of the air are perfectly equipped for the highly specific ways they go about making a living. Over millions of years, Mother Nature has eliminated all the ill-suited candidates for each niche in the natural world.

One major difference between most other creatures and human beings is that all the individuals of most other species are pretty much alike. There are small differences between individuals, but, essentially, each giraffe is pretty much like all the others. On the other hand, every person is a unique individual, different in many ways from all the others. We are different from the other people around us not only in personality, temperament, and interests but also in our innate talents. Each of us is genetically dealt a very specific hand of talent/ability cards that gives us a knack for playing a narrow range of roles in the working world with natural ease and mastery.

When you see someone wind surfing gracefully, like a dancer in a high wind, moving quickly and powerfully across the sea, you are viewing the result of extensive training and a commitment to improve a body that was born with a special gift for balance and agility. People who were born with less coordinated bodies are rarely the ones out there in the stronger winds. It is more difficult for them to master the skills and usually not as much fun as it is for someone with natural talent.

Everyone is born with a unique group of talents that are as individual as a fingerprint or a snowflake. These talents give each person a special ability to do certain kinds of tasks easily and happily, yet also make other tasks seem like pure torture. Talents are completely different from acquired knowledge, skills, and interests. Your interests can change. You can gain new skills and knowledge. Your natural, inherited talents remain with you, unchanging, for your entire life. They are the hand you have been dealt by Mother Nature. You can't change them. You can, however, learn to play the hand that you have been dealt brilliantly and to your best advantage. The better you understand your unique genetic gifts, the more likely you will be to have a satisfying and successful career.

Most of what we usually think of as special talents, such as music, writing, math, science, and business management, are each actually constellations of deeper, more elemental abilities that, when well combined, play together in harmony like instruments in a band. Let's use an example. Suppose that you need an operation and want to pick the best possible surgeon, someone with a real "gift." Obviously, other factors, such as quality of training and length of experience, are extremely important. But since you are looking for someone who is truly excellent, you want a surgeon who combines excellent training and experience with natural talent. What would be the elements of that special gift?

First of all, you would want someone with high spatial ability, a talent for thinking in three dimensions. How would you feel about going under the blade of a surgeon who viewed your body as an abstract philosophical concept? You would want your surgeon to be a natural in something called diagnostic reasoning. This is a talent for being able to leap to accurate conclusions based on just a few clues. If something went wrong during your operation, the surgeon would use this talent to figure out what to do quickly. Another talent to look for is something we call "low idea flow." Some people have minds that move quickly, restlessly, seemingly at a hundred miles an hour. These folks are great at improvising but have difficulty in concentrating on one thing for long periods of time. Their brains are just zooming along too quickly. They have "high idea flow." You would want a surgeon who naturally and easily kept his or her mind totally concentrated on the task at hand. You would also want someone with "great hands." Manual dexterity is an innate gift. If you had a choice between a surgeon with superb, average, or low hand dexterity, which would you pick? There are several more aspects of what constitutes the natural talents of a great surgeon. But, hopefully, now you have a sense of what I mean when I speak of innate talents.

Getting to the Source of Career Difficulties

The difference between a career that is just okay and one that is a perfect fit depends on fitting together many elements, all of which are important and all of which we cover in the course of *The Pathfinder*. When people complain about work, they usually bitch about fairly obvious problems they face in their jobs: the boss, the money, the hours, boredom, stress, and so on. They don't realize that what stands between them and a truly satisfying career may be more complex. The obnoxious boss and the long hours are usually just the tip of the iceberg. When you are willing to put up with an okay career, then solving the obvious problems may be all that matters. But when it is important to have a fit between you and your work, you have to deal with the whole iceberg.

Over the years, Rockport Institute has worked with thousands of clients. Many of them come to us in midcareer with the goal of changing to a new occupation. When they describe why their present careers are less than perfect, they report various factors that they believe are the main causes of their dissatisfaction. As a part of their Rockport Institute Career Choice Program, they take a testing program that measures natural talents and aptitudes. Ninety percent of the time, there turns out to be a substantial mismatch between their abilities and their work. So even if they were to solve the problems that they believe are the source of their difficulties, they would still continue to feel less than satisfied with their work.

What happens when there is a mismatch between your talents and your work? For creatures other than us humans, the answer to this question is extinction. Because we are so adaptable, we survive, but at a terrible cost. What gets extinguished is the pure joy of doing something that comes perfectly naturally. The further you get from fully expressing your talents and abilities, the less likely it is that you will enjoy your day on the job.

When important abilities go unused, people become bored with their work. When the job requires talents they do not possess, people find their work frustrating and difficult. Sometimes, having only one element out of whack can ruin the chance for career satisfaction.

When someone performs less than optimally at work, his or her supervisor often makes inaccurate assumptions. The supervisor thinks the problem is that the employee doesn't have the right personality for the job, isn't "motivated," isn't smart enough, or has some sort of personal flaw. Sometimes supervisors correctly diagnose the problem. But often they fail to understand that what's really going on is that the employee's innate talents don't fit well with his or her job. The supervisor's attempts to correct the situation only make things worse. What would happen if your car's fuel pump was broken but you misdiagnosed the problem and began to adjust the carburetor? You would then have both a broken fuel pump *and* a carburetor problem.

The workplace has no monopoly on difficulties caused by talent mismatches. Imagine a bright high school student with a wild, fast-flowing imagination and a talent for powerful, critical diagnostic thinking. Some kids with this combination may join the debate team, a perfect outlet for these talents that can be a great deal of fun while building self-esteem. Others, just as worthy, just as gifted, will make a different set of assumptions. They may get rightfully bored in Miss Peabody's drone-it-right-out-of-the-book history class. To preserve their personal dignity, they may decide to opt out of school and mainstream society. This solution leads to drugs, early pregnancy, and crime.

The Mystery of Human Talents

Until recently, the entire subject of innate talents and aptitudes was a mystery to scientists. The theories of intelligence that have dominated scientific thinking until recently essentially boiled down to slightly different versions of one single premise: Some people are smart and some people aren't. Intelligence was thought of as a single scale, like a thermometer. Either you had it or you didn't. At the same time, the psychological community promoted the notion that the differences between individuals are mostly the by-products of parenting, environment, and other forces that influenced our upbringing. If you were smart and well brought up, you did well in school. If you had a less than spectacular academic record, you were thought to be either lacking in brains or somehow psychologically impaired.

In the last few years, scientists have made major breakthroughs in understanding the human mind. The old theories of why each of us is a distinct and special individual are being blown down like straw houses by gale-force winds of brain research. This new thinking has not yet trickled down to reach the man on the street, partly because the old-fashioned theories are so entrenched and their proponents are so stubborn. The scientists who led the field in the study of intelligence for most of the twentieth century, endlessly arguing the color of the emperor's cloak, had in their ponderous majesty vastly overrated their own intelligence. IQ tests were, and still are, thought of as an accurate barometer of intellectual firepower. However, this narrow interpretation of intelligence does not even begin to recognize the enormous range of human abilities.

Forward-looking scientists have recognized that there are different kinds of intelligence. Instead of having one big mental computer that can be measured by IQ tests, it turns out that each of us has a unique collection of smaller, highly specialized "brains" that are the reason why you are better than your friend at some things and he or she is better than you at others. Harvard psychologist Howard Gardner has sorted out seven different intelligences that, he says, everyone possesses to a greater or lesser degree. In his excellent book *Frames of Mind: The Theory of Multiple Intelligences*, he argues that each person has a unique cognitive profile that comes from differing strengths in these intelligences. The different intelligences he recognizes include linguistic, musical, logical-mathematical, spatial, body kinesthetic, interpersonal, and intrapersonal.

Other researchers have come up with their own lists of multiple intelligences.

While the lists are different, the central theme of multiple intelligences is the same. With the newer brain scans, it is possible to see regions of the brain light up when a particular talent is used. While this is all relatively new thinking to the scientific community, it is really just good old basic common sense. While the great old men of psychology were busy having enormous thoughts about minuscule differences between their theories, the average high school kid was tuned in to a more accurate viewpoint on human ability. Most kids intuitively realize that their fellow students are naturally good at different things: getting good grades, tinkering with cars, athletics, babeology, organizing people or events, and so forth. No high school kid in his or her right mind would ever think of putting the introverted computer genius in charge of selling ads for the yearbook or asking the wild, frenetic class clown to be the proofreader for the school paper.

When someone really stands out in any particular area, we recognize that he has a "gift." In the last few years, we have begun to understand that all people have their own gifts. We now know that each individual's gift is made up of several innate abilities playing together in harmony like instruments in a band. Now that we have the knowledge and the tools to understand your multiple intelligences, it is possible for you to do a much better job of choosing a career that makes use of these abilities.

Intelligence: A Natural Gift for Doing Anything Well

One of the reasons that many of the scientists never caught up with the average high school student in understanding human ability is that scientists never managed to agree on what the word *intelligence* means in the first place. Right now they're probably out there somewhere locked in horn-to-horn combat over this weighty issue. You and I have a very practical reason for learning more about innate abilities. Since your goal in reading this book, and mine in writing it, is for you to wind up in a career that you love, let's look at the question of intelligence and ability from a practical and observable viewpoint. First of all, let's use a broader definition of *intelligence*. If you consider intelligence to be "an innate capacity for doing something well," it is pretty clear that academic ability is only a small part of the total picture. Some people have a natural gift for music, athletics, invention, interpersonal relationships, and so forth. These gifts are just as real and just as important as the combination of abilities that we call "academic ability." Usually the talents we consider gifts are a combination of both the learned and the innate. Some may have the innate talent to be a great violinist but never have the opportunity to learn to play. Or they may be taught in a way that is so contrary to their learning style that they abandon the instrument before discovering their talent.

Our conventional way of assessing ability is old-fashioned and constrained. You might find it extremely useful to open up your perspective about what you are naturally good at doing. Anything you have a knack for is a talent, an aptitude, a kind of intelligence to be appreciated and considered as a possible component in designing your career.

What About Learned Skills?

There are two kinds of learned skills: basic and specialized. Basic learned skills consist of all the stuff we have to learn to function successfully as human beings. If we were born with our brains full size and fully developed, women would have to have hips like a rhinos. Thankfully, nature thought slimmer hips was a better idea. So we are born with some of our software already installed. Then our brain grows for a few years while our parents and our tribe fill it with what we need to know. For millions of years, hominids have taught their children well how to prosper in the environment and the tribe. More than 50 percent of the software we have as adults comes to us this way, through learning basic skills. Almost all humans have the natural talent to learn these basic skills.

Nowadays, we are also trained in highly specialized skills. Most of what you are good at doing is the result of long practice and acquired skill. If you are a "talented" skier, you have spent years learning to master a technically difficult skill. The technical skills you have acquired are supported by a foundation of innate, inherited ability. Anyone, even a person with one leg, can learn to become an intermediate skier and have a wonderful, magical time on the slopes. Unless you were raised next door to a ski course and skied constantly, it would be unlikely that you would ever get much beyond the intermediate level unless you had a natural gift for the sport. If you dedicated yourself single-mindedly to becoming an expert, I suppose you could do it. But every time you turned a hard-fought corner in increasing your skills, you would immediately face another difficult challenge. Moving each step up the skill ladder would be very difficult.

In general, people enjoy doing that which they do well. When someone becomes highly skilled at anything he was not forced to learn, it is fairly safe to assume that he is expressing a natural gift. It is also safe to assume that if someone regularly spends many hours happily engaged in some hobby activity, she is expressing a natural gift. For someone born with the collection of innate abilities it takes to be a master skier—or, for that matter, a master at anything—each progressive skill corner is turned much more easily. The same amount of energy and commitment that would take a less gifted person around one corner would take someone with a natural gift around ten. So the way to really get your work life flying is to choose a career for which you have exceptional natural talent and then put in the time and energy to become a real master. Talent and acquired skill are an unbeatable combination.

Are Innate Talents Completely Fixed and Unchangeable?

You can improve on genetically derived abilities by learning to use them fully. You can acquire a body of knowledge, experience, and training that turns ability potential into actuality. You may discover talents you did not know you possessed. But, at this point in time, you cannot create a natural gift in yourself that does not exist. Innate talent can be improved in very young children. With rigorous, expert training, children can learn at a level so deep that some acquired abilities are indistinguishable from inherited talents. But if you are reading this book, it's too late for you.

There is evidence coming to light that indicates that we may, in the future, discover a way for adults to learn at a level of depth that duplicates innate ability. But we are not there yet, and we won't be anytime soon. The most important year for learning and development is the first year of life; the next most important is the second year, and so on.

The Problem with the Solution

Most creatures are not very adaptable. The birds that live in the woods behind your house would disappear if you were to cut down the trees. If you were to cut down all similar forest environments, the other birds of that species might disappear as well. Many creatures inhabit such a narrow ecological niche that a seemingly insignificant change in their habitat can doom their species to extinction. Our fellow inhabitants of planet Earth are the ultimate job specialists. Human beings, on the other hand, are not only the smartest of creatures but also by far the most adaptable. We dominate the earth partially because of that amazing adaptability. We seem to be able to make do with whatever Mother Nature throws at us. In the working world, this translates into each of us being able to fill a wide range of jobs. Given sufficient intelligence, the average human can do just about anything with reasonable competence. But there is a big difference between being able to do something and a perfect fit between you and your work. A four-hundred-pound man was once discovered clinging to the top of a tall palm tree in Florida after a close encounter with an alligator. With typical human adaptability, he had managed to stretch his capabilities way beyond the usual limits.

Our versatility does have its downside, however. Because we are so amazingly adaptable, we've embraced a set of beliefs that causes untold mischief, particularly in our choice of careers. In general, it is believed that if you are intelligent, have the right opportunities, and are interested in the subject matter, you could just as easily be satisfied and successful as a doctor, teacher, computer programmer, or stockbroker. That point of view was perfectly valid in the past, when success was defined primarily by financial security. Now that people are waking up to the possibility that work can be deeply fulfilling, challenging, and fun as well as a means to financial security, we need to take a closer look at the assumptions that have guided our career choices.

Throughout history, people have had little opportunity to select their careers freely. They have been constrained by attitudes and circumstantial limitations. To start with, there were a limited number of occupations from which to choose. During most of human history, only a small number of occupations were necessary for the smooth functioning of a society. A few thousand years ago, there were approximately five occupations to choose from. By 1900, the grand total rose to nearly one hundred different occupations. Only recently, and only in the developed world, has the complexity of the social fabric given rise to almost unlimited career possibilities. The US government now identifies more than ten thousand different job titles. In the past, people were limited to choices from within the narrow set of options available to members of their caste. In the narrower paradigm of earlier times, most people made career choices based on basic survival. You wanted to be as far away as possible from having the wolf at your door. People often were mostly concerned with picking a career that was secure, made good money, and was looked upon favorably by fellow caste members. Because of human adaptability, they were able to succeed in careers that fulfilled these requirements but had little connection with their individual natural traits. This tendency continues today. Parents whose young lives were affected by hardship still counsel their children that "you're not supposed to like it, just pick something with a secure future."

Consequently, people accept the daily discomfort of a career that does not really fit their talents. They tend to put up with unsuitable, ill-fitting careers because they don't realize that their suffering is unnecessary. I have seen woodpeckers land on a metal flagpole and start tapping away, looking for supper. Each time it took only a few seconds for the bird to realize that it was in the wrong place and fly off. We human beings put up with careers that are, in some ways, as ill suited for us as the metal flagpole is for a woodpecker. We can get by. We can survive. But if you want your life to really soar, you have to find a way to match your natural abilities with your work. Otherwise you will keep banging away at the metal flagpole, with an empty stomach, wondering why you keep getting migraines.

An Elegant Fit

It is an obvious, empirical truth that when people are doing something they enjoy and do it extremely well, they get more done and they do it better. When someone is able to perform at a level of mastery, it is usually a function of making use of acquired skills and experience in conjunction with a strong foundation of natural talent. What is most important is the role of natural talents. People who are both highly successful and continue to love their work, year after year, spend most of their time at work engaged in activities that make use of their strongest abilities. They spend very little time performing functions for which they have no special gift. Their lives are concentrated on doing what they do best. If you think about it, everything on earth, except human beings, does exactly that. What could be more elegant than the fit between duck and pond, tiger and jungle? The people you envy because they are both successful and happy in their work have found their pond, their jungle. Their talents are perfectly matched with what they do.

You are probably not one of those rare people with a big, sensitive career antenna who unerringly made the perfect career decision early on, or you would not be reading this book. So you are faced with a question: How can you go about doing the best possible job of matching your talents and your work? How can you come closest to duplicating what the people who have succeeded in finding a perfect match for their talents have accomplished?

Self-Assessing Your Natural Talents and Aptitudes

Our culture accidentally provides the tools to learn about some aspects of our individual abilities. For example, after years of gym classes, with the opportunity to participate in almost every imaginable kind of athletic activity, you probably know a great deal about your innate athletic talents or the lack thereof. Because you have had such a wide exposure to different athletic activities, you can self-assess fairly accurately. You might have a harder time accurately assessing the talents and abilities that would allow you to perform brilliantly in some jobs, only competently in others, and less well in still others. Few of us have done more than scratch the surface with regard to recognizing and appreciating our unique profile of talents.

In addition to the problem of not having superaccurate talent-sensing antennae, there are also a couple of other problems. What you know of your talents is based only on what you have done before. If you are in midcareer and plan to choose a new career direction, you probably do not want to limit yourself to choices suggested by what you have learned from your previous experiences. It makes sense to look at a broader and deeper range of possible career options than would be evident by simply reshuffling the deck. If you are a young person making your first career decisions, it is very unlikely that you have the range of experience to even self-assess the basics accurately.

Often people are most proud of skills they possess that took a great deal of effort to develop. At the same time, they may take for granted the things they are best at doing, because these things come so naturally and easily to them. If you met a fish who could play the piano, it would most likely be extremely proud of its skill, especially since it doesn't have hands. The fish would probably not consider its gift for swimming and breathing underwater as anything special, because these talents come so naturally to it. All of these influences tend to confuse the picture we have of our innate abilities.

Constellations of Talents

The other problem with self-assessing is that what we think of as our talents are usually collections of innate abilities working together rather than the individual talents themselves. People say that John Lennon was a genius. They say he had a gift, an extraordinary natural talent. If you think about it, he had many individual talents and personality characteristics that combined, like stars in a constellation, to make up what we think of as his genius. First of all, on the most basic level, he had the underlying musical aptitudes needed by any reasonably competent musician: tonal memory, which is a memory for complex melodies; an accurate sense of pitch; and a great sense of rhythm. These are inherited abilities. If you were born lacking in one of them, forget about making your living as a musician.

Imagine what it would be like if you were trying to make it as a musician, but you couldn't remember the tune or sing on key or had no sense of rhythm. In addition to these basics, John Lennon had many special gifts, just a few of which I will mention. He had the soul of the true revolutionary artist, always true to his vision, never compromising. On the one hand, he had a great, sage heart, constantly giving everything he had, and on the other, a streak of rebelliousness and playful cynicism. He had a great gift for language, for subtle wordplay. He had an ability to communicate from the core of the most profound aspects of life, while taking it all lightly. He never lost a sense of wonder. He had a lightning-fast imagination and wit. He could pierce to the heart of people and issues and situations, see them clearly and from a perspective unlike anyone else's. I could go on, but the point is to idolize *you*, not John. Just as he had a marvelous collection of individual traits that combined into genius, so do you. One big difference between you and him is that he found a way to have all his abilities play together in perfect harmony, and get paid for it.

When people say they are good at math, or solving problems with people, or writing, they are not describing a single ability, but several working in concert. We see the loaf of bread, not the ingredients. If you think about it, there is not much you can do with a loaf of bread: make sandwiches and French toast, feed the birds. But there are innumerable ways you can combine the basic ingredients: flour, yeast, water, oil, and salt. On the shelves of your supermarket, there are hundreds of items made from these few ingredients.

Mother Nature dealt each of us a very specific hand of natural talent and personality cards. Throughout our lives, we play various combinations of these cards in our work and elsewhere. These combinations are what we recognize as our talents and strengths. Recognizing and understanding the individual "cards" allow us to combine them in new ways instead of limiting ourselves to replaying the combinations we have used successfully in the past. This is especially useful for people considering heading in a new direction.

The best way to understand your innate abilities in a way that helps you design a career that will fit perfectly is to get down to the deepest level; to the basic abilities that combine to make up your unique profile of talents. And the one way to do that well is to go through an in-depth career testing program. The value is not just in understanding individual abilities, but knowing how they combine. When you mix personality traits into the recipe, there are hundreds of different profiles, each perfectly suited to some careers and less so to the great majority of jobs.

Career Testing Programs

I personally think it makes no sense to attempt to make career decisions without being absolutely clear about your talents and aptitudes. You can access all the other areas to investigate through the inquiries in this book. The best way to get absolutely clear about this most important area is through scientific assessment of your talents. Programs that test innate abilities are very different from the kinds of tests traditionally given by career counselors. Most people who have taken old-fashioned career interest tests say that they contribute little to their ability to make life/work decisions. Programs that test abilities give you an edge in making excellent career decisions.

Going through a testing program that measures natural talents and abilities is such a powerfully effective tool that we recommend it to all of our clients. Time after time, they say they are amazed that they could learn so much about themselves from a series of tests. Midcareer clients quickly realize why they have not achieved the satisfaction or success they wanted. Again and again people say, "I wish I had done this years ago." Younger people say that, for the first time, they understand which careers would fit their talents. Clients of all ages learn how to use all their important talents in harmony to create a future that is not a compromise.

Several organizations, including Rockport Institute, provide this type of testing. Two things to look for in selecting the organization are: (1) Make sure that it measures not only natural talents but also personality traits, and (2) You are not a plug-and-play machine, so you don't want a robotic test interpretation. The traditional approach looks at the high scores and prescribes careers typically associated with those scores. One thing we have discovered over the past thirty years is that no one is "typical." I recommend using an organization with a more personalized, holistic approach, communicating results to you in a way that makes sure you can see for yourself how the various talents and combinations have shown up in your life so far. Your own recognition and sense of certainty about what is most important are far more useful in defining definite components than information alone. The cost of most good testing programs is around $550.

Some people do a perfectly adequate job of self-assessing their talents and how they combine without taking a testing program. Inquiry 15, "What Comes Naturally to Me?," is a simple self-assessment of your perceived strengths. Inquiry 16, "Natural Talents and Abilities Self-Assessment," is designed to provide some basic information and insights about your natural gifts. It may be all you need.

INQUIRY 15

What Comes Naturally to Me?

In this inquiry, you will take a look into what you now perceive as your natural gifts.

1. Write down everything that comes naturally to you, for which you seem to have a "knack." Include everything, both work related and otherwise. Don't include those areas where you think you have developed a skill but have no real natural talent. For example, as a boy, I swam competitively on a national level. It would seem, at first glance, that I was a talented swimmer. Actually, I was there because I happened to be on a great team with a great coach and because my dad forced me to go to a very rigorous team practice every morning. Just list those areas in which you feel you are a natural. What were you known for in school? What do you excel in at work? What do you enjoy most? What work activities do you not consider to be work but fun? What projects have you enjoyed? What do other people say you were especially good at? Ask your spouse, your boss, your parents, and others who may have different points of view from yours. Include personality trait strengths as well. They are just as much elements of your talent profile as special knacks you may have.

2. Look back over this inquiry for clues.

3. Add whatever you find to your Clues list. Ask, "Is there anything I am willing to choose as a definite component?" Add anything you choose to your Definite Career Design Components. Do any new careers or jobs come to mind? If so, add them to your Career Ideas.

INQUIRY 16

Natural Talents and Abilities Self-Assessment

This inquiry provides a way for you to assess your natural abilities. Read the following descriptions of talents and abilities and rate yourself in each talent area. You can do this right in the pages of this book. Don't rush. Spend some time looking back over your life to see how much evidence you find for each talent and/or natural ability.

1. Rate your talents and abilities. To help with rating yourself in the natural talents listed below, remember situations that came easily and naturally to you at work and in the rest of your life, both in recent times and in the distant past. After reading about each ability, check one of the circles to rate yourself in that ability: ① for low, ② for midrange, ③ for high. If you're not sure, check the diamond with the question mark. Don't guess. If you aren't sure, check the diamond. Don't worry about how many categories you checked. After you've finished assessing your talents, further instructions will tell you what to do next.

Problem-Solving Talents

① ② ③ ◈ Diagnostic Reasoning

Diagnostic reasoning is a gift for quickly seeing a relationship between apparently unrelated facts; for forming an accurate conclusion from a few scattered bits of evidence. It is the ability to leap to accurate conclusions without using a logical, step-by-step approach. It allows a person who possesses it to perceive instantly a link between seemingly unrelated bits of information. It is especially useful in situations where there is no way to solve the problem logically; where an accurate diagnosis must be made without having all of the facts available. Scientists use this ability to create new theories by perceiving relationships and connections between discrete bits of evidence. Sir Isaac Newton used diagnostic reasoning when he discovered gravity on that fateful day when the apple fell on his head. If his talent had been in analytical reasoning, his conclusion would more likely have been:

You should not sit under apple trees when the apples are ripe and the wind is blowing.

A physician uses this ability to quickly and accurately pinpoint the illness at the root of a group of symptoms. A critic uses it to critique a movie or restaurant; to come to a conclusion that unifies many individual impressions. Diagnostic reasoning is a powerfully active ability that can cause as many problems as it solves. People with this talent need to have a constant flow of new problems. They may have a fascination with learning a new job or skill and then get bored as soon they have it figured out and are not presented with a new problem to tackle. When high scorers have a career that does not use it regularly, diagnostic reasoning keeps on running and critiques whatever gets in its path: the workplace, the boss, and all too often turns to self-criticism. In many careers, this ability is a liability. For example, in traditional corporate management and other careers that place a premium on maintaining the status quo, the diagnostic problem solver's drive to ferret out unworkability, get to the heart of every problem, and bring these problems, along with suggested solutions, to the attention of senior management—who didn't even recognize there was a problem—is usually considered to be unwanted boat rocking and complaining.

Career fields that use diagnostic reasoning: physical, life, and social sciences; emergency medicine and all medicine specialties that present a constant flow of new, nonroutine problems; consulting of all kinds; litigation and criminal law; investigative journalism; forensic science; critiquing professions (comedy, art critic, food critic, social satire); political pundits, op-ed columnists; innovators (inventors, entrepreneurs, all design fields); troubleshooting technical problems; persuasive fields such as advertising and marketing, product buying; quality improvement; copy editing, coaching.

---

① ② ③ ◈ Analytical Reasoning

People high in analytical reasoning ability think systematically and logically. Analytical people can easily organize information within a set of *existing* rules and theories. People who have this ability solve problems by organizing concepts, information, or things in a logical sequence. They bring order to chaos, analyze, systematize, organize, prioritize, solve logical puzzles, synthesize, categorize, schedule, plan, and boil down information to the most important components. Most people with this talent have gifts for some but not all the different ways of expressing it. Just as great legs are the key to admission to the Rockettes, analytical reasoning is an absolutely essential aptitude for careers such as engineering, computers, and editing.

Analytical reasoning is the most used and trusted problem-solving talent in our computer-centered world. Practically every aspect of business, science, and technology requires planning, systematizing, and organizing people, information, and things. Scientists and engineers use mathematical equations to make sense of data, while executives plan and implement new strategies. Writers use the ability to organize ideas and information.

Career fields that use analytical reasoning: business management, engineering, science, mathematics, law, social sciences, research and writing, editing, planning, strategizing, accounting, finance, technical writing, computer programming, journalism.

Specialized Talents

Spatial/Tangible/Nonspatial Orientation

Each of us is born with our own natural way of understanding the world around us. The spatial/nonspatial scale provides some important basic information about how you experience and understand your environment, how you perceive the world, and what you understand and work with most naturally and easily. Deciding on a career without being aware of this important distinction has caused untold havoc in the careers of millions of people.

The range of this ability is best described on a continuum from nonspatial to tangible to spatial, as below:

NONSPATIAL	TANGIBLES	SPATIAL (3-D)

You may or may not be able to pin down where you fit on this scale. Look at what you do well, what you think about, what you talk about, your hobbies, and so on. Women often score very high in spatial orientation, yet they may not easily find evidence of this talent if, as children, they were not encouraged to pursue activities considered more "boyish"—building things, for example. A rough but still helpful way to look into this for women is to remember how you played with dolls. Girls on the spatial side tend to concentrate on the physical world their dolls inhabit: the Barbie Beach Bungalow with real pink sand and tiny margaritas. The nonspatial girl usually gets into acting out doll relationships: "Ken! Malibu Stacy and I are leaving. We are moving to her place on the beach without you."

① ② ③ ⟨❧⟩ Spatial Orientation

High spatial orientation is an aptitude for visualizing in 3-D. People with this talent are usually happiest in careers where the work is concerned mainly with thinking about or working directly with "things" (objects), especially where they spend significant time solving three-dimensional problems. Both a biologist and an architect spend most of their time at work thinking about three-dimensional objects even though they may not come into physical contact with the actual objects. Architects without a natural talent for perceiving and working with three-dimensional reality would, in time, almost certainly grow to dislike their careers. Most people with this talent would experience a profound lack of fit with careers that are not spatial.

In the field of medicine, surgery is spatial, as is radiology, where it is important to think three-dimensionally. Most medical specialties fit someone who is either in the tangible part of the continuum or somewhat spatial. A dermatologist spends her day with real, tangible skin, but she does not need the degree of spatial ability a surgeon does.

Businesses appropriate for a spatially gifted person include landscaping and construction management. Even though the manager of a construction company performs many of the same functions as any other businessperson, much of the construction manager's day involves three-dimensional thinking.

Career fields that use spatial orientation: some medical specialties, forensic science, physical therapy, chiropractic, dentistry, speech pathology, architecture, most engineering disciplines, physics, microbiology, organic chemistry, robotics, computer architecture, computer game design, microelectronics, most design fields, hair styling, farming, culinary arts, sports (gymnastics, golf, basketball, football, and many others), construction, kitchen and bath design, auto mechanics, carpentry, navigating, battlefield command, manufacturing, dance and choreography, special effects in film, sculpture, and other fields that require an ability to mentally visualize in 3-D. Careers that fit people with a tangible orientation are sometimes appropriate for spatial people as well.

---

① ② ③ ◈ Tangible Orientation

A tangible orientation, in the middle of the continuum between spatial and nonspatial, often suggests work involving the physical (tangible) world that does not require continual 3-D problem solving. Detectives use this ability to pull together real-world facts and evidence to solve a criminal case. Most medical specialties do not require thinking in 3-D and may be a good fit for some people with a tangible orientation. Antiques dealers choose and surround themselves with objects. Criminal attorneys and prosecutors depend on physical evidence and a chain of tangible events. Some people in this range, especially those with humanistic personality types, enjoy careers that do not involve the physical world but concentrate on the practical application of fields such as psychology. In recent years, real-world-oriented neuroscientists have moved the understanding of human behavior forward far beyond the contributions of traditional theoretical, nonspatial psychologists.

> *Career fields that use a tangible orientation: computer programming, IT and network engineering, database design, electrical engineering, industrial engineering, wildlife biology, zoology, botany, naturalist, some medical specialties, nursing, web design, display design, product development and brand management, cosmetology, business management in manufacturing and product distribution, retail store and restaurant management.*

① ② ③ ◈ Nonspatial Orientation

To many, life occurs mainly as concepts that have little to do with three-dimensional reality. This ability is the opposite of spatial talent. Those scoring high on the nonspatial scale are especially gifted in understanding nonphysical, conceptual reality. When spatial people look at a house, they usually concentrate their perceptions on the structural, physical aspects of the house, whereas the nonspatial person may think mainly about the lives of the people who live in the house, its value as an investment, the feeling it projects, or any number of nonphysical perceptions or concepts about the house. People with an MBA use this ability to run and improve business operations. Most lawyers test as nonspatial, with constitutional lawyers fitting on the far end of the nonspatial scale. Sociologists work with ideas about group behavior, and economists construct conceptual models of consumer trends.

We've met trained surgeons and engineers who tested as nonspatial and said that they had to work extremely hard to perform even moderately well. Some left their field for fear of making a major mistake or becoming ill from high stress.

> *Career fields that use nonspatial reasoning:* all business disciplines: marketing, advertising, public relations, finance, accounting, human resources, sales, management; social sciences: economics, sociology, psychology, political science, demographics, actuarial mathematics, statistics, politics, cultural anthropology, gender studies, social history; humanities: philosophy, religion, language, literature, diplomacy, international relations, public policy; counseling, psychology, organizational behavior; journalism, publishing, editing, poetry.

① ② ③ ◈ Abstract _____ ① ② ③ ◈ Mixed _____ ① ② ③ ◈ Concrete

Some people are naturally results oriented and driven to seek concrete results. This is obviously an important trait for anyone in a "get the job done" business. Others are perfectly happy to cogitate forever on abstractions. People who score on the abstract end of the scale are usually happiest in work that is theoretical or concept oriented. Their work does not need to produce tangible results in the world of physical reality. For example, many economists are unperturbed when their predictions about trends turn out to be inaccurate. Their interest is in a reality so abstract that their thinking does not need to refer directly to any practical aspect of reality. When you combine this scale with the spatial-nonspatial scale, you get some excellent clues as to what sorts of careers would fit you best.

Someone with a spatial talent could be concrete, which would be appropriate for an engineer or someone in construction; or he could be abstract, like Albert Einstein. A nonspatial person could be oriented toward producing results, such as a stockbroker or corporate manager, or she could be abstract, like a philosopher or Jungian psychologist. Of course, there are many other possible positions on these scales. Career difficulties are almost a certainty if you and your work do not mesh well in these important areas. Doing business with people whose profiles do not mesh with your expectations also causes untold grief. For example, many people who become psychotherapists are nonspatial abstracts. A therapist with this profile might be helpful to someone seeking more understanding or a sounding board. But she would not be of much help to someone seeking to produce real concrete changes rapidly.

Here is a grid that combines abstract-concrete talents with the spatial-nonspatial continuum to show sample career paths:

NATURAL TALENTS

	NONSPATIAL	TANGIBLE	SPATIAL
CONCRETE	Business executive Stockbroker Tax auditor	Tech sales Pharmacist Electrical engineer	Dentist Surgeon Mechanical engineer
MIXED	Advertising director Psychologist Federal judge	Brand manager Documentary filmmaker FBI analyst	Environmental "green" architect Neuroscientist Human-computer interaction designer
ABSTRACT	Poet Economist Constitutional lawyer	Composer: film Science journalist Criminal lawyer	Astrophysicist Thematic sculptor (like Rodin) Patent lawyer

① ② ③ ◈ Rate of Idea Flow

Have you noticed that some people never seem to run out of new ideas, plans, or things to say? Idea flow involves the rate at which your mind generates thoughts and ideas. Idea flow is a gauge of the quantity, not the quality, of your ideas. Like water coming out of a faucet, there could be a tremendous flow of polluted water or just a trickle of the tastiest water you've ever had. A fast flow of ideas doesn't mean that you necessarily have brilliant thoughts or ideas; it just means they come quickly.

Your position on this scale is a good indicator of how much "flow" you need in your work during the course of each day. People with high idea flow feel more at home with, and are usually better at, work that lets this swift flow of thoughts continue unimpeded most of the time. Low-scoring people usually enjoy work that involves focus and concentration. As with the other abilities, there is no good or bad score. Whatever your score, it can be a powerful clue about what sort of work would fit best.

People with high idea flow are especially prolific at coming up with spur-of-the-moment ideas. They have minds that move quickly from one thought to another, from one idea to the next. They often have trouble concentrating on one thing for too long, especially if they aren't particularly interested in the task at hand. They have more difficulty than other people in concentrating on repetitive tasks. In school, they often have more trouble keeping their attention focused on the professor who drones on and on. Many high-idea-flow people have a gift for improvisation and enjoy conversations that involve a continual flow from subject to subject. They are often good at thinking on their feet and responding quickly, although introverted people with this trait may not see themselves that way. Introverts sometimes don't notice they possess this ability because it operates inside their heads. In the arts, a modern artist who painted spontaneously and quickly, like Pablo Picasso, would be a good example of quick idea flow. At the other, low-idea-flow end of the spectrum would be an engraver, who would benefit from a mind that naturally and easily focused for long periods of time.

People with a lower rate of idea flow can be just as creative as people with a fast flow. It simply means that the ideas come more slowly. Often the best ideas come from thinking things out carefully. People with lower idea flow can concentrate their energies on a particular task for a longer period of time. For many jobs in the business world, a rapid flow of ideas is a hindrance. Thomas Edison experimented with hundreds of filaments before he came up with one that led to the lightbulb. Someone with high idea flow might have given up and gone on to other projects.

Career fields that use high idea flow: advertising, marketing, comedy, acting, emergency medicine, teaching, consulting, improvisational music and arts, cartooning, newspaper journalism, sales.

Midrange idea flow: business management, design engineering, architecture, some sales, project management.

Low idea flow: dentistry, surgery, banking, accounting, auditing, insurance, computer programming, house painting, engraving.

① ② ③ ◈ Interpersonal Intelligence

There are several kinds of interpersonal, or social, intelligence. You may have a gift for one or more of them. One form is the ability to accurately perceive and understand others' moods, motives, and intentions. Someone with this talent has a kind of interpersonal X-ray vision that enables them to read other people, even if their subjects are attempting to conceal their true thoughts and feelings. Some people have a variety of this ability that works only with individuals, one-on-one. This is an extremely useful ability for counselors, salespeople, employment interviewers, managers, and police detectives. Others have a gift for understanding and affecting groups. The best politicians, seminar speakers, religious leaders, and teachers possess this "group reading" aptitude. A third form of social intelligence is an ability to get along with others. Some people possess all three varieties of social intelligence. Truly excellent managers have a gift for all three. They can "read people like a book." They pick up subtle signals that allow them to manage employees with sensitivity and to understand the ever-changing dynamics of the group they lead. They also get along with people easily and naturally.

> *Career fields that use interpersonal intelligence: film directing, acting, screenwriting, creative writing, psychology fields, counseling and coaching fields, nursing, physical therapies, child care, teaching K–12, mentoring, diplomacy, training, organizational development, people management, marketing, sales, advertising, humanities, social sciences, public policy, politics.*

① ② ③ ◈ Intrapersonal Intelligence

This is your degree of access to your inner life and feelings, a natural ability to perceive and understand your own moods, motives, and behaviors. Some people have almost no access to their inner life. They can distinguish pleasure from pain but are completely unaware of the constantly changing tides of their inner life. At the other end of the spectrum are people who are aware of every subtle emotional nuance and who can call upon these distinctions to guide their actions and choices. This keen intrapersonal intelligence is found in the best poets, novelists, actors, painters, therapists, and mentors.

> *Career fields and occupations that use intrapersonal intelligence:* poet, playwright, novelist, musician, fine artist, actor, journalist, mediator, counselor, coach, therapist, teacher, professor, social scientist.

Sensory and Perception Abilities

① ② ③ ◈ Intuition

Intuition is an imaginative way of perceiving the world around you. While your five senses see factual detail, your intuition sees the nuances, or shades, of meaning. For intuitives, the world is full of possibilities, and exploring new ideas, people, places, and things is what gives life its zest. They love to seek what's possible in the future; they aim to understand whole systems rather than just the parts. This is the aptitude used by scientists to raise new questions and think outside the box. Poets employ intuition to create metaphors and playfully manipulate the commonsense meaning of words. Actors use it to imagine the inner lives and motives of the characters they portray.

> *Career fields that use intuition:* physical sciences, life sciences, social sciences, humanities, abstract arts, poetry, acting, filmmaking, advertising, marketing, design, psychology, investigative journalism, media studies, entrepreneurs, trend forecasters.

① ② ③ ◈ Sensing

Sensing is a factual way of perceiving the world. Strong sensors trust the literal details perceived by their eyes, ears, and sense of touch more than the more vague impressions and hunches that come from intuition. Rather than speculating about possible futures, sensors jump in and get the job done. They feel at home with practical ideas and things. As sensors, accountants precisely apply detailed and static rules. Police officers use this ability as rigorous observers of the physical world.

Career fields that use sensing: engineering, medicine, dentistry, business administration, dance, physical therapy, cooking, cinematography, sales, accounting, landscape architecture, information technology, broadcast journalism, social work.

① ② ③ ◈ Visual Dexterity

A high score in visual dexterity indicates a gift for working quickly and accurately with the clerical tasks and the pen-and-paper details of the working world. It indicates a special ability to deal with the mounds of paperwork that are a part of professions such as editing, accounting, secretarial work, banking, and law. If you have a high score in this aptitude, you won't necessarily have a passionate love affair with paperwork, but you will be good at getting it done quickly. Those with high scores are terrific proofreaders and extremely detail oriented. Those with low scores are less gifted in noticing typos and dealing with details. As students, they are often penalized for their difficulty in crossing every *t* and dotting every *i* correctly. People with a high score often "miss the forest for the trees." They tend to divide life into pieces and parts, thereby missing the big picture. They think of the forest as made up of a specific, measurable number of trees. Someone with a lower score will usually have a more holistic viewpoint. He or she will easily grasp the impact of the forest but have less ability to view the forest as individual trees. Most physicians are very high in visual dexterity. They tend to look at ailments of the body as specific symptoms caused by the malfunction of a specific organ. Physicians with an interest in preventive medicine or with a more holistic mind-body interpretation of illness usually score somewhat lower in this measure.

Career fields that use visual dexterity: accounting, auditing, banking, biotechnology, business management, computer programming, finance, forensic science, informatics, language translation, law, legal research, library science, medical research, microbiology, nanotechnology, public administration, publishing and editing.

Memories

① ② ③ ◈ Associative Memory

This is an aptitude for learning vocabulary in other languages and memorizing by association. It can be used to learn foreign languages, technical jargon, or computer languages. It is also a useful ability for politicians and others who need to easily remember the names of many people. If you have a low or midrange score in this ability, it does not mean that you cannot learn languages. It will simply take longer for you to memorize vocabulary. A very low score suggests that you should avoid work that involves heavy doses of memorization, such as computer programming.

> *Career fields that use associative memory: acting, ad copywriting, computer science, curriculum design, consulting, creative writing, education/ teaching, humanities, journalism, language, law, medicine, museum staff, physical sciences, life and social sciences, politics, sales, training and development.*

① ② ③ ◈ Number Memory

A talent for remembering numbers and details easily is useful in accounting, banking, tax law, and statistics. People with a very high score are usually gifted at remembering a vast range of encyclopedic facts and details. They are often terrific at games like Trivial Pursuit. This ability is useful to tax lawyers, inventory workers, and all others who need to commit to memory a vast quantity of detailed information.

> *Career fields that use number memory: accounting, allied health, anesthesiology, auditing, banking, bioinformatics, business journalism, business management, computer science, engineering, finance and investing, financial planning, information technology, library and information science, mathematics, management information systems, nursing, retail sales (e.g., auto parts, grocery cashier), physical and earth sciences, sports journalism, statistics, tax law.*

① ② ③ ◈ Design Memory

Design memory is the ability to memorize visual information and tangible forms in the world around you. It also plays a role in navigating. Many people who are high in it quickly learn their way around a new city.

> *Career fields that use design memory: architecture, adventure guide, antiques appraiser, archivist, botany, chemistry, dance and performance arts, dentistry, earth sciences, engineering, graphic arts, fashion design, filmmaking, forensic science, interior design, industrial design, law enforcement, mechanical engineering, materials science, microbiology, patent law, aircraft piloting, physical science, medicine (especially surgery), tour guide, sports coaching (playing field strategy), surveying, taxi and truck driving, visual arts.*

Other Specialized Abilities

① ② ③ ◈ Mathematical Ability

People who display a natural talent for a specific niche of math may have a mix of several natural abilities working together. For example, mathematics used to solve 3-D problems such as geometry and advanced calculus (used in engineering fields) engages a combination of high analytical reasoning, high spatial reasoning, high number memory, and a logical temperament—the perfect recipe of strengths for math talent. Adding intuition to this mix of talents can suggest the ability for abstract mathematics such as differential calculus used in theoretical research fields in the physical and life sciences.

> *Career fields that use mathematical ability: actuary science, architecture, computer science, engineering, financial engineering and investing, marketing research, mathematics, physical sciences, earth sciences, economics, operations research, statistics, and probability.*

① ② ③ ⟨?⟩ Language Ability

People who display a natural talent for learning and using language usually have a mix of several natural abilities working together. People with high associative memory and high analytical reasoning tend to learn languages easily. Adding in some musical talent provides the mix of abilities necessary for speaking a second language with perfect inflection.

> *Career fields that use language ability:* acting, screenwriting, print journalism, languages, law, poetry and literary arts, literary agents and editors, social sciences and humanities, politics, publishing, technical writing, scientific writing and research, science journalism.

① ② ③ ⟨?⟩ Artistic and Musical Abilities

Each artistic expression (music, performance art, dance, and other visual arts) engages a different set of innate abilities. In all art forms, from the classical and traditional to the contemporary and improvisational, different talent combinations tend to pull the artist in a direction that comes easily and naturally.

> *Career fields that use artistic and musical abilities:* acting, advertising and commercial arts, architecture, computer video game design, dance performance arts, most design fields, filmmaking, film editing and production, film scoring, film special effects, graphic arts, music composition, musical performance arts, photography and photojournalism, literary arts, sound engineering, speech therapy, visual arts, website design.

① ② ③ ⟨?⟩ Body Kinesthetic Ability

People who excel at gymnastics, athletic sports, dance and performance arts, and martial arts have just the right mix of kinesthetic talents for their specific field of performance. Other fields that require regular use of kinesthetic talents include modeling, acting, circus performing, exploring, diving, search and rescue, and law enforcement.

Choosing a sport that fits your talents is more complex that it seems. It involves a number of factors, including musculoskeletal makeup, heart-lung capacity, mental-sensory perception, and other traits. A world-class cross-country skier needs larger lung capacity than a top-notch tennis player. The skier needs more endurance muscle fiber, whereas the tennis player needs explosive sprint muscle fiber. Both skiers and tennis players benefit if they have a lower center of gravity, which means that their legs are somewhat short in proportion to their upper bodies. Someone who excels at swimming butterfly would find the broad chest and shoulders that are such an advantage in that sport a disadvantage in bicycle racing because they would create wind resistance.

Career fields that use body kinesthetic ability: acting, dance and performance arts, farming, fashion modeling, law enforcement, firefighting, heavy equipment operation and construction, military, paramedic/EMT, sports, search and rescue, trades.

---

2. Search for the Best Clues. Transfer your self-assessments to your notebook or the grid on the following page by checking the box that you think best represents your strength in each area. If you're not sure of your strength in a certain area, check the "Not Sure" column to remind yourself to look for more clues about that ability. Think about the abilities you think may represent strong natural talents. Spend some time paying attention to your activities, noticing which talents you use often and what you do well. Also, notice what you do not do well naturally.

3. Look back over this inquiry for clues. Add whatever you find to your Clues list. Ask, "Is there anything I am willing to choose as a definite component?" Add anything you choose to your Definite Career Design Components. Do any new careers or jobs come to mind? If so, add them to your Career Ideas. Remember to keep working with your clues, moving them toward selecting new definite components.

4. If you have completed this chapter as well as chapter 15, "Temperament and Personality," and chapter 16, "Your Core Personality," you may enjoy checking out chapter 29, "Rockport Type and Talent Indicator," which uses the results of the inquiries in these three chapters to suggest possible careers.

Natural Talents and Abilities	High	Mid	Low	Not Sure	Definite Career Components
Diagnostic Reasoning					
Analytical Reasoning					
Spatial Orientation					
Tangible Orientation					
Nonspatial Orientation					
Abstract Orientation					
Concrete Orientation					
Rate of Idea Flow					
Interpersonal Intelligence					
Intrapersonal Intelligence					
Intuition					
Sensing					
Visual Dexterity					
Associative Memory					
Number Memory					
Design Memory					
Mathematical Ability					
Language Ability					
Artistic and Musical Ability					
Body Kinesthetic Ability					

5. If you want to start comparing a few specific careers based on clues or components you have chosen, do the "Eight Great Careers" inquiry in chapter 24, "Which Careers Fit Best?" Doing "Eight Great Careers" at this point is a preliminary exploration. There are still other factors to consider. You will most likely use the "Eight Great Careers" inquiry later on as well. You might check it out now and use it anytime you think it will prove valuable.

CHAPTER 18

•

NATURAL ROLES

We tend to think of ourselves as a permanent, unchanging entity, that person we call "me." Look a little more closely and you may discover that there is more to you and "me" than is obvious. We all play multiple roles in our lives. Some of these may be temporary or simply the result of circumstance. Most of the roles we play are permanent, natural expressions of our character—or, I should say, characters. Each of us is inhabited by a cast of characters who appear onstage during the course of our lives, sometimes in a lead role and other times in a lesser role. Even as children, we exhibited some of these roles. Think of kids you knew who were natural leaders, comedians, rebels, risk takers, or artists. These roles, also called archetypes, stay with us for our entire lives. Each of us has several roles that come to us most naturally. They are almost like different characters who take turns having lead roles in chapters of our lives. These roles don't necessarily have any consistency or relationship among them. For example, a Mafia hit man may be absolutely ruthless at work and a loving, devoted parent at home.

The kid who was the class president is likely to take on leadership roles in his or her adult life. The class clown will probably play that role throughout life. It may continue to be a lead role. Most comedians say they inhabited that role from an early age. On the other hand, it may recede in later life and appear only after a couple drinks or with close friends. Still, unless it somehow is squished by circumstances, it is likely to continue as a cast member throughout life.

Most of these roles have a genetic component: They choose you, not the other way around. For example, one of the roles described in this chapter is risk taker. Scientists have linked risk-taking behavior in mice to a single gene. Some mice with a particular genetic structure are willing to walk along an unprotected walkway high above the ground, while most seek a safer, more secure path. Like the men and women willing to walk unprotected on narrow steel beams to build the great skyscrapers, or extreme-sport athletes joyfully performing dangerous feats, some people are born risk takers.

Recognizing these natural inclinations can provide some powerful clues for deciding what to do with your life. Someone whose dominant roles are networker and marketer might fit best in a very different career from someone whose main roles are healer and animal lover. Since there is no single, unchanging "me," knowing your main roles is one of the best ways to know yourself and where you best fit in the world of work. If you imagine people you know working in situations that are completely alien to their dominant roles, it is easy to see how important it is to choose work where your best roles are cast as the leading characters in your life.

Roles differ in power, importance, and expression. Some are major players; others take on a smaller part in your life. A role that is healthy in moderation may take on a different character when it dominates. For example, most people at least occasionally attempt to influence the people around them. This characteristic may lose its innocence when manipulation becomes a major role.

Your challenge in this chapter is to sort out your own unique collection of roles, how you function in the more dominant roles, and how roles combine. Because we tend to go through life more conscious of *what* we do than *why* we do it, you may not have given much thought to the roles you play. We all take ourselves for granted, so it's going to take looking at yourself with new eyes.

There is no simple formula for turning roles into careers that fit you. Please remember that this inquiry provides another kind of access to who you are and some more clues and puzzle pieces about how you and the working world will best fit together.

INQUIRY 17

My Natural Roles

There are two different ways of doing this inquiry. The short and simple way is to do it yourself, just you and this book, without involving anyone else. Another way is to involve some people who know you intimately—perhaps close friends or family members. Doing it this way often reveals things about you that you might not notice if you didn't include other people's assessments. One woman, who gave herself a zero for the role of Hero, saw herself in a new light after everyone else gave her high marks.

How to Identify Your Natural Roles

1. Read through this chapter, marking the appropriate circle for each role. Strong, dominant roles get the ③ checked. Less dominant but still important roles get a ②. If you are not completely sure whether a certain role is part of your repertoire, give it a ①. And if it seems to play no part in your life, mark that ⓪. Identify roles you actually play rather than ones you like. Wanting to be a visionary doesn't make you one. Some roles may not

be completely obvious. That's why it is useful to make some copies of this chapter and pass them out to others who know you well.

Roles are divided into groups. Four of these groups are based on the middle two letters of your personality type. Pay particular attention to roles listed under the letters that fit you. For example, if you determined that you are an ENFP in chapter 15, the middle letters of your personality type would be NF, so you should pay special attention to roles listed in the category called "Roles Common with Intuitive-Feelers (NF)." These roles that are often linked with personality-type roles may or may not prove useful but are definitely worth a bit of special attention.

Okay. Ready? Go ahead. The rest of the instructions are at the end of the chapter, after you have done this first part of the inquiry.

Basic Universal Roles

___ ⓪ ① ② ③ Child

We all inhabit this role. To some degree, we all carry our childhood with us, for better or worse, throughout our lives. The positive side of this role is the eternal child; the person who remains eternally young at heart. He or she is lighthearted and fun to be around, preserving a charming innocence, a spirit of playfulness, and a vital, energetic youthfulness.

On the negative side, some people never fully grow up, remaining irresponsible as a childish adult. Afraid to face the unknowns and unpredictable aspects of life, the Child yearns to be protected and taken care of by others. He may care only about fulfilling his own needs. He may be bratty, need to always be the center of attention, or be unable to form mature relationships. When it comes to career choices, the eternal Child wants someone else to decide for him or just hopes it all works out rather than treating career choice as one of life's most important decisions. When times get tough, nearly everyone has bouts of the Child role; the hope of being rescued from tough choices and dangers is woven deeply into human nature.

___ ⓪ ① ② ③ Mother

The nurturer, the vital giver of life. The Mother is protective, devoted, caring, and unselfish. Although most women can biologically function as a mother, this role describes people of either sex who embody these characteristics in their everyday life. They may have their own children or passionately look forward to having a family, or this role may show up in many other ways:

for example, in a devotion to protecting the environment or the well-being of anything else they care about.

___ ⓪ ① ② ③ Father

Even beyond the immediate family, some people embody the bold and courageous male patriarch. The Father initiates, takes charge, and leads through the tough decisions in life. People who embody the spirit of the Father role will find ways to apply this talent in the workplace as the wise manager, on the playing field as the nurturing sports coach, and as a parent to their own children as the ultimate "cool" dad (or mom). On the dark side, the Father may also abuse his authority by being overly controlling, dictatorial, or a know-it-all.

___ ⓪ ① ② ③ Warrior

The Warrior takes a stand and fights for something. The adversary can be anything: other Warriors, an injustice, a disease, a shortcoming of society, a personal weakness, a belief system, an unfulfilled goal. The Warrior is willing to do what it takes to reach the goal, no matter what obstacles arise, no matter how uncomfortable he or she feels. The more evolved Warrior seeks to win without a fight, the objective being the goal rather than the need to go to battle. Men and women drawn to defend their country on the battlefield embody the physical Warrior, willing to put life on the line for a cause. Others manifest the Warrior in fighting for social injustices, or on the proverbial battlefield of the competitive business world. On the dark side is the Warrior who can't stop; who loves the battle more than the goal.

___ ⓪ ① ② ③ Hero

The Hero arises in many forms. The true hero begins as an ordinary person, called to a mission beyond his or her present capacities. Out of dedication to the goal, the Hero undergoes difficulties and emerges transformed by the experience. Many tales handed down to us from ancient days follow this theme. The character Frodo in *The Lord of the Rings* is the perfect embodiment of this role in modern literature. The Hero's journey can involve an adventure in the external world or an inner quest for wisdom or personal transformation. The Hero's quest always involves overcoming those very weaknesses or inner demons holding him or her back. Many of you reading this book with a strong desire to find a career you love are on a Hero's journey: You are working against a prevailing belief that not enjoying work is normal. ("If it was fun, they wouldn't call it work.")

___ ⓪ ① ② ③ Comedian

The consummate class clown, prankster, fool, and jokester. The Comedian thrives on making people laugh, cry, or think about things differently. He sees the humor and absurdity in everyday life. He makes us laugh at ourselves and our "foolish" ways. Some are court jesters, a role that gives them special permission to reveal the truth that most of us, caught up in trying to be politically (or otherwise) correct, aren't seeing.

___ ⓪ ① ② ③ Leader/King/Queen

Without much effort, some people carry an air of authority, confidence, clarity, vision, or majesty; they are recognized by others as natural leaders. As if born with royal blood, they have natural authority. While Managers administer projects and work the details, Leaders see the whole forest while maintaining a practical eye on the trees. They are at their best when they know the difference between power and force. A truly powerful Leader is benevolent, using wisdom, persuasion, and the example of his actions. People follow him because they want to. The best leaders direct their kingdom, company, organization, family, or team without needing to use force and domination.

___ ⓪ ① ② ③ Prince/Princess

Deserving, entitled, Princes and Princesses need to be taken care of. They think of themselves as special, born to be honored and adored. They are vulnerable, seek attention, and usually find others to worship them, dote on them, and generally treat them as royalty. Rarely independent or self-sufficient, they often trap themselves in relationships and situations where they are completely reliant on others and never fully develop their own powers to live independently in the real world.

___ ⓪ ① ② ③ Money Person

Since the dawn of civilization, some people have had a strong affinity for money: acquiring it, saving it, investing it, understanding the complexities of it, and working with it. Just because you want a lot of it doesn't mean this role is one of yours. Look instead for a real affinity. This may be one of your natural roles if you spend a lot of time looking for the good deal or reading about investing, and enjoy the financial intricacies of business, balancing your checkbook, or doing financial spreadsheets.

Public or "Social Face" Roles

__ ⓪ ① ② ③ Extrovert

Naturally talkative, outgoing, sociable, the Extrovert's world revolves around engaging with people. Most Extroverts have a rich outer world of relationships; they'd rather be on the go and meeting new people than reading a book. Extroversion is not the same as friendliness and, despite social conventions, is not any more "normal" than introversion. Stronger Extroverts do their best work with people, in careers such as salesperson, manager, teacher, broadcast journalist, and the like. Everyone is a combination of both introversion and extroversion; it's a matter of degree.

__ ⓪ ① ② ③ Group Worker/Team Member

The loyal teammate who works with and through other people, contributing her part to the larger group goal. Whether introverted or extroverted, leader or follower, about 75 percent of the population is team oriented, preferring to work as part of a company, team, or tribe. She is happiest being one of a group, in a role where she doesn't stand out as a unique specialist or expert. Employees often claim this role, including senior management of service and retail businesses and corporations, government workers, and military personnel.

__ ⓪ ① ② ③ Insider

Insiders get much of their identity from their membership in a certain group. Insiders are loyal to the group's values and goals, and measure their success using the group's yardstick. They usually are very protective of the group's values and fiercely defend its traditions.

__ ⓪ ① ② ③ Outsider

Their identity is based on *not* being part of the group. Some Outsiders' motivation stems from an individualistic or unconventional viewpoint; others turn their exclusion from a group into a badge of honor; and still others simply don't like joining anything.

__ ⓪ ① ② ③ Marketeer

The natural promoter, public relations, and public affairs expert. Marketers enjoy communicating the value of an idea, product, or service to their audience and persuading others to jump on board. They enjoy getting across the benefits and making the sale, which may involve actually selling something or convincing others of something.

___ ⓪ ① ② ③ Networker

These folks continually create and manage relationships with other people who may prove useful in furthering their goals. The skillful Networker gives as much as he gets, so that his relationships are characterized by shared resources and support. Some act as go-betweens to bring people together; they effortlessly move in and out of different groups, clubs, social cliques, and associations, and introduce people to each other.

___ ⓪ ① ② ③ Bullshooter

Shooting the bull is the ancient role of storyteller. To the Bullshooter, the story is the reality. They don't let the facts get in the way of a good tale. They enjoy holding forth, gaining the rapt attention of others. Some are happy as salespeople; others are inspiring teachers. Before the advent of writing, the Bullshooter was the carrier and keeper of the tribe's history.

___ ⓪ ① ② ③ Politician

Their most basic attribute is their relentless drive toward attaining a position of power and/or influence. At their best, politicians are statesmen and stateswomen, dedicated to the public good, able to set aside their own survival strategies in favor of forwarding society. Great politicians express a complex combination of several roles, such as the Leader, Marketeer, Deal Maker, and Networker. On the dark side, many of them are dedicated to partisan causes and personal gain, and are willing to scheme, maneuver, and lie to gain power.

___ ⓪ ① ② ③ Deal Maker

Part Networker, Politician, and Marketeer, the Deal Maker can get the deal done and the contract signed. Some are gifted at making friends, building relationships, and proposing the "win-win" deal. Others have a talent for getting people to agree to deals that favor only the Deal Maker. They understand what makes people tick and know what it takes to motivate others to make up their minds and sign on the dotted line. They often become salespeople and also excel as marketing executives, politicians, and diplomats.

__ ⓪ ① ② ③ Introvert

Naturally quiet, introspective, reserved, talks little but thinks constantly. Introverts have a rich inner life and do their best work in their heads or with their hands, such as writers, craftspeople, accountants, lawyers, researchers, scientists, artists, and so on. Introversion is not shyness or a lack of confidence. Introverts have an inward focus, which is just as normal as extroversion. Everyone is a combination of both introversion and extroversion; it's a matter of degree. Some may try to hide their natural tendency and force themselves into more extroverted careers. Introversion is not a weakness; it's a natural trait that, if not taken into account, can lead to exhaustion on the job.

__ ⓪ ① ② ③ Hermit

A small percentage of people are happy to live in solitude. Most introverts are not Hermits. The difference is that introverts have a social life. Hermits don't. Rather, they prefer to live and work alone and consider contact with other people a bother.

Adventurer Roles

__ ⓪ ① ② ③ Free Spirit

Live and let live, try anything twice, the world is a playground to explore. Open-minded, socially liberal, artistic, uninhibited by social conventions and traditions, Free Spirits don't want to be tied down, resist or avoid authority, and avoid the domination of others. Careerwise, they are attracted to professions such as the arts, entertainment, and travel, as well as consulting and self-employment. On the negative side, they can have trouble settling on something long enough to master it.

__ ⓪ ① ② ③ Naturewise Person

These folks pay attention to the natural world and its sights, sounds, smells, and potential dangers. This is an ancient role, one that our hunter-gatherer ancestors lived every day. Like the Streetwise Person, they are keenly aware of their surroundings. As the Streetwise Person is often clueless in the natural environment, the Naturewise Person may be unaware of the complexities and dangers of the city. Many a Naturewise Person becomes a bird-watcher, hunter, or hiker as a hobby. This role calls some people so strongly that they become foresters, land conservationists, geologists, ecologists, marine biologists, and so on.

__ ⓪ ① ② ③ Seeker

In search of truth and wisdom, the Seeker looks into the unknown, asking, "Who am I?" "What is the truth?" "What is the nature of reality?" Endlessly curious, the Seeker wanders, wonders, and explores. On the dark side, Seekers may wander on an endless, aimless journey to nowhere and avoid finding whatever they seek for fear that finding will end their search.

__ ⓪ ① ② ③ Humanitarian

Concerned with helping to improve the lives or alleviating the suffering of others, they are the good Samaritans. Sometimes practical and sometimes naïve do-gooders, Humanitarians are generous in their devotion to making the world a better place.

__ ⓪ ① ② ③ Rule Breaker/Rebel

The outsider and maverick who questions conventions and deviates from the norm. Rebel energy often helps society break out of habits that no longer work. Social activists and critics, scientists, comedians, artists and poets, visionary leaders, and change agents who move the world to see things anew or challenge the status quo have the Rule Breaker in their makeup. Matt Groening, creator of *The Simpsons*, is an example of the artistic, comedic Rule Breaker. On the dark side, some Rebels are on a path of destruction, bringing harm to themselves or society as professional criminals, con artists, tricksters, and scammers. This group's white-collar representatives often show up in the news: Politicians and Criminals with MBAs and law degrees, manipulating the public for their own ends.

__ ⓪ ① ② ③ Risk Taker

The daredevil, willing to do things that most people would consider dangerous, chancy, speculative, or foolhardy. The Risk Taker may take physical risks, like the mountain climber or stunt person, or thrive on beating the odds, like the day trader or the entrepreneur. Much of human history has been made by successful Risk Takers. Many of the advances and advantages we most cherish exist only because someone took a big risk and won. On the dark side, some get their kicks by trying to beat the system. At the farther end of that spectrum lies the Criminal roles.

__ ⓪ ① ② ③ Innovator/Pioneer

Goes where no man or woman has gone before, exploring the unknown territories of inner or outer worlds. Innovators bring new ideas, systems, theories, technologies, and discoveries into being. The ultimate "paradigm shifters," Innovators are drawn to operate on the edge of the unknown. Pioneers are similar, with one difference: Their focus is less on creating something new than on exploring unknown territory or making use of a new technology as an early adopter. Both can operate without the agreement of society. Some play this role on the world's stage, others in their own lives. They are often subject to criticism from defenders of the status quo.

Antisocial Roles

Much of what is commonly considered antisocial may be just pushing the boundaries of what is known or accepted; and that is the engine that moves humanity forward. The roles in this category are different, however. They have no intention of making a contribution to society. Their impulse is narrow, in service to the ignoble in humanity or to cause intentional harm.

__ ⓪ ① ② ③ Sellout

At one time or another, each of us plays this role. Whether it is a dominant role for you depends on how much time you devote to playing it. Sellouts make choices that they know are based on expediency and what's easy rather than right, cashing in their values and dreams for money, power, comfort, security, or status. Common expressions of this role occur when you choose a career you don't enjoy, or marry someone you don't love for security or status. Selling out damages not only you but also the fabric of life around you.

__ ⓪ ① ② ③ Criminal

This role is somewhat different from the everyday use of the word. Most people in prison fit the common definition: someone who commits acts against the law. But not all fit the role described here. The Criminal role includes people without much moral or ethical concern about the damage they inflict on other people as they pursue their own advancement, power, or wealth. They may have antisocial or psychopathic tendencies or simply not care how their actions affect others. The bad guy in the movies and the mercenary soldier of fortune fill this role, but so do some perfectly respectable citizens who happily rob you with a fountain pen. Computer virus creators fall into this category. Wherever you find hired guns, you also will find people playing the Criminal role: some lawyers, lobbyists, politicians, senior corporate managers, financial finaglers, and so forth.

__ ⓪ ① ② ③ Bully

The bully dominates others through force—either physical force or just a dominating personality focused on getting its way no matter what.

Roles Grouped by Personality Type

From this point on, the roles listed are grouped by the personality types that are often linked with them. Any of these roles could be one of yours, no matter what your personality type. The reason I put them in groups is because these roles are especially common in people of certain personality types. Please consider all of these as possible roles you play and pay special attention to those especially listed under your personality type, but check them all out to see if they describe one of your dominant roles.

Roles Common with Sensor-Thinkers (ST)

The next group of natural roles could fit you no matter what your personality type but is especially common in people with a sensor-thinker (ST) personality (ESTJ, ISTJ, ESTP, and ISTP). If yours is one of these personality types, you should read this group of roles with special care.

__ ⓪ ① ② ③ Manager

The natural organizer and administrator of people and projects. Although often in a leadership position, a Manager is not necessarily a natural authority or visionary leader. Supervisor, captain of a team, gets the job done. Whether in the workplace, at home, or planning a vacation or dinner party, the Manager brings order to chaos, sets the agenda, plans the project, orchestrates the activities, and manages the resources to make it all happen.

__ ⓪ ① ② ③ Builder/Designer

The natural engineer, born to build, tinker, and find practical solutions to tangible problems. Builders show signs of their gift early in life, engineering things out of Lego blocks that often astound their parents. All engineering specialties, the trades, architecture, and the hardware and software sides of information technology are playgrounds for Builders. They are the toolmakers and tool users who build and improve the efficiency of our everyday lives, following in the footsteps of the Henry Fords and Alexander Graham Bells. Crafting and shaping the physical world of objects to serve human purposes is their joy.

__ ⓪ ① ② ③ Athlete

The embodiment of strength, character, commitment, and determination to push the human body and mind to its limits. The Athlete's spirit is expressed in the relentless pursuit of physical and mental mastery, and in someone less competitive is sometimes expressed as simply loving a sport or other athletic activity for the sheer joy of it. Olympic and professional athletes, classical musicians, circus performers, dancers, stunt people, soldiers, fighter pilots, explorers, rescue personnel, and outdoor adventurers are careers enjoyed by Athletes.

__ ⓪ ① ② ③ Streetwise Person

Walks the urban landscape keenly aware of what's going on, the intentions of people he encounters, and potential threats. The Streetwise Person's movements and actions are consistent with survival; he knows when to cross to the other side of the street. This is one of the most ancient roles. Imagine that you and your tribe are walking down the trail twenty thousand years ago and suddenly come upon a strange group of people. You would want to have someone in your group who could pick up the vibes of the other people and know instinctively if they meant you harm. People with this trait are often attracted to police work, undercover intelligence, firefighting, and emergency medic/paramedic fields, including animal rescue and disaster relief.

__ ⓪ ① ② ③ Protector

Keeper of traditions, guardian of the rules, laws, customs, and socially accepted morals, the Protector sees the world through a lens of shoulds and shouldn'ts, judging rights and wrongs, holding life as black and white. Plays by the rules. Defending homeland and honor, Protectors are usually loyal to whatever they identify as their tribe: country, organization, belief system. Usually socially conservative, they strive to maintain important values and ways of life. Protectors are attracted to professions that enforce and make more rules, as law enforcement personnel, federal agency regulators, and armed forces.

__ ⓪ ① ② ③ Right-hand Person
(Helper/Sidekick/Companion/Server)

The ultimate "right hand" who gets the job done. Their strength, dedication, loyalty, and supportive nature are often the real backbone of an organization. Some vice presidents, chief operating officers, general managers, executive assistants, and secretaries often say they are not interested in being the main person out front, but they thrive as the one who makes it all work behind the scenes. Some are Companions or Sidekicks with a giving nature who find joy in serving, hosting, and pleasing others. Some become waiters or work in other hospitality industry careers; others work as cooks, manage a bed-and-breakfast, drive a taxi, or run a hotel. Helpers are often grossly underappreciated.

Roles Common with Sensor-Feelers (SF)

The next group of natural roles could fit you no matter what your personality type. They are especially common in people with a sensor-feeler (SF) personality (ESFJ, ISFJ, ESFP, and ISFP). If yours is one of these personality types, you should read this group of roles with special care.

__ ⓪ ① ② ③ Teacher/Mentor

Drawn to educate, instruct, and pass on knowledge or wisdom to students and apprentices. Teachers instruct groups of students, whereas Mentors take an individual apprentice under their wing to pass on their mastery.

__ ⓪ ① ② ③ Healer

The modern-day descendant of our hunter-gatherer ancestors' shaman. The healer is called to heal the sick and restore well-being to those suffering. Strangely enough, many modern physicians do not identify with this as a dominant role. They practice medicine in another role.

__ ⓪ ① ② ③ Caregiver/Helper

An innate desire to take care of other people or animals is the main characteristic of this role. The Caregivers' nonjudgmental, responsive, and nurturing spirit calms people who come into contact with them. With their power of empathy, they nurse others back to health, help them through a crisis, and care for the elderly. They make the perfect nurse, hospice counselor, or physical therapist. The Helper is a somewhat different role characterized by the need to help whether or not it is needed or wanted. The Helper can't help but help.

__ ⓪ ① ② ③ Animal Lover

Able to bond with the animal kingdom. They enjoy spending time with animals and often have a special ability to communicate with them. People with this temperament will go out of their way to train, care for, or rescue animals in distress. Naturalists, zookeepers, ecologists, racehorse trainers, jockeys, search-and-rescue dog trainers, ASCPA officers, veterinarians, and avid pet owners usually inhabit the Animal Lover role.

__ ⓪ ① ② ③ Artisan

The Artisan is the craftsperson who makes beautiful and functional objects by hand. Many have a designer's aesthetic; their finely tuned senses are sensitive to subtleties of design, color, form, taste, touch. Chefs, fashion designers, interior designers, landscape designers, home remodelers, stonemasons, historic preservationists, antique appraisers, furniture makers, instrument makers, vintners, musicians, makeup artists, massage therapists, and hairstylists often embody the Artisan role.

__ ⓪ ① ② ③ Hedonist

The pleasure seeker whose philosophy is "Why put off what you can enjoy now?" and who lives for the moment. Hedonists are the ultimate shoppers; the impulse buyers. The dark side of hedonism is when it interferes with living sensibly, attaining long-range goals, and forming lasting relationships.

__ ⓪ ① ② ③ Sensualist

Considers life a grand feast for the senses, finds delight in the sensual world. Sensualists may love music, art, food, touch, nature, physical pleasures, scent, or beauty. This is a different role from the Hedonist in that it lacks the compulsive "pleasure, now, now, now" quality of the Hedonist.

Roles Common with Intuitive-Thinkers (NT)

The next group of natural roles could fit you no matter what your personality type. They are especially common in people with an intuitive-thinker (NT) personality (ENTJ, INTJ, ENTP, INTP). If yours is one of these personality types, you should read this group of roles with special care.

___ ⓪ ① ② ③ Scientist

Seeking understanding and drawn to experiment, Scientists inquire into the mysteries of life to understand and explain the laws of nature or the universe. Some are interested in the physical universe, others in social or psychological science.

___ ⓪ ① ② ③ Academic

Often found working at a university or similar setting as researchers and sometimes as teachers. Traditionally considered to have their "head in the clouds," in fact, some academics have their feet very much on the ground. Most are interested in subjects with a significant theoretical component. When combined with a streak of independence, this role may result in independent academic types who work outside the system.

___ ⓪ ① ② ③ Investigator

Some detectives solve homicides; others seek a cure for cancer. What all Investigators have in common is a nose for a good clue and a mind that can't help looking under the surface to figure out the truth. They constantly pay attention to their environment with a critiquing ability that allows them to discover clues that might not be obvious to others. Detectives, scientists, inventors, mystery writers, counselors, lawyers, and crime scene investigators sometimes embody this gift.

___ ⓪ ① ② ③ Analyst

Uses an analytical approach to life and work. Whether or not Analysts have a strong natural gift for analytical reasoning, this is how life occurs for them. They tend to give more credence to logic than feelings and believe that life can and should be organized and rational.

___ ⓪ ① ② ③ Entrepreneur

Innovative by nature, Entrepreneurs build businesses from the ground up. They make use of a wide range of natural talents, calling on multiple abilities to create something that didn't exist before. They take pride in being able to do it on their own, counting on their own resources, talents, and know-how.

_ ⓪ ① ② ③ Amateur

He delights in some specialty without the drive (or sometimes talent) to become a professional. Inspired Amateurs may love sports, the arts, cooking, cars, or any other area. They are often passionately engaged in their interest but happy to let others do it for a living. Sometimes their passion takes so much of their attention that they fail to develop the same level of interest in their career. It is especially useful to claim this role if it fits you so that you don't get overwhelmed by your hobbies or feel you have failed because your hobby is not your profession.

_ ⓪ ① ② ③ Critic

The Critic has the eye of the hawk, the nose of a dog, the sonar of a bat. Nothing gets by him or her. Critics are born to find flaws or get to the truth under the surface appearances. They look for "what's wrong with this picture," sleuth out the hidden agenda, the design flaws, let us know why we shouldn't bother to see that movie. They have a built-in lie detector and tend to critique everything that crosses their radar screen.

_ ⓪ ① ② ③ Perfectionist, Stickler

Demands the highest standards of excellence and rejects anything less, in himself, in others, and in his projects. Perfectionists believe that perfection is obtainable—a good trait for someone on the bomb disposal squad. The dark side of this role is setting unrealistically demanding goals. Some find very little in their lives satisfying, because, for them, one less-than-perfect detail ruins everything.

_ ⓪ ① ② ③ Geek

Geeks have their attention focused on scientific or technical pursuits, often to the exclusion of other interests. At one time, *geek* was an insult by non-Geeks confusing geekdom with social ineptitude. These days, the fact that many of those former "Geeks" are billionaires has warmed public perception of the role.

_ ⓪ ① ② ③ Lifelong Learner

The perennial student, always curious to learn more. You should hope that your doctor is one of these people.

Roles Common with Intuitive-Feelers (NF)

The next group of natural roles could fit you no matter what your personality type. They are especially common in people with an intuitive-feeler (NF) personality (ENFJ, INFJ, ENFP, INFP). If yours is one of these personality types, you should read this group of roles with special care.

__ ⓪ ① ② ③ Guide/Coach/Counselor/Therapist

These four roles are similar in some ways. They all involve working with a person or group to help them reach a goal or learn something new.

The Guide is the highest, most evolved form of teacher. The guide communicates wisdom, based on personal mastery of a subject that comes from a lifetime of experience. Guides transmit principles, the heart of the matter, and are often the most creative contributors to their field.

The coach assists a talented, committed person in reaching a goal. Twenty-five years ago, I coined the term "career coach" because I thought that the term "career counselor" was insufficient, implying a prescriptive relationship mostly offering information and advice. A Coach, on the other hand, figures out what it will take for you to reach your goal, elicits your strengths and wisdom, assigns appropriate tasks, and makes sure that you get to your goal. You do the work, whether that means practicing your sport every day or moving toward some important personal goal. A relationship with a Coach is a partnership between you and your Coach. Today there are personal, life, romance, business, career, and spiritual Coaches in addition to the original: the athletic Coach.

The Counselor provides advice and information, such as a lawyer, psychologist, the more capable physicians, and some of the best professors. They rely on a deep well of knowledge and years of experience to give you the best advice.

The Therapist works with people needing some form of help, who are suffering from some problem, and who take on the role of patient. What distinguishes this role is that the Therapist helps resolve or cure something that is perceived as a problem or shortcoming.

__ ⓪ ① ② ③ Charming Enchanter

The person who enchants others with a tale, a tune, an idea, a look. Enchanters are often quick-witted, articulate persuaders who easily influence others with their charisma, charm, or wit. Some, like John F. Kennedy and Ronald Reagan, combine the Enchanter with the Leader roles into a powerful political personality. Others use this role to persuade people to buy what they're selling, from CEO to salesperson to the museum director who uses charm to raise funds. On the dark side, Enchanters manipulate or seduce others into their web with selfish designs.

___ ⓪ ① ② ③ Romantic

The passionate lover of life, people, culture, art, music, food, sex, science, technology, the unknown, the mysterious, or whatever his or her fancy may be. Floating in a starry sky, Romantics are rarely realistic, always hopeful, forever seeking passion and connection. They may find reality tiresome.

___ ⓪ ① ② ③ Artist/Poet

The artistic visionary who sees through everyday existence into the hidden world of truth, beauty, comedy, and tragedy, and who expresses that vision as a communication to us through many media. William Shakespeare, Mark Twain, Pablo Picasso, e. e. cummings, Bob Dylan, John Lennon, and Abraham Lincoln all expressed and communicated their passionate, subjective, sensitive intuitions and truths through their art, whether poetry, drama, lyrics, paintings, photography, film, architecture, or other media, and, once in a great while, in politics. The genius of our greatest creative thinkers, such as Albert Einstein, often comes from their ability to combine the roles of Scientist and Artist.

___ ⓪ ① ② ③ Visionary

The dreamer who sees beyond the commonplace, everyday reality and imagines new possibilities. These possibilities may be new ideas, points of view, paradigms, methods, forms of self-expression.

___ ⓪ ① ② ③ Advocate

Committed to furthering an ideal or coming to the defense of a person, group, or cause, the Advocate goes to battle as the champion of something he or she believes in. Many Advocates are idealistic and attracted to fighting injustice and the shortcomings of society. Nonprofit directors, philanthropists, environmentalists, legislators, and district attorneys often embody this role. Others, like lawyers or lobbyists, are paid Advocates who may or may not believe in what they are fighting for.

___ ⓪ ① ② ③ Mediator/Peacemaker

These good-hearted souls find a bridge between the different sides of a dispute. Usually gifted with a diplomatic talent and a knack for bringing people and groups together, they are facilitators who move people toward resolving conflicts.

Now That You Have Identified Your Roles, Continue with the Instructions That Follow

2. *Zero in on the real you.* Once you have gone through this chapter and marked your roles, go through the list again, narrowing it down to the main players. Select a few main roles by making a check mark in the line before the circled numbers, most likely ones chosen from roles you marked as a ③. Since you are looking for clues that may relate to choosing your career, some roles such as Mother, Father, Child may be a big part of your life but not serve as useful career clues.

   You are looking for roles that you actually play as a regular and significant part of your life. The younger you are, the less likely it is that you will have had much actual experience playing some roles. In that case, what to look for is the connection, the recognition, the sense of familiarity.

3. *Prioritize.* Now dig in deeper and look for the biggest, strongest, most compelling roles—ones that will help to describe what sort of work will be the best fit. Prioritize your top roles, with number one being the strongest. See if you can separate out roles that you might want to play somewhere in your life other than your career. For example, one of my roles is Nature Man. I grew up playing in the woods, had many wild animal pets, and am a sucker for a good nature show on TV. Now I live in a forest, where I see and interact with wild animals that eat my flowers every day. This satisfies that role, but I wouldn't want a nature-centered career.

   Designate your main role or roles. Of your top natural roles, which one or two do you think would be the top roles that express you best or take the lead most often? If you're not sure, ask friends or family members for their opinions and give it some time to become clearer. There may not be one that takes the lead. Instead there may be two or more dominant roles that work together. For example: Abraham Lincoln might select *Leader, Hero, Father, Politician,* and *Deal Maker,* among others. No single role describes him. Only when you consider all of these roles together do you get more than a glimpse of his life. That may be the case with you too. But you are best served by whittling it down to one or two dominant roles.

How are your main roles expressed in your life? For instance, you probably have one or more roles that influence your major choices in life. Are some of your biggest goals or common concerns and behaviors shaped by your main roles? For example, someone whose dominant role is *Mother* may not put much thought into a career choice; anything will do, so long as it leads to motherhood and family. Another person with *Mother* as a lead role may feel a passion for work caring for other people. The *Naturewise Person* may dislike working indoors. The *Critic* may find fault with almost everything.

Remember that you aren't a robot. You have the choice to promote or demote some roles. If you discover that one of your roles does not contribute to moving your life forward or is not always appreciated, you may choose to lock it up under the cellar stairs some of the time. However, your main, dominant roles are likely to describe your best means of self-expression, so, by all means, play them to the hilt. Give them a big stage and a major part to play in your life and work.

4. Look back over this inquiry for clues. Add whatever you find to your Clues list. Ask, "Is there anything I am willing to choose as a definite component?" Add anything you choose to your Definite Career Design Components. Do any new careers or jobs come to mind? If so, add them to your Career Ideas. Remember to keep working with your clues, moving them toward selecting new definite components.

CHAPTER 19

•

THE GAMES OF LIFE

*Seek above all for a game worth playing . . . Having found the game,
play it with intensity—play it as if your life depended on it.*

—ROBERT DE ROPP

This chapter is another way to discover clues about your personality and behavior. Like the other inquiries in this book, it is not the whole truth but merely a model to use for discovery—a template to place over your life to notice useful clues. In chapter 18, you considered roles, the characters you play in the day-to-day drama of your life. This chapter provides another useful viewpoint by supposing that our lives consist of a group of games we play.

What is a game? It is an activity in which there is a set of rules and an objective, and a way to win or lose. You make some things more important than others. In poker, a royal flush is better than a pair. In Monopoly, hotels are better than houses. Why? Because the rules say so. If it doesn't matter whether you have more properties or money, there is no game. The game starts when you decide to play and accept a set of rules. In Monopoly, you agree that it is better to have more money than the other players. If nothing is more important or meaningful than anything else, there is no game.

If you know you are playing a game, you can make up new rules or decide to play a new game. *It is completely up to you!* You are not stuck with the rules printed on the box or imprinted on your brain. For example, in Monopoly, you could decide that the first person to go broke wins, the most generous player wins, whoever lands on Baltic Avenue wins, or you could just declare everyone a winner. On the other hand, if you think the game you are playing represents the one true reality, you are stuck with it forever.

You always have a choice. One would think that everyone living in cultures on the edge of survival, where droughts and famines are a constant threat, would be forced to play only the most ancient games—eat, procreate, seek shelter from the storm, and take care of yourself before all others—but this is not the case. There are people who, on the brink of starvation, are enormously generous, sharing what little they have with others.

One way to make life really exciting is to forget it is a game. It is like going to the movies and seeing a film that is so compelling that your identity as a separate observer disappears. You become so entranced by the action on-screen that nothing else exists. You become so completely plugged in to experiencing all the adventures, joys, and tragedies that you forget it is a film. Playing our various life games, the same thing happens. We become so entranced with playing the game that we do not notice it is a game. We forget that whatever we are playing is not the only possible game.

The particular games you play reflect your own individual life strategies and aims. They vary from person to person because we have different personalities, backgrounds, experiences, and levels of inner development.

This chapter consists of two inquiries that were designed to look into the games we play. The first inquiry, "What Am I Playing For?," provides an opportunity to identify the games you play and notice which of them you play most often. In the second inquiry, "What Games Will I Play?," you get to tinker with them, noticing how well they are working for you and whether they are worth continuing to play. Then you can choose, change, modify, or abandon the rules.

INQUIRY 18

What Am I Playing For?

Most of us go through life unaware that we are in the midst of endlessly playing games for stakes we never consciously chose. Please spend a few minutes and take inventory of your game collection. Some games may remind you of roles you selected in the previous chapter. There is some overlap between these two distinctions. What is most useful is finding clues about your behavior, whether you consider them to be roles or games.

1. Go through the following list of games. Mark all the games you play or have ever played during the course of your life. Don't forget the games you play only occasionally. You may notice that you play most of them at one time or another. Even the most conscious, self-aware, positive person may occasionally play a few hands of Zombie. The instructions continue after the games list.

Zombie: Lives a completely mechanical existence; just goes through the motions of living.

Sufferer: Lives in darkness. Can always find something to suffer about every day. Small hint: The Buddha said that this is the primary game everyone plays. Whenever we think anything (including ourselves, others, the world) should be other than it is, we suffer.

Criminal: Sees others as a "mark" or as an asset to manipulate. This includes the professional criminals and many supposedly upstanding, more socially acceptable people who use others for their own ends and hardly notice the suffering they cause. Throughout history, there have been plenty of industrial magnates, lawyers, politicians, and many others who belong in this category.

Tribal Primate: Lives exactly the same way that people did one hundred thousand years ago. Gets up in the morning, fulfills a gender role, raises kids, chats with other tribe members, goes to bed. This is the human variation on the basic ancient game of life: eat, procreate, seek shelter from the storm, and survive.

Leaf in the Wind: Goes whichever way life leads. Reacts automatically to whatever circumstances arise.

Comfort Junkie: Does anything to remain at equilibrium and avoid uncomfortable emotions and thoughts. This game is often at the core of addictive behaviors, couch potatodom, and risk avoidance. "Always return to equilibrium ASAP" is one of the most basic strategies of nature. No wonder it is one of the most favored games of the human race. You play this one often. So does everyone else.

Hog in the Trough: Get more, have more, buy a bigger one.

Power and Domination: Played in innumerable ways. Can involve controlling territory, people, or information. A game played by people from every walk of life: from the child having a tantrum to the macho man, from cops to serial killers.

Security: Protection from loss and from negative changes in circumstance is the key. The goal of the game is to store lots of nuts against the possibility of famine and to keep the wolf away from the door.

Driven: Participants in this game run endlessly on whatever treadmill they are on—never finished, never complete, never at peace.

In Control or Not Out of Control: Must always control their environment, inside and out. One of the most prevalent games. Avoids loss of control at all costs.

The Social Animal: The game is about relationships and interplay with other people. The players of this game invest more energy in social interaction than others do.

Looking Good, or "I'm Cool": Get their sense of self from peering in the mirror of what they perceive others think of them. "I am what I think I see reflected in the eyes of other people."

Compliance and Rebellion: Two sides of the same coin. They do what others want, or exactly the opposite.

Always Seeking Love: The game is to fill a perceived deficit of love, affection, acceptance.

I'm the Boss: Runs the show, may be the commander in chief of an empire or just one small goldfish.

Know-it-all: Knows everything about everything.

Kid at Play: Carpe diem, perennial kid.

Hedonism: If it feels good, do it. If it doesn't feel good, don't do it.

Adventurer: Plays daring games, seeks new experiences, unknown territory. This can be played in the external world or within one's own internal world.

Dreamer: Perfectly happy floating in his internal cosmos without needing to bring his dreams down to earth.

Householder: Raise a family.

Knowledge: Learning, education, acquisition of information, understanding, and/or know-how.

Dedicated to Truth: The philosopher, seeker of the grail of understanding.

Wise One: A fountain of wisdom, learning, knowledge, intelligence.

Art and/or Beauty: Devoted to appearance, fashion, design, lovely things, art appreciation.

Problem Solver: Everything is a problem to be solved.

The Performer: Always onstage.

The Artist: The self-expressed person who communicates through works of art. The art may be a traditional art or the art of ideas.

Celebrity: The goal is fame and the special treatment that comes with celebrity.

Religion: The goal is salvation or an equivalent.

Personal Growth: Attention is turned inward toward self-discovery and improvement. Their psyches and souls are the works of art they are sculpting. Perhaps this one could be listed under the games of the Contribution category below, but working on one's own self does not necessarily make a contribution to anyone else.

Awakening: Players discover that they are rarely present, mainly functioning on autopilot, and take on the game of waking up.

Creativity: This game has nothing to do with the field in which it is played. It can be expressed in sports or business as well as in the arts. At its essence are visionary magic and the inspired genesis of creating something new.

Excellence: The game of producing extraordinary results at whatever you are doing and whoever you are being.

Contribution: Make the world a better place, give a gift of well-being to others.

Service (Agent of the Universe): The rules of this game ask that a person take on a new identity as a commitment to serve instead of identifying oneself primarily as a psychological being concerned mainly with one's own strategies and desires. People who play this game still have all the concerns, considerations, and emotions as everyone else. What is different is that they have chosen to give less command-and-control value to their personal strategies.

2. Go through the games again, putting a different identifying mark next to those you play often, the ones that are a regular part of your daily life.

3. Go through the list a third time and see if you can identify one or two main games. Which game or games run the show? This should not be too difficult to identify, because our main game or games are the central strategies, the organizing principles of our lives. If more than one or two are vying for the championship, you may be able to sort this out by asking, "Which of these do I play all the time, in most situations?" Identify which ones actually run the show, not which ones you would like to play. If you are not excited about the one that you discover has been running the show, you can always make up a new main game. But, for the time being, just do your best to get to the truth.

4. One of the central principles of the concept of "game" is that in a game, the rule book defines one destination as more desirable than the others. Every game has an objective. In Monopoly it is to be the only player who has not gone bankrupt. If there is no destination, there is no game. How do you win the games you play? What is the main objective of your biggest and most dominant games? What do you get from playing that game? At this very moment, you are asking yourself one of the most powerful questions a human being can ask himself or herself: *What am I playing for?* You are revealing the core of what runs your life. It is not something deep and mysterious. It may be so obvious that you haven't noticed it before. It may be the perfect game for you, or it may not be. It may or may not be as noble and idealistic as you would wish. But who said you had to be noble and idealistic, anyway? You may discover that you want to keep it or change it. Don't worry about that right now. Just keep asking, "What am I playing for? What is the objective? What is the strategy?" The answer may appear right away, or it may take a few days of inquiry. After all, "What am I playing for?" and "What is the meaning of (my) life?" are the same question. Since philosophers have been working on this one for thousands of years, it wouldn't hurt to spend some time on this.

5. Look back over this inquiry for clues. Add whatever you find to your Clues list. Ask, "Is there anything I am willing to choose as a definite component?" Add anything you choose to your Definite Career Design Components. Do any new careers or jobs come to mind? If so, add them to your Career Ideas.

    Remember to keep working with your clues, moving them toward selecting new definite components.

INQUIRY 19

What Games Will I Play?

Now you know that you are a player of multiple games. You've identified them and understand the rules and the objectives. The moment of choice has arrived.

1. Ask yourself these questions:

    *   Are my main games worth playing?

    *   How well is it working for me to play the games I do?

    *   Do I want to keep playing them?

    *   Do I want to promote or demote any of them?

    *   Will I take on any new games that are more worthy of playing?

2. If your most dominant games are not the ones you want to play most, why not? What is missing?

3. What games would you like to wake up to in the morning and play wholeheartedly, every day?

4. What sort of work would best serve to help you to win the main games you intend to play? Give some time to this question.

5. What are some of the qualities, functions, activities, and rewards that a job might offer that would help you win the games you intend to play?

6. What might interfere with winning the games you most want to play?

7. Would you be willing at this time to take on a new game, to reorder the priorities of the ones you play, to make up some new rules? If so, turn to your Definite Components document and add whatever you have decided.

8. Look back over this inquiry for clues. Add whatever you find to your Clues list. If there is anything that you are willing to choose as a definite career component, add it to your Definite Career Design Components. If any new career or job comes to mind, add it to your Career Ideas. Ask yourself why that career appeals to you and see if that suggests more clues. If you now know that a career on your Career Ideas list does not fit, remove it. See if that suggests any additional clues. Remember to keep recording and working with your clues, moving them toward definite career components.

When you cease to make a contribution, you begin to die.

—ELEANOR ROOSEVELT

Once we recognize that our lives consist of playing multiple games, a powerful transformation can occur. Until now, we have been dangling on strings controlled by the rules of whatever games we've been playing. Once we know this, we can choose either to keep playing those games, and play them consciously, or pick some new ones. If we keep the ones we already have, we can then play them 100 percent, without reservation. We can keep the old rules or make up new ones. If we pick new games or new rules, we alter our lives forever.

CHAPTER 20

•

THEY PAY YOU TO PERFORM SPECIFIC JOB FUNCTIONS

No matter what your job, you are paid for just one thing: performing some functions in order to produce specific results. Nearly all of those who operate at a high skill level and love their work spend their days performing functions that express their strongest talents. They do what comes naturally.

Most careers concentrate on performing a very few specialized functions. Some of these functions are *directly people oriented*. Customer-service representatives, supervisors, therapists, and teachers all perform people-related functions. Some functions are centered on *data, information, and ideas*. Songwriters, computer programmers, editors, and secretaries all perform functions that mainly involve data, information, and/or ideas. Other careers center on *things, objects, and the physical world*: sculptors, surgeons, biologists, carpenters, and architects.

Many careers involve multiple functions. But most use one or two senior functions, the most central parts of the job. Other functions have a supporting, or secondary, role. For example, a journalist's primary function is writing news stories— a "data/information" function. Even though journalists may spend significant time interviewing people, the final product and central focus of the job is data/information—the story. Take a minute to consider the careers of people you know and work you have done. Look for the central function. What are the supporting functions?

Some careers involve multiple senior functions. A professor of mechanical engineering may engage in all these categories. He or she teaches groups of students, advises and supports individual students, researches, writes, and thinks about 3-D subject matter. Even though all the functional categories can be elements of this career, one function often stands out as most important. The professor could particularly love working with the students directly or have a passion for the world of things, or information might predominate.

In the past, many physicians considered themselves healers first and foremost—a people function. Nowadays, the practice of medicine is primarily a things function. The modern physician is a mechanic, a technical expert in the diagnosis and treatment of disease, the repair of body parts. Even though the thrust of medical education is to produce highly trained mechanics, an individual can always choose to be a healer above all else. However, if you are considering a career in medicine and are mainly interested in being a healer, you might find yourself in an alien environment in a modern hospital or medical practice. Remember to be realistic when you design the functions of your future career. If you are not deeply interested in the highly technical diagnosis and repair of body parts, don't become a physician. If you don't love selling, don't become a salesperson or fund-raiser. It is not enough to love the product or interacting with people. Since you will be selling a product or service all day, every day, the senior function of all sales jobs is selling, not advising, consulting, or knowing a great deal about some service or product.

People often make the mistake of choosing a career with interesting subject matter but that requires spending the day in activities that are not a great fit. Just because you love carpets woven by nomads in the Persian deserts doesn't necessarily mean you will love selling them, or studying them, or weaving them. The trick is to find a way to have it all: work where you perform a set of functions you really enjoy, using your best talents in a career that fits with your personality and values, combined with subject matter that you care about.

In the following inquiry, you are going to have a chance to get clear about which functions are your best and most natural forms of self-expression. This is an especially important inquiry because, if you can pin down the functions you will perform, you will have solved some big pieces of the puzzle. If you had a huge key on your back like a windup toy, and they wound you up each morning and turned you loose, what would you do? What do you do naturally, without being asked? What are the functions you just can't help doing when an opportunity is presented? People stuck in careers that don't really fit often find ways to do what comes naturally, either at work or after work. Someone whose natural functions lean toward teaching but who is stuck in a secretarial job may find a way to function as an educator on the job or after work. Another secretary with a gift for counseling may be the one everyone trusts to listen to their problems and advise them. Your activities and interests outside of work also provide clues about what functions express you most naturally.

Some folks hate to "box themselves in" by narrowing the field to just a few functions. They say they want to perform a wide range of functions in their work. Almost everyone, no matter how creative, brilliant, or successful, does work that concentrates mainly on a very few functions, rarely more than three. Even the multitalented Leonardo da Vinci concentrated his work on a few functions: creating art, designing three-dimensional objects, and investigating the physical world. Yes, he did many, many things. But most of them expressed these few functions or played a lesser role in his extraordinary career. This doesn't mean that you will not get to do many other things as significant parts of your work or your life outside of work. In fact, I suppose there is no reason why you cannot do everything in the following functions list, if you so desire. But use this inquiry to pin down just a few major functions.

```
┌─────────────────────────────┐
│        INQUIRY 20           │
└─────────────────────────────┘
```

Job Functions

1. Start at the beginning of the job functions list. Place a check mark in front of the functions that come naturally to you or express what you do best. Be selective and just mark the most important stuff. Do your best to limit your selections to just a few. Some entries have several versions of a function on one line. If one or more really stands out, circle it. When you have finished, go to the end of the functions list, where the instructions will continue.

PEOPLE-ORIENTED FUNCTIONS AND ACTIVITIES: PRIMARILY ONE-ON-ONE

Problem Solving, Providing Expert Advice

___ ① ② ③ ④ ⑤   Mentoring, one-on-one teaching, instructing, training, tutoring

___ ① ② ③ ④ ⑤   Counseling, coaching, guiding, empowering

___ ① ② ③ ④ ⑤   Healing, treating the diseases or problems of, rehabilitating

___ ① ② ③ ④ ⑤   Advising, consulting with

___ ① ② ③ ④ ⑤   Assessing, evaluating

___ ① ② ③ ④ ⑤   Diagnosing, analyzing, or understanding an individual's needs, mood, motives, responses, behavior, and so on

___ ① ② ③ ④ ⑤   Using intuition or nonverbal clues to understand individuals

___ ① ② ③ ④ ⑤   Observing, studying behaviors

___ ① ② ③ ④ ⑤   Other _____

Supporting, Enabling, Hosting, Entertaining

___ ① ② ③ ④ ⑤   Encouraging, supporting

___ ① ② ③ ④ ⑤   Providing emotional support

___ ① ② ③ ④ ⑤   Promoting, being an agent for others

___ ① ② ③ ④ ⑤   Listening

_ ① ② ③ ④ ⑤   Being understanding and patient with others
_ ① ② ③ ④ ⑤   Enabling, assisting other people to locate information
_ ① ② ③ ④ ⑤   Helping, serving, providing needs of individuals
_ ① ② ③ ④ ⑤   Assisting, caretaking
_ ① ② ③ ④ ⑤   Hosting
_ ① ② ③ ④ ⑤   Entertaining, amusing, conversing with
_ ① ② ③ ④ ⑤   Giving pleasure to
_ ① ② ③ ④ ⑤   Using your personal charisma
_ ① ② ③ ④ ⑤   Other _____

Managing, Informing, Selling, General Administrative Activities

_ ① ② ③ ④ ⑤   Cultivating and maintaining relationships
_ ① ② ③ ④ ⑤   Selecting, screening, hiring
_ ① ② ③ ④ ⑤   Managing, supervising
_ ① ② ③ ④ ⑤   Giving instructions, providing information to
_ ① ② ③ ④ ⑤   Persuading, selling, motivating, influencing, enrolling, recruiting
_ ① ② ③ ④ ⑤   Interviewing
_ ① ② ③ ④ ⑤   Communicating verbally with
_ ① ② ③ ④ ⑤   Bringing together, introducing
_ ① ② ③ ④ ⑤   Networking, building alliances and relationships
_ ① ② ③ ④ ⑤   Negotiating between individuals, arbitrating
_ ① ② ③ ④ ⑤   Other _____

PEOPLE-ORIENTED FUNCTIONS AND ACTIVITIES: PRIMARILY WITH GROUPS, ORGANIZATIONS, THE PUBLIC, OR HUMANITY

Problem Solving, Providing Expert Advice to a Group

_ ① ② ③ ④ ⑤   Empowering, enabling a group
_ ① ② ③ ④ ⑤   Instructing, teaching, training a group
_ ① ② ③ ④ ⑤   Guiding a group through a healing process
_ ① ② ③ ④ ⑤   Diagnosing, analyzing, or understanding a group's existing or potential needs, mood, motives, responses, behavior
_ ① ② ③ ④ ⑤   Using intuition or nonverbal clues to understand a group or individuals in a group setting
_ ① ② ③ ④ ⑤   Consulting to affect a group's or organization's productivity, behavior
_ ① ② ③ ④ ⑤   Advising a group, providing expertise

___ ① ② ③ ④ ⑤   Designing events or educational experiences
___ ① ② ③ ④ ⑤   Creating activities, games
___ ① ② ③ ④ ⑤   Other _____

Managing, Leading, Interacting with a Group

___ ① ② ③ ④ ⑤   Managing, leading a group, organization, company
___ ① ② ③ ④ ⑤   Initiating, creating, founding a group of people or a company
___ ① ② ③ ④ ⑤   Supervising, captaining a group or team
___ ① ② ③ ④ ⑤   Being a team member such as a member of a work group, athlete, orchestra member
___ ① ② ③ ④ ⑤   Leading a group in recreation, games, exercise, travel, rehabilitation
___ ① ② ③ ④ ⑤   Negotiating between groups, resolving conflicts or disputes, bringing conflicting groups together
___ ① ② ③ ④ ⑤   Inspiring a group
___ ① ② ③ ④ ⑤   Facilitating, guiding a group
___ ① ② ③ ④ ⑤   Other _____

Influencing and Persuading a Group

___ ① ② ③ ④ ⑤   Persuading, motivating, convincing, or selling to a group
___ ① ② ③ ④ ⑤   Using personal charisma
___ ① ② ③ ④ ⑤   Networking with groups
___ ① ② ③ ④ ⑤   Communicating verbally with groups, public speaking, or communicating verbally through the media
___ ① ② ③ ④ ⑤   Communicating with people via art, music, writing, film, or other art forms
___ ① ② ③ ④ ⑤   Other _____

Entertaining and Hosting Group Functions

___ ① ② ③ ④ ⑤   Hosting, entertaining socially
___ ① ② ③ ④ ⑤   Amusing, providing entertainment or pleasure
___ ① ② ③ ④ ⑤   Performing, acting
___ ① ② ③ ④ ⑤   Presenting to people via TV, films, seminars, speeches
___ ① ② ③ ④ ⑤   Selecting, screening prospective members or employees
___ ① ② ③ ④ ⑤   Assisting, serving, helping
___ ① ② ③ ④ ⑤   Other _____

INFORMATION-ORIENTED FUNCTIONS AND ACTIVITIES: PRIMARILY WITH IDEAS, DATA, MEDIA, KNOWLEDGE, WISDOM, OR ART

Creating, Designing, and Using Imagination

_ ① ② ③ ④ ⑤ Generating ideas, creating, inventing, imagining
_ ① ② ③ ④ ⑤ Asking new questions, pioneering new ideas
_ ① ② ③ ④ ⑤ Brainstorming
_ ① ② ③ ④ ⑤ Drawing, painting, filming, photographing
_ ① ② ③ ④ ⑤ Creating original works of art, including music
_ ① ② ③ ④ ⑤ Creating visual or written presentations, or presentations using other media
_ ① ② ③ ④ ⑤ Creating marketing materials, advertisements, promotional campaigns
_ ① ② ③ ④ ⑤ Creating activities, games, or other experiential learning activities
_ ① ② ③ ④ ⑤ Designing events or educational experiences
_ ① ② ③ ④ ⑤ Writing fiction, creative writing (poetry, essays, novels, scripts)
_ ① ② ③ ④ ⑤ Performing, acting
_ ① ② ③ ④ ⑤ Presenting to people via TV, films, seminars, speeches
_ ① ② ③ ④ ⑤ Information engineering, database design, computer programming
_ ① ② ③ ④ ⑤ Information architecture, such as in website design
_ ① ② ③ ④ ⑤ Creating software or similar works
_ ① ② ③ ④ ⑤ Designing research experiments to make new discoveries
_ ① ② ③ ④ ⑤ Other _____

Problem Solving, Researching, Investigating

_ ① ② ③ ④ ⑤ Diagnosing by seeing the relationship between clues
_ ① ② ③ ④ ⑤ Analyzing by perceiving patterns in data, events, or processes, or accurately evaluating information
_ ① ② ③ ④ ⑤ Seeing through masses of information to the central principles or most important facts
_ ① ② ③ ④ ⑤ Breaking down masses of data into component parts, analyzing
_ ① ② ③ ④ ⑤ Synthesizing: combining parts to form a whole
_ ① ② ③ ④ ⑤ Systematizing, prioritizing, categorizing, or organizing information
_ ① ② ③ ④ ⑤ Deciding what data or information to collect
_ ① ② ③ ④ ⑤ Conducting research to develop new ideas, theories

___ ① ② ③ ④ ⑤   Researching by observing behavior or phenomena
___ ① ② ③ ④ ⑤   Researching by gathering or compiling information
___ ① ② ③ ④ ⑤   Making decisions based on the meaning of data or information
___ ① ② ③ ④ ⑤   Other _____

Reading, Learning, Mastering a Body of Knowledge

___ ① ② ③ ④ ⑤   Reading, learning, gathering information
___ ① ② ③ ④ ⑤   Interpreting other people's concepts, ideas
___ ① ② ③ ④ ⑤   Adapting information to suit another purpose
___ ① ② ③ ④ ⑤   Combining existing ideas or concepts into new ones
___ ① ② ③ ④ ⑤   Mastering a specialized body of knowledge, expertise, wisdom, lore
___ ① ② ③ ④ ⑤   Other _____

Critiquing, Evaluating, Making Recommendations

___ ① ② ③ ④ ⑤   Critiquing other people's ideas
___ ① ② ③ ④ ⑤   Critiquing works of art, such as in script reading, book reviews, film reviews
___ ① ② ③ ④ ⑤   Critical writing, such as nonfiction, journalism, and science writing
___ ① ② ③ ④ ⑤   Technical writing, such as in business, law, technology, medicine, public policy
___ ① ② ③ ④ ⑤   Judging, evaluating, or appraising information
___ ① ② ③ ④ ⑤   Using physical senses to evaluate
___ ① ② ③ ④ ⑤   Process improvement, making systems more efficient
___ ① ② ③ ④ ⑤   Risk and opportunity cost analysis
___ ① ② ③ ④ ⑤   Making recommendations, providing solutions
___ ① ② ③ ④ ⑤   Troubleshooting, debugging, and maintaining software
___ ① ② ③ ④ ⑤   Editing to improve content
___ ① ② ③ ④ ⑤   Using mathematics, numbers, statistics, working with formulas to evaluate
___ ① ② ③ ④ ⑤   Other _____

Organizing, Planning, Improving, Other General Administrative Activities

___ ① ② ③ ④ ⑤   Organizing information, projects, or events
___ ① ② ③ ④ ⑤   Project management, setting goals and milestones, budgeting, status reporting

_ ① ② ③ ④ ⑤ Planning, strategizing, forecasting
_ ① ② ③ ④ ⑤ Translating, interpreting information to another language, medium, or style
_ ① ② ③ ④ ⑤ Copy editing to improve grammar, syntax
_ ① ② ③ ④ ⑤ Retrieving or finding information, researching, compiling information
_ ① ② ③ ④ ⑤ Entering data into a computer, data entry, word processing
_ ① ② ③ ④ ⑤ Comparing, proofing
_ ① ② ③ ④ ⑤ Accounting, bookkeeping, business mathematics
_ ① ② ③ ④ ⑤ Record keeping, storing, filing
_ ① ② ③ ④ ⑤ Other _____

"THING"-ORIENTED FUNCTIONS AND ACTIVITIES: PRIMARILY WITH OBJECTS, TOOLS, THE HUMAN BODY, OR THE PHYSICAL WORLD

Problem Solving and Understanding Complex Physical Systems

_ ① ② ③ ④ ⑤ Understanding complex physical systems such as in the physical sciences, medicine, engineering, and technology
_ ① ② ③ ④ ⑤ Diagnosing and analyzing complex mechanical systems, like a mechanic, engineer, physician, or veterinarian does
_ ① ② ③ ④ ⑤ Repairing or improving complex mechanical systems
_ ① ② ③ ④ ⑤ Other _____

Creating, Designing, Inventing Physical Objects, Including Art

_ ① ② ③ ④ ⑤ Designing complex physical systems
_ ① ② ③ ④ ⑤ Creating new theories, understanding or interpreting physical systems
_ ① ② ③ ④ ⑤ Inventing, creating, designing original devices or objects
_ ① ② ③ ④ ⑤ Directing films or plays, choreographing scenes, storyboarding
_ ① ② ③ ④ ⑤ Creating works of three-dimensional art
_ ① ② ③ ④ ⑤ Other _____

Evaluating, Critiquing, Fixing, and Repairing Objects and Things

_ ① ② ③ ④ ⑤ Evaluating and critiquing physical objects, including food, arts, design, or the human body

___ ① ② ③ ④ ⑤   Appraising and judging physical objects, including food, arts, design, or the human body

___ ① ② ③ ④ ⑤   Repairing, restoring, or maintaining things

___ ① ② ③ ④ ⑤   Assembling

___ ① ② ③ ④ ⑤   Other _____

Crafting, Beautifying, Using Tools to Produce Objects

___ ① ② ③ ④ ⑤   Sculpting, shaping, tooling

___ ① ② ③ ④ ⑤   Crafting (combining artistic and motor skills to fashion things)

___ ① ② ③ ④ ⑤   Employing fine hand dexterity (as used by surgeon, dentist, craftsman, artist, musician)

___ ① ② ③ ④ ⑤   Precision use of tools

___ ① ② ③ ④ ⑤   Manufacturing or mass-producing objects

___ ① ② ③ ④ ⑤   Cooking, preparing, or displaying food

___ ① ② ③ ④ ⑤   Choosing, arranging objects artistically

___ ① ② ③ ④ ⑤   Utilizing eye for design, color, texture, or proportion

___ ① ② ③ ④ ⑤   Sensual acuity of sight, sound, smell, taste, or feel

___ ① ② ③ ④ ⑤   Other _____

Athletics, Performing Expertly with the Body, Manipulating the Human Anatomy

___ ① ② ③ ④ ⑤   Dancing or choreographing dance routines

___ ① ② ③ ④ ⑤   Use physical agility, fine sensory-motor skills, strength, and dexterity in athletics and other fields such as law enforcement, firefighting, emergency medicine

___ ① ② ③ ④ ⑤   Using spatial visualization for gymnastics, figure skating, diving, and other sports that require visualizing body movements

___ ① ② ③ ④ ⑤   Performing stunts or other extreme physical feats

___ ① ② ③ ④ ⑤   Massaging, adjusting, touching, hands-on healing

___ ① ② ③ ④ ⑤   Other _____

Operating Machines and Equipment

___ ① ② ③ ④ ⑤   Operating an airplane, ship or boat, truck or car, motorcycle or bicycle

___ ① ② ③ ④ ⑤   Using large tools such as bulldozers and other construction machinery, tanks

___ ① ② ③ ④ ⑤ Constructing buildings or other large objects, such as bridges and roads
___ ① ② ③ ④ ⑤ Operating, controlling, or guiding machines
___ ① ② ③ ④ ⑤ Tending machines
___ ① ② ③ ④ ⑤ Fighting, using firearms or other weapons
___ ① ② ③ ④ ⑤ Installing
___ ① ② ③ ④ ⑤ Cleaning, preparing, washing, dusting
___ ① ② ③ ④ ⑤ Moving, storing, warehousing, carrying, lifting, handling
___ ① ② ③ ④ ⑤ Other _____

Interacting with the Physical World, Including Nature

___ ① ② ③ ④ ⑤ Navigating, orienteering, pathfinding, exploring
___ ① ② ③ ④ ⑤ Farming, gardening, growing or tending plants or animals
___ ① ② ③ ④ ⑤ Acute awareness of surroundings, physical environment, nature
___ ① ② ③ ④ ⑤ Using street wisdom, acute alertness to threats to survival
___ ① ② ③ ④ ⑤ Hunting, trapping, fishing
___ ① ② ③ ④ ⑤ Other _____

Inquiry 20-1: Job Functions (continued)

2. Go back over the functions again. Examine all the ones you marked and rate your estimated natural ability for each by marking the numbered circles. One ① is the lowest rating; five ⑤ is the highest. This way you will have a guide to your top functions based on your sense of fit, appeal, and talent.

3. Next, narrow down your top functions to a maximum of ten.

4. Then narrow down from ten to somewhere around five final, most important, most fitting functions. Get to the real essentials. If you have many functions marked and have difficulty selecting a few, it may be that you do not want to toss out things you like to do or give up on having work with diverse activities. You don't have to surrender anything, just find the ones that describe the major activities you will do every day.

5. Look over your selections. Are there any themes or clusters of similar functions? Do most of your highest-rated functions involve people, information, or things? Are there any clusters of functions such as "Problem Solving," "Providing Expert Advice," or "Managing, Leading, Interacting with a Group"? (If one section dominates, that's a pretty good clue that your work should concentrate in that area.) Delve deep to see what else you can discover.

    One way to begin narrowing things down is to look for clusters of functions that work together. If you selected a group of activities that can operate as a series of steps in a process, you can group them into a single function. For example, a cluster of functions such as using intuition or nonverbal clues to understand individuals, observing behaviors, listening, assessing, diagnosing moods and motives, and making recommendations can be grouped under a single combined function such as advising or counseling. Perhaps a group of functions from different categories combines in some way, such as running a particular kind of business. Another way to reduce the number of your selections is to imagine performing them for several hours each day forever. Do any of them lose their appeal when put to the volume test? Push yourself to get past the romance of functions that may sound good, but only for a few hours a week or less.

6. Primary job function. Most careers and/or jobs have one primary function and some secondary ones. A surgeon's primary function is all about blades and blood, a musician's is playing an instrument, a mutual fund manager's is picking stocks. Their primary function is what they are paid to do. It is possible to have more than one or two primary functions, but this is much more common in nontraditional jobs and entrepreneurial ventures. See if you can pick one or two of your final five as your primary function or functions. If you can't, don't worry. Do the next step in this inquiry.

7. Secondary job functions. Are any of your final five functions obviously secondary or supporting functions? For example, someone who sells high-end audio gear may have selling as a primary function, with teaching, advising, and learning about new gear as secondary.

    Having difficulty sorting out what's primary and what's not? Try this: List your final five. Then try out some playful scenarios. For example: Imagine that you died and woke up in heaven with an angel wringing her hands and saying that she had made a terrible mistake. The person who was supposed to get run over by the truck was right behind you and wearing the same clothes. You get to go back to earth, and you can pick four of your top five functions to use in your job. So you have to drop or demote one of the five. Which one would it be? Now imagine it is the year 2050, you are the same age that you are now, and you were just blown to smithereens by a space alien. Medical science can rebuild you, but it can rebuild only three main functions. Which one would get demoted from your final four? Keep it light. Play around with different scenarios to discover what are likely to be your primary and secondary functions. Want a more serious approach? Try the next method.

8. Simulate your workday. Use pie charts to visually represent how much of your day might make use of your top functions. Each slice represents the percentage of the day you would perform each function. The following example illustrates a workday breakdown of an actual career, someone who runs her own arts-and-crafts business. There is one primary function and three secondary ones. Notice that the primary function, crafting beautiful objects, takes up about half the workday, and the secondary tasks and activities are support functions that are performed less often but are just as important to the job. Create some experimental pie charts, simulating several possible workday scenarios by varying the percentage of time for each function. Explore different combinations until one clicks for you.

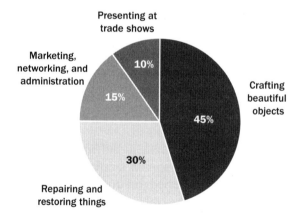

Look back over this inquiry for clues. Add whatever you find to your Clues list. Ask, "Is there anything I am willing to choose as a definite component?" Add anything you choose to your Definite Career Design Components. Do any new careers or jobs come to mind? If so, add them to your Career Ideas.

Part 2

WHY WORK? MEANING, PURPOSE, GOALS, REWARDS

CHAPTER 21

•

PASSION, MEANING, MISSION, PURPOSE

A vision without a task is but a dream, a task without a vision is drudgery; a vision and a task is the hope of the world.

—FROM AN INSCRIPTION ON AN OLD ENGLISH CHURCH

Why do you get up in the morning and go to work? Do you wake up with the same enthusiasm on workdays as you do on the weekend? Even if your career fits your personality and uses your talents fully, it won't be truly satisfying if you go to work because you have to. Working because you have to pay the bills is a form of bondage, like slavery. The chains are subtle, invisible, the servitude accepted without much of a struggle. Wage slaves are forced to report to work every weekday morning against their will, or else face the lash of their mortgage company and credit bureau. There are two practical ways out of this life of servitude. The first is to make so much money that you can buy your freedom. The second is to choose a career you care about. Although you still have to pay your bills and meet your monthly expenses, you do not go to work because you must but because you want to.

Ensconced in more meaningful or more interesting work, you discover that you actually look forward to going to work. Sure, you are still a human being. Little pink wings have not sprouted from your back. There will be days when you fall out of the wrong side of a bed of nails, days when wild horses could not drag you out of your funk. However, much more often there is a sense of excitement and enthusiasm for the day ahead.

In the next few pages, you will have an opportunity to look at what really matters to you, decide how important it is to have work you care about, and to design some important components of your future career. Before we can talk about any of these, we have to lay a little groundwork.

Although many of us already know what we care about and what we find interesting, we may have trouble making the journey from knowledge to actually living our lives as an expression of what matters to us. This next section provides an opportunity to bring the ideal of meaningful work down to earth, where it can grow and flourish.

In this chapter, we are going to investigate how important it is for you to do "meaningful" work, as well as what you mean by "meaningful." Each of us has our own definition of "meaningful work," so we will investigate the several ways this can be expressed through your work. First we will delve into work that fulfills a personal passion or interest. Next we will consider work that is meaningful to you because it makes a positive difference in the world or in others' lives. Then we will look at work driven by a sense of mission, and, finally, discuss living from a created purpose.

INQUIRY 21

Passions and Interests

You may be passionate about your work, some special activity you do in your spare time, or perhaps something you care about but just follow on the Internet or watch on TV. You may feel strongly about the subject matter itself or the state of mind you find yourself in when you are engaged in it. In this inquiry, you will have a chance to sort out what you feel passionate about, what is the source of the passion, and whether it needs to be a part of your work.

1. Start a new document, "Passions and Interests."

2. Under the heading "Passions," write down everything you feel passionate about. Do not limit your entries to areas you think you could turn into a career. If you are wildly passionate about some new technology but do not envision it as a career opportunity, write it down anyway. Your passion may be for some specific subject matter, such as antiques, art, or history. It could be for a field such as mathematics, robotics, or engineering. It could be for an activity, such as sailing, football, reading, or using spreadsheets to solve problems. This could turn out to be a long list, or it may contain just a few items or none at all. It is perfectly fine if you do not have any strong passions or if your passions seem to have no connection with possible future careers. Some people just feel more naturally passionate than others do. If you do not feel the raging exultation of Zorba the Greek, that does not mean something is wrong. If that is so, just go on to the next instruction, where we will look at your interests.

What you are passionate about and what is meaningful to you can be completely different. I am passionate about old Martin guitars and sailing, but, to me, they are not particularly meaningful. It may turn out that you want a meaningful career, or one that engages a passionate interest, or both or none of the above.

3. Under a heading titled "Interests, Preferences, and Activities I Enjoy," list areas of interest or preference that do not qualify as passions. Include both subject matter, fields, and activities. For example, at work you may not be particularly interested in the subject matter but look forward to getting out of the office and visiting clients. You may look forward to shutting the office door and messing around with your computer, or you may like to fix things around your home. If you like it, write it down. Write it all down.

   If you have difficulty coming up with any interests and preferences, then either you don't have strong preferences—so this inquiry will not be an important part of designing your future—or your passions and interests have been beaten into submission. If you used to have more passions and interests than you do now, it is likely that the latter is the cause. If that is so, you might consider finding a way to regenerate your sense of passion, starting with paying more attention to what you enjoy, remembering what you used to do that brought enjoyment, and trying out new activities. I suggest that you plan one day or evening each week dedicated to experimenting with new activities, subjects, events, places, and people. Your assignment is to have ten times as much fun as you usually do, without winding up in jail.

4. Ask yourself these questions: "How passionate must I feel about my work?" "Is it enough to be doing interesting activities?" "Must I also have a personal interest in the subject matter?" "If so, what interests, passions, and subjects might play a big part in my future career?"

5. Look back over this inquiry for clues. Add whatever you find to your Clues list. Ask, "Is there anything I am willing to choose as a definite component?" Add anything you choose to your Definite Career Design Components. Do any new careers or jobs come to mind? If so, add them to your Career Ideas. Remember to keep working with your clues, moving them toward selecting new definite components.

Meaningful Work

We all want to do work we care about, that we find inherently interesting. Even people who say it doesn't matter would pick doing something they care about over something they didn't. Everyone would rather spring out of bed looking forward to a workday filled with interesting projects than trudge off to the salt mine. Each of us has our own internal model of what matters, what is interesting and worthwhile. It is highly personal and can be completely different from one person to the next. By "meaningful," you might mean working toward fulfilling your highest ideals, or you might be perfectly satisfied simply doing something you like or feel is especially interesting. Most of us, although we might deny it, believe that what is personally significant to us is what is truly and universally meaningful. We tend to think our own taste in music, our political point of view, and our understanding of life are just slightly more in touch, and hence more meaningful, than those people who look from a different pair of eyes. Bodybuilders cannot understand how ninety-eight-pound weaklings could be perfectly satisfied with their lives. People interested in personal growth may consider folks who do not share their sense of meaning to be less evolved.

If each of us has a different viewpoint about what is meaningful, and other people's points of view are just as real and valid as yours and mine, then whatever is meaningful to you derives that meaning from your personal interpretations. If you were to travel across the entire universe and explore every corner of it, you might return to tell us that the physicists and mystics got it right, that everything in the universe is exactly as meaningful as everything else. Some stuff is bigger. Other stuff is smaller. Some is closer. Some farther away. There is fast stuff and slow stuff. But what if nothing means anything by itself? What if each of us gives everything the meaning it has for us? Perhaps Gandhi and Elvis are not inherently more meaningful than a lamp. Yes, one or both of them may be more meaningful to you, but not necessarily to your lamp-worshipping next-door neighbors. But, you say, Elvis has done so much more for the world than my lamp. Ah, very true. Good point. But that is more meaningful only to people who believe it is better to do more. The lamp worshippers next door may believe that doing less is better.

Let's look at this from a bigger perspective. Imagine the entire universe stretching out forever in all directions with billions of galaxies each containing billions of stars. How meaningful would it be on a cosmic scale if we humans really screwed up completely and turned our beautiful little blue planet into a cinder? Every time we glance up at the stars, we may be looking directly toward millions of planets where the inhabitants used up all their resources and lie mummified on the surface of their former paradise. Tell the truth now: Which is more meaningful to you, millions of mummified civilizations or that your credit card is topped out?

If each of us has our own idea of what is meaningful, then there are literally billions of somewhat different realities coexisting with one another. If you have any doubt that this is true, see if you can find one single person whose idea of what is meaningful is exactly like yours. Could it be possible that each of these points of view, no matter how radically different from our own, could be just as valid as ours? Could it be that what is meaningful to the family next door is just as intrinsically meaningful as what is important to you and me? The enormous variety of different interpretations is what makes us such a rich and varied tribe. The point of this is not to convert you to the physicists' or mystics' philosophy but to give you more room to choose meaningful work. We each have in us a very specific list of what is meaningful to us. For some of us, this list consists of our highest ideals and our most passionate beliefs.

If you recognize that what matters to you isn't the one-and-only true list of goodness, righteousness, and evolved consciousness, and realize that it is simply your list, you may find that you have more room to broaden the range of what you would consider meaningful work. You might find that you are more able to expand your definition of "meaningful" and consider other possibilities that were not on your list.

INQUIRY 22

What Does "Meaningful Work" Mean to Me?

Now we're going to look from a somewhat different viewpoint. As I mentioned before, meaning is not necessarily the same as passion or interest. Doing what is meaningful to you is motivated partly or mostly by self-fulfillment and self-interest. There may be noble objectives, an ideal fulfilled, evil conquered, and a major contribution to the world made. However, the primary motive of doing meaningful work is for you, not for others. The Episcopalian church ladies I know who volunteer their time in a soup kitchen for homeless people are a perfect example. They are lovely, generous women who care deeply about others. In no way do I mean to demean them when I say that they do what they do to fulfill themselves. Yes, they are also motivated by a commitment to making a contribution. But if serving soup didn't make them feel like the good people they are, they would hang up their ladles and find something else to do.

When you honestly embrace the perfectly normal selfishness that is inherent in doing meaningful work, you can look more clearly at what it will take to fulfill you without feeling guilty that you are not living up to some ideal.

If you choose to serve your highest ideals, great. If you want to play professional Ping-Pong, affect history by being the prime minister's secret lover, or make world-class cheesesteaks, great. If that is what is most meaningful to you, go for it. You do not have to spend the rest of your life feeling guilty because you did not choose to become Jim or Joan of Arc. What is important is to make your own choices as a free agent. What is best for you is what you decide is best for you.

To design a career that is meaningful requires that you be completely honest in appraising your motives. It is not enough to simply look off to the stratospheric heights of your most lofty ideals. You've gotta get down and dirty, be straight with yourself, and design your career so that you get what you want as well as make whatever contribution you choose to make. It is better to give *and* to receive. (For more about this, see chapter 12, "Right Livelihood."

There is nothing obscure about meaning. If you want to know what matters to someone, just ask. What is meaningful or important to any individual is right there on the surface, not hidden in the murky depths of the unconscious. Let's take a look. Answer as many of these questions as you find useful to identify strong clues and definite components.

Note: This inquiry requires time and consideration. Some people take weeks to do it. They want time to explore this area or to let this inquiry simmer on the back burner for a while.

1. Start a new document titled "Meaning and Work." First answer the question "What do I mean by meaningful?" Do you mean that you want to do something you enjoy or work in a field in which you have an interest? Do you mean that you want your work to provide you with certain kinds of rewards or challenges? Do you mean that you want to do work that you believe in, that you think is important or makes some sort of social contribution? Define what *meaning* means to you and write it down. Be as specific as possible. A big, wide generality or ideal won't be as useful as a more pointed, specific statement.

2. List everything that is most meaningful to you. Include things that you might consider doing for a living as well as things that you consider to be highly significant, important, or meaningful but unlikely to be the centerpiece of your career. Be specific. "Everything" could include specific fields of endeavor, problems that need to be solved, social ills, things you like to do, places you like to go, activities you are especially passionate about, functions you love to perform, and anything else that falls within the range of what you consider meaningful. Meaningful does not have

to seem noble or idealistic. We once worked with a client who said that what was meaningful to her was the kind of friendly, interactive environment and popularity she enjoyed in high school. She did not care about saving the world or making some specific contribution to a field or interest. She just wanted to re-create her happy high school days. (By the way, she found the perfect job.) Make sure to write down what is really meaningful to you, not what you think should be meaningful. If you are shocked that what you chose seems shallow or self-interested, let me suggest that perhaps honesty has depth and self-deception doesn't.

3. How important is it for you to do work that is personally meaningful to you?

4. For some people, it is vitally important that the central focus of their work be a direct expression of their highest ideals. Others want to do something they find interesting. Some want to work in a field that does not have a destructive impact. How important is it that your work be directly or indirectly related to something that is personally meaningful to you? If so, how directly related?

5. If it is important that you make a direct impact or contribution in an area important to you, what kind of an impact? How much of an impact? Could you be happy in a job that does not directly make a contribution you care about but in an organization that does?

6. What stands in your way of actually doing meaningful work? Write down all important obstacles. For example, here are two common Yeahbuts shared by many people who find that working for socially responsible nonprofit organizations is meaningful: "I will have to work long hours for very little money" and "There are many jobs for people who want to rape, pillage, and loot but few for people who want to do something meaningful." Afterward, consider each obstacle separately. Brainstorm possible ways of handling the obstacle. Do not listen to your Yeahbuts. Write down everything, even possibilities that seem far-fetched. After you have finished brainstorming, go over all the possible solutions, considering carefully, "Would this work? Is it possible? How could I make it happen?" Do not act as the agent for your Yeahbuts but rather as an enthusiastic supporter of your ability to handle any challenge, any obstacle.

7. What is sufficiently meaningful that you would actually consider dedicating your work life to it? Make a vertical list of everything that you might

consider meaningful enough to choose as a central component of your future work, prioritized so that the most likely meaningful things are at the top of the list and things with less significance are at the bottom. You could list different job names, specific fields of endeavor, things you feel would be good to accomplish, or whatever else you think fits into this list. Go through the list again. Reorder it so it is in an absolute hierarchy. In other words, you want each item on the list to be more important to you than the item directly below it.

8. Now draw a line at the point that separates those things that would be meaningful enough to make a central component of your work from those that wouldn't. There is no way to do this other than just make the choice yourself. You want to wind up with all the items above the line being things that would be sufficiently meaningful to do as a central element of your career. In this inquiry, you are looking only at what would be sufficiently meaningful. The careers that wind up at the top of this list do not have to be practical. They do not have to be something you would want to do. They just have to be sufficiently meaningful. Here's a sample:

> population control
> educating children in a way that preserves their sense of wonder
> educating children to be ready for the challenges of the future
> publishing good books
> creative educational television
> creating technology to reduce stress
> ecological balance
>
> ---
>
> creating tools appropriate for the third world
> helping homeless people
> helping families in trouble
> marketing ecologically appropriate products
> providing opportunities for people to reduce stress in the country

9. Go through this list one more time and see if you can shorten it further. Are there any that, although they are meaningful, you know in your heart you would really never follow through on? Do your best to trim down your list to a few entries, but don't delete anything that truly belongs on the list.

10. What are the elements that make the ones above the line suitable to you? Is it the subject matter, the furthering of a specific ideal, an elegant fit

between aspects of you and the work, or is it simply that these options seem more realistic? Are there other things you could add now that you have looked at the top contenders above the line? If so, write them in. What makes the ones that are not high on your list fail to fully satisfy your requirements?

11. Do you need to produce results in those areas that are meaningful to you? To what degree do you need to produce results? What sort of results would be meaningful? What kind of results would it take for you to be able to declare yourself successful? Must they be tangible? If so, how tangible?

12. Can you narrow down your selection to one or more top candidates? If so, great. If not, don't worry. You may be perfectly content working in one of several meaningful areas.

13. Do you need to do some research, talk with people, or otherwise find out more about any of your top contenders? If so, what do you need to do? Be specific. What do you need to know to decide or to further narrow down the range of possibilities? What questions do you need to ask and answer? Go do the research and meet me back here when you are ready.

14. Look back over this inquiry for clues. Add whatever you find to your Clues list. Ask, "Is there anything I am willing to choose as a definite component?" Add anything you choose to your Definite Career Design Components. Do any new careers or jobs come to mind? If so, add them to your Career Ideas. If your work must be meaningful, commit to that. If it must be one of the areas above the line, commit to that. Nail down as much as you can. If you can, create a commitment to have your career be about something above the line. If not, what do you have to learn, consider, or decide in order to commit? If you are unable to go all the way to the point of commitment now, go on, do other parts of *The Pathfinder*, and come back here later. Keep inquiring into this area. Work to develop more clarity and definition. Making decisions about other pieces of the puzzle may help you narrow it down further. For example, if you decide that you are not willing to learn a completely new discipline, that might automatically cross some items off your list.

That's all there is to it. If you have wanted to find work with meaning, or what is important to you, you may have found it. It is not the great mystery it sometimes seems. Some folks spend their lives searching for meaning when it was right there within reach all the time.

Look back over this inquiry for clues. Add whatever you find to your Clues. Ask, "Is there anything I am willing to choose as a definite component?" Add anything you choose to your Definite Career Design Components. Do any new careers/jobs come to mind? If so, add them to your Career Ideas. Remember to keep working with your clues, moving them toward selecting new definite components.

On a Mission

When you are on a mission, your energy is directed outward toward producing an outcome. Meaningful work does not necessarily require that you make anything happen. A career with a mission is often an action-oriented extension of having a meaningful career. For others, having a mission is central, and the nature of that mission is less important. Some of us would be perfectly satisfied to work in a particular field, concentrate on a personal interest, or use certain abilities without the need to produce some result in the world around us. Having a mission could mean converting the cannibals to your religion, saving the whales, working for peace and human rights, becoming a successful editor or family physician, making a few million bucks, becoming the first female president, or winning an Olympic gold medal. When you are considering what is meaningful to you, it is very useful to get clear whether having a sense of mission is important. If right now you aren't thinking, "Yeah, this mission stuff is exactly what I want!" just skip this inquiry.

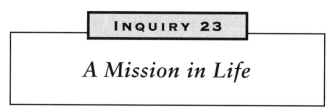

INQUIRY 23

A Mission in Life

1. How important is it that your work involve having a mission, directing your energy toward achieving long-term specific goals?

2. Whom do you admire who have or had a mission? Write it down. If they were asked what that mission is or was, what do you think their answer would be?

3. What sorts of missions would you find personally inspiring? Use this question to brainstorm. Write down whatever surfaces. Don't edit out things that seem beyond your reach or impossible for some reason or

another. Some examples: bring back art and music to the classrooms in your area; amass a fortune; have a number one hit album; bring world population growth down to a sustainable level; build a business, keep green areas from becoming parking lots; or edit many wonderful books so that they are even better.

4. Go over the previous list and cross out whatever you know you will not actually dedicate yourself to. Be completely honest with yourself. You might cross out some because, as noble or interesting as they seem, they just aren't something you can imagine actually dedicating yourself to. Others may miss the mark for other reasons.

5. Ask yourself why you crossed out the ones you did. What is it about them that made you take them off the list? This is important information. It may help guide you to focus on which of the ones remaining best fulfill what is important to you. (Good clues here.)

6. Which of the remaining ones are most fitting, most attractive? Which ones sing your song loud and clear? Mark the ones that rise to the top like cream.

7. What are the elements that make the ones you just marked so attractive to you? Is it the subject matter, the furthering of an ideal, an elegant fit between aspects of you and the work the mission would entail?

8. Can you narrow down your selection to one or more top candidates?

9. Do you need to do some research, talk with people, or otherwise find out more about any of your top contenders? If so, what do you need to do? Be specific. What do you need to know to decide or to further narrow down the range of possibilities? What questions do you need to ask and answer? Go do the research and come back here when you are complete.

10. Look back over this inquiry for clues. Add whatever you find to your Clues list. If there is anything that you are willing to choose as a definite career component, add it to your Definite Career Design Components. If any new career or job comes to mind, add it to your Career Ideas. Ask yourself why that career appeals to you and see if that suggests more clues. If you now know that a career on your Career Ideas list does not fit, remove it. See if that suggests any clues. Remember to keep recording and working with your clues, moving them toward definite career components.

Purpose

You do not belong to you. You belong to the universe. The significance of you will remain forever obscure to you, but you may assume you are fulfilling your significance if you apply yourself to converting all your experience to the highest advantage of others.

—R. BUCKMINSTER FULLER

Several years ago, I noticed something unusual about an older man who worked on the garbage truck that serviced my neighborhood. Come rain, shine, or particularly ripe offerings from his clients, he always had boundless enthusiasm and a smile for everyone he met along the way. As time passed, my curiosity soared. Did he love working outdoors? Was he just a naturally cheerful fellow, or was he a bit of a lunatic? Finally, I asked. He said that he had worked on a trash truck all of his life. When he was a young man, he had always thought that someday he would hang up his trash can and move on to something more in keeping with his dreams. He woke up middle-aged one day and realized that he would spend the rest of his life on the trash truck. He felt that his life didn't amount to anything. After a bout of self-pity, he realized that the reason he felt his life didn't amount to anything had nothing to do with working as a trashman. It was because his life had no purpose. He saw for the first time that he was just a cog in the wheel. Somehow he realized that it was within his power to invent a purpose for his life, to literally create himself as something other than just a trashman. He decided that he would dedicate his life to one thing: "to bring a little ray of sunshine into the lives of everyone I meet."

How can I be useful, of what service can I be?
There is something inside me, what can it be?

—VINCENT VAN GOGH

Each of us has his or her own definition of "purpose." This discussion defines it in a particular way. Not truth—just access to an interpretation you may find useful. Looking from the point of view or template we are using in this book, having meaningful work or work with a mission is essentially a process of satisfying yourself as you are now, finding something you like to do, something that matters to you.

Living from a purpose is quite different. It exists in the realm of pure creation and invention. *A purpose is an ongoing commitment to a principle that becomes who you are. It is not a belief or a goal to be achieved, but a place to come from. It is not what you do, but who you are being.* A strange definition, to be sure. Before my trashman created his purpose, he was answering the calls of nature and the bill collector, reacting to whatever habitual noise was playing in his brain that morning. When he created his purpose, he literally reinvented himself as someone new. Now, when he rose in the morning, no matter what mood he awoke to, he found that he could reinvent himself as the guy fulfilling the purpose of bringing a little sunshine into the lives of everyone he met.

> *I don't know what your destiny will be, but one thing I know:*
> *The only ones among you who will be really happy are*
> *those who have sought and found how to serve.*

—ALBERT SCHWEITZER

Please remember that there is a difference between "meaning" or "mission" and "living from a purpose." The statement you use to describe any of the three could be exactly the same. For example, "to end world hunger" could be a statement of what is meaningful to you, a statement of an objective that you are very actively working toward achieving (a mission), or a broad vision that you have literally given your life to and have made more important than getting what you want and being the center of your own personal universe.

What exactly does it mean to live from a purpose? What does it require? *A purpose is an ongoing commitment to a principle that becomes who you are.* The essence of purpose is contribution. You invent a commitment to a principle outside of yourself and larger than yourself. You dedicate yourself to furthering that principle. You literally give yourself to that commitment. It becomes your innermost self, your reason for being.

It is not a belief or a goal to be achieved, but a place to come from. It is not what you do, but who you are being. A person with the purpose of bringing a little ray of sunshine into people's lives is never finished. You wouldn't say, "Well, I finally did it. I brought sunshine to five thousand lives. My job is finished. I'm retiring from the sunshine business." It is a commitment to a principle and is therefore a place to come from into your life and work. Purpose becomes the organizing principle of your life or of a part of your life. Instead of checking with your mood or opinions to know what to do, you check in with your purpose. The trashman experienced the same moods that you and I do. But he didn't usually indulge in them. His actions were enlightened by his purpose.

It does not descend on you from high above. You don't find or discover a purpose. The only way to have one is to choose one. Were you born with a purpose? Who knows? I have worked with a steady stream of clients who say they want to discover their purpose in life. They say they feel sure that each person is born for some specific purpose, if only they could discover it. Many of them have been look-ing for that purpose for a long, long time. I expect that some of them will go to their graves still searching. Then again, I have worked with many people who have created a purpose for their work.

Make your work in keeping with your purpose.

—Leonardo da Vinci

When my mentor Bucky Fuller was a young man, a business failure left him feeling that the best thing he could do for the people he loved was to commit suicide. Just as he was about to end it all, he looked up at the stars and had a revelation. He later said that he realized that he did not own himself, so therefore he had no right to kill himself. He then dedicated his life to using what he had to offer to make the big-gest contribution he could. Then he asked himself what he had to offer, what was he gifted at? As a result of giving his all, Fuller made so many breakthroughs and dis-coveries that, eventually, his entry in *Who's Who* became the most voluminous of all.

He chose his purpose by looking at what he had to offer. You can wait for the angels to whisper in your ear, or you can live a purpose-centered life now. If you were born with a purpose, it seems to me that it would be to use what you have been given to make the fullest contribution you can to your world.

It is not an exalted state. It makes you no better than anyone else. It is, however, a lot more fun than the way that many of us spend our lives.

You do not have to be a Gandhi, a Mother Teresa, or a Martin Luther King Jr. to create a purpose for your work and live fully from that commitment. If the trashman can do it, so can you. Your purpose can be something lofty: advocating a worldview or faith or consciousness that inspires hope in a benevolent cosmos and leads to greater planetary well-being. Or it can be much more down-to-earth. As a matter of fact, there are probably plenty of people around you who live from a purpose. Their purpose may be to teach your kids in a way that helps them preserve their sense of wonder, to make the best widgets, or to make your world a better place in some other way. To have a purpose for your work does not mean dedicating yourself to widely agreed-upon ideals. Some of the finest actors and artists, creative business leaders, and scientists live from a purpose. In fact, many of the people who get to play a big part on the world stage in any area live from a purpose bigger than themselves. Greatness is often born of the passionate dance between a rare talent and a noble purpose.

The world is filled with many thousands of unknown people who, because they live from purpose, contribute in their own very special ways to our world. I know a man whose life is completely dedicated to creating the finest steel string guitars that have ever existed. With this purpose, he does not get to compromise or cut corners, even when it would save him many hours and no one else would likely ever notice. I know people dedicated to selling with total integrity. With this purpose, they have turned the usual manipulative sales relationship with customers into one of contribution. What they represent contributes something that they believe makes a difference. They are often very successful because people trust them.

You must be ready, willing, and able to live a life that is not informed mainly by your own needs and desires. As Gandhi said, "Even God cannot talk to a hungry man except in terms of bread." When you live from a created purpose, you transform yourself from psychological being to philosophical being. Instead of looking to your personality for your identity and to guide your actions, you look to your commitment to your chosen purpose. Your highest commitment shifts from self-fulfillment to contribution. You begin to invent who you are. When you ask, "Who am I?" you are not stuck with your historical identity. The trashman was able to be deeply, profoundly enthusiastic and loving because, rather than succumb to whatever mood blew in with the wind, he was willing to become his own new creation every day.

> ***When we quit thinking primarily about ourselves and our own self-preservation, we undergo a truly heroic transformation of consciousness.***
>
> —JOSEPH CAMPBELL

It is extraordinary to be able do something you care about, something meaningful. That is sufficient for most people who seek full self-expression in their work. Working from purpose is not better, loftier, or more important than anything else. It is simply another game, just like all the other games of life that some people choose to play when they have won whatever games they have been playing in the past. Once people have found themselves, or have become passionately committed to some principle, they may discover that their next step is to reinvent themselves, making service to that principle a more senior part of their identity than the need to seek fulfillment. If that is what you are seeking, this section on purpose is for you.

> ***You must be the change you wish to see in the world.***
>
> —MOHANDAS GANDHI

You can create a purpose for any domain of your life. When you dedicate your life to a purpose, it transforms who you are in the most fundamental way possible. But you do not have to go all the way over the edge and surrender to the void to have the power of purpose transform various domains of your life. For example, you could have a purpose for your leisure time, your workout, your personal growth, your friendships, your marriage. Since purpose is about contribution, why not create purposes that contribute to you as well?

Couples, Groups of People, and Organizations Can Have Purposes Too

Just as an individual can invent purposes, so can groups of people. A marriage can be dedicated to a shared ideal, to making some sort of contribution or anything else that extends the intentions of the relationship beyond the usual boundaries. A group of friends can create a purpose so that their interactions are more than just hanging out together. Some examples:

Marriage: to be a model for other people, including our children, of just how great a relationship can be; to contribute to the world around us.

A group of friends: to be family to one another; to support one another to have all of our lives be happy and successful.

A few of the best-run, most successful companies have purposes. They are not just moneymaking machines. Of course, money is an absolute requirement, but not the reason for the company's existence. As Tom Peters and Robert Waterman wrote in *In Search of Excellence: Lessons from America's Best-Run Companies*: "Every excellent company we studied is clear on what it stands for."

A company's purpose might be to create technological breakthroughs that contribute to humanity; to be the best in its field; to serve the creative spirit of our people so that it can express itself fully through leading-edge products; superior service. On the downside, companies that are founded to be inspired and led by a purpose usually devolve to a more typical ambition, especially if they become public companies. Hopefully, in the near future, the business world will learn from the ones that have stayed true to a lofty purpose.

The Benefits of Living from a Purpose

When you are inspired by some great purpose, some extraordinary project, all your thoughts break their bounds: Your mind transcends limitations, your consciousness expands in every direction, and you find yourself in a new, great, and wonderful world. Dormant forces, faculties, and talents become alive, and you discover yourself to be a greater person by far than you ever dreamed yourself to be.

—PATANJALI

Singleness of purpose is the most powerful way to move mountains. Normally, folks do what is within their comfort zone, or at least within the limits of what they think is possible. When your reference point is your purpose rather than your psyche, you seek solutions outside your usual boundaries. You do what works rather than what you want and feel like doing. You become almost an unstoppable force of nature. Your effectiveness is not impeded by having to keep your psycho psyche happy and comfortable.

Things work brilliantly more of the time. To illustrate: Some of the best, most exciting, and most profoundly satisfying marriages I know of are dedicated to a purpose. Why does this contribute to having a marriage work? In most marriages, the quality of the relationship depends mostly on chance. There are precious few commitments that effectively shape the quality of the relationship into something truly extraordinary. It is so easy to let a me-first mentality erode what began as a passionate tango. Little problems tend to pile up in the dark. Uncommunicated things and unresolved transactions form walls that reduce intimacy. When a marriage is dedicated to furthering a purpose, it is imperative to keep it well oiled and working smoothly if the relationship itself is to make a contribution. You discover that if you want the marriage to make a difference, you have to give up playing all these little games that create friction and distance. Instead of hiding problems in the closet, you resolve them, in service of your purpose. A couple who has dedicated their marriage to "being a model for other people, including our children, of just how great a relationship can be" may find it easier to avoid getting stuck in the inevitable problems that arise—because they keep referring back to their purpose.

You notice when things are not working much more quickly. You tend to be awake and sensitive to how well you are playing the game of life to a degree that is nearly impossible otherwise. If you notice that you are heading down a blind alley quickly, you can change course posthaste. The faster you are able to make course corrections in any journey, the better.

Life becomes an exciting adventure. I love those Indiana Jones movies where Harrison Ford swings on a vine across the bottomless chasm. It is even more fun to do the swinging yourself. Talk about light-speed personal growth! It is exciting enough to grow and improve gradually, to become slowly, steadily more able to face the slings and arrows of life with flexibility and joy. It is terrific to be able to make goals come true. But if you want to have excitement, challenges, and deep fulfillment, you've got to jump from the frying pan into the fire. Up the ante from doing something you believe in to giving yourself to a purpose larger than you.

This is the true joy in life, being used for a purpose recognized by yourself as a mighty one: being a force of nature instead of a feverish, selfish little clod of ailments and grievances, complaining that the world will not devote itself to making you happy. I am of the opinion that my life belongs to the whole community, and as long as I live, it is my privilege to do for it whatever I can. I want to be thoroughly used up when I die, for the harder I work, the more I live. I rejoice in life for its own sake. Life is no "brief candle" to me. It is a sort of splendid torch that I have got hold of for the moment, and I want to make it burn as brightly as possible before handing it on to future generations.

—GEORGE BERNARD SHAW

A person starts to live when he can live outside of himself.

—ALBERT EINSTEIN

INQUIRY 24

Choose a Purpose,
Then Go Live It

1. First of all, decide if you are willing to live from a purpose. This is a way of life much like mountain climbing: It is very exciting, you often tingle from head to toe with the sheer joy of life, and you get to see the world and yourself from a place you could not otherwise reach. It is, however, much more demanding than the way we are used to living. You find that you are often hanging from a cliff with an endless drop below. Before you take this on, make sure that you are not fooling yourself. If you want to live from a purpose mainly to get some benefit or reward for yourself, you are looking for meaningful work, not purposeful work. You do not, however, have to be selfless or humble to live from a purpose. Throughout history, most of the people who demonstrate the best examples of purposeful living have had big, healthy egos. As long as the purpose is bigger than the ego, fine.

2. Find a principle to which you would be willing to dedicate yourself. Pick something where the ongoing fulfillment of the purpose uses you fully and naturally. Your talents and personality together form a tool that has the best chance of moving mountains. It also helps if you have a very strong natural passion for making a contribution in this area. Choose the area you care about most, or use some other selection criteria of your own. If you find that selecting a principle to which to dedicate yourself is extremely difficult, you are probably not quite ready to live from a purpose.

3. Use the power of language to craft your purpose precisely. Keep working on it until, when you say it, it can almost burn a hole through the wall with its clarity and power. Remember, a purpose is not a goal. It is the expression of a principle. Craft the words so that they remind you that your purpose is a place to come from, not somewhere to get to. "To make a million a year" is a mission, a goal, not a purpose. "To be a great example to my children" can be a purpose. If you can invent it now, you can live it now, and from it can issue an endless stream of appropriate actions, then it could be a purpose.

4. Declare it as your purpose. Make a definite commitment to your purpose as a big part of your identity. For example: "I am a commitment to bringing together East and West through communication and media." "I am a commitment to people having careers that fit them perfectly so that their lives will be creative, purposeful, and fun." "I am a commitment to using ethical salesmanship to get products to people that make a real difference in their lives." Perhaps you could even have a little ceremony to induct yourself into your purpose.

5. Work out the best possible ways to express your purpose. Then get to work. From a clear purpose come potent actions. Sit down and figure out what would move things most powerfully in the direction of your purpose. Then get to work and do whatever it takes.

6. Manage your life day by day and moment to moment so that you are "on purpose" as much as possible. Find ways to remind yourself of your purpose. You will constantly forget that you are living from a purpose and get lost in the day-to-day routine. Purpose has to be continually renewed.

7. If there is anything you are willing to choose as a definite career component, add it to your Definite Career Design Components list. If any new career or job comes to mind, add it to your Career Ideas. Ask yourself why that career appeals to you and see if that suggests more clues. If you now know that a career on your Career Ideas list does not fit, remove it.

CHAPTER 22

•

VALUES AND REWARDS

Like the dog who performs tricks for a biscuit or a pat on the head, we work primarily to earn rewards. Some of them are obvious, like a paycheck; others less so. In the right career, you get much more than a paycheck from your work. If your work rewards you by fulfilling your most important values, you are well on the way to a very satisfying life. Values and rewards are two sides of the same coin. Still, our clients have found it very useful to look at both of these areas separately, since doing so generates a broader perspective and makes it much less likely that they will overlook something vitally important. In this chapter, you will pinpoint your most important work-related values and clarify how your work needs to reward you if it is to give you a life of satisfaction and success.

INQUIRY 25

Values

1. Please take a few minutes to go through the following values checklist. Put a mark in the circle in front of all the values that are personally important to you. Don't worry about the boxes and columns that appear after a particular value. We'll get to those later. Mark all of your values, not just ones that are related to work. This list is just a starting point. Your most important values may not be on this list. Write in other important values that are not listed. *Please do this now.* Please do not read further until you have completed this step.

Values Chart

	VALUE	Ideal	Standard	Want	True Value	Life Value	Work Value	Priority
○	ACHIEVEMENT OR ACCOMPLISHMENT							
○	ACKNOWLEDGEMENT							
○	ADVANCEMENT							
○	ADVENTURE							
○	AFFECTION							
○	ALIVENESS / VITALITY							
○	ART OR THE ARTS							
○	AUTONOMY							
○	AVOID BEING DOMINATED							
○	AVOID PAIN							
○	BE A GOOD MEMBER OF MY RELIGION							
○	BE A GOOD PARENT OR CHILD							
○	BE A VALUED MEMBER OF THE TEAM							
○	BE ENGAGED FULLY WITH LIFE							
○	BE IN CONTROL							
○	BE RIGHT							
○	BE THE BEST							
○	BE TRUSTED							
○	BEAUTY							
○	BELONG TO THE GROUP							
○	BUILD A BUSINESS							
○	CARING							
○	CHALLENGE							
○	CHALLENGE STATUS QUO							
○	CHILDREN							
○	COMPETING							
○	CONNECTION							
○	CONTRIBUTE TO OTHERS							
○	CONTROL MY ENVIRONMENT							
○	COOPERATION							
○	COURAGE							
○	CREATIVITY							
○	CULTURE							
○	DARING							
○	DIGNITY							
○	DO GOOD							

Values Chart

VALUE	Ideal	Standard	Want	True Value	Life Value	Work Value	Priority
DO THE RIGHT THING							
DO THINGS MY WAY							
DIE WITH THE MOST TOYS							
ELEGANCE							
EMPOWERMENT							
ENLIGHTENMENT							
ENTREPRENEURSHIP							
EQUALITY							
EQUITY							
ESTEEM (OF OTHERS)							
EXCELLENCE							
EXCITEMENT							
EXPRESS MY SEXUALITY FULLY							
FAME							
FAMILY HAPPINESS							
FEEL GOOD							
FINANCIAL SECURITY							
FIX BROKEN THINGS OR SYSTEMS							
FRANKNESS/CANDOR							
FREEDOM							
FRIENDSHIP							
FUN AND LAUGHTER							
FULFILLMENT							
GETTING AHEAD							
GIVE OF MYSELF							
GOODNESS (OR BADNESS)							
HAPPINESS							
HARD WORK							
HARMONY OF RHETORIC AND ACTION							
HEALTH							
HELPING							
HELPING THE LESS FORTUNATE							
HONESTY							
HUMOR							
ICONOCLASM							
I'LL SHOW THEM							

Values Chart

VALUE	Ideal	Standard	Want	True Value	Life Value	Work Value	Priority
○ INCLUSIVITY							
○ INDEPENDENCE							
○ INNER HARMONY							
○ INNOVATION							
○ INTEGRITY							
○ INTERESTING EXPERIENCES							
○ INTIMACY							
○ INVENTING							
○ JOY							
○ JUSTICE							
○ KEEP THINGS THE SAME							
○ LEADERSHIP							
○ LEARNING							
○ LEISURE TIME							
○ LOOK GOOD							
○ LOVE							
○ LOYALTY							
○ MAKE MONEY							
○ MARRIAGE							
○ MASTERY							
○ OPPORTUNITY							
○ ORDER							
○ PEACE							
○ PERSEVERANCE							
○ PERSONAL APPEARANCE							
○ PERSONAL DEVELOPMENT							
○ PLAY							
○ PLAYFULNESS							
○ PLEASURE/SENSUAL GRATIFICATION							
○ PREPARE FOR RETIREMENT							
○ PRIVACY							
○ QUALITY							
○ REACH FOR THE STARS							
○ RECOGNITION							
○ RE-CREATE THE CAREER OF A PARENT							
○ RELIABILITY							

Values Chart

VALUE	Ideal	Standard	Want	True Value	Life Value	Work Value	Priority
○ RESPECT							
○ REVOLUTION							
○ SAFETY							
○ SAVING/INVESTING							
○ SECURITY							
○ SEEK TRUTH							
○ SELF-CONTROL							
○ SELF-ESTEEM							
○ SELF-EXPRESSION							
○ SELF-RELIANCE							
○ SELF-RESPECT							
○ SERVICE							
○ SET AN EXAMPLE FOR OTHERS							
○ SEX							
○ SIMPLICITY							
○ SOCIALIZING							
○ SOCIAL ADVANCEMENT							
○ SOLVING PROBLEMS							
○ SPIRITUAL DEVELOPMENT							
○ SPIRITUAL VALUES							
○ SPONTANEITY/IMPROVISATION							
○ STRENGTH							
○ SYNERGY							
○ TEAM SPIRIT							
○ TRUTH							
○ UNIQUENESS							
○ USING MY TALENTS							
○ WEALTH							
○ WINNING							
○ WISDOM							
○ WORLD HOPPING							
○ YOUTH							
○ OTHER							
○ OTHER							
○ OTHER							
○ OTHER							

WHAT ARE VALUES?

Many career-counseling programs are based on "human values." You are asked to consider what values are important to you and then to design a career based on them. But what exactly is a value? According to the dictionary, a value is a *principle, standard, or quality held by an individual, group, or society.* Notice that the definition does not make any mention of the individual, group, or society actually living by its values. American society holds certain traditional values, including equal rights for each individual, freedom of speech, truth, justice, fair play, and so forth. The comic-book heroes live by these values. How about the rest of us? Our foreign policy record suggests that we sometimes live by an entirely different set of values. When individuals are polled about their values, their answers rarely reflect the ones they actually live by. What's going on here? Are these people consciously lying? I don't think so. The problem is that the very concept of values is fuzzy. Let's see if we can sort this out in a way that gets our hands on the steering wheel.

The point of this present discussion is to encourage you to become aware of, separate, and distinguish the several very different elements that we lump together and call "values." Attempting to become clear about your values and then making career decisions appropriate to them is difficult so long as what you call your values is an undifferentiated mass. When you separate them into categories, you'll be able to choose which values will enhance your life and provide a sense of direction. You can decide which to keep, which to discard, which to alter or reconfigure. Then you will be the source of—the creator—of the values by which you live.

VALUES, DISSECTED AND CLASSIFIED

When people go through a typical, old-fashioned values exercise, the result may seem reminiscent of the Boy Scouts law, which, if I remember correctly, is to be trustworthy, loyal, helpful, friendly, courteous, kind, obedient, cheerful, thrifty, brave, clean, and reverent. All wonderful values, but not necessarily ones that will provide you with clarity in choosing the perfect career. The reason for this is that we lump together our ideals, wants, standards, preferences, and the true values we live by day after day. What we are going to do now is separate these categories so that you know which is which and can focus on designing the ones that matter most into your future work.

Ideals

An ideal is *a conception or model of something perfect that exists only in concept, not in reality.* It is the ultimate aim, not how we actually live. The ideal person always strives toward his or her ideals. Extraordinary people often do. Many of us do little more than complain about how other people don't live up to the ideals that *we* don't live up to either.

Having ideals gives us a vision of a perfect life to strive for and to come from. If you use your ideals as a reference point to pull you up toward an ideal life, so much the better. One of the most powerful commitments you could ever make would be to dedicate yourself to continual improvement in the direction of fulfilling your ideals. It would transform your life again and again and again.

On the other hand, expecting that you will always live up to your ideals is a recipe for disaster. You will never live up to your ideals. You're not supposed to. That's why they are called ideals. If you indulge in demeaning your present reality by comparing it with your ideals, you nullify the opportunity that having ideals offers. If you are a musician, what gets accomplished by selling yourself short by comparing yourself with Mozart or Dylan?

Standards

A standard is *a level of performance or attainment used as a measure of adequacy.* When applied to personal values, it is a judgment or conclusion that something should be other than the way it actually is. For example, many people subscribe to a standard that "life should be fair." Whenever life isn't fair, they get upset, disturbed. They feel that something is wrong. But, in fact, life is usually randomly unfair. It has always been that way. The good guys don't necessarily finish first, except in the movies. Bad people do not usually get their comeuppance. Expecting that our standards should be met, by ourselves and others, is a form of self-righteousness of which we are all guilty. We have standards about almost everything—standards about how people should look, dress, and behave, how the government should work, how people should raise their children. We have standards about haircuts and bread, music, and manners. We have standards about ourselves, our work, our relationships. The only things we don't have standards about are the things we haven't thought about yet.

How do you recognize a standard? Simple! It always contains a "should." If you "should" be taller, better looking, further along in life, better educated, younger, older, more successful, richer, more caring, have more or better friends, or have a better sex life, you are face-to-face with a standard. If you think the world "should" be more peaceful, more just, or less polluted, there's a standard lurking about. The problem is that nothing is ever the way it should be. It's always the way it is. "Should" exists only when something doesn't come up to your measure of adequacy.

Wants and Preferences

Some values may simply be wants and preferences. For example, you may have marked "adventure" as one of your values in the previous exercise. This may not be an important ideal, or a "should." It may simply be something that you want or prefer to have as a part of your career, if possible. What's the difference between a want and a preference? A want has more of a charge behind it, more need, more urgency, more attachment than a preference does.

True Values

Your true values are those that you live by or are willing to commit to live by and then strive to express. They may be virtuous or noble, but many of them were passed on to you by your family and culture. The real opportunity is to be able to choose your own set of true values.

Some of your true values apply universally to all aspects of your life. You may, for example, hold honesty and integrity as important values that are just as important at work as they are in the rest of your life. Some other life values may be very important to you but need not necessarily be fulfilled or expressed at work. For example, you may get enough adventure in your leisure-time activities, such as skydiving.

To help you gain a clearer perspective as you go through this inquiry, let's also divide values into work-related values and ones that are not work related:

Work Values

These are the values that are intimately connected with your work. Some of them may be universal life values and others may apply only to work. Sometimes your work values may be completely different from those in the rest of your life. For example, you may be highly competitive at work, always going for victory and staying ahead of the pack, while at home you are docile and totally noncompetitive.

Nonwork Values

These are values that you do not need to fulfill or express at work.

Let's get back to the inquiry we started at the beginning of this chapter:

2. Go through the previous values checklist. Of the ones you marked as values important to you, consider which of your values are actually ideals, standards, or wants, the first three boxes. Mark the appropriate box with a check. *Please do not read further until you have completed this step.*

3. Go through your list of values again. Check the "True Value" box after each of the values that you actually live by every day. If one of your most important values is not on the list, write it in. Don't mark the ones you think you should have, the best or most noble ones. Mark only the ones that actually, truly guide your life.

   Here's how you can tell. If saving for a rainy day is one of your top values, you will be actively engaged in saving, or you will be consistently striving to change your circumstances to make saving possible. If you are in pain about not saving and you're not fully engaged in resourceful, creative action to remedy the situation, then saving is only a standard or an ideal.

   This is not the time to attempt to "look good" to yourself by marking idealistic values that you wish drove your daily life but in reality don't. For example, according to advertising psychologists, there are five reasons that people are motivated to buy what they buy and do what they do. These are powerful background motivators that people forget when they make up values lists. We tend to forget about them because we don't "feel good" admitting that we are motivated by these things. These powerful motivators are: looking good, feeling good, being right, feeling safe, avoiding pain or discomfort. And let's not forget the most basic value of all—survival. If you do not have at least some of these and other less than ideal-seeming values in your true value list, you may be fooling yourself.

4. Go through your true values and mark the ones that are also important work values. For example, spending time in nature may be an important personal value but not a central work value. Now you have some information that will be very valuable to your career design project: a clear accounting of your real, work-related values.

5. Now that you have sorted out the values you actually live by and from, you may wish to create some new ones. Look to see if you would be

willing to add any new values to your list. Please, no New Year's resolutions! Add only those values that you have not been living from that you are now willing to adopt fully and completely as your own. For example, you may have recognized that "saving for a rainy day" has actually been a standard, not a true value. You can forge it into a true value by choosing it and then living it from this moment hence. There may also be values that you have lived by in the rest of your life, but not at work, that you are now willing to forge into work values as well.

6. Prioritize your work values. Here's how to do it. Values are hierarchical. People will usually sacrifice a lower but still very important value to protect or uphold a higher value. Some basically honest senior government officials have in the past resorted to lying when faced with a choice between loyalty to their administration and honesty. That's because loyalty, keeping their jobs, or some other value was higher on their scales than honesty.

Go over the work values you have marked. Which is your number one, most important true work value? Which value would you never sacrifice under any circumstances? Mark it number one in the "Priority" column of your values checklist. Which is next most important? Which is third, and so forth? Write down the appropriate number in the "Priority" column. Continue to prioritize your top work values. Don't worry if you can't absolutely prioritize them. Just do the best you can.

If your top values are all noble and high-minded, you may be fooling yourself. Could you be counted on to be completely honest even if you would be terminally embarrassed if you told the truth? What if you would lose your job if you told the truth? What if you would lose your life? For many people, avoiding losing their jobs is a higher value than honesty. That does not mean they are devoid of integrity. They may always be honest except when confronted with the possible loss of their jobs. Dig in and get face-to-face with your top work values now. You may want to take a few days to work on this exercise.

7. It is useful to get more specific. Dig into each true work value and get clear what you really mean. For example, if one of your values is security, what exactly does security mean to you? Do you mean $10 million in the bank, a job that's impossible to be fired from, headhunters constantly knocking at your door, or working in a safe neighborhood?

8. Look back over this inquiry for clues. Add whatever you find to your Clues list. Ask, "Is there anything I am willing to choose as a definite

component?" Add anything you choose to your Definite Career Design Components. Do any new careers or jobs come to mind? If so, add them to your Career Ideas.

INQUIRY 26

Rewards

We go to work to get rewarded. At the most basic level, we work to fulfill physical needs such as food and shelter. If those are met, we then seek security rewards that keep the wolf far from our door. Then, if those are met, we seek the next level of rewards, things such as self-esteem, approval, power, a position higher on the chimpile than the other apes, and the acquisition of symbols of success. Finally, at the top of the heap are rewards such as self-expression, achievement, fulfillment, creativity, fun, freedom, contribution. A secret to having a career you love is to have a job that rewards you on all levels. (Personally, I'm for both self-expression and food.)

One of the rewards you get from your work is a paycheck. If the only work-related value that mattered to you was money, you could simply pick the career that provided you with the biggest bucks. But for work to be fulfilling, it must contribute much more than money. It must reward or express your most important true work values, both the external ones like income and security, and the internal ones such as personal satisfaction or making a difference. The rewards that mean the most are not necessarily the ones society says are important. They aren't necessarily the ones offered by organizations to entice you to work there. They are yours. Many years ago, when I used to spend time around the Harvard campus, my student friends built plenty of internal rewards into their game plans. Nowadays, a distressing percentage of students there think mainly of the external rewards, almost guaranteeing that they will be both rich and miserable. Rewards are highly personal. Fortunately, you have just finished naming and sorting out your true work values. In terms of the workplace, values and rewards are two sides of the same coin. In truth, you get two paychecks. One has some numbers and a dollar sign printed on it. The other consists of other top values adequately rewarded. These rewards are the answer to the question "Why work?" If your job fails to adequately reward even one of your top true work values, it may greatly diminish your level of workplace fulfillment. If, for example, "positive acknowledgment" is an important workplace value, you will not perform at your best or experience an ongoing sense of satisfaction in a job where the management style is to criticize mistakes rather than recognize accomplishment.

1. Create a new document, "Rewards." Look through your values. Reword your most important values into language that communicates them as rewards. For example, if *respect* is a top work value, you might reword it to something like: "I will be respected for my high level of mastery and dedication to producing extraordinary results." If *integrity* is a top value, you might say, "I will work for an organization that has a high level of integrity, in how it interacts with customers and how it treats employees." Notice that in doing this, you are declaring how it will be in your future. You are making a bold statement of intention. Many of these rewards may be ripe to turn into definite career design components. Others may be useful clues.

2. Look back over this inquiry for clues. Add whatever you find to your Clues list. If there is anything you are willing to choose as a definite career component, add it to your Definite Career Design Components. If any new career or job comes to mind, add it to your Career Ideas. Ask yourself why that career appeals to you, and see if that suggests more clues. If you now know that a career on your Career Ideas list does not fit, remove it. See if that suggests any clues. Remember to keep recording and working with your clues, moving them toward definite career components.

Part 3

WORK WHERE?
WORKPLACE ENVIRONMENT

CHAPTER 23

•

WORKPLACE ENVIRONMENT

Workplace Ecology

When the subject of ecology comes up, it is usually in reference to environmental deterioration or how we are destroying an ecological niche by altering its delicate balance. In the suburban jungle, to archetypal white-collar Bob, it all seems a little abstract, like bad news from far away. He turns off the TV, vaguely distressed by the news feature about syringes floating up on the shore again. He goes to bed and dreams of beaches. In the morning, he is off on his one-hour, bumper-to-bumper commute in a sea of fellow drivers. Many of them, like Bob, are feeling both competitive and benumbed. All the way to work, he worries that he may fall victim to the downsizing that has reduced his department by 50 percent. His stomach churns. Because the workload hasn't diminished, he has been ordered to shoulder twice the responsibility. He is still tired and stressed out from the pressure and isn't thinking clearly. Every day, it gets a little more difficult. It seems like the workday never ends. Plus, no matter how much he does, he never gets any praise. His supervisor seems to have learned his skills at the Cotton Fields School of Management, where the Boss sits on a big white horse and points out all the mistakes his employees make while instilling as much fear and uncertainty as possible.

In the midst of all this turmoil, Bob has not noticed that he is part of an ecosystem. He is an organism in the midst of various environments that alter the course and quality of his every moment. He attributes his exhaustion and grumpiness to some of the parts of his environment: the boss, the long hours. He never recognizes that it is not quite as simple as that. It's not just one thing or another. It is the impact his entire ecosystem has on him. The stressors he notices and complains about are just the tip of the iceberg. Beneath the surface are other, more subtle environmental factors that affect his peace of mind, clarity of thought, creativity, and physical health. How does he deal with it? He simply accepts his fate with a shrug and pays the price that his personal ecological disaster zone exacts. So, to some degree, do many of us. Once again, our adaptability and resilience are our downfall. If, in order to be reasonably productive, we humans needed an environment almost perfectly designed for us, there would be more human ecologists working in big business than accountants. But every day, we humans continue to prove we can survive nearly anything except total starvation.

We put up with destructive environments because we think we must. In career planning, the quality of the workplace environment is often the first thing to be sacrificed for the sake of other goals. "I'll put up with any degree of discomfort to reach my goal" is considered an admirable philosophy. Sometimes the traditional climb up the career ladder requires you to temporarily pay heavy dues. *Temporarily* is the key word. For every person who temporarily puts up with an ill-suited environment as part of a clearly focused plan, there are ten who wind up permanently stuck, glued by stasis like flies on flypaper. People end up in these ecological cesspools permanently because they were not sufficiently committed to working in a supportive environment, or because they did not understand the impact an adverse work environment would have on the overall quality of their lives.

Sometimes it's just good old crazy thinking that gets people into a mess. I know a man who wakes up at four thirty in the morning, does the chores on his ten-acre country place, drives a two-hour commute into the city, works a ten-hour day at a job he doesn't like, arrives back home at eight o'clock in the evening, and enjoys living in the country for two hours before he falls asleep. Nearly every weekend, he brings a big pile of work home. Is it worth it? Speaking from the shade of his furrowed brow, he says it is. I can't help thinking that he pays a hefty price for his few hours of pleasure. Instead of designing a career from the ground up that included living in the country and the time to enjoy it, he just added the farm on top of an already stressful career, thinking it would be the cure. The real subject of this chapter is stress. The point of considering your workplace environment is more than just hanging around in a place you like. It is to design a personal ecosystem that manages stress well.

Low-Stress Living

Nobody ever has anything good to say about stress. It is right up there with mosquitoes on the list of Mother Nature's major nuisances. Nevertheless, it is virtually impossible to have a life that is stress free. Life becomes stress free the moment you die. When we sit in a sylvan glade and absorb the peace of the deep forest, we do not realize that all balanced ecosystems have numerous stressors. One component of a balanced system is its ability to process stress successfully. As your own personal career ecologist, you want to design a career ecosystem that melts, dissolves, and dissipates stress so that it doesn't build up inside of you.

Stress is not a complicated subject. Picture yourself as a talking tube with a hole in each end, like this:

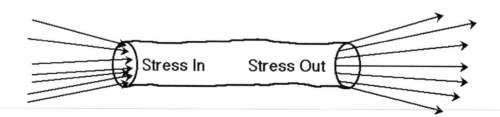

Stress In   Stress Out

The stress goes in one end and, hopefully, out the other. So long as the exit is as big as the entrance, everything is fine. The stress that enters gets back out again. When the amount of stress coming in is more than the system can handle, it builds up and is stored in the body and brain, like this:

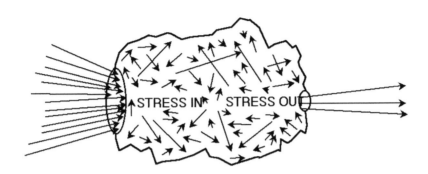

If you choose a career that is reasonably low stress, you will not have to master processing stress through your system. If you pick work that involves a lot of challenge, it will most likely generate more stress. If this is the case, or if getting to your goal involves spending a few years in a stressful environment, you will have to design into your career plan a way to deal with it. There are just three ways to deal with stress:

Minimize the stressors in your environment. The very best way is to choose a career that fits you perfectly in as many areas as possible: talents, personality, and so forth. Or you could just pick a career that is naturally low in stress.

Keep the stresses in the environment from getting to you. Close your office door, wear earplugs and dark sunglasses, or develop some compassion for your boss.

Learn ways to let out the stress that gets in. There are many ways to dissipate career-related stress, to actually dissolve it by opening up the exit sphincter so that the stress flows out of your system: have nurturing relationships, a sense of humor, a home environment that melts stress. Live a balanced life. Do daily aerobic exercise. Make use of stress-relieving practices such as mindfulness meditation or yoga.

If you remember that you are an energetic tube with a hole in each end, it should be easier to figure out how to reduce the stress-in sphincter or enlarge the stress-out one.

Designing Your Workplace Ecosystem

Are you ready to become your own personal ecologist? Human ecology is the science concerned with understanding the relationships between humans and their physical and social environments. To design a career that fits, you need to consider both the physical and social environments of your work life. The physical environment ranges from the big geographical picture (where you live) to the micro (the noise level and the color of the paint in your office). The social environment includes everything from the socioeconomics of where you live to the customary mood of the people you work with (including you). To be your own human ecologist takes more observation than study. Your heart knows what fits and what doesn't. You could easily sit down right now and invent a workplace environment that would be perfect for you. On the other hand, many of us make unnecessary compromises because it seems too difficult and challenging to have it all fit together perfectly. As usual, it is a question of commitment. If it is important that you love your work, you will definitely need to make the environment just as important as all the other vital pieces of the puzzle.

These days, you have to think not only about designing a career by considering the present workplace environments but also about what will likely take place in the future. Years ago, while trapped in a small tent by a howling blizzard, my friend Andy read a story to me where people living in an icy wilderness had to spend all their lives searching for enough firewood to barely heat their huts. It was an ultimate horror story that now seems more a part of the real world as populations soar and resources become ever more precious. It now takes a couple to have the same kind of lifestyle my parents enjoyed with only Dad bringing home a paycheck. So think about the future and design it into your plan.

It is one thing to pay some dues now for a wonderful future you have carefully planned. It is yet another to fool yourself that you are paying temporary dues, when, in reality, you are just in a bad place. When I founded Rockport Institute many years ago, I put every penny into research. That meant living at the office for a while. The office was in downtown Washington, DC, four blocks up Pennsylvania Avenue from the White House. Whenever the president needed a pack of gum in the middle of the night, a whole fleet of vehicles would go screaming by just a few feet below with the sirens going full tilt. There was a big, noisy student bar close by, and the young dudes used my corner for late-night games of chest thumping, hurling, and yelling. I used earphones, shades, exercise, and meditation to deal with that incredibly stress-provoking corner. All the while, I knew it was temporary. Now, many years later, I'm sitting in my office overlooking a lake and flower gardens and listening to mockingbirds and wood thrushes sing. Was it worth it to put up with that terrible downtown environment in the beginning? Oh yes! Would I have gone berserk if I had not had a clear vision of where I was going? Oh yes!

INQUIRY 27

Designing Your Own
Workplace Ecosystem

The long list of questions in chapter 9, "Questions," contains many that are environment related. Go back through them. What environmental elements are most important to you? What affects you negatively? What would be the ideal environment? What stressors would you be willing to deal with in your work environment? How much? How often? Remember that it is impossible to have a stress-free environment. Your job is to design your environment so that it fits in with what you can and are willing to handle. For example, it might be ideal for you to work at home and never have to deal with rush-hour traffic. Are you willing to commit to this perfect situation, or will you make some sort of compromise? If so, how far will you drive? Make sure you assess carefully. What shape would you be in after a commute of fifteen minutes? A half hour? An hour? What about after five years? Please look at all the other environment-related questions in this same way.

Look back over this inquiry for clues. Add whatever you find to your Clues list. Ask, "Is there anything I am willing to choose as a definite component?" Add anything you choose to your Definite Career Design Components. Do any new careers or jobs come to mind? If so, add them to your Career Ideas. Remember to keep working with your clues, moving them toward selecting new definite components.

Part 4

PUTTING IT ALL TOGETHER

CHAPTER 24

WHICH CAREERS FIT BEST?

This chapter consists of two inquiries that will help you home in on careers that may fit your specifications. The first is "Eight Great Careers," an inquiry in which you can describe, compare, and contrast several careers. There are two different ways to use this inquiry.

You can use it early in your career design project as a purely speculative exercise to explore careers to find clues and build definite components.

Or use it later in the process, to narrow the field of careers worthy of your consideration. In this inquiry, you compare and contrast several careers to gain further clarity about what is most important to you. It may be that none of these eight careers turns out to be your final choice.

The second inquiry—"Which Careers Fit Best?"—helps you compare potentially fitting careers with your specifications.

INQUIRY 28

Eight Great Careers

1. Start a new document in your notebook or download a template from www.rockportinstitute.com.

2. Think of eight careers that are as close as possible to being a perfect fit with everything important to you: your talents, personality, dreams, plans, goals, and so on. Most of these careers should be a practical possibility as well. Don't use impossible dreams that you are unwilling to stretch to attain. You can use this inquiry in different ways, depending on how far you've come in designing your career:

   • Early in the process, when you may be considering a wide variety of careers, use the inquiry as a speculative exercise to compare each with the others. The goal is to discover some great clues. Use careers from your Career Ideas list, or simply brainstorm eight careers that seem the most attractive, based on what you know about your talents and personality, and so forth. You could also use careers that fit a particular ability or characteristic you possess, or something you found through research.

- Later in the career design process, after you have developed a handsome collection of definite components, use the inquiry for a practical, real-world comparison of careers you can seriously consider. *Take the time and effort to come up with a great list.* Make sure they meet the criteria of being as close to a perfect fit and as free of unpalatable compromises as possible. You may have to spend many hours online or in other research to come up with eight good ones. If you can't come up with eight after putting in a serious effort, include some that are a bit less than perfect. You want the variety that eight provides to fully compare and contrast each with the others to come up with the most useful clues and definite components.

  Make them as varied as possible. Write the name of each career in your Eight Great Careers document. If you are using a paper notebook, you will need two pages for each career. Work on this inquiry one career at a time. Explore the various steps of this inquiry for one of the eight careers. Then come back and work on another. Repeat until you have done all eight *completely.*

3. Write a description of the first career on your list. Write this description in a way that breathes life into this career. You want a rich and multisensory description so that you can visualize yourself actually doing this job. You want to be able to see, feel, hear, and touch it. Write down day-to-day activities, the nature and purpose of the work, functions performed, the physical location, and the abilities and traits you would use every day. The more practical and down-to-earth you make your description, the more real it will be for you.

   - If you are doing this early in your career design project and using it as a speculative exercise, it is not necessary to know the real nature of the careers you are describing. It is more about uncovering what is important to you. Just do your best in describing what you think the work would be like.

   - If you do this once you have a well-developed list of definite career components, then take an even more practical approach. Make sure you know what people in these careers actually do in the course of an average day. You may have to do some research. If you haven't spent significant time observing people actually performing this career, I recommend finding out by talking with several people who know. You would be amazed at the percentage of unhappy lawyers who based their choice on movies and TV.

4. Do a Hot and Not Hot comparison for the career. If you are using a paper notebook, draw a vertical line down the middle of a page for each of the eight careers. Above the left column, write "Hot." Write "Not Hot" above the right-hand column. Then begin to look critically at all aspects of the career. First answer the question "What's hot?" Write down everything positive about the career, what is attractive to you, what fits, what feels good, what fulfills your goals, and so forth. Dig deep. Don't just take the obvious, easy answers. Consider everything about this potential career and how it might contribute to you, and you to it. The point of this is to mine all the gold from every possible vein. If one of your "hots" involves working with people, ask yourself other questions concerning people. How many people? Doing what? How often? What sort of people? Why be with them? What's the result of our interactions? Next do the same thing with everything that is "not hot" about the potential career. Spend enough time to explore fully. You may want to use the long list of questions at the back of the "Questions" chapter to help you work on this inquiry. *The exercise should take at least a couple of hours to complete if you don't need to do any research.*

5. Collect all the important "hots" from all the individual pages on one master "hots" page. Do the same with the "nots." Then prioritize the most important entries in each master list.

6. Go back over the eight careers. Compare and contrast each with the others. How are they different? What "hots" and "nots" run through several of them as themes? How important are these themes to you? What careers have risen to the top? Which have sunk to the bottom? Why? Ask yourself what further questions this inquiry brings to light.

7. Look back over this inquiry for clues. Add whatever you find to your Clues list. Ask, "Is there anything I am willing to choose as a definite component?" Add anything you choose to your Definite Career Design Components. Do any new careers or jobs come to mind? If so, add them

to your Career Ideas. Remember to keep working with your clues, moving them toward selecting new definite components.

8. If you are using this later in your career design project, go on to the following inquiry.

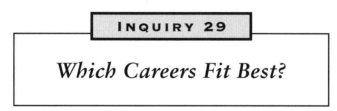

INQUIRY 29

Which Careers Fit Best?

The goal of this inquiry is to check out how well your various career ideas fit your specifications.

1. For this inquiry, you need worksheets similar to the example below. Make your own or use the templates on the Rockport Institute website.

2. Across the top of the page, list careers that you think might be the best fit with all your definite career design components. Write your most important definite career design components down the left side of the worksheet.

3. Starting with the first career, go down the column of components and rate how well you think the components match from 1 to 5, with 5 signifying an excellent match.

4. Do the same thing for the other careers. Notice that in the abbreviated sample, brain surgeon fits all the components listed, whereas burger flipper does not. Don't guess. If you don't know whether something fits, do some research. It may take time to do this inquiry.

5. Total the scores for each career. Remember that this is an inquiry, not a final Super Bowl score. The point is to explore, compare, and move closer to making your own informed choice. Just because a particular career "wins" the high score does not mean you have to pick it. It is your choice to make.

6. If there is anything you are willing to choose as a definite career component, add it to your Definite Career Design Components list.

7. Even better, you could choose your career now!

CAREER COMPARISON WORKSHEET

Career Design Components	Brain Surgeon	Burger Flipper	Career #3	Career #4	Career #5	Career #6
		Mark columns to show where components match up with a career				
3-D spatial	5	3				
Make 400K	5					
Use my hands	5	3				
Respected	5					
Total check marks	20	6				

•

CHAPTER 25

FINAL RESEARCH AND MAKE THE CHOICE

You are close to the finish line. At this point, you should have narrowed your choices to two to four finalists.

Final In-Depth Research

The average American male spends more time researching and considering his first new car purchase than in designing his career. Remember, you are going to be driving this career for a long, long time. So please put in the time.

The point of this research is twofold: to find out enough about a career to predict how well it will fit you, and to move beyond any romantic fantasies to the real deal. To make sure that the career satisfies all or most of your career design components, you have to turn over a lot of rocks and learn everything you can about your final few contenders. You need to find out what each career is really like, flushing out all the details down to an hour-by-hour flow of a typical workday. I assume you have already used chapter 11, "The Bottom Line—Research," to do basic research. Now is the time to get your remaining questions answered and make the final choice.

1. List your unknowns. Identify the major unknowns and concerns you have for each career you need to research. You may have incomplete knowledge, missing information, distorted generalizations, and flawed understandings about the careers you are considering.

2. Ask sharp questions. Ask, "What do I need to know to make a final choice?" Sharpen your questions to make them more specific. You may want to use chapter 9, "Questions," to help with this. Decide where you will find the answers. It is always one of these three:

- *Look inside.* Sometimes the best answers are internal, such as "Am I willing to live near a big city?"

- *Look outside.* You need information from external sources. Use all the resources you can find, including the Internet, libraries, company websites, professors, people who work in the field, alumni networks, seminars and conventions in the field, professional associations, professional journals and trade magazines, and anything else you can think of. Talk to as many people as possible who do the job you are considering (a minimum of ten who do *exactly* the job you are researching).

- *Make up an answer.* Sometimes you won't find the answer internally or externally. Perhaps the career you want most is less predictably attainable than others are. In that case, you may just have to take a leap into the unknown and make a bold declaration, like the guys who signed the Declaration of Independence. For example, the question "Can I make 200K as a green architect?" may be hard to answer definitively; there may be no "right" answer. Some green architects make that much, but many don't. It may be a matter of making an existential choice—just making the choice you know is right for you. Obviously, before you can make a bold statement like that, it pays to do some preliminary external research to make sure that your declaration is within the range of what you deem possible and within the range of how far you are willing to stretch.

- Keep at it until you have answered all your important questions.

4. Manage your research. You could make a table like the one on the following page or use the template available on the Rockport Institute website. Create a chart like this for each career you want to research. For each career, investigate the three major design areas as shown on the chart.

5. Keep it realistic. Give sufficient attention to the availability of the work you are considering, how far you are willing to stretch, and how much of a risk you are willing to take.

CAREER TITLE: MECHANICAL ENGINEER

Research Steps	Talents and Personality	Subject Matter and Meaning	Workplace Environment
1. Unknowns	Do I have the right talents to excel in this field?	Do I care enough about the problems that mechanical engineers solve?	Not sure of the range of companies that hire mechanical engineers
2. Questions	Who can I talk with to learn what talents are needed in this field?	What are the major problems they solve and niche areas they work in?	Which are the innovative companies, and where are they geographically?
	How do I know whether I have the right talents?	What industries hire mechanical engineers?	With what type of company do my talents and personality traits fit best?
	What kind of people go into this field, and am I like them?	Why am I attracted to this field? What am I trying to get out of it?	What kind of human and work culture setting would be best for me?
	What job functions do they typically perform?	Do I care about this subject matter enough?	What are the typical pay and benefits?
3. Resources and Research to Do	Talk to three college professors, and at least ten mechanical engineers. Read engineering journals and websites. Visit an engineering library on campus.	Find professional associations; get recommendations for books to read. Read books to learn about the niches and problems solved in this field. Ponder internally as to my true motivations; get clear why I would care to do this kind of work. What are my metagoals here?	Find out about about engineering companies and their work environments from talking with engineers.
4. Answers and Findings	Mechanical engineers are high in spatial reasoning and analytical reasoning talents. Most are strong introverts with logical, practical mind-sets. I am exactly like this; I would be in my element in this field.	A large percentage of jobs in this field are in the aerospace, defense, home appliance, and automotive industries. I love cars and am very excited about helping to develop technology like alternative-fuel engines.	Work environments vary widely; it depends on whether they are innovating new products or mass-producing them. I am an innovator, so a small, dynamic firm that designs new products is where I fit best.

Make the Choice

For some, the final decision will not be too challenging. The choice may be obvious. It could be that you now have to choose between more than one career that fits your specifications. If that is the case and you have reached the moment of choice, you may want to reread chapter 7, "Making Decisions—A Short Course," to help you get off the horns of your dilemma. This is your life, and your choice to make.

I suggest that after all the work you have done, you are the one person in the universe who is capable and prepared to make this choice. All you have to do is do it. It is your final created commitment: "I will be a . . ."

The Yeahbuts may be telling you to leave your options open. If you do, you will still be in the midst of uncertainty. There are only a few special situations when it may be appropriate to have your final choice include more than one specific career:

- More than one very similar job would be equally appealing, and you are willing to split your job search between them.

- You are a college student or otherwise in a situation where you feel that you have narrowed your choice sufficiently for the present, and you want to get some more experience or maturity under your belt before you make the final decision.

- You have decided to have more than one career and divide your time between them. This is usually a bad idea, since it usually takes a 100 percent effort to get a single career off the ground. However, some people run several part-time businesses and make it work.

Unless your situation is similar to one of these scenarios, reluctance to make one final choice is probably just an attack of Yeahbuts. So take a deep breath and go for it!

When the choice is made, you may not feel excited or relieved. If your choice extends you out into new territory, you may feel apprehensive or suffer an even more massive attack of Yeahbuts than usual. There is a phenomenon all salespeople know about that they call "buyer's remorse." This is a special form of Yeahbut that attacks once a decision has been made. It famously occurs with expensive purchases, like cars. After lots of research, you buy what you've decided is the right car. Driving it home, you start to wonder if you made a mistake. You see a different car on the street and wonder if it might have been a better choice. If this happens, don't let it sway your resolve. In fact, you may have doubts surface regularly. This is perfectly normal. If you read the biographies of people who have accomplished extraordinary feats, you realize that doubts are inevitable. Once I asked my explorer friend John Goddard if he suffered from attacks of doubt in the midst of expeditions into new territory. He said that sometimes the doubts were constant, especially at times of great difficulty and duress. I suggest that you treat them like mosquitoes. Know that you will have to put up with them and that they will draw some blood. But do not let them keep you from your destination.

You did it!

If you are reading this paragraph, you have reached the end of the journey and designed your perfect career—or at least you have chosen work that is a big improvement. If so, congratulations. You did it! I know how much time, energy, and hard work you have put into this project. You kept going when the going got tough, when there was no light at the end of the tunnel, when the Yeahbuts were doing their best to shoot you down. You persisted through all of it to arrive here. I wish you the best: a life you love, a passion for your own personal growth and development, and, most of all, a commitment to make your world a better place for everyone.

Remember, the final step is to celebrate. Go have yourself an amazing party. You deserve it!

•

CHAPTER 26

WHAT IF NOTHING FITS OR I CAN'T DECIDE?

Sometimes it all clicks together perfectly. You generate definite components that point toward one or more fitting careers. Then it is just a matter of research and whittling down the possibilities to make the best choice. Other people have a harder time.

What If Nothing Fits All of My Specifications?

Occasionally no career fits every specification. Don't get discouraged if you can't find the perfect match. Remember, you are defying the odds with your commitment to have a great career. The taller an order your career components add up to, the bigger the challenge to find everything you want. Let's see what may be going on.

Perhaps you haven't searched thoroughly enough to uncover the perfect fit. One way to widen your search is to pare down your definite components to the most important ones, reword them in simple, powerful language, and then see if anything fits this tighter list. You could ask everyone you know what fits these specifications. One of our clients who wanted to explore less obvious options narrowed down his specifications to a short, focused, powerfully worded list and stapled posters downtown offering a reward for the winning career idea. He found a career that fit everything—one that nobody had thought of before.

You may need to alter your design. Perhaps alter or drop some specifications. Compromise does not necessarily equal sacrifice. If you've followed the Rockport Career Design Method fully, you have taken the high road and sought perfection—or close to it. This method has a huge advantage over the way most people make a choice. They usually take the middle road, with compromises unconsciously built into the design. Their Yeahbuts were a vocal member of the design team, warning against considering anything beyond the most reasonable. You, on the other hand, have been wonderfully unreasonable, reaching for the stars in your career design. By seeking perfection, you have more room to adjust and still wind up successful and satisfied. If nothing fits perfectly, you do have to alter your design components a little. Identify the snag—the component or components that push your design into the "nothing fits" territory. See if you can drop or alter this specification. Loosen up a little. Add a little more flexibility into your design or tweak some other components.

Redefine/reframe. Sometimes it is necessary to redefine your way into a fit. For example, one client's sticking point was security. This was a critical component for him, but the way he had defined security meant that he would have to work for a large, soulless, bureaucratic company. By expanding his definition of security, far more attractive possibilities instantly opened up.

Too many career design components? One surefire way to make it nearly impossible to find anything that fits is to have a large number of definite components. Trying to connect too many data points can overwhelm you. Neuroscientists find that the brain is not very good at dealing with so much simultaneous input. The cereal aisle in a huge supermarket is enough to boggle the mind. The brain likes just two or three things to think about at once. Simplify your design. Choose a few of the most important design components, the ones you would never give up, and then see if anything matches.

You may have to invent yourself a new career. If all the careers you've found are too narrow in scope, and you want to use a broad range of talents, don't worry: You're not going crazy or asking too much. Most jobs do not provide a lot of breadth. Even complex, high-level jobs often force the worker into a narrow range of functions. These days many people want more than a cookie-cutter job, and they're willing to custom-design one. If you can't find a career that has everything you're committed to, perhaps you'll have to make one up. You would be amazed how many people have persuaded a decision maker to hire them for a job that didn't previously exist.

There are a few organizations in which employees define the parameters of their projects and daily functions. Since this approach produces the happiest employees, in time it is likely that more organizations will adopt a more flexible approach. But you are dealing with reality today. If you want to make full use of a broad palette of talents, traits, and functions, and have the most say in how and what you do, the obvious solution is the self-designed job, whether this translates into convincing someone to let you do what you want in his or her organization, starting a business, or working on your own. One bored lawyer created a career triumvirate by adding his hobbies of property and antiques: real estate law, commercial rentals, and estate appraisal.

You may need to take interim steps to reach that perfect job. You may need to reach the goal indirectly by working in a bridge job that takes you partway there or by getting more education and training.

What If I Can't Decide?

If you have trouble deciding on your future career, it's not a character flaw, nor is it peculiar to you. Most people, including those revered for great leadership, wrestle with decisions that have far-reaching consequences. There are also consequences, however, for sitting on the fence. There's an old saying in the military that *a* decision is better than *no* decision. You might find it useful to reread chapter 10, "When You Get Stuck." Now let's look at some common causes of indecision about a career.

I might make a mistake and pick the wrong career. It is certainly possible to make the wrong decision about anything: where to live, with whom to spend your life, and what to do with that life. There are few guarantees. One thing you can count on, however, is that we all will make many mistakes. Given that the US divorce rate hovers around 50 percent, certain areas seem more susceptible to mistakes than others.

Insufficient preparation is by far the main reason people wind up in careers that do not fit. They selected their work with too little thought, using methods unlikely to produce the intended result. You can, most likely, make a choice you won't regret if you apply the tools in *The Pathfinder*. If you break down the process into smaller pieces, find good clues, fully investigate those clues, ask and answer the important questions, build strong definite components, do the research, and talk with many people engaged in the same work you intend to do, you have a high probability of success.

Career choice is not like an algebra problem. There is no guarantee. You may just have to take the leap.

I'm not sure I will get it right on my own. Earlier in the book, I suggested going through a career design coaching program that includes in-depth testing of innate natural talents. I did not write that to sell our services at Rockport Institute, but because I strongly believe that career design is a complex process for which most of us have no training. It remains a do-it-yourself project for most of us out of cultural habit; we think we *should* do it on our own. And we believe this in the face of dismal evidence from career satisfaction surveys suggesting that conventional career decision methods have resulted in 40 to 70 percent of people either "unengaged" or actively unhappy at their work. But we keep trying to do it ourselves because that's the way people have always done it.

Using professional coaching is by far the most effective way to design your future career. If you find it difficult to reach certainty and total specificity about your future work, check out the career design coaching programs at www.rockportinstitute.com. Or use another organization that offers similar programs. If one-on-one coaching is not for you, form a small group of fellow adventurers with similar goals to work with you through this project. In any event, if possible, don't go it alone.

This book has worked for many of the hundreds of thousands of people who used it as their coach, although it works less well for those who do not follow the Rockport Career Design Method meticulously. It won't work at all if you read it like a novel or dabble your way through it, just doing the parts that seem interesting. If you were an athlete with the goal of winning an Olympic medal, you would do what your coach recommended—even the parts you didn't want to do.

You may not have sufficient high-quality components. Remember that in the Rockport Career Design Method, we ask you to designate clues and definite components as gold, silver, or bronze. You assess clues and components based on how useful they will be in pointing toward specific kinds of work. Check out your components to see if you have sufficient golds and silvers to point to just a few careers. It is possible to have a long list of components that do not point to anything definite. You may have decided you are going to live in Chicago and wear casual clothes to work in a cutting-edge but noncompetitive environment that values individual contribution more than seniority *and* has a good health care plan. It uses your planning talent with your outgoing personality. Hmmm, what fits those specifications? I have no idea. A list like that can go on and on and create more confusion the longer it gets. Here is a useful test of the quality of your components: If you read your list to a large audience, are they able to make a few specific suggestions? Try this out on some friends. If they come up with ideas that are all over the map or can't think of anything specific, you've got to develop more gold and silver definite career design components to help narrow down the possibilities.

Here's the kind of specificity you're looking for: "financial industry in a consultative capacity." When combined, those components turn to gold, since they point to a very limited number of jobs. They are specific enough to generate a few strong possibilities. What about analytical problem solving working with three-dimensional objects? If you were to try out either of those two on an audience, people would offer specific suggestions that you could research and pare down to an even more specific few to seriously consider. Some other gold/gold combinations: teaching/training adults, administrator in academic or nonprofit, marketing concepts/ideas.

Definite components form the structure from which you build your future career. It is impossible to design a car, a bridge, or a vacation without them. If you have good clues but insufficient definite career design components, go back a few steps. Do you see gold shining from your design components? Do you have enough of them to point to specific work? If not, you need to go back to working on clue development. Focus on practical matters: functions, subject matter, and what would get you out of bed with enthusiasm. Work on turning clues into definite specifications.

Do you have enough skill in effective decision making? If you avoid making decisions because you aren't sure you will make the best ones, reread chapter 7, "Making Decisions—A Short Course."

You may be deciding not to decide. When people say, "I want to think about it for a while" or, "I need to process this further," they are sometimes fooling themselves. In reality, they may be making an unconscious decision to not decide. Not deciding is a valid choice, but it would be useful to raise it to a conscious level, where you can be a powerful player in your own life, responsible for the consequences of your decisions.

Not to decide is to decide.

—HARVEY COX

Are you wired to keep your options open? Some temperament types prefer to wait and see, let the situation develop, keep all possibilities open, or adapt as the situation changes. They naturally resist deciding. If your four-letter personality type has a *P* on the end, you may fit into this group, and deciding is not as natural for you as it is for people with big, strong decision-making muscles. If your nature is to let it all flow, choose a career where that characteristic fits the work. But to do that—to have a career that fits you perfectly—you have to push yourself to choose.

If you feel that you are cutting off other wonderfully attractive options when you make a decision, it's true. But you make decisions all day long without a great deal of angst. Right now you are reading this book when you could be making love or racing motorcycles or writing your own book. You could be doing a million other things. You are an expert at picking one thing to the exclusion of countless others. Not one waking moment goes by that you could not spend doing something else. You constantly make decisions about what you are going to do that exclude everything else.

I want to do so many things. The fact of the matter is that we cannot do it all now. We are human beings with limited time, limited energy, and a limited life span. Doing something you love, doing it brilliantly, and getting paid well for it is a lot better than avoiding choosing one direction. It takes such a big chunk of a person's life and energy to master one thing and make a success of it. Most of the people you admire do one thing well. They sing or create businesses or make discoveries or whatever. Only a very few people succeed in multiple arenas. Most of them completely mastered one game and then expanded into a new area. Then again, there is nothing wrong with having multiple careers at the same time. But it can be a bit like dating ten people at once.

Do you know enough about what jobs exist out there in the real world? If you have solid gold and silver components but still have trouble coming up with specific careers that fit them, it may be that you don't know enough about what careers might fit, or it could be possible that nothing fits. Get to work on uncovering jobs that would fit. By far, the best resource is other people. Run your career design components by as many people as it takes to discover some likely possibilities. It might be useful to simplify the list to a few components—just the most important ones. Ask people until you have a list of practical possibilities. Take their suggestions, write them down, and investigate. Even if one idea doesn't appeal, perhaps something else will show up in the investigation. You may have to ask many people. There is no other method nearly as effective. If you have notions of broad, general areas or fields that may fit, you could join online groups of people interested in those particular areas and ask the participants to help you get more specific.

Sometimes there are valid reasons to hold off on making the final choice. There are times when you need to know more than it is possible to know at the time. If you are a younger person, you may need more experience or maturity to provide a framework to weave a choice. You need to take some courses or take on some internships to explore options, or spend a year backpacking around the world to gain breadth and perspective. If you are a person of any age who just had a major tragedy that demands much of your attention and energy, holding off may be a good call. As one of the world's most ancient books, the *I Ching*, says, "Strength in the face of danger does not plunge ahead but bides its time, whereas weakness in the face of danger grows agitated and has not the patience to wait."

What I Want Seems Unobtainable

Maybe it is impossible. If you want to be president of the United States and you were born in Norway, you need to find a new dream. If you are not very strong or agile and weigh ninety-eight pounds, you are not going to play pro football. Most of the time, however, thinking the dream is impossible is just a Yeahbut: Jiminy Lizard whispering in your ear, telling you to resist stretching too far. What seems impossible is usually just difficult. You have to decide whether you are willing to do what it takes.

Are you willing and able to do what is necessary to get from here to there? At Rockport Institute, we occasionally have clients who can define what they want but falter when it looks difficult to turn the dream into reality. Sometimes they haven't been sufficiently realistic about how far they are willing to stretch into new territory. It is one thing to take a peek outside the box but quite another to actually jump out. One way to deal with this apparent impasse is to assess the benefits and costs of leaving the old box far behind. For example, continuing on your present path may risk a life of stress, boredom, or lack of fulfillment. A change involves different risks, such as uncertainty. Both options are risky. The easy road of staying where you are may bring continual, long-term, chronic stress along with the subsequent risks to your health, longevity, and relationships. On the other hand, the seemingly more difficult road of making a difficult choice may result in massive short-term stress, which, if you have chosen well, will disappear. Which risk do you choose?

Are you having an attack of the Yeahbuts? Our primary mind-set is to do whatever seems most likely to increase our chances to survive. Considering any new direction drives up fear and uncertainty and sets off the alarms and defensive behaviors of our survival system. It is likely that, no matter what new option you come up with, you are going to face an attack of Yeahbuts. Go back and read chapter 5, "Why You Don't Get What You Want," and chapter 6, "The Power of Commitment." Get to know your Yeahbuts as what they are: automatic survival-system reactions to potential change, not necessarily the truth. Turn your doubts and fears into specific questions to consider and resolve. Don't let the voice of Jiminy Lizard talk you back into the old box. Do your best to determine which obstacles that arise in Yeahbut attacks are serious and insurmountable and which are not.

Section 4

MARKETING AND JOB SEARCH

•

CHAPTER 27

PERSONAL MARKETING PRINCIPLES

Now that you have decided what to do, it is time to get out there and make it happen. This short chapter covers two basic principles of personal marketing. The chapter that follows this one is all practical advice about the job search. If you use the principles in this chapter, you will be more effective, whether you are job hunting or trying to gain admittance to the perfect graduate school program.

Abundance

Scarcity and abundance are opposing states of mind. I used to visit all the old folks in a nursing home in Camden, Maine, on Christmas Day. Each of these folks had an identical room, with identical furniture and an identical view. When I walked into one room, I heard a torrent of complaints: The room was too small, the view inadequate, and so forth. In the next room, I found a cheerful person saying how great the room was and admiring the terrific view. A state of mind of abundance produces a completely different worldview than scarcity, and, as a result, generates different results. It allows you to create circumstances that otherwise could never occur. Your ideas and actions will be more restrained and your expectations lowered if you view a job search project from the point of view of scarcity. You will be more willing to compromise and grab the first decent job offer. Why not set your goal much higher at the very beginning? Why not something like "Have several excellent job offers to choose from within the next three months"? If you are fully committed to multiple offers, you will get out there and kick up a bigger storm of creativity and action than you would if you were looking for one.

Creating Agreement

Career changers ask, "Why would an employer hire me when I have no experience in the field I want to go into? Even if they did, wouldn't I have to go all the way back to square one, compete with younger people for a low-level job, and take a big pay cut? How can I deal with this problem?"

First-time career choosers ask, "How can I increase my chances of being the person who gets the job? How can I stand out from the crowd as an exceptional candidate?"

What makes a movie star a star? How did a madman like Adolf Hitler take over the minds of an entire nation? Why is a diamond worth more than a grain of sand? Why is a swan more beautiful than a chicken (except to another chicken)? All of these questions are answerable when you understand the principle of "agreement." A diamond is worth more than a grain of sand because we agree that it is. Most cultures agree that uncommon objects are more valuable than plentiful things. There are also agreements about what is beautiful and what isn't. What makes a dandelion a weed is that people agree that it is. Isn't it more sensible and beautiful to cultivate a lawn speckled with thousands of beautiful yellow dandelions than to spend endless hours devoted to wiping out every one?

No matter how deeply and passionately a president of the United States may want to chart a course that makes significant changes and improves the lives of the citizenry, the reality is that he or she has to make decisions that generate agreement. This person, who has more power than anyone else in the world, has to be more circumspect in what he says than anyone else, because he cannot risk saying things that drain his hard-won reservoir of agreement.

Agreement is one of the most powerful forces in the world, not only in shaping our culture but also in defining who we are, what we believe, and how we behave. I was told about an experiment where a researcher brought subjects, one at a time, into a specially constructed, completely dark room, where the floor, walls, and ceiling had been painted flat black. Each person was guided to sit in the one chair in the room and look at the far wall, on which two dots of laser light were projected. Because the air was filtered to be free of dust, all the subject could see was two distant points of light. The subject was asked to estimate how far apart the two dots were. Some of them guessed the lights were two feet apart; others guessed twenty feet apart. Since they had no clues to help them estimate how far away the wall was, their answers varied widely. Later on, the researcher repeated the same experiment with several people in the room at the same time. They were asked to give their estimates out loud so the other participants could hear them. The first person guessed that the points of light were four feet apart, the next person said five feet, and another person three feet. Gone was the wide-ranging diversity of opinion. Without attempting to influence the group, the first participant unknowingly set the standard for the others, who unknowingly went along with an estimate in the narrow range.

You gain admittance into any group, social or professional, by creating agreement. If the group members think you have the right stuff, you get to join. Some fields, such as medicine or law, require a piece of paper, a license to practice, that automatically generates agreement that you are an insider in that field. Without the paper, you are excluded.

Fortunately for you, most careers do not demand specific paper credentials. There are more subtle credentials. Whether you are seen as an insider or an outsider in that field is a matter of perception, even though sometimes that perception can be very finely tuned. Here's how it works:

Let's say your hobby is underwater photography, and you find yourself on a plane sitting next to someone who is also an inveterate scuba photographer. Soon you are deep into a conversation that would be difficult for an outsider to understand. You both see the other as an "insider," make certain assumptions about the person, and use language in a special insider's code. Without thinking about it, both of you have included the other inside a "sphere of agreement." Every field of endeavor has around it a similar sphere of agreement. When two chefs, two cops, or two film directors meet and present the right credentials (the right dress, speech, attitude, and so forth), they do exactly the same thing as the underwater photographers: make some assumptions and automatically include the other as an insider.

Let's say that you started to date a kayaker and felt left out of the conversation whenever another kayaker was around. You might resolve the problem by "creating agreement." You might go kayaking a few times with your friend, read some books, start to act like a kayaker, look like one, think like one, talk like one, and move like one. Then you would be included within the kayakers' sphere of agreement, because you had actually become a kayaker. They would think of you as an insider; an accepted member of the group. Now let's say that you were a spy who wanted to get close to the kayaker for some nefarious purpose. You wouldn't waste time taking kayak voyages. You would just read the right books and magazines, and talk with other kayakers to get a feel for the sport and its jargon. Then you could speak the language well enough to pass yourself off briefly as a kayaker and gain admission into the sphere of agreement. I'm not suggesting that you deceive anyone. What is useful to take from these examples is that people consider you an "insider" or a "member" based on agreement, not necessarily on your long years of experience.

The way to gain entrance into a new career area is to create agreement. Take a look at the illustration. The domelike structure represents a sphere of agreement. Notice that it has many layers, like an onion. The outermost layer is the beginners' circle. It is where new graduates, or novices, begin the journey toward the innermost layer. Within that inner circle are the people who have generated the most agreement. They are the leaders or masters of this particular field. Remember, they are not necessarily the most experienced, the wisest, or the most capable. Many people who permanently inhabit the middle layers of the sphere of agreement in any field of endeavor may be just as wise and experienced as those who reach the inner circle. Members of the inner circle are there mostly because of one thing: Other people in the field agree that they should be there. What these people are good at is creating agreement.

Most of us seek to enter a new field in the least effective way possible. It goes something like this: You, shown bowing to the guardian of the gate in the illustration (the HR department), with résumé in hand, present yourself to the dragon, who guards the door into the new field. The door leads to the outermost beginners' circle. We use this method first as newly minted college graduates, when we prostrate ourselves, with degree and résumé in hand, before various job interviewers and ask them to please, please let us in. Our résumés and degrees clearly communicate that the only agreement we have collected so far consists of the college courses we took.

Recent graduates have one thing in their favor. Organizations expect to populate the beginners' circle with people who will work long hours for little compensation, so the traditional path through the guardian's door works for the ones with the best degrees, résumés, and interviewing skills. Midcareer changers have a more difficult problem. Since they do not have any direct work experience in the field they wish to enter, they do not fit within the standard guidelines.

The guardian of the gate selects potential candidates mechanically, by comparing résumé data. He is sieving a vast pool of minnows, looking for the biggest and best ones that fit the specs perfectly. He will then pass on these plump, energetic minnows to a decision maker, who will make the final selection. You might get dumped back in the pool, even though you might be perfect for the job, because the company doesn't want to take a chance on anything outside of its list of specs. Remember, HR is part of the administrative function, usually one of the most risk-averse parts of any organization. The people in human resources want to make sure their butts are covered. If you come to work one day with an Uzi and blow away everyone on the fourth floor, they want to be able to explain that it was not their fault. You did, after all, have the best résumé.

If the pathway through the front door into the beginners' circle is not the best way in, what is? I once had a fifteen-year-old high school student come to me as a client. He was mathematically gifted and had decided to become a math professor. He told me that only one-third of the people who earn a PhD in math actually find what he called "real math jobs." He wanted to get a head start and make sure he was one of the people who found the right job. Together we came up with a plan. He did a little research and identified the three best-known mathematicians in the area; the ones in the middle of the inner circle. Then he called each of them and asked if he could meet with them for a few minutes to make a proposal. At the first meeting, with the mathematician he most respected, he offered to work for him for two hours every Saturday. All he wanted in exchange was a half hour each week to ask him questions about math. This was an offer impossible to refuse. Even the most exalted mathematicians have the same grungy messes in their garages and basements as the rest of us. In addition, the mathematician was pleased to help this gifted and innovative kid in the field they both loved. Soon my client had a mentor and supporter. Eventually, through his mentor, he met some of the other leading mathematicians, who were reminded of themselves at an earlier age. They too became his boosters and stuck with him through his college career. During his undergraduate years, he looked from the point of view that he was already a mathematician and already in the middle of the sphere of agreement, rather than a lowly math student. He took on creative projects, while the other students just did what they were told. The rest, as they say, is history. He combined the following methods to increase his chances of being selected. These apply equally to career changers and first-time job hunters.

Practical Tips for Getting in the Sphere

Here are a few suggestions to help you create agreement that you are already in the sphere:

- **Be what you want to do.** Most people who make a career change and then seek a job in the new field walk into interviews with the point of view that "I am not a [*fill in job title here*]. But maybe they will hire me so I can learn to become one." If that is where you are coming from, they will hear your message loud and clear. But there is another possibility. It is to absorb everything about your intended career thoroughly so that you know it like a pro. If you know it as well as a pro, then declare yourself a pro. You simply say, "I am a corporate trainer," and mean it. This is not a matter of making up some words. You have to fill yourself completely with the new career. You have to live it and breathe it and do everything you need to do to know it well as a brand-new insider. Once you declare yourself to be a corporate trainer, begin doing the things that trainers do. If you act like a trainer, walk like a trainer, talk like a trainer, read what they read, hang out where they hang out, have friends who are trainers, join trade associations, attend conventions and seminars, get a friend who owns a company to let you train her people gratis, then all that's left to do is to get a job as a trainer. Your motive is not to fool anyone but to simply do what works and have the steel filings of agreement line up behind your magnet.

  When my young mathematician friend got to college, he immediately did what is natural for someone *being* a mathematician rather than *trying to learn to be a mathematician* like the other students. He made friends with the math professors and became a part of their circle. He was soon engaged in creative, independent, advanced studies. When he finished his undergraduate years, he had no trouble gaining admission to the best PhD program because he was already deep within the sphere of agreement, had demonstrated real mastery, and had built a powerful network of supporters that began when he was in high school. *The best way to get in is to be in.*

Being what you want to do is one big secret to gaining entry into any sphere of agreement. Instead of going in the front door to gain entrance to the outer circle, beam yourself up into the middle of the inner circle.

- **Read extensively about your new field.** Learn it thoroughly by reading all pertinent books, including academic texts, how-to books, trade journals, and books by leaders in the field.

- **Attend conventions and seminars.** Conventions offer perfect opportunities to meet people. Everyone you meet will automatically confer insider status on you because you're there. You will be surrounded by the key players. All of them are just a handshake away from becoming a member of your network of support. In addition, the seminars, panel discussions, and access to vendors will provide an extraordinary educational experience.

- **Create a network of supporters in the field.** This is so important that it deserves an in-depth discussion. See the inquiry "The Networking Game" in the next chapter.

- **Do projects that place you inside the sphere.** Your résumé should show you as an insider, if possible. A creative résumé can focus attention on your strengths in a way that beams you aboard, but it always helps to have actual experience in the field you wish to enter. There is no better way to demonstrate being inside than having actual work experience. Perhaps you could volunteer or persuade a friend who owns a business to let you do whatever you want to do for his company without financial compensation. Create cooperative, nonadversarial relationships and transactions. A job interview usually has an adversarial component. You are trying to sell something to them: namely, yourself. You and the interviewer are psychologically on opposite sides of the table. Learn to create relationships that do not have an adversarial component. Notice how different it feels when you look at the left side of the illustration on page 360 than when you look at the right side. When you must enter an adversarial transaction, learn to turn it to a cooperative one.

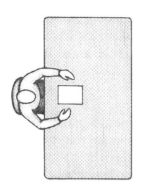 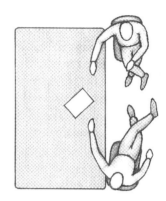

There are many ways you could create relationships that are cooperative and help to beam you aboard. For example, you could write an article for a trade magazine or newsletter, most of which are always hungry for good articles. Pick an interesting, slightly controversial topical subject. Interview several people in the middle of the inner circle, placed just slightly below God, and preferably in a position to hire you. Quote them extensively in your article.

These relationships start off on a completely different footing than if you were asking them for a job. You are on the same side of the psychological desk, asking them questions that show just how far inside the sphere you are. In this relationship, you are perceived as an insider who will further cement their position in the middle of the inner circle by lionizing them in print. Once you have established a friendly, cooperative relationship, ask them to support you—or at the very least, ask them for names of people you might contact.

Then, when you call the people they suggested, you can say, "Mr. X [just slightly below God] suggested that I call you." If you interview several people, you are likely to have good chemistry with at least one of them. They may be willing to do more and really go to bat for you. This and other similar methods don't work nearly as well if you cheat. You really have to thoroughly prepare. You have to "be" inside the sphere. You have to do so much reading and research that you know both the theoretical and practical aspects of the field. You should have a couple of projects you have done in the field as a volunteer on your résumé, if possible.

Turn around situations like job interviews by recognizing that an adversarial component is counterproductive, for both you and the interviewer. Turn it around with your attitude and actions. Your best chance for achieving this is to create a personal relationship with interviewers by sharing yourself, by being honest and forthright. They are used to interviewing people who are on the defensive, smile frozen on face, trying their best to answer every question perfectly while revealing as little as possible. Revealing yourself does not mean airing your dirty laundry. You do not have to tell them about your foibles or about the two years you spent wandering in the Himalayas if you don't want to. To reveal yourself means being who you are rather than some persona you manufactured to look good in the interviewer's eyes. People usually hire someone they get along with instead of the candidate with the best résumé. If you treat them like a close friend of your best friend, that should break the adversarial ice.

- Use creative approaches. These few tips just scratch the surface of what is possible. You need to develop your own creative solutions that fit your situation. Don't be afraid to be outrageous. Once there was a man who had trouble getting by the secretaries of the high-powered people he wanted to reach. He wanted to speak with them to offer something he thought would be a unique opportunity for them. Secretary troubles didn't stop him, however. A few days later, each of the high-powered folks received a box delivered by courier. On it was a note that said: "I have been trying to get through to you to tell you about ___, which I think you will be very interested in hearing about. In the attached box is a trained homing pigeon. If you want to hear more about our offer, just take the box to your window and release the pigeon. It will bring a message to me that I should contact you right away. If you aren't interested, please accept the pigeon as my gift to you." He had a 100 percent response rate. Every single one of his potential customers released the pigeon. Most were amused and quite willing to speak with him.

CHAPTER 28

•

THE JOB SEARCH

Forget about the traditional approaches to job searching. They are woefully ineffective. Don't waste your time combing the literature for tips that will make your search fast and painless. It will not be painless. You will have to deal with rejection repeatedly. You may have to spend hundreds of hours over the course of several months engaged in activities that are outside your comfort zone. Don't panic. When I say hundreds of hours, I just mean that as a wake-up call. You may not have to spend that much time. The more focused and effective the job search method you use, the sooner you will have the job you want.

The ideal situation in any job search is to have several potential employers lined up at your door, making high-quality job offers. Does this scenario seem unrealistic? If it does, you have hampered your efforts before you are even out of the gate. Thousands of job seekers have used the practical job searching skills that make up the rest of this chapter to increase the effectiveness of their job search.

Job Search Effectiveness

The one most basic principle of job searching is that every step in the process is a form of personal marketing. The person who gets the job is often the one who does the best job of marketing himself or herself, rather than the person most qualified. To compete successfully, you have to understand why one person gets selected over another and design your campaign so that you will be that person. Each phase of the job search provides an opportunity for you to come up with a creative strategy to boost the effectiveness of your campaign.

Presenting yourself in the best possible light takes a lot more than the right clothes and a great résumé. Your success in the job search depends on the two axes of the chart on page 364. The horizontal axis is the Number of Transactions. Job search is a numbers game. If you speak with two hundred people who might turn out to be your next boss, you will have ten times the chance of landing one than if you talk with twenty. If you spend thirty hours a week engaged in an effective search, you will have ten times the chance of landing a job than if you do it three hours a week. Double the transactions, double your chances. It's that simple.

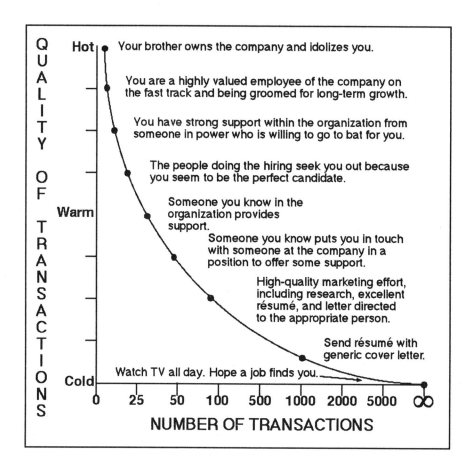

The other axis is the Quality of Transactions. "Hot," high-quality transactions all depend on creating and managing relationships with people who can hire you, will help you, or can recommend you as an exceptional candidate. At the top of the chart, you have a relative who owns the company and idolizes you. In this case, you have everything going for you: There is a strong sense of relatedness and the perception that you are the best candidate. If you are operating in this "blazing hot" zone, you probably will get a job offer with only one transaction. The higher you operate on the Quality scale, the fewer transactions it will take per job offer. Conversely, as you descend the Quality scale, the number of transactions needed to land a job multiplies at an enormous rate. Once you have descended into the pits of traditional job hunting, leaving it up to your résumé, you are now up to an average of at least one thousand transactions per offer. Before this method lands you the right job, you'll probably be ready to retire. Notice that increasing the quality of your marketing effort has a powerful effect on reducing the number of transactions necessary. One step up the quality ladder brings down the number of transactions to approximately one hundred. This chart makes an important point. In reality, though, things are not quite so simple. What counts as a transaction? Anything that leads to conversations with a decision maker who might be your next boss. A conversation with your potential boss counts as a megatransaction. Writing a letter is more of a minitransaction, but it's still a useful part of your search.

Turn Your Job Search into a Project

When you design your search as a project and make a commitment to achieve exceptional results, you will almost certainly have to do some things that don't come easily. Within the context of a project, your actions are driven by your commitment to results rather than by your feelings. Once you have made a definite commitment to a specific result, planned how to get there, and listed all the steps in their logical order, all you have to do is wake up each morning and do what your list tells you to do. Implementing a creative action plan is what gets you to your goal—not doing what is in your everyday bag of tricks. In job searching, the ends *do* justify the means, even if the means make you uncomfortable.

What you want to do is to raise your effectiveness as high as possible, reduce mistakes, and position yourself to succeed as soon as possible, with a minimum of difficulty and distress. Doing that means learning a lot about the art of designing and implementing your job search project.

Step 1: Write a Description of Exactly What You Are Looking for

How can you get there if you don't know where *there* is? If you don't have a clear picture, you have not completed your career design project. Go back a few steps. Keep working on career design until you are certain of your objective. Describe everything you can about what you will be doing. Name the specific job title. If you don't know what you're looking for, you won't know where to look.

Step 2: Define and List Your Target Market

"Target market" in advertising terms refers to people a company aims to turn into customers. In your job search, your target is the collection of specific organizations that might hire you to do what you want where you want to do it. You choose the organizations that make it to your target list. If you have no geographical requirements, your market could include the world. If you plan to stay in Seattle, get a map and draw a line around the geographical limits of your search. Within that area, you target the type(s) of companies you want: profit-making companies, nonprofits, or government agencies. What business or industry? What size organization? If you have other specifications, include those. Once you have identified organizations that might hire you, find out everything about them. What is it like to work there? How well do they do what they do? What's their history and likely future, their financials, their strengths and weaknesses? What are their main concerns? What kind of people do they prefer to hire? Do they seek the best candidate or take a hire-the-one-with-the-best-résumé approach? Who are the decision makers? What are they like? How could you get to them? Whom do you know who might have access to them? Do you have the qualifications they require? What's their hiring philosophy? How well do you fit it? This takes a lot of detective work. The main value of the Internet in job searching is this kind of research. Networking is, by far, the best way to find out what you need to know.

Prioritize your target organizations once you have developed your target list and done some research. You want to put the bulk of your effort into the most likely places you might work.

Step 3: Write an Effective, Targeted Résumé

Your résumé is not the history of your life. It is an ad and, like all good ads, it says, "If you buy this product, you will get these benefits." It tells them what you have done, but more than that, it communicates why you are the perfect person for the job. Check out the section of the Rockport Institute site (www.rockportinstitute .com) called "How to Write a Masterpiece of a Résumé." It is a guide to writing your résumé as a marketing document. Don't consider your résumé to be a major component of your job search. A great one won't land the job, but a poorly written résumé will hurt your chances.

Step 4: Plan Your Job Search Project

Plan your search campaign and the steps you will take. Make up a daily and weekly plan of action. What will you accomplish each day? Be specific: Instead of "Ask friends . . ." note exactly whom you will talk to about what. And your plan should include talking to people, not emailing them. How much time will you spend? How will you keep track?

Step 5: Get in Action. Concentrate on the Most Effective Activities

Most job seekers spend too little time each week on their job search. Once again, this is a numbers game. You get twice the results from twice the effort. When someone tells me that he has been searching for a job for more than a year, I ask how much time he has spent on his search in the last week. The person usually admits to spending very few hours. The few who have put in sufficient time have usually spent that time on low-payback activities. If possible, make finding your new job a full-time job. If you are not working full-time now, plan to work close to full-time on your search. If you are working, you still have to find a way to spend several hours each week on your search. If you don't, it might take forever. Since networking should be your main focus, the fact that you are at work all day may be less of a disadvantage than you think. One strategy is to arrange to work fewer hours each day or fewer days each week, take a lot of sick days, or spend your free time at your current job searching for a new one. Unless you are very financially secure, quitting your job to make time to job search may be counterproductive. Unemployed people tend to get a bit desperate and are therefore more likely to pick the wrong job. After giving so much thought to designing your future career, you do not want to con yourself into accepting the wrong job because you feel vulnerable.

> *I'm a great believer in luck, and I find that the harder I work,*
> *the more of it I have.*

> —THOMAS JEFFERSON

Target all your job search actions toward speaking with people who could make the decision to hire you. Anything else is a waste of time. Passive job search activities rarely produce results. Adding your résumé to Internet databases rarely produces job offers. Even if you have impeccable, perfect qualifications, background, and keywords, people hire other people, not data. People rarely hire the perfect candidate. They hire someone they like, someone who fits in, someone with enthusiasm who works hard and gets the job done. You can't communicate any of these qualities on a résumé. In person is always best. Telephone is next best. When I first moved to the Washington, DC, area more than thirty years ago, I befriended a woman whose brother was the head of a huge organization. We spent a couple of evenings at his place, enjoying the warm glow of good company, conversation, and fine scotch whiskey. The number two person in one of his two divisions had suddenly quit. He did not particularly like the potential candidates and asked if I would take the job. I refused. I was an unqualified and completely unlikely candidate. He offered me the job because he liked me.

If the decision maker is an avid sailor, your love of sailing will likely be a much more important factor in his or her choice than where you went to school or your history in the same job somewhere else. This may not fit the everyday wisdom floating around, but it is how people get hired. If you take this approach to your job search, you need to find ways to give decision makers a chance to know you, to discover your sterling qualities.

There are plenty of other things you need to do: plan your job search campaign, research organizations, learn more about decision makers, write letters, and keep track of your search project. The goal is always to come face-to-face with as many decision makers as possible. Each step in the job search prepares you, in one way or another, for the one thing vital to this process: talking directly with people who can offer you the job. Not just one or two people, but many of them. The more the better. Sort out which activities are most effective by asking yourself how directly they lead to talking with someone who could hire you. If speaking with them is the goal, then gaining access to them should be the goal of all other campaign activities. To talk directly with decision makers, find inside sources who work for the same organization—preferably people who know the decision maker and can recommend you, such as friends and colleagues of the decision maker, people she respects, people she likes. Networking is the secret. Make a game out of it. Play the networking game in this chapter, and play it to win. If you are an introvert, you still need to talk with decision makers. It may be less comfortable for you than for someone who is more extroverted, but you need to do what works, not what is comfortable.

Here is the biggest job search gold nugget: Forget about trying to land existing job offerings. Since decision makers prefer and most often hire someone they know or are in some way connected to, your best chance to land a job may exclude existing job openings. No extraordinary manager wants to hire through HR unless there is no other alternative. If you are unemployed and desperate to get a job to pay the mortgage now, you might resort to searching for existing openings, but avoid it if you can. The best way to land a job is to concentrate 100 percent of your effort on creating relationships with decision makers. Then, when a job that fits you becomes available, you are a likely candidate. The chart in this chapter shows why this works. When you place yourself higher up the Quality of Transactions axis, you are aiming closer to the target. This is not some slick, new strategy. It is pure common sense.

Step 6: Track Your Progress

Keep a record of your actions every day and every week: the number of decision makers you speak with, the number of inside sources you speak with, the number of letters you send, and so forth. Tracking your progress keeps you aware of your actions and reduces any tendency to slack off. Since many of the most effective job search activities are likely to be outside your comfort zone, your natural inclination may be to avoid discomfort by avoiding the more difficult things, especially if one or two didn't work out. Tracking your activities and progress also allows you to assess exactly what is working and what isn't, and then to adjust your actions to increase your effectiveness.

Step 7: Keep at It Until You Reach Your Goal

This seems obvious, but so often people give up because their inner survival system interprets the job search as a threat.

Rejection

Most of us job search from a point of view that saps our effectiveness from the very beginning. Take a few moments to imagine what it would be like if you were offered every job you applied for. Then the search would just be a matter of sorting: meeting with potential employers to clarify whether there would be a perfect fit between you and the job, negotiating benefits, and accepting the one you wanted. It would be like shopping for anything else. Remember how it felt to shop for something you were excited about: a special gift, a book, clothes, a car, a guitar, or whatever.

The difference between those mental exercises and the reality of a job search is the possibility of rejection. You probably won't be offered every job. Many organizations will probably reject you before you land the job you want. It happens to everyone, and no one likes it. Years ago, a woman I was dating broke up with me just as I was going to break up with her. I felt betrayed and rejected even though I got exactly what I wanted. My feelings made no sense, but that didn't reduce their impact one bit. Because feelings arise automatically, you cannot call up some inner force that makes them go away. If you search for a job, you will be rejected and feel rejected. The key is to transform the search by approaching it from the point of view that you are the cause, rather than the effect, of the stream of events. Instead of being a leaf in the wind, hoping to run across a job that wants you, become an active force of your intentions and seek to create multiple excellent job offers to choose from. Rejection is part of the process. And it works both ways.

Success is the ability to go from one failure
to another with no loss of enthusiasm.

—SIR WINSTON CHURCHILL

If you design and plan your job search carefully, taking into consideration all the realities, as well as the twists and turns of circumstance and fate, you can concentrate on effective action rather than reacting to discomfort and potential rejection. Remember that some of the most powerful criteria driving human behavior are: feeling safe, being right, feeling good, looking good, and avoiding pain. In a traditional job search, all of these criteria take a beating. You don't feel safe, because you are exposing yourself to rejection. You don't experience being right when you are not chosen for the team. You don't feel good about all the uncertainty inherent in the search. You don't look good to yourself if they don't want you. Many people unconsciously conduct their job search based on these criteria. A stiff and uncomfortable dance with rejection means that job searchers concentrate on avoiding having their toes stepped on rather than really swinging out. They say something like "I'm not comfortable calling people I don't know." That may be a perfectly valid statement, but when it rules their actions, they lose. When the commitment is to results, you may voice the same complaint, but you do so while dialing the phone. (Even better: Stop voicing the complaint. You don't need self-hypnosis of that variety.)

It's all a matter of perspective. If you were shopping for a special article of clothing, you might try on many candidates before you picked the final one. Are you rejecting the clothes that don't fit or look right, or are they rejecting you? Most job searchers feel more like clothes on the rack than someone shopping for the perfect fit. There is nothing personal about job search rejection. By turning your job search into an intentional project, a game of your own design, potential employers become the candidates instead of you. They become part of your movie, rather than you a bit player in theirs. One job search expert suggests using a piece of graph paper to deal with rejections. Start at the top. Make an *X* in one box every time you get rejected. He says that before you have filled the paper, you will have the job.

INQUIRY 31

The Networking Game

The purpose of the Networking Game is to create a powerfully effective network. You can use this method in many areas of your life. Early in your career design project, use it to learn more about careers you are considering. In this chapter, use it as a tool that leads to high-quality job offers. Remember that the two axes on the Job Search Effectiveness graph earlier in this chapter are Number of Transactions and Quality of Transactions. This game is concerned with generating some sizzling heat in the quality of your transactions. It transforms networking from something difficult and confusing into a game that many people find they enjoy. Even those who don't like the game can generate results out of networking in places they would never ordinarily go.

A typical job hunter's marketing methods focus efforts on transactions close to the bottom of the Quality of Transactions axis. Notice that job-hunting effectiveness depends directly on the warmth and strength of your relationships with people who can help you and on their degree of interest in and commitment to your cause. That automatically puts you in the Networking Game, whether you wish to play or not. Your style of play may be to say "I pass" every time your turn rolls around, but you are in the game nevertheless, like it or not. If you are willing to send out résumés only to job listings you found somewhere, or to use other cold approaches near the bottom of the effectiveness scale, your turn may come thousands of times before you win the game. Or, more likely, you will get desperate and accept a job you don't really want.

No matter how reluctant you are to market yourself by putting forth an effective networking campaign, that's what there is to do if you want to land a really excellent job. Since you are already in the game, you might as well play it consciously and play it to win. Ask people who are masters of networking. They will tell you that they do exactly the same things this game asks of you, with only minor stylistic differences. Although there are folks who are natural-born schmoozers with networking flowing in their veins, you can learn to play extremely well, so long as you don't let yourself get trampled by Yeahbut-type thoughts and feelings. It comes down to the same old question: Which is more important, safety and comfort, or getting results?

Finding Players for Your Networking Game

1. Make a list of people you know who could possibly help you. Write down absolutely everyone who might be able to help you directly or refer or recommend you to someone who could. No editing. Let's say, for example, that you want to break into documentary films. You should write down everyone you know except those who you are absolutely sure do not know anyone who *knows* anyone in documentary films. (In other words, someone who has said specifically, "I do not know anyone who knows anyone who works in documentary films. Plus, I wouldn't help you if you were the last person on earth.") Otherwise, include everyone. In building a network, it is better to be active, intentional, and inclusive than smart. Being too smart is deciding in advance that the guy who works in your next-door neighbor's garden doesn't know anything about filmmaking. For all you know, he also works in the garden of an award-winning independent-film producer-director. Include college and high school classmates, your family, friends of your family, your friends, your friends' friends, former professors, former employers, sports partners, neighbors, the parents of the kids on your kid's team. Obviously, decision makers and people who have access to them are ideal participants in

your network. When you are finished, you have created a network. You may think it doesn't look like much, but it is better than no network or a tiny one made up of your three best friends. After all, you've got to start somewhere.

2. Keep adding people to your network. Increase the quality of people participating in your network while at the same time keeping up the numbers. What you want is both quality and quantity. To make sure your network does not shrink to zero, you have to have a certain critical mass of participants. If you have only ten people to tap, your network is always face-to-face with extinction. It is the same with endangered species. If there are only a few individuals left of a particular animal, the first project is to initiate a breeding program to get the numbers up.

How many people did you write down as possible players? If you came up with more than, say, fifty people, you have a small but manageable network. If you came up with one hundred or more, you are in great shape. If you have fewer than fifty, you need to get to work building numbers right away. Later on, as you play the Networking Game, if your numbers fall below fifty, you know that your team is headed for extinction. The point here is to make sure your boat is not sinking.

3. Create a "super list" of stars in this field. The point of this list is to remind you to be unreasonable. One of the most effective networking methods is to increase the quality of participants as you build numbers. Seek out people who can help you in some substantial way. Even though your original network may have the neighbor's gardener as a possible supporter, the chances are pretty slim that the gardener will be of much help. The people who could be most helpful are the most central luminaries in the field you seek to enter. They are the people in the middle of the sphere of agreement we discussed in the previous chapter. These anointed ones could, with one phone call, get you the job you want.

Take a few minutes to create a list titled "Powerful People." Include people who are leaders in the field you want to enter, people who would be most able to help you, regardless of other factors. Though six degrees of separation is really just a trivia game, you may be only one or two steps away from the decision makers who could hire you.

If you want to break into films, put some big-time directors and a few other major players at the top. Think big. The people who inhabit the inner circles of the sphere of agreement will be the same people whose support would rate most highly on the Job Search Effectiveness chart. Why not spend your time going after their support? Next get the support of some of these major players. I haven't searched for a job for many years, but I use the same networking principle. When I had an ant problem years ago, I called E. O. Wilson, one of the great scientific minds of our time and the world's leading ant expert.

Does this sound completely out of the question? Imagine for a minute that the three people you love most have been kidnapped by the forces of evil. You find a note that says, "You have one month to get a great job in your new field, or else your loved one will be fed to the crocodiles." Wouldn't your reservations about contacting the most potentially helpful people disappear instantly? Wouldn't you do whatever it took to save them? Well, this is exactly the situation you are in right now, except it is the quality of your life that is at stake!

Even if what I have just said seems completely outrageous, the point is still valid. Put your networking energy into finding, contacting, getting to know, and generating agreement about how terrific you are with people as close to the inner circles as you possibly can. Communicating with the gods of your chosen field is never out of the question. If playing at a certain level of the inner circle seems impossibly huge, work at a level that is as far into the sphere of agreement as you can muster the courage to handle. Put your energy into getting to know the head of the department you want to work in, not the file clerk; the project director, not the most junior engineer. In making your participant list, you may discover that you don't know who could be most helpful, in which case it is time for some research.

People building a network often lament that they are not as fortunate as those folks who have a "good old boy" or "good old girl" network. These networks are mostly fantasy. A network is a network is a network. Your job is to create a hot network of support. Old school chums are just one kind of support you can call on. These old friends may be hot contacts. But there are many other ways to generate equivalent support. Someone you meet tomorrow may become a big player in your cause and do far more to help you than any old school friend.

The more creative you are, the better it will work out. Loosen up. Think of some outrageous ways to build your network. For example, if you still like the idea of an old boy or old girl network, get creative about it. Don't just rely on the people you knew at school. Every alumnus who went to your college whose heart is still beating is a potential source of support. Many of them would be willing to help when they find out that you both went to the same school. Seek out the alumni contact lists. Call the alumni office. Find out who works in the field you are entering. If they won't tell you, do further research. Get a complete list of alumni.

Find out who is the chair of the reunion committee for each class. Call each of them. They will know who is doing what or who would know the answers to your inquiries. You are definitely not going to feel like calling one hundred fellow alums you have never spoken to before. But, as they say, feel the fear and do it anyway. Practice with a friend or in front of a mirror until you reduce the butterflies to a manageable level.

4. Rate your team of supporters. Take a look at the quality of your network. Rate each person on the list. Remember that this is the Networking Game. In all games, some things have more value than others. In Monopoly, hotels rate more than houses. Don't rate people based on your feelings but on these criteria: one star, two stars, or three stars.

   A *three-star* supporter. Some three-star supporters may be people with extraordinary resources they are willing to provide to help you reach your goal. They could be decision makers in the field you want to enter, or trusted friends or colleagues of a targeted decision maker. They could be people who care about your success and have access to some extraordinary asset, such as their own appropriate network of contacts, knowledge of the field you want to enter, or a television show or popular website that would feature you. They could be in the inner circle of your intended field. Also include everyone with a high level of interest in your success, people who will work in your favor without your having to prod them and without constant management. They will champion your cause. They are your most solid, proactive supporters. These most valuable people do not necessarily have contacts or other special access. Some three-star participants may just be people who love you to death and will stand for you, support you to be your best, act as a sounding board or a shoulder to cry on. Your father, mother, husband, wife, or best friends could already be three-star supporters.

   Two-star supporters are people with a personal interest in you. They will go to bat for you or perhaps spend some time helping, but they need active management to remain a useful resource. Two-stars need a phone call or written communication every couple of weeks. Otherwise they will forget about your job search.

   A *one-star* is someone who, for one reason or another, is a potentially useful member of your network but is not participating at the level of the two- and three-star people. Most people have a network of support that consists almost entirely of one-star contacts: old college buddies who might answer some questions about their organizations, give you some names of useful people to contact, or go to bat for you in a limited way. The difference between a one-star and a two-star is that the two-star will go further for you, put more energy into helping you, make more phone calls, strongly recommend you to a decision maker, or provide ongoing personal support or coaching.

Then there are the *unborn*, people who are not yet playing in your network. Each represents a spark of possibility not yet tapped. They are people you have not yet contacted and, so far, are not a part of your network. There are approximately eight billion of them. When someone tells me he doesn't know anyone who might be a useful contact, I think of those eight billion. There is never "no one" out there. Either you don't know how to stir up a relationship with them, don't know how to find appropriate people, or you are a little shy about meeting them.

The final category is the *dead*. You would never contact these people. You are sure they would not help you. They are people you have killed off as potential supporters for one reason or another. Most of them are dead only in your imagination. They are just people you are unwilling to contact. Most are actually members of the ranks of the unborn. People tend to bury many of their potential supporters in unmarked graves because they fear rejection. There is no reason you cannot ask people you used to date or work with for some support. There is no reason you should not call the film producer whose car you totaled or the former boss who fired you. There is no reason you cannot find a way to contact and get support from the most powerful people in the field you want to get into—except for fear of rejection. The worst they can do is say no.

5. Play the game by making requests. You win the Networking Game by making requests of the people in your network that wind up with your having several excellent job offers. Most people network in a very timid way. When they have a contact in a powerful position in the organization they wish to work for, they waste this influential contact by asking them for information. You don't want information. You want a job! Requests are one of the most powerful tools you have to move your life forward. "Will you marry me?" is a request. Applications to colleges as well as cover letters sent along with your résumé are all requests. Designing requests is a learned skill. Most people do not realize the power of designing and communicating potent requests. Each of us has a built-in, internal, automatic request designer. Our programming comes up with safe, comfortable, reasonable requests. When you design a request, ask yourself, "What do I really want? If I had no qualms at all, what would I ask of this person?" "If I was sure this person would say yes, what would I ask for?"

The only reason people avoid making more outrageous requests is fear of rejection. "I don't want to impose on people," "I don't want to be pushy," "I'm not that kind of person," "I would feel uncomfortable." "I don't want to make them uncomfortable." All of these thoughts are just Yeahbuts provided to you by your friendly internal survival system, to avoid the near-death experience of rejection. We tend to take "no" personally. If you make a big request of someone and he says no, it doesn't mean you are unworthy. It just means he declines. Period. A good networker will then make another, smaller request. If you remove all the significance from the process of making requests, here's what happens:

You make a request. The person you ask does one of three things. She agrees to fulfill your request, she says no, or she makes a counteroffer. Most people fold their cards when they get a no. Don't do it. Make a smaller request instead.

Request:	"Will you be my love slave forever?"
Reply:	"Not a chance."
Request:	"How about just for tonight?"
Reply:	"Nope."
Request:	"Want to go have a cup of coffee together?"
Reply:	"Okay, let's do it!"

The secret of getting favorable responses to your requests is the ability to create a sense of relatedness. The more related you and the other person become, the more likely he or she is to fulfill your requests. If you ask random people on the street to give you $100, you will get few takers. If you ask your best friend, he or she would not refuse. Relatedness is not a function of time previously spent together. You and your boss may have inhabited the same office for the last ten years yet have no real relatedness. On the other hand, some people create relatedness almost instantly. Even though many of the people who do this naturally are expressing an innate talent, you can learn to do it too. The best way to create relatedness is to communicate with other people and assume relatedness. Share yourself with them. Let them find out who you are. Lighten up. Be friendly, personal. Be more interested than interesting. Listen more than talk. Really listen. Don't pretend. You don't need to impress them. Instead let them get to know you. Even though they may expect a certain businesslike formality, break through it as quickly as you can.

When you communicate with people you do not know, or know well, your real objective is to create a relationship, a friendship, a mutual concern. Only within a state of relatedness will people be willing to go out of their way for you. There is no way you can fake it. You need to start looking at relatedness in a new way, as a state that can be created and built upon rather than something that just develops by itself over time. Since the basis for relatedness is intimacy and generosity, they are what you have to offer the other person. Don't be a taker. The way to be a great networker is to be a willing and generous participant in other people's lives and networks. If you are always willing to give more than you get and don't give in to your Yeahbuts, you will turn yourself into a spectacular networker.

As a networker, you are in the relationship business. These people do not need you, and they will help you only to the extent that they experience being related with you. If this "creating relatedness" is all a new concept to you, go out and practice creating relationships with everyone you meet for the next week. When you buy a pack of gum, create a state of relatedness with the clerk. Find common ground with him. Acknowledge him. Assume the best. Call him by name. Communicate with enthusiasm. Offer him a stick of gum. When the cop stops you for speeding, create a friendship instead of arguing.

Before you begin playing the Networking Game actively, get clear exactly what you want the people in your network to do for you. Sit down and brainstorm a list of ideas for possible outcomes. At one end of the spectrum, you could ask them to hire you or become your champion and strongly advocate your candidacy to a decision maker. At the other end, you could ask them for a little information on what they do in their job. There are many requests you could make somewhere between the two polar ends of the spectrum. Before you pick up the phone or meet with someone, have a definite goal for the call in mind. Make each conversation a powerful expression of playing the Networking Game. Make sure you know what you want. Make sure you ask for what you want. One request to make of every single person you contact is "Who do you know who might . . . ?" Always work on building your network. After each transaction, rate the conversation. What worked? What didn't work? How can you improve next time?

Chess players guard their most powerful pieces carefully. If they have to put a piece in danger, they sometimes sacrifice a pawn. You want to do the same thing. Marshall your forces strategically. Make use of the people in your network appropriately. Reserve the most useful participants until it is time to use them to maximum benefit. Otherwise you will waste them on trivia. If your best friend's brother is the decision maker at an organization where you want to work, do not call him while you are doing basic information gathering. Don't let him see you as a know-nothing outsider. Wait until you have thoroughly mastered everything you need to handle to enter your new field. Wait until you are extremely knowledge-able and sure of yourself. Then make a big request. Ask him to champion your cause; to go to bat for you.

6. Manage your network. Manage your network by creating more one-star participants in your game from the endless sea of the unborn. At the same time, work on transforming one-star participants into two-star and three-star players. It is a little like increasing the number of houses you own in Monopoly, heading toward owning hotels. You raise the number of stars of a participant in your network by generating an upgraded commitment to your success in finding that great job. Commitment isn't lip service. It is dedication and action.

When you begin the game, your network may be small and consist mostly of one-star participants. Still, I suggest that you play the game as if you were in the Olympics. If the neighbor's gardener is not likely to be able to help you, why even ask him? Because you never know: He might prove helpful. Work with the resources you have available. Second, and most importantly, you are learning to play a game where you must do what is needed, not what you feel like doing. You want to get to the point where you do what is next on your list wholeheartedly rather than listen to the endless chorus of internal Yeahbuts.

CHAPTER 29

•

ROCKPORT TYPE AND
TALENT INDICATOR

Note: This chapter depends on your having finished all three of these chapters: 15, "Temperament and Personality"; 16, "Core Personality"; and 17, "Natural Talents." It consists of charts that list careers that may fit the combination of your personality type and some of your talents. It combines your personality type with whether you are more Maestro/Tribal and with the spatial/nonspatial scale. For example, if you are an ENFJ, it has a list of careers that may fit Maestro ENFJs and another for Tribal ENFJs. Then it takes it a step further and divides those lists into careers that fit spatial, tangible, and nonspatial people. So if you are a spatial Maestro ENFJ, you will find a list of careers that might be a good fit for you.

It works only if you know your personality type and whether you are Maestro or Tribal. And it works best if you know where you fit on the spatial/nonspatial scale. If you aren't sure, I suggest that you get absolutely sure about your personality and natural talents and then come back to this chapter.

The best way to use these lists is to check out the list of careers that fit your type and talents. Notice what the careers have in common. Notice which ones are attractive to you and ask yourself why. Notice which ones are not attractive to you and what it is about them that makes them so. The intent is to help you find good clues. For example, if you notice that the careers in your category that appeal to you involve solving abstract puzzles or using your hands, you might have found a powerful clue. This also might provide some good ideas for your Career Ideas list.

Very important note: The following career lists are no more than suggestions to help you understand yourself. Do not take any of this too literally. The goal is to give you ideas, not a list to pick from. More than one type and talent profile fits each of these careers. Some fit several profiles. You may fit careers that are suggested for other types. You may not be attracted to any of the careers listed for your combination. Study the whole set of careers for your personality type. For example, if you are a Maestro spatial ENTP but don't like the careers suggested in the spatial column for your type, see what you find interesting in the Maestro tangible ENTP column. Get to know what fits people somewhat like you. You may be attracted to careers that fit combinations closely connected to your own. For example, a Maestro ENTP may feel an attraction to some Tribal ENTP careers.

Maestro ENFP

Nonspatial	Tangible	Spatial
actor: theater	*adventure education: program designer, instructor*	*alternative medicine practitioner*
....	*alternative therapist: biofeedback, virtual reality therapy*	*primatologist*
coach: personal growth, career change, life planning	....	*evolutionary biologist, sociobiologist*
consultant: communications, education, HR	*cognitive scientist: personality, psychobiology*	*film director: independent production*
drama coach	*documentary filmmaker*	*fine artist*
law: entertainment, media	....	*wilderness skills instructor*
motivational speaker, self-help seminar leader	*photojournalist*	*life sciences professor*
organizational development consultant	*professor: humanities, film, arts*	*neuropsychologist*
psychologist: relationship, spiritual, career	*psychologist: sports psychology*	*performing arts: dance instructor*
social entrepreneur	*theater director*	*physician: family, psychiatry, preventive*

social scientist: emphasis on teaching	therapist: neurolinguistic programming (NLP)	therapeutic humorist
....	....	yoga and meditation instructor

Tribal ENFP

Nonspatial	Tangible	Spatial
admissions counselor: college	buyer: educational products, arts, books, music	art therapist
activist: education reform, health care reform, peace	film producer: feature films	athletic coach
agent for actors, artists, writers	internal consultant: HR, organization development	dance/movement therapist
clergy in low-dogma faiths	music therapist	design arts (team leader): set design, new urbanism
counselor: career center staff, outplacement firm	nonprofit director: public health, international development	film director: Hollywood production
diplomat: senior level	nurse: counseling, psychiatric	neurotherapist
journalist: human interest	passenger service representative	nurse: midwifery, psychiatric
fund-raiser	political campaign manager	physician assistant: family practice, preventive
lobbyist: social causes	recreation leader	teacher: spatial arts, computer graphics, dance
marketing/ communications director	recreation therapist	team leader: life sciences, technology projects
marketing research	religious activities director	trainer: technology fields, sciences, engineering

meeting facilitator	*teacher: high school social studies, history, English*	....
nonprofit director: social issues, arts/ culture advocacy	*trainer: applied social sciences, counseling, education*	....
ombudsman: corporations, universities, government agencies	....	....
public relations director	....	....
school psychologist	....	....
social marketer	....	....
training and development: program designer, trainer	....	....

Maestro INFP

Nonspatial	Tangible	Spatial
actor	*cognitive scientist: personality, psychobiology*	*alternative medicine practitioner: naturopath, bodywork*
attorney: social change, international human rights	*documentary filmmaker*	*archaeologist*
coach: career, life, personal growth	*evolutionary biologist*	*architectural historian*
consultant: education, organizational behavior	*fine artist: impressionist, abstract*	*choreographer: dance, performing arts*
counselor: relationship, spiritual, career change	*forensic psychologist*	*dancer: jazz, improvisational*
creative writer: poet, novelist, playwright	*historian: history of science*	*engineer: human-computer interaction, ergonomics*

cultural anthropologist, ethnographer

curriculum designer

drama coach

economist: family, public, labor, health, education

historian: social, art

humanities scholar

independent scholar: social sciences, humanities

law professor: psychology of human emotions

linguist

mythologist

nonfiction writer: self-help, personal growth

professor: humanities, social sciences

psychology: evolutionary, educational, organizational

researcher: social sciences, humanities

social entrepreneur

social scientist: sociology, social policy, regional studies

songwriter/musician

life scientist: wildlife biology, sociobiology

photojournalist

psychologist

science journalist

software designer: educational application

software developer: graphical user interface

survey methodologist

fine artist: sculpture

industrial designer

music video filmmaker

performer, gymnast, acting

physical anthropologist

physician: psychiatrist, family, holistic

primatologist

screenwriter: independent feature

set designer

somatic psychologist

symphony conductor

yoga and meditation instructor

Tribal INFP

Nonspatial	Tangible	Spatial
activist	commercial arts: greeting card designer, advertising	architect: green design, monuments, memorials
advertising: copywriter, web content writer	foreign service officer: US State Department	artist: 3-D animation, spatial arts
campaign strategist	human-computer interface designer	athletic coach (mental and physical game)
clergy in low-dogma faiths	human factors engineer	design artist: feng shui, interior design, historic parks
fiction writer: historical novels, memoirs, romance	IT: database designer, graphical user interface	screenwriter: educational, sitcom, TV, Hollywood
human resources: training specialist, career coaching	military officer: human intelligence, psychology ops	set design: theater, film, costume
journalist: editor, staff writer, freelance	nurse: psych, counseling	urban planning: new urbanism designer
librarian: specialized in social sciences, arts, humanities		video game designer
mediator		website designer: graphic design and information architecture
nonprofit researcher: societal issues		
speechwriter: politics		
training and development: program designer, trainer		

Maestro ENFJ

Nonspatial	Tangible	Spatial
career coach	art historian: emphasis on teaching	alternative medicine practitioner
communications consultant: meeting facilitator	art therapist	athletic coach: college level
communications director	documentary filmmaker	film director: independent production
consultant: HR, training program design specialist	music therapist: neurobiological disorders	naturopath
drama coach	professor: life sciences, medicine	neurotherapist
humanities professor	sports psychologist	physician: family, holistic, preventive
law: mental health, race relations, disability rights	....	professor, instructor: architecture and design
life coach: personal development, relationships	....	yoga instructor
psychologist	....	....
public speaker: social causes	....	....
social sciences professor	....	....
social work counselor: addiction disorders	....	....
trainer: leadership development, team building	....	....

Tribal ENFJ

Nonspatial	Tangible	Spatial
administrator: health care, adult education	camp director	athletic coach: high school level
admissions counselor: college	nurse manager	design arts manager
advertising account executive	outplacement counselor	film director: Hollywood production
agent for actors, artists, writers	producer: films, TV programs, television promotions	military officer: broadcasting director
association executive	speech pathologist	physician assistant
clergy	supervisor, manager, team leader	urban planning: project manager
counselor: career, public health, student advisor	website producer	....
dean, university president	teacher: visual arts, graphic arts	....
diplomat: senior level	information architect: project manager	....
fund-raiser	....	....
human resources director	....	....
marketing director	....	....
mediator	....	....
newscaster: human interest	....	....

nonprofit director: social causes, arts promotion	....	....
political consultant: campaign strategist	....	....
politician: state senator, US senator	....	....
public relations	....	....
recruiter	....	....
sales manager	....	....
teacher: high school English, history, music	....	....

Maestro INFJ

Nonspatial	Tangible	Spatial
coach: career, life, personal growth	art appraiser	acupuncturist
consultant: education, human resources	art historian	alternative medicine practitioner: naturopath
counselor: relationship, spiritual, career	composer: film scores	archaeologist
drama coach	information science specialist	architectural historian
entrepreneur: education- and human-development-related	IT: database designer	artist: sculptor
humanities scholar: history, literature, musicology	playwright	challenge course designer: outdoor adventure

law professor

training and development: program designer, presenter

computer game designer

lawyer: art, civil, employment, comparative family law

website design: information architect

engineer: human-computer interface, ergonomics

nonprofit: director of writing and research

....

geographer: economic, political, cultural, historical

organizational behavior and development specialist

....

holistic therapist: mind-body connection

politician: US senator

....

organic farmer: environmental educator

psychologist/therapist: narrative therapy, Neuro-Linguistic Programming

....

screenwriter: feature-length screenplay

researcher: political think tank

....

symphony conductor

social scientist

....

....

social work: researcher, program development

....

....

songwriter/musician

....

....

writer: biographer

....

....

Tribal INFJ

Nonspatial	Tangible	Spatial
activist	commercial artist: graphic arts, advertising	architect: sustainable development, green
advertising: copywriter, website content writer	film editor	design arts: designer of sets, monuments, historic parks

clergy in low-dogma faiths

director: education or social service nonprofit

editor: book, magazine, newspaper journalist

grant writer

human resources: career planning and leadership trainer

meeting facilitator, mediator

paralegal: researcher, law librarian

public policy analyst

public relations/ communications: writer, researcher

researcher/writer: advocacy, nonprofit, policy think tank

social marketer

speechwriter

strategic planner

TV sitcom writer

résumé writer

human-computer interface designer

human factors engineer

information architect

jury consultant

marketing research analyst

nurse: psych, counseling, midwife

physician: psychiatrist, family, preventive

reference librarian: college library

script reader: film

exhibit designer: museum, living history exhibits

industrial design artist

physician assistant: psychiatric, preventive

screenwriter: TV, sitcom

software developer: graphical user interface

urban planning: landscap architect

Maestro ENTP

Nonspatial	Tangible	Spatial
academic professor: law, social sciences, public policy	academic professor: mathematics, computer science	architecture: sustainable development consultant
consultant: change management, social change projects	consultant: MIS, telecommunications, business systems	academic professor: engineering, physical and life sciences
foreign service officer: US State Department	documentary filmmaker	consultant: engineering, medicine, science applications
humanities scholar	entrepreneur: new technologies, scientific research	ecologist
investment broker	epidemiologist	evolutionary scientist
investment fund manager: emerging markets	executive coach	inventor
lawyer: constitutional, intellectual property	math tutor: coach high schoolers how to pass SATs	life and physical scientist: chief researcher
political pundit, columnist	social entrepreneur	neuropsychologist, neuroscience, neurology
political scientist		physician: medical scientist, preventive medicine
social critic		software and engineering design: technical team leader
social policy researcher: think tank, nonprofit		space exploration: NASA scientist
social scientist: emphasis on teaching		
venture capitalist		

Tribal ENTP

Nonspatial	Tangible	Spatial
agent: literary, film	*advertising, creative director*	*architect: marketing role, educator*
campaign strategist	*business systems analyst*	*construction manager*
journalist: investigative reporter	*CEO: high-tech companies*	*design engineer: research and development (all fields)*
lobbyist	*corporate executive: special-projects developer*	*industrial designer: new-product innovation*
manager: leading-edge company	*design arts: project manager*	*instructor/professor: medicine, science, engineering*
marketer	*film producer*	*physician assistant: neurology, cardiology*
political analyst	*intelligence agent: US homeland security, Central Intelligence Agency, Federal Bureau of Investigation*	*project manager: physical sciences, engineering*
politician: US senator, US congressman, US president	*intelligence analyst: CIA, FBI, Defense Intelligence Agency, National Security Agency, Drug Enforcement Administration*	*real estate developer: green buildings* ....
public relations publicist	*military officer: counterintelligence, interrogator*	*science/math teacher: high school AP courses*
strategic planner	....	....

Maestro INTP

Nonspatial	Tangible	Spatial
comedian: comedy writer, performer	artificial intelligence research	archaeologist
cultural anthropologist	bioinformatics	biologist: all subspecialties
economist: international, development, game theory	computer programmer	biomedical engineering: virtual-reality engineer
historian: prehistory, ancient, world	documentary filmmaker	chemist: all subspecialties
independent scholar: social sciences, humanities	economist: environmental and natural resource	computer scientist
judge: federal courts and Supreme Court	epidemiologist	design engineer: research and development (all fields)
law: constitutional, intellectual property	evolutionary scientist: sociobiology	ecologist: global warming research
linguistic scientist	fiction writer: sci-fi, horror, screenwriter	film: special effects and animation artist
mathematician: theoretical, operations research	fine artist	forensic artist
musician: jazz/classical guitarist, violinist, pianist	law: international environmental law	forensic paleontologist ....
musicologist	political cartoonist	forensic scientist: biochemist, geneticist
nonfiction writer: sciences, politics, technology	psychologist: psychometrics, cognitive science	geneticist
philosopher	researcher: computer science, new technology	inventor

political pundit, columnist	*social entrepreneur: new technologies*	*lawyer: patent*
political scientist		*life and physical scientist: emphasis on research*
psychiatrist	....	*nanotechnology scientist*
researcher: social sciences	....	*neuroscientist, neuropsychologist*
social critic	....	*optical engineer: lasers, holography*
social policy researcher: think tank, nonprofit	....	*physician: medical scientist, academic research*
social sciences professor	....	*physicist: all subspecialties*
sociologist	....	*researcher: life science, physical science*
statistician	....	*robotics research*
		software architect, designer, developer
....	....	*surgeon: plastics, neurology, cardiology*

Tribal INTP

Nonspatial	Tangible	Spatial
editor: social sciences, public health, public policy	*advertising artist*	*architect: green technologies, new urbanism*
financial analyst	*environmental planner*	*industrial designer*
grant writer	*intelligence agent: US homeland security, CIA, FBI*	*interior design, interior planner*
investment analyst: mutual fund, stock/ bond analyst	*intelligence analyst: CIA, FBI, DIA, NSA, DEA*	*physician assistant: surgery, oncology, neurology*

journalist: media criticism, politics, science, health

military officer: counterintelligence, interrogator

urban designer

law: researcher, district attorney, military lawyer (JAG)

technical writer

video game animator

marketing researcher

urban planner

yacht and marine designer

public policy: researcher, analyst

strategic planner

Maestro ENTJ

Nonspatial	Tangible	Spatial
college professor: economics, law, political science	*college professor: IT, MIS, computer science*	*architect: consultant*
credit investigator	*consultant: management, business systems, IT, MIS*	*college professor: engineering, physical sciences*
economic consultant	*engineering executive*	*computer security specialist*
Federal Reserve: economic analyst, board member	*entrepreneur*	*engineering consultant*
financial planner	*epidemiologist*	*medicine: environmental, virology, immunology*
judge: federal courts and Supreme Court	*executive coach*	*sales rep: pharmaceutical, medical equipment*
law: ethics, health policy, trial	....	....
lobbyist	....	....
military officer: lawyer, judge	....	....

mortgage banker	....	....
Securities and Exchange Commission analyst	....	....
stockbroker	....	....
strategic planner	....	....

Tribal ENTJ

Nonspatial	Tangible	Spatial
administrator: college dean, university president	*business manager: high-tech, engineering*	*architect: project manager*
corporate leadership: CEO, board of directors	*business systems analyst*	*athletic coach*
journalist: reporter	*chief information officer (CIO)*	*computer systems analyst*
manager: sales, marketing	*federal agency director: Federal Emergency Management Agency, Environmental Protection Agency, Food and Drug Administration, Federal Communications Commission*	*construction manager*
mutual fund manager	*general manager, senior level*	*design engineer: technical team leader*
mutual fund trader	*intelligence agent: US homeland security, CIA, FBI*	*manufacturing executive*
nonprofit: director, program designer	*intelligence analyst: CIA, FBI, DIA, NSA, DEA*	*patent agent, attorney*
politician: US president, US senator	*law: public defender, district attorney*	*project manager: engineering, software, IT*

project team leader	*sales: high-tech*	*shop foreman: auto repair service*
public policy analyst	....	*US foreign service: medical officer*
sales: banking, securities	....	*US surgeon general*

Maestro INTJ

Nonspatial	Tangible	Spatial
curriculum designer	*artificial intelligence scientist*	*acoustic engineer: concert hall, recording studio designer*
economist: financial, business, history of economics	*bioinformatics expert*	*biologist: all subspecialties*
forensic accounting expert	*computer programmer: software development consultant*	*biomedical engineer*
historian	*consultant: business, information technology*	*chemist: all subspecialties*
journalist: technology, political columnist	*forensic psychiatry*	*computer forensics specialist*
judge: federal courts and Supreme Court	*information technology: network and database design*	*computer hardware engineer*
law professor	*lawyer: housing, criminal, health care, public health*	*computer security specialist*
law: constitutional, immigration, international finance	*mathematician: applied problem solving*	*design engineer: all fields*
musicologist	*psychologist: research, psychometrics, cognitive science*	*economist: urban and rural, agricultural, development*

political science professor	science writer	environmental engineer
psychiatrist	....	forensic scientist: biochemist, geneticist
social policy researcher: think tank, nonprofit	....	genetic engineer
sociologist	....	inventor
statistician	....	lawyer: patent, antitrust, technology, land use, cyberlaw
....	....	pharmacologist
....	....	physician: neurology, cardiology, facial reconstruction
....	....	physicist: all subspecialties
....	....	robotics engineer
....	....	software architect, designer, developer

Tribal INTJ

Nonspatial	Tangible	Spatial
CEO, high-tech	computer programmer: banking, financial applications	architect ....
financial analyst	electronics engineer, technician	computer programmer: engineering, manufacturing applications
grant writer	environmental planner	computer systems analyst
investment analyst: mutual fund, stock/ bond analyst	intelligence analyst: CIA, FBI, DIA, NSA	industrial designer

journalist: editor, staff writer	lawyer: public defender	landscape architect
loan officer: banking, mortgage, small business	military enlisted: electronic technician	patent agent, examiner
marketing researcher	urban planner	physician assistant: cardiovascular surgery
military officer: lawyer, judge	....	structural engineer
public policy analyst	....	transportation planner
SEC analyst	....	urban designer
strategic planner	....	....

Maestro ESFP

Nonspatial	Tangible	Spatial
actor	animal trainer, pet psychologist	art appraiser
comedian	athlete	athlete: gymnast
entrepreneur: specialty products and services	botanist	chiropractor
language professor	Outward Bound instructor	cinematographer
music teacher	public health scientist	dance instructor, choreographer
pharmaceutical sales representative	recreational therapist	dermatologist
singer, performer	restaurant manager, host, hostess	makeup artist
social worker: young adults, teens at risk	sports psychologist	midwife

	wellness and fitness nutrition expert	*naturopathic doctor*
	wine steward, sommelier	*sports medicine practitioner wildlife biologist*

Tribal ESFP

Nonspatial	Tangible	Spatial
advertising account executive	*B and B owner, manager*	*athletic coach*
communications director: associations, nonprofits	*entrepreneur: restaurant, hospitality, retail*	*cheerleader*
diplomat	*health promotion manager*	*chef*
foundation manager	*health spa manager*	*firefighter*
fund-raiser	*merchandiser, product buyer*	
marketing director	*personal shopper, image consultant*	*gym teacher*
mediator	*personal trainer*	*hairstylist*
military officer: public affairs officer, broadcast manager	*police officer*	*kindergarten teacher*
newscaster	*politician: city council, mayor*	*nurse: emergency, sexual assault forensics*
press secretary	*sales rep: manufacturers, distributors, service providers*	*paramedic*
producer/promoter: film, TV	*salesperson: fashion, housewares*	*physical therapist*
public relations,	*teacher: elementary*	*US foreign service: health*

public affairs specialist

salesperson

talk show host: travel, food, entertainment

school, science, physical ed

travel: agent, tour guide, TV program host

website producer

practitioner

Maestro ISFP

Nonspatial	Tangible	Spatial
actor	*animator: film, video games, cartoons*	*animal rescue officer*
animal trainer, pet psychologist	*art therapist*	*art and antiques appraiser*
entertainer	*bodybuilder*	*art conservator*
meditation and relaxation teacher	*botanist*	*artisan, craftsman*
music teacher	*cartoonist*	*athlete*
musician, performer, singer	*cheese maker*	*baker, cake maker*
occupational/vocational counselor	*color specialist*	*chef*
social work: teens at risk, inmate rehab	*dietitian*	*cinematographer*
songwriter	*fashion model*	*dancer, ballerina, figure skater, gymnast*
special education tutor	*fitness trainer*	*fine artist: portrait, mural, landscape, sculpture*
training and development specialist	*graphic artist, multimedia specialist*	*forester*
travel writer	*nutritionist: clinical specialist*	*gardener, plant nursery, landscaper*

	painter: ornaments, fine wood, home interiors	luthier: instrument maker/repairer
....	pastry chef	makeup artist
....	perfumer	massage therapist: sport, Rolfing
....	photographer: fashion, nature, advertising, travel	military: plastic surgeon, dietitian, counselor
....	poet	naturopathic doctor, holistic medicine
....	public health scientist	performer, gymnast, acrobat
....	wildlife biologist: nature photographer, conservationist	performing arts medicine: musician injuries
....	wine and cheese shop owner	physician: plastic surgeon, audiologist, emergency, sports MD
....	wine steward, sommelier	potter, glassblower, stained glass maker
....	yoga instructor	restoration specialist: historical homes and buildings
....	....	stonemason, woodworker
....	....	veterinarian

Tribal ISFP

Nonspatial	Tangible	Spatial
communications expert: PR, public affairs, public outreach	advertising artist: photography, 2-D art	advertising artist: 3-D graphics

customer service representative	bartender, waiter/waitress	aerobics instructor
editor	child care provider: day care center	bodywork: massage, Rolfing, etc.
employment counselor	children's book writer, artist	drafting technician: computer-aided design
guidance counselor	entrepreneur: retail, personal services, B and B owner	dressmaker: wedding, special occasions
interpreter	fashion buyer, sales	firefighter
language teacher	interior decorator	hairstylist
matchmaker: dating service	personal assistant	interior designer
mediator	police officer	jewelry designer
recruiter, staffing advisor	product buyer	landscape architect
student advisor, admissions counselor	secret shopper	nurse: emergency, psych, first-assist
teacher: preschool, K–12, ESL	US foreign service: health practitioner	set designer, costume designer, film location scout

Maestro ESFJ

Nonspatial	Tangible	Spatial
genetic counselor	antiques dealer	animal rescue officer
hospice counselor	caterer	chiropractor
job counselor: unemployment office	food service specialist	medical technologist: allied health
language professor	health educator	personal trainer
religious educator	nutritionist	physician: gynecologist, obstetrician, pediatrician

social work counselor: mental health, drug rehab	recreation therapist	physician: palliative care, pain management, geriatrics
special education teacher	sales rep: manufacturers, distributors, service providers	physician's assistant
trainer: customer service, sales	shopkeeper: specialty items	space planner: retail, grocery, commercial
weight management counselor	special event designer	sports physician
....	....	veterinarian (primary care)

Tribal ESFJ

Nonspatial	Tangible	Spatial
account executive: sales, marketing	assisted-living attendant	athletic coach
administrator: social services, public health	bartender, host/hostess, waiter/waitress	dental hygienist
advertising sales: hospitality, human resources, health	funeral home director	engineering manager
concierge	grocery store manager	food service manager
customer care liaison	hospitality manager: hotel, restaurant, innkeeper, health spa	general contractor
diplomat	interior decorator	hairstylist
health care administrator	nurse manager	health club manager
human resources manager	office manager	hospitality manager: restaurant, hotel, B and B, resort

marketing manager	*personal shopper*	*household/holiday crafts maker*
military: public affairs officer, personnel manager, recruiter	*politician: city mayor, municipal government council*	*nurse: gerontology, midwife, pediatric*
news reporter, broadcaster	*real estate agent*	*occupational therapist*
personal secretary	*retail management*	*physical therapist: recreational, pediatric*
receptionist	*sales engineer*	*police officer*
recruiter	*teacher: preschool, kindergarten, elementary, ESL*	*property manager*
retail sales	*travel agent, planner*	*window display designer: retail*
sales party host: cookware, cosmetics, jewelry	*wedding planner*	
school principal		

Maestro ISFJ

Nonspatial	Tangible	Spatial
counselor: drug rehab, hospice, geriatric, crisis hotline	*animal trainer*	*acupuncturist*
language professor	*art and antiques appraiser*	*animal rescue officer*
law: family, divorce, human resources, tort, and accident	*art therapist*	*art restoration specialist*
librarian: information science specialist	*baker*	*artisan, craftsman*

mediator	botanist	chef
meditation teacher	calligrapher	curator, conservator
religious educator, scholar	cheese maker	dentist: orthodontics, endodontics
special education tutor	color specialist	food scientist
training and development specialist	entrepreneur: retail, personal services, B and B owner	forester
....	gardener	furniture maker
....	nutritionist: clinical specialist	industrial designer
....	organic farmer	instrument maker
....	perfumer	medical technologist: allied health technician
....	sports psychologist	midwife
....	technical sales support	military officer: plastic surgeon, dietitian
....	trainer: hardware/ software technologies	nurse: research
....	wine and cheese shop owner	optometrist
		pastry chef
....	....	physician: family practice, pediatrician, internist

Tribal ISFJ

Nonspatial	Tangible	Spatial
administrative assistant, secretary	child care provider: day care center	anesthesiologist
customer service representative	children's book writer	dental hygienist

editor	clinical dietitian: home health, rehab facility	fashion designer
educational administrator	dietetic technician	firefighter
guidance counselor	health service worker	graphic artist, multimedia specialist
human resources administrator, generalist	innkeeper	hairdresser, cosmetologist
insurance agent	interior decorator	interior designer
interpreter, translator	IT network administrator	jewelry designer
librarian, archivist	librarian: multimedia management	landscape architect
magazine editor	manager: restaurant, retail, personal services	massage therapist
matchmaker: dating service	PC technician: help desk	nurse: generalist, rehab, hospice, occupational
medical transcriptionist	personal chef	occupational therapist
paralegal	pet groomer	paramedic
personal assistant	police officer	physical therapist, exercise physiologist, kinesiologist
priest/minister/ rabbi/monk/nun	product buyer	respiratory therapist
receptionist	retail store clerk, cashier	speech pathologist
....	teacher: preschool, K–12, ESL	veterinary assistant
social worker administrator: adoption, foster care	....	website designer
student advisor, admissions counselor	....	zookeeper

Maestro ESTP

Nonspatial	Tangible	Spatial
business consultant	athletic coach	astronaut
corporate lawyer	auctioneer	athlete
entrepreneur: specialized products and services	ecotourism guide	driver: tank, truck, construction and heavy equipment
financial planner	fitness instructor	earth sciences: geology, volcanology, seismology
negotiator	lawyer: military, sports	explorer
stockbroker	outdoor-challenge course guide	home inspector
tax consultant	pharmacist	IT: PC and network troubleshooter, problem solver
	photographer: adventure, wartime correspondent	physician: internist, oncologist, physiatrist
	retail store owner: specialty products	pilot: military training
		racer: auto, boat, motorcycle
		real estate developer
		resource extraction engineer: mining, petroleum
		special forces
		stunt actor
		surgeon: emergency medicine, battlefield ER
		veterinarian

Tribal ESTP

Nonspatial	Tangible	Spatial
actuarial manager	agriculture: farm manager	air traffic control manager
auditing manager, supervisor	bicycle tour guide	construction manager
broadcast news reporter	drug enforcement agent (DEA)	firefighter: urban, forest
lawyer: corporate	engineering manager: all specialties, field and test	food service manager
marketing presenter	executive: hands-on, operations, manufacturing	forestry: land manager
retail business manager	field agent: CIA, FBI	mechanic supervisor
sales manager	insurance adjuster: natural disaster claims	military officer: artillery, missile systems, tank
tax manager	law enforcement: detective, CSI, police officer	paramedic: ambulance driver, EMT, helicopter pilot
white-collar-crime investigator	project manager: business, technical	physical therapist: sports medicine
....	real estate agent: commercial	search and rescue worker: FEMA, National Guard
....	recreational therapist	trades: carpenter, plumber, HVAC technician
....	Secret Service agent	....
....	teacher: math, physics, chemistry	....
....	technical sales: engineering, medical, heavy equipment	....
....	travel tour manager	....

Maestro ISTP

Nonspatial	Tangible	Spatial
accountant: forensic, auditing, forecasting, tax	agriculture: organic farmer, beekeeper, farm manager	adventure education: outdoor-challenge course designer
actuary	animal scientist	astronaut
business consultant	diplomatic security: special agent	athlete: golf, baseball, basketball
entrepreneur: practical products and services	ecotourism guide	chef
financial planner	horticulture: botanist, wine maker, gardener	construction: surveyor, landscaper
lawyer: mergers and acquisitions, securities regulation	IT: PC and network troubleshooter, problem solver	dentist: emergency surgeon, forensic dentistry
statistician	operations research scientist	driver: tank, truck, construction and heavy equipment
stock analyst	Outward Bound guide	earth sciences: geology, volcanology, seismology, geomorphology
tax consultant	personal services: barber, personal chef	forestry: forester, arborist, ecologist, land manager
technical writer	pharmacist	gemologist
venture capital analyst	photographer: news, wartime correspondent	home inspector
....	soil scientist	hunter, fisherman
....	....	lifeguard
....	....	martial arts instructor
....	....	mechanic: general, race car, motorcycle, aircraft

....   *military: fighter pilot, infantry officer, machine gunner*

....   *mining engineer, mineralogist*

....   *mountain medicine: altitude illness, hypothermia, frostbite*

....   *nurse: ICU, emergency room*

....   *optometrist*

....   *petroleum engineer: offshore drilling, geochemistry*

....   *physician: ophthalmologist, orthopedic surgeon, forensic pathologist*

....   *pilot: military, news, stunt, recreational*

....   *racer: auto, boat, motorcycle*

....   *scuba diver: industrial underwater welder*

....   *special forces*

....   *sports physician*

....   *stunt actor*

....   *surgeon: ER, military flight or field surgeon*

....   *surveyor/mapper*

Tribal ISTP

Nonspatial	Tangible	Spatial
chief financial officer (CFO)	athletic coach	dental assistant
chief information officer (CIO)	bicycle tour guide	engineer: all specialties, field and test, Army Corps
chief operations officer (COO)	drug enforcement agent (DEA)	firefighter: urban, forest
corporate executive (all levels)	executive: hands-on, operations, construction	paramedic: ambulance driver, EMT, helicopter pilot
executive secretary	insurance adjuster	search and rescue worker: FEMA, National Guard
financial analyst	intelligence field agent	teacher: high school physics, geometry, shop
lawyer: corporate, contracts, copyright	law enforcement: detective, CSI, police officer	trades: carpenter, electrician, plumber, mason
	production operations analyst	
	project manager: business, technical	
	recreational attendant	
	Secret Service agent	
	teacher: math, biology, chemistry	
	technician: allied health, lab, IT, telecom, TV/radio	
	video camera technician	
	white-collar-crime investigator	

Maestro ESTJ

Nonspatial	Tangible	Spatial
auditor	computer programmer: technical team leader	chef
business consultant: accounting, auditing	dietitian	computer security analyst
business systems analyst	FBI field agent	computer systems analyst
certified public accountant (CPA)	funeral director	conservationist
entrepreneur: practical products	industrial engineer	earth science: geologist, hydrologist
financial planner	IT consultant	engineering consultant (all specialties)
insurance agent, broker, or underwriter	pharmaceutical sales representative	field technician: HVAC, telecom, cable TV
IRS agent	technical sales: engineering, medical, heavy equipment	medical equipment representative
judge: municipal court	....	physical therapist: speech pathologist, occupational
lawyer: corporate, tax, real estate, estate planning	....	physician: oncology, urology, orthopedic
stockbroker	....	quality inspector: USDA, FDA, EPA, indoor air, safety
....	....	space planner

Tribal ESTJ

Nonspatial	Tangible	Spatial
actuarial manager	business operations manager: all industries	construction manager
administrator: health, school, government	engineering manager	dental hygienist
audit supervisor	event planner	engineer: team-centered
bank manager	food service manager	fireman, paramedic, EMT
cashier	homeland security analyst	general contractor
chief executive officer (CEO)	immigration officer	manufacturing foreman, supervisor
chief information officer (CIO)	insurance adjuster	military manager: communications, supplies
chief operations officer (COO)	project manager: all industries	nurse: RN, case manager, rehab manager
corporate executive (all levels)	office manager	patent agent
executive assistant	purchasing agent	physician assistant: orthopedics
loan officer	police chief	production operations manager
mutual fund trader	real estate agent	shop foreperson: auto repair
sales manager	real estate management	....
school principal	retail store manager	....
stockbroker	sales rep: manufacturers, distributors, service providers	....
tax manager	teacher of practical material: math, gym, shop, technical	....
....	travel tour manager	....

Maestro ISTJ

Nonspatial	Tangible	Spatial
actuary: health, life, annuities, property, pensions insurance	computer programmer	adventure guide
auditor	conservationist	airline pilot
business consultant	defense intelligence analyst	applied mathematician
business systems analyst	dietitian	chemist: inorganic
certified public accountant (CPA)	electrical engineer	computer security analyst
compliance analyst	entrepreneur: practical products	dentist: general, periodontics
financial planner	historian: military, Civil War	earth science: geologist, hydrologist
forensic accountant	industrial engineer	engineering consultant: civil, mechanical, reliability
lawyer: business, tax, real estate, estate planning, mergers	IT: database and network administration, PC technician	entomologist
mutual fund accountant	operations research scientist	environmental engineering
statistician	pharmacist	farmer, hunter, fisherman
stock analyst	compliance specialist: pharmaceuticals, biotech, chemistry	field technician: HVAC, telecomm, cable TV
tax analyst	quality assurance specialist: engineering, biotech	forest ranger
technical writer: business-related	technical writer: computer, software-related	green architecture specialist
....	....	heavy equipment operator

....	....	*historic restoration specialist*
....	....	*lawyer: patent, property, land use*
....	....	*machinery operator*
....	....	*metallurgist*
....	....	*meteorologist*
....	....	*physical therapist: speech pathologist, occupational*
....	....	*physician: surgeon, pathologist, podiatrist, radiologist*
....	....	*technical writer: engineering related*
....	....	*woodworking specialist: furniture maker*

Tribal ISTJ

Nonspatial	Tangible	Spatial
accountant: general	*chef: short-order cook, line chef*	*athletic coach*
administrator: public health, school, health care, government	*clinical research librarian*	*auto-CAD technician*
bank teller	*event and travel planner*	*combat engineer: U.S. Army*
business manager: Fortune 500	*FBI analyst*	*computer systems analyst*
chief financial officer (CFO)	*Homeland Security analyst*	*construction manager*
chief information officer (CIO)	*immigration officer*	*engineer: all specialties, field and test*

chief operations officer (COO)	insurance adjuster	engineering manager
corporate executive (all levels)	manager: retail store, operations, projects	firefighter, paramedic, EMT
executive assistant	property management	materials engineer
financial analyst	purchasing manager, inventory control, supply chain	mechanic: aircraft, auto, diesel, heavy equipment
government employee	quality inspector: USDA, FDA, EPA, indoor air, safety	military: resource management analyst, aircraft navigator
IRS agent	real estate manager	nurse: OR, radiology, generalist
lawyer: corporate, business law, bankruptcy	reference librarian: business research	patent examiner
librarian	security engineering officer: U.S. State Department	police officer: civil servant, military police
office manager	security guard	production operations manager
paralegal	summer camp director	roadway engineer
school principal	teacher: math, gym, shop	teacher: shop, vocational
....	....	technician: lab, science, engineering, health, TV/radio
....	....	trades: carpenter, electrician, mason, plumber
....	....	wastewater/drainage engineer

RESOURCES AND CONTACT INFORMATION

On the Rockport Institute website, you will find resources to assist you in working through this book. This includes downloadable templates to use with this book, other information for readers, and the world's most-used résumé-writing guide, "How to Write a Masterpiece of a Résumé." You can also find out about Rockport's programs and services to help you change to a new career and test your natural talents, to help younger people make an original career choice, and to assist entrepreneurs to choose the right business.

You can find us online at
www.rockportinstitute.com;
or write to us at: info@rockportinstitute.com.

Rockport Institute LTD, 10124 Lakewood Drive, Rockville, MD 20850

A request: If you liked this book, please write or video a review of it where you buy books online.

Thanks,
Nick Lore

Acknowledgments

My Phenomenal Supporters

My wife, Mitra Mortazavi Lore, whose boundless love and support make everything possible.

Nancy Chek, for her wisdom and keen sensibilities, who edited and improved this immeasurably.

Anthony Spadafore for curiosity, ideas, and exceptional contributions.

My son, Neema Moraveji, who brings new paradigms and love by the truckload.

Michelle Howry, my editor, for her support and for being an all-around terrific person; and editorial assistant Kiele Raymond.

My agent and friend Loretta Barrett, who never gives up on me.

Becky Cabaza, who edited the first edition and helped a first-time author craft a best seller.

Stephanie Tade, who made it all happen.

My brother, Mac Lore, whose illustrations add another dimension.

You are all Hot! Hot! Hot!

My Mentors

My mom, for love and genes; my dad, for uncompromising ethics that guide my life.

John Sebastian, itinerant jug-band musician, who opened the doors to the magic world beyond Wallingford.

Sam Lightnin' Hopkins, great friend, long gone, still missed. Po' me.

Werner and Randy MacNamara, thank you, thank you, for everything and nothing.

Bucky Fuller, who got me into this.

I. J. Grandes del Mazo, foxy Peruvian Yoda. Thank you, Toto.

Our 14,000-plus clients, who taught me everything I know.

My Inspirations

Erin, Newsha, and Neema; Kyle, Maia, Azi, Jeff, and Mac; Yoghoub and Azar; Roya, Sam Boogandoo, Crip, Muggleduffy, Curly, and all the crew in pet heaven. John Goddard, great adventurer and loving soul, the Beatles, who showed me how mastery, magic, joy, commitment, and irreverence can play together in perfect harmony. Dylan, Robert Johnson, Rembrandt, Vermeer, W. Edwards Deming, Sid Gautama, and Yeshua the carpenter (two career changers).

Additional thanks to Trish Todd, Susan Kohm, Rick Duff, Julie Myers, and Monica Rose.

INDEX

Page numbers in *italics* indicate illustrations, charts, scales, and graphs.

ABOUT THE AUTHOR

Nicholas Lore created and named the field of career coaching and developed many of the leading-edge methods used in the field. He has been personally commended for excellence by two U.S. presidents. His message is that you can live a life you love and have a career that fits you perfectly. As the director of Rockport Institute, he has directly helped more than fourteen thousand clients choose a new career.

He has been a CEO, manufacturing plant manager, entrepreneur, researcher in the field of psychology, blues singer and guitar player, organic farming and green energy pioneer, market gardener, well driller, weave room fixer, and paperboy.

STOCKS FOR THE LONG RUN

Fourth Edition

STOCKS FOR THE LONG RUN

The Definitive Guide to Financial Market Returns and Long-Term Investment Strategies

JEREMY J. SIEGEL
Russell E. Palmer Professor of Finance
The Wharton School
University of Pennsylvania

New York   Chicago   San Francisco
Lisbon   London   Madrid   Mexico City
Milan   New Delhi   San Juan   Seoul
Singapore   Sydney   Toronto

5 6 7 8 9 0 DOC/DOC 1 5 4 3 2 1 0

ISBN   978-0-07-149470-0
MHID 0-07-149470-7

This publication is designed to provide accurate and authoritative information in regard to the subject matter covered. It is sold with the understanding that neither the author nor the publisher is engaged in rendering legal, accounting, futures/securities trading, or other professional service. If legal advice or other expert assistance is required, the services of a competent professional person should be sought.

> —*From a Declaration of Principles jointly adopted by a Committee*
> *of the American Bar Association and a Committee of Publishers*

McGraw-Hill books are available at special quantity discounts to use as premiums and sales promotions, or for use in corporate training programs. For more information, please write to the Director of Special Sales, Professional Publishing, McGraw-Hill, Two Penn Plaza, New York, NY 10121-2298. Or contact your local bookstore.

This book is printed on acid-free paper.

Library of Congress Cataloging-in-Publication Data
Siegel, Jeremy J.
  Stocks for the long run / by Jeremy Siegel.—4th ed.
     p. cm.
  Includes index.
  ISBN 978-0-07-149470-0
  MHID 0-07-149470-7
  1. Stocks.   2. Stocks—History.   3. Rate of return.   4. Stocks—Rate of return.   I. Title.
HG4661.S53   2007
332.63'22—dc22

                                    2007042478

CONTENTS

Chapter 8

The Impact of Economic Growth on Market Valuation and the Coming Age Wave   123

PART 3

HOW THE ECONOMIC ENVIRONMENT IMPACTS STOCKS

Chapter 11

Gold, Monetary Policy, and Inflation   187

Chapter 12

Stocks and the Business Cycle   207

Chapter 16

Market Volatility   269

Chapter 17

Technical Analysis and Investing with the Trend   289

Chapter 21

Structuring a Portfolio for Long-Term Growth   359

Index   367

F O R E W O R D

Some people find the process of assembling data to be a deadly bore. Others view it as a challenge. Jeremy Siegel has turned it into an art form. You can only admire the scope, lucidity, and sheer delight with which Professor Siegel serves up the evidence to support his case for investing in stocks for the long run.

But this book is far more than its title suggests. You will learn a lot of economic theory along the way, garnished with a fascinating history of both the capital markets and the U.S. economy. By using history to maximum effect, Professor Siegel gives the numbers a life and meaning they would never enjoy in a less compelling setting. Moreover, he boldly does battle with all historical episodes that could contradict his thesis and emerges victorious—and this includes the crazy years of the 1990s.

With this fourth edition, Jeremy Siegel has continued on his merry and remarkable way in producing works of great value about how best to invest in the stock market. His additions on behavioral finance, globalization, and exchange-traded funds have enriched the original material with fresh insights into important issues. Revisions throughout the book have added valuable factual material and powerful new arguments to make his case for stocks for the long run. Whether you are a beginner at investing or an old pro, you will learn a lot from reading this book.

Jeremy Siegel is never shy, and his arguments in this new edition demonstrate he is as bold as ever. The most interesting feature of the whole book is his twin conclusions of good news and bad news. First, today's globalized world warrants higher average price-earnings ratios than in the past. But higher P-Es are a mixed blessing, for they would mean average returns in the future are going to be lower than they were in the past.

I am not going to take issue with the forecast embodied in this viewpoint. But similar cases could have been made in other environments of the past, tragic environments as well as happy ones. One of the great lessons of history proclaims that no economic environment survives the long run. We have no sense at all of what kinds of problems or victories lie in the distant future, say, 20 years or more from now, and what influence those forces will have on appropriate price-earnings ratios.

That's all right. Professor Siegel's most important observation about the future goes beyond his controversial forecast of higher aver-

age P-Es and lower realized returns. "Although these returns may be diminished from the past," he writes, "there is overwhelming reason to believe stocks will remain the best investment for all those seeking steady, long-term gains."

"[O]verwhelming reason" is an understatement. The risk premium earned by equities over the long run *must* remain intact if the system is going to survive. In the capitalist system, bonds cannot and should not outperform equities over the long run. Bonds are contracts enforceable in courts of law. Equities promise their owners nothing—stocks are risky investments, involving a high degree of faith in the future. Thus, equities are not inherently "better" than bonds, but we demand a higher return from equities to compensate for their greater risk. If the long-run expected return on bonds were to be higher than the long-run expected return on stocks, assets would be priced so that risk would earn no reward. That is an unsustainable condition. Stocks must remain "the best investment for all those seeking steady, long-term gains" or our system will come to an end, and with a bang, not a whimper.

Peter Bernstein

P R E F A C E

I wrote the first edition of *Stocks for the Long Run* with two goals in mind: to document the returns on the major classes of financial assets over the past two centuries and to offer strategies that maximize long-term portfolio growth. My research definitively showed that over long periods of time, the returns on equities not only surpassed those on all other financial assets but were far safer and more predictable than bond returns when inflation was taken into account. I concluded that stocks were clearly the asset of choice for investors seeking long-term growth.

I am both honored and flattered by the tremendous reception that the core ideas of *Stocks for the Long Run* have received. Since the publication of the first edition 13 years ago, I have given hundreds of lectures on the markets and the economy both in the United States and abroad. I have listened closely to the questions that audiences pose, and I have contemplated the many letters, phone calls, and e-mails from readers. My responses have formed the basis of much of the new material that has been added to the fourth edition of *Stocks for the Long Run*.

NEW MATERIAL IN THE FOURTH EDITION

The fourth edition not only updates all the data from the third edition, but it also introduces completely new material on such topics as *which* stocks have done well in the long run and what will be the distribution of world output and equity values in the middle of this century. A whole new chapter has been added on the history of the firms in the S&P 500 Index, which celebrated its fiftieth anniversary in March 2007.

A recurring theme in this edition of *Stocks for the Long Run* is that "growth does not imply return." This principle can be applied to individual stocks, industries, and even countries. I show the superiority of high-dividend-yield and low-P-E strategies for the stocks in the S&P 500 Index. Sector growth turns out to play only a minor role in determining returns. These findings support the conclusion that value stocks outperform growth stocks in the long run, a phenomenon that has been well documented in the finance literature.

In the preface to the 2002 edition of *Stocks for the Long Run*, I wrote, "Although I still believe that [capitalization-weighted] indexed investments should constitute the core of every investor's long-term portfolio,

. . . [s]ome indexes, such as the Standard & Poor's (S&P) 500 Stock Index, have become so popular that entry to the index carries with it a price premium that may reduce future returns."

Further research has supported this contention. The chapter on the history of the S&P 500 Index shows that the new firms added to the index have generally had lower returns than the original firms that were chosen in 1957. In this edition, I introduce the "noisy market hypothesis," an alternative to the efficient market hypothesis that explains why value stocks outperform growth stocks. In Chapter 20, I describe "fundamentally weighted" indexes as an efficient alternative to capitalization-weighted indexes for capturing the value premium.

Any analysis of the stock market today must be international in scope, and in this edition I have greatly expanded the material on international markets. I detail the role of the developing economies in mitigating the aging crisis that will soon envelop the United States, Europe, and Japan as the ranks of retirees swell. I believe that Asia and other developing countries will, by the middle of this century, play a dominant role in the world's economy and capital markets. I conclude that Americans face a crucial choice—allow the influx of foreign capital or face poor financial returns and a far more difficult retirement period.

All this makes investing in international equities not only important but critical to developing a comprehensive investment strategy. The chapter on global economics shows that despite the increased short-term correlation between country returns, global diversification is still an essential part of today's investment strategy. Without doubt, the portion of the world's equity capital that is located outside the United States will grow rapidly in the coming years.

The fourth edition also reevaluates the findings reported in the previous editions. Such topics as calendar anomalies (for example, the January Effect), the impact of Fed interest rate changes on the stock market, and the importance of investor sentiment in predicting future market returns are given a new look. I determine whether there have been any systematic changes in the response to these factors since the first edition of *Stocks for the Long Run* was published in 1994.

There are some surprising results: some of the calendar anomalies hold up very well while others disappear altogether. For example, Fed rate cuts, although having a powerful immediate impact on stock prices, do not have as predictable an intermediate-term impact as they once had. Other topics examined include the "Gordon model" of stock valuation and economic growth, the increasing advantage of exchange-traded funds over mutual funds, momentum investing, and why many "bears"

have misinterpreted historical evidence on dividend growth and corporate profits.

CONCLUDING REMARKS

Since the publication of the first edition of *Stocks for the Long Run*, there have been some extraordinary events in the capital markets. The greatest bull market in the 200-year history of U.S. equities ended in 2000 when the surging technology stocks crashed and U.S. stocks entered a severe bear market. And the terrorist attacks of 9/11 closed the exchange for four days, the longest period since the Great Depression.

Yet the public, once regarded as fickle and quick to abandon stocks in difficult times, stuck with equities. There appeared to be much less public disenchantment with stocks in the last bear market than in previous downturns, and surveys showed that most retained their faith that stocks were still the best long-term investment. If earlier editions of *Stocks for the Long Run* played some small part in stock investors' newfound tenacity, I take great satisfaction.

Nevertheless, all who strive to be successful investors must exercise patience. In 1937, John Maynard Keynes stated in *The General Theory*: "Investment based on genuine long-term expectation is so difficult today as to be scarcely practicable." Seventy years later, long-term investing is as difficult as ever, but with today's growing global economy, there is overwhelming evidence that stocks will remain the best investment for all those seeking long-term gains.

Jeremy J. Siegel

ACKNOWLEDGMENTS

It is never possible to list all the individuals and organizations that have praised *Stocks for the Long Run* and encouraged me to update and expand past editions. Many who provided me with data for the first three editions of *Stocks for the Long Run* willingly contributed their data again for this fourth edition, including the Vanguard Group, Morgan Stanley, Smithers & Co., and Randell Moore of Blue Chip Economic Indicators.

Jeremy Schwartz, who was my principal researcher for the third edition of *Stocks for the Long Run* as well as for *The Future for Investors*, provided invaluable assistance for the fourth edition. More than a year ago he and I sketched the outline for the new edition, and his participation, despite the heavy demands of his own new career, was essential to this edition's success. As with previous editions, this work would not have been possible without the help of Wharton students. In particular, I wish to thank Winston Liu, Peter Yi Wang, Anthony Massaro, and Adam Freedman for their invaluable help. Adam Freedman especially provided critical research support during the final stages of this manuscript, and without his dedicated work, this edition would not have been completed in a timely manner.

A special thanks goes to the thousands of financial advisors from dozens of financial firms, such as Merrill Lynch and Morgan Stanley, who have provided me with invaluable feedback on earlier editions of *Stocks for the Long Run* in seminars and open forums. As senior investment strategy advisor to WisdomTree Investments, I have been better able to articulate the value-based strategies discussed in this book.

Again, I am honored that Peter Bernstein has written a foreword for this fourth edition. I strive to attain the clarity that he has achieved in his bestselling books about the history and practice of investing.

For a manuscript to become a finished book requires an editor, and I can honestly say that Leah Spiro of McGraw-Hill took over the responsibility from Jeffrey Krames, my editor for the last two editions, with both skill and enthusiasm. Her input helped focus the material, and her encouragement spurred me to meet the tight deadlines. As with the last edition, Jane Palmieri did a superb job as editing manager.

As before, the support of my family was critical in my being able to produce this edition. Now that my sons are grown and out of the house, it was my wife Ellen who had to pay the whole price of the long hours

spent producing this book. She convinced me to completely clear my summer schedule so that I could complete the first draft before the school year—and my extensive lecturing schedule—began. That superb advice enabled us to take a weeklong vacation in Scotland before beginning the demanding job of editing the final drafts of the book. I am hopeful that my efforts will bring us even more time together in the future.

STOCKS FOR THE LONG RUN

PART 1

THE VERDICT OF HISTORY

CHAPTER 1

STOCK AND BOND RETURNS SINCE 1802

I know of no way of judging the future but by the past.

PATRICK HENRY, 1775[1]

"EVERYBODY OUGHT TO BE RICH"

In the summer of 1929, a journalist named Samuel Crowther interviewed John J. Raskob, a senior financial executive at General Motors, about how the typical individual could build wealth by investing in stocks. In August of that year, Crowther published Raskob's ideas in a *Ladies' Home Journal* article with the audacious title "Everybody Ought to Be Rich."

In the interview, Raskob claimed that America was on the verge of a tremendous industrial expansion. He maintained that by putting just $15 per month into good common stocks, investors could expect their wealth to grow steadily to $80,000 over the next 20 years. Such a return—24 percent per year—was unprecedented, but the prospect of effortlessly amassing a great fortune seemed plausible in the atmosphere

---

[1] Speech in Virginia Convention, March 23, 1775.

3

of the 1920s bull market. Stocks excited investors, and millions put their savings into the market seeking quick profit.

On September 3, 1929, a few days after Raskob's ideas appeared, the Dow Jones Industrial Average hit a historic high of 381.17. Seven weeks later, stocks crashed. The next 34 months saw the most devastating decline in share values in U.S. history.

On July 8, 1932, when the carnage was finally over, the Dow Industrials stood at 41.22. The market value of the world's greatest corporations had declined an incredible 89 percent. Millions of investors' life savings were wiped out, and thousands of investors who had borrowed money to buy stocks were forced into bankruptcy. America was mired in the deepest economic depression in its history.

Raskob's advice was ridiculed and denounced for years to come. It was said to represent the insanity of those who believed that the market could rise forever and the foolishness of those who ignored the tremendous risks inherent in stocks. Senator Arthur Robinson of Indiana publicly held Raskob responsible for the stock crash by urging common people to buy stock at the market peak.[2] In 1992, 63 years later, *Forbes* magazine warned investors of the overvaluation of stocks in its issue headlined "Popular Delusions and the Madness of Crowds." In a review of the history of market cycles, *Forbes* fingered Raskob as the "worst offender" of those who viewed the stock market as a guaranteed engine of wealth.[3]

Conventional wisdom holds that Raskob's foolhardy advice epitomizes the mania that periodically overruns Wall Street. But is that verdict fair? The answer is decidedly no. If you calculate the value of the portfolio of an investor who followed Raskob's advice in 1929, patiently putting $15 a month into stocks, you find that his accumulation exceeded that of someone who placed the same money in Treasury bills after less than 4 years! By 1949 his stock portfolio would have accumulated almost $9,000, a return of 7.86 percent, more than double the annual return in bonds. After 30 years the portfolio would have grown to over $60,000, with an annual return rising to 12.72 percent. Although these returns were not as high as Raskob had projected, the total return of the stock portfolio over 30 years was more than 8 times the accumulation in bonds and more than 9 times that in Treasury bills. Those who never bought stock, citing the Great Crash as the vindication of their

[2] Irving Fisher, *The Stock Market Crash and After*, New York: Macmillan, 1930, p. xi.
[3] "The Crazy Things People Say to Rationalize Stock Prices," *Forbes*, April 27, 1992, p. 150.

caution, eventually found themselves far behind investors who had patiently accumulated equity.[4]

The story of John Raskob's infamous prediction illustrates an important theme in the history of Wall Street. This theme is not the preva-
lence of foolish optimism at market peaks; rather, it is that over the last
century, accumulations in stocks have always outperformed other financial assets for the patient investor. Even such calamitous events as the
Great 1929 Stock Crash did not negate the superiority of stocks as long-
term investments.

FINANCIAL MARKET RETURNS FROM 1802

This chapter analyzes the returns on stocks and bonds over long periods of
time in both the United States and other countries. This two-century history is divided into three subperiods. In the first subperiod, from 1802
through 1870, the United States made a transition from an agrarian to an
industrialized economy, comparable to the transition that the "emerging
markets" of Latin America and Asia are making today.[5] In the second subperiod, from 1871 through 1925, the United States became the foremost political and economic power in the world.[6] The third subperiod, from 1926
to the present, contains the 1929 to 1932 stock collapse, the Great Depression, and the postwar expansion. The data from this period have been analyzed extensively by academics and professional money managers and
have served as benchmarks for historical returns.[7] The story is told in Figure 1-1. It depicts the total return indexes for stocks, long- and short-term
bonds, gold, and commodities from 1802 through 2006. *Total return* means
that all returns, such as interest and dividends and capital gains, are automatically reinvested in the asset and allowed to accumulate over time.

---

[4] Raskob succumbed to investors in the 1920s who wanted to get rich quickly by devising a scheme
by which investors borrowed $300, adding $200 of personal capital, to invest $500 in stocks. Al-
though in 1929 this was certainly not as good as putting money gradually in the market, even this
plan beat investment in Treasury bills after 20 years.

[5] A brief description of the early stock market is found in Appendix 1 at the end of this chapter. The
stock price data during this period are taken from Schwert (1990), and I have added my own dividend series. G. William Schwert, "Indexes of United States Stock Prices from 1802 to 1987," *Journal
of Business*, vol. 63 (July 1990), pp. 399–426.

[6] The stock series used in this period are taken from the Cowles indexes as reprinted in Robert
Shiller, *Market Volatility*, Cambridge: MIT Press, 1989. The Cowles indexes are capitalization-
weighted indexes of all New York Stock Exchange stocks, and they include dividends.

[7] The data from the third period are taken from the Center for Research in Security Prices (CRSP)
capitalization-weighted indexes of all New York stocks, and starting in 1962, they include American
and Nasdaq stocks.

FIGURE 1–1

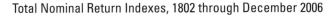

Total Nominal Return Indexes, 1802 through December 2006

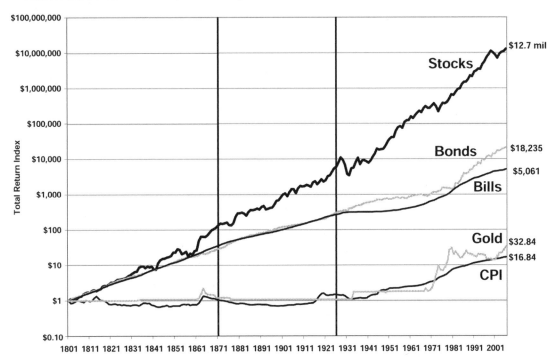

It can be easily seen that the total return on equities dominates all other assets. Even the cataclysmic stock crash of 1929, which caused a generation of investors to shun stocks, appears as a mere blip in the stock return index. Bear markets, which so frighten investors, pale in the context of the upward thrust of total stock returns. One dollar invested and reinvested in stocks since 1802 would have accumulated to over $12.7 million by the end of 2006. This sum can be realized by an investor holding the broadest possible portfolio of stocks in proportion to their market value and is calculated to include those companies that do not survive.[8]

By extension, the above analysis indicates that $1 million invested and reinvested during these more than 200 years would have grown to the incredible sum of $12.7 trillion by the end of 2006, nearly three-quarters the entire capitalization of the U.S. stock market!

One million dollars in 1802 is equivalent to roughly $16.84 million in today's purchasing power. This was certainly a large, though not

---

[8] Analysis of *survivorship bias* issues in computing returns is discussed in Chapter 20.

overwhelming, sum of money to the industrialists and landholders of the early nineteenth century.[9] But total wealth in the stock market, or in the economy for that matter, does not accumulate as fast as the total return index. This is because investors consume most of their dividends and capital gains, enjoying the fruits of their past saving.

It is rare for anyone to accumulate wealth for long periods of time without consuming part of his or her return. The longest period of time investors typically hold onto assets without touching the principal and income occurs when they are accumulating wealth in pension plans for their retirement or in insurance policies that are passed on to their heirs. Even those who bequeath fortunes untouched during their lifetimes must realize that these accumulations are often dissipated in the next generation or spent by the foundations to which the money is bequeathed.[10] The stock market has the power to turn a single dollar into millions by the forbearance of generations—but few will have the patience or desire to endure the wait.

THE LONG-TERM PERFORMANCE OF BONDS

Bonds are the most important financial assets competing with stocks. Bonds promise fixed monetary payments over time. In contrast to equity, the cash flows from bonds have a maximum monetary value set by the terms of the contract. Except in the case of default, bond returns do not vary with the profitability of the firm.

The bond series shown in Figure 1-1 are based on long- and short-term U.S. Treasury bonds, when available; if they were not available, other highest-grade municipal bonds were chosen. Default premiums were removed from all interest rates in order to obtain a comparable series over the entire period.[11]

The interest rates on long-term bonds and short-term bonds, called *bills*, over the 200-year period are displayed in Figure 1-2. Interest rate fluctuations during the nineteenth and early twentieth centuries re-

---

[9] Blodget, an early-nineteenth-century economist, estimated the wealth of the United States at that time to be nearly $2.5 billion so that $1 million would be only about 0.04 percent of the total wealth: S. Blodget, Jr., *Economica, A Statistical Manual for the United States of America*, 1806 edition, p. 68.

[10] One of the world's largest foundations, the Bill and Melinda Gates Foundation to which Warren Buffett has left the bulk of his money, has announced that all of its money must be spent within 50 years of their deaths.

[11] See Jeremy Siegel, "The Real Rate of Interest from 1800–1990: A Study of the U.S. and the U.K.," *Journal of Monetary Economics*, vol. 29 (1992), pp. 227–252, for a detailed description of the process by which a historical yield series was constructed.

FIGURE 1–2

U.S. Interest Rates, 1800 through December 2006

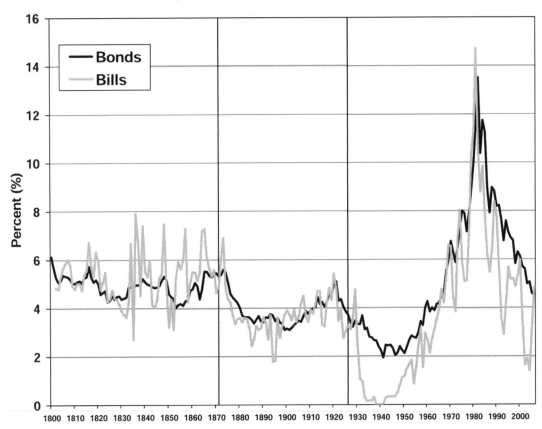

mained within a narrow range. But from 1926 to the present, the behavior of both long- and short-term interest rates changed dramatically. During the Great Depression of the 1930s, short-term interest rates fell nearly to zero, and yields on long-term government bonds fell to a record low of 2 percent. In order to finance record wartime borrowings, the government maintained low rates during World War II and the early postwar years. Deposit rates were also kept low by strict limits, known as Regulation Q,[12] imposed by the Federal Reserve on bank deposit rates through the 1950s and 1960s.

---

[12] Regulation Q was a provision in the Banking Act of 1933 that imposed ceilings on interest rates and time deposits.

The 1970s marked an unprecedented change in interest rate behavior. Inflation reached double-digit levels, and interest rates soared to heights that had not been seen since the debasing of the continental currency in the early years of the republic. Never before had inflation been so high for so long.

The public clamored for government action to slow rising prices. Finally, by 1982, the restrictive monetary policy of Paul Volcker, chairman of the Federal Reserve System since 1979, brought inflation and interest rates down to more moderate levels. One can see that the level of interest rates is closely tied to the level of inflation. Understanding the returns on fixed-income assets therefore requires knowledge of how inflation is determined.

THE END OF THE GOLD STANDARD AND PRICE STABILITY

Consumer prices in the United States and the United Kingdom over the past 200 years are depicted in Figure 1-3. In each country, the price level at the end of World War II was essentially the same as it was 150 years earlier. But after World War II, the nature of inflation changed dramatically. The price level rose almost continuously during that 60-year period, often gradually, but sometimes at double-digit rates as in the 1970s. Excluding wartime, the 1970s witnessed the first rapid and sustained inflation ever experienced in U.S. history.

The dramatic changes in the recent inflationary trend can be easily explained. During the nineteenth and early twentieth centuries, the United States, United Kingdom, and the rest of the industrialized world were on a gold standard. As described in detail in Chapter 11, a gold standard restricts the supply of money and hence the inflation rate. But from the Great Depression through World War II, the world shifted to a paper money standard. Under a paper money standard there is no legal constraint on the issuance of money, so inflation is subject to political as well as economic forces. Price stability depends on the ability of the central banks to limit the growth of the supply of money in order to counteract deficit spending and other inflationary policies implemented by the federal government.

The chronic inflation that the United States and other developed economies have experienced since World War II does not mean that the gold standard was superior to the current paper money standard. The gold standard was abandoned because of its inflexibility in the face of economic crises, particularly during the banking collapse of the 1930s. The paper money standard, if properly administered, can prevent the

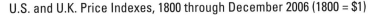

FIGURE 1-3

U.S. and U.K. Price Indexes, 1800 through December 2006 (1800 = $1)

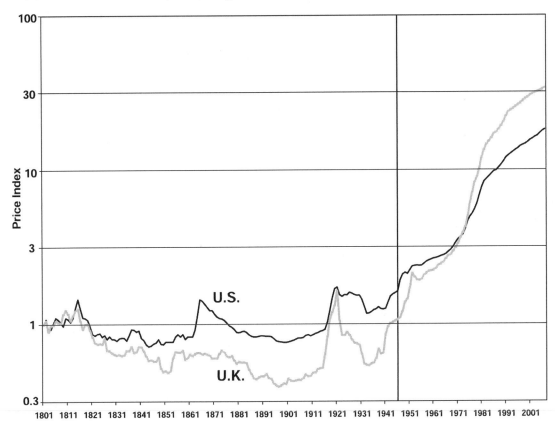

banking panics and severe depressions that plagued the gold standard and still bring inflation down to very moderate levels, as we have seen in the last two decades.

It is not surprising that the price of gold has closely followed the trend of overall inflation over the past two centuries. Its price soared to $850 per ounce in January 1980, following the rapid inflation of the preceding decade. When inflation was brought under control, its price fell. One dollar of gold bullion purchased in 1802 was worth $32.84 at the end of 2006. In the long run, gold offers investors protection against inflation, but little else. Whatever hedging property precious metals possess, holding these assets will exert a considerable drag on the return of a long-term investor's portfolio.[13]

TOTAL REAL RETURNS

The focus of every long-term investor should be the growth of purchasing power—that is, monetary wealth adjusted for the effect of inflation. Figure 1-4 shows the growth of purchasing power, or total real returns, in the same assets that were graphed in Figure 1-1: stocks, bonds, bills, and gold. These data are constructed by taking the dollar returns and correcting them by the changes in the price level shown in Figure 1-3.[14]

The growth of purchasing power in equities not only dominates all other assets but also shows remarkable long-term stability. Despite ex-

---

[13] Ironically, despite the inflationary bias of a paper money system, well-preserved paper money from the early nineteenth century is worth many times its face value on the collectors' market, far surpassing gold bullion as a long-term investment. An old mattress found containing nineteenth-century paper money is a better find for an antiquarian than an equivalent sum hoarded in gold bars!

[14] Total returns are graphed on a ratio, or logarithmic scale. Economists use this scale to graph virtually all long-term data since equal vertical distances anywhere in the chart represent equal percentage changes in return. As a result, a constant slope represents a constant after-inflation rate of return.

FIGURE   1–4

Total Real Return Indexes, 1802 through December 2006

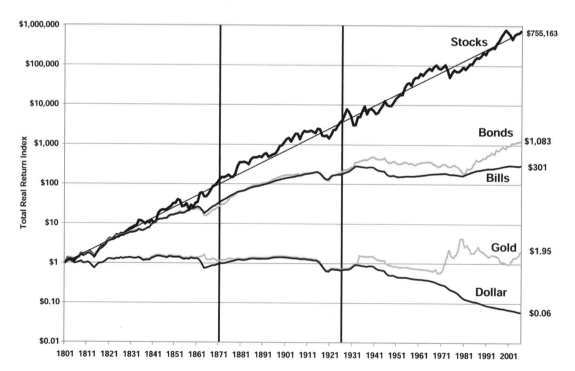

traordinary changes in the economic, social, and political environment over the past two centuries, stocks have yielded between 6.6 and 7.0 percent per year after inflation in all major subperiods.

The wiggles on the stock return line represent the bull and bear markets that equities have suffered throughout history. The long-term perspective radically changes one's view of the risk of stocks. The short-term fluctuations in the stock market, which loom so large to investors when they occur, are insignificant when compared to the upward movement of equity values over time.

In contrast to the remarkable stability of stock returns, real returns on fixed-income assets have declined markedly over time. In the first and even second subperiods, the annual returns on bonds and bills, although less than those on equities, were significantly positive. But since 1926, and especially since World War II, fixed-income assets have returned little after inflation.

INTERPRETATION OF RETURNS

Long-Term Returns

The annual returns on U.S. stocks over the past two centuries are summarized in Table 1-1.[15] The shaded column represents the real after-inflation, compound annual rate of return on stocks. The real return on equities has averaged 6.8 percent per year over the past 204 years. This means that purchasing power has, on average, doubled in the stock market about every 10 years. If past trends persist—that is, if inflation averages 2½ percent per year and equities offer a 6½ percent forward-looking annual real return—this increase in purchasing power would translate into about a 9 percent per year nominal or money return on stocks.

Note the extraordinary stability of the real return on stocks over all major subperiods: 7.0 percent per year from 1802 through 1870, 6.6 percent from 1871 through 1925, and 6.8 percent per year since 1926. Even since World War II, during which all the inflation that the United States has experienced over the past 200 years occurred, the average real rate of

---

[15] The dividend yield for the first subperiod has been estimated by statistically fitting the relation of long-term interest rates to dividend yields in the second subperiod, yielding results that are closer to other information we have about dividends during the period. See Walter Werner and Steven Smith, *Wall Street*, New York: Columbia University Press, 1991, for a description of some early dividend yields. See also a recent paper by William Goetzmann and Phillipe Jorion, "A Longer Look at Dividend Yields," *Journal of Business*, vol. 68, no. 4 (1995), pp. 483–508, and William Goetzmann, "Patterns in Three Centuries of Stock Market Prices," *Journal of Business*, vol. 66, no. 2 (1993), pp. 249–270.

T A B L E 1–1

Annual Stock Market Returns, 1802 through December 2006

Comp = compound annual return
Arith = arithmetic average of annual returns
Risk = standard deviation of arithmetic returns
All Data in Percent (%)

		Total Nominal Return			Nominal Capital Appreciation			Div Yld	Total Real Return			Real Capital Appreciation			Real Gold Retn	Consumer Price Inflation
		Comp	Arith	Risk	Comp	Arith	Risk		Comp	Arith	Risk	Comp	Arith	Risk		
Periods	1802-2006	8.3	9.7	17.5	2.9	4.3	17.4	5.1	6.8	8.4	18.1	1.5	3.0	17.8	0.3	1.4
	1871-2006	8.9	10.5	18.5	4.2	5.8	18.3	4.5	6.7	8.4	18.8	2.1	3.9	18.5	0.4	2.0
Major Subperiods	I 1802-1870	7.1	8.1	15.5	0.3	1.3	15.4	6.4	7.0	8.3	16.9	0.1	1.4	16.4	0.2	0.1
	II 1871-1925	7.2	8.4	15.7	1.9	3.1	16.1	5.2	6.6	7.9	16.8	1.3	2.7	17.1	-0.8	0.6
	III 1926-2006	10.1	12.0	20.1	5.8	7.7	19.5	4.0	6.8	8.8	20.1	2.7	4.6	19.5	1.2	3.0
Postwar Period	1946-2006	11.2	12.5	16.9	7.4	8.6	16.3	3.6	6.9	8.4	17.4	3.2	4.6	16.8	0.5	4.0
	1946-1965	13.1	14.3	19.5	8.2	9.2	18.7	4.6	10.0	11.4	18.7	5.2	6.5	18.1	-2.7	2.8
	1966-1981	6.6	8.3	17.2	2.6	4.3	16.6	3.9	-0.4	1.4	17.1	-4.1	-2.4	16.7	8.8	7.0
	1982-1999	17.3	18.0	12.5	13.8	14.5	12.4	3.1	13.6	14.3	12.6	10.2	10.9	12.6	-4.9	3.3
	1985-2006	12.4	13.6	15.6	9.8	11.0	15.1	2.4	8.4	10.3	15.4	6.6	7.7	14.9	0.3	3.0

return on stocks has been 6.9 percent per year. This is virtually identical to the previous 125 years, which saw no overall inflation. This remarkable stability is called the *mean reversion* of equity returns, which means that returns can be very unstable in the short run but very stable in the long run.

Mean reversion can also be seen by noting how the total real return in stocks "cling" to the statistical trend line fitted through the 204 years of stock market data in Figure 1-4. When the total real return on stocks was substantially above the trend line, such as during the late 1960s and 1990s, the market was at risk for a correction, as forces of mean reversion eventually worked to bring total returns down. Similarly, periods during which the market fell below the trend line, such as during the early 1980s, pointed to promising future returns.

The long-term stability of stock returns is all the more surprising when one reflects on the dramatic changes that have taken place in our society during the last two centuries. The United States evolved from an agricultural to an industrial economy and then to the postindustrial, service- and technology-oriented economy it is today. The world shifted from a gold-based standard to a paper money standard. And information, which once took weeks to cross the country, can now be instanta-

neously transmitted and simultaneously broadcast around the world. Yet despite mammoth changes in the basic factors generating wealth for shareholders, equity returns have shown an astounding stability.

Short-Term Returns and Volatility

The bull market from 1982 through 1999 gave investors an extraordinary after-inflation return of 13.6 percent per year, which is double the historical average. This constituted the greatest bull market in U.S. stock market history. The superior equity returns over this period followed the dreadful stock returns realized in the previous 15 years, from 1966 through 1981, when the real rate of return was –0.4 percent. Nevertheless, this bull market carried stocks too high, as total real returns in Figure 1-4 reached 81 percent above the trend line. The subsequent bear market and recovery have brought stocks, as of the end of 2006, near their long-term trends.

REAL RETURNS ON FIXED-INCOME ASSETS

As stable as the long-term real returns have been for equities, the same cannot be said of fixed-income assets. The nominal and real returns on both short-term and long-term bonds are reported in Table 1-2 covering the same time periods as in Table 1-1. The real return on bills has dropped precipitously from 5.1 percent in the early part of the nineteenth century to a bare 0.7 percent since 1926, a return only slightly above inflation.

The real return on long-term bonds has shown a similar pattern. Bond returns fell from a generous 4.8 percent in the first subperiod to 3.7 percent in the second, and then to only 2.4 percent in the third. If the returns from the last 80 years were projected into the future, it would take 32 years to double one's purchasing power in bonds and nearly 100 years to do so in Treasury bills. In contrast, it takes about 10 years to double purchasing power in stocks.

The decline in the average real return on fixed-income securities is striking. In any 30-year period beginning with 1889, the average real rate of return on short-term government securities has exceeded 2 percent only three times. Since the late nineteenth century, the real return on bonds and bills over any 30-year horizon has seldom matched the average return of 4.5 to 5 percent reached during the first 70 years of our sample. From 1880, the real return on long-term bonds over every 30-year period has never reached 4 percent, and it has exceeded 3 percent during only 22 such periods.

T A B L E   1–2

Fixed-Income Returns, 1802 through December 2006

Comp = compound annual return
Arith = arithmetic average of annual returns
Risk = standard deviation of arithmetic returns
All Data in Percent (%)

			Long-Term Governments						Short-Term Governments			
		Coupon Rate	Nominal Return			Real Return			Nominal Rate	Real Return		
			Comp	Arith	Risk	Comp	Arith	Risk		Comp	Arith	Risk
Periods	1802-2006	4.8	5.0	5.1	6.2	3.5	3.9	8.8	4.3	2.8	3.0	6.0
	1871-2006	4.7	5.0	5.3	7.4	2.9	3.3	8.9	3.8	1.7	1.8	4.5
Major Subperiods	I 1802-1870	4.9	4.9	4.9	2.8	4.8	5.1	8.3	5.2	5.1	5.4	7.7
	II 1871-1925	4.0	4.3	4.4	3.0	3.7	3.9	6.4	3.8	3.2	3.3	4.8
	III 1926-2006	5.2	5.5	5.8	9.2	2.4	2.9	10.3	3.8	0.7	0.8	4.0
Postwar Periods	1946-2006	6.0	5.7	6.2	10.2	1.6	2.2	10.9	4.7	0.6	0.6	3.2
	1946-1965	3.1	1.6	1.7	7.1	-1.2	-1.0	8.1	2.0	-0.8	-0.7	2.1
	1966-1981	7.2	2.5	2.8	12.0	-4.2	-3.9	12.9	6.9	-0.2	-0.1	2.4
	1982-1999	8.5	12.1	12.9	13.8	8.5	9.3	13.6	6.3	2.9	2.9	1.8
	1985-2006	7.0	10.4	11.0	12.3	7.2	7.7	12.0	4.9	1.7	1.8	2.1

You have to go back more than 1½ centuries to the period from 1831 through 1861 to find any 30-year period during which the return on either long- or short-term bonds exceeded that on equities. The dominance of stocks over fixed-income securities is overwhelming for investors with long horizons.

THE FALL IN FIXED-INCOME RETURNS

Although the returns on equities have fully compensated stock investors for the increased inflation since World War II, the returns on fixed-income securities have not. The change in the monetary standard from gold to paper had a far greater impact on the returns of fixed-income assets than on stocks. It is clear that the buyers of long-term bonds in the 1940s, 1950s, and early 1960s did not recognize the inflationary consequences of the change in monetary regime. How else can you explain

why investors voluntarily purchased 30-year bonds with 3 and 4 percent coupons ignoring a government policy that favored inflation?

But there must have been other reasons for the decline in real returns on fixed-income assets. Theoretically, the unanticipated inflation of the postwar period should have had a significantly smaller effect on the real return of short-term bonds, such as Treasury bills. This is because short-term rates may be reset frequently to capture expected inflation. But, as noted previously, the decline in the real return on short-term bonds actually exceeded the decline in the real return on long-term bonds.

Another explanation for the fall in bond returns is investors' reaction to the financial turmoil of the Great Depression. The stock collapse of the early 1930s caused a whole generation of investors to shun equities and invest in government bonds and newly insured bank deposits, driving bond returns downward. Finally, many investors bought bonds because of the widespread but incorrect predictions that another depression would follow the war.

But it was not just the risk preferences of investors that kept fixed rates low. The Federal Reserve actively supported the bond market through much of the 1940s to keep the government's interest expense low. This support policy was abandoned in 1951 because it led to interest rates that were inconsistent with one of its primary goals of maintaining low inflation.

And finally, one should not ignore the transformation of a highly segmented market for short-term instruments in the nineteenth century into one of the world's most liquid markets today. Treasury bills satisfy certain fiduciary and legal requirements that no other asset can match. But the premium paid for these services has translated into a meager return for investors, who have paid a high price for gaining *short-term* stability of their assets.

THE EQUITY PREMIUM

Whatever the reasons for the decline in the real return on fixed-income assets over the past century, it is very likely that the real returns on bonds will be higher on average in the future than they have been since the end of World War II. As a result of the inflation shock of the 1970s, bondholders have incorporated an inflation premium in the coupon on long-term bonds. In most major industrialized nations, if inflation does not increase appreciably from current levels (2 to 3 percent), real returns of about 2 percent will be realized from government bonds whose nom-

inal rate is between 4 and 5 percent. These projected real returns are lower than the 3½ percent average compound real return on U.S. long-term government bonds over the past 205 years, but they are not as low as they were during the postwar period.

The excess return for holding equities over short-term bonds is plotted in Figure 1-5, and it is referred to as the *equity risk premium,* or simply the *equity premium.*[16] The equity premium, calculated as the difference in 30-year compound annual real returns on stocks and bills, averaged 1.4 percent in the first subperiod, 3.4 percent in the second subperiod, and 5.9 percent since 1926.

The abnormally high equity premium since 1926 is certainly not sustainable. It is not a coincidence that the highest 30-year average eq-

---

[16] For a rigorous analysis of the equity premium, see Jeremy Siegel and Richard Thaler, "The Equity Premium Puzzle," *Journal of Economic Perspectives,* vol. 11, no. 1 (Winter 1997), pp. 191–200, and more recently, "Perspectives on the Equity Risk Premium," *Financial Analysts Journal,* vol. 61, no. 1 (November/December 2005), pp. 61–73, reprinted in Rodney N. Sullivan, *Bold Thinking on Investment Management,* CFA Institute, 2005, pp. 202–217.

F I G U R E   1–5

Equity Risk Premium (30-Year Compound Annual Moving Average, 1831 through December 2006)

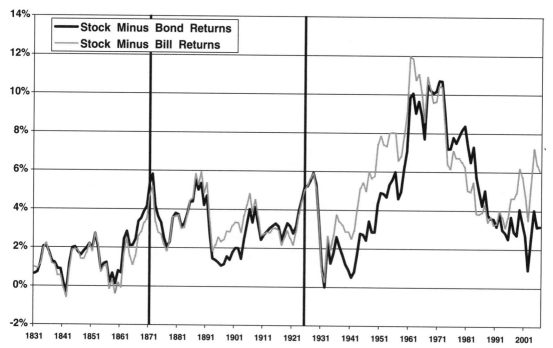

uity return occurred in a period marked by very low real returns on
bonds. Since firms finance a large part of their capital investment with
bonds, the low cost of obtaining such funds increased returns to shareholders. The period of the 1930s and 1940s marked an extremely undervalued period for equities and overvalued period for government
bonds, leading to unusually high returns for stocks and low returns for
bonds. As stocks and bonds become more correctly priced, the equity
premium will certainly shrink. Chapter 8 will further discuss the equity
premium and its implications for future returns.

WORLDWIDE EQUITY AND BOND RETURNS: GLOBAL STOCKS FOR THE LONG RUN

When I published *Stocks for the Long Run* in 1994, some economists questioned whether my conclusions, drawn from data from the United
States, might overstate equity returns measured on a worldwide basis.

Several economists emphasized the existence of a *survivorship bias*
in international returns, a bias caused by the fact that long-term returns
are intensively studied in successful equity markets, such as the United
States, but ignored in countries, such as Russia or Argentina, where
stocks have faltered or disappeared outright.[17] This bias suggested that
stock returns in the United States, a country that over the last 200 years
has been transformed from a small British colony into the world's greatest economic power, are unique and historical equity returns in other
countries would be lower.

Three U.K. economists subsequently examined the historical stock
and bond returns from 16 countries over the past century and put to bed
concerns about survivorship bias. Elroy Dimson and Paul Marsh, professors at the London Business School, and Mike Staunton, director of
the London Share Price Database, published their research in a book entitled *Triumph of the Optimists: 101 Years of Global Investment Returns*. This
book provides a rigorous yet readable account of worldwide financial
market returns in 16 separate countries.

Despite the major disasters visited on many of these countries, such
as war, hyperinflation, and depressions, all 16 countries offered substantially positive, after-inflation stock returns. Furthermore, fixed-income
returns in countries that experienced major wartime dislocations, such
as Italy, Germany, and Japan, were decidedly negative, so that the supe-

---

[17] See Stephen J. Brown, William N. Goetzmann, and Stephen A. Ross, "Survival," *Journal of Finance*,
vol. 50 (1995), p. 853–873.

riority of equities relative to other financial assets was decisive in all countries.

The average annual real stock, bond, and bill returns of the 16 countries analyzed from 1900 through 2006 are shown in Figure 1-6.[18] Real equity returns ranged from a low of 2.7 percent in Belgium to a high of almost 8 percent in Sweden and Australia. Stock returns in the United States, although quite good, were not exceptional. U.S. stock returns were exceeded by the returns in Sweden, Australia, and South Africa. And the average real-world return on stocks is not far from the U.S. return.

---

[18] Elroy Dimson, Paul Marsh, and Mike Staunton, "Global Investment Returns Yearbook 2007," ABN-AMRO Bank NV, February 2007.

FIGURE 1–6

Average Annual Real Stock, Bond, and Bill Returns of the 16 Countries Analyzed from 1900 through December 2006

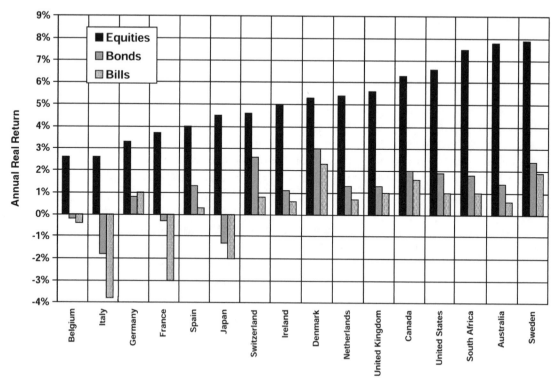

SOURCE: Based on information from Elroy Dimson, Paul Marsh, and Michael Staunton, *Triumph of the Optimists: 101 Years of Global Investment Returns*, (Princeton, N.J.: Princeton University Press, 2002).

When all the information was analyzed, the *Triumph of the Optimists* concluded "that the US experience of equities outperforming bonds and bills has been mirrored in all sixteen countries examined. . . . Every country achieved equity performance that was better than that of bonds. Over the 101 years as a whole, there were only two bond markets and just one bill market that provided a better return than our *worst* performing equity market."

Furthermore, "While the US and the UK have indeed performed well, . . . there is no indication that they are hugely out of line with other countries. . . . Concerns about success and survivorship bias, while legitimate, may therefore have been somewhat overstated [and] investors may have not been materially misled by a focus on the US."[19,20]

This last statement is significant. More studies have been made of the U.S. equity markets than the equity markets of any other country in the world. Dimson, Marsh, and Staunton are saying that the results found in the United States have relevance to all investors in all countries. The superior performance of U.S. equities over the past two centuries is not a special case. Stocks have outperformed fixed-income assets in every country examined and often by an overwhelming margin. International studies have reinforced, not diminished, the case for equities.

CONCLUSION: STOCKS FOR THE LONG RUN

Over the past 200 years the compound annual real return on a diversified portfolio of common stock is nearly 7 percent in the United States, and it has displayed a remarkable constancy over time. The reasons for the persistence and long-term stability of stock returns are not well understood. Certainly the returns on stocks are dependent on the quantity and quality of capital, productivity, and the return to risk taking. But the ability to create value also springs from skillful management, a stable political system that respects property rights, and the capacity to provide value to consumers in a competitive environment. Swings in investor sentiment resulting from political or economic crises can throw stocks off their long-term path, but the fundamental forces producing economic growth enable equities to regain their long-term trend. Perhaps that is why long-

---

[19] Elroy Dimson, Paul Marsh, and Michael Staunton, *Triumph of the Optimists: 101 Years of Global Investment Returns*, Princeton, N.J.: Princeton University Press, 2002, pp. 52–53 and 175.

[20] In fact, *Triumph of the Optimists* may have actually *understated* long-term international stock returns. The U.S. stocks markets and other world markets for which we have data did very well in the 30 years prior to 1900, when their study begins. U.S. returns measured from 1871 outperform those returns taken from 1900 by 32 basis points. Data from the United Kingdom show a very similar pattern.

term stock returns have displayed such stability despite the radical political, economic, and social changes that have impacted the world over the past two centuries.

Yet one must be aware of the political and legal framework in which these returns were generated. The superior returns to equity over the past two centuries might be explained by the growing dominance of nations committed to free-market economics. Who might have expected the triumph of market-oriented economies during the Great Depression of the 1930s and the tumult following World War II? The robustness of world equity prices in recent decades might reflect the emergence of the golden age of capitalism—a system in ascendancy today but whose fortunes could decline in the future. Yet even if capitalism declines, it is unclear which assets, if any, will retain value. In fact, if history is any guide, government bonds in our paper money world may fare far worse than stocks in any political or economic upheaval. As the next chapter shows, the risks in bonds actually outweigh those in stocks over long horizons.

APPENDIX 1: STOCKS FROM 1802 TO 1870

The first actively traded U.S. stocks, floated in 1791, were issued by two banks: the Bank of New York and the Bank of the United States.[21] Both offerings were enormously successful and were quickly bid to a premium. But they collapsed the following year when Alexander Hamilton's assistant at the Treasury, William Duer, attempted to manipulate the market and precipitated a crash. It was from this crisis that the antecedents of the New York Stock Exchange were born on May 17, 1792.

Joseph David, an expert on the eighteenth-century corporation, claimed that equity capital was readily forthcoming not only for every undertaking likely to be profitable but also, in his words, "for innumerable undertakings in which the risk was very great and the chances of success were remote."[22] Although over 300 business corporations were chartered by the states before 1801, fewer than 10 had securities that traded on a regular basis. Two-thirds of those chartered before 1801 were

---

[21] Until recently, the oldest continuously operating firm was Dexter Corp., founded in 1767, a Connecticut maker of special materials that was purchased in September 2000 by Invitrogen Corp. The current oldest is Bowne & Co. (1775), which specializes in printing; the second is Wachovia Bank, which acquired First Union, the successor of the First National Bank of Pennsylvania founded in 1782; and the third is the Bank of New York Corp., founded in 1784, which was involved in the successful 1791 stock offering with the Bank of the United States that was eventually involved in the crash of 1792.

[22] Werner and Smith, *Wall Street*, p. 82.

connected with transportation: wharves, canals, turnpikes, and bridges. But the important stocks of the early nineteenth century were financial institutions: banks and, later, insurance companies. Banks and insurance companies held loans and equity in many of the manufacturing firms that, at that time, did not have the financial standing to issue equity. The fluctuations in the stock prices of financial firms in the nineteenth century reflected the health of the general economy and the profitability of the firms to whom they lent. The first large nonfinancial venture was the Delaware and Hudson Canal, issued in 1825, which also became an original member of the Dow Jones Industrial Average 60 years later. In 1830, the first railroad, the Mohawk and Hudson, was listed, and for the next 50 years railroads dominated trading on the major exchanges.

APPENDIX 2: ARITHMETIC AND GEOMETRIC RETURNS

The average arithmetic return r_A is the average of each yearly return. If r_1 to r_n are the n yearly returns, $r_A = (r_1 + r_2 + \ldots + r_n)/n$. The average geometric, or compound, return r_G is the nth root of the product of one-year total returns minus 1. Mathematically this is expressed as $r_G = [(1 + r_1)(1 + r_2) \ldots (1 + r_n)]^{1/n} - 1$. An asset that achieves a geometric return of r_G will accumulate to $(1 + r_G)^n$ times the initial investment over n years. The geometric return is approximately equal to the arithmetic return minus one-half the variance σ^2 of yearly returns, or $r_G \approx r_A - \frac{1}{2}\sigma^2$.

Investors can be expected to realize geometric returns only over long periods of time. The average geometric return is always less than the average arithmetic return except when all yearly returns are exactly equal. This difference is related to the volatility of yearly returns.

A simple example demonstrates the difference. If a portfolio falls by 50 percent in the first year and then doubles (up 100 percent) in the second year, "buy-and-hold" investors are back to where they started, with a total return of zero. The compound or geometric return r_G, defined above as $(1 - 0.5)(1 + 1) - 1$, accurately indicates the zero total return of this investment over the two years.

The average annual arithmetic return r_A is +25 percent = (−50 percent + 100 percent)/2. Over two years, this average return can be turned into a compound or total return only by successfully "timing" the market, specifically increasing the funds invested in the second year, hoping for a recovery in stock prices. Had the market dropped again in the second year, this strategy would have been unsuccessful and resulted in lower total returns than achieved by the buy-and-hold investor.

CHAPTER 2

RISK, RETURN, AND PORTFOLIO ALLOCATION

Why Stocks Are Less Risky Than Bonds in the Long Run

As a matter of fact, what investment can we find which offers real fixity or certainty income? . . . As every reader of this book will clearly see, the man or woman who invests in bonds is speculating in the general level of prices, or the purchasing power of money.

IRVING FISHER, 1912[1]

MEASURING RISK AND RETURN

Risk and return are the building blocks of finance and portfolio management. Once the risk and expected return of each asset are specified, modern financial theory can help investors determine the best portfolios. But

---

[1] Irving Fisher et al., *How to Invest When Prices Are Rising*, Scranton, Pa.: G. Lynn Sumner & Co., 1912, p. 6.

the risk and return on stocks and bonds are not physical constants, like the speed of light or gravitational force, waiting to be discovered in the natural world. Despite the overwhelming quantity of historical data, one can never be certain that the underlying factors that generate asset prices have remained unchanged. One cannot, as in the physical sciences, run repeated controlled experiments, holding all other factors constant while estimating the value of the parameter in question. As Nobel laureate Paul Samuelson is fond of saying, "We have but one sample of history."

Yet one must start by analyzing the past in order to understand the future. The first chapter showed that not only have fixed-income returns lagged substantially behind those on equities but, because of the uncertainty of inflation, bonds can be quite risky for long-term investors. In this chapter one shall see that because of the changing nature of risk over time, portfolio allocations depend crucially on the investor's planning horizon.

RISK AND HOLDING PERIOD

For many investors, the most meaningful way to describe risk is by portraying a "worst-case scenario." The best and worst after-inflation returns for stocks, bonds, and bills from 1802 over holding periods ranging from 1 to 30 years are displayed in Figure 2-1. Here stock returns are measured by dividends plus capital gains or losses available on a broad capitalization-weighted index of U.S. small and large stocks.

Note that the height of the bars, which measures the difference between best and worst returns, declines far more rapidly for equities than for fixed-income securities as the holding period increases.

Stocks are unquestionably riskier than bonds or Treasury bills over one- and two-year periods. However, in every five-year period since 1802, the worst performance in stocks, at –11 percent per year, has been only slightly worse than the worst performance in bonds or bills. And for 10-year holding periods, the worst stock performance has actually been *better* than that for bonds or bills.

For 20-year holding periods, stock returns have never fallen below inflation, while returns for bonds and bills once fell as much as 3 percent per year below the inflation rate for two decades. This wiped out almost one-half the purchasing power of a bond portfolio. For 30-year periods, the worst returns for stocks remained comfortably ahead of inflation by 2.6 percent per year, a return that is not far from the *average* return on fixed-income assets.

F I G U R E 2–1

Maximum and Minimum Real Holding Period Returns, 1802 through December 2006

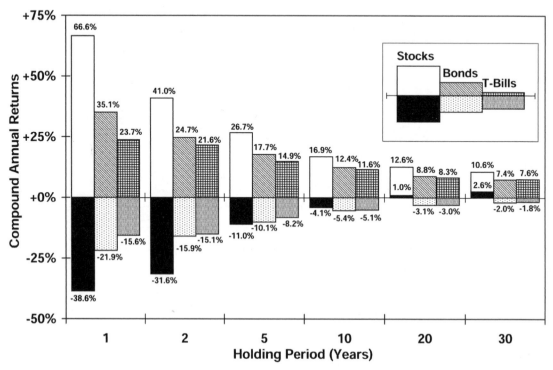

It is very significant that stocks, in contrast to bonds or bills, have never delivered to investors a negative real return over periods of 17 years or more. Although it might appear to be riskier to accumulate wealth in stocks rather than in bonds over long periods of time, precisely the opposite is true: the safest long-term investment for the preservation of purchasing power has clearly been a diversified portfolio of equities.

Some investors question whether holding periods of 10 or 20 or more years are relevant to their planning horizon. But one of the greatest mistakes that investors make is to underestimate their holding period. This is because many investors think about the holding periods of a particular stock, bond, or mutual fund. But the holding period that is relevant for portfolio allocation is the length of time the investors hold *any* stocks or bonds, no matter how many changes are made among the individual issues in their portfolio.

The percentage of times that stock returns outperform bond or bill returns over various holding periods is shown in Table 2-1. As the hold-

TABLE 2–1

Holding Period Comparisons: Percentage of Periods When Stocks Outperform Bonds and Bills

Holding Period	Time Period	Stocks Outperform Bonds	Stocks Outperform T-Bills
1 Year	1802-2006	61.0	62.0
	1871-2006	60.3	64.7
2 Year	1802-2006	65.2	65.7
	1871-2006	65.4	69.9
3 Year	1802-2006	67.2	70.2
	1871-2006	68.7	73.3
5 Year	1802-2006	69.2	72.6
	1871-2006	71.3	75.0
10 Year	1802-2006	80.1	80.6
	1871-2006	82.4	85.3
20 Year	1802-2006	91.9	94.6
	1871-2006	95.6	99.3
30 Year	1802-2006	99.4	97.2
	1871-2006	100.0	100.0

ing period increases, the probability that stocks will outperform fixed-income assets increases dramatically. For 10-year horizons, stocks beat bonds and bills about 80 percent of the time; for 20-year horizons, it is over 90 percent of the time; and over 30-year horizons, it is virtually 100 percent of the time.

As noted in the last chapter, the last 30-year period in which bonds beat stocks ended in 1861, at the onset of the U.S. Civil War. This is a point worth remembering: never in any of the past 175 years would a buyer of newly issued 30-year government bonds (had they been issued on an annual basis) have outperformed an investor in a diversified port-folio of common stocks held over the same period.

Although the dominance of stocks over bonds is readily apparent in the long run, it is also important to note that over one- and even two-year periods, stocks outperform bonds or bills only about three out of every five years. This means that nearly two out of every five years a

stockholder's return will fall behind the return he or she would get on Treasury bills or bank certificates. The high probability that bonds and even bank accounts will outperform stocks in the short run is the primary reason why it is so hard for many investors to stay in stocks.[2]

INVESTOR RETURNS FROM MARKET PEAKS

Many investors, although convinced of the long-term superiority of equity, believe that they should not invest in stocks when stock prices appear high. But this is not true for the long-term investor. The after-inflation total return over 10-, 20-, and 30-year holding periods after the eight major stock market peaks of the last century is shown in Figure 2-2.

Even from major stock market peaks, the wealth accumulated in stocks is more than four times that in bonds and more than five times that in Treasury bills if the holding period is 30 years. If the holding period is 20 years, stock accumulations beat those in bonds by about two-to-one. Even 10 years after market peaks, stocks still have an advantage over fixed-income assets. Unless investors believe there is a high probability that they will need to liquidate their savings over the next 5 to 10 years to maintain their living standard, history has shown that there is no compelling reason for long-term investors to abandon stocks no matter how high the market may seem.

Of course, if investors can identify peaks and troughs in the market, they can outperform the buy-and-hold strategy that is advocated in this book. But, needless to say, few investors can do this. And even if an investor sells stocks at the peak, this does not guarantee superior returns. As difficult as it is to sell when stock prices are high and everyone is optimistic, it is more difficult to buy at market bottoms when pessimism is widespread and few have the confidence to venture back into stocks.

A number of "market timers" have boasted that they yanked all their money out of stocks before the 1987 stock crash or the 2000 bear market. But in 1987 many did not get back into the market until it had already passed its previous highs. And many of the bears of the most recent decline are still out of the market, despite the fact that most market averages have hit all-time highs. In the long run, getting out of the market at the peak does not guarantee that you will beat the buy-and-hold investor.

---

[2] Chapter 19 on behavioral economics analyzes how investors' aversion to taking losses, no matter how small, affects portfolio performance.

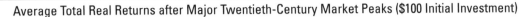

F I G U R E   2–2

Average Total Real Returns after Major Twentieth-Century Market Peaks ($100 Initial Investment)

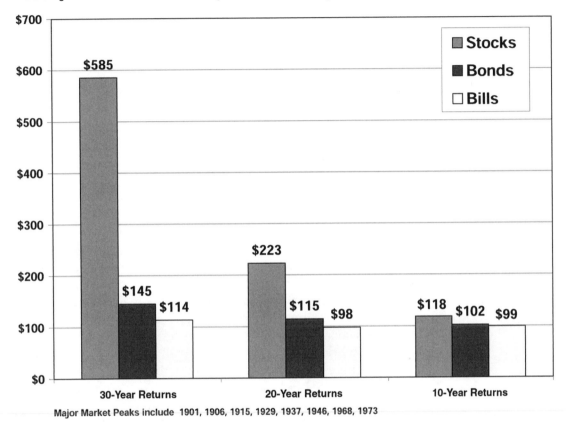

Major Market Peaks include 1901, 1906, 1915, 1929, 1937, 1946, 1968, 1973

STANDARD MEASURES OF RISK

The risk—defined as the standard deviation of average real annual returns—for stocks, bonds, and bills based on the historical sample of over
200 years is displayed in Figure 2-3. Standard deviation is the measure of
risk used in portfolio theory and asset allocation models.

Although the standard deviation of stock returns is higher than for
bond returns over short-term holding periods, once the holding period
increases to between 15 and 20 years, stocks become less risky than
bonds. Over 30-year periods, the standard deviation of a portfolio of equities falls to less than three-fourths that of bonds or bills. The standard
deviation of average stock returns falls nearly twice as fast as for fixed-
income assets as the holding period increases.

F I G U R E   2–3

Risk for Average Real Return over Various Holding Periods, 1802 through December 2006 (Historical Risk versus Risk Based on Random Walk Hypothesis)

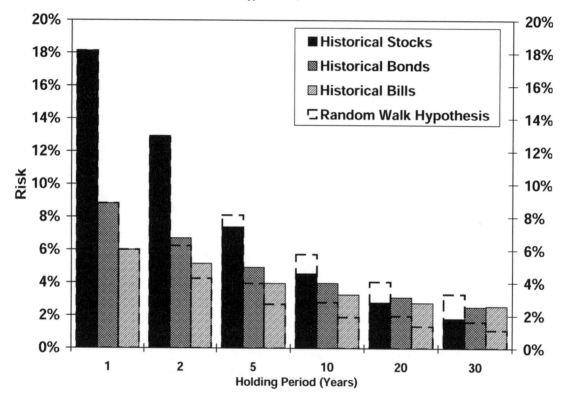

Theoretically the standard deviation of average annual returns is inversely proportional to the holding period if asset returns follow a random walk.[3] A *random walk* is a process whereby future returns are considered completely independent of past returns. The dashed bars in Figure 2-3 show the decline in risk predicted under the random walk assumption.

But the historical data show that the random walk hypothesis cannot be maintained for equities. This is because the actual risk of stocks declines far faster than the predicted rate, indicated by the dashed bars. This occurs because of the mean reversion of equity returns that I described in Chapter 1.

---

[3] In particular, the standard deviation of average returns falls as the square root of the length of the holding period.

The standard deviation of returns for fixed-income assets, on the other hand, does not fall as fast as the random walk theory predicts. This is a manifestation of mean aversion of bond returns. *Mean aversion* means that once an asset's return deviates from its long-run average, there is an increased chance that it will deviate further, rather than return to more normal levels. Mean aversion of bond returns is especially characteristic of hyperinflations, such as those that impacted Japanese and German bonds, but it is also present in the more moderate inflations that have hit the United States and the United Kingdom. Once inflation begins to accelerate, the inflationary process becomes cumulative and bondholders have virtually no chance of making up losses to their purchasing power. In contrast, stockholders who hold claims on real assets rarely suffer a permanent loss due to inflation.

VARYING CORRELATION BETWEEN STOCK AND BOND RETURNS

Even though the returns on bonds fall short of that on stocks, bonds may still serve to diversify a portfolio and lower overall risk. This will be true if bond and stock returns are *negatively correlated*, which means that bond yields and stock prices move in opposite directions. The diversifying strength of an asset is measured by the correlation coefficient. The *correlation coefficient*, which theoretically ranges between –1 and +1, measures the correlation between an asset's return and the return of the rest of the portfolio. The lower the correlation coefficient, the better the asset serves as a portfolio diversifier. Assets with negative correlations are particularly good diversifiers. As the correlation coefficient between the asset and portfolio returns increases, the diversifying quality of the asset declines.

The correlation coefficient between *annual* stock and bond returns for six subperiods between 1926 and 2006 is shown in Figure 2-4. From 1926 through 1965 the correlation was only slightly positive, indicating that bonds were fairly good diversifiers for stocks. From 1966 through 1989 the correlation coefficient jumped to +0.34, and from 1990 through 1997 the correlation increased further to +0.55. This means that the diversifying quality of bonds diminished markedly from 1926 to 1997.

There are good reasons why the correlation became more positive during this period. Under the gold-based monetary standard of the 1920s and early 1930s, bad economic times were associated with falling commodity prices; when the real economy was sinking, stocks declined and the real value of government bonds rose.

Under a paper money standard, bad economic times are more likely to be associated with *inflation*, not deflation, as the government at-

FIGURE 2–4

Correlation Coefficient between Monthly Stock and Bond Returns

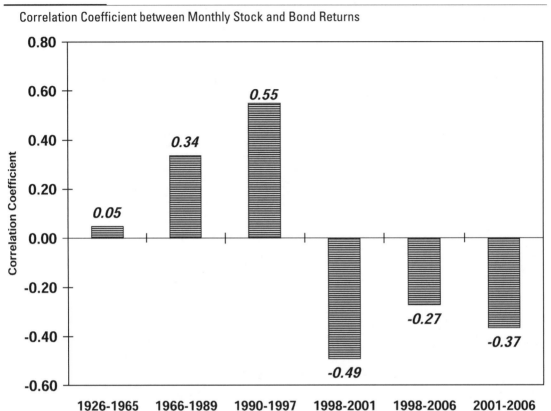

tempts to offset economic downturns with expansionary monetary policy. This inflationary policy accompanies a weak real economy, such as occurred during the 1970s. The negative short-term effects of inflation on equity returns are detailed in Chapter 11.

But this has changed in recent years. Since 1998 there has been a dramatic reversal in the short-term correlation between stock and bond prices, as shown in Figure 2-4. Over the past decade stock prices have been *negatively* correlated with government bond prices. From 1997 through 2001 the world markets were roiled by economic and currency upheavals in Asia, the deflationary economy in Japan, and then the events of September 11.[4] The collapsing currency markets, combined with falling commodity prices, had an eerie resemblance to the 1930s,

---

[4] The causes and consequences of these events are discussed in Chapter 10.

when deflation ruled and government bonds were the only appreciating assets. As a result international investors fled to the U.S. government security market when turmoil hit equities and other currencies. Long-term U.S. government bonds became "safe havens" for investors fearing a meltdown in the stock market.[5]

This tendency for investors to hide in long-term U.S. Treasury issues when equities experienced sudden declines persisted, despite the Asian recovery and the improving Japanese economy. As central banks have held firm against inflation, government bonds can be an island of stability when there is financial stress.

But it is an open question whether bonds will be good *long-term* diversifiers, especially if the specter of inflation looms once again. Nevertheless, the premium now enjoyed by Treasury issues generated by investors seeking *short-term* safe havens means that the return on government bonds will be low and they will become less desirable to long-term investors.

EFFICIENT FRONTIERS[6]

Modern portfolio theory describes how investors may alter the risk and return of a portfolio by changing the mix between assets. Figure 2-5, based on the 200-year history of stock and bond returns, displays the risks and returns that result from varying the proportion of stocks and bonds in a portfolio over various holding periods ranging from 1 to 30 years.

The square at the bottom of each curve represents the risk and return of an all-bond portfolio, while the cross at the top of the curve represents the risk and return of an all-stock portfolio. The circle falling somewhere on the curve indicates the minimum risk achievable by combining stocks and bonds. The curve that connects these points represents the risk and return of all blends of portfolios from 100 percent bonds to 100 percent stocks. This curve, called the *efficient frontier*, is the heart of modern portfolio analysis and is the foundation of asset allocation models.

Investors can achieve any combination of risk and return along the curve by changing the proportion of stocks and bonds. Moving up the

---

[5] Short-term Treasury securities such as bills have often enjoyed safe-haven status. Rising bond prices in a tumultuous equity market also occurred during the October 19, 1987, stock market crash, but much of the rise then was predicated on the (correct) belief that the Fed would lower short-term rates.

[6] This section, which contains some advanced material, can be skipped without loss of continuity.

F I G U R E   2–5

Risk-Return Trade-Offs for Various Holding Periods, 1802 through December 2006

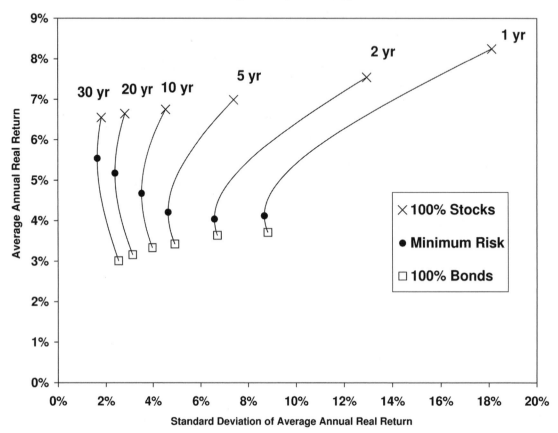

curve means increasing the proportion in stocks and correspondingly reducing the proportion in bonds. As stocks are added to the all-bond
portfolio, expected returns increase and risk decreases, a very desirable
combination for investors. But after the minimum risk point is reached,
increasing stocks will increase the return of the portfolio but only with
extra risk.

   The slope of any point on the efficient frontier indicates the risk-return trade-off for that allocation. By finding the points on the longer-
term efficient frontiers that have a slope equal to the slope on the
one-year frontier, one can determine the allocations that represent the
same risk-return trade-offs for all holding periods.

RECOMMENDED PORTFOLIO ALLOCATIONS

What percentage of an investor's portfolio should be invested in stocks? The answer can be seen in Table 2-2, which is based on standard portfolio models incorporating both the risk tolerance and the holding period of the investor.[7] Four classes of investors are analyzed: the ultraconservative investor who demands maximum safety no matter the return, the conservative investor who accepts small risks to achieve extra return, the moderate-risk-taking investor, and the aggressive investor who is willing to accept substantial risks in search of extra returns.

The recommended equity allocation increases dramatically as the holding period lengthens. Based on the 200 years of historical returns on stocks and bonds, ultraconservative investors should hold nearly three-quarters of their portfolio in stocks over 30-year holding periods. This allocation is justified since stocks are safer than bonds in terms of purchasing power over long periods of time. The historical data suggest that even conservative investors should hold nearly 90 percent of their portfolio in stocks for these long horizons, while the analysis indicates moderate and aggressive investors should have over 100 percent in equity. Borrowing or leveraging an all-stock portfolio can achieve this allocation, although if such borrowing is not desired, investors with these preferences would do quite well to hold 100 percent of their long-term portfolio in stocks.

Given these striking results, it might seem puzzling that the holding period has almost never been considered in portfolio theory. This is

---

[7] The one-year proportions (except minimum risk point) are arbitrary and are used as benchmarks for other holding periods. Choosing different proportions as benchmarks does not qualitatively change the analysis.

T A B L E   2–2

Portfolio Allocation: Percentage of Portfolio Recommended in Stocks Based on All Historical Data

Risk Tolerance	Holding Period			
	1 Year	5 Years	10 Years	30 Years
Ultraconservative (Minimum Risk)	9.0%	22.0%	39.3%	71.4%
Conservative	25.0%	38.7%	59.6%	89.5%
Moderate	50.0%	61.6%	88.0%	116.2%
Aggressive Risk Taker	75.0%	78.5%	110.1%	139.1%

because modern portfolio theory was established when the academic profession believed in the random walk theory of security prices. As noted earlier, under a random walk, the *relative* risk of various securities does not change for different holding periods, so portfolio allocations do not depend on how long one holds the asset. The holding period becomes a crucial issue in portfolio theory when the data reveal the mean reversion of stock returns.[8]

INFLATION-INDEXED BONDS

Until the last decade, there was no U.S. government bond whose return was guaranteed against changes in the price level. But in January 1997, the U.S. Treasury issued the first government-guaranteed inflation-indexed bond. The coupons and principal repayment of this inflation-protected bond are automatically increased when the price level rises, so bondholders suffer no loss of purchasing power when they receive the coupons or final principal. Since any and all inflation is compensated, the interest rate on this bond is a *real*, or inflation-adjusted, interest rate.

When these bonds were first issued, their real yields were about 3½ percent, and they rose to over 4 percent at the height of the 2000 bull market. However, these yields have declined markedly since 2001, and at the end of 2006, their real yields fell to about 2 percent, less than one-third the historical return on equity. Nevertheless, these bonds may be an attractive alternative for investors who do not want to assume the short-term risks of stocks but fear loss of purchasing power in bonds. In 20 percent of all 10-year periods from 1926, stocks have fallen short of a 2.0 percent real return. For most long-term investors, inflation-indexed bonds should dominate nominal bonds in a portfolio.

---

[8] For an excellent review of this literature see Luis M. Viceira and John Y. Campbell, *Strategic Asset Allocation: Portfolio Choice for Long-Term Investors*, New York: Oxford University Press, 2002. Also see Nicholas Barberis, "Investing for the Long Run When Returns Are Predictable," *Journal of Finance*, vol. 55 (2000), pp. 225–264. Paul Samuelson has shown that mean reversion will increase equity holdings if investors have a risk aversion coefficient greater than unity, which most researchers find is the case. See Paul Samuelson, "Long-Run Risk Tolerance When Equity Returns Are Mean Regressing: Pseudoparadoxes and Vindications of 'Businessmen's Risk'" in W. C. Brainard, W. D. Nordhaus, and H. W. Watts, eds., *Money, Macroeconomics, and Public Policy*, Cambridge: MIT Press, 1991, pp. 181–200. See also Zvi Bodie, Robert Merton, and William Samuelson, "Labor Supply Flexibility and Portfolio Choice in a Lifecycle Model," *Journal of Economic Dynamics and Control*, vol. 16, no. 3 (July–October 1992), pp. 427–450. Bodie, Merton, and Samuelson have shown that equity holdings can vary with age because stock returns can be correlated with labor income.

CONCLUSION

No one denies that in the short run stocks are riskier than fixed-income assets. But in the long run, history has shown that stocks are actually less risky investments than bonds. The inflation uncertainty that is inherent in the paper money standard that the United States and the rest of the world have adopted indicates that "fixed income" does not mean "fixed purchasing power." Despite the dramatic gains in price stability seen over the past decade, there is still much uncertainty about what a dollar will be worth two or three decades from now. Historical evidence indicates that we can be more certain of the purchasing power of a diversified portfolio of common stocks 30 years in the future than the principal on a 30-year U.S. government bond.

CHAPTER 3

STOCK INDEXES

Proxies for the Market

It has been said that figures rule the world.

JOHANN WOLFGANG GOETHE, 1830

MARKET AVERAGES

"How's the market doing?" one stock investor asks another.

"It's having a good day—it's up over 70 points."

For most of the past century, no one would ask, "What's up 70 points?" Everyone knew the answer: the Dow Jones Industrial Average, the most quoted stock average in the world. This index, popularly called the Dow, was so renowned that the news media often called the Dow "the stock market." No matter how imperfectly the index describes the movement of share prices—and virtually no money manager pegs his or her performance to it—the Dow was the way virtually all investors thought of the stock market.

But today the Dow does not go unchallenged as an indicator of market prices. The S&P 500, first published by Standard & Poor's, now a division of The McGraw-Hill Companies, in March 1957, has become the uncontested benchmark index for large U.S. stocks. And the Nasdaq,

an automated electronic market that began in 1971, has become the exchange of choice for technology companies. The Nasdaq index measures the performance of such large technology firms as Microsoft, Intel, Cisco Systems, Google, and Apple.

The rise of the Nasdaq did not go unnoticed at Dow Jones. In 1999, for the first time in over 100 years, Dow Jones ventured off the Big Board, as the New York exchange is called, and selected two Nasdaq stocks—Microsoft and Intel—to join its venerable list. Here's the story of these three very different indexes with three unique reflections of the stock market.

THE DOW JONES AVERAGES

Charles Dow, one of the founders of Dow Jones & Co. that also publishes the *Wall Street Journal*, created the Dow Jones averages in the late nineteenth century. On February 16, 1885, he began publishing a daily average of 12 stocks (10 railroads and 2 industrials) that represented active and highly capitalized stocks. Four years later, Dow published a daily average based on 20 stocks—18 railroads and 2 industrials.

As industrial and manufacturing firms succeeded railroads in importance, the Dow Jones Industrial Average was created on May 26, 1896, from the 12 stocks shown in Table 3-1. The old index created in 1889 was reconstituted and renamed the Rail Average on October 26, 1896. In 1916, the Industrial Average was increased to 20 stocks, and in 1928 the number was expanded to 30. The Rail Average, whose name was changed in 1970 to the Transportation Average, is composed of 20 stocks, as it has been for over a century.

The early Dow stocks were centered on commodities: cotton, sugar, tobacco, lead, leather, rubber, and so on. Six of the 12 companies have survived in much the same form, but only one—General Electric, which in the summer of 2007 boasted the second-highest market value on U.S. exchanges—has retained both its membership in the Dow Industrials and its original name.[1]

Almost all of the original Dow stocks thrived as large and successful firms, even if they did not remain in the index (see the chapter appendix for details). The only exception was U.S. Leather Corp., which was liquidated in the 1950s. Shareholders received $1.50 plus one share of Keta Oil & Gas, a firm acquired earlier. But in 1955, the president, Lowell Birrell, who later fled to Brazil to escape U.S. authorities, looted

---

[1] Chicago Gas Company, an original member of the 12 Dow stocks, became Peoples Energy, Inc., and was a member of the Dow Utilities Average until May 1997.

T A B L E   3–1

Firms in the Dow Jones Industrial Average

1896	1916	1928	1965	2007
American Cotton Oil	American Beet Sugar	Allied Chemical	Allied Chemical	3M
	American Can	American Can	Aluminum Company of America	Alcoa Inc
American Sugar		American Smelting	American Can	Altria Group Inc
	American Car & Foundry	American Sugar	American Tel. & Tel.	American Express
	American Locomotive	American Tobacco	American Tobacco	American International Group
American Tobacco		Atlantic Refining	Anaconda Copper	AT&T Inc
	American Smelting	Bethlehem Steel	Bethlehem Steel	Boeing Co
Chicago Gas	American Sugar	Chrysler	Chrysler	Caterpillar Inc
		General Electric	DuPont	Citigroup Inc
	American Tel & Tel	General Motors	Eastman Kodak	Coca-Cola
Distilling & Cattle Feeding	Anaconda Copper	General Railway Signal	General Electric	DuPont
		Goodrich	General Foods	Exxon Mobil
	Baldwin Locomotive	International Harvester	General Motors	General Electric
General Electric		International Nickel	GoodYear	General Motors
	Central Leather	Mack Trucks	International Harvester	Hewlett-Packard
	General Electric	Nash Motors	International Nickel	Home Depot
Laclede Gas		North American	International Paper Company	Honeywell Int'l
	Goodrich	Paramount Publix	Johns-Manville	Intel
National Lead	Republic Iron & Steel	Postum, Inc.	Owens-Illinois Glass	IBM
		Radio Corp.	Procter & Gamble	Johnson & Johnson
	Studebaker	Sears, Roebuck	Sears, Roebuck	JPMorgan Chase
North American	Texas Co.	Standard Oil (N.J.)	Standard Oil of California	McDonald's Corp
		Texas Corp.	Standard Oil (N.J.)	Merck
	U.S. Rubber	Texas Gulf Sulphur	Swift & Company	Microsoft Corp
Tennessee Coal & Iron	U.S. Steel	Union Carbide	Texaco Incorporated	Pfizer
		U.S. Steel	Union Carbide	Procter & Gamble
U.S. Leather Pfd.	Utah Copper	Victor Talking Machine	United Aircraft	United Technologies
	Westinghouse	Westinghouse Electric	U.S. Steel	Verizon Communications
		Woolworth	Westinghouse Electric	Wal-Mart Stores
U.S. Rubber	Western Union	Wright Aeronautical	Woolworth	Walt Disney Co

Keta's assets. Shares in U.S. Leather, which in 1909 was the seventh-largest corporation in the United States, became worthless.

Computation of the Dow Index

The original Dow Jones averages were simply the sum of the prices of the component shares divided by the number of stocks in the index. However, this divisor had to be adjusted over time to prevent jumps in the index when there were changes in the companies that constituted the average and stock splits. In December 2006, the divisor was about 0.1248, so that a 1-point rise in any Dow stock caused the average to increase about 8 points.[2]

---

[2] The procedure for computing the Dow Jones averages when a new (or split) stock is substituted is as follows: the component stock prices are added up before and after the change, and a new divisor is determined that yields the same average as before the change. Because of stock splits, the divisor generally moves downward over time, but the divisor could increase if a higher-priced stock is substituted for a lower-priced one in the average.

The Dow Industrials is a *price-weighted index*, which means that the prices of the component stocks are added together and then divided by the number of firms in the index. As a result, proportional movements of high-priced stocks in the Dow averages have a much greater impact than movements of lower-priced stocks, regardless of the size of the company. A price-weighted index has the property that when a component stock splits, the split stock has a reduced impact on the average, and all the other stocks a slightly increased impact.[3]

Price-weighted indexes are unusual since the impact of the firm's price on the index has nothing to do with the relative size of the company. This is in stark contrast to a capitalization-weighted index, such as Standard & Poor's 500 Index, which is described later in the chapter. As of December 2006, the 30 Dow stocks were valued at $4.2 trillion, which is about 25 percent of the capitalization of the entire U.S. market. Out of the 10 largest U.S.-based capitalization stocks, all but Bank of America are in the Dow Industrials. But not all the Dow stocks are large. Two Dow stocks are not even in the top 100: Alcoa and General Motors. And the smallest, General Motors, is ranked below 200 and has about 4 percent of the market value of Exxon Mobil, which is the largest component.

Long-Term Trends in the Dow Jones

Figure 3-1 plots the monthly high and low of the Dow Jones Industrial Average from its inception in 1885, corrected for changes in the cost of living. The inset shows the Dow Industrial Average uncorrected for inflation.

A *trend line* and a *channel* are created by statistically fitting the Dow on a time trend. The upper and lower bounds are 1 standard deviation, or 50 percent, above and below the trend. The slope of the trend line, 1.85 percent per year, is the average compound rate at which the Dow stocks have appreciated, excluding inflation, since 1885. The Dow Jones average, like most other popular averages, does not include dividends, so the change in the index greatly understates the total return on the Dow stocks. Since the average dividend yield on stocks was about 4.3 percent during this time, the total annual real compound return on the Dow stocks was 6.2 percent over this period, a bit below the long-term real stock return reported in Chapter 1.

---

[3] Before 1914, the divisor was left unchanged when a stock split, and the stock price was multiplied by the split ratio when computing the index. This led to rising stocks having greater weight in the average, something akin to value-weighted stock indexes today.

FIGURE 3–1

The Real Dow Jones Industrial Average, February 1885 through December 2006 (in 2006 Dollars)

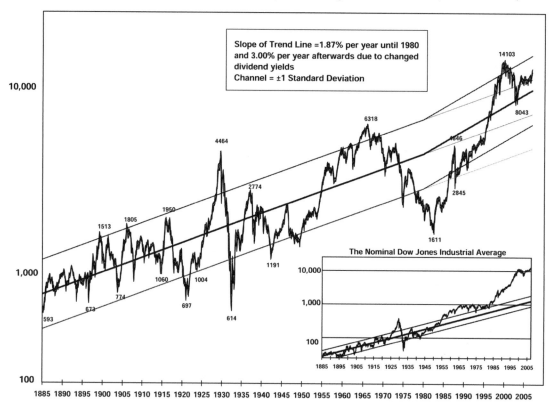

The inflation-corrected Dow has stayed within the channel about three-quarters of the time. When the Dow broke out of the channel to the upside, as it did in 1929 and again in the mid-1960s, stocks subsequently suffered poor short-term returns. Likewise, when stocks penetrated the channel on the downside, they subsequently experienced superior short-term returns.

BEWARE THE USE OF TREND LINES TO PREDICT FUTURE RETURNS

Using channels and trend lines to predict future returns, however tempting, can be misleading. Long-standing trends have been broken in the past. Uncorrected for inflation, the Dow Industrials broke and stayed above the trend line in the mid-1950s, as shown in the inset of Figure 3-1. This is because inflation, caused by the shift to a paper money standard,

propelled nominal stock prices justifiably above their previous, noninflationary trend. Those who used trend-line analysis and who failed to analyze stock prices in real, instead of nominal, terms would have sold in 1955 and *never* reentered the market.[4]

But there is now another justification why the channel may be penetrated on the upside. Stock indexes record only capital appreciation, and they therefore understate total returns, which must include dividends. But firms have been paying an ever-lower fraction of their earnings as dividends. More of the return is being pushed into capital gains through stock buybacks and reinvestment of earnings. Since the average dividend yield on stocks has fallen 2.88 percentage points since 1980, a new channel has been drawn in Figure 3-1 with a 2.88 percentage point higher slope to represent increased capital gains. By that measure the Dow level at the end of 2006, although at a peak, was within 1 standard deviation of the mean.

VALUE-WEIGHTED INDEXES

Standard & Poor's Index

Although the Dow Jones Industrial Average was published in 1885, it was certainly not a comprehensive index of stock values, covering at most 30 stocks. In 1906 the Standard Statistics Co. was formed, and in 1918 it began publishing the first index of stock values based on each stock's performance weighted by its capitalization, or market value. This technique is now recognized as giving the best indication of the overall market, and it is almost universally used in establishing market benchmarks. In 1939, Alfred Cowles, founder of the Cowles Commission for Economic Research, constructed indexes of stock values back to 1871 that consisted of all stocks listed on the New York Stock Exchange using Standard & Poor's market-weighting techniques.

The Standard & Poor's stock price index began in 1923, and in 1926 it became the Standard & Poor's Composite Index containing 90 stocks. The index was expanded to 500 stocks on March 4, 1957, and it became the S&P 500 Index. At that time, the value of the S&P 500 Index comprised about 90 percent of the value of all NYSE-listed stocks. The 500 stocks contained exactly 425 industrial, 25 railroad, and 50 utility firms. Before 1988, the number of companies in each industry was restricted to these guidelines.

---

[4] For a related situation in which a long-standing benchmark was broken because of inflation, see the first section in Chapter 7, "An Evil Omen Returns."

A base value of 10 was chosen for the average value of the S&P index from 1941 to 1943 so that when the index was first published in 1957, the average price of a share of stock (which stood between $45 and $50) was approximately equal to the value of the index. An investor at that time could easily identify with the changes in the S&P 500 Index since a 1-point change approximated the price change for an average stock.

The S&P 500 Index does not contain the 500 largest stocks, nor are all the stocks in the index U.S.-based corporations. For example, Warren Buffett's Berkshire Hathaway, which S&P considers a holding company, is not in the S&P 500 Index. On the other hand, the S&P 500 Index has a few firms that are quite small, representing companies that have fallen in value and have yet to be replaced. As of March 2007, the total value of all S&P 500 companies was about $12.7 trillion, but this constituted less than 75 percent of the value of all stocks traded in the United States, significantly less than 50 years ago when the index comprised almost 90 percent of the market. A history of the S&P 500 Index and the insights that come from analyzing these stocks in this world-famous index is described in the next chapter.

Nasdaq Index

On February 8, 1971, the method of trading stocks underwent a revolutionary change. On that date, an automated quotation system called the *Nasdaq* (for National Association of Securities Dealers Automated Quotations) provided up-to-date bid and asked prices on 2,400 leading "over-the-counter" (OTC) stocks. Formerly, quotations for these unlisted stocks were submitted by the principal trader or by brokerage houses that carried an inventory. The Nasdaq linked the terminals of more than 500 market makers nationwide to a centralized computer system.

In contrast to the Nasdaq, stocks traded on the New York or American Stock Exchanges are assigned to a single specialist, who is charged with maintaining an orderly market in that stock. The Nasdaq changed the way quotes were disseminated and made trading these issues far more attractive to both investors and traders.

At the time that the Nasdaq was created, it was clearly more prestigious to be listed with an exchange (and preferably the New York Stock Exchange) than be traded on the Nasdaq. Nasdaq stocks tended to be small or new firms that had recently gone public or did not meet the listing requirements of the larger exchanges. However, many young technology firms found the computerized Nasdaq system a natural home.

Some, such as Intel and Microsoft, chose not to migrate to the Big Board, as the NYSE was termed, even when they qualified to do so.

The Nasdaq Index, which is a capitalization-weighted index of all stocks traded on the Nasdaq, was set at 100 on the first day of trading in 1971. It took almost 10 years to double to 200 and another 10 years to reach 500 in 1991. It reached its first major milestone of 1,000 in July 1995.

As the interest in technology stocks grew, the rise in the Nasdaq Index accelerated, and it doubled its value to 2,000 in just three years. In the fall of 1999, the technology boom sent the Nasdaq into orbit. The index increased from 2,700 in October 1999 to its all-time peak of 5,048.62 on March 10, 2000.

The increase in popularity of Nasdaq stocks resulted in a tremendous increase in volume on the exchange. At the onset, the volume on the Nasdaq was a small fraction of that on the New York Stock Exchange. By 1994 share volume on the Nasdaq exceeded that on the NYSE, and five years later dollar volume on the Nasdaq surpassed the NYSE as well.[5]

No longer was the Nasdaq the home of small firms waiting to qualify for Big Board membership. By 1998 the capitalization of the Nasdaq had already exceeded that of the Tokyo Stock Exchange. At the market peak in March 2000, the total market value of firms traded on the Nasdaq reached nearly $6 trillion, more than one-half that of the NYSE and more than any other stock exchange in the world. At the peak, Nasdaq's Microsoft and Cisco had the two largest market values in the world, and Nasdaq-listed Intel and Oracle were also among the top 10. By 2007 Microsoft was the only Nasdaq stock among U.S. stocks ranked in the top 10 by market value.

When the technology bubble burst, trading and prices on the Nasdaq sunk rapidly. The Nasdaq Index declined from over 5,000 in March 2000 to 1,150 in October 2002 before rebounding to 2,400 at the end of 2006. Trading also fell off from an average of over 2.5 billion shares when prices peaked to approximately 2 billion shares in 2007. Despite the decline in the Nasdaq Index, the Nasdaq still trades in some of the world's most active stocks.

Although there is a lively rivalry between the Nasdaq and the NYSE, most investors should not be concerned about what exchange a

---

[5] There is admittedly some double counting of volume in the Nasdaq dealer system due to the fact that the dealer buys the security rather than acting as an auctioneer. See Anne M. Anderson and Edward A. Dyl, "Trading Volume: NASDAQ and the NYSE," *Financial Analysts Journal*, vol. 63, no. 3 (May/June 2007), p. 79.

stock is listed on. Small stocks may be better served by having a specialist provide liquidity, but the spread between the price a stock sells for
and the price it can be bought for may be lower on active stocks under
the Nasdaq market maker system. There is now rapid consolidation
among exchanges, and cross-listing of issues is now becoming common.
The importance of what exchange a stock is listed on will decline even
more in the future.[6]

Other Stock Indexes: The Center for Research in Security Prices (CRSP)

In 1959, Professor James Lorie of the Graduate School of Business of the
University of Chicago received a request from the brokerage house Merrill
Lynch, Pierce, Fenner & Smith. The firm wanted to investigate how well
people had done investing in common stock and could not find reliable
historical data. Professor Lorie teamed up with colleague Lawrence Fisher
to build a database of securities data that could answer that question.

With computer technology in its infancy, Lorie and Fisher created
the Center for Research in Security Prices (CRSP, pronounced "crisp")
that compiled the first machine-readable file of stock prices dating from
1926 that was to become the accepted database for academic and professional research. The database currently contains all stocks traded on the
New York and American Stock Exchanges and the Nasdaq.

At the end of 2006, the market value of the 6,744 stocks was $18
trillion.

The largest comprehensive index of U.S. firms, Figure 3-2 shows
the size breakdown and total market capitalization of the stocks in this
index. The top 500 firms, which closely mirror the S&P 500 Index, constitute 74.6 percent of the market value of all stocks. The top 1,000 firms
in market value, which are virtually identical to the Russell 1000 and
published by the Russell Investment Group, comprise 85.4 percent of the
total value of equities. The Russell 2000 contains the next 2,000 largest
companies, which adds an additional 11.7 percent to the market value of
the total index. The Russell 3000, the sum of the Russell 1000 and 2000
indexes, comprises 97.1 percent of all U.S. stocks. The remaining 3,744
stocks constitute 2.9 percent of the value.

Closely related to the CRSP Total Return indexes is the Dow Jones
Wilshire 5000 Index, which was founded in 1974 and contains approximately 5,000 firms.

---

[6] Institutions have their own ways of dealing with big blocks of stock no matter what exchange the
stock is listed on.

FIGURE 3–2

CRSP Total Market Index (Value at $18.12 trillion in September 2007)

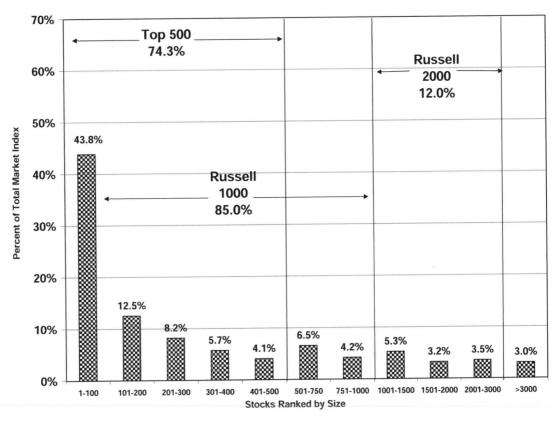

RETURN BIASES IN STOCK INDEXES

Because stock indexes such as the S&P 500 Index constantly add new firms and delete old ones, some investors believe that the return calculated from these indexes will be higher than the return that can be achieved by investors in the overall market.

But this is not the case. It is true that the best-performing stocks will stay in the S&P 500 Index, but this index misses the powerful upside move of many small and mid-sized issues. For example, Microsoft was not added to the S&P 500 Index until June 1994, eight years after going public. While small stock indexes are the incubators of some of the greatest growth stocks, they also contain those "fallen angels" that dropped out of the large-cap indexes and are headed downward.

An index is not biased if its performance can be replicated or matched by an investor. To replicate an index, the date of additions and deletions to the index must be announced in advance so that new stocks can be bought and deleted stocks can be sold. This is particularly important for issues that enter into bankruptcy: the postbankrupt price (which might be zero) must be factored into the index. All the major stock indexes, such as Standard & Poor's, Dow Jones, and the Nasdaq, can be replicated by investors.[7] Consequently, there is no statistical reason to believe that capitalization-based indexes give a biased representation of the return on the market.

APPENDIX: WHAT HAPPENED TO THE ORIGINAL 12 DOW INDUSTRIALS?

Two stocks (General Electric and Laclede) retained their original name (and industry); five (American Cotton, American Tobacco, Chicago Gas, National Lead, and North American) became large public companies in their original industries; one (Tennessee Coal and Iron) was merged into the giant U.S. Steel; and two (American Sugar and U.S. Rubber) went private—both in the 1980s. Surprisingly, only one (Distilling and Cattle Feeding) changed its product line (from alcoholic beverages to petrochemicals, although it still manufactures ethanol), and only one (U.S. Leather) liquidated. Here is a rundown of the original 12 stocks (market capitalizations as of March 2007):

> *American Cotton Oil* became Best Food in 1923, Corn Products Refining in 1958, and finally, CPC International in 1969—a major food company with operations in 58 countries. In 1997, CPC spun off its corn-refining business as Corn Products International and changed its name to Bestfoods. Bestfoods was acquired by Unilever in October 2000 for $20.3 billion. Unilever (UN), which is headquartered in the Netherlands, has a current market value of $43.2 billion.

> *American Sugar* became Amstar in 1970 and went private in 1984. In September 1991 the company changed its name to Domino Foods, Inc., to reflect its world-famous Domino line of sugar products.

---

[7] The original Value Line Index of 1,700 stocks, which was based on a geometric average of the changes in the individual stocks, was biased downward. This eventually led Value Line to abandon the geometric average in favor of the arithmetic one, which could be replicated.

American Tobacco changed its name to American Brands (AMB) in 1969 and to Fortune Brands (FO) in 1997, a global consumer products holding company with core business in liquor, office products, golf equipment, and home improvements. American Brands sold its American Tobacco subsidiary, including the Pall Mall and Lucky Strike brands, to one-time subsidiary B.A.T. Industries in 1994. The current market value is $12.1 billion.

Chicago Gas became Peoples Gas Light & Coke Co. in 1897, and then Peoples Energy Corp., a utility holding company, in 1980. Peoples Energy Corp. (PGL) was bought by WPS Resources and changed its name in 2006 to Integrys Energy Group (TEG). It has a market value of $4.1 billion. PGL was a member of the Dow Jones Utility Average until May 1997.

Distilling and Cattle Feeding went through a long and complicated history. It changed its name to American Spirits Manufacturing and then to Distiller's Securities Corp. Two months after the passage of prohibition, the company changed its charter and became U.S. Food Products Corp. and then changed its name again to National Distillers and Chemical. The company became Quantum Chemical Corp. in 1989, a leading producer of petrochemicals and propane. Nearing bankruptcy, it was purchased for $3.4 billion by Hanson PLC, an Anglo-American conglomerate. It was spun off as Millennium Chemicals (MCH) in October 1996. Lyondell Chemical (LYO) bought Millennium Chemicals in November 2004. The current market value of Lyondell is $7.7 billion.

General Electric (GE), founded in 1892, is the only original stock still in the Dow Industrials. GE is a huge manufacturing and broadcasting conglomerate that owns NBC and CNBC. Its market value of $359 billion is the second highest in the world.

Laclede Gas (LG) changed its name to Laclede Group, Inc., and it is a retail distributor of natural gas in the St. Louis area. The market value is $647 million.

National Lead (NL) changed its name to NL Industries in 1971, and it manufactures titanium dioxide and specialty chemicals. The market value is $4.96 billion.

North American became Union Electric Co. (UEP) in 1956, providing electricity in Missouri and Illinois. In January 1998, UEP merged with Cipsco (Central Illinois Public Service Co.) to form Ameren (AEE) Corp. The market value is $10.5 billion.

Tennessee Coal and Iron was bought out by U.S. Steel in 1907, and it became USX-U.S. Steel Group (X) in May 1991. In January 2002, the company changed its name back to U.S. Steel Corp. U.S. Steel has a market value of $10.2 billion.

U.S. Leather, one of the largest makers of shoes in the early part of this century, liquidated in January 1952, paying its shareholders $1.50 plus stock in an oil and gas company that was to become worthless.

U.S. Rubber became Uniroyal in 1961, and it was taken private in August 1985. In 1990 Uniroyal was purchased by the Michelin Group, which has a market value of €13 billion.

THE S&P 500 INDEX

A Half Century of U.S. Corporate History

Most of the change we think we see in life is due to truths being in and out of favor.

ROBERT FROST, "THE BLACK COTTAGE," 1914

Out of the three stock market indexes, the Dow, the Nasdaq, and the S&P 500, only one became the world standard for measuring the performance for U.S. stocks. It was born on February 28, 1957, and it grew out of Standard & Poor's Composite Index, a capitalization-weighted index begun in 1926 that contained 90 large stocks. Ironically, the 1926 index excluded the largest stock in the world at that time, American Telephone and Telegraph, because S&P did not want to let the performance of such a large firm dominate the index. To correct this omission and to recognize the growth of new firms in the 1950s, Standard & Poor's compiled an index of 500 of the largest industrial, rail, and utility firms that traded on the New York Stock Exchange.

The S&P 500 Index comprised about 85 percent of the total value of firms traded on the Big Board in 1957. It soon became the standard against which the performance of institutions and money managers in-

vesting in large U.S. stocks was compared. The S&P 500 Index originally contained exactly 425 industrial, 25 rail, and 50 utility firms, but these groupings were abandoned in 1988 in order to maintain, as S&P claimed, an index that included "500 leading companies in leading industries of the economy."

Since its creation, the index has been continually updated by adding new firms that meet Standard & Poor's criteria for market value, earnings, and liquidity while deleting an equal number that fall below these standards.[1] The total number of new firms added to the S&P 500 Index from its inception in 1957 through 2006 was 987, an average of about 20 per year. On average the new firms constitute about 5 percent of the market value of the index.

The highest number of new firms added to the index in a single year occurred in 1976, when Standard & Poor's added 60 firms including 15 banks and 10 insurance carriers. Until that year, the only financial stocks in the index were consumer finance companies because banks and insurance companies were traded in the "over-the-counter" (OTC) market and timely price data were not available until the Nasdaq Exchange began in 1971. In 2000, at the peak of the technology bubble, 49 new firms were added to the index, the highest since Nasdaq stocks were included in 1976. In 2003, just after the bottom of the subsequent bear market, the number of additions fell to a record-tying low of 8.

SECTOR ROTATION IN THE S&P 500 INDEX

The evolution of the U.S. economy during the past half century has brought about profound changes in its industrial landscape. Steel, chemical, auto, and oil companies once dominated our economy. Today healthcare, technology, finance, and other consumer services firms hold sway.

Increasingly, active investors are using sector analysis to allocate their portfolios. The most popular industry classification system was formulated in 1999 when Standard & Poor's joined Morgan Stanley to create the Global Industrial Classification Standard (GICS). This system arose from the earlier Standard Industrial Code (SIC) system devised by the U.S. government that had grown less suited to our service-based economy.[2]

---

[1] Criteria for listing and other information are found on Standard & Poor's Web site www2.standard andpoors.com/spf/pdf/index/500factsheet.pdf.

[2] In 1997 the SIC codes were expanded to include firms in Canada and Mexico, and the revised listing was renamed the North American Industrial Classification System (NAICS).

The GICS divides the economy into 10 sectors: **materials** (chemicals, papers, steel, and mining), **industrials** (capital goods, defense, transportation, and commercial and environmental services), **energy** (exploration, production, marketing, refining of oil and gas, and coal), **utilities** (electric, gas, water, and nuclear generating or transmission firms), **telecommunication services** (fixed line, cellular, wireless, and bandwidth), **consumer discretionary** (household durables, autos, apparel, hotels, restaurants, media, and retailing), **consumer staples** (food, tobacco, personal products, retailing, and hypermarkets), **healthcare** (equipment producers, healthcare providers, pharmaceuticals, and biotechs), **financial** (commercial and investment banking, mortgages, brokerage, insurance, and real estate [REITs]), and **information technology** (software services, Internet, home entertainment, data processing, computers, and semiconductors).

The share of the market value of each of these sectors in the S&P 500 Index from 1957 through 2006 is displayed in Figure 4-1. Many of the

F I G U R E   4–1

Changes in Sector Weighting, 1957 through December 2006

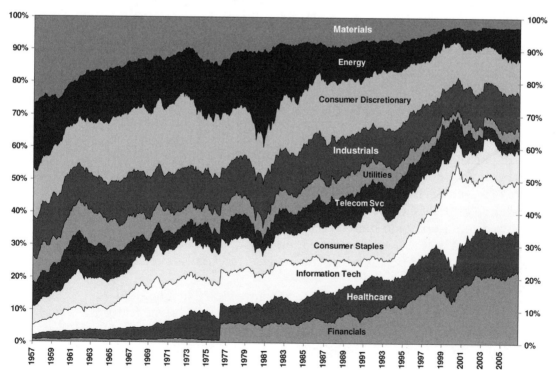

changes have been dramatic. The materials sector, by far the largest in 1957, has become the smallest today. The materials and energy sectors made up almost one-half of the market value of the index in 1957, but today these two sectors together constitute only 12 percent of the index. On the other hand, the financial, healthcare, and technology sectors, which started off as the three smallest sectors and comprised only 6 percent of the index in 1957, held one-half of the market value of all S&P 500 firms in 2007.

It is important to realize that when measured over long periods of time, the rising or falling market shares do not necessarily correlate with rising or falling investor returns. That is because change in sector shares often reflects the change in the *number* of firms, not just the change in the *value* of individual firms. This is especially true in the financial sector, as commercial and investment banks, insurance companies, brokerage houses, and government-sponsored enterprises such as Fannie Mae and Freddie Mac have been added to the index since 1957. The technology share has also increased primarily because of the addition of new firms. In 1957, IBM was two-thirds the technology sector; in 2007, IBM was only the third largest in a sector that contains 74 firms.

The returns of the 10 GICS sectors against the *change* in their market share over the past 50 years are plotted in Figure 4-2. The fast-growing financial and technology sectors have had only mediocre returns. The weight of their sectors has increased not because the prices of individual firms have risen but because many new firms have been added to the index.

In contrast, the energy sector shrunk from 22 to 8 percent of the market weight of the index, yet its return of 12.87 percent is well above the S&P 500 Index. Statistical analysis shows that over the past 50 years only 20 percent of the return to a sector is related to whether the sector is expanding or contracting. This means that 80 percent of the investor return of a sector is based on the valuation of the firms in the sector, not the relative growth of the industry. Rapidly expanding sectors often induce investors to pay too high a price, which results in lower returns. As a result, the best values are often found in stagnant or declining sectors that are ignored by investors and whose price is low relative to fundamentals.

The performance of the 20 largest companies that Standard & Poor's put into their first list in 1957 is shown in Table 4-1. One feature that stands out is that all 9 oil companies on the list finished in the top 10, with only General Electric nudging ahead of Phillips Petroleum and Texaco for eighth place. The returns on all the oil companies beat the S&P

FIGURE 4–2

Change in Sector Weights and Returns, 1957 through December 2006

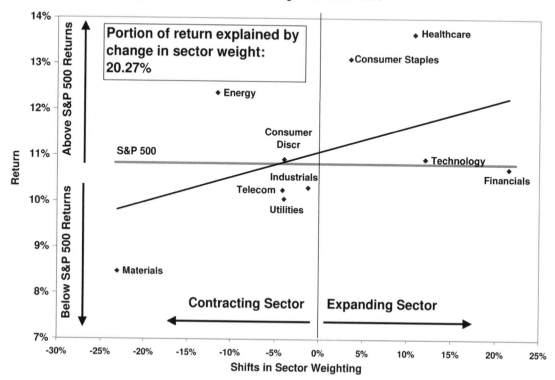

500 by between 80 and 310 basis points *per year* despite the rapid shrinkage of the oil sector relative to the rest of the market.

The top-performing stock of the original 20 largest was Socony Mobil Oil, which dropped the Socony, which stood for Standard Oil of New York, in 1966 and merged with Exxon in 1999. The second-best-performing stock was Royal Dutch Petroleum, a firm founded in the Netherlands, and one of the companies that Standard & Poor's deleted from its index in 2002 when it purged all foreign-based firms. The third-best performer was Standard Oil of New Jersey, which changed its name to Exxon in 1972 and is currently the largest-market-value stock not only in the United States but in the entire world.

Fourth-best performing stock was Shell Oil, a U.S.-based company that was purchased by Royal Dutch in 1985. Next was Standard Oil of Indiana, which merged into BP Amoco in 1998. Sixth-ranking Gulf Oil, seventh-ranking Standard Oil of California, and tenth-ranking Texas Co. (Texaco) eventually merged to form ChevronTexaco, while ninth-

T A B L E   4–1

50-Year Returns of the 20 Largest Companies in 1957

Return Rank	Original Company	1957-2006 Return	1957 Mkt. Cap Rank
1	SOCONY MOBIL OIL	13.85%	13
2	ROYAL DUTCH PETR	13.75%	12
3	STANDARD OIL NJ	13.31%	2
4	SHELL OIL	13.28%	14
5	STD OIL IND	13.01%	16
6	GULF OIL	12.78%	6
7	STD OIL CALIF	12.29%	10
8	GENERAL ELECTRIC	12.02%	5
9	PHILLIPS PETR	11.98%	20
10	TEXACO	11.63%	8
11	SEARS, ROEBUCK	11.52%	15
12	IBM	11.35%	11
13	AT&T	10.77%	1
14	UNION CARBIDE	9.99%	7
15	DUPONT	8.26%	4
16	EASTMAN KODAK	7.88%	19
17	ALCOA	7.18%	17
18	GENERAL MOTORS	7.05%	3
19	U.S. STEEL	6.55%	9
20	BETHLEHEM STEEL	---	18
	AVERAGE TOP 10	11.37%	
	AVERAGE TOP 20	11.78%	
	S&P 500	10.88%	

ranking Phillips Petroleum, merged with Conoco (Continental Oil Co.) to form ConocoPhillips in 2002.

The only firm to beat any oil firm is General Electric, founded in 1892 as a result of the merger of Thomson Houston and Edison General Electric, the latter founded by Thomas Edison. As noted in the last chapter, General Electric is the only member of the original Dow Jones Industrial Average that has survived intact today. Although GE is listed in the industrial sector, about one-half its revenue comes from its financial and healthcare divisions and NBC.

Two other companies of the original largest 20 bested the performance of the S&P 500 Index over the last half century. They are Sears and Roebuck, thanks to the transformation wrought by Eddie Lampert, who changed the stodgy retailer into a dynamic hedge fund operation. The other is IBM, a firm that in 1957 was two-thirds of the value of the tech sector and has just been able to beat the S&P's return since 1957.[3]

Eight of the original 20 largest companies lagged the performance of the S&P 500 Index. Two deserve attention. U.S. Steel and AT&T were at one time the largest corporations in the world. Through industrial changes and corporate divestments, they shrunk to a tiny fraction of their former size, but they have been revived, and as of 2007 they are expanding rapidly.

U.S. Steel was formed in 1901 from the merger of 10 steel companies, led by Andrew Carnegie and financed by J. P. Morgan. After the merger, it was the first billion-dollar-sales company in history, and it controlled two-thirds of the U.S. market. To cushion itself against rising energy costs, it bought Marathon Oil Company in 1982 and renamed itself USX Corporation. In 1991, U.S. Steel was spun off as a separate firm, and in 2003, the value of its shares sank to just over $1 billion, the same size as it was a century earlier. Aggressive cost cutting has brought U.S. Steel back, and it is now the second-biggest steel producer behind Mittal Steel USA, which purchased, among other steel firms, the bankrupt assets from Bethlehem Steel, the eighteenth-largest company in the S&P 500 Index in 1957.

American Telephone and Telegraph Co. was the largest company in the world when it joined the S&P 500 Index in 1957, and it remained that way until 1975. The company boasted a market value of $11.2 billion in 1957, a capitalization that would rank in the bottom 200 of the S&P 500 firms in 2007. The telephone monopoly known as "Ma Bell" was broken up in 1984, giving birth to the "Baby Bell" regional providers. But the

---

[3] Today IBM is only 7 percent of the technology sector, and its market value is eclipsed by both Microsoft and Cisco.

stripped-down AT&T was bought by one of its children, SBC Communications, in 2005, and through other acquisitions, it worked itself back to the top 20 in market value in the United States by 2007. The 50-year return on AT&T, had you also held all the Baby Bells when Ma Bell spun them off 23 years ago, would have given you a 10.77 percent annual return, virtually matching the index.

General Motors, which was formed by the consolidation of 17 auto companies in 1908, was destined to become the largest auto producer in the world, a title that in 2007 it still owns. And until it was surpassed by Toyota in 2007, General Motors was the world leader in sales. But foreign competition and healthcare obligations to its retired labor force have drained GM's resources and reduced the creditworthiness of its once-grade-A obligations to "junk" status. Despite its trouble, it is the largest foreign car manufacturer in China, the world's fastest-growing automotive market. The world is waiting to see whether GM, like U.S. Steel and AT&T, can regain its predominant position in the automobile market.

The returns of three—Union Carbide (now part of Dow Chemical), DuPont, and Alcoa—of the remaining four firms all belong to the materials industry and have lagged the market significantly over the past half century. The fourth firm, Eastman Kodak, failed to make a successful transition to digital photography. Unionization and foreign competition are some reasons behind the poor performance of these firms. Whether these erstwhile giant corporations will be able to reinvent themselves is yet to be seen.

TOP-PERFORMING FIRMS

The 20 best-performing firms of the original S&P 500 that have survived with their corporate structure intact are shown in Table 4-2. Table 4-3 lists the 20 best-performing firms whether they have survived intact or have been merged into another firm.

By far the best-performing stock was Philip Morris, which in 2003 changed its name to Altria Group.[4] Philip Morris introduced the world to the Marlboro Man, one of the world's most recognized icons, two years before the formulation of the S&P 500 Index. Marlboro cigarettes subsequently became the world's best-selling brand and propelled Philip Morris stock upward.

The average annual return on Philip Morris over the past half century, at 19.88 percent per year, almost doubled the 10.88 percent annual

---

[4] The firm retained its ticker symbol MO, or "Big Mo," as traders affectionately call Philip Morris.

TABLE 4–2

The 20 Best-Performing S&P 500 Firms That Have Survived Intact, 1957 through December 2006

Rank	1957 Name	2007 Name	1957-2006 Return	Sector
1	PHILIP MORRIS	ALTRIA GROUP	19.88%	Con. Staples
2	ABBOTT LABS	ABBOTT LABS	15.86%	Healthcare
3	CRANE CO	CRANE CO	15.47%	Industrials
4	MERCK	MERCK	15.43%	Healthcare
5	BRISTOL MYERS	BRISTOL-MYERS SQUIBB	15.43%	Healthcare
6	PEPSI-COLA CO.	PEPSICO INC	15.40%	Con. Staples
7	SWEETS CO OF AMER.	TOOTSIE ROLL INDS	15.12%	Con. Staples
8	COCA-COLA CO	COCA-COLA CO	15.05%	Con. Staples
9	COLGATE-PALMOLIVE	COLGATE-PALMOLIVE	14.99%	Con. Staples
10	AMERICAN TOBACCO	FORTUNE BRANDS INC	14.92%	Con. Disc.
11	HJ HEINZ CO.	HJ HEINZ CO	14.48%	Con. Staples
12	PFIZER	PFIZER INC	14.48%	Healthcare
13	MCGRAW-HILL BOOK CO	MCGRAW-HILL COS.	14.31%	Con. Disc.
14	SCHERING	SCHERING-PLOUGH	14.22%	Healthcare
15	WM WRIGLEY	WRIGLEY WM JR	14.15%	Con. Staples
16	SCHLUMBERGER	SCHLUMBERGER LTD	14.06%	Energy
17	PROCTER & GAMBLE	PROCTER & GAMBLE CO	14.05%	Con. Staples
18	HERSHEY CO	HERSHEY	14.02%	Con. Staples
19	KROGER	KROGER CO	14.01%	Con. Staples
20	MELVILLE SHOE	CVS CORP	13.85%	Con. Staples

return on the S&P 500 Index. This return means that $1,000 invested in Philip Morris on March 1, 1957, would have accumulated to over $8.25 million by the end of 2006, nearly 50 times the $170,000 accumulation in the S&P 500 Index.

Philip Morris's outstanding performance does not just date from mid-century. Philip Morris was also the best-performing company since 1925, the date when comprehensive returns on individual stocks were first compiled. From the end of 1925 through the end of 2006, Philip Morris delivered a 17.2 percent compound annual return, 7.4 percent greater than the market indexes. If you had invested $1,000 in this firm in 1925, it would be worth, with dividends reinvested, almost $380 million in 2007!

Philip Morris's bounty did not extend to only its own stockholders. Philip Morris eventually became the owner of *10* other original S&P 500

T A B L E   4–3

The 20 Best-Performing Firms of the Original S&P 500 Index, 1957 through December 2006

Return Rank	Original Company	Surviving Company	1957-2006 Return
1	PHILIP MORRIS	ALTRIA GROUP	19.88%
2	THATCHER GLASS	ALTRIA GROUP	18.61%
3	DR. PEPPER	CADBURY SCHWEPPES	17.92%
4	CELANESE CORP.	CELANESE AG	17.91%
5	LANE BRYANT	LIMITED INC.	17.84%
6	NATIONAL CAN	PECHINEY SA	17.81%
7	GENERAL FOODS	ALTRIA GROUP	17.14%
8	LORILLARD	LOEWS CORP.	17.13%
9	CALIFORNIA PACKING CO.	ALTRIA GROUP	16.71%
10	STANDARD BRANDS	ALTRIA GROUP	16.60%
11	NATIONAL DAIRY	ALTRIA/KRAFT	16.24%
12	R.J. REYNOLDS TOBACCO	ALTRIA GROUP	15.90%
13	NABISCO	ALTRIA GROUP	15.90%
14	ABBOTT LABS	ABBOTT LABS	15.86%
15	PENICK & FORD	ALTRIA GROUP	15.75%
16	RICHARDSON MERRELL	PROCTER & GAMBLE	15.52%
17	FLINTKOTE	BRITISH AMER. TOB.	15.50%
18	VIRGINIA CAROLINA CHEM.	EXXON MOBIL	15.48%
19	CRANE CO.	CRANE CO.	15.47%
20	HOUDAILLE INDUSTRIES	*PRIVATIZED*/IDEX	15.44%

firms. Many investors became enormously wealthy because the shares of their firms were exchanged with shares of successful companies such as Philip Morris. Riding on the coattails of such winners is an unexpected gift for many stockholders.

HOW BAD NEWS FOR THE FIRM BECOMES GOOD NEWS FOR INVESTORS

Some readers may be surprised that Philip Morris is a top performer for investors in the face of the onslaught of governmental restrictions and legal actions that have cost the firm tens of billions of dollars and have threatened the cigarette manufacturer with bankruptcy.

But in the capital markets, bad news for the firm often can be good news for investors who hold onto the stock and reinvest their dividends. If investors become overly pessimistic about the prospects for a stock, the low price enables stockholders who reinvest their dividends to buy the company on the cheap. These reinvested dividends have turned its stock into a pile of gold for those who stuck with Philip Morris.

TOP-PERFORMING SURVIVOR FIRMS

Philip Morris is not the only firm that has served investors well. The return on the other 19 best-performing surviving companies has beaten the return on the S&P 500 Index by between 3 and 5 percent per year. Of the top 20 firms, 16 are dominated by two industries; consumer staples, represented by internationally well known consumer brand-name companies, and healthcare, particularly large pharmaceutical firms.[5] Hershey chocolate, Heinz ketchup, and Wrigley gum, as well as Coca-Cola and Pepsi-Cola, have built up wide brand equity and consumer trust. The four other winner stocks are Crane, a manufacturer of engineered industrials products founded in 1855 by Richard Crane; Fortune Brands, formerly American Tobacco, founded in 1910, which has since divested its tobacco holding; McGraw-Hill, a global information provider, founded by James H. McGraw in 1899 and now the owner of Standard & Poor's; and Schlumberger, an oil service company begun by the Frenchman Conrad Schlumberger in 1919. All these firms have, despite significant changes in the economic and political landscapes, expanded aggressively into international markets.

One firm of particular note is CVS Corporation, which in 1957 entered the S&P 500 Index as Melville Shoe Corp., a company whose name was taken from the founder, Frank Melville, who started a shoe company in 1892 and incorporated as Melville Shoe in 1922.

Shoe companies have been among the worst investments over the past century, and even Warren Buffett bemoans his purchase of Dexter Shoe in 1991. But Melville was fortunate enough to buy the Consumer Value Store chain in 1969, specializing in personal health products. The chain quickly became the most profitable division of the company, and in 1996 Melville changed its name to CVS. So a shoe manufacturer, destined to be a bad investment, turned to gold as a result of the management's fortuitous purchase of a retail drug chain.

---

[5] About one-half of the products of Fortune Brands qualify as consumer staples, but because of its ventures in golf equipment and home improvement products, it is now classified in the consumer discretionary index.

There are similar stories for firms taken from Table 4-3, which lists the 20 best-performing stocks whether they have survived in their original corporate form or have been merged into another firm. Thatcher Glass was the second best performing of all original S&P 500 stocks behind Philip Morris and was the leading milk bottle manufacturer in the early 1950s. But as the baby boom turned into the baby bust and glass bottles were replaced by cardboard cartons, Thatcher's business sank. Fortunately for Thatcher shareholders, in 1966 the firm was purchased by Rexall Drug, which became Dart Industries, which merged with Kraft in 1980 and was eventually bought by Philip Morris in 1988. An investor who purchased 100 shares of Thatcher Glass in 1957 and reinvested the dividends would have owned 140,000 shares of Philip Morris stock, worth almost $13 million by the end of 2006!

OTHER FIRMS THAT TURNED GOLDEN

As the medical, legal, and popular assault on smoking accelerated through the 1980s, Philip Morris, as well as the other giant tobacco manufacturer, RJ Reynolds, diversified into brand-name food products. In 1985 Philip Morris purchased General Food, and in 1988 it purchased Kraft Foods for $13.5 billion, which had originally been called National Dairy Products and was an original member of the S&P 500 Index. Philip Morris completed its food acquisitions with Nabisco Group Holdings in 2000.

Nabisco Group Holdings was the company the Kohlberg Kravis Roberts & Co. (KKR) spun off in 1991 after taking RJR Nabisco private in 1989 for $29 billion, at that time the largest leveraged buyout in history. Under our methodology for computing long-term returns, if a firm is taken private, the cash from the buyout is assumed to be invested in an S&P 500 Index fund until the company is spun off, at which point the shares are repurchased in the new IPO.[6] RJ Reynolds Tobacco Co. had previously absorbed six original S&P companies: Penick & Ford, California Packing, Del Monte Foods, Cream of Wheat (purchased in 1971 by Nabisco), Standard Brands, and finally National Biscuit Co. in 1985. All these companies became top-20 performers in large part because of their ultimate purchase by Philip Morris.

Also on the list of best-performing stocks is Richardson Merrell, which was purchased by Procter & Gamble in 1985, and Flintkote, which

---

[6] If the firm remains private, the returns are assumed to accumulate at the same level as the S&P 500 Index.

was founded in 1901 and produced roofing materials. In 1980 an owner-ship stake was bought by Genstar, which was then absorbed by Imasco, and finally bought by British American Tobacco in 2000. The purchase was lucky for shareholders because Flintkote went bankrupt in 2004 as a result of asbestos litigation.

Virginia Carolina Chemicals was bought by Mobil Oil, best per-former of the largest 20 corporations. Houdaille Industries, founded by the Frenchman Maurice Houdaille before World War I, was bought by KKR in 1979; at the time, it was the first leveraged buyout over $100 mil-lion. Its 17.78 percent average return from 1957 through 1979 was high enough to give the firm the twentieth position.[7]

OUTPERFORMANCE OF ORIGINAL S&P 500 FIRMS

One of the most remarkable aspects of these original 500 firms is that the investor who purchased the original portfolio of 500 stocks and never bought any of the nearly 1,000 additional firms that have been added by Standard & Poor's in the subsequent 50 years would have outperformed the dynamic updated index. The return of the original 500 firms was 11.72 percent versus 10.83 percent for the updated index. This annual difference results in a 50 percent higher accumulation in the original stocks than those updated in the index.

Why did this happen? How could the new companies that fueled our economic growth and made America the preeminent economy in the world underperform the older firms? The answer is straightforward. Al-though the earnings and sales of many of the new firms grew faster than those of the older firms, the price investors paid for these stocks was simply too high to generate good returns.

Stocks that qualify for entry into the S&P 500 Index must have suf-ficient market value to be among the 500 largest firms. But a market value this high is often reached because of unwarranted optimism on the part of investors. During the energy crisis of the early 1980s, firms such as Global Marine and Western Co. were added to the energy sector, and they subsequently went bankrupt. In fact, 12 of the 13 energy stocks that were added to the S&P 500 Index during the late 1970s and early 1980s did not subsequently match the performance of either the energy sector or the S&P 500 Index.

---

[7] However, one can trace the firm further. In 1987 IDEX was formed to buy back six units of Houdaille that had been sold to a British firm. IDEX, an acronym for Innovation, Diversification, and Excellence, has outperformed the S&P 500 Index by 1.5 percent per year, and if that return were appended to Houdaille, its half-century return would be even higher.

About 30 percent of the 125 firms that have been added to the technology sector of the S&P 500 Index since 1957 were added in 1999 and 2000. Needless to say, most of these firms have greatly underperformed the market. The telecommunications sector added virtually no new firms from 1957 through the early 1990s. But in the late 1990s, firms such as WorldCom, Global Crossing, and Quest Communications entered the index with great fanfare, only to collapse afterward.

Of all 10 industrial sectors, only the consumer discretionary sector has added firms that have outperformed the first firms put into the index. This sector was dominated by the auto manufacturers (GM, Chrysler, and then Ford), their suppliers (Firestone and Goodyear), and large retailers, such as JCPenney and Woolworth's.

CONCLUSION

The superior performance of the original S&P 500 firms surprises most investors. But value investors know that growth stocks often are priced too high and often induce investors to pay too high a price. Profitable firms that do not catch investors' eyes are often underpriced. If investors reinvest the dividends of such firms, they are buying undervalued shares that will add significantly to their final accumulation.

The study of the original 500 companies also gives you an appreciation of the dramatic changes that the U.S. economy has undergone in the past half century. Notwithstanding, many of the top performers are producing the same brands that they did 50 years earlier. Most have aggressively expanded their franchise internationally. Brands such as Heinz ketchup, Wrigley gum, Coca-Cola, Pepsi-Cola, and Tootsie Rolls are as profitable today as they were when these products were launched, some over a hundred years ago.

But we also see that many companies make good investments by being merged into a stronger company. And four of the top-performing original companies—Dr. Pepper, Celanese, National Can, and Flintkote—are now owned by foreign companies. In fact, it is more likely than not that the future winners among companies that are currently American based will not be headquartered in the United States. Foreign firms, clearly secondary when the S&P 500 Index was founded in 1957, are apt to be the ultimate owners of many of today's top firms.

CHAPTER

THE IMPACT OF TAXES ON STOCK AND BOND RETURNS

Stocks Have the Edge

In this world nothing is certain but death and taxes.

BENJAMIN FRANKLIN[1]

The power to tax involves the power to destroy.

JOHN MARSHALL[2]

For all long-term investors, there is only one objective—maximum total real return after taxes.

JOHN TEMPLETON[3]

---

[1] Letter to M. Leroy, 1789.

[2] *McCulloch v. Maryland*, 1819.

[3] Excerpts from "The Templeton Touch" by William Proctor, quoted in Charles D. Ellis, ed., *Classics*, Homewood, Ill.: Dow Jones-Irwin, 1989, p. 738.

John Templeton's objective to maximize total real return after taxes is an essential investment strategy. And stocks are very well suited to this purpose. In contrast to fixed-income investments, both the capital gains and now the dividends are treated favorably by the U.S. tax code. So in addition to having superior before-tax returns, stockholders often hold an even larger after-tax advantage over bondholders.

HISTORICAL TAXES ON INCOME AND CAPITAL GAINS

Figure 5-1a plots the marginal tax rate on dividend and interest income for investors at three income levels: the highest tax bracket, the tax rate for real 2006 income of $150,000, and the tax rate for real income of $50,000. The tax rates on capital gains are shown in Figure 5-1b.

Until the dividend tax rate reductions were put into effect in 2003, the tax rates on dividend and interest income were identical, although in the past, small amounts of dividends were often exempt from tax. From 1930 to 2003 the capital gains tax rate was generally below the dividend tax rate; then in 2003 the tax rates on qualified dividends and capital gains were made equal. A history of the tax code applicable to stock investors is provided in the appendix at the end of this chapter.

A TOTAL AFTER-TAX RETURNS INDEX

A total real returns index for stocks, bonds, bills, and gold is presented in Figure 1-4 in Chapter 1. The effect of taxes on these returns is shown in Figure 5-2.

- The upper line of the stock range equals the before-tax real stock returns shown in Figure 1-4. These returns would be applicable to tax-exempt individuals or institutions.
- The lower line of the stock range in Figure 5-2 assumes that investors pay the highest tax rate on dividend, interest, and capital gains income, with no deferral of capital gains taxes.
- The shaded area shows the range of total real returns from the lowest- to the highest-taxed investor.

These calculations include only federal taxes; no state, local, or estate taxes are considered.

The difference between the before- and after-tax total returns is striking. Total before-tax real stock returns accumulate to $755,163, while after-tax accumulation for someone in the highest bracket is about $30,018—less than 5 percent of the before-tax accumulation. Similar

F I G U R E 5-1

Federal Tax Rates, 1913 through December 2003

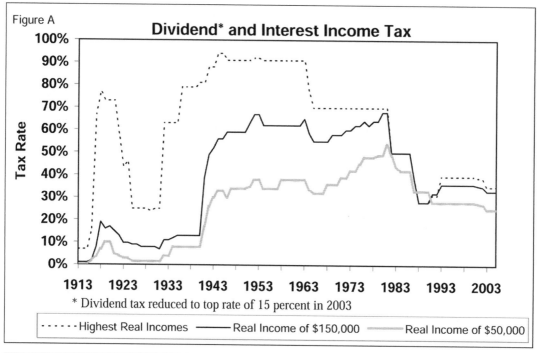

Figure A

Dividend* and Interest Income Tax

* Dividend tax reduced to top rate of 15 percent in 2003

·····Highest Real Incomes   ——Real Income of $150,000   ——Real Income of $50,000

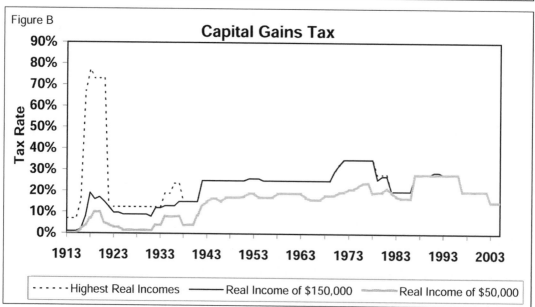

Figure B

Capital Gains Tax

·····Highest Real Incomes   ——Real Income of $150,000   ——Real Income of $50,000

FIGURE 5-2

After-Tax Real Return for Various Federal Tax Brackets, 1802 through December 2006

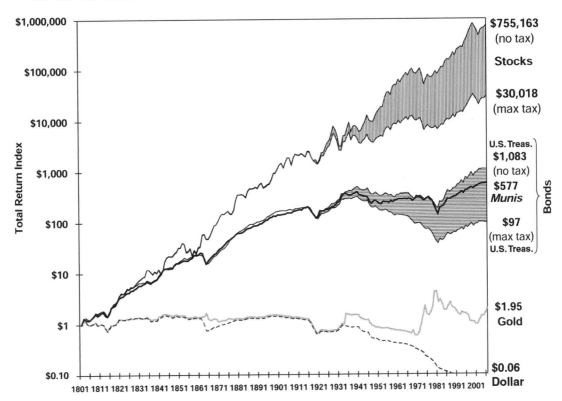

ranges for the total real returns on Treasury bonds and the total real returns on municipal bonds, which are exempt from federal taxes, are displayed. Since municipal bond yields are generally lower than Treasury bond yields, the total return on Treasuries is higher than municipal bonds for untaxed investors, but lower for most taxable investors.

The historical real after-tax returns for four tax brackets are displayed in Table 5-1. Since 1913, when the federal income tax was instituted, the after-tax real return on stocks has ranged from 6.3 percent for untaxed investors to 2.8 percent for investors in the highest bracket who do not defer their capital gains. For taxable bonds, the real annual return ranges from 1.9 to –0.7 percent, and in bills from 0.5 to –2.3 percent, depending on the tax bracket. Municipal bonds have yielded a 0.9 percent annual real return since the income tax was instituted.

TABLE 5–1

After-Tax Real Asset Returns, 1802 through December 2006: Compound Annual Rates of Return (%)*

		Stocks Tax Brackets				Bonds Tax Brackets				Bills Tax Brackets				Muni Bds	Gold	CPI
		$0	$50K	$150K	Max	$0	$50K	$150K	Max	$0	$50K	$150K	Max			
Period	1802-2006	6.8	5.9	5.6	5.2	3.5	2.8	2.6	2.3	2.8	2.3	1.8	1.5	3.0	0.3	1.4
	1871-2006	6.7	5.4	4.9	4.2	2.8	1.8	1.5	1.0	1.7	0.9	0.2	-0.3	2.0	0.4	2.1
	1913-2006	6.3	4.4	3.7	2.8	1.9	0.5	0.0	-0.7	0.5	-0.6	-1.6	-2.3	0.9	0.4	3.3
Major Subperiods	I 1802-1870	7.0	7.0	7.0	7.0	4.8	4.8	4.8	4.8	5.1	5.1	5.1	5.1	5.0	0.2	0.1
	II 1871-1925	6.6	6.5	6.4	6.2	3.7	3.7	3.6	3.4	3.2	3.1	3.0	2.7	3.4	-0.8	0.6
	III 1926-2006	6.6	4.4	3.7	2.8	2.2	0.6	0.0	-0.6	0.7	-0.6	-1.6	-2.3	1.1	1.2	3.0
Postwar Periods	1946-2006	6.8	4.3	3.4	2.9	1.4	-0.6	-1.2	-1.7	0.6	-1.1	-2.5	-3.2	0.5	0.5	4.0
	1946-1965	10.0	7.0	5.2	3.8	-1.2	-2.0	-2.7	-3.5	-0.8	-1.5	-2.3	-2.7	-0.6	-2.7	2.8
	1966-1981	-0.4	-2.2	-3.0	-3.3	-4.2	-6.1	-7.0	-7.5	-0.2	-3.0	-5.2	-6.1	-1.0	8.8	7.0
	1982-1999	13.6	9.4	9.1	9.1	8.4	4.9	4.5	4.4	2.9	0.8	-0.8	-1.7	2.7	-4.9	3.3
	1982-2006	9.0	6.4	6.3	6.2	7.3	4.5	4.2	4.0	2.1	0.4	-0.9	-1.7	2.2	-1.2	3.1

*Federal income tax only. Assume one-year holding period for capital gains portion of return.

Despite the debilitating effect of taxes on equity accumulations, taxes cause the greatest damage to the returns on fixed-income investments. On an after-tax basis, an investor in the top tax bracket who put $1,000 in Treasury bills at the beginning of 1946 would have $138 after taxes and after inflation today, a *loss* in purchasing power of more than 86 percent. Instead, a highest-bracket investor would have turned $1,000 into over $5,719 by buying stocks, a 470 percent increase in purchasing power.

In fact, for someone in the highest tax bracket, short-term Treasury bills have yielded a negative after-tax real return since 1871, even lower if state and local taxes are taken into account. In contrast, top-bracket taxable investors would have increased their purchasing power in stocks 269-fold over the same period.

THE BENEFITS OF DEFERRING CAPITAL GAINS TAXES

In May 2003 President George W. Bush signed the Jobs and Growth Reconciliation Act of 2003, which reduced the highest tax rate on qualified

dividends and capital gains to 15 percent. Nevertheless, effective taxes on capital gains are still lower than on dividends since taxes on capital gains are paid only when the asset is sold, not as the gain is accrued. The advantage of this tax deferral is that the return from capital gains accumulates at the higher before-tax rates rather than the after-tax rates as in the case of dividends. I call the advantage of capital gains over dividend income the "deferral benefit."[4]

For long-term investors the advantage of the deferral benefit can be substantial. For example, take two stocks, one yielding 10 percent per year in dividend income and the other yielding 10 percent solely in capital gains. Assume an individual is in a 30 percent taxable bracket, and the capital gains and dividend tax rate is 15 percent. For an untaxed investor, both investments would yield identical 10 percent returns. But the after-tax yield on the dividend-paying stock is 8.5 percent per year, while, if the investor waits for 30 years before selling the capital-gains-paying stock, the after-tax return is 9.41 percent per year. This is only 59 basis points less than the return of an untaxed investor.

Therefore, from a tax standpoint, there is still bias for firms to deliver capital gains as opposed to dividend income. This is unfortunate since, as we shall note in Chapter 9, dividend-paying stocks generally yield better before- and after-tax returns than non-dividend-paying stocks. Dividends can be put on the same tax basis as capital gains if investors who reinvest their dividends back into the stock are allowed to obtain a tax deferral on reinvested dividends until the stock is sold.

INFLATION AND THE CAPITAL GAINS TAX

In the United States, capital gains taxes are paid on the difference between the price of an asset when it is purchased (its *nominal price*) and the value (price) of that asset when it is sold, with no adjustment made for inflation. This nominally based tax system means that an asset that appreciates by less than the rate of inflation—resulting in a loss of purchasing power—will nevertheless be taxed upon sale.

Although the appreciation of stock prices generally compensates investors for increases in the rate of inflation, especially in the long run, a tax code based on *nominal* prices penalizes investors in an inflationary environment. For a given real return, even a moderate inflation rate of 3 percent causes an investor with a five-year average holding period to

---

[4] It may be that firms that pay higher dividends have better incentives to provide shareholders with higher total returns. This possibility is not explored in this chapter.

lose 31 basis points per year compared with the after-tax return that would result if the inflation rate were zero. If the inflation rate rises to 6 percent, the decline in annual return is more than 65 basis points per year. I call this effect the "inflation tax." The inflation tax for various inflation rates and various holding periods under the current tax system are displayed in Figure 5-3.[5]

The inflation tax has a far more devastating effect on after-tax real returns when the holding period is short than when it is long. This is because the more frequently an investor buys and sells assets, the more frequently the government can tax the capital gains. But even for long-term investors, the inflation tax reduces after-tax returns.

---

[5] Figure 5-3 assumes a total real return of 7 percent (real appreciation of 5 percent, a dividend yield of 2 percent), and tax rates of 15 percent on capital gains and dividend income. If inflation is 3 percent, the total before-tax return on stocks will be 10 percent in nominal terms.

F I G U R E 5-3

Impact of Holding Period on Real After-Tax Returns

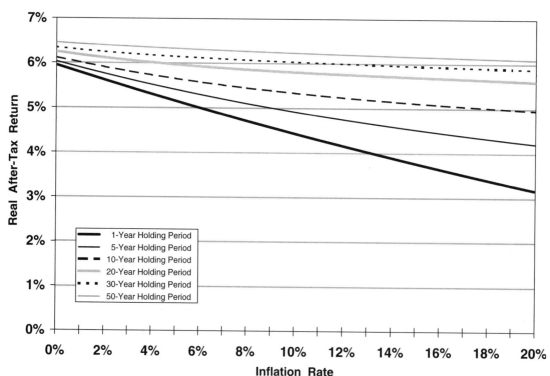

There is considerable support, both inside and outside government, to make some adjustment for inflation in the tax system. In 1986,
the U.S. Treasury proposed the indexation of capital gains, but this provision was never enacted into law. In 1997, the House of Representatives
included capital gains indexation in its tax law, but it was removed by
House-Senate conferees under threat of a presidential veto. Under these
plans, investors would pay taxes on only that portion of the gain (if any)
that exceeded the increase in the price level over the holding period of
the asset. Although this legislation is currently dormant, in recent years
the Federal Reserve has kept inflation low, and this has reduced the impact of the inflation tax.

INCREASINGLY FAVORABLE TAX FACTORS FOR EQUITIES

In recent years there have been some very favorable tax developments
for stocks. They include the following:

1. Reduction in dividend and capital gains tax rates
2. Lower inflation, which reduces the inflation tax imposed on
   nominal capital gains,
3. Switch to capital gains from dividends, which increases the deferral benefit

The capital gains tax rate has been reduced from a maximum of 35
percent in 1978 to 15 percent in 2003. Until 2003, when the tax rate on
dividends was for the first time decoupled from the tax rate on ordinary
income, the tax rate on dividends ranged from a high of 90 percent in the
immediate post–World War II years to 33 percent in 1998 and then to the
special rate of 15 percent in 2003. (See the appendix at the end of the
chapter for the history of the tax code.)

Since the tax law is based on only nominal values uncorrected for
inflation, inflation imposes an additional tax on capital gains. The inflation rate has fallen from double-digit levels in 1979 to the 2 to 3 percent
level in 2007. Since tax brackets are indexed to inflation, the tax rate on
dividends is not directly affected by inflation. Furthermore, since the
capital gains tax is based on realizations instead of accruals, firms have
been buying back shares in lieu of paying dividends and generating
more capital gains income. As a result, the average dividend yield has
fallen from about 5 percent before 1980 to only 2 percent in 2007.

It can be calculated that all these factors have increased the real
after-tax return on stocks by more than 2 percentage points over the past
30 years for a *given* before-tax return. Although the real after-tax return

on bonds has also increased as a result of the drop in the tax rates on ordinary income, the increase in the real return on stocks has been greater. In any equilibrium model of asset pricing, the favorable tax factors for equities suggest that stocks should be priced at a higher multiple of earnings. This will be discussed in Chapter 8.

STOCKS OR BONDS IN TAX-DEFERRED ACCOUNTS?

The most important savings vehicles for many individuals are their tax-deferred accounts (TDAs) such as Keogh, IRA, and 401(k) plans. Many investors hold most of their stock (if they hold any at all) in their tax-deferred accounts, while they hold primarily fixed-income assets in their taxable accounts.

Yet many of the recent changes in the tax laws argue that investors should do the opposite. Dividends will enjoy the lower tax rates and appreciation on shares will gain the lower capital gains tax advantage only if they are held in taxable accounts. This is because when a tax-deferred account is cashed out at retirement, an individual pays the full ordinary income tax on the entire withdrawal regardless of how much of the accumulation has been realized through capital gains and how much through dividend income.

The above counsel, however, ignores two factors. First, if you are an active trader or buy mutual funds that actively trade, then there may be significant capital gains realized, some short run, that would be best kept in a tax-deferred account. Trading in tax-deferred accounts also does not require complicated tax computations since there are no taxes paid until money is withdrawn and the source of the money is of no consequence.

Second, although the government taxes your capital gains and dividends at ordinary rates when withdrawn from a TDA, the government also shares more of the risk. If you realize a capital loss in a taxable account, the government limits your ability to offset this loss against ordinary income. However, when funds are withdrawn from a tax-deferred account, the full withdrawal is treated as taxable income, so that all losses become totally deductible from taxable income. Therefore, there is less after-tax risk putting your money in tax-deferred accounts.

When all the factors are considered, it is better for most investors to hold stocks in their taxable accounts, unless they are active traders. If you have a long horizon, the possibility that you will have a loss in your stock accounts is minimal, so the loss-sharing aspect of TDAs is less important. It is advisable, however, to hold stocks that do not pay tax-

qualified dividends, such as REITs and other income trusts, in one's tax-deferred account to avoid current taxes. However, some risk-averse investors who are reluctant to hold stocks in their personal accounts because of short-term volatility find it easier to hold stocks in their retirement accounts where they have a longer-term perspective and may be better able to tolerate short-term losses.

CONCLUSION

Tax planning is important to maximize returns from financial assets. Because of favorable dividend and capital gains tax rates and the potential to defer those capital gains taxes, stocks hold a significant tax advantage over fixed-income assets. These advantages have risen in recent years as the capital gains and dividend tax has been reduced, inflation has remained low, and firms have repurchased shares to increase capital gains. These favorable developments have increased the after-tax return of equities by more than 2 percentage points over the average after-tax return of the past 50 years. As favorable as stocks are over bonds for long-term investors, the advantage of equities is even greater for the taxable investor.

APPENDIX: HISTORY OF THE TAX CODE

Federal income tax was first collected under the Revenue Act of 1913, when the Sixteenth Amendment to the U.S. Constitution was ratified. Until 1921 there was no tax preference given to capital gains income. When tax rates were increased sharply during World War I, investors refrained from realizing gains and complained to Congress about the tax consequences of selling their assets. Congress was persuaded that such "frozen portfolios" were detrimental to the efficient allocation of capital, and so in 1922 a maximum tax rate of 12.5 percent was established on capital gains income. This rate became effective when taxable income reached $30,000, which is equivalent to about $240,000 in today's dollars.

In 1934, a new tax code was enacted that, for the first time, excluded a portion of capital gains from taxable income. This exclusion allowed middle-income investors, and not just the rich, to enjoy the tax benefits of capital gains income. The excluded portion of the gain depended on the length of time that the asset was held; there was no exclusion if the asset was held 1 year or less, but the exclusion was increased to 70 percent if the asset was held more than 10 years. Since marginal tax rates

ranged up to 79 percent in 1936, the effective maximum tax on very-long-term gains was reduced to about 24 percent.

In 1938, the tax code was amended again to provide for a 50 percent exclusion of capital gains income if an asset was held more than 18 months, but in no case would the tax exceed 15 percent on such capital gains. The maximum rate on capital gains income was raised to 25 percent in 1942, but the holding period was reduced to 6 months. Except for a 1 percent surtax that raised the maximum rate to 26 percent during the Korean War, the 25 percent rate held until 1969.

In 1969, the maximum tax rate on capital gains in excess of $50,000 was phased out over a number of years, so ultimately the 50 percent exclusion applied to all tax rates. Since the maximum rate on ordinary income was 70 percent, this meant the maximum tax rate on capital gains rose to 35 percent by 1973. In 1978, the exclusion was raised to 60 percent, which lowered the effective maximum tax rate on capital gains to 28 percent. When the maximum tax rate on ordinary income was reduced to 50 percent in 1982, the maximum tax rate on capital gains was again reduced to 20 percent.

In 1986, the tax code was extensively altered to reduce and simplify the tax structure and ultimately eliminate the distinction between capital gains and ordinary income. By 1988, the maximum tax rates for both capital gains and ordinary income were identical, at 33 percent. For the first time since 1922, there was no preference for capital gains income. In 1990, the top rate was lowered to 28 percent on both ordinary and capital gains income. In 1991, a slight wedge was reopened between capital gains and ordinary income: the top rate on the latter was raised to 31 percent, while the former remained at 28 percent. In 1993, President Clinton raised tax rates again, increasing the top rate on ordinary income to 39.6 percent while keeping the capital gains tax unchanged. In 1997, Congress lowered the maximum capital gains tax to 20 percent for assets held more than 18 months and the following year returned to the 12-month capital gains period. Starting in 2001, investors could take advantage of a new 18 percent top capital gains rate for assets held at least 5 years.

In 2003 President Bush signed into law legislation that lowered the top rate on capital gains and qualified dividend income to 15 percent. Qualified dividend income must come from taxable enterprises, not "flow through" organizations such as real estate investment trusts or investment companies.

CHAPTER 6

THE INVESTMENT VIEW OF STOCKS

How Fickle Markets Overwhelm Historical Facts

The "new-era" doctrine—that "good" stocks (or "blue chips") were sound investments regardless of how high the price paid for them—was at the bottom only a means of rationalizing under the title of "investment" the well-nigh universal capitulation to the gambling fever.

BENJAMIN GRAHAM AND DAVID DODD, 1934[1]

Investing in stocks has become a national hobby and a national obsession. To update Marx, it is the religion of the masses.

ROGER LOWENSTEIN, 1996[2]

---

[1] Benjamin Graham and David Dodd, *Security Analysis*, New York: McGraw-Hill, 1934, p. 11.
[2] Roger Lowenstein, "A Common Market: The Public's Zeal to Invest," *Wall Street Journal*, September 9, 1996, p. A11.

It was a seasonally cool Monday evening on October 14, 1929, when Irving Fisher arrived at the Builders' Exchange Club at 2 Park Avenue in New York City. Fisher, a professor of economics at Yale University and the most renowned economist of his time, was scheduled to address the monthly meeting of the Purchasing Agents Association.

The Yale economist, often called the founder of modern capital theory, was no mere academic. He actively analyzed and forecast financial market conditions, wrote dozens of newsletters on topics ranging from health to investments, and created a highly successful card-indexing firm based on one of his own patented inventions. Despite hailing from a modest background, his personal wealth in the summer of 1929 exceeded $10 million.[3]

Association members and the press crowded the meeting room. Fisher had intended to defend investment trusts, the forerunner of today's mutual funds. But the audience was most eager to hear his views on the stock market, as they had been nervous since early September when Roger Babson, businessman and market seer, predicted a "terrific" crash in stock prices.[4] Fisher had dismissed Babson's pessimism, noting that he had been bearish for some time. But the public sought to be reassured by the great man who had championed stocks for so long.

The audience was not disappointed. After a few introductory remarks, Fisher uttered a sentence that, much to his regret, became one of the most-quoted phrases in stock market history: "Stock prices," he proclaimed, "have reached what looks like a permanently high plateau."[5]

On October 29, two weeks to the day after Fisher's speech, stocks crashed. His "high plateau" turned instead into a bottomless abyss. The next three years witnessed the most devastating market collapse in history. Like Neville Chamberlain's proud claim that the "agreement" Adolph Hitler signed in Munich in September 1938 guaranteed "peace in our time," Fisher's stock market prediction stands as a memorial to the folly of great men who failed to envision impending disaster.

After the crash, it made little difference to the public that Fisher had earlier correctly forecast the bull market in the 1920s, or recognized the importance of the Federal Reserve in creating a favorable economic climate, or properly defended investment trusts, the forerunners of today's mutual funds, as the best way that the public could participate in the stock market. After 1929, his reputation was shattered.

---

[3] Robert Loring Allen, *Irving Fisher: A Biography*, Cambridge: Blackwell, 1993, p. 206.

[4] *Commercial and Financial Chronicle*, September 7, 1929.

[5] "Fisher Sees Stocks Permanently High," *New York Times*, October 16, 1929, p. 2.

But one should hesitate to render too harsh a judgment on Fisher's analysis. By the end of 1929, stock prices had recovered nearly 50 percent of their losses, and they would have likely continued upward had it not been for the disastrous performance of the Federal Reserve, an institution into which Fisher and many investors put their faith.

As the central bank stood by when the financial system collapsed around it, the most vicious bear market in history took hold. The 1930s would leave an indelible mark on the psyches of all investors. As happened so often throughout history, the data that confirmed the long-term superiority of stocks and served as the rationale for the market advance were dismissed as investors dumped stocks regardless of their intrinsic value. Public and professional opinions about stocks are as volatile as the markets themselves.

EARLY VIEWS OF STOCK INVESTING

Throughout the nineteenth century, stocks were deemed the province of speculators and insiders but certainly not conservative investors. It was not until the early twentieth century that researchers came to realize that stocks, as a class, might be suitable investments under certain economic conditions for investors outside those traditional channels. In the early 1920s, Irving Fisher maintained that stocks would indeed be superior to bonds during inflationary times although common shares would likely underperform bonds during periods of declining prices.[6] This view became the conventional wisdom of the early twentieth century.

Edgar Lawrence Smith, a financial analyst and investment manager of the 1920s, exploded this popular conception. Smith was the first to demonstrate that accumulations in a diversified portfolio of common stocks outperformed bonds not only when commodity prices were rising but also when prices were falling. Smith published his studies in 1925 in a book entitled *Common Stocks as Long-Term Investments*. In the introduction he stated:

> These studies are a record of a failure—the failure of facts to sustain a preconceived theory, . . . [the theory being] that high-grade bonds had proved to be better investments during periods of [falling commodity prices].[7]

By examining stock returns back to the Civil War, Smith found that not only did stocks beat bonds whether prices were rising or falling but there was also a very small chance that you would have to wait a long

---

[6] Irving Fisher, *How to Invest When Prices Are Rising*, Scranton, Pa.: G. Lynn Sumner & Co., 1912.

[7] Edgar L. Smith, *Common Stocks as Long-Term Investments*, New York: Macmillan, 1925, p. v.

time (which he put at 6 and, at most, 15 years) before being able to sell your stocks at a profit. He concluded:

> We have found that there is a force at work in our common stock holdings which tends ever toward increasing their principal value. . . . [U]nless we have had the extreme misfortune to invest at the very peak of a noteworthy rise, those periods in which the average market value of our holding remains less than the amount we paid for them are of comparatively short duration. Our hazard even in such extreme cases appears to be that of time alone.[8]

Smith's conclusion was right not only historically but also prospectively. It took just over 15 years to recover the money invested at the 1929 peak, following a crash far worse than Smith had ever examined. And since World War II, the recovery period for stocks has been better than Smith's wildest dreams. The longest it has ever taken since 1945 to recover an original investment in the stock market (including reinvested dividends) was the five-year, eight-month period from August 2000 through April 2006.

The Influence of Smith's Work

Smith wrote his book at the outset of one of the greatest bull markets in our history. Its conclusions caused a sensation in both academic and investing circles. The prestigious weekly *The Economist* stated, "Every intelligent investor and stockbroker should study Mr. Smith's most interesting little book, and examine the tests individually and their very surprising results."[9]

Irving Fisher saw Smith's study as a confirmation of his own long-held belief that bonds were overrated as safe investments in a world with uncertain inflation. Fisher summarized the new findings:

> It seems, then, that the market overrates the safety of "safe" securities and pays too much for them, that it underrates the risk of risky securities and pays too little for them, that it pays too much for immediate and too little for remote returns, and finally, that it mistakes the steadiness of money income from a bond for a steadiness of real income which it does not possess. In steadiness of real income, or purchasing power, a list of diversified common stocks surpasses bonds.[10]

---

[8] Ibid., p. 81.

[9] "Ordinary Shares as Investments," *The Economist*, June 6, 1925, p. 1141.

[10] From the Foreword by Irving Fisher in Kenneth S. Van Strum, *Investing in Purchasing Power*, New York: Barron's, 1925, p. vii. Van Strum, a writer for Barron's weekly, followed up and confirmed Smith's research.

Smith's ideas quickly crossed the Atlantic and were the subject of much discussion in Great Britain. John Maynard Keynes, the great British economist and originator of the business cycle theory that became the accepted paradigm for future generations, reviewed Smith's book with much excitement. Keynes stated:

> The results are striking. Mr. Smith finds in almost every case, not only when prices were rising, but also when they were falling, that common stocks have turned out best in the long-run, indeed, markedly so. . . . This actual experience in the United States over the past fifty years affords prima facie evidence that the prejudice of investors and investing institutions in favor of bonds as being "safe" and against common stocks as having, even the best of them, a "speculative" flavor, has led to a relative over-valuation of bonds and under-valuation of common stocks.[11]

Money managers were also quick to realize the impact of Smith's work. Hartley Withers wrote in the *London Investors Chronicle* and *Money Market Review*:

> Old-fashioned investors and their old-fashioned advisers have so long been in the habit of looking on all holdings of ordinary shares or common stocks as something rather naughty and speculative, that one feels a certain amount of hesitation in even ventilating the view that is now rapidly gaining acceptance that ordinary shares, under certain conditions, are really safer than [bonds], even though the latter may be of the variety which is commonly called "gilt-edged."[12]

Smith's writings were published in such prestigious journals as the *Review of Economic Statistics* and the *Journal of the American Statistical Association*.[13] Further research confirmed his results. Smith acquired an international following when Siegfried Stern published an extensive study of returns in common stock in 13 European countries from the onset of World War I through 1928. Stern's study showed that the advantage of investing in common stocks over bonds and other financial investments extended far beyond America's financial markets.[14]

---

[11] John Maynard Keynes, "An American Study of Shares versus Bonds as Permanent Investments," *The Nation & The Athenaeum*, May 2, 1925, p. 157.

[12] Quoted by Edgar Lawrence Smith in *Common Stocks and Business Cycles*, New York: William-Frederick Press, 1959, p. 20.

[13] Edgar Lawrence Smith, "Market Value of Industrial Equities," *Review of Economic Statistics*, vol. 9 (January 1927), pp. 37–40, and "Tests Applied to an Index of the Price Level for Industrial Stocks," *Journal of the American Statistical Association*, Supplement (March 1931), pp. 127–135.

[14] Siegfried Stern, *Fourteen Years of European Investments*, 1914–1928, London: Bankers' Publishing Co., 1929.

Common Stock Theory of Investment

The research demonstrating the superiority of stocks became known as the "common stock theory of investment."[15] Smith himself was careful to not overstate his findings. He wrote:

> *Over a period of years* the principal value of a *well-diversified holding* of common stocks of *representative* corporations in essential industries tends to increase in accordance with the operation of compound interest. . . . Such stock holding may be relied upon *over a term of years* to pay an average income return on such increasing values of something more than the average current rate on commercial paper.[16]

Yet Chelcie C. Bosland, a professor of economics at Brown University in the 1930s, claimed that the common stock theory was often misused to justify any investment in stocks no matter what the price. Bosland stated:

> The purchase of common stocks after 1922 was more likely to result in profit than in loss. Even though this was largely a cyclical up-swing, many believed that it was a vindication of the theory that common stocks are good long-term investments. Participation in this profit-making procedure became widespread. The "boom psychology" was everywhere in evidence. No doubt the "common stock theory" gave even to the downright speculator the feeling that his actions were based upon the solid rock of scientific finding.[17]

A RADICAL SHIFT IN SENTIMENT

But the glorious days for common stocks did not last. The crash pushed the image of stocks as safe and fundamentally sound investments into the doghouse and with it Smith's contention that stocks were the best long-term investments. Lawrence Chamberlain, an author and well-known investment banker, stated, *"Common stocks, as such, are not superior to bonds as long-term investments, because primarily they are not investments at all. They are speculations."*[18]

The common stock theory of investment was attacked from all angles. In 1934, Benjamin Graham, an investment fund manager, and

---

[15] Chelcie C. Bosland, *The Common Stock Theory of Investment, Its Development and Significance*, New York: Ronald Press, 1937.

[16] Smith, *Common Stocks as Long-Term Investments*, p. 79, emphasis added.

[17] Bosland, *The Common Stock Theory of Investment*, p. 4.

[18] Lawrence Chamberlain and William W. Hay, *Investment and Speculations*, New York: Henry Holt & Co., 1931, p. 55, emphasis his.

David Dodd, a finance professor at Columbia University, wrote *Security Analysis,* which became the bible of the value-oriented approach to analyzing stocks and bonds. Through its many editions, the book has had a lasting impact on students and market professionals alike.

Graham and Dodd clearly blamed Smith's book for feeding the bull market mania of the 1920s by proposing plausible-sounding but fallacious theories to justify the purchase of stocks. They wrote:

> The self-deception of the mass speculator must, however, have its element of justification. . . . In the new-era bull market, the "rational" basis was the record of long-term improvement shown by diversified common-stock holdings. [There is] a small and rather sketchy volume from which the new-era theory may be said to have sprung. The book is entitled *Common Stocks as Long-Term Investments* by Edgar Lawrence Smith, published in 1924.[19]

THE POSTCRASH VIEW OF STOCK RETURNS

As the news spread about all the people who lost their life savings in the market, the notion that stocks could still beat other financial assets sounded ludicrous.

In the late 1930s, Alfred Cowles III, founder of the Cowles Commission for Economic Research, constructed capitalization-weighted stock indexes back to 1871 of all stocks traded on the New York Stock Exchange. Cowles examined stock returns including reinvested dividends and concluded:

> During that period [1871–1926] there is considerable evidence to support the conclusion that stocks in general sold at about three-quarters of their true value as measured by the return to the investor.[20]

Yet Cowles placed the blame for the crash of 1929 squarely on the shoulder of the government, claiming that increased taxation and government controls drove stock prices downward.

As stocks slowly recovered from the Depression, their returns seemed to warrant a new look. In 1953, two professors from the University of Michigan, Wilford J. Eiteman and Frank P. Smith, published a study of the investment returns on all industrial companies with trading

---

[19] Benjamin Graham and David Dodd, *Security Analysis,* 2d ed., New York: McGraw-Hill, 1940, p. 357.

[20] Alfred Cowles III and associates, *Common Stock Indexes 1871–1937,* Bloomington, Ind.: Pricipia Press, 1938, p. 50.

volume over 1 million shares in 1936. By regularly purchasing these 92 stocks without any regard to the stock market cycle (a strategy called *dollar cost averaging*), they found that the returns over the next 14 years, at 12.2 percent per year, far exceeded those in fixed-income investments. Twelve years later they repeated the study, using the same stocks they had used in their previous study. This time the returns were even higher despite the fact that they made no adjustment for any of the new firms or new industries that had surfaced in the interim. They wrote:

> If a portfolio of common stocks selected by such obviously foolish methods as were employed in this study will show an annual compound rate of return as high as 14.2 percent, then a small investor with limited knowledge of market conditions can place his savings in a diversified list of common stocks with some assurance that, given time, his holding will provide him with safety of principal and an adequate annual yield.[21]

Many dismissed the Eiteman and Smith study because it did not include the Great Crash of 1929 to 1932. But in 1964, two professors from the University of Chicago, Lawrence Fisher and James H. Lorie, examined stock returns through the stock crash of 1929, the Great Depression, and World War II.[22] Fisher and Lorie concluded that stocks offered significantly higher returns (which they reported at 9.0 percent per year) than any other investment media during the entire 35-year period, 1926 through 1960. They even factored taxes and transaction costs into their return calculations and concluded:

> It will perhaps be surprising to many that the returns have consistently been so high. . . . The fact that many persons choose investments with a substantially lower average rate of return than that available on common stocks suggests the essentially conservative nature of those investors and the extent of their concern about the risk of loss inherent in common stocks.[23]

Ten years later, Roger Ibbotson and Rex Sinquefield published an even more extensive review of returns in an article entitled "Stocks, Bonds, Bills, and Inflation: Year-by-Year Historical Returns (1926–74)."[24] They acknowledged their indebtedness to the Lorie and Fisher study and confirmed the superiority of stocks as long-term investments. Their summary statistics, which are published annually in yearbooks, are fre-

---

[21] Wilford J. Eiteman and Frank P. Smith, *Common Stock Values and Yields*, Ann Arbor: University of Michigan Press, 1962, p. 40.

[22] "Rates of Return on Investment in Common Stocks," *Journal of Business*, vol. 37 (January 1964), pp. 1–21.

[23] Ibid., p. 20.

[24] *Journal of Business*, vol. 49 (January 1976), pp. 11–43.

quently quoted and have often served as the return benchmarks for the securities industry.[25]

THE BEGINNING OF THE GREAT BULL MARKET

The Ibbotson and Sinquefield findings were first published in the teeth of the worst bear market since the Great Depression. Because of the Vietnam War, surging inflation, and the OPEC oil embargo, real stock returns were negative from the end of 1966 through the summer of 1982. But as the Fed successfully squeezed out inflation and interest rates fell sharply, the stock market began its greatest bull market run in August 1982. From a level of 790 the Dow began to shoot skyward, surging past 1,000 to a new record by the end of year.

Amid much skepticism, some analysts took the correct view of the markets. Robert Foman, president and chairman of E.F. Hutton, proclaimed in October 1983 that we are "in the dawning of a new age of equities" and boldly predicted the Dow Jones average could hit 2,000 or more by the end of the decade.

But even Foman was too pessimistic, as the Dow Industrials broke 2,000 in January 1987. Except for the great stock crash that occurred that October, which is documented in Chapter 16, stocks marched steadily upward, and the Dow broke 3,000 just before Saddam Hussein invaded Kuwait in August 1990. The Gulf War and a real estate recession precipitated a second bear market, but this one, like the crash in 1987, was short-lived.

Iraq's defeat in the Gulf War ushered in one of the most fabulous decades in stock market history. The world witnessed the collapse of communism and diminished threat of global conflict. The transfer of resources from military expenditures to domestic consumption enabled the United States to experience increased economic growth and low inflation. The interests of Americans turned inward, and the postwar baby boomers became preoccupied with career enhancement and retirement security.

The Dow Industrials quickly scaled 3,000 in March 1991. Few thought the trend would last. In 1992, *Forbes* warned investors in a cover story "The Crazy Things People Say to Rationalize Stock Prices" that stocks were in the "midst of a speculative buying panic" and cited Raskob's foolish advice to invest at the market peak in 1929.[26]

---

[25] *Stocks, Bonds, Bills, and Inflation Yearbooks*, 1983–1997, Chicago: Ibbotson and Associates.

[26] William Baldwin, "The Crazy Things People Say to Rationalize Stock Prices," *Forbes*, April 27, 1992, pp. 140–150.

But such caution was ill advised. After a successful battle against inflation in 1994, the Fed eased interest rates and the Dow subsequently moved above 4,000 in early 1995. When the Dow was at 4,300, *Business-Week* defended the durability of the bull market in an article on May 15, 1995, entitled "Dow 5000? Don't Laugh." The Dow quickly crossed that barrier by November and then reached 6,000 eleven months later.

By late 1995, the persistent rise in stock prices caused many more analysts to sound the alarm. Michael Metz of Oppenheimer, Charles Clough of Merrill Lynch, and Byron Wein of Morgan Stanley expressed strong doubts about the underpinnings of the rally. In September 1995, David Shulman, chief equity strategist for Salomon Brothers, wrote an article entitled "Fear and Greed," which compared the current market climate to that of similar stock market peaks in 1929 and 1961. Shulman claimed intellectual support was an important ingredient in sustaining bull markets, noting Edgar Smith's and Irving Fisher's work in the 1920s, the Fisher-Lorie studies in the 1960s, and my *Stocks for the Long Run*, published in 1994. Shulman's own long-term studies, based on dividend growth, reinforced his long-term bearish views on stocks.[27]

WARNINGS OF OVERSPECULATION

By 1996 price-earnings ratios on the S&P 500 Index reached 20, considerably above its average postwar level. More warnings were issued. Roger Lowenstein, a well-known author and financial writer, asserted in the *Wall Street Journal*:

> Investing in stocks has become a national hobby and a national obsession. People may denigrate their government, their schools, their spoiled sports stars. But belief in the market is almost universal. To update Marx, it is the religion of the masses.[28]

Floyd Norris, lead financial writer for the *New York Times*, echoed Lowenstein's comments by penning an article in January 1997 "In the Market We Trust."[29] Henry Kaufman, the Salomon Brothers guru whose pronouncements on the fixed-income market had frequently rocked bonds in the 1980s, declared that "the exaggerated financial euphoria is

---

[27] Three months later, in December 1995, Shulman capitulated to the bullish side, claiming his long-time emphasis on dividend yields was incorrect.

[28] Roger Lowenstein, "A Common Market: The Public's Zeal to Invest," *Wall Street Journal*, September 9, 1996, p. A1.

[29] Floyd Norris, "In the Market We Trust," *New York Times*, January 12, 1997.

increasingly conspicuous," and he cited assurances offered by optimists equivalent to Irving Fisher's utterance that stocks had reached a permanently high plateau.[30]

Warnings of the end of the bull market did not emanate just from Wall Street. Academicians were increasingly investigating this unprecedented rise in stock values. Robert Shiller of Yale University and John Campbell of Harvard wrote a scholarly paper showing that the market was significantly overvalued and presented this research to the board of governors of the Federal Reserve System in early December 1996.[31]

With the Dow surging past 6,400, Alan Greenspan, chairman of the Federal Reserve, issued a warning in a speech before the annual dinner for the American Enterprise Institute (AEI) in Washington on December 5, 1996. He asked, "How do we know when irrational exuberance has unduly escalated asset values, which then become subject to unexpected and prolonged contractions as they have in Japan over the past decade? And how do we factor that assessment into monetary policy?"

His words had an electrifying effect, and the phrase "irrational exuberance" became the most celebrated utterance of Greenspan's tenure as Fed chairman. Asian and European markets fell dramatically as his words were flashed across computer monitors. The next morning Wall Street opened dramatically lower. But investors quickly regained their balance, and stocks closed in New York with only moderate losses.

From there it was onward and upward, with the Dow breaking 7,000 in February 1997 and 8,000 in July. Even *Newsweek*'s cautious cover story "Married to the Market," depicting a Wall Street wedding between America and a bull, did nothing to quell investor optimism.[32]

The market became an ever-increasing preoccupation of middle- and upper-income Americans. Business books and magazines proliferated, and the all-business cable news stations, particularly CNBC, drew huge audiences. Television sets in bars, airports, and other public places were invariably tuned to an all-business network. Electronic tickers and all-business TV stations were broadcast in lunchrooms, bars, and even lounges of the major business schools throughout the country. Cruise

---

[30] Henry Kaufman, "Today's Financial Euphoria Can't Last," *Wall Street Journal*, November 25, 1996, p. A18.

[31] Robert Shiller and John Campbell, "Valuation Ratios and the Long-Run Stock Market Outlook," *Journal of Portfolio Management*, vol. 24 (Winter 1997).

[32] *Newsweek*, April 27, 1998. Cover stories about the stock market in major newsweeklies have often been poorly timed. *BusinessWeek*'s cover article "The Death of Equities" on August 13, 1979, occurred 14 years after the market had peaked and 3 years before the beginning of the greatest bull market in stocks.

ships and resorts in some of the world's most isolated locations were sure to carry all-financial stations. Air travelers could view up-to-the-minute Dow and Nasdaq averages flying 35,000 feet above the sea as they were flashed from monitors on phones anchored to the back of the seat in front of them.

Adding impetus to the already surging market was the explosion of communications technology. Internet service providers such as AOL allowed investors to stay in touch with markets and their portfolio from anywhere in the world. Whether it was from Internet "chat rooms," financial Web sites, or e-mail newsletters, investors found access to a plethora of information at their fingertips. CNBC became so popular that major investment houses made sure that all their brokers watched the station on television or their desktop computers so that they could be one step ahead of clients calling in with breaking business news.

The bull market psychology appeared impervious to financial and economic shocks. The first wave of the Asian crisis, discussed further in Chapter 10, sent the market down a record 554 points on October 27, 1997, and closed trading temporarily. But this did little to dent investors' enthusiasm for stocks.

The following year, the Russian government defaulted on its bonds, and Long-Term Capital Management, considered the world's premier hedge fund, found itself entangled in speculative positions measured in the *trillions* of dollars that it could not trade. Markets temporarily seized up, and the Federal Reserve facilitated a rescue of the fund in order to resuscitate financial markets. These events sent the Dow Industrials down almost 2,000 points, but three quick Fed rate cuts sent the market soaring again. On March 29, 1999, the Dow closed above 10,000, and it then went on to a record close of 11,722.98 on January 14, 2000.

THE TOP OF THE BUBBLE

As always, the bull market gave birth to those who envisioned much higher stock prices. In 1999, two economists, James Glassman and Kevin Hassett, published a book entitled *Dow 36,000*. They claimed that the Dow Jones Industrial Average, despite its meteoric rise, was still grossly undervalued, and its true valuation was nearly three times higher at 36,000. They incorrectly asserted that the theoretical underpinning for their analysis came from my book *Stocks for the Long Run*! Since I showed that nominal (nonindexed) bonds were as risky as stocks over long horizons, they improperly claimed that stock prices should rise sufficiently

to reduce their returns to those of bonds, which implied an astronomical level for stock prices.[33]

Despite the pundits' preoccupation with the Dow Industrials, the real action in the market was in the Nasdaq. The once sleepy over-the-counter market in unlisted stocks soared to preeminence as the public's fascination with computers, the Internet, mobile communications, and networking firms blossomed. Volume on the Nasdaq eclipsed the New York Stock Exchange, as investors feverishly traded shares in Cisco, Sun Microsystems, Oracle, JDS Uniphase, and other companies that were scarcely in existence a decade earlier. The most heated pace of trading centered on the Internet stocks, where a dot-com index of 24 online firms soared from 142 in November 1997 to a high of 1,350 on March 10, 2000.

THE BEAR MARKET AND ITS AFTERMATH

The date March 10, 2000, marked the peak not only of the Nasdaq but also of many Internet and technology stock indexes. When capital expenditures in technology unexpectedly slowed, the bubble burst and a severe bear market began. Measured by the S&P 500 Index, the market declined by 49.15 percent between March 10 and October 9, 2000, eclipsing the 48.2 percent decline in the 1972 to 1974 bear market and the worst since the Great Depression. There were some redeeming features to the devastation. Since inflation had been far lower during the recent bear market, the after-inflation decline was considerably more moderate, and small stocks did not fall nearly as much in the 2002 bear market as they did in the 1970s.

Still, the decline in stock values exceeded $9 trillion, by far the greatest loss in history. The bear market came in two waves. The first was the popping of the technology bubble, which sent the Nasdaq index plummeting by nearly 70 percent by the summer of 2001. Nontech stocks held up very well until the second wave of the bear market, which was sparked by the spectacular crash of Enron and allegations of accounting irregularities at many firms, including such blue chips as General Electric.

Just as the bull market brought out the optimists, the collapsing stock prices brought out the bears in droves. In September 2002, Bill

---

[33] I immediately wrote a rebuttal in the *Wall Street Journal* ("Are Internet Stocks Overvalued? Are They Ever," April 19, 1999, p. A22) stating that their analysis was faulty and that stocks must have returns exceeding those on U.S. Treasury inflation-protected bonds, whose yield had reached 4 percent at that time.

Gross, the legendary head of the PIMCO bond trading department and head of at that time the largest mutual fund in existence, came out with an piece entitled "Dow 5,000" in which he said that despite the market's awful decline, stocks were still nowhere near as low as they should be on the basis of economic fundamentals. As will be discussed in the next chapter, this analysis was wrong since it concentrated on historical growth of earnings, failing to take into account changes in dividend and investment policies that impacted future growth. Here, within a period of a couple years, you had economists claiming the right value for the Dow was as high as 36,000 and as low as 5,000.

The bear market squelched the public's fascination with stocks. Televisions in public venues were no longer tuned to CNBC but instead switched on sports and Hollywood gossip. As one bar owner colorfully put it, "People are licking their wounds and they don't want to talk about stocks anymore. It's back to sports, women, and who won the game."[34]

The bear market also left many professionals skeptical of stocks. Yet bonds did not seem an attractive alternative, as their yields had declined below 4 percent. Many looked to other, nontraditional assets that might lead the way.

David Swensen, chief investment officer at Yale University since 1985, seemed to provide that answer. At the peak of the bull market, he wrote a book, *Pioneering Portfolio Management: An Unconventional Approach to Institutional Investment*, that espoused the qualities of "nontraditional" (and often illiquid) assets, such as private equity, venture capital, real estate, timber, and hedge funds. Hedge funds—pools of investment money that can be invested in any way the fund managers see fit, often in the nonconventional assets Swensen advocated—enjoyed a boom.[35] From a mere $100 billion in 1990, assets of hedge funds grew to over $1.5 trillion by 2007.

But the surge of assets into hedge funds drove the prices of many unconventional assets to levels never before seen. Jeremy Grantham, a successful money manager at GMO and a one-time big booster of unconventional investing, stated in April 2007, "After these moves, most diversifying and exotic assets are badly overpriced."[36] In comparison, in

---

[34] Paul Sloan, "The Craze Collapses," *US News and World Report Online*, November 30, 2000.

[35] The word *hedge* means "to offset," as someone making an investment in a foreign market may want to hedge, or offset, adverse currency movements with a transaction in the forward market. Hedge funds often, but not always, took positions that were contrary to the stock market.

[36] Jeremy Grantham, "A Global Bubble Warns against the Stampede to Diversify," *Financial Times*, April 24, 2007, p. 38.

early 2007 the valuation of stocks, particularly large-capitalization equities, was near its historical average, and many hedge funds were bidding well above the market for large, publicly traded companies.

Despite the bursting of the bubble and the success of nontraditional investors, many individual investors ignored these bears and retained their long-term faith in stocks as the best long-term investments. Data collected by Robert Shiller of Yale University confirmed that despite the severe bear market of 2001 to 2002, as of January 2007, three-quarters of investors believed that stocks were the best long-term investment.[37]

And with good reason. Stocks have returned a very healthy 15 percent per year measured from the market lows reached in October 2002 through the end of 2006. By 2007, stocks as measured by the popular capitalization-weighted indexes were at or near all-time highs, having recovered all their losses sustained in the bear market.

The bull and bear markets of the last decade were no different from the bull and bear markets that preceded them. As stocks rose, the bulls came out of the woodwork, and at the top they fabricated theories that would support even higher prices. In the subsequent down markets, the bears would pounce with justifications for even lower prices. Nearly all would discard the long-term historical evidence that supports the case for equities. How can investors avoid these fickle prognosticators and accurately assess the future returns on the market? This is the topic of our next chapter.

---

[37] Robert Shiller, Yale School of Management Stock Market Confidence Indexes, http:// icf.som.yale.edu/confidence.index.

PART 2

VALUATION, STYLE INVESTING, AND GLOBAL MARKETS

STOCKS: SOURCES AND MEASURES OF MARKET VALUE

Even when the underlying motive of purchase [of common stocks] is mere speculative greed, human nature desires to conceal this unlovely impulse behind a screen of apparent logic and good sense.

BENJAMIN GRAHAM AND DAVID DODD, 1940[1]

AN EVIL OMEN RETURNS

In the summer of 1958, an event of great significance took place for those who followed long-standing indicators of stock market value. For the first time in history, the interest rate on long-term government bonds rose above the dividend yield on common stocks.

BusinessWeek noted this event in an August 1958 article entitled "An Evil Omen Returns," warning investors that when yields on stocks approached those on bonds, a major market decline was in the offing.[2] The stock market crash of 1929 occurred in a year when stock dividend

---

[1] "The Theory of Common-Stock Investment," *Security Analysis*, 2d ed., New York: McGraw-Hill, 1940, p. 343.

[2] *BusinessWeek*, August 9, 1958, p. 81.

yields fell to the level of bond yields. The stock crashes of 1891 and 1907 also followed episodes when the yield on bonds came within 1 percent of the dividend yield on stocks.

Until 1958, as Figure 7-1 indicates, the yearly dividend yield on stocks had always been higher than long-term interest rates, and financial analysts thought that this was the way it was supposed to be. Stocks were riskier than bonds and therefore should yield more in the marketplace. Under this reasoning, whenever stock prices went too high and sent dividend yields below the yields on bonds, it was time to sell.

But things did not work that way in 1958. Stocks returned over 30 percent in the 12 months after dividend yields fell below bond yields, and stocks continued to soar into the early 1960s.

It is now understood that there were good economic reasons why this well-respected valuation indicator fell by the wayside. Inflation increased the yield on bonds to compensate lenders for rising prices, while investors bought stocks against the eroding value of money. As early as September 1958, *BusinessWeek* noted, "The relationship between stock

F I G U R E   7–1

Dividend and Nominal Bond Yields, 1871 through December 2006

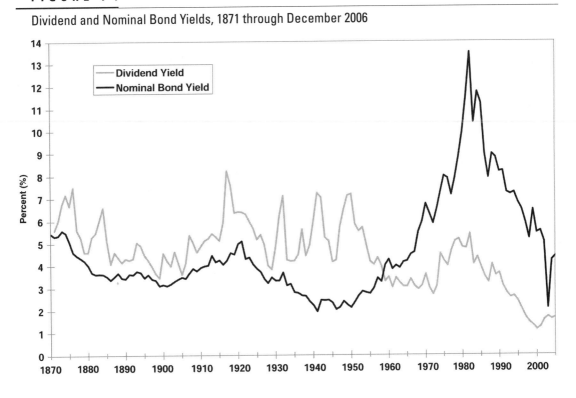

and bond yields was clearly posting a warning signal, but investors still believe inflation is inevitable and stocks are the only hedge against it."[3]

Yet many on Wall Street were puzzled by the "great yield reversal." Nicholas Molodovsky, vice president of White, Weld & Co. and editor of the *Financial Analysts Journal*, observed:

> Some financial analysts called [the reversal of bond and stock yields] a financial revolution brought about by many complex causes. Others, on the contrary, made no attempt to explain the unexplainable. They showed readiness to accept it as a manifestation of providence in the financial universe.[4]

Imagine the investor who followed this well-regarded indicator and pulled all his or her money out of the stock market in August 1958 and put it into bonds, vowing never to buy stocks again unless dividend yields rose above bond yields. Such an investor, if he or she were still alive, would still be waiting to get back into stocks. After 1958, stock dividend yields *never again* exceeded those of bonds. Yet over the last half century, stock returns overwhelmed the returns on fixed-income securities.

This episode illustrates that valuation benchmarks are valid only as long as underlying economic and financial conditions do not change. The chronic postwar inflation, resulting from a switch to a paper money standard, changed forever the way investors judged the investment merits of stocks and bonds. Stocks were claims on real assets whose prices rose with inflation, while bonds were not. Those investors who clung to the old ways of valuing equity never participated in the greatest bull market for stocks in history.

VALUATION OF CASH FLOWS FROM STOCKS

The fundamental sources of stock valuation derive from the earnings and dividends of firms. In contrast to a work of art—which can be bought both for an investment and for its viewing pleasure—stocks have value only because of the cash flows that current investors receive or the appreciation caused by cash flows that future investors hope to receive. These cash flows may come from the payment of dividends out of earnings or from cash distributions resulting from the sale of the firm's

---

[3] "In the Markets," *BusinessWeek*, September 13, 1958, p. 91.

[4] "The Many Aspects of Yields," *Financial Analysts Journal*, vol. 18, no. 2 (March–April 1962), pp. 49–62.

assets. One can estimate the investment value of shares by forecasting and valuing these expected cash flows.[5]

More generally, the value of any asset—stock, bond, real estate, or any other property—is determined by the discounted value of all expected future cash flows. Future cash flows are *discounted* because cash received in the future is not worth as much as cash received in the present. The reasons for discounting are (1) the innate *time preferences* of most individuals to enjoy their consumption today rather than wait for tomorrow; (2) *productivity*, which allows funds invested today to yield a higher return tomorrow; and (3) *inflation*, which reduces the future purchasing power of cash received in the future. A fourth reason, which applies primarily to the cash flows from risky assets such as equities, is the *uncertainty* associated with the magnitude of future cash flows.

Sources of Shareholder Value

For the stockholder, earnings are the source of future cash flows. Earnings, profits, and net incomes are the cash flows that remain after the costs of production are subtracted from the sales revenues of the firm. The costs of production include labor and material costs, interest on debt, corporate taxes, and allowances for depreciation.

Firms can create value for shareholders by using their earnings in a number of ways. The first and historically the most important is this one:

- Payment of cash dividends

Earnings that are not used for dividends are called *retained earnings*. Retained earnings can be used to create value in the following ways:

- Retirement of debt
- Investment in securities or other assets or acquisition of other firms
- Repurchase of the firm's own shares (which is known as a *buyback*)
- Investment in capital projects designed to increase future profits

If a firm retires its debt, it reduces its interest expense and therefore increases the cash flow available to shareholders. If a firm buys assets, the income from these assets is available to pay future dividends

---

[5] There might be some psychic value to holding a controlling interest in a firm. In that case, the owner values the stock more than minority shareholders value it.

or otherwise increase value. If a firm repurchases its shares, it reduces the number of shares outstanding and thus increases future *per share* earnings. Finally, retained earnings can be used to expand the capital of the firm in order generate higher future revenues and/or reduce costs.

Some people believe that shareholders value cash dividends the most, and that assertion is probably true in a tax-free world. But from a tax standpoint, share repurchases are superior to dividends. As discussed in Chapter 5, share repurchases generate capital gains whose tax can be deferred until the shares are sold. Recently an increasing number of firms have been engaging in share repurchases. Nevertheless, the commitment to pay a cash dividend often focuses management on delivering profits to shareholders and reduces the probability that earnings will be spent in a less productive way.

Others might argue that debt repayment lowers shareholder value because the interest saved on the debt retired is generally less than the rate of return earned on equity capital. They might also claim that by retiring debt, they lose the ability to deduct the interest paid as an expense (the interest tax shield).[6] But debt entails a fixed commitment that must be met in good or bad times, and, as such, the use of debt increases the volatility of earnings. Reducing debt therefore lowers the volatility of future earnings and may not diminish shareholder value.[7]

Some investors claim the investment of earnings is an important source of value. But this is not always the case. If retained earnings are reinvested profitably, value will surely be created. But retained earnings, especially if they are accumulated in liquid investments, might tempt managers to overbid to acquire other firms or to spend these funds on perquisites and other activities that do not increase the value to shareholders. Therefore, the market often views the buildup of cash reserves and marketable securities with suspicion and often discounts their value.

If the fear of misusing retained earnings is particularly strong, it is possible that the market will value the firm at less than the value of its

---

[6] Whether debt is a valuable tax shield depends on whether interest rates are bid up enough to offset that shield. See Merton H. Miller, "Debt and Taxes," Papers and Proceedings of the Thirty-Fifth Annual Meeting of the American Finance Association, Atlantic City, N.J., September 16–18, 1977, *Journal of Finance*, vol. 32, no. 2 (May 1977), pp. 261–275.

[7] Meeting interest payments may also be a good discipline for management and reduce the tendency to waste excess profits. See Michael Jensen, "The Takeover Controversy: Analysis and Evidence," in John Coffee, Louis Lowenstein, and Susan Rose-Ackerman, eds., *Takeovers and Contests for Corporate Control*, New York: Oxford University Press, 1987.

reserves. Great investors, such as Benjamin Graham, made some of their most profitable trades by purchasing shares in such companies and then convincing management (sometimes tactfully, sometimes with a threat of takeover) to disgorge its liquid assets.[8]

One might question why management would not employ assets in a way to maximize shareholder value since managers often hold a large equity stake in the firm. The reason is that a conflict often exists between the goal of the shareholders, which is solely to increase the return on their shares, and the goals of management, which may include prestige, control of markets, and other objectives. Economists recognize the conflicts between the goals of managers and shareholders as *agency costs*, and these costs are inherent in every corporate structure where ownership is separated from management. Payment of cash dividends or committed share repurchases often lowers management's temptation to pursue goals that do not maximize shareholder value.

Finally, capital expenditures are certainly necessary in a growing firm, yet many studies show that firms often overexpand and spend too much on capital, which reduces profits and forces retrenchment by management.[9] Often young, fast-growing companies may create more value by spending on capital expenditures, while companies in older, more mature industries, in which agency costs are most severe, pay dividends or repurchase shares, which is better for shareholders.

The Value of Stock as Related to Dividend Policy

Management determines its dividend policy by evaluating many factors including the tax impact on shareholders; the need to generate internal funds to retire debt, invest, or repurchase shares; and the desire to maintain a stable dividend level in the face of fluctuating earnings. Since the price of a stock depends primarily on the present discounted value of all expected future dividends, it appears that dividend policy is crucial to determining the value of the stock.

But as long as one specific condition holds—*that the firm earns the same return on its retained earnings as shareholders demand on its stock*—then future dividend policy does not impact the market value of the firm. This is because dividends not paid today become retained earnings that

---

[8] Benjamin Graham and Seymour Chatman (ed.), *Benjamin Graham: The Memoirs of the Dean of Wall Street*, New York: McGraw-Hill, 1996, Chap. 11.

[9] See Jeremy Siegel, "Capital Pigs," *The Future for Investors: Why the Tried and the True Triumph over the Bold and the New*, New York: Crown Business, 2005, Chap. 7.

generate higher dividends in the future, so that the present value of those dividends is unchanged, notwithstanding when they are paid.[10]

The management can, of course, influence the time path of dividends. The lower the *dividend payout ratio*, which is the ratio of cash dividends to earnings, the smaller the dividends will be in the near future. But over time, dividends will rise and eventually exceed the path of dividends associated with a higher dividend payout ratio. Assuming the firm earns the same return on investment as the investors require from the equity, the present value of these dividend streams will be identical no matter what payout ratio is chosen.

Although earnings drive the dividend policy of the firm, the price of the stock is always equal to the present value of all future *dividends* and not the present value of future earnings. Earnings not paid to investors can have value only if they are paid as dividends or other cash disbursements at a later date. Valuing stock as the present discounted value of future earnings is manifestly wrong and greatly overstates the value of a firm.[11]

John Burr Williams, one of the greatest investment analysts of the early part of the last century and the author of the classic *Theory of Investment Value*, argued this point persuasively in 1938:

> Most people will object at once to the foregoing formula for valuing stocks by saying that it should use the present worth of future earnings, not future dividends. But should not earnings and dividends both give the same answer under the implicit assumptions of our critics? If earnings not paid out in dividends are all successfully reinvested at compound interest for the benefit of the stockholder, as the critics imply, then these earnings should produce dividends later; if not, then they are money lost. Earnings are only a means to an end, and the means should not be mistaken for the end.[12]

A simple example should illustrate this proposition. Assume a company's stock is selling for $100 per share and earns 10 percent, or $10 per share each year, which, given its risk, is equal to the return investor's demand on its stock. If it paid all its earnings as dividends, it would pay $10 per share every year into the future. This stream of dividends, if discounted at 10 percent, yields a $100 share price.

---

[10] Differential taxes between capital gains and dividends are an exception to this rule. If taxes are higher on dividends, a high-dividend policy will reduce the value of shares.

[11] Firms that pay no dividends, such as Warren Buffett's Berkshire Hathaway, have value because their assets, which earn cash returns, can be liquidated and disbursed to shareholders in the future.

[12] John Burr Williams, *The Theory of Investment Value*, Cambridge, Mass.: Harvard University Press, 1938, p. 30.

If instead the company did not pay a dividend but invested its earnings in assets whose return is the identical 10 percent, the value of the company would remain the same. Yet its earnings would grow to $11 per share in the second year, $12.10 in the third, and so on. The present value of these per share earnings, discounted at a 10 percent rate of return, is infinite—clearly a nonsensical value for the firm. This is because discounting earnings that are not paid out as dividends is wrong and overstates the value of the firm. Under the assumptions given, the firm is always worth $100, whether the firm reinvests the earnings at a 10 percent rate of return or pays dividends to the shareholders.

The assumption that the firm earns the same rate of return on its retained earnings as the market demands on its stock is a strong one, despite the fact that it is often assumed in capital market theory to result from optimal investment behavior of the firm. But the firm does not always invest optimally, as the previous section suggests. Frequently management engages in expenditures that have a lower return, and in that case a policy of paying dividends will result in higher returns to shareholders.

EARNINGS CONCEPTS

Despite the dependence of firm value on current and future dividends, dividends are not possible on a sustained basis without positive earnings. As a result, it is critical that a concept of earnings be developed that gives investors the best possible measure of the sustainable cash that is available for the payment of dividends.

Earnings, which are sometimes called *net income*, or *profit*, are simply the difference between revenues and costs. But the determination of earnings is not just a cash-in-minus-cash-out calculation since many costs and revenues, such as capital expenditures, depreciation, and contracts for future delivery, extend over many years. Furthermore, some expenses and revenues are one-time or "extraordinary" items, such as capital gains and losses or major restructurings, and they do not add meaningfully to the picture of the ongoing or sustainable earnings that are so important in valuing a firm. Because of these issues, there is no single "right" concept of earnings.

Earnings Reporting Methods

There are two principal ways that firms report their earnings. *Net income* or *reported earnings* are those earnings sanctioned by the Financial Ac-

counting Standards Board (FASB), an organization established in 1973 to establish accounting standards. These standards are called the *generally accepted accounting principles* (GAAP), and they are used to compute the earnings that appear in the annual report and are filed with government agencies.[13]

The other more generous concept of earnings is called *operating earnings*. Operating earnings represent ongoing revenues and expenses, omitting unusual items that occur on a one-time basis. For example, operating earnings often exclude restructuring charges (for example, expenses associated with a firm's closing a plant or selling a division), investment gains and losses, inventory write-offs, expenses associated with mergers and spin-offs, and depreciation of "goodwill."

Operating earnings are what Wall Street watches and what analysts forecast. The difference between the operating earnings a firm reports and what analysts expect it to report is what drives stocks during the "earnings season," which occurs in the few weeks following the end of each quarter. When we hear that XYZ Corporation "beat the Street," it invariably means that its earnings came in above the average (or consensus) forecast of *operating* earnings.

In theory, operating earnings gives a more accurate assessment of the long-term sustainable profits of a firm than reported earnings gives. But the concept of operating earnings is not formally defined by the accounting profession, and its calculation involves much management discretion. As management has come under increasing pressure to beat the Street's earnings forecasts, they are motivated to "stretch the envelope" and exclude more expenses (or include more revenues) than are appropriate.

The data show the increased gap between reported and operating earnings in recent years. From 1970 to 1990, reported earnings averaged only 2 percent below operating earnings. Since 1991, the average difference between operating and reported earnings has widened to over 18 percent, nine times the previous average.[14] In 2002, the gap between the two earnings concepts widened to a record 67 percent. However, in 2006, this earnings gap had narrowed to about 7 percent.[15]

During the later phases of the bull market of the 1990s, some firms, particularly those in the technology sector, were rightly criticized for ex-

---

[13] Although earnings filed with the IRS may differ from these.

[14] It was partly the favorable reaction of investors themselves that spurred management to increase write-offs. In the 1990 to 1991 recession, investors bought firms that had large write-offs because the investors believed that those firms would drop losing divisions and become more profitable.

[15] See the S&P 500 Web site on earnings.

cluding too many expenses. For example, Cisco Systems wrote off inventories that the firm couldn't sell and used accounting techniques that made its acquisitions appear far more favorable than they were. Some firms advanced pro forma earnings concepts that involved even more extreme assumptions. Amazon.com declared it was profitable in 2000 on a pro forma basis if the interest on nearly $2 billion of debt were ignored.

The Employee Stock Option Controversy

One of the most controversial issues is accounting for employee stock options. Employee stock options give workers a right to buy stock at a given price if they have worked for the firm a given period of time, usually five years. The proliferation of stock options given as a part of employee compensation began after the IRS ruled that payment by options did not violate the compensation limitations set by Congress.

But options were popular not only because they bypassed restrictions on management compensation but also because most stock options, when granted, did not have to be accounted for as expenses in the firm's profit statements. Instead, these options were expensed only if and when they were exercised.

Although the FASB approved this treatment many years ago, there were many vociferous critics. Nobody put the case for expensing options better than Warren Buffett who stated in 1992, well before this issue took center stage:

> If stock options are not a form of compensation, what are they? If compensation is not an expense, what is it? And if expenses shouldn't go into the income statement, where in the world should they go?[16]

Buffett is perfectly correct. Options should be expensed when issued because earnings should reflect the firm's best determination of the "sustainable flow of profits," profits that could be paid out as dividends to shareholders. If employees were not issued options, their regular cash compensation would have to be raised by the value of the options forgone. Whether the compensation is paid by cash, options, or candy bars, it represents an expense to the firm.

When an option is exercised, the firm sells new shares to the option holder at a discounted price determined by the terms of the option. These new shares will reduce the *per share* earnings and is called the *dilution* of earnings. Current shareholders are giving up part of the firm's

---

[16] Berkshire Hathaway 1992 Annual Report.

profits to new shareholders who, through options, purchased the shares at below market prices.

In 2000 the FASB reversed its position and, following the lead of the International Accounting Standards Board (IASB), decided that options should be expensed when granted.

Technology firms, heavy users of options, lobbied Congress to block the FASB from instituting those rules. But after the technology bubble broke, there was clear professional sentiment that options should be expensed, and the FASB set 2006 as the year that firms must expense options. Many firms began expensing options earlier, and by the middle of 2004, 176 firms in the S&P 500, representing over 40 percent of the market capitalization, expensed options.

Employee Stock Options Lower Risks to Stockholders

The issuance of employee stock options increases the risk borne by shareholders. If the firm experiences poor earnings and the share price declines, then many employee options will expire worthless and the firm, since it had expensed them, will realize a gain by reversing the expense. On the other hand, if there is good news and the share price rises, then the options will be exercised and per share earnings will decline because of the dilution.

The risk that employees shoulder when they accept options instead of cash compensation thereby reduces the risk to the outside shareholders. This means that a firm that fully expenses the fair value of options paid to employees should, all other things equal, be valued slightly more than firms that pay an equivalent amount of cash in lieu of options.

But this also means that much of the upside of technology stocks is enjoyed first by employees exercising their options, which dilutes the interest of outside shareholders. This is an important consideration not always appreciated by those buying stocks in this options-saturated sector.

Controversies in Accounting for Pension Costs

Defined Benefit and Defined Contribution Plans

Almost as contentious as the treatment of options is the accounting treatment of pension costs. There are two major types of pension plans: defined benefit (DB) plans and defined contribution (DC) plans.

Defined contribution plans, which gained enormous popularity in the 1990s' bull market, place both the employees' and employer's pension

contributions directly into assets that are owned by the employees. In these plans, the firm does not guarantee any benefits. In contrast, in *defined benefit plans* the employer spells out the income and healthcare benefits that will be paid, and the assets backing these plans are not chosen by or directly owned by the employees.

Under government regulations, DB plans must be *funded*—that is, the firm must place assets in a separate account that will cover the expected benefits associated with these plans. In DC plans, the risk that the value of the plan at retirement will not cover retirement expenses is taken by the employees instead of the employers, and it is the employees who must decide where to place their investment dollars.

There were two reasons for the tremendous increase in the popularity of the DC plans over the past two decades. One was the great bull market of the 1990s that made many employees believe that they could obtain a better return on their own investments than the returns promised by the firm.

The second reason was that contributions in a DC plan were immediately *vested*—that is, they became the property of the employee. If an employee left the firm, he could take his DC assets with him. In contrast, it takes a number of years before the benefits of a DB plan belong to the employee. If an employee leaves the firm before these benefits become vested, then the employee receives no benefit.

Problems and Risks in Defined Benefit Plans

Current rules for calculating the returns on the assets backing DB plans are generous to the corporations. The FASB allows firms to choose their own estimate of the rate of return on the assets in their portfolio, and often these estimates are too high. Furthermore, if the value of the assets falls below the pension liabilities (and the fund is called *underfunded*), the FASB allows firms to close this gap over a substantial period of time. Although the government shortened the period over which firms must restore underfunded pensions in the Pension Protection Act of 2006, firms are still allowed to choose their own return estimates.

While the government requires firms to build a fund for retirement income benefits, it does *not* require them to fund other pension-related benefits, particularly health benefits. In 2003 a Goldman Sachs analyst estimated that the healthcare liabilities of the three Detroit automakers amount to $92 billion, roughly 50 percent greater than their combined market capitalizations.[17]

---

[17] David Stires, "The Breaking Point," *Fortune*, February 18, 2003.

Most investors are fully cognizant of these unfunded liabilities and have taken down the value of the auto manufacturers as well as other firms that have large underfunded pension plans. The bankruptcy of the steel manufacturers and airlines over the last decade are related to their inability to meet their pension obligations. By mid-2007, because of rising stock prices and interest rates (which help reduce the magnitude of the pension obligation), overall the S&P 500 firms were fully funded with respect to their pension obligations but still were about $300 billion underfunded in health and other postretirement employee benefits (OPEB).[18]

Since virtually all pension plans started in the last 20 years have been set up as DC plans and have sharply cut back or eliminated retiree health benefits, the corporate pension problem will disappear over time as the risk of funding retirement is shifted to individuals instead of corporations. Nevertheless, it behooves investors to take a close look at the stock of firms with large DB plans as they can be a serious drain on future earnings.

Standard & Poor's Core Earnings

The dismay over the treatment of pensions and options and the ever-widening definition of *operating earnings* led the Standard & Poor's corporation in 2001 to propose a uniform method of calculating earnings that they called *core earnings*. The objective was to define and measure earnings from a firm's principal or "core" businesses and to exclude from earnings revenues or expenses that are incurred for other reasons. Core earnings expenses employee stock options, recalculates pension costs, and excludes unrelated capital gains and losses, goodwill impairments, and one-time litigations gains and losses, among others.

This unusual and bold stance was taken by the nonregulatory, private sector firm that is the keeper of the world's most replicated benchmark, the S&P 500 Index. The *New York Times* called it one the best ideas in 2002.[19] Warren Buffett applauded the S&P's stance, stating in an open letter to David Blitzer, managing director of Standard & Poor's, "Your move is both courageous and correct. In the future, investors will look back at your action as a milestone event."[20]

---

[18] This was communicated to me by Howard Silverblatt of Standard & Poor's in an e-mail on June 5, 2007.

[19] Tim Carvell, "The Year in Ideas," *New York Times Magazine*, December 15, 2002.

[20] Warren Buffett, open letter to David Blitzer, managing director of Standard & Poor's, May 15, 2002.

I believe that adopting the concept of core earnings makes a significant move in the direction of standardizing profit statements and is currently the best way to measure a firm's earnings potential.[21] One should not underestimate how important this is. A typical firm in today's market sells for about 20 times yearly earnings. This means that only one-twentieth, or 5 percent, of its price depends on what happens in the next 12 months and 95 percent of its price depends on what happens after that. That is why when we calculate earnings, accounting decisions should distinguish between any one-time gains and losses that are not expected to be repeated and those that have implications for future profitability. This is what Standard & Poor's accomplished with core earnings.

EARNINGS QUALITY

Going beyond Standard & Poor's core earnings, another way to measure the quality of earnings is by examining a firm's *accruals*, which is defined as accounting earnings minus cash flows.

A firm with high accruals may be manipulating its earnings, and this could be a warning of problems in the future. Alternatively, low accruals may be a good sign that earnings are being conservatively estimated by the firm.

There is strong evidence that firms with low accruals have much higher stock returns than firms with high accruals. Richard Sloan, a professor at the University of Michigan, was the first to determine that a high level of accruals was related to subsequent poor earnings and low stock returns.[22]

Sloan found that from 1962 through 2001, the difference between the firms with the highest-quality earnings (lowest accruals) and those with the poorest-quality earnings (highest accruals) was a staggering 18 percent *per year*. Further research indicated that despite the importance of accruals, Wall Street analysts did not take this into account when forecasting future earnings growth.

---

[21] The core earnings concept is the brainchild of David Blitzer, managing director and chairman of the Index Committee, Robert Friedman, Howard Silverblatt, and others.

[22] Richard Sloan, "Do Stock Prices Reflect Information in Accruals and Cash Flows about Future Earnings?" *Accounting Review*, vol. 71 (1996). High levels of accruals are also associated with more SEC enforcement actions, earnings restatements, and class action lawsuits, all of which have negative implications for stock returns. Also see Richard Sloan, Scott Richardson, Mark Soliman, and Irem Tuna, "Accrual Reliability, Earnings Persistence and Stock Prices," *Journal of Accounting and Economics*, vol. 39 (2005).

Determining earnings will always be fraught with estimates, even if made in good faith. The bottom line is that cash flows, as well as dividends, are much harder to manipulate than earnings.

DOWNWARD BIASES IN EARNINGS

Although some accounting conventions work in a favorable direction for the firm, there are many that work in the opposite direction. For example, research and development costs are routinely expensed although there is good reason to capitalize these expenditures and then depreciate them over time.[23] This means that the earnings of firms with a high level of R&D expenditures, such as the pharmaceutical industry, may be understating their earnings.

Take Pfizer, the largest drug stock in the world and one of the 10 largest companies in the S&P 500 in March 2007. In 2006, Pfizer spent $7.6 billion on research and development for drugs and slightly over $2 billion on plants and equipment. Governed by current accounting rules, Pfizer subtracted from its earnings only 5 percent of the $2 billion it spent on plant and equipment as depreciation because the remainder would be deducted over the useful life of these assets.

But 100 percent of the $7.6 billion Pfizer spent on research and development was subtracted from its earnings. This is because Pfizer's R&D is not considered an asset under these accounting definitions, and it must be expensed when the expenditures are made.

Does this make sense? Is Pfizer's R&D less of an asset than its property, plants, and equipment? Considering that Pfizer's value largely stems directly from the patents it gains through its research and development expenditures, this accounting treatment seems to cast too negative a shadow on Pfizer's performance.

Leonard Nakamura, an economist at the Federal Reserve Bank of Philadelphia, believes this is the case. "It's really those [R&D] expenditures that are going to drive long-run corporate performance," he has stated.[24] Thus, in many ways, especially for industries with intensive research and development, current earnings measures understate the future earnings potential of the corporation and economic reality.

Another understatement comes from the treatment of interest expense. Interest expenses are deducted from corporate earnings even

---

[23] Leonard Nakamura, "Investing in Intangibles: Is a Trillion Dollars Missing from GDP?" *Business Review*, Federal Reserve Bank of Philadelphia, Fourth Quarter 2001, pp. 27–37.

[24] Cecily Kump, "Innovation," *Forbes*, July 5, 2004.

though inflation, which raises interest costs, causes a corresponding reduction in the real value of corporate debt. In inflationary times the impact of rising prices on fixed corporate liabilities could be substantial.

The bottom line is that some accounting practices understate the
true earnings of firms.

HISTORICAL YARDSTICKS FOR VALUING THE MARKET

Many yardsticks have been used to evaluate whether stock prices are
overvalued or undervalued. Most of these measure the market value of
the shares outstanding relative to economic *fundamentals*, such as earnings, dividends, or book values, or to some economic aggregate, such as
the gross domestic product (GDP) or total replacement cost of the capital stock. Stock prices are often said to be "high" if these ratios exceed
their historical average value. Yet one has to be very careful when exercising this judgment. The following are a set of commonly used valuation measures.

Price-Earnings Ratios

The most basic and fundamental yardstick for valuing stocks is the *price-
earnings ratio*. The price-earnings ratio (or *P-E ratio*) of a stock is simply
the ratio of its price to its annual earnings. The price-earnings ratio of the
market is the ratio of the aggregate earnings of the market to the aggregate value of the market. The P-E ratio measures how much an investor
is willing to pay for a dollar's worth of current earnings.

The single most important variable determining the P-E ratio for an
individual stock is the expectation of future earnings growth. If investors believe future earnings growth is going to be high, they will pay
at a higher P-E ratio than they will pay if they expect earnings to stag-
nate or decline. But earnings growth is not the only factor influencing
the P-E ratio. P-E ratios are also influenced by other factors such as interest rates, risk attitudes of investors, taxes, and liquidity.

The P-E ratio of the entire market, based on the most recent 12
months of reported earnings, is shown in Figure 7-2. It has fluctuated between a low of 5.31 in 1917 and a high of 46.71 in 2002. Its average historical level is 14.45.

The very high number recorded for 2002 is due to very special circumstances. It is not the "bubble" in market prices that prevailed at the
end of the last century. Instead, as we will discuss in the next chapter, it is
related to the collapse in reported earnings caused by a few technology

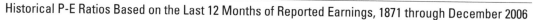

FIGURE 7-2

Historical P-E Ratios Based on the Last 12 Months of Reported Earnings, 1871 through December 2006

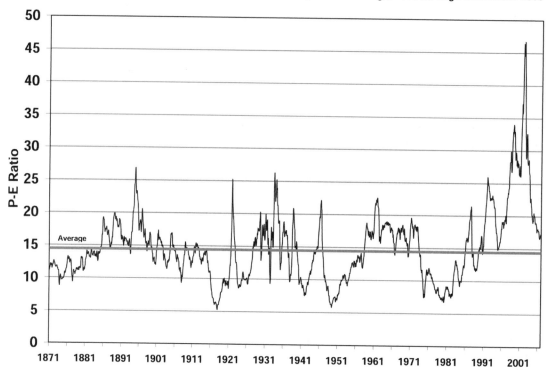

firms, such as JDS Uniphase and AOL, that took huge write-offs related to overpriced stocks that were purchased at the height of the bubble.

P-E Ratios and Future Stock Returns

Although the P-E ratio can be a misleading indicator of future stock returns in the short run, in the long run the P-E ratio is a very useful predictor. The reasons may be understood by analyzing how stock and bond returns are calculated.

The *current yield* of a bond is the ratio of the interest received over the price paid, and it is a good measure of future return if the bond is not selling at a large premium or discount to its maturity value. A similar computation can be made with stocks by computing the *earnings yield*, which is the earnings per share divided by the price. The earnings yield

is the inverse of the price-earnings ratio, and it would be the current yield on a stock if all earnings were paid out as dividends.[25]

Since the underlying assets of a firm are real, the earnings yield is a *real*, or inflation-adjusted, return. Inflation raises the prices of the output and hence the cash flows from the underlying assets. As a result real assets tend to rise in value when the price level increases. The increasing cash flow from equities contrasts to the *fixed* return earned from bonds, where the coupons and the final payment are fixed in money terms and do not rise with inflation.

The long-run data certainly bear out this contention. As noted above, the average historical P-E ratio has been 14.45, so the average earnings yield on stocks has been 1/14.45, or 6.8 percent. This earnings yield is virtually identical to the 6.7 percent real return on equities from 1871 taken from Table 1-1.

When using the earnings yields to predict forward-looking real returns, it is advisable to take some average of past earnings to smooth out temporary increases and decreases in earnings that may be due to such factors as the business cycle. The earnings yield based on a five-year average of past earnings against the next five years of real returns is plotted in Figure 7-3.

Although there is significant noise in the data, the plot does show a significant relation between earnings yields and subsequent returns. The very high earnings yields (and low P-E ratios) of over 0.2 were associated with the highest subsequent five-year returns, while the two lowest earnings yields (and highest P-E ratios) of 0.0291 and 0.0293 are associated with low subsequent returns. Almost one-quarter of the subsequent five-year returns can be explained by the earnings yields.

But one must be very careful about using a historical average of earnings. Although such a procedure will remove some of the cyclical bias in the data, it is not robust to changes in dividend yield policy. As noted in Chapter 3 in discussing the trend line of the Dow Jones Industrials, and as will be discussed in the next chapter, a change in dividend policy will change the rate of earnings growth so that average earnings yields are not directly comparable. A fall in the payout ratio, which accelerates capital gains, will lead to an *underestimate* of future real returns if an average of past earnings is used.

---

[25] If all earnings are not paid as dividends, then the return on the stock will be the sum of the dividend yield plus the capital gain, which, under the assumptions about the invariance of the value of the firm to the dividend policy noted earlier, will equal the earnings yield on the stock.

FIGURE 7-3

Plots of the Earnings Yields Based on a Five-Year Average of Past Earnings, January 1876 through December 2001, versus the Next Five Years of Real Returns

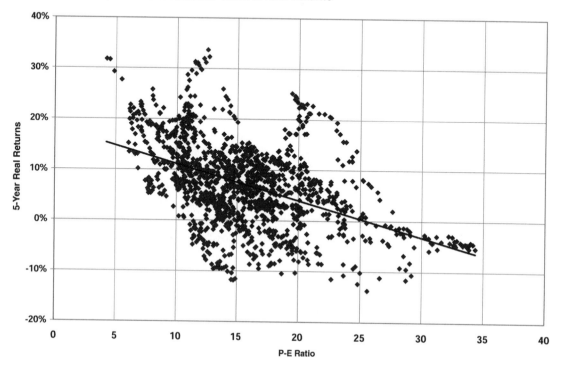

The Fed Model, Earnings Yields, and Bond Yields

In early 1997, in response to Federal Reserve Chairman Alan Greenspan's increasing concern about the impact of the rising stock market on the economy, three researchers from the Federal Reserve produced a paper entitled "Earnings Forecasts and the Predictability of Stock Returns: Evidence from Trading the S&P."[26] This paper documented the remarkable correspondence between the earnings yields on stocks and the 30-year government bond rates.

Greenspan supported the results of this paper and suggested that the central bank regarded the stock market as "overvalued" whenever

---

[26] Joel Lander, Athanasios Orphanides, and Martha Douvogiannis, "Earnings Forecasts and the Predictability of Stock Returns: Evidence from Trading the S&P," Federal Reserve, January 1997. Reprinted in the *Journal of Portfolio Management*, vol. 23 (Summer 1997), pp. 24–35. It refers to an earlier version that was presented in October 1996.

this earnings yield fell below the bond yield and "undervalued" whenever the reverse occurred. The analysis showed that the market was most overvalued in August 1987, just before the October 1987 stock market crash, and most undervalued in the early 1980s, when the great bull market began.

The basic idea behind the Fed model is that bonds are the chief alternative for stocks in investors' portfolios. When the bond yields rise above the earnings yields, stock prices fall because investors shift their portfolio holdings from stocks to bonds. On the other hand, when the bond yields fall below the earnings yields, investors shift to stocks from bonds.

Figure 7-4 shows that the Fed model appeared to work fairly well beginning in 1970. When interest rates fell, stocks rallied to bring the earnings yields down, and the opposite occurred when interest rates rose.

What is surprising is that this relation held despite the fact that stocks and bonds are very different assets. Government bonds have ironclad guarantees to pay a specified number of dollars over time but bear the risk of inflation. Stocks, on the other hand, are real assets whose prices will rise with inflation, but they bear the risk of the uncertainty of

F I G U R E   7–4

Fed Model of Stock Market Valuation, 1926 through December 2006

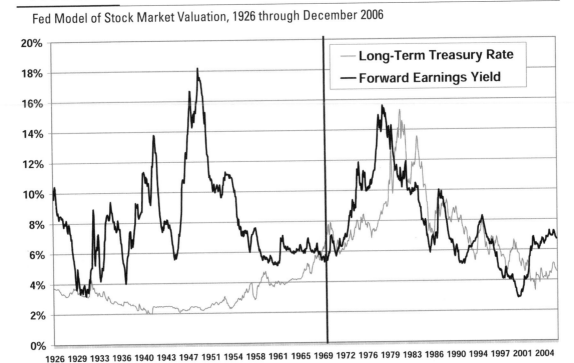

earnings. The reason why the Fed model worked is that the market rated these two risks as approximately equal during this period.

There is no question that both bonds and stocks do badly when inflation increases. Bond prices fell in the late 1960s and 1970s because rising inflation forced interest rates up to offset the depreciating value of money. Stocks fall during inflationary periods for other reasons, such as poor monetary policy, low productivity, and a tax system that is only partially indexed to inflation. These are detailed in Chapter 5.

But these two risks are not equal when inflation is low or when deflation threatens. In those circumstances, bonds (especially U.S. government bonds) will do very well, but deflation undermines firms' pricing power and is bad for corporate profits. Figure 7-4 shows that before inflation became a major concern in the 1970s, there was no relation between bond yields and earnings yields and the Fed model broke down.

In order to put stock and bond valuations on an equivalent valuation, one should compare the earnings yields on stocks with the yields on Treasury inflation-protected securities (TIPS) and bonds. TIPS have absolute certainty of purchasing power return and are the safest assets. Stocks are of course riskier, and they should bear a risk premium above TIPS.

There is considerable debate on what constitutes a "normal" risk premium between stocks and inflation-protected bonds, as is discussed in Chapter 2. Generally the equity risk premium is taken between 2 and 3 percent, but it could certainly be higher in times of great uncertainty or lower when investors are very bullish on stocks.

Corporate Profits and National Income

Another indicator of stock market valuation is the ratio of corporate profits to national income (GDP). Its rise in recent years has alarmed some stock market analysts who worry that if the share of profits to national income falls to its long-term average, stock prices will suffer.

Closer examination of this claim should put those fears to rest. Figure 7-5 displays the ratio of after-tax corporate profits and after-tax profits plus proprietors' income, and their sum since 1947. Proprietors' income is profits of nonincorporated businesses, including profits to partnerships and individual owners.

One can see the long-term downtrend of proprietors' income share from the 1940s to the 1980s, which has recovered only slightly since then. Over this period many brokerage houses, investment banks, and other firms became publicly traded corporations, and some government-

FIGURE 7–5

Market Value, Replacement Cost, and the GDP

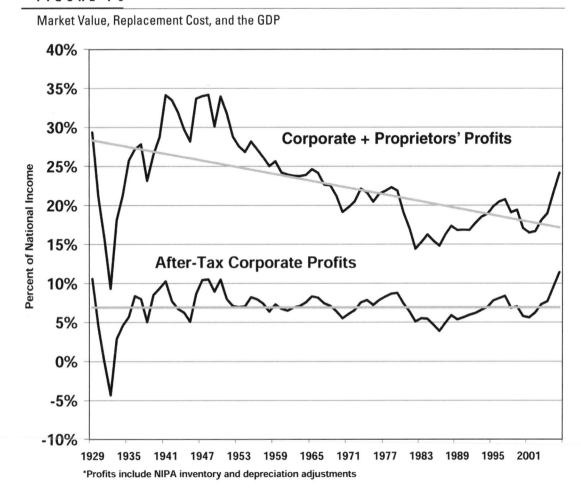

*Profits include NIPA inventory and depreciation adjustments

sponsored firms such as Fannie Mae and Freddie Mac also became public corporations. The sum of corporate profits and proprietors' income is
only slightly higher than its long-term average.

Another consideration is that the fraction of corporate profits of
U.S.-based firms that come from abroad has also been increasing. In
2006, over 44 percent of the sales of S&P 500 companies were foreign. As
the U.S. economy shrinks relative to the size of the world economy, the
corporate profits of U.S. multinational corporations should rise relative
to the GDP.

Book Value, Market Value, and Tobin's Q

The *book value* of a firm has often been used as a valuation yardstick. The book value is the value of a firm's assets minus its liabilities, evaluated at historical costs. The use of aggregate book value as a measure of the overall value of a firm is severely limited because book value uses *historical* prices and thus ignores the effect of changing prices on the value of the assets or liabilities. If a firm purchased a plot of land for $1 million that is now worth $10 million, examining the book value will not reveal this. Over time, the historical value of assets becomes less reliable as a measure of current market value.

To help correct these distortions, James Tobin, a professor at Yale University and a Nobel laureate, adjusted the book value for inflation and computed the "replacement cost" of the assets and liabilities on the balance sheet.[27] He developed a theory that the "equilibrium" or "correct" market price of a firm should equal its assets minus its liabilities adjusted for inflation. If the aggregate market value of a firm exceeds the cost of capital, it would be profitable to create more capital, sell shares to finance it, and reap a profit. If the market value falls below the replacement cost, then it would be better for a firm to dismantle and sell its capital, or stop investment and cut production.

Tobin designated the ratio of the market value to the replacement cost with the letter Q, and he indicated that its ratio should be unity if the stock market was properly valued. The historical values of "Tobin's Q," as the theory has become known, are shown in Figure 7-6. The ratio has fluctuated between a high of 1.84 in 1999 to a low of 0.27 in 1920, with the average being 0.70.

In 2000 Andrew Smithers and Stephen Wright of the United Kingdom published the book *Valuing Wall Street*,[28] which maintained that Tobin's Q was the best measure of value and that the U.S. markets as well as the U.K. and many other European markets were extremely overvalued by this criterion. There are some who maintain that Q should generally be less than unity because older capital is not as productive as newly installed capital.[29] If this is true, then the market was even more overvalued in the late 1990s.

---

[27] James Tobin, "A General Equilibrium Approach to Monetary Theory," *Journal of Money, Credit, and Banking*, vol. 1 (February 1969), pp. 15–29.

[28] Andrew Smithers and Stephen Wright, *Valuing Wall Street: Protecting Wealth in Turbulent Markets*, New York: McGraw-Hill, 2000.

[29] This is also because in equilibrium the marginal productivity of capital should be treated as being equal to the cost of new capital, while the stock market measures the average productivity of both old and new capital.

F I G U R E   7–6

Tobin's Q = Ratio of Market Value to Replacement Cost of Capital

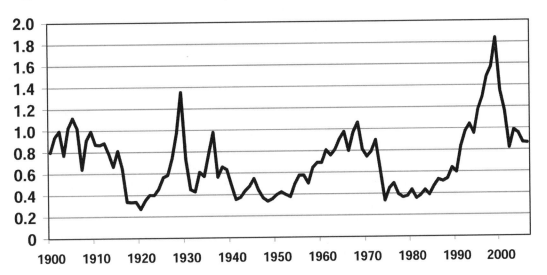

But there are critics of the Q theory. Capital equipment and structures lack a good secondary market, and hence there is no realistic way
to value much of the physical capital stock. The inability to value intellectual capital is a perhaps more significant drawback. Microsoft has a
book value of about $40 billion but a market value over seven times as
large. In fact, the value of most technology firms is composed of their intellectual capital.

Smithers maintains that the existence of intellectual capital should
not be used to justify any gap between the book and market values. Although firms may own trademarks and patents, they do not own the entrepreneurs, engineers, or other employees that generate ideas. As long
as there is a competitive labor market, accounting allowances for human
factors of production must be calculated by their market values, just as
physical capital. The stock options lavished on employees during the
technology boom of the late 1990s to keep key personnel from being bid
away by other firms are an example of this.

This point is well taken, but some firms are more successful than
others at creating and maintaining productive groups of talented individuals. Often employees can create more firm value by working together than they can by working separately, and other firms may not be
able to create the same creative environment. The ability of the United

States to draw talent from the rest of the world may create shareholder value in excess of the cost of hiring these workers.[30]

It may be that in the very long run the market value of the tangible and intangible capital must equal the cost of reproducing it. But book value is a construct of the past; market value derives from prospective earnings and looks to the future. These prospective earnings more accurately establish the basis of stock valuation than the historical costs at which the firms purchased these assets.

Market Value Relative to the GDP and Other Ratios

The gross domestic product (GDP) is universally regarded as the best measure of the overall output in the economy. It would be reasonable to assume that the market value (MV) of firms should bear some normal relation to the size of the economy. Figure 7-7 shows the ratio of the market value of stocks to the GDP since 1900.

---

[30] Of course, one can reply that for every firm that creates a more productive environment, there is another firm that creates an unsuccessful one and ends up overpaying and wasting intellectual resources.

FIGURE 7–7

Market Value of Equities as Percent of Total GDP

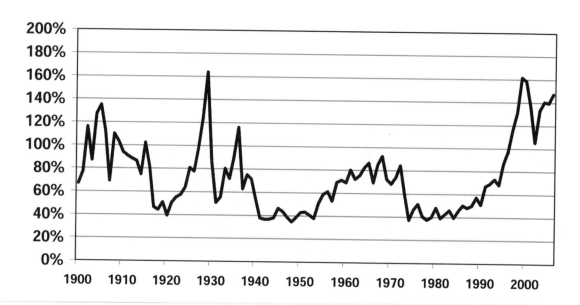

The ratio of the market value of equity to the GDP can both theo-retically and empirically exceed 1. Equity valuation is a balance sheet item, while the GDP is an annual flow. Many firms have capital that far exceeds their annual sales, so it is not at all unusual for the value of an economy's capital to be greater than its output.

But more importantly, equity capital is only a part of total capital. Both debt and equity finance the capital stock, and the ratio between them changes over time. In the 1990s as interest rates fell, many firms re-tired high-coupon bonds and reduced their leverage, a process called *deleveraging*. Deleveraging increases the value of equity and decreases the value of debt but leaves the total value of the firms unchanged. As the market has risen, more firms have become public companies. This will increase the market value of stocks even if the total value of firms, public and private, remains unchanged.

Moreover, the ratio of the market capitalization to the GDP differs widely among countries. Multinational firms might be headquartered in a particular country while their sales span the globe. As international trade increases, it should not be surprising if the market value of firms deviates from the GDP of the country in which they are headquartered. Table 7-1 shows that the market value of shares traded in Hong Kong are over 600 percent of its GDP, while in Germany, Italy, and Japan the ratio is less than 100 percent. The variation between countries results from large differences in the leverage, the fraction of firms that are publicly traded, and the international scope of the firms headquartered there.

One ratio that has very little meaning but is often seen in the press is a time series of the ratio of a stock index such as the S&P 500 or the Dow Jones Industrials to the GDP. Stock indexes report the average prices of individual shares, not the total value of such shares that will

T A B L E   7–1

Summary Market Statistics for Various Countries as of February 2007: Market Value (MV) to Gross Domestic Product (GDP); P-E Ratio; and Dividend Yield

Statistic	U.S.	Japan	Germany	Britain	Hong Kong	Switzerland	Italy
MV/GDP*	136%	74%	53%	159%	602%	270%	47%
P-E†	19.0	24.1	15.9	18.9	14.9	17.6	14.8
Div. Yld.†	1.67%	0.97%	2.29%	3.54%	2.78%	1.62%	3.53%

*Data for market value (MV)/GDP are for February 17, 2007.
†P-E and dividend yield are based on last 12 months of earnings and dividends.

increase over time as new firms go public. Another misleading time series is a representative stock index against average housing prices. The flow of housing services, or rental income, is not included in the price of homes, while stock price indexes include capital gains caused by reinvested earnings.

CONCLUSION

The fundamental determinant of stock values remains the earnings of a corporation, from which dividends are paid, and the interest rate that discounts those dividends. The best concept of earnings is the "core earnings" concept developed by Standard & Poor's in 2002, which was the first to fully expense options and make adjustments to pension income. The earnings yield, which is the reciprocal of the P-E ratio, is a good predictor of future *real* stock returns.

One of the most difficult issues in economics is to know when there has been a basic structural shift in the economy and when there has not. Admittedly, there are too many times, such as the technology bubble at the end of the last century, when speculators used "new era" economics to justify unreasonably high prices. But there are also times when there has been an important structural shift, such as in the 1950s when the dividend yields on stocks fell below the interest rates on long-term Treasury bonds.

There have been some important shifts in recent years. The fall in the dividend payout ratio has shifted stock returns from dividends to capital gains, impacting the growth rates of future earnings and dividends. Furthermore, the dramatic fall in transactions costs combined with the increase in macroeconomic stability may also change the P-E ratio of stock prices to valuation metrics. How these events will impact future stock returns will be discussed in the next chapter.

CHAPTER 8

THE IMPACT OF ECONOMIC GROWTH ON MARKET VALUATION AND THE COMING AGE WAVE

The term "new economy" has become, beginning in 2000, a fad in itself. It appears suddenly as a new name for our hopes and for economic progress due to recent technological advances, notably the Internet, and for our reasons to think that the future growth prospects are ever so brilliant.

ROBERT SHILLER, 2001[1]

What are the most important macrotrends in the economy that influence future stock market returns? Economic growth immediately comes to mind. But economic growth has nowhere near as big an impact on stock returns as most investors believe. However, other important trends do have a positive impact on stock valuation: the stability of the overall economy, the reduction in transactions costs, and the change in taxes on stock market income.

---

[1] Robert Shiller, *Irrational Exuberance*, New York: First Broadway Books, 2001, Afterword to the paperback edition, p. 249.

Yet all of these factors may be eclipsed by the most important macroeconomic trend of the next two decades—the hundreds of millions of baby boomers from the developed world that are planning to finance their retirement by selling their financial assets. This chapter will analyze all these issues, coming to the conclusion that the long-term future of equity returns looks bright *if* the United States keeps its capital markets open to the rest of the world.

GDP GROWTH AND STOCK RETURNS

Some very surprising results are shown in Figure 8-1. In Chapter 1 we reported on the long-term stock returns of 16 major markets around the world from 1900 through 2006. The long-term dollar returns of each country reported against the average real growth of its GDP are plotted in Figure 8-1a. The results are striking. Real GDP growth is *negatively* correlated with stock market returns.[2] That is, higher economic growth in individual countries is associated with lower returns to equity investors.[3] Similarly, the stock returns for the developing countries against their GDP growth are plotted in Figure 8-1b.[4] Again, despite the huge returns chalked up to developing markets in recent years, there is a negative relation between the returns to individual countries and the growth rates of their GDP.

Why does this occur? Since stock prices are the present value of future dividends, it would seem natural to assume that economic growth would positively impact future dividends and hence increase stock prices. But the determinants of stock prices are earnings and dividends on a *per share* basis. Although economic growth influences *aggregate* earnings and dividends favorably, economic growth does not necessarily increase the growth of *per share* earnings or dividends. This is because economic growth requires increased capital expenditures, and this capital does not come freely.

Implementing and upgrading technology requires substantial investment. These expenditures must be funded either by borrowing in the debt market (through the banks, trade credit, or by selling bonds) or

---

[2] This is an update of the chart that was presented in the second edition of *Stocks for the Long Run* (1998) as Figure 9-2 but omitted from the third edition.

[3] Elroy Dimson, Paul Marsh, and Michael Staunton confirm my findings in the *Triumph of the Optimists: 101 Years of Global Investment Returns* (Princeton, N.J.: Princeton University Press, 2002), but they do not provide an explanation for it.

[4] This is an updated version of Chart 16 in Jeremy Siegel, *The Future for Investors: Why the Tried and the True Triumph over the Bold and the New*, New York: Crown Business, 2005.

FIGURE 8–1a

Long-Term Dollar Returns Reported for 16 Countries against Each Country's Average Real GDP Growth, 1900 through December 2006

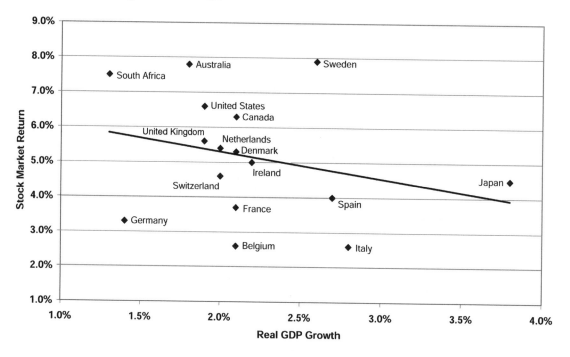

by floating new shares. The added interest costs (in the case of debt financing) and the dilution of earnings (in the case of equity financing) reduce the growth of per share earnings.

It is possible that growth can occur in the short term without capital expansion by using the existing plant more intensely. But the long-run historical evidence strongly suggests that capital must be expanded to support higher growth. One of the signal characteristics of long-term historical data is that the level of the capital stock—the total value of all physical capital such as factories and equipment as well as intellectual capital—has grown over time roughly in proportion to the level of aggregate output. In other words, a 10 percent increase in GDP ultimately requires a 10 percent increase in the capital stock.[5]

---

[5] For a good summary of all this literature, see Jay R. Ritter, "Equity Growth and Equity Returns," *Pacific-Basin Finance Journal*, vol. 13 (2005), pp. 489–503.

F I G U R E   8–1b

Long-Term Stock Returns for 25 Developing Countries against Each Country's Average Real GDP Growth, Various Starting Years through December 2006

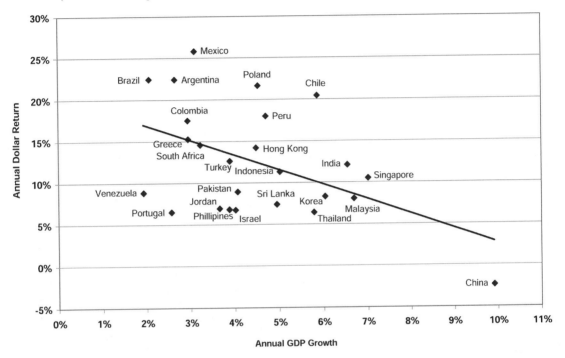

The Gordon Dividend Growth Model

The belief that growth automatically boosts stock prices grows out of the misuse of a popular model for valuing stocks—namely, the *Gordon dividend growth model* developed by Roger Gordon in 1962.[6] In Chapter 7 we noted that the price of a stock is the present value of all the future dividends. It can be easily shown that if dividends grow in the future at a constant rate g, then the price per share of a stock P can be written as follows:

$$P = \frac{d}{r - g}$$

---

[6] Myron J. Gordon, *The Investment, Financing, and Valuation of the Corporation*, Homewood, Ill.: Irwin, 1962.

where d is next period's dividend per share, g is the constant rate of future growth of dividends per share, and r is the discount rate that investors apply to stock.

From this model, it appears as if an increase in growth g unambiguously raises the price of shares. But the g in the Gordon equation refers to the growth in *per share* dividends, not the growth in aggregate dividends, and the two concepts can deviate substantially, as the historical data confirm.

ECONOMIC GROWTH AND STOCK RETURNS

The summary statistics for dividends per share, earnings per share, and stock returns for the U.S. economy from 1871 through December 2006 are shown in Table 8-1. The data show that real per share earnings growth over the entire 135 years has averaged a paltry 1.88 percent, considerably below the growth rate of real GDP, which is about twice that number. As noted above, because shares and/or debt must be used to finance capital expenditures, earnings per share growth do not match aggregate economic growth over the long run.

It is also of interest that the growth of earnings and dividends per share is higher since World War II than before even though the GDP growth is lower. The cause of the higher earnings growth in the last 60 years is the decline in the dividend-payout ratio and subsequent increase in the use of retained earnings to finance growth.

As explained in Chapter 7, the valuation of a firm is independent of the dividend policy chosen as long as the rate of return on retained earnings is identical to that demanded by shareholders. This can be shown

TABLE 8-1

Summary Statistics for Dividends per Share, Earnings per Share, and Stock Returns for the U.S. Economy, 1871 through December 2006

	Real GDP Growth	Real per Share Earnings Growth	Real per Share Dividend Growth	Dividend Yield*	Payout Ratio*
1871-2006	3.57%	1.88%	1.32%	4.58%	58.17%
1871-1945	3.97%	0.66%	0.74%	5.29%	66.78%
1946-2006	3.09%	3.40%	2.03%	3.53%	51.38%

*Denotes median.

by the Gordon model. If a firm cuts its dividend d and uses the proceeds to earn a rate of return r, the growth of future dividends g will rise by just enough to keep price of the stock P, unchanged under the lower dividend.

The low growth of real historical earnings per share has caused some economists to predict low future real returns for the stock market. In 2002, at the bear market low, Robert Arnott and Peter Bernstein predicted that the current low dividend yield when added to the historical growth of real earnings will yield future real stock returns of between 2 and 4 percent.[7]

But these pessimistic predictions proved wrong because they ignored the impact of the lower dividend-payout ratio on earnings growth.[8] As noted above, a reduction in the dividend increases retained earnings, and if the return that management earns of its retained earnings is identical to the return demanded by shareholders on its stock, then the increase in earnings per share growth will exactly offset the decrease in the dividend yield.[9] One must not forecast future real returns from historical earnings growth rates when the payout ratio has changed.

FACTORS THAT RAISE VALUATION RATIOS

We have noted that the historical real return on equity has been between 6½ and 7 percent per year over long periods and that this has coincided with an average P-E ratio of approximately 15. But there have been structural changes in the economy in recent years that may change that ratio.

Two of these changes relate directly to the expected rate of the return on equities and one to the equity risk premium.

---

[7] Robert D. Arnott and Peter L. Bernstein, "What Risk Premium Is 'Normal'?" *Financial Analysts Journal*, vol. 58 (2002), pp. 64–85. As noted in Chapter 6, Bill Gross from PIMCO (Pacific Investment Management Company, Newport Beach, Calif.) also used this analysis to predict "Dow 5000" in September 2002.

[8] Robert Arnott and Cliff Asness disputed the claim that higher retained earnings means higher dividend growth and issued a pessimistic forecast in "Surprise! Higher Dividends = Higher Earnings Growth," *Financial Analysts Journal*, January/February 2003, pp. 70–87.

[9] A simple example will illustrate the point. If the P-E ratio of the market is 15, then the earnings yield is 6.8 percent, which is also a prediction of its real return. If the dividend yield is set at 5 percent, then the accumulation of retained earnings will allow the rate of growth of real earnings per share to be 1.8 percent per year. If the dividend yield is set at 2 percent, then the increase in per share real earnings will be 4.8 percent per year.

Factors That Impact Expected Returns

We have shown in Chapter 5 that the reduction in taxes on equity return due to the reduction in marginal and capital gains tax rates and inflation have added more than 2 percentage points to the return over the last half century. This is substantially more than the increase in the after-tax return on fixed-income assets.

But there has been a second significant factor increasing expected return on stocks—the reduction in transactions costs. Chapter 1 confirmed that the real return on equity *as measured by stock indexes* was near 7 percent in the nineteenth and twentieth centuries. But over the nineteenth century and the early part of the twentieth century, it was extremely difficult, if not impossible, for an investor to replicate the stock returns calculated from these stock indexes.

Charles Jones of Columbia University has documented stock trading costs over the last century.[10] These costs include both the fees paid to brokers and the "bid-asked spread," or the difference between the buying and selling costs for stocks. His analysis shows that the average one-way cost to either buy or sell a stock has dropped from over 1 percent of value traded as late as 1975 (before the deregulation of brokerage fees) to under 0.18 percent today.

The fall in transactions costs suggests that the price of obtaining and maintaining a diversified portfolio of common stocks, which is necessary to replicate index returns, could have easily cost from 1 to 2 percent per year over much of the nineteenth and twentieth centuries. Because of these costs, investors in earlier years purchased fewer stocks than in an index and were less diversified, thereby assuming more risk than implied by stock indexes. Alternatively, if investors attempted to buy all the stocks, their real returns could have been as low as 5 percent per year after deducting transactions costs.

The collapse of transactions costs over the past two decades means that stockholders can now acquire and hold a completely diversified portfolio at an extremely low cost.[11] It has been well established that liquid securities—that is, those assets that can be sold quickly and at little cost on short notice in the public market—command a premium over illiquid securities. Through most of the past two centuries, stocks were far less liquid than today, and therefore they were sold at a significant

---

[10] Charles M. Jones, "A Century of Stock Market Liquidity and Trading Costs," working paper, May 23, 2002.

[11] The cost of some index funds for even small investors is only 0.1 percent per year. See Chapter 20.

discount to such safe and liquid assets as government bonds. As stocks become more liquid, their valuation relative to earnings and dividends should rise.[12]

The Equity Risk Premium

Over the past 200 years the average compound rate of return on stocks in comparison to safe long-term government bonds—the *equity premium*—has been between 3 and 3½ percent.[13] In 1985, economists Rajnish Mehra and Edward Prescott published a paper entitled "The Equity Premium: A Puzzle."[14] In their work they showed that given the standard models of risk and return that economists had developed over the years, one could not explain the large gap between the returns on equities and fixed-income assets found in the historical data. They claimed that economic models predicted that either the rate of return on stocks should be lower, or the rate of return on fixed-income assets should be higher, or both. In fact, according to their studies, an equity premium as low as 1 percent or less could be justified.[15]

Mehra and Prescott were not the first to believe that the equity premium derived from historical returns was too large. Fifty years earlier Professor Chelcie Bosland of Brown University had stated that one of the consequences of the spread of knowledge of superior stock returns in the 1920s as a result of Edgar Lawrence Smith's contributions would be a narrowing of the equity premium:

> Paradoxical though it may seem, there is considerable truth in the statement that widespread knowledge of the profitability of common stocks, gained from the studies that have been made, tends to diminish the likelihood that correspondingly large profits can be gained from stocks in the future. The competitive bidding for stocks which results from this knowledge causes prices at the time of purchase to be high, with the attendant smaller possibilities of gain in the principal and high yield. The discount process may do away with a large share of the gains from common stock

---

[12] John B. Carlson and Eduard A. Pelz, "Investor Expectations and Fundamentals: Disappointment Ahead?" Federal Reserve Bank of Cleveland, *Economic Commentary*, May 1, 2000.

[13] This is based on the difference in *compound*, or geometric, average rates of return. The premium is higher based on arithmetic average returns.

[14] Rajnish Mehra and Edward C. Prescott, "The Equity Premium: A Puzzle," *Journal of Monetary Economics*, vol. 15 (March 1985), pp. 145–162.

[15] Mehra and Prescott used the Cowles Foundation data going back to 1872. In their research, they did not even mention the mean reversion characteristics of stock that would have shrunk the equity premium even more.

investment and returns to stockholders and investors in other securities may tend to become equalized.[16]

More Stable Economy

There is much literature that attempts to justify the 3 to 3½ percent risk premium found in the historical data in the context of standard macro-economic models.[17] Some of these are based on very high aversion by individuals to lowering their consumption. Others are based on the myopic behavior of those who dislike taking short-term losses on their investments even when they have substantial long-run gains.

Even if we assume that the historical level of the equity risk premium is justified, there is a reason why that premium might narrow in the future: increasing stability of the real economy.

Examine Figure 8-2, which displays the changes in U.S. industrial production since 1884. One can see a major reduction in economic volatility over time, particularly after the Great Depression and again following 1980. Furthermore, by examining industrial production alone, one may *underestimate* the reduced volatility of the entire economy because of the increase in the importance of the more stable service sector.

The swings in the GDP have also become more muted. Recessions have become shorter and milder and expansions longer. The last economic expansion in the United States lasted a record 10 years from March 1991 to March 2001. Economic expansions in Europe have lasted even longer: the last recession in the United Kingdom ended in 1995 and much of the Eurozone has been recession free for more than a decade.

Economists call this trend toward greater macroeconomic stability "The Great Moderation."[18] The moderation has been attributed to better monetary policy; a larger service sector, which is inherently more stable than the goods sectors; and better inventory and production control, enabled in part by the information revolution.

Whatever the reasons, greater macroeconomic stability should lead to greater stability of earnings and a lower equity premium. The lower

---

[16] Chelcie C. Bosland, *The Common Stock Theory of Investment*, New York: Ronald Press, 1937, p. 132.

[17] See Jeremy Siegel, "Perspectives on the Equity Risk Premium," *Financial Analysts Journal*, vol. 61, no. 1 (November/December 2005), pp. 61–73. Reprinted in Rodney N. Sullivan, ed., *Bold Thinking on Investment Management, The FAJ 60th Anniversary Anthology*, Charlottesville, Va.: CFA Institute, 2005, pp. 202–217.

[18] James H. Stock and Mark W. Watson, "Has the Business Cycle Changed and Why?" *NBER Macroeconomics Annual*, 2002, pp. 159–218.

FIGURE 8–2

Monthly Percentage Change in Industrial Production, 1884 through December 2006

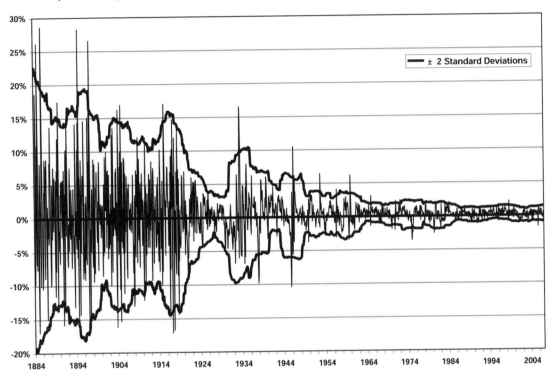

the equity premium, the higher will be the valuation of stocks relative to economic fundamentals, such as earnings and dividends. In this more stable economic environment, firms may wish to boost their earnings by increasing their leverage, using lower-cost debt to substitute for higher-cost equity.[19]

New Justified P-E Ratios

What do all these favorable developments mean for the stock market? First, they mean that the average historical P-E ratio of 15 may no

---

[19] Lower economic volatility also means that labor income has become more predictable and workers can be persuaded to put a larger share of their savings in riskier assets such as equities. This is because workers will not need to accumulate as many fixed-income assets to protect themselves in case unemployment arises, which will also have a favorable impact on equity prices. See John Heaton and Deborah Lucas, "Portfolio Choice in the Presence of Background Risk," *Economic Journal*, vol. 110 (January), pp. 1–26.

longer be appropriate in today's market. If the real risk-free rate of interest on long-term TIPS bonds is 2 percent, then a 3 percent equity premium will yield a 5 percent real return on equities, equivalent to a price-to-earnings ratio of 20. If the equity premium shrinks to 2 percent, then the price-to-earnings ratio can rise to 25 to yield a 4 percent real, forward-looking return on equities. If the real risk-free rate rises to 3 percent, the real return on equities will be 5 percent with a 2 percent risk premium, implying a P-E ratio of 20. Therefore, if inflation stays low, the tax policy remains favorable for equities, and the business cycle remains muted, one can justify price-to-earnings ratios in the low 20s for the equity market.

THE AGE WAVE

Inflation, tax policy, macroeconomic stability, and the drop in transactions costs are important factors influencing the valuation of equities. But looking into the future, there is one factor that is apt to be even more important: the *age wave.*

The reality is that the United States and the rest of the developed world stand at a precipice. Over the next two decades, nearly a quarter *billion* Americans, Europeans, and Japanese—members of the prosperous baby-boom generation that was born following World War II—will leave the labor force. Many are expecting a long and comfortable retirement by relying on government and private pension plans as well as tax-supported medical services.

But unless we can exploit the dramatic demographic and economics changes that lie before us, our future may be much poorer. Instead of stepping into an easy retirement, many retirees will tumble into a retirement marked by bankrupt government social programs and declining asset values that will quickly deplete their cherished nest eggs.

This forecast is not based on an unpredictable future but on events that have already transpired. Aside from immigration, we know almost exactly how many people over the next 20 years are going to reach the working age of 20 and the retirement age of 65. "Demography," as the great management sage Peter Drucker once remarked, "is the future that has already happened."[20]

---

[20] This quote was the title of Peter F. Drucker's *Harvard Business Review* (HBR) article published in HBR's September 1997 edition marking its seventy-fifth anniversary year. Drucker's article was part of the journal segment "Looking Ahead: Implications of the Present."

Demography Is Destiny

The latest data from the U.N. Demographic Commission, displayed in Figure 8-3, show clearly the aging of the developed world. In the United States in 1950 there were seven people of working age (20 to 65) for every retiree, and even today, there are almost five. But by 2030, when the last of the baby-boom generation retires, that ratio will fall by nearly one-half, down below three to one.

   The aging of the population in Europe and Japan is even more extreme than in the United States. In Japan by midcentury, the ratio of workers aged 20 to 65 to retirees will fall to just over one for one. At that time the most populated five-year age segment in Japan will be those aged 75 to 80, and the same will be true in such European countries such as Italy. The demands of the retirees from Europe and Japan will raise the prices of goods bought and sold in international markets, so there is no way the United States, despite its younger population, can shield itself from the demands arising from the aging populations abroad.

FIGURE 8–3

Ratio of Population Aged 20 to 65 to Population Aged 65 and Over

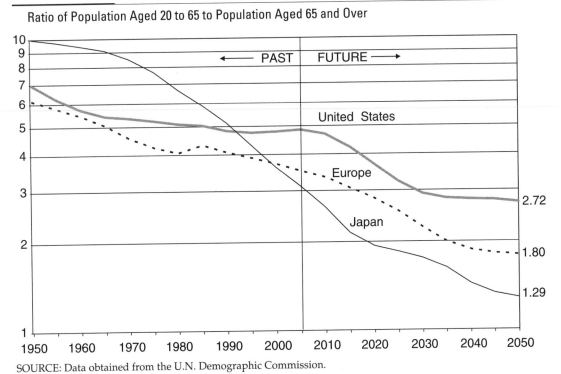

SOURCE: Data obtained from the U.N. Demographic Commission.

The Bankruptcy of Government *and* Private Pension Systems

Although it is widely known that our Social Security and Medicare programs are threatened by these demographic trends, there are many who believe that they have accumulated sufficient private wealth to fund their retirement.

But this may not be so. The same crisis that strikes the public pension programs can overwhelm private pensions as well. Since there will not be enough workers earning income, there will not be enough savings generated to purchase the assets the retirees must sell to finance their retirement.

The reasons why retirees cannot turn their savings into consumption is because the assets of wealth can be transformed into goods and services only if they are sold to those willing to defer their consumption. In a modern economy, wealth does not represent "stored consumption," such as a cache of acorns that squirrels bury to bide them through a long winter. You cannot consume your stock certificates but must sell them to someone else who wants a chance to consume at a later date. If there is a shortage of these savers, this may cause a long and painful bear market in stocks, bonds, and real estate that will leave retirees with insufficient assets to enjoy retirement.

There are some who maintain that so much wealth in stocks is passed on through bequests that the lack of demand from future workers will not have much impact. But the heirs and foundations who are bequeathed these fortunes often spend their wealth far faster than did their wealthy benefactors, and this spending often requires the sale of substantial stock. Furthermore, the large volume of bank accounts, bonds, and other fixed-income securities that must be liquidated to finance the retirements of ordinary retirees could sharply raise interest rates and depress equity prices.

Reversal of a Century-Long Trend

Without enough demand and too much supply, asset prices will sink and the long-standing trend to an earlier retirement will be halted dead in its tracks. When Social Security was passed in 1935, the average retirement age was 69. That age fell to 67 by 1950, and to 62 today. In 2003, for the first time, more Americans chose the reduced Social Security benefits at age 62 than the full benefit that starts at 65. Despite improving health, surveys indicate that the bulk of Americans and Europeans want to retire *earlier*, not later.

But that will not be possible. Because of our aging population, it is most likely that future increases in the age of retirement will actually exceed the increase in the life expectancy and will cause—for the first time in history—an absolute reduction in the number of years in retirement.

The Global Solution: An Opportunity to Make a Trade

There is no easy solution. To be sure, rising productivity brings higher income, but it also brings higher benefits in retirement since benefits are based on income earned in the last several working years. Increased immigration of high-income workers would ease the situation, but the numbers would need to be prodigious to keep the retirement age from rising.

Nevertheless, there is a solution that can help aging economies. The developing world has a much younger age profile than the developed world. This difference in age establishes an opportunity to make a trade: goods produced by the younger developing world can be exchanged for assets of the older developed world.

This trade is not new. The transfer of goods for assets has taken place throughout history, first between family members (parents giving to children in exchange for old-age support), and then extending to clans, communities, and finally whole nations. Soon it can be done on a worldwide basis. The developing world has the capability of simultaneously providing us with goods and acquiring our assets, filling the gap left by our aging workers.

I call this the "Global Solution" to the age wave. How effective this solution will be depends on two factors: the growth rate in the developing world and the degree to which world trade and capital markets are kept open. The average retirement and life expectancy in the United States since 1950 and projections that I have made to 2050 are shown in Figure 8-4. Note how crucial the growth rate of the developing world is to future retirees. If the growth in the developing world grinds to a halt, the lack of goods will force the retirement age up to 75, and it will shrink the time in retirement to less than 8 years from nearly 16 today. If the growth rate rises to 2 percent, which is slightly below the rate in the developed world, this will improve matters somewhat, but if growth can proceed at 4 percent or faster, the effect on the retirement age is dramatic.

An overall average growth rate of the developing world of 4 percent is highly likely. China has been growing at 8 to 10 percent for more than 20 years, and India is nearing that rate. Most certainly, as these countries grow richer, their growth rates will slow. Africa and the

FIGURE 8–4

Average Retirement and Life Expectancy in the United States Since 1950 and Projected to 2050

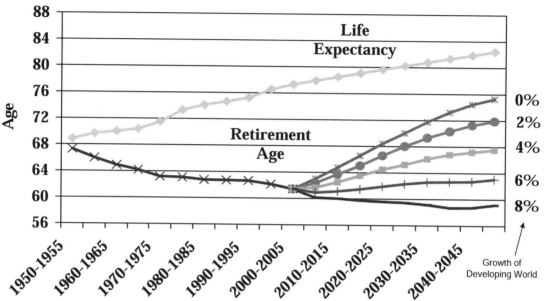

Mideast, outside of oil, have not been growing rapidly. If the entire developing world increases its growth to 6 or even 8 percent, then there would be sufficient productivity in the rest of the world to provide the goods that the baby boomers need and then buy the assets the boomers will have to sell; the retirement age can remain at 62 or even decline, continuing its pattern over the past century.

Attraction of U.S. Capital

Why would the developing world wish to acquire our capital when their countries are expanding so rapidly? At the beginning of this chapter, we learned that the best returns are rarely found in countries that grow the fastest. Witness China's dismal returns for so many years despite being the fastest-growing country in the last 20 years. Investors can often find better returns in slow-growing countries and industries.

To that end, U.S. capital markets have many attractive attributes. Our country is still viewed as the fountainhead of innovation, discovery, invention, and entertainment, and our institutions of higher education are second to none. Our capital markets are deep, easy to access, and

willing to provide capital to those who wish to innovate. Equally important is that many U.S. brand names have great appeal worldwide so the growth of consumer markets abroad holds high promise for many U.S. firms.

For these capital movements to occur, we must be viewed as receptive to international capital. Although there has already been a large number of cross-country mergers, there has also been increasing opposition, such as the Congressional rebuff of the Chinese National Offshore Oil Company's (CNOOC) bid for Unocal and the Dubai Ports fiasco. Furthermore, some indicate that London is already replacing New York as the world's financial capital. The United States cannot rest; resisting these globalizing trends will lower our future returns and living standards.

CONCLUSION

In this chapter we have shown that faster economic growth in no way guarantees higher returns. In fact, based on the historical data, slow-growing countries, because of their more reasonable valuations, have tended to have higher returns than fast-growing countries.

Higher stock returns follow periods of low price-to-earnings ratios, and lower stock returns follow high price-to-earnings ratios. Although the historical average price-to-earnings ratio is about 15, there are persuasive reasons why future valuation measures may be higher. Lower transactions costs, lower taxes, and increased economic stability argue for higher ratios in the future, although this will ultimately mean lower future stock returns if share prices reach these higher levels. Although these returns may be diminished from the past, there is overwhelming reason to believe stocks will remain the best investment for all those seeking steady long-term gains.

In the far future, the aging of the population is a critical issue impacting financial market returns. We cannot escape from our demographic realities. But we can take actions that will lead to a much brighter outcome. The integration of the world's economies and capital markets is the key to our future well-being. If we shun this path, our future will in no way be as bright as our past.

OUTPERFORMING THE MARKET

The Importance of Size, Dividend Yields, and Price-to-Earnings Ratios

Security analysis cannot presume to lay down general rules as to the "proper value" of any given common stock. . . . The prices of common stocks are not carefully thought out computations, but the resultants of a welter of human reactions.

BENJAMIN GRAHAM AND DAVID DODD, 1940[1]

STOCKS THAT OUTPERFORM THE MARKET

What criteria can investors use to choose stocks with superior returns that will outperform the market? Earnings, dividends, cash flows, book values, capitalization, and past performance, among others, have been put forward as important factors for investors to consider.

---

[1] Benjamin Graham and David Dodd, "Price Earnings Ratios for Common Stocks," *Security Analysis*, 2d ed., New York: McGraw-Hill, 1940, p. 530.

Yet finance theory has shown that if capital markets are "efficient" in the sense that known valuation criteria are already factored into prices, investing on the basis of these fundamentals factors will not improve returns. In an efficient market, only higher risk will enable investors to receive higher returns. The *capital asset pricing model* (CAPM) has shown that the correct measure of a stock's risk is the correlation of its return with the overall market, known as *beta*.[2,3]

Beta can be estimated from historical data, and it represents the fundamental risk of an asset's return that cannot be eliminated in a well-diversified portfolio and for which investors must be compensated. If beta is greater than 1, the stock requires a return greater than the market, and if it is less than 1, a lesser return is required. Risk that can be eliminated through diversification (called *diversifiable* or *residual risk*) does not warrant a higher return. The "efficient market hypothesis" and the CAPM became the basis for stock return analysis in the 1970s and 1980s.

Unfortunately, as more data were analyzed, beta did not prove successful at explaining the differences in returns among individual stocks or portfolios of stocks. In 1992, Eugene Fama and Ken French wrote an article, published in the *Journal of Finance*, which determined that there are two factors, one relating to the size of the stocks and the other to the valuation of stocks, that are far more important in determining a stock's return than the beta of a stock.[4]

After further analyzing returns, they claimed that the evidence against the CAPM was "compelling" and that "the average return anomalies . . . are serious enough to infer that the [CAPM] model is not a useful approximation" of a stock's return, and they suggested researchers investigate "alternative" asset pricing models or "irrational asset pricing stories."[5]

---

[2] The capital asset pricing model was developed by William Sharpe and John Lintner in the 1960s. See William Sharpe, "Capital Asset Prices: A Theory of Market Equilibrium under Conditions of Risk," *Journal of Finance*, vol. 19, no. 3 (September 1964), p. 442, and John Lintner, "The Valuation of Risk Assets and the Selection of Risky Investment in Stock Portfolios and Capital Budgets," *Review of Economics and Statistics*, vol. 47, no. 1 (1965), pp. 221–245.

[3] Greek letters are used to designate the coefficients of regression equations. Beta, the second coefficient, is calculated from the correlation of an individual stock's (or portfolio's) return with a capitalization-weighted market portfolio. The first coefficient, alpha, is the average historical return on the stock or portfolio above the return on the market.

[4] Eugene Fama and Ken French, "The Cross Section of Expected Stock Returns," *Journal of Finance*, vol. 47 (1992), pp. 427–466.

[5] Eugene Fama and Ken French, "The CAPM Is Wanted, Dead or Alive," *Journal of Finance*, vol. 51, no. 5 (December 1996), pp. 1947–1958.

Fama and French's findings have prompted financial economists to classify the stock universe along two dimensions: *size*, measured by the market value of the stock, and *valuation*, or the price relative to "fundamentals" such as earnings and dividends. The emphasis on valuation to gain an investment edge did not originate with Fama and French. Valuation formed the cornerstone of the principles that Benjamin Graham and David Dodd put forth more than 70 years ago in their investment classic *Security Analysis*.[6]

SMALL- AND LARGE-CAP STOCKS

Cracks in the capital asset pricing model's predictions of stock returns appeared well before Fama and French's research. In 1981, Rolf Banz, a graduate student at the University of Chicago, investigated the returns on stocks using the database that had been recently compiled by the Center for Research in Security Prices (CRSP) located at the university. He found that small stocks systematically outperformed large stocks, even after adjusting for risk as defined within the framework of the capital asset pricing model.[7]

To illustrate this point, the returns from 1926 through 2006 on 10 groups of 4,252 stocks sorted by market capitalization are shown in Table 9-1. The largest 168 stocks comprising 61.64 percent of total market value had a compound annual return of 9.60 percent, and even though the beta of these stocks was less than 1, the return trailed the CAPM prediction. On the other hand, smaller stocks had a higher beta, but their return increased more than predicted by the CAPM. The smallest 1,744 companies—each of which had a market value less than $314 million and comprised less than 1½ percent of the market capitalization of all stocks—had a compound return of 14.03 percent, which was 627 basis points above what would have been predicted by the CAPM.[8]

Some maintain that the superior historical returns on small stocks are compensation for the higher transaction costs of acquiring or disposing of these securities, especially in the earlier years of the sample. But for long-term investors, transactions costs should not be of great importance. The outperformances of these small stocks, although variable,

---

[6] Benjamin Graham and David Dodd, *Security Analysis*, 1st ed., New York: McGraw Hill, 1934.

[7] Rolf Banz, "The Relationship between Return and Market Value of Common Stock," *Journal of Financial Economics*, vol. 9 (1981), pp. 3–18.

[8] These data are adapted from *Stocks, Bonds, Bills, and Inflation (SBBI) 2007 Yearbook*, Chicago: Morningstar Publications, Chap. 7.

T A B L E   9–1

Returns on 10 Groups of 4,252 Stocks Sorted by Market Capitalization, 1926 through December 2006

Decile	Number of Companies	Largest Company Cap.	% of Total Cap.	Compound Return	Beta	Excess Return over CAPM
Largest	168	$371,187,368	61.64%	9.60%	0.91	-0.36%
2	179	$16,820,566	13.81%	11.00%	1.04	0.65%
3	198	$7,777,183	7.24%	11.35%	1.10	0.81%
4	184	$4,085,184	4.02%	11.31%	1.13	1.03%
5	209	$2,848,771	3.17%	11.69%	1.16	1.45%
6	264	$1,946,588	2.76%	11.79%	1.18	1.67%
7	291	$1,378,476	2.15%	11.68%	1.23	1.62%
8	355	$976,624	1.83%	11.88%	1.28	2.28%
9	660	$626,955	1.92%	12.09%	1.34	2.70%
Smallest	1,744	$314,433	1.47%	14.03%	1.41	6.27%
Total	4,252	$371,187,368	100.00%	10.31%	1.00	0.00%

have persisted over time and are difficult to explain in an efficient market model.

Trends in Small-Cap Stock Returns

Although the historical return on small stocks has outpaced large stocks since 1926, the magnitude of the small-cap stock outperformance has waxed and waned unpredictably over the past 80 years. A comparison of the cumulative returns on small stocks with those of the S&P 500 Index is shown in Figure 9-1.[9]

Small stocks recovered smartly from their beating during the Great Depression, but they still underperformed large stocks from the end of World War II until almost 1960. In fact, the cumulative total return on small stocks (measured by the bottom quintile of market capitalization) did not overtake large stocks even once between 1926 and 1959. Even by the end of 1974, the average annual compound return on small stocks exceeded large stocks by only about 0.5 percent per year, not nearly enough to compensate most investors for their extra risk and trading costs.

But between 1975 and the end of 1983, small stocks exploded. During these years, small stocks averaged a 35.3 percent compound annual return, more than double the 15.7 percent return on large stocks. Cumulative returns in small stocks during these nine years exceeded 1,400 percent. Figure 9-1 shows that if the nine-year period from 1975 through

---

[9] The small-cap stock index is the bottom quintile (20 percent) size of the NYSE stocks until 1981, then it is the performance of Dimensional Fund Advisors (DFA) Small Company fund from 1982 through 2000, and then it is the Russell 2000 Index from 2001 onward.

FIGURE 9-1

Small Stocks and S&P 500 Returns, 1926 through December 2006 (Including and Excluding 1975–1983)

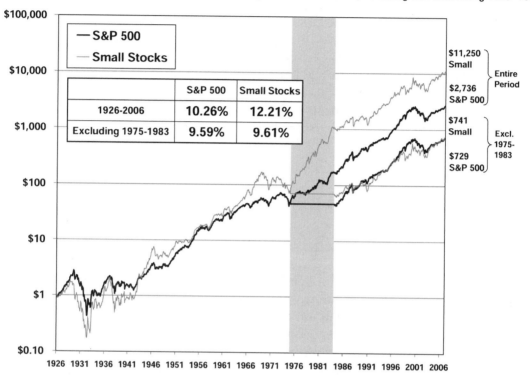

1983 is eliminated, the total accumulation in large stocks over the entire period from 1926 through 2006 is virtually the same.

After 1983, small stocks hit a long dry period that lasted 17 years as they underperformed large stocks, especially in the late 1990s as the technology boom gained momentum. But when the technology bubble burst, small stocks strongly outperformed once again. From the March 2000 peak through 2006, despite the severe intervening bear market, small stocks enjoyed a 7.2 percent annual return, while large stocks, represented by the S&P 500 Index, returned less than 1 percent per year.

What caused the tremendous performance of small stocks during the 1975 to 1983 and 2000 to 2006 periods? In the earlier period, pension and institutional managers found themselves attracted to smaller stocks following the collapse of the large-growth stocks, known as the "Nifty Fifty," that were so popular in the preceding bull market. In addition, the enactment of the Employee Retirement Income Security Act (ERISA) by Congress in 1974 made it far easier for pension funds to diversify into small

stocks, boosting their holdings of these issues. The 2000 to 2006 small stock surge followed the collapse of large-cap tech stocks in the bubble of the late 1990s, which again turned investors' attention to smaller issues.

Whatever the reasons for the small stock surges, the trendiness of small stock returns does not mean that investors should avoid these firms. Small- and mid-cap stocks not in a big capitalization index such as the S&P 500 Index constitute about 20 percent of the market value of all U.S. stocks. One should be warned, however, that the existence of the small stock premium does not mean that small stocks will outperform large stocks every year, or even every decade.

VALUATION

Value Stocks Offer Higher Returns Than Growth Stocks

The second dimension along which stocks are classified is by *valuation*— that is, factors relating the price of the stock relative to some fundamental metric of firm worth, such as dividends, earnings, book values, and cash flows. Like small-cap stocks, Fama and French determined that stocks that were cheap relative to these fundamentals had higher returns than would be predicted by the capital asset pricing model.

Stocks whose prices are low relative to these fundamentals are called *value* stocks, while those with prices high relative to these fundamentals are called *growth* stocks. Prior to the 1980s, value stocks were often called *cyclical stocks* because low-P-E stocks were often found in those industries whose profits were closely tied to the business cycle. With the growth of style investing, equity managers that specialized in these stocks were uncomfortable with the "cyclical" moniker and greatly preferred the term "value."

Value stocks generally occur in such industries as oil, motor, finance, and utilities where investors have low expectations of future growth or believe that profits are strongly tied to the business cycle, while growth stocks are generally found in such industries as high technology, brand-name consumer products, and healthcare where investors expect profits either to grow quickly or to be more resistant to the business cycle.

Of the 10 largest U.S.-based corporations by market value at the end of 2006, Exxon Mobil, Citigroup, and Bank of America had a low price relative to fundamentals and were considered "value stocks" while Microsoft, Procter & Gamble, and Johnson & Johnson had higher prices, consistent with "growth stocks."

Although value stocks might sound unattractive, these stocks should not be shunned by investors. First, investors' expectations of low growth may be incorrect. But, more importantly, even if these expectations are correct, these stocks might offer superior returns if their price is low enough to compensate for the lower growth. In fact, as we shall show below, value stocks generally give investors higher returns than growth stocks.

DIVIDEND YIELDS

Dividends have always been an important criterion for choosing stocks as Graham and Dodd stated in 1940:

> Experience would confirm the established verdict of the stock market that a dollar of earnings is worth more to the stockholder if paid him in dividends than when carried to surplus. The common-stock investor should ordinarily require both an adequate earning power and an adequate dividend.[10]

Graham and Dodd's claim has been supported by more recent research. In 1978, Krishna Ramaswamy and Robert Litzenberger established a significant correlation between dividend yield and subsequent returns.[11] And more recently, James O'Shaughnessy has shown that in the period 1951 through 1994, the 50 highest-dividend-yielding large-capitalization stocks had a 1.7 percentage point higher return than the market.[12]

The historical analysis of the S&P 500 Index supports the case for using dividend yields to obtain higher stock returns. Using December 31 of each year from 1957 onward, I sorted the firms in the S&P 500 Index into five groups (or quintiles) ranked from the highest to the lowest dividend yields, and then I calculated the total returns over the next calendar year.

The striking results are shown in Figure 9-2. In strictly increasing order, the portfolios with higher dividend yields offered investors higher total returns than portfolios of stocks with lower dividend yields. If an investor put $1,000 in an S&P 500 Index fund at the end of Decem-

---

[10] Graham and Dodd, *Security Analysis*, 2d ed., p. 381.

[11] See Robert Litzenberger and Krishna Ramaswamy, "The Effects of Personal Taxes and Dividends on Capital Asset Prices: Theory and Empirical Evidence," *Journal of Financial Economics*, 1979, pp. 163–195.

[12] James P. O'Shaughnessy, *What Works on Wall Street*, 3rd ed., New York: McGraw-Hill, 2003.

FIGURE 9–2
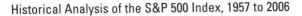

Historical Analysis of the S&P 500 Index, 1957 to 2006

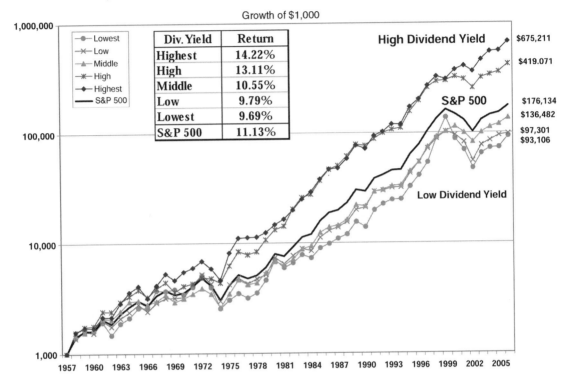

Growth of $1,000

Div. Yield	Return
Highest	14.22%
High	13.11%
Middle	10.55%
Low	9.79%
Lowest	9.69%
S&P 500	11.13%

ber 1957, she would have accumulated $176,134 by the end of 2006, for an annual return of 11.13 percent. An identical investment in the 100 highest dividend yielders accumulated to over $675,000, with a return of 14.22 percent.

The highest dividend yielders also had a beta below unity, indicating these stocks were more stable over market cycles, as shown in Table 9-2. The lowest-dividend-yielding stocks not only had the lowest return but also the highest beta. The annual return of the 100 highest dividend yielders in the S&P 500 Index over the past 50 years was 3.78 percentage points per year above what would have been predicted by the efficient markets model while the return of the 100 lowest dividend yielders would have had a return that was 1.68 percentage points per year lower.

TABLE 9–2

S&P 500 Stocks Sorted by Dividend Yield

Dividend Yield	Geometric Return	Arithmetic Return	Standard Deviation	Beta	Excess Return over CAPM
Highest	14.22%	15.71%	18.81%	0.9336	3.78%
High	13.11%	14.24%	16.22%	0.8559	2.86%
Middle	10.55%	11.71%	16.02%	0.9085	-0.04%
Low	9.79%	11.35%	18.21%	1.0460	-1.36%
Lowest	9.69%	12.20%	23.17%	1.2130	-1.68%
S&P 500	11.13%	12.39%	16.52%	1.0000	0.00%

Other Dividend Yield Strategies

There are other high-dividend-yield strategies that have outperformed the market. A well-known one is called the "Dogs of the Dow," or the "Dow 10" strategy, and is chosen from high-yielding stocks in the Dow Jones Industrial Average.

The Dow 10 strategy has been regarded by some as one of the simplest and most successful investment strategies of all time. James Glassman of the *Washington Post* claimed that John Slatter, a Cleveland investment advisor and writer, invented the Dow 10 system in the 1980s.[13] Harvey Knowles and Damon Petty popularized the strategy in their book *The Dividend Investor*, written in 1992, as did Michael O'Higgins and John Downes in *Beating the Dow*.

The strategy calls for investors at year-end to buy the 10 highest-yielding stocks in the Dow Jones Industrial Average and to hold them for the subsequent year and then repeat the process each December 31. These high-yielding stocks are often those that have fallen in price and are out of favor with investors. For this reason the Dow 10 strategy is often called the "Dogs of the Dow."

Another natural extension of the Dow 10 strategy is to choose the 10 highest-yielding stocks from among the 100 largest stocks in the S&P 500. The 100 largest stocks in the S&P 500 Index comprise a much higher percentage of the entire U.S. market than the 30 stocks in the Dow Jones Industrial Average.

---

[13] John R. Dorfman, "Study of Industrial Averages Finds Stocks with High Dividends Are Big Winners," *Wall Street Journal*, August 11, 1988, p. C2.

Indeed, both of these strategies have excelled, as Figure 9-3 shows.[14] The Dow 10 strategy returned 14.08 percent per year over the past half century, and the S&P 10 returned a dramatic 15.71 percent per year, more than 3 and 4½ percentage points a year above their respective benchmarks. And both these strategies have a lower beta than either the Dow Jones Industrial Average or the S&P 500 Index, as shown in Table 9-3.

The worst year for both the Dow 10 and S&P 10 strategies relative to the benchmark indexes was 1999, when the high-capitalization tech stocks reached their bubble peak. The Dow 10 underperformed the S&P 500 Index by 16.72 percent that year, and the S&P 10 underperformed by over 17 percentage points. It is during the later stages of a bull market,

---

[14] Interestingly, an equal investment in the 30 Dow Jones Industrial stocks beats the performance of the S&P 500 Index from 1957 through 2006 by 73 basis points even though the Dow's beta is less than 1. The managing editor of the *Wall Street Journal* has the primary responsibility for the selection of the Dow stocks. As noted in Chapter 4, the companies in the S&P 500 Index are chosen primarily on the basis of market value, assuming that the firm is profitable.

FIGURE 9–3

Dow and S&P 500 High-Dividend Yield Strategies

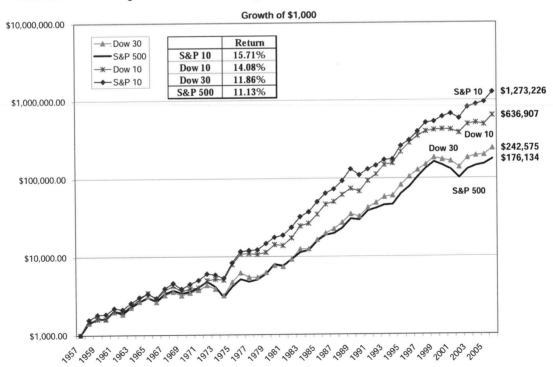

T A B L E 9–3

Dow and S&P 500 High-Dividend Strategies

High-Yield Strategy	Geometric Return	Arithmetic Return	Standard Deviation	Beta	Excess Return Over CAPM
S&P 10	15.71%	17.00%	17.53%	0.9092	5.25%
Dow 10	14.08%	15.32%	17.06%	0.8532	3.95%
Dow 30	11.86%	13.05%	16.31%	0.9341	1.12%
S&P 500	11.13%	12.39%	16.52%	1.0000	0.00%

when growth stocks catch the eye of speculative investors, that these value-based strategies will underperform capitalization-weighted strategies.

But these strategies have gained these back—and more—during subsequent bear markets. The Dow 30 was down by 26.5 percent, and the S&P 500 Index was down 37.3 percent during the 1973 to 1974 bear markets. But the S&P 10 strategy fell only 12 percent while the Dow 10 strategy actually gained 2.9 percent in these two years.

These dividend strategies also resisted the 2000 to 2002 bear market. From the end of 2000 through the end of 2002, when the S&P 500 Index fell by more than 30 percent, the Dow 10 strategy fell by only less than 10 percent, and the S&P 10 strategy fell by less than 5 percent.[15] These high-dividend strategies have provided investors with higher returns and lower volatility over the past five decades.

PRICE-TO-EARNINGS (P-E) RATIOS

Another important metric of value that can be used to formulate a winning strategy is the P-E ratio, or the price of a stock relative to its earnings. The research into P-E ratios began in the late 1970s, when Sanjoy Basu, building on the work of S. F. Nicholson in 1960, discovered that stocks with low price-to-earnings ratios have significantly higher returns than stocks with high price-to-earnings ratios, even after accounting for risk.[16]

---

[15] After 2003 the Dow 10 strategy lagged the Dow 30 for several years, mostly because of the poor performance of General Motors, which continued to pay a dividend until it was cut in half in 2005.

[16] S. F. Nicholson, "Price-Earnings Ratios," *Financial Analysts Journal*, July/August 1960, pp. 43–50, and Sanjoy Basu, "Investment Performance of Common Stocks in Relation to Their Price-Earnings Ratio: A Test of the Efficient Market Hypothesis," *Journal of Finance*, vol. 32 (June 1977), pp. 663–682.

Again, these results would not have surprised the value investors Graham and Dodd, who, in their classic 1934 text *Security Analysis*, stated the following:

> Hence we may submit, as a corollary of no small practical importance, that people who habitually purchase common stocks at more than about 16 times their average earnings are likely to lose considerable money in the long run.[17,18]

In a manner analogous to the research on dividend yields among S&P 500 stocks, I computed the P-E ratios for all 500 firms in the index on December 31 of each year by dividing the last 12 months of earnings by the year-end prices. I then ranked these firms by P-E ratios and divided them into five quintiles, computing their subsequent return over the next 12 months.[19]

The results of this research are similar to that reported on the dividend yield and are shown in Figure 9-4. Stocks with high P-Es (or low earnings yields) are, on average, overvalued and have given lower returns to investors. A portfolio of the highest-P-E stocks had a cumulative return of $65,354, earning an annual return of 8.90 percent, while the lowest-P-E stocks had a return of 14.30 percent and accumulated to almost $700,000.

In addition to a higher yield, the standard deviation of low-P-E stocks was lower, and the beta was much lower than that of the S&P 500 Index stocks, as shown in Table 9-4. In fact, the return on the 100 lowest-P-E stocks in the S&P 500 Index was about 5½ percentage points per year above what would have been predicted on the basis of the capital asset pricing model.

PRICE-TO-BOOK RATIOS

Price-to-earnings ratios and dividend yields are not the only value-based criteria. A number of academic papers, beginning with Dennis Stattman's in 1980 and later supported by Fama and French, suggested

---

[17] Graham and Dodd, *Security Analysis*, 1st ed., p. 453. Emphasis theirs.

[18] Yet even Graham and Dodd must have felt a need to be flexible on the issue of what constituted an "excessive" P-E ratio. In their second edition, published in 1940, the same sentence appears with the number 20 substituted for 16 as the upper limit of a reasonable P-E ratio! (Graham and Dodd, *Security Analysis*, 2d ed., p. 533.)

[19] Firms with zero or negative earnings were put into the high-P-E-ratio quintile. Returns were calculated from February 1 to February 1 so that investors could use actual instead of projected earnings for the fourth quarter.

FIGURE   9–4

P-E Ratios for the S&P 500 Index Companies, 1957 through December 2006

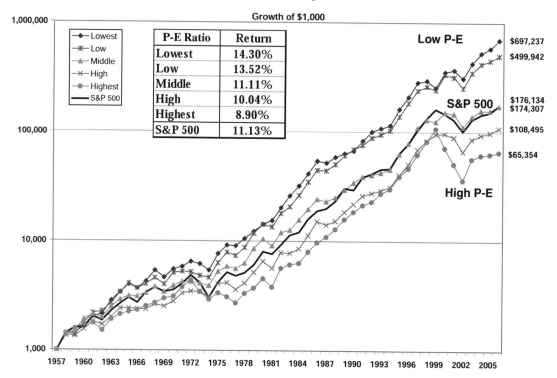

TABLE   9–4

Returns on the S&P 500 Stocks Sorted by P-E Ratios

P-E Ratio	Geometric Return	Arithmetic Return	Standard Deviation	Beta	Excess Return over CAPM
Lowest	14.30%	15.35%	15.50%	0.6347	5.51%
Low	13.52%	13.52%	15.79%	0.6067	4.99%
Middle	11.11%	11.11%	14.59%	0.6230	2.30%
High	10.04%	10.04%	14.95%	0.7077	0.70%
Highest	8.90%	8.90%	18.84%	0.8546	-0.78%
S&P 500	11.13%	12.39%	16.52%	1.0000	0.00%

that price-to-book ratios might be even more important than price-to-earnings ratios in predicting future cross-sectional stock returns.[20]

Like P-E ratios and dividend yields, Graham and Dodd considered book value to be an important factor in determining returns:

> [We] suggest rather forcibly that the book value deserves at least a fleeting glance by the public before it buys or sells shares in a business undertaking. . . . Let the stock buyer, if he lays any claim to intelligence, at least be able to tell himself, first, how much he is actually paying for the business, and secondly, what he is actually getting for his money in terms of tangible resources.[21]

Although Fama and French found that the ratio of book to market value was a slightly better value metric than the dividend yield or P-E ratio in explaining cross-sectional returns in their 1992 research, there are conceptual problems with using book value as a value criterion. Book value does not correct for changes in the market value of assets, nor does it capitalize research and development (R&D) expenditures. In fact, over the time period 1987 through 2006, our studies showed that book value underperformed either dividend yields, P-E ratios, or cash flows in explaining returns.[22] Since it is likely that an increasing fraction of a firm's worth will be captured by intellectual property, book value may become an even more imperfect indicator of firm value in the future.

COMBINING SIZE AND VALUATION CRITERIA

The compound annual returns on stocks sorted into 25 quintiles along size and book-to-market ratios from 1958 through 2006 are summarized in Table 9-5.[23] Historical returns on value stocks have surpassed growth stocks, and this outperformance is especially true among smaller stocks. The smallest value stocks returned 19.59 percent per year, the highest of any of the 25 quintiles analyzed, while the smallest growth stocks returned only 5.97 percent, the lowest of any quintile. As firms become larger, the difference between the returns on value and growth stocks be-

---

[20] Dennis Stattman, "Book Values and Expected Stock Returns," unpublished MBA honors paper, University of Chicago, and Fama and French, "Cross Section of Expected Stock Returns."

[21] Graham and Dodd, *Security Analysis*, 1st ed., pp. 493–494.

[22] Unpublished work estimating the alpha from quintile selection of value strategies from 1987 through 2006 using the data on the Fama-French Web site http://mba.tuck.dartmouth.edu/pages/faculty/ken.french/data_library.html.

[23] These data come from the Fama-French Web site cited in the preceding footnote.

TABLE 9-5

Compound Annual Returns by Size and Book-to-Market Ratio, January 1, 1958, to December 31, 2006

Entire Period		Size Quintiles				
		Small	2	3	4	Large
Book-to-Market Quintiles	Value	19.59%	18.29%	17.58%	16.10%	13.17%
	2	18.37%	17.53%	16.20%	16.15%	12.25%
	3	15.06%	16.00%	13.90%	14.72%	12.16%
	4	13.90%	12.78%	13.92%	11.43%	11.11%
	Growth	5.97%	8.30%	8.85%	10.62%	9.87%

Excluding 1975-1983		Size Quintiles				
		Small	2	3	4	Large
Book-to-Market Quintiles	Value	15.52%	14.86%	14.64%	13.67%	12.04%
	2	14.80%	13.98%	13.49%	14.50%	10.69%
	3	10.91%	13.23%	10.92%	12.43%	11.18%
	4	9.61%	9.11%	10.75%	9.26%	9.94%
	Growth	1.46%	4.62%	5.91%	8.73%	9.56%

comes much smaller. The largest value stocks returned 13.17 percent per year while the largest growth stocks returned about 9.87 percent.

When the 1975 to 1983 period is removed, the return to small stocks shrinks, as expected. But it is noteworthy that the *difference* in the returns to small value and growth stocks remains large and virtually unchanged.

The dramatic difference in the cumulative return to smallest quintile growth and value stocks over the period from 1957 through 2006 are shown in Figure 9-5. Small growth stocks have a cumulative return of only 5.97 percent per year over the period, and $1,000 invested in December 1957 accumulated to $17,121 by the end of 2006. In contrast, small value stocks have a cumulative return of 19.59 percent per year, and a $1,000 investment grows to $6.42 million.

Accentuating the difference in the performance of small growth and value stocks is that the risk measured by the beta of the small-cap value stocks is about 1, while that of the small growth stocks is over 1½.

FIGURE 9–5

Cumulative Returns to Smallest Quintile Growth and Value Stocks, 1957 through December 2006

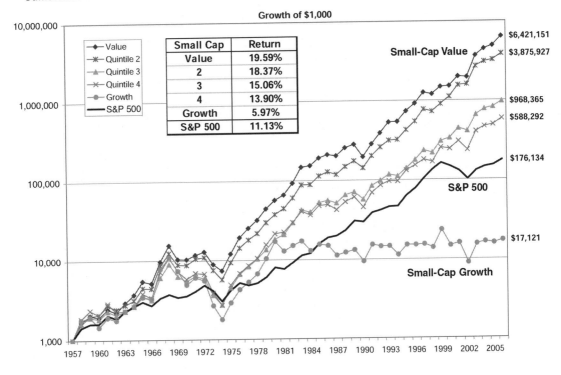

This means that the historical return to small value stocks is nearly *10* percentage points above the "efficient market" prediction, while the historical return to small growth stocks has been 4.4 percentage points below its predicted level.

INITIAL PUBLIC OFFERINGS: THE DISAPPOINTING OVERALL RETURNS ON NEW SMALL-CAP GROWTH COMPANIES

Some of the most hotly sought after small stocks are initial public offerings (IPOs).

New companies are launched with enthusiasm that excites investors, who dream that the upstarts will turn into the next Microsofts or Intels. The large demand for IPOs causes most IPOs to surge in price after they are released into the secondary market, offering those investors who were able to buy the stock at the offering prices immedi-

ate gains.[24] As a result, the vast majority of these IPOs are classified as "growth" stocks.

Certainly there have been some big winners among past IPOs. Wal-Mart, which went public in October 1970, turned a $1,000 investment into more than $1,370,000 by the end of 2006. Investors who put $1,000 into Home Depot and Intel when they went public also turned into millionaires—if they held on to their stock. Cisco Systems was another winner. Floated to the public in February 1990, the networking supplier has delivered an average of 40 percent annual returns to investors through December 2006, although all of the gains were made in the first 10 years.

But can these big winners compensate for all the losers? To determine whether IPOs are good long-term investments, I examined the buy-and-hold returns of almost 9,000 IPOs issued between 1968 and 2001. I calculated the returns whether investors purchased the IPOs either at the end of the first month of trading or at the IPO offer price and held these stocks until December 31, 2003.[25]

There is no question that the losing IPOs far outnumber the winners. Of the 8,606 firms examined, the returns on 6,796 of these firms, or 79 percent, have subsequently underperformed the returns on a representative small stock index, and almost half the firms have underperformed by more than 10 percent per year.

Unfortunately, the huge winners like Cisco and Wal-Mart *cannot compensate* for the thousands of losing IPOs. The *differences* in the returns to a portfolio that buys an equal dollar amount of all the IPOs issued in a given year and a portfolio in which an investor puts an equivalent dollar amount into a Russell 2000 small-cap stock index are featured in Figure 9-6. Returns are computed from two starting points: (1) from the end of the month when the IPO was first issued and (2) from the usually lower IPO offer price.

The returns on all yearly IPO portfolios issued from 1968 through 2000 were examined to December 31, 2003, to allow for at least three years of subsequent returns to be calculated. The results are clear. From 1968 through 2000, the yearly IPO portfolios, measured from the end of the price of the first month of trading, underperformed a small-cap stock index in 29 out of 33 years when measured *either* from the last day of trading in the month they were issued *or* from the IPO issue price.

---

[24] Obtaining IPOs at the offering prices, especially ones that are in great demand, is very difficult as investment banks and brokerage firms ration these shares to their best customers.

[25] About one-third of these firms survived in their current corporate form through December 31, 2003. If they did not, I substituted the return on the Ibbotson small-cap stock index (see footnote 9).

FIGURE 9–6

Buy-and-Hold Returns of Almost 9,000 IPOs Issued between 1968 and 2001

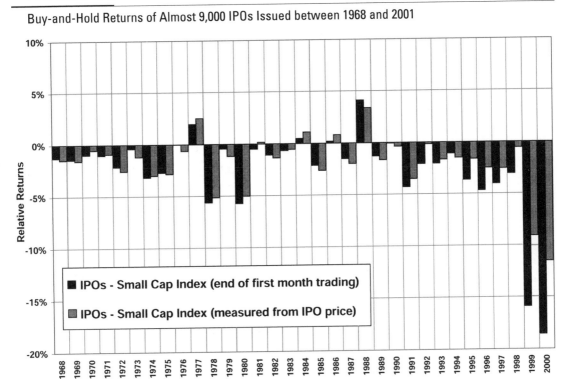

Even in years such as 1971 when the big-winning stocks Southwest Airlines, Intel, and The Limited Stores all went public, a portfolio of all the IPOs issued that year trailed the returns on a comparable small-cap stock index when measured through 2003, and the same happened in 1981 when Home Depot went public.

Even in the banner year 1986, when Microsoft, Oracle, Adobe, EMC, and Sun Microsystems all went public and delivered 30 percent plus annual returns over the next 16 years, a portfolio of all the IPOs from that year just barely managed to keep up with the small-cap stock index.

The performance of the mostly technology IPOs issued in the late 1990s were disastrous. The yearly IPO portfolios in 1999 and 2000 underperformed the small-cap stock index by 8 and 12 percent per year, respectively, if measured from the IPO price and 17 and 19 percent per year if measured from the end of the first month of trading.

Even stocks that doubled or more on the opening of trading were very poor long-term investments. Corvis Corporation, which designs

products for the management of Internet traffic, went public on July 28, 2000. At the time of the offering, the firm had never sold a dollar's worth of goods and had $72 million in operating losses. Nevertheless, Corvis had a market value of $28.7 billion at the end of the first trading day, a capitalization that would place it in the top 100 most valuable firms in the United States.

It is sobering to contrast Corvis Corporation with Cisco Systems, which went public 10 years earlier. By the time of its IPO in February 1990, Cisco had already been a profitable company, earning healthy profits of $13.9 million on annual sales of $69.7 million. The market value of Cisco's IPO at the end of the first trading day was $287 *million*, exactly one-hundredth of the market value of Corvis Corporation, which at the time had not yet had either sales or profits. Cisco would be classified as a "growth" company in 1990 with a higher-than-average P-E ratio, but Corvis was a "hypergrowth" company.

Corvis Corporation, with an IPO price of $360 (split adjusted) on July 28, 2000, opened trading at $720 and later rose to $1,147 in early August. Subsequently the stock fell to $3.46 in April 2005.

THE NATURE OF GROWTH AND VALUE STOCKS

When choosing "growth" and "value" stocks, investors should keep in mind that these designations are not inherent in the product the firm produces or the industry that the firm is in. The designations depend solely on the market value relative to some fundamental measure of enterprise value, such as earnings or dividends.

Therefore, a firm in the technology sector, which is considered to be an industry with high growth prospects, could actually be classified as a value stock if it is out of favor with investors and sells for a low price relative to fundamentals. Alternatively, a promising auto manufacturer in a mature industry with limited growth potential could be classified a growth stock if its stock is in favor with investors and priced high relative to fundamentals. In fact, over time many firms and even industries are alternately characterized as "value" or "growth" as their market price fluctuates.

EXPLANATIONS OF SIZE AND VALUATION EFFECTS

There have been many attempts to explain the size and valuation factors in the data. Fama and French had hypothesized that there might be unusual financial stresses in value stocks that only appear during periods

of extreme crisis, and that investors demand a premium to hold value stocks in case those circumstances arise. Indeed, value stocks did underperform growth stocks during the Great Depression and the stock market crash of 1929 through 1932. But since then, value stocks have actually done *better* than growth stocks during both bear markets and economic recessions, so it is doubtful this is the answer.[26]

Another possible reason why value stocks outperform growth stocks is that the use of beta to summarize the risk of a stock is too narrow. Beta is derived from the capital asset pricing theory, a static pricing model that depends on an unchanged set of investment opportunities. In a dynamic economy, real interest rates proxy changes in the opportunity set for investors, and stock prices will respond not only to earnings prospects but also to changes in interest rates.

In an article entitled "Good Beta, Bad Beta," John Campbell separates the beta related to interest rate fluctuations (which he called "good beta") from the beta related to business cycles (which he called "bad beta")[27] based on historical evidence. But recent data are not supportive of this theory as growth stocks rose from 1997 to 2000 when real interest rates were rising and fell subsequently as real interest rates dropped.

Another theory about why growth stocks have underperformed value stocks is behavioral: investors get overexcited about the growth prospects of firms with rapidly rising earnings and bid them up excessively. "Story stocks" such as Intel or Microsoft, which in the past provided fantastic returns, capture the fancy of investors, while those firms providing solid earnings with unexciting growth rates are neglected.[28]

The Noisy Market Hypothesis

A more general theory for the outperformance of value stocks is that stock prices are constantly being impacted by buying and selling that is unrelated to the fundamental value of the firm. These buyers and sellers are called "liquidity" or "noise" traders in the academic literature. Their transactions may be motivated by taxes, fiduciary responsibilities, rebalancing of their portfolio, or other personal reasons. In order to explain the value

---

[26] John Y. Campbell (with Jens Hilscher and Jan Szilagyi), "In Search of Distress Risk," revision of National Bureau of Economic Research (NBER) Working Paper No. 12362, Cambridge, Mass., March 2007.

[27] John Y. Campbell and Tuomo Vuolteenaho, "Bad Beta, Good Beta," *American Economic Review*, vol. 94, no. 5 (December 2004), pp. 1249–1275.

[28] Behavioral finance is the topic of Chapter 19.

and size effects we see in the historical data, another assumption needs to be added: that price movements caused by these liquidity traders are not *immediately* reversed by those trading on fundamental information.

This assumption is a deviation from the efficient markets hypothesis that claims that at all times the price of a security is the best unbiased estimate of the underlying value of the enterprise. I have called the alternative assumption the "noisy market hypothesis" because the actions of noise or liquidity traders often obscure the fundamental value of the firm.[29]

The noisy market hypothesis can provide an explanation for the size and value effects.[30] A positive liquidity shock raises the price of the stock above its fundamental value and makes that stock more likely to be classified as a "large" or "growth" stock. When this positive shock disappears, these large growth stocks decline in price and thus have lower returns. On the other hand, a negative liquidity shock lowers the price and makes it more likely a stock will belong to the "small" or "value" category, which is likely to be underpriced relative to its fundamentals. When the negative shock disappears, these value stocks have higher returns.

CONCLUSION

Historical research shows that investors can achieve higher long-term returns without taking on increased risk by focusing on the factors relating to the size and valuation of companies. Dividend yield has been one such factor and the price-to-earnings ratio has been another. Over time, portfolios of stocks with higher dividend yields and lower P-E ratios have outperformed the market more than would be predicted by the efficient markets hypothesis or the capital asset pricing model.

Nevertheless, investors should be aware that there is no strategy that will outperform the market all the time. Small stocks exhibit periodic surges that have enabled their long-term performance to beat that of large stocks, but most of the time their performance has fallen behind large stocks. Furthermore, value stocks have tended to do very well in bear markets, but often underperform growth stocks in the latter stages of bull markets. This means that investors must exercise patience if they decide to pursue these return-enhancing strategies.

---

[29] See Jeremy Siegel, "The Noisy Market Hypothesis," *Wall Street Journal*, June 14, 2006.

[30] See Robert Arnott, Jason Hsu, Jun Liu, and Harry Markowitz, "Does Noise Create the Size and Value Effects?" unpublished manuscript, September 2006.

CHAPTER 10

GLOBAL INVESTING AND THE RISE OF CHINA, INDIA, AND THE EMERGING MARKETS

Today let's talk about a growth industry. Because investing world-wide is a growth industry. The great growth industry is international portfolio investing.

JOHN TEMPLETON, 1984[1]

Chapter 1 demonstrated that the superior long-term returns of stocks were not unique to the United States. Investors in many other countries have accumulated substantial wealth in equities. Until the late 1980s, however, foreign markets were almost exclusively the domains of native investors and were considered too remote or risky to be entertained by outsiders.

But no longer. The *globalization* of financial markets is not just a prediction for the future; it is a fact right now. The United States, once the unchallenged giant of capital markets, is today only one of many coun-

---

[1] Transcript of address delivered to the Annual Conference of the Financial Analysts Federation, May 2, 1984.

tries in which investors can accumulate wealth. At the end of World War
II, U.S. stocks comprised almost 90 percent of the world's equity capitalization; in 1970, they still comprised two-thirds. But today, the U.S. market constitutes considerably less than half of the world's stock value, and
that fraction is shrinking. To invest only in the United States is to ignore
the majority of the world's equity capital.

THE WORLD'S POPULATION, PRODUCTION, AND EQUITY CAPITAL

Despite the growth abroad, the equity markets are still heavily represented by the developed countries in the world.[2] The lopsidedness of the
world economy is illustrated in Figures 10-1a through 10-1c. The developed world contains less than 15 percent of the world's population. Yet
it produces over 50 percent of the world's goods and headquarters over
93 percent of the world's equity capital.[3]

---

[2] North America (the United States and Canada); Western Europe; Japan; Australia and New
Zealand; Singapore, South Korea, and Taiwan; and Hong Kong.

[3] The equity capital is based on the free float shares, and for China only those shares issued in Hong
Kong.

F I G U R E   10–1a

The 2005 World Population

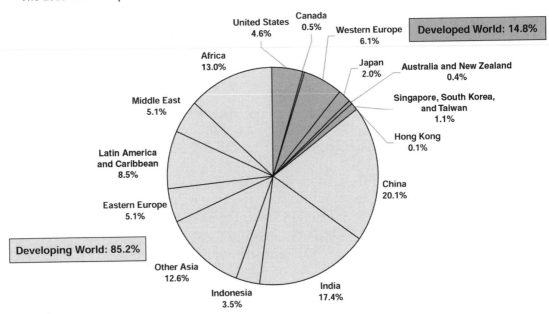

FIGURE 10–1b

The 2006 World GDP

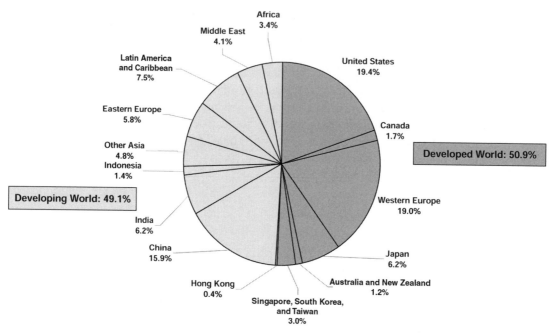

FIGURE 10–1c

The 2007 World Equity

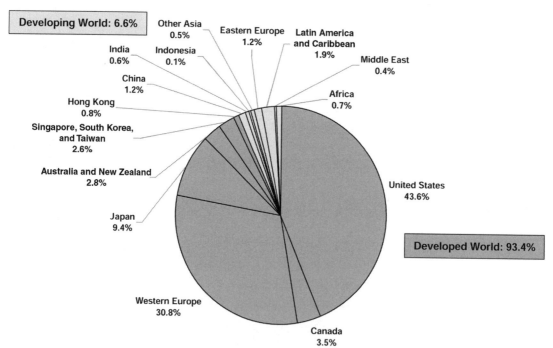

But this very unequal distribution of output and capital will not last. The emerging nations' share of output and equity capital has been rising rapidly and will continue to do so. As we shall see, the forces unleashed by the communications revolution and market capitalism will push countries such as China and India to the forefront of the world economy.

Nevertheless, investors should not become too enchanted with economic growth. We learned in Chapter 8 that growth does not guarantee good returns. A look at history shows that there have been many times when investor hopes of superior returns were dashed by subsequent events.

CYCLES IN FOREIGN MARKETS

In the past, strong U.S. markets were often coupled with weak foreign markets and vice versa. In the 1970s and 1980s, U.S. stock returns lagged behind both Europe and Japan, then surged to the head of the pack in the 1990s, only to lag behind again this decade, as shown in Table 10-1.

T A B L E   10–1

Compound Annual Dollar Returns in World Stock Markets, 1970 through December 2006 (Standard Deviations in Parentheses)

Country or Region	1970-2006	1970-1979	1980-1989	1990-1999	2000-2006
World*	10.81%	6.96%	19.92%	11.96%	4.65%
	(17.07)	(18.09)	(14.59)	(13.94)	(20.76)
EAFE†	11.57%	10.09%	22.77%	7.33%	7.08%
	(21.93)	(22.77)	(23.28)	(16.93)	(23.85)
USA	10.84%	4.61%	17.13%	19.01%	2.45%
	(17.10)	(19.01)	(12.52)	(14.39)	(18.35)
Europe	12.27%	8.57%	18.49%	14.50%	7.34%
	(20.95)	(20.97)	(25.89)	(12.71)	(24.33)
Japan	11.47%	17.37%	28.66%	-0.69%	4.28%
	(34.69)	(45.41)	(28.57)	(28.90)	(25.71)

*World = Morgan Stanley Capital International (MSCI) Value-Weighted World Index.
†EAFE is the MSCI index for Europe, Australasia, and the Far East.

These differences in returns emphasize the importance of maintaining a well-diversified world portfolio.

The Japanese Market Bubble

The 1980 bull market in Japan stands as one of the most remarkable bubbles in world stock market history. In the 1970s and 1980s, Japanese stock returns averaged more than 10 percentage points per year above U.S. returns and surpassed those from every other country. The bull market in Japan was so dramatic that by the end of 1989, for the first time since the early 1900s, the market value of the American stock market was no longer the world's largest. Japan, a country whose economic base was totally destroyed in World War II and had only half the population and 4 percent of the land mass of the United States, became the home to the world's most highly valued stock market.

The superior returns in the Japanese market attracted billions of dollars of foreign investment. By the end of the 1980s, valuations on many Japanese stocks reached stratospheric levels. Nippon Telephone and Telegraph, or NTT, the Japanese version of America's former telephone monopoly AT&T, was priced at a P-E ratio above 300. This company alone had a market valuation of hundreds of billions of dollars, dwarfing the aggregate stock values of all but a handful of countries. Valuations reached and in some cases exceeded those attained in the great technology bubble of 2000 and were far above anything known in the U.S. or European markets.

During his travels to Japan in 1987, Leo Melamed, president of the Chicago Mercantile Exchange, asked his hosts how such remarkably high valuations could be warranted. "You don't understand," they responded. "We've moved to an entirely new way of valuing stocks here in Japan." And that is when Melamed knew Japanese stocks were doomed, for it is when investors cast aside the lessons of history that those lessons come back to haunt them.[4]

The Nikkei Dow Jones, which had surpassed 39,000 in December 1989, fell to nearly 14,000 by August 1992 and below 8,000 in 2002—a decline worse than any experienced by the U.S. or European stock markets since the great 1929 to 1932 crash. The shares of NTT fell from 3.2 million yen to under 500,000. The mystique of the Japanese market was broken.

---

[4] Martin Mayer, *Markets*, New York: Norton, 1988, p. 60.

The Emerging Market Bubble

The collapse of the Japanese market shifted the emphasis of global enthusiasts to *emerging markets*—markets in developing countries. Investors had already witnessed the stock booms of Taiwan, South Korea, and Thailand. Now India, Indonesia, and even China were set to join the club.

And Asian countries were not the only markets put into play. Latin America, long a backwater of authoritarian, anti-free-market regimes (of both the right and left) had turned full circle and aggressively sought foreign investment. Equity gains were impressive in such countries as Argentina, Brazil, and Mexico.

Even China, the last major country ruled by communist leaders, developed stock markets. The opening of the first Chinese stock market in Shenzhen in 1998 was met with a riot as thousands stood days in lines waiting to be allocated shares in firms in the world's most populated country. And who would have imagined that investors in Hong Kong would beat those in the United States during the last decade, despite the fact that the island nation was handed over to communist China, once the sworn enemy of capitalism?

The term *emerging markets* evokes the image of a beautiful butterfly rising from its chrysalis, ready to soar to the heavens. But a more accurate name might have been "submerging markets." The enthusiasm that greeted these markets far exceeded their performance. Just as birds eat most butterflies soon after they take wing, the bears devoured many of these newly emerging markets soon after investors rushed in.

The year 1997 marked the beginning of the worst collapse in the history of emerging markets. The emergent Asian economies, idolized by many investors who had sent their shares skyward, saw their currencies and equity prices plummet. In 1998, the bearish contagion spread beyond the Pacific Basin to Latin America, Eastern Europe, and Russia.

In that two-year period, virtually no emerging market was safe. Most, if not all, of the countries' stock markets fell by at least 50 percent in dollar terms, and many fell much more. Measured in U.S. dollars, the Indonesian, Thai, and Russian markets fell more than 90 percent, and those in the Philippines and South Korea fell more than 80 percent. Even stocks in the strongest and most advanced of these developing countries, Singapore and Hong Kong, fell 70 percent.

The collapse of these economies dimmed investors' enthusiasm for foreign investing. But troubles were also brewing for U.S. investors seeking gains in the developed markets. As the U.S. stock market and the U.S. dollar soared, the dollar returns in European and Japanese markets fell behind the United States. The advantage that U.S. investors had gained through many years of investing abroad vanished, leaving many questioning the wisdom of international investing.

The New Millennium and the Technology Bubble

The last three years of the twentieth century, marked by the emergence of a huge technology bubble, saw strong gains in all of the world stock markets, with the European and American markets surging to all-time highs. But this was not to last.

A few months into the new millennium, the technology bubble burst and stocks fell into a severe bear market. All of the developed countries' markets fell by at least 50 percent: from March 2000 through October 2002, the U.S. market fell by one-half, matching its record post-Depression decline in the ferocious 1972 to 1974 bear market, while European and Japanese markets, which suffered declines of 60 and 63 percent, respectively, bottomed in March 2003—five months after the U.S. market bottomed and just prior to the U.S.-led invasion of Iraq.

As the world economy recovered from the 9/11 terrorist attacks and the recession, stocks in the United States and Europe pushed upward, and by 2007 they hit new all-time highs. But the dollar changed direction sharply. After appreciating strongly from 1995 through 2001, the greenback sank precipitously, falling by one-third of its value through the end of 2004. As a result, dollar-based investors saw their international stocks far outperform their domestic holdings in a reversal of the pattern set in the previous decade.

Emerging stock markets, which usually fare far worse than developed markets in downturns, held up surprisingly well in the 2000 to 2002 bear market, a good portent for future performance. Indeed, when the world economy had recovered, emerging markets soared once again, surpassing their highs of a decade earlier.

What have these market cycles taught us about international stocks? No single market is always dominant, and the globalization of the world markets affords investors more opportunities for spreading their risk than are available in the domestic markets.

DIVERSIFICATION IN WORLD MARKETS

Principles of Diversification

It might surprise investors that the principal motivation for investing in foreign stocks is not that foreign countries are growing faster and therefore will provide investors with better returns. We learned in Chapter 8 that faster growth in no way guarantees superior returns.

Rather, the reason for investing internationally is to diversify your portfolio and reduce risk.[5] Foreign investing provides diversification in the same way that investing in different sectors of the domestic economy provides diversification. It would not be good investment policy to pin your hopes on just one stock or one sector of the economy. Similarly it is not a good policy to buy the stocks only in your own country, especially when developed economies are becoming an ever smaller part of the world's market.

International diversification reduces risk because the stock prices of one country often rise at the same time those of another country fall, and this asynchronous movement of returns dampens the volatility of the portfolio. However, in recent years, world markets have moved more in sync with each other, particularly in the short run, which I will discuss later in this chapter.

An asset with a low correlation with the rest of the market provides better diversification than an asset with a high correlation. The correlation of returns between stocks or portfolios of stocks is measured by the *correlation coefficient*. A good case for investors is if there is no correlation between the stock returns of two countries, and the correlation coefficient is equal to zero. In this case, an investor who allocates his or her portfolio equally between each country can reduce his or her risk by almost one-third, compared to investing in a single country. As the correlation coefficient increases, the gains from diversification dwindle, and if there is perfect synchronization of returns, the correlation coefficient equals 1 and there is no gain (but no loss) from diversification.

"Efficient" Portfolios: Formal Analysis

How do you determine how much should be invested at home and abroad? As the above analysis suggests, the amount invested in each country can be derived from one's assessment of the expected risk and

---

[5] *Risk* here is defined as the standard deviation of the returns on the portfolio.

expected return in each country and the expected correlation between returns of the U.S. market and these emerging countries. One way of estimating these expected returns, risks, and correlations is by analyzing the historical return data. Once these expectations have been determined, the "best" or most "efficient" risk-return portfolio can be determined by mathematical techniques of formal portfolio analysis.

The historical risks and returns for U.S. and foreign markets are shown in Table 10-2. One can see that from 1970 through 2006, the dollar returns on Morgan Stanley's EAFE Index, an index of the developed world stocks,[6] actually surpassed that of the United States, offering dollar-based investors compound annual returns of 11.57 versus 10.84 percent in U.S. stocks.

Although the return was higher in foreign stocks, the risk was also higher. The risk of these returns to dollar investors in foreign markets is composed of two sources: fluctuations in foreign stock markets themselves, called *local risk*, and fluctuations in the exchange rate that translates foreign returns back to dollars, or *exchange-rate risk*.

It is very important to note that the total risk of holding foreign equities is substantially less than the sum of the local and exchange-rate

---

[6] The countries in the EAFE portfolio are Australia, Austria, Belgium, Denmark, Finland, France, Germany, Greece, Hong Kong, Ireland, Italy, Japan, the Netherlands, New Zealand, Norway, Portugal, Singapore, Spain, Sweden, Switzerland, and the United Kingdom.

T A B L E   10–2

Dollar Returns and Risks in Stocks, January 1970 through December 2006

Country or Region	U.S. $ Returns		Domestic Risk	Exchange Risk	Total Risk	Correlation Coefficient*
	Compound	Arithmetic				
World	10.81%	12.17%	16.57%	5.07%	17.07%	84.27%
EAFE	11.57%	13.64%	19.30%	10.25%	21.93%	57.42%
USA	10.84%	12.21%	17.10%	——	17.10%	100.00%
Europe	12.27%	14.10%	20.18%	11.27%	20.95%	70.57%
Japan	11.47%	16.05%	28.34%	12.71%	34.69%	29.90%

*Correlation between U.S. dollar returns and foreign market U.S. dollar returns.

risks. This is because these variables are not perfectly correlated, so movements in the exchange rate and the local stock market frequently offset each other.

The standard deviation of dollar returns in foreign markets is nearly 22 percent, about 5 percentage points higher than found in the U.S. market. The historical correlation between the annual returns in U.S. and non-U.S. markets has been about 57 percent, which means that 57 percent of the variation in non-U.S. markets is also seen in U.S. stock returns.

Using these historical data allows us to construct Figure 10-2, which shows the risk-return trade-off (called the *efficient frontier*) for dollar-based investors depending on varying the proportions that are invested in foreign markets (measured by the EAFE Index) and U.S. markets. The minimum risk for this world portfolio occurs when 22.5 percent is allocated to EAFE stocks and thus 77.5 percent to U.S. stocks.

But the "best" risk-return portfolio, called the *efficient portfolio*, is not the one with the lowest risk but the one that optimally balances risk and return. This "best" portfolio is found at a much higher 37.8 percent foreign stock allocation.[7] For comparison, in July 2007 the EAFE stocks

FIGURE 10–2

Portfolio Allocation between U.S. and EAFE Stocks

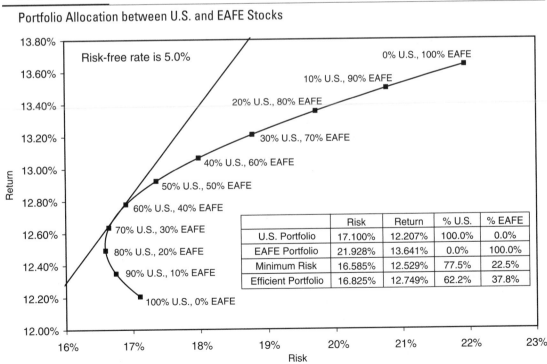

	Risk	Return	% U.S.	% EAFE
U.S. Portfolio	17.100%	12.207%	100.0%	0.0%
EAFE Portfolio	21.928%	13.641%	0.0%	100.0%
Minimum Risk	16.585%	12.529%	77.5%	22.5%
Efficient Portfolio	16.825%	12.749%	62.2%	37.8%

represented about 57 percent, and the U.S. stocks represented 43 percent of this world portfolio based on market values.

The estimation of the best combination of U.S. and foreign stocks is very dependent on the risk and return assumptions. For example, if foreign exchange risk is ignored, as might be justified for an investor or institution that buys goods in many different countries, so that translation back to dollars is not necessary, the optimal foreign portfolio rises to 52.6 percent, just slightly short of the 2007 market value weight.

The impact of changes in the risk and return assumptions on the allocation between U.S. and foreign stocks is shown in Table 10-3. For every increase of 100 basis points in U.S. expected returns—or fall in expected returns in the EAFE Index—there is about an 11.1 percentage point rise in the allocation to U.S. stocks. For every percentage point increase in the expected risk of U.S. returns or decrease in the expected risk of EAFE returns, the U.S. allocation falls 6.5 percentage points. And a 0.10 increase in the correlation coefficient between EAFE and U.S. returns will lower the EAFE allocation by just over 2 percentage points.[8]

---

[7] Readers who wish to understand risk-return analysis can go to Richard A. Brealey, Stewart C. Myers, and Franklin Allen, *Principles of Corporate Finance,*" 8th ed., New York: McGraw-Hill, 2006.

[8] The impact of a change in the correlation coefficient is highly nonlinear. If the correlation rises to 0.77, the U.S. allocation will rise over 6 percentage points; if it rises to 0.87, the U.S. share will rise by over 17 percentage points.

T A B L E   10–3

Efficient Portfolio for Varying Assumptions

	U.S. Share	EAFE Share	Shift to (+) from (-) US
Historical Data*	62.20%	37.80%	-
Add 100 bps to US Return	73.30%	26.70%	+11.10%
Add 100 bps to EAFE Return	52.30%	47.70%	-9.90%
Add 100 bps to US Risk	55.70%	44.30%	-6.50%
Add 100 bps to EAFE Risk	67.10%	32.90%	+4.90%
Add 10% to Corr. Coefficient	64.50%	35.50%	+2.30%

*U.S. Return = 12.21%, U.S. Risk = 17.10%, EAFE Return = 13.64%, EAFE Risk = 21.93%, Correlation = 57.42%

This last result is of particular note. Using historical data, an increase in correlation between U.S. and EAFE returns lowers the attractiveness of foreign investing. And there is evidence that the short-run correlations between U.S. and foreign markets have been increasing. A two-year moving average of the correlation coefficient between the United States and the EAFE is shown in Figure 10-3. The correlation rose dramatically in the early 2000s, and it has dropped a bit since. Critics of foreign investing often cite high correlations as a reason to keep foreign stock exposure low.

But this is not necessarily so. The impact of increased correlation on the allocation can be reversed with only a slight change in assumptions. If EAFE returns are expected to be only 60 basis points higher than their historical average, or the expected risk of foreign stocks slightly lower, then an increased correlation will actually *raise* your foreign allocation. This occurs because under these altered assumptions, investors would be receiving a better risk-return trade-off in foreign stocks than they receive in U.S. stocks. Hence, the more correlated foreign and U.S. markets, the less attractive U.S. stocks are.

FIGURE 10–3

The Correlation between U.S. and EAFE Stock Returns

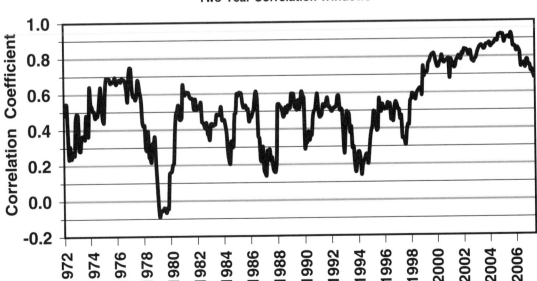

Two-Year Correlation Windows

Should You Hedge Foreign Exchange Risk?

Since foreign exchange risk does add to the dollar risk of holding foreign securities, it could be desirable for an investor in foreign markets to hedge against currency movements. *Currency hedging* means entering into a currency contract that offsets unexpected changes in the price of foreign currency relative to the dollar.

Although currency hedging seems like an attractive way to offset exchange risk, in the long run it is often unnecessary and could be detrimental. This is because the cost of hedging depends on the difference between the interest rate in the foreign country and the domestic country, and that could be high.

For example, the British pound depreciated from $4.80 to about $2.00 over the past century. But since British interest rates were, on average, substantially higher than interest rates in the United States, the cost of hedging exceeded the depreciation in the pound. Thus investors' dollar returns were higher if they owned British stocks without hedging them than their dollar returns if they owned British stocks and paid to hedge them.

Furthermore, for investors with long-term horizons, hedging currency risk in foreign stock markets is not important. In fact, there is some evidence that in the long run, currency hedges might actually increase the volatility of dollar returns.[9] In the long run, exchange-rate movements are determined primarily by differences in inflation between countries, a phenomenon called *purchasing power parity*. Since equities are claims on real assets, their long-term returns have compensated investors for changes in inflation and thus protected investors from exchange-rate risk. Therefore, it is not worth the cost for long-term stock investors to hedge their currency risk.

Sector Diversification

Although the returns between foreign and U.S. stocks might be increasingly correlated, the returns between international industrial sectors are not becoming more correlated. The trends in correlations between the major world industry sectors as classified by the Morgan Stanley Capital Market Indexes are shown in Figure 10-4.

Sector correlation sunk rapidly in the late 1990s and reached a low point in 2000 when the technology stocks soared while other sectors fell

[9] See Kenneth A. Froot, "Currency Hedging over Long Horizons," National Bureau of Economic Research (NBER) Working Paper No. 4355, Cambridge, Mass.: NBER, May 1993.

F I G U R E   10–4

Correlations of International Sectors and World Stock Returns

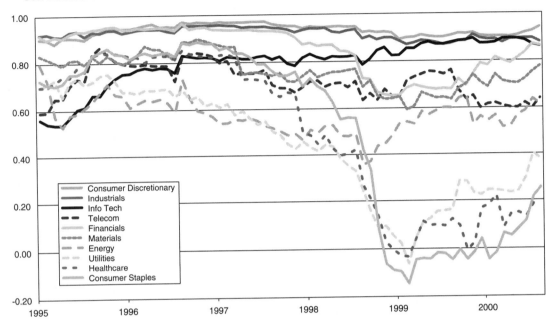

in price. But even after the tech bubble popped, sector correlations were lower than before. One reason for the decreased correlation between sectors is the moderation of the business cycle, which means that shifts in sector demands, rather than changes in the overall economy, become the primary sources of changes in firm profitability. What does it mean that sector returns are not as correlated as in the past?

I believe that a sector approach to international investing may supplant a country approach in coming years. It is true that government regulations and legal structures will still matter, even when most of the firm's sales, earnings, and production come from abroad. But these home-country influences will very likely diminish as globalization advances. In fact, I envision a future of *international incorporations*, where firms choose to be governed by a set of international rules agreed upon among nations. This will be similar to the growing popularity of the accounting standards adopted by the International Accounting Standards Board (IASB) over country-based standards. If international incorporation gained prominence, there would be no meaning to "headquartered country," and investment allocations would have to be made on the

basis of global sectors, or by regions of production and distribution. In that case, a U.S.-only portfolio would be very narrow indeed.

Sector Allocation around the World

Let's take a closer look at the importance of these industrial sectors by region and by country. The 10 Global International Classification (GIC) industrial sectors in five geographic regions (United States, EAFE, Europe, Japan, and the emerging markets)[10] are shown in Table 10-4, by the respective weight of each industrial sector. The 20 largest firms by market value headquartered in and outside the United States are shown in Table 10-5.[11]

The financial sector is the largest sector in *every* region of the world. This demonstrates how commercial and investment banks, insurance companies, and brokerages are critical to economic growth. The largest share of the financial market value sector is found in Europe, belonging to companies such as HSBC, UBS, and the Royal Bank of Scotland. The partial privatization of the Bank of China, the Industrial and Commercial Bank, and the China Construction Bank have also made this sector the largest in the emerging markets. In the United States, the largest financial firms are Citigroup, Bank of America, and AIG.

---

[10] The United States is represented by the S&P 500 Index, and the non-U.S.-developed regions are represented by the EAFE Index (described in footnote 6), Europe (iShares S&P Europe 350, symbol IEU), and the emerging market (iShares MSCI Emerging Markets Index, symbol EEM).

[11] The chapter appendix gives a brief discussion of the 10 largest non-U.S.-based stocks, ranked by market capitalization. All these are ranked by total market value, including all government holdings.

T A B L E 10–4

Sector Allocation in World Regions

	S&P 500	EAFE	Europe	Japan	Emerging Markets
Consumer Discretionary	10.2%	12.0%	9.0%	20.0%	4.3%
Consumer Staples	9.4%	7.9%	9.2%	4.5%	3.8%
Energy	10.6%	7.2%	9.9%	1.1%	15.2%
Financials	21.3%	29.2%	31.1%	20.7%	21.1%
Healthcare	11.8%	6.4%	7.4%	5.5%	2.0%
Industrials	11.3%	12.0%	8.4%	18.4%	4.8%
Information Technology	15.2%	5.3%	3.5%	12.7%	16.2%
Materials	3.1%	9.4%	8.2%	9.8%	15.3%
Telecommunication Services	3.8%	5.3%	6.4%	3.0%	12.5%
Utilities	3.5%	5.4%	6.9%	4.3%	4.8%

TABLE 10–5

Top 20 U.S. and Foreign Companies by Total Market Value in June 2007

Rank	American Companies	Sector	Market Cap (Bil. US$)	Foreign Companies	Sector	Country	Market Cap (Bil. US$)
1	Exxon Mobil	Energy	505	PetroChina	Energy	China	282
2	General Electric	Industrial	413	Gazprom	Energy	Russia	272
3	Microsoft	Info. Tech.	287	Royal Dutch Shell	Energy	The Netherlands	271
4	Citigroup	Financial	258	BP	Energy	United Kingdom	237
5	AT&T	Telecom	248	China Mobile	Telecom	China	233
6	Bank of America	Financial	220	Toyota	Consumer Disc.	Japan	227
7	Wal-Mart	Consumer Staples	201	Ind. and Comm. Bank of China	Financial	China	226
8	Procter & Gamble	Consumer Staples	199	HSBC	Financial	United Kingdom	218
9	Chevron	Energy	198	Total S.A.	Energy	France	205
10	Johnson & Johnson	Healthcare	185	EDF	Utilities	France	198
11	Pfizer	Healthcare	183	Vodafone	Telecom	United Kingdom	175
12	AIG	Financial	181	China Construction	Financial	China	168
13	Cisco	Info. Tech.	181	Bank of China	Financial	China	160
14	Google	Info. Tech.	172	Roche	Healthcare	Switzerland	159
15	Berkshire Hathaway	Financial	170	Nestle	Consumer Staples	Switzerland	158
16	JPMorgan Chase	Financial	170	ENI	Energy	Italy	156
17	IBM	Info. Tech.	162	GlaxoSmithKline	Healthcare	United Kingdom	152
18	Intel	Info. Tech.	151	Novartis	Healthcare	Switzerland	150
19	Altria	Consumer Staples	150	Petrobras	Energy	Brazil	141
20	ConocoPhillips	Energy	142	Sinopec	Energy	China	136

In the consumer discretionary sector, Japan has by far the highest weight of all geographic regions, primarily because of the presence of Toyota Motors, one of the largest non-U.S.-based corporations in the world. This sector covers companies that produce products that consumers generally buy with discretionary income. Sony Corporation, Honda Motor, and Matsushita Electric Industrial also contribute to this sector. In the United States, the largest firms in the consumer discretionary sector are Comcast, Time Warner, and Home Depot while in Europe DaimlerChrysler is the largest.

The United States has the largest weight in the consumer staples sector, closely followed by Europe. Here the big firms in the United States are Procter & Gamble, Altria, and Wal-Mart, while in Europe the dominant firms are Nestlé, Unilever, and British American Tobacco. The emerging markets have few entries in this sector while Japan has virtually no presence relative to the size of its market.

The energy sector has a large value everywhere but in Japan, which has very little in energy resources. In the United States the integrated oil producers such as Exxon Mobil, Chevron, and ConocoPhillips dominate, while in Europe the largest firms are BP (British Petroleum), Total in France, and ENI in Italy. Energy firms in the emerging markets are dominated by the Chinese PetroChina, the largest foreign firm, and Russian Gazprom, the second largest. Both these firms are only partially privatized.

Healthcare has the largest share of U.S. firms and the smallest share in the emerging markets. In the United States, the largest firms are Pfizer, Johnson & Johnson, and Merck; in Europe, GlaxoSmithKline, AstraZeneca, Roche, and Novartis; while in Japan, Takeda Pharmaceutical is predominant.

The share of industrial firms is largest in Japan and smallest in the emerging markets. Mitsubishi and Mitsui dominate in Japan; Siemens and Deutsche Post in Europe, and General Electric in the United States.

Information technology has the highest share in the emerging markets, but this is almost entirely due to the Asian giants Samsung Electronic from South Korea and Taiwan Semiconductor. If we exclude firms from South Korea and Taiwan, then India has nearly 80 percent of the remaining market value of technology firms with Infosys and Wipro being the largest.

By far the largest sector share for telecommunications firms is found in the emerging markets, due to Chunghwa Telecom of Taiwan, América Móvil, S.A.B. de C.V. of Mexico, and China Mobile. In Europe Vodafone is the largest telecommunications firm, followed by the Spanish Telefonica and Deutsche Telekom. In the United States the largest firms are AT&T and Verizon.

Finally, utility firms have a small share of only 3½ percent in the U.S. market (led by Exelon Corp.), an electric utilities firm, to nearly 7 percent in Europe led by Enel of Italy and Electricité de France, the tenth-largest foreign firm.

Private and Public Capital

Exxon Mobil may be the largest company by market value in the world, and it has the largest reserves of oil and gas (20 billion barrels) of any

private company. But if one includes government-owned companies, this U.S. giant is only the fourteenth largest.[12] Saudi Arabia's Aramco and Iran's NIOC have reserves of about 300 billion barrels! If one were to value these reserves at only $3.30 a barrel, or 5 percent of the 2007 price, that would make each company worth about $1 trillion. That shows how much wealth is still owned by governments around the world. In many countries, gas, electric, and water facilities are still owned and operated by government, and in many other industries, governments have a large, if not a controlling, interest.

Even in such privatized countries as the United States, the federal, state, and local governments own trillions of dollars of wealth in such forms as land, natural resources, roads, dams, schools, and parks. There is strong disagreement about how much of this wealth, if any, should be privatized. But there is increasing awareness that privatized firms often do experience efficiency gains. Growth of the world's capital stock will come not only from private entrepreneurs but from the privatization of many government-owned assets.

THE WORLD IN 2050

We began this chapter with a look at the distribution of population, output, and equity capital worldwide. Through most of the twentieth century, the developed world produced most of the world's output and generated an even larger share of its capital.

But this dominance will not last. The success of market-oriented economies in the last century provided a blueprint for the next. Twenty-five years ago, China came around to accept the benefits of a market economy. Fifteen years later, India did the same. The collapse of communism in the former Soviet Union and Eastern Europe has broadened the list even further. And many countries in Latin America, although not all, have adopted the free-market principles that have given Chile the second highest per capita income on the continent.

The Middle East and Africa have most certainly lagged. The Middle East is addicted to oil revenue and sectarian strife, and Africa is slowly emerging from a dark period of misrule and exploitation. But here too there has been some progress: the remarkable growth of Dubai has shown the Arab world that oil need not be the cornerstone of prosperity, and Africa is experiencing increased economic activity. There is

---

[12] From Steve Forbes, "Fact and Comment," *Forbes*, April 16, 2007, pp. 33–34.

even a freshly minted acronym for this region: MENA, or Middle East and North Africa.

These developments will lead the world to be a very different place by midcentury. By making conservative projections of productivity growth throughout the world and combining these assumptions with the population data compiled by the U.N. Demographic Commission, we can project the distribution of population, GDP, and equity capital by midcentury, as shown in Figures 10-5a, b, and c.[13]

As one can see in Figure 10-5b, the share of economic output in the developed world will shrink dramatically: from more than one-half of the world's output to about one-quarter by midcentury. The United States' share will shrink from 19 to 12 percent, Western Europe's from 19 to 9 percent, and Japan's from 6 to 2 percent. Well before midcentury,

---

[13] Average productivity growth from 2006 through 2050 in the developed world, 2.5 percent ; China and Indonesia, 5.0 percent; India, 5.5 percent; other Asia and Eastern Europe, 4.5 percent; Latin America and Caribbean, 4.0 percent; Middle East and Africa, 3.5 percent. The value of equity was determined by regression analysis of equity markets against the GDP.

F I G U R E   10–5a

The 2050 World Population

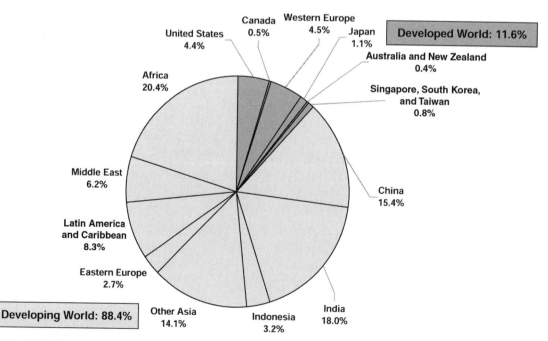

FIGURE   10–5b

The 2050 World GDP

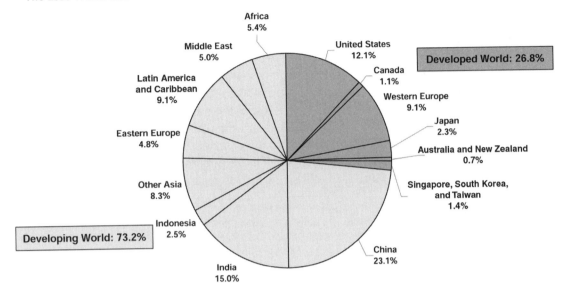

FIGURE   10–5c

The 2050 World Equity

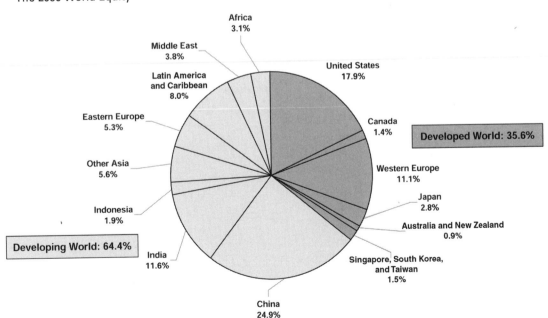

China will become the world's largest economy (projections range from 2025 to 2030), and in 2050, it will command 23 percent of the world's output, equal to the combined production of the United States, Western Europe, and Japan. India will not be far behind with an economic share of 15 percent, and India and China will be producing more than one-third of the world's output.

Although the overall economy of China will eclipse that of the West, this does not mean that the average Chinese worker will be better off than the average European, Japanese, or American. China's population is projected to be about 3½ times that of the United States, and its *per capita income* at about one-half that level. If Chinese productivity growth exceeds expectations and per capita income rises to 60 percent of the U.S. level, China's GDP will increase to over 25 percent of the world total.

The astounding rise of China and India will bring the distribution of output more in line with the distribution of population. It has been estimated by economic historians that in the seventeenth and eighteenth centuries, the combined economies of India and China were about one-third that of the entire world.[14] But for political reasons, both these giants went into eclipse, while the Industrial Revolution began in Europe and was exported to the United States. Now India and China may once again become economic leaders of the twenty-first century.

The radical shift in the distribution of output will also bring about a redistribution of capital. Based on my analysis of the relation between the size of a country's equity markets and its GDP, I was able to project where the world's equity capital will be headquartered at midcentury.

The developed world, which now comprises over 90 percent of the world's total stock market value, will shrink to slightly more than one-third. Not only will large amounts of capital be created abroad but, as noted in the last chapter, Western capital will be sold to the emerging nations in exchange for the goods that aging economies will need.

Investors should be warned that the increase in a country's share of world capital shown from Figure 10-1c to Figure 10-5c does not necessarily represent capital appreciation of existing shares. Rather, most of the increases come from the flotation of new capital as well as the acquisition of old capital. As we learned in the last chapter, economic growth does not guarantee good returns, and in fact, the evidence indicates that investors pay too high a price for stocks in fast-growing countries.

---

[14] Angus Maddison, *Chinese Economic Performance in the Long Run*, Organisation for Economic and Co-operation Development, Paris: OECD Development Centre, 1998.

CONCLUSION

The inexorable trend toward integration of the world's economies and markets will certainly continue in this new millennium. No country will be able to dominate every market, and industry leaders are apt to emerge from any place on the globe. The globalization of the world economy means that the strength of management, product lines, and marketing will be far more important factors in achieving success than where the firm is domiciled.

Sticking only to U.S. equities is a risky strategy for investors. No advisor would recommend investing only in those stocks whose name begins with the letter A. But sticking only to U.S. equities would be just such a bet since U.S.-based equity will likely shrink to less than 18 percent of the world market by midcentury. And equity in China and India will grow to more than one-third of the world's equity market and be twice the size of the United States. Only those investors who have a fully diversified world portfolio will be able to reap the best returns with the lowest risk.

APPENDIX: THE LARGEST NON-U.S.-BASED COMPANIES

Table 10-5 lists the top 20 U.S. and non-U.S. companies by total market value, based on *all* shares outstanding (not float adjusted, whether partially owned by the government or not).

1. PetroChina (China)

PetroChina is a subsidiary of the state-owned China National Petroleum Corporation, and it produces two-thirds of China's oil and gas. The company has 11.5 billion barrels of oil reserves and has interests in over 15,900 gas stations. PetroChina was created in 2000 to manage China's domestic petroleum production. As of October 2007, its market value has soared to $438 billion, second in the world to Exxon Mobil.

2. OAO Gazprom (Russia)

Gazprom, Russia's largest company, is an oil and gas giant that controls 25 percent of the world oil reserves. Its revenues account for 25 percent of the Russian government's tax revenues. Initially a state-owned natural gas monopoly, Gazprom was converted into a joint-stock company in

1993. The state first had a 40 percent share, which was boosted to 51 percent in 2003. Gazprom offered 1 percent of its stock to foreigners in 1996.

3. Royal Dutch Shell (the Netherlands)

The company known today as Royal Dutch Shell was formed from the merger of two global oil conglomerates in 2003—Royal Dutch Petroleum (founded by a Dutchman in 1890) and Shell Transport and Trading (founded by an Englishman in 1897)—that have been in a close relationship for over a century. Royal Dutch has oil and gas operations in over 27 countries, and it sells its products to over 130 companies. Its 2006 sales were over $320 billion.

4. BP (British Petroleum) (United Kingdom)

Like its competitors Royal Dutch Shell, Exxon Mobil, and ConocoPhillips, today's BP comes from the recent merger in 1993 of two massive oil conglomerates—British Petroleum, founded in 1911, and Amoco, a spin-off of the Standard Oil Trust in 1911. BP is a multinational, earning 29 percent of its revenue from its native United Kingdom, 31 percent from the United States, and 22 percent from Continental Europe. As Britain has very few oil reserves, production is accomplished almost entirely abroad. Its 2006 sales were over $260 billion.

5. China Mobile (China)

China Mobile serves almost 300 million subscribers in China, and it enjoys a 67 percent market share. It's the world's leading wireless company by subscribers. Like many other modern Chinese corporations, China Mobile was once part of a state-owned monopoly but is now publicly traded. As of October 2007, its total market value soared to $370 billion.

6. Toyota Motor Corporation (Japan)

The largest foreign company by market value is Toyota Motor, founded in 1926 as Toyoda Loom Works by Sakichi Toyoda. In 1950 the company was reorganized into Toyota Motor Corporation, and in 2008 it will overtake General Motors as the leading automobile manufacturer in the world. Toyota, which has recently expanded into financial services, produces automobiles in 27 different countries, and only 37 percent of its automobiles are produced in Japan.

7. Industrial and Commercial Bank of China (ICBC) (China)

For most of its history, ICBC was the state-owned commercial bank in the People's Republic of China. On October 28, 2005, ICBC was transformed from a state-owned enterprise to a shareholding company, with the Chinese Ministry of Finance and SAFE Investments Limited each holding 124 billion shares. In 2006, ICBC set the record for the largest initial public offering in history, with a $21.9 billion sale on the Hong Kong and Shanghai exchanges; 83.5 percent of the shares are still government owned.

8. HSBC Holdings (United Kingdom)

HSBC was founded as the Hong Kong and Shanghai Bank by a group of Hong Kong businessmen led by Thomas Sutherland in 1865. In 1955 the Shanghai office was closed, and in 1993 the bank moved its official headquarters to London in anticipation of the Chinese takeover of Hong Kong. HSBC has over 10,000 offices in over 80 countries and assets of over $1.8 trillion.

9. Total (France)

The French oil company Total began in 1924 as the Compagnie Française des Pétroles (CFP). It created the brand name Total in 1954 and adopted it as the name of the company in 1991. Total is a vertically integrated oil company with reserves in Indonesia, Argentina, Colombia, and the North Sea. The oil company has operations in over 130 companies and earns less than one-quarter of its revenue from France.

10. Electricité de France (EDF) (France)

EDF was formed from the nationalization of private utilities in 1946. The French government sold 15 percent of EDF to the public in 2005, and it deregulated 70 percent of the market. EDF was primarily a hydroelectric producer, but it now operates many nuclear power plants. The company earns 63 percent of its revenues from France and about one-third from other European countries, including the United Kingdom.

P A R T

HOW THE ECONOMIC ENVIRONMENT IMPACTS STOCKS

CHAPTER 11

GOLD, MONETARY POLICY, AND INFLATION

In the stock market, as with horse racing, money makes the mare go. Monetary conditions exert an enormous influence on stock prices.

MARTIN ZWEIG, 1990[1]

If Fed Chairman Alan Greenspan were to whisper to me what his monetary policy was going to be over the next two years, it wouldn't change one thing I do.

WARREN BUFFETT, 1994[2]

On September 20, 1931, the British government announced that England was going off the gold standard. It would no longer exchange gold for an account at the Bank of England or for British currency, the pound sterling. The government insisted that this action was only "temporary," that it had no intention of forever abolishing its commitment to exchange its money for gold. Nevertheless, it was to mark the beginning of

---

[1] Martin Zweig, *Winning on Wall Street*, updated ed., New York: Warner Books, 1990, p. 43.
[2] Linda Grant, "Striking Out at Wall Street," *U.S. News & World Report*, June 30, 1994, p. 59.

the end of both Britain's and the world's gold standard—a standard that had existed for over 200 years.

Fearing chaos in the currency market, the British government ordered the London Stock Exchange closed. New York Stock Exchange officials decided to keep the U.S. exchange open but also braced for panic selling. The suspension of gold payments by Britain, the second-greatest industrial power, raised fears that other industrial countries might be forced to abandon gold. Central bankers called the suspension "a world financial crisis of unprecedented dimensions."[3] For the first time ever, the New York Exchange banned short selling in an effort to shore up stock share prices.

But much to New York's surprise, stocks rallied sharply after a short sinking spell, and many issues ended the day higher. Clearly, British suspension was not seen as negative for American equities.

Nor was this "unprecedented financial crisis" a problem for the British stock market. When England reopened the exchange on September 23, prices soared. The AP wire gave the following colorful description of the reopening of the exchange:

> Swarms of stock brokers, laughing and cheering like schoolboys, invaded the Stock Exchange today for the resumption of trading after the two-day compulsory close-down—and their buoyancy was reflected in the prices of many securities.[4]

Despite the dire predictions of government officials, shareholders viewed casting off the gold standard as good for the economy and even better for stocks. As a result of the gold suspension, the British government could expand credit by lending reserves to the banking system, and the fall in the value of the British pound would increase the demand for British exports. The stock market gave a ringing endorsement to the actions that shocked conservative world financiers. In fact, September 1931 marked the low point of the British stock market, while the United States and other countries that stayed on the gold standard continued to sink into depression. The lessons from history: liquidity and easy credit feed the stock market, and the ability of the central banks to provide liquidity at will is a critical plus for stock values.

A year and a half later, the United States joined Britain in abandoning the gold standard, and finally every nation eventually went to a fiat, paper money standard. But despite the new standard's inflationary bias,

---

[3] "World Crisis Seen by Vienna Bankers," *New York Times*, September 21, 1931, p. 2.

[4] "British Stocks Rise, Pound Goes Lower," *New York Times*, September 24, 1931, p. 2.

the world has become comfortable with the new standard and enjoys the flexibility it accords policymakers.

MONEY AND PRICES

In 1950, President Truman startled the nation in his State of the Union address with a prediction that the typical American family income would reach $12,000 by the year 2000. Considering that median family income was about $3,300 at the time, $12,000 seemed like a princely sum and implied that America was going to make unprecedented economic progress in the next half century. In fact, President Truman's prediction has proved quite modest. The median family income in 2000 was $41,349. However, that sum buys less than $6,000 in 1950 prices, a testament to the inflation of the last half-century. So instead of the typical family income soaring over 12 times, from $3,300 to $41,349 in roughly half a century, real incomes have only doubled, from $3,300 to $6,000, because of the inflation bite.

Inflation and deflation, which is defined as falling prices, have characterized economic history as far back as economists have gathered data. However, in the last 60 years there has never been a single year in which the U.S. consumer price index has declined. What has changed over the past half century that makes inflation the rule rather than the exception? The answer is simple: control of the money supply has shifted from gold to the government. With this shift, a whole new system has come into being that connects money, government deficits, and inflation.

The overall price level in the United States and Great Britain over the last 200 years is displayed in Figure 1-3 in Chapter 1. It is striking how similar the general trends are in these two countries: no overall inflation until World War II and then protracted inflation after. Before the Great Depression, inflation occurred only because of war, crop failures, or other crises. But the behavior of prices in the postwar period has been entirely different. The price level has almost never declined: the only question is at what rate will prices rise.

Economists have long known that one variable is paramount in determining the price level: the amount of money in circulation. The robust relation between money and inflation is strongly supported by the evidence. Take a look at Figure 11-1, which displays money and prices in the United States since 1830. The overall trend of the price level has closely tracked that of the money supply normalized for the level of output.

F I G U R E   11-1

Money and Price Indexes in the United States, 1830 through December 2006

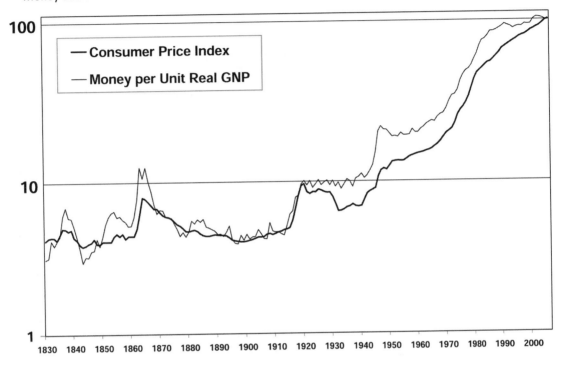

The strong relation between the money supply and consumer prices is a worldwide phenomenon. No sustained inflation is possible without continuous money creation, and every hyperinflation in history has been associated with an explosion of the money supply. There is overwhelming evidence that countries with high monetary growth experience high inflation, while countries with restrained money growth have low inflation.

Why is the quantity of money so closely connected to the price level? Because the price of money, like any good, is determined by supply and demand. The supply of dollars is printed by the central bank. The demand for dollars is derived from the demand of households and firms transacting billions of dollars of goods and services in a complex economy. If the supply of dollars increases more than the number of goods produced, this leads to inflation. The classic description of the inflationary process—"too many dollars chasing too few goods"—is as apt today as ever.

THE GOLD STANDARD

For the nearly 200 years prior to the Great Depression, most of the industrialized world was on a gold standard. This meant that, for example, the U.S. government was obligated to exchange dollars for a fixed amount of gold. To do this, the U.S. and other governments had to keep gold reserves in sufficient quantity to assure money holders that they would always be able to make good on this exchange. Since the total quantity of gold in the world was fixed—new gold discoveries were relatively small and contributed insignificantly to the world's total gold supply—prices of goods generally remained relatively constant.

The only times the gold standard was suspended was during crises, such as wars. Great Britain suspended the gold standard during both the Napoleonic Wars and World War I, but in both cases it returned to the gold standard with the original parity price. Similarly, the United States temporarily suspended the gold standard during the Civil War, but it returned to the standard after the war ended.[5]

The adherence to the gold standard is the reason why the world experienced no overall inflation during the nineteenth and early twentieth centuries. But overall price stability was not achieved without a cost. By equating the money in circulation to the quantity of gold available, the government essentially relinquished control over monetary conditions. This meant that the central bank was unable to provide additional money during economic or financial crises or when the economy grew in size. In the 1930s, adherence to the gold standard turned from being an exercise in government restraint and responsibility to being a straitjacket from which the government sought to escape.

THE ESTABLISHMENT OF THE FEDERAL RESERVE

Periodic liquidity crises caused by strict adherence to the gold standard prompted Congress in 1913 to pass the Federal Reserve Act that created the Federal Reserve System (the Fed) to be the country's central bank. The responsibilities of the Fed were to provide an "elastic" currency, which meant that in times of banking crises the Fed would become the lender of last resort. In trying times, the central bank would provide

---

[5] When the government issued non-gold-backed money during the Civil War, the notes were called "greenbacks" because the only "backing" was the green ink printed on the notes. Yet just 20 years afterward, the government redeemed each and every one of those notes in gold, completely reversing the inflation of the Civil War period.

currency to enable depositors to withdraw their deposits without forc-
ing banks to liquidate loans and other assets.

In the long run, money creation by the Fed was still constrained by
the gold standard since the government's paper currency, or Federal Reserve notes, promised to pay a fixed amount of gold. But in the short
run, the Federal Reserve was free to create money as long as it did not
threaten the convertibility of Federal Reserve notes to gold at the exchange rate of $20.67 per ounce. Yet the Fed was never given any guid-
ance by Congress or by the Federal Reserve Act on how to conduct
monetary policy and determine the right quantity of money.

THE FALL OF THE GOLD STANDARD

This lack of guidance had disastrous consequences just two decades
later. In the wake of the stock crash of 1929, the world economies entered
a severe downturn. Falling asset prices and failing businesses made depositors suspicious of banks' assets. When word was received that a few
banks were having problems meeting depositors' withdrawals, this
started a bank panic.

In an astounding display of institutional ineptitude, the Federal Reserve failed to provide extra reserves in order to stem the banking panic
and prevent a crash of the financial system, even though the Fed had the
explicit power to do so under the Federal Reserve Act. In addition, those
depositors who did receive their money sought even greater safety by
turning their notes back to the Treasury in exchange for gold, a process
that put extreme pressure on the government's gold reserves. The banking panic soon spread from the United States to Great Britain and Continental Europe.

To prevent a steep loss of gold, Great Britain took the first step and
abandoned the gold standard on September 20, 1931, suspending the
payment of gold for sterling. Eighteen months later, on April 19, 1933,
the United States also suspended the gold standard as the Depression
and financial crisis worsened.

The financial markets loved the government's new-found flexibility, and the reaction of the U.S. stock market to gold's overthrow was
even more enthusiastic than that in Great Britain. Stocks soared over 9
percent on April 19 and almost 6 percent the next day. This constituted
the greatest two-day rally in stock market history. Investors felt the government could now provide the extra liquidity needed to stabilize commodity prices and stimulate the economy, which they regarded as a
boon for stocks. Bonds, however, fell, as investors feared the inflationary

consequences of leaving the gold standard. *Business Week*, in a positive editorial on the suspension, asserted:

> With one decisive gesture, [President Roosevelt] throws out of the window all the elaborate hocus-pocus of "defending the dollar." He defies an ancient superstition and takes his stand with the advocates of managed money. . . . The job now is to manage our money effectively, wisely, with self-restraint. It can be done.[6]

POSTDEVALUATION MONETARY POLICY

Ironically, while the right to redeem dollars for gold was denied U.S. citizens, it was soon reinstated for foreign central banks at the devalued rate of $35 per ounce. As part of the Bretton Woods agreement, which set up the rules of international exchange rates after the close of World War II, the U.S. government promised to exchange all dollars for gold held by foreign central banks at the fixed rate of $35 per ounce as long as these countries fixed their currency to the dollar.

In the postwar period, as inflation increased and the dollar bought less and less, gold seemed more and more attractive to foreigners. U.S. gold reserves began to dwindle, despite official claims that the United States had no plans to change its gold exchange policy at the fixed price of $35 per ounce. As late as 1965, President Johnson stated unequivocally in the *Economic Report of the President*:

> There can be no question of our capacity and determination to maintain the gold value of the dollar at $35.00 per ounce. The full resources of the Nation are pledged to that end.[7]

But this was not so. As the gold reserves dwindled, Congress removed the gold-backing requirement for U.S. currency in 1968. In next year's *Economic Report of the President*, President Johnson declared:

> Myths about gold die slowly. But progress can be made—as we have demonstrated. In 1968, the Congress ended the obsolete gold-backing requirement for our currency.[8]

Myths about gold? Obsolete gold-backing requirement? What a turnabout! The government finally admitted that domestic monetary policy would not be subject to the discipline of gold, and the guiding

---

[6] "We Start," *Business Week*, April 26, 1933, p. 32.

[7] *Economic Report of the President*, Washington, D.C.: Government Printing Office, 1965, p. 7.

[8] *Economic Report of the President*, Washington, D.C.: Government Printing Office, 1969, p. 16.

principle of international finance and monetary policy for almost two centuries was summarily dismissed as a relic of incorrect thinking.

Despite the removal of gold backing, the United States continued to redeem gold at $35 an ounce for foreign central banks, although individuals were paying over $40 in the private markets. Seeing that the end of this exchange option was near, foreign central banks accelerated their exchange of dollars for gold. The United States, which held almost $30 billion of gold at the end of World War II, was left with $11 billion by the summer of 1971, and hundreds of millions more were being withdrawn each month.

Something dramatic had to happen. On August 15, 1971, President Nixon, in one of the most extraordinary actions since Roosevelt's 1933 declaration of a Bank Holiday, announced the "New Economic Policy": Freezing wages and prices and closing the "gold window" that was enabling foreigners to exchange U.S. currency for gold. The link of gold to money was permanently—and irrevocably—broken.

Although conservatives were shocked at that action, few investors shed a tear for the gold standard. The stock market responded enthusiastically to Nixon's announcement, which was also coupled with wage and price controls and higher tariffs, by jumping almost 4 percent on record volume. But this should not have surprised those who studied history. Suspensions of the gold standard and devaluations of currencies have witnessed some of the most dramatic stock market rallies in history. Investors agreed that gold was a monetary relic.

POSTGOLD MONETARY POLICY

With the dismantling of the gold standard, there was no longer any constraint on monetary expansion, either in the United States or in foreign countries. The first inflationary oil shock from 1973 to 1974 caught most of the industrialized countries off guard, and all suffered significantly higher inflation as governments vainly attempted to offset falling output by expanding the money supply.

Because of the inflationary policies of the Federal Reserve, the U.S. Congress tried to control monetary expansion by passing a congressional resolution in 1975 that obliged the central bank to announce monetary growth targets. Three years later, Congress passed the Humphrey-Hawkins Act, which forced the Fed to testify on monetary policy before Congress twice annually and establish monetary targets. It was the first time since the passage of the Federal Reserve Act that Congress instructed the central bank to take the control of the stock of

money. To this day, the financial markets closely watch the Fed chairman's biannual testimony, which takes place in February and July.[9]

Unfortunately, the Fed largely ignored the money targets it set in the 1970s. The surge of inflation in 1979 brought increased pressure on the Federal Reserve to change its policy and seriously control inflation. On Saturday, October 6, 1979, Paul Volcker, who had been appointed in April to succeed G. William Miller as chairman of the board of the Federal Reserve System, announced a radical change in the implementation of monetary policy. No longer would the Federal Reserve set interest rates to guide policy. Instead, it would exercise control over the supply of money without regard to interest rate movements. The market knew that this meant sharply higher interest rates.

The prospect of sharply restricted liquidity was a shock to the financial markets. Although Volcker's Saturday night announcement (later referred to as the "Saturday Night Massacre") did not immediately capture the popular headlines—in contrast to the abundant press coverage devoted to Nixon's 1971 New Economic Policy that froze prices and closed the gold window—it roiled the financial markets. Stocks went into a tailspin, falling almost 8 percent on record volume in the 2½ days following the announcement. Stockholders shuddered at the prospect of sharply higher interest rates that would be necessary to tame inflation.

The tight monetary policy of the Volcker years eventually broke the inflationary cycle. European central banks and the Bank of Japan joined the Fed in calling inflation "public enemy number 1," and they consequently geared their monetary policies toward stable prices. Restricting money growth proved to be the only real answer to controlling inflation.

THE FEDERAL RESERVE AND MONEY CREATION

The process by which the Fed changes the money supply and controls credit conditions is straightforward. When the Fed wants to increase the money supply, it buys a government bond in the *open market*—a market where billions of dollars in bonds are transacted every day. What is unique about the Federal Reserve is that when it buys government bonds in what is called an *open market purchase*, it pays for them by crediting the reserve account of the bank of the customer from whom the Fed bought the bond—thereby creating money. A *reserve account* is a deposit

---

[9] In 2000, Congress allowed to lapse the Humphrey-Hawkins Act, but legislation still required the Federal Reserve chairman to report biannually to Congress.

a bank maintains at the Federal Reserve to satisfy reserve requirements and facilitate check clearing.

If the Federal Reserve wants to reduce the money supply, it sells government bonds from its portfolio. The buyer of these bonds instructs his or her bank to pay the seller (the Fed) from his or her account. The bank then instructs the Fed to debit the bank's reserve account bank, and that money disappears from circulation. This is called an *open market sale*. The buying and selling of government bonds are called *open market operations*.

HOW THE FED'S ACTIONS AFFECT INTEREST RATES

We have seen that when the Federal Reserve buys and sells government securities, it influences the amount of reserves in the banking system. There is an active market for these reserves among banks, where billions of dollars are bought and sold each day. This market is called the *federal funds market,* and the interest rate at which these funds are borrowed and lent is called the *federal funds rate.*

Although this market is called the "federal funds market," the market is not run by the government, nor does it trade government securities. The fed funds market is a private lending market among banks where rates are dictated by supply and demand. However, the Federal Reserve has powerful influence over the federal funds market. If the Fed buys securities, then the supply of reserves is increased and the interest rate on federal funds goes down because banks then have ample reserves to lend. Conversely, if the Fed sells securities, the supply of reserves is reduced and the federal funds rate goes up because banks scramble for the remaining supply.

Although federal funds are lent overnight so the funds rate is an overnight rate, the interest rate on federal funds forms the anchor to all other short-term interest rates. These include the prime rate, which is the benchmark for most consumer and much commercial lending, as well as short-term Treasury securities. The federal funds rate is the basis of literally trillions of dollars of loans and securities.

Interest rates are an extremely important influence on stock prices because interest rates discount the future cash flows from stocks. Therefore, bonds compete with stocks in investment portfolios. Bonds become more attractive when interest rates rise, so investors sell stocks until the returns on stocks again become attractive relative to the returns on bonds. The opposite occurs when interest rates fall.

Over most of the past 50 years, changes in the fed funds rates have been a very good predictor of future stock prices. This is shown in Table 11-1,

TABLE 11–1

Federal Funds Rates and Subsequent Stock Returns (Number of Changes in Parentheses)

1955-2006	3-month	6-month	9-month	12-month
Increases (116)	1.4%	3.3%	6.0%	7.4%
Decreases (108)	5.0%	9.5%	11.8%	15.3%
Benchmark*	2.9%	5.8%	8.8%	11.8%
1955-1959				
Increases (18)	5.0%	7.0%	10.1%	11.8%
Decreases (8)	6.4%	17.4%	27.8%	36.0%
Benchmark*	3.3%	6.4%	8.9%	11.4%
1960-1969				
Increases (22)	-1.2%	1.2%	1.4%	2.6%
Decreases (17)	3.5%	6.1%	7.4%	8.6%
Benchmark*	2.2%	4.1%	6.2%	8.4%
1970-1979				
Increases (29)	-1.9%	-1.2%	3.7%	4.8%
Decreases (26)	6.5%	11.1%	13.8%	17.7%
Benchmark*	1.9%	4.3%	6.7%	9.3%
1980-1989				
Increases (16)	3.9%	4.2%	9.1%	8.6%
Decreases (23)	6.5%	12.9%	14.9%	21.1%
Benchmark*	4.3%	8.8%	13.0%	16.9%
1990-1999				
Increases (11)	3.3%	8.8%	13.4%	20.2%
Decreases (22)	6.1%	10.6%	14.3%	17.6%
Benchmark*	4.5%	9.0%	13.9%	18.9%
2000-2006				
Increases (20)	2.7%	4.7%	4.1%	4.6%
Decreases (12)	-1.7%	-3.2%	-7.4%	-9.8%
Benchmark*	0.6%	1.0%	1.2%	1.9%

* Average of all time periods in selected sample

which displays the return on the S&P 500 Index from the beginning of the month after the fed funds rate has been changed to a date 3, 6, 9, and 12 months later.

The effects of Fed actions on stock prices are dramatic: following increases in the fed funds rate, the subsequent returns on stocks are significantly less than average; when the fed funds rate is decreased, stock returns are significantly higher than average. Since 1955, the total return on stocks has been 7.5 percent in the 12 months following the 112 increases in the fed funds rate, while it has been 15.3 percent following the 108 times the fed funds rate has been reduced. This compares to an average 12-month return over the period of 11.8 percent. If these results persist in the future, investors could significantly beat a buy-and-hold strategy by increasing their stock holdings when the Fed is easing credit conditions and reducing stocks when the Fed is tightening.

But this may not be the case. Although this strategy has worked well from the 1950s through the 1990s, since 2000, the impact of Fed rate changes on the stock market has been the absolute opposite of the historical record. The market has experienced negative returns following interest rate decreases and positive returns after increases.

This is what has happened. To slow the rate of increasing inflation, the Fed initiated a series of rate hikes in June 1999 that extended through May 2000. But the stock market ignored these increases, and it did not start falling in earnest until September 2001, more than 15 months after the Fed began raising rates. As the economy suddenly slowed, the Fed began easing in January 2001, but the market continued downward and didn't bottom until October 2002. The Fed eased a final 25 basis points (bps) in June 2003, to reach a 50-year low of 1 percent, which it maintained for one year.

The market moved upward strongly in 2003, but in June 2004, as the economy was recovering, the Fed began the first of 17 consecutive ¼-point increases that ended in the summer of 2006. Despite these increases, stocks continued to rise. Buying when the Fed begins to ease and selling when they start to tighten has been a poorly performing strategy over the past decade.

There could be a number of reasons why stocks are not reacting to Fed rate movements as they have in the past. Perhaps investors have become so geared to watching and anticipating Fed policy that the effect of its tightening and easing is already discounted in the market so that the impact of Fed actions extend over a period of a few days rather than over several months. If investors expect the Fed to do the right thing to stabilize the economy, this will be built into stock prices far before the

Fed even begins to take its stabilizing actions. Whatever the reasons, Fed policy actions, at least since 2000, have not evoked the same responses in the equity market as they had in the past.

STOCKS AS HEDGES AGAINST INFLATION

Although the central bank has the power to moderate (but not eliminate) the business cycle, its policy has the greatest influence on inflation. As noted above, the inflation of the 1970s was due to the overexpansion of the money supply, which was an action the central bank took in the vain hope that it could offset the contractionary effect of the OPEC oil supply restrictions. This expansionary monetary policy brought inflation to double-digit levels in most industrialized economies peaking at 13 percent per year in the United States and exceeding 24 percent in the United Kingdom.

In contrast to the returns of fixed-income assets over long periods of time, the historical evidence is convincing that the returns on stocks over the same time periods have kept pace with inflation. Since stocks are claims on the earnings of real assets—assets whose value is intrinsically related to labor and capital—it is reasonable to expect that their long-term returns will not be influenced by inflation. For example, the 60-year period since World War II has been the most inflationary long-term period in our history, yet the real returns on stocks have exceeded that of the previous 150 years. The ability of an asset such as stocks to maintain its purchasing power during periods of inflation makes equities an *inflation hedge*.

Indeed, stocks were widely praised in the 1950s as hedges against rising consumer prices. As noted in Chapter 7, many investors stayed with stocks, despite seeing the dividend yield on equities fall below the interest rate on long-term bonds for the first time. In the 1970s, however, stocks were ravaged by inflation, and it became unfashionable to view equity as an effective hedge against inflation.

What does the evidence say about the effectiveness of stocks as an inflation hedge? The annual compound returns on stocks, bonds, and Treasury bills against inflation over 1-year and 30-year holding periods from 1871 to 2006 are shown in Figure 11-2.

These figures indicate that neither stocks nor bonds nor bills are good short-term hedges against inflation. Short-term real returns on these financial assets are highest when the inflation rates are low, and their returns fall as inflation increases. But the real returns on stocks are virtually unaffected by the inflation rate over longer horizons. Bonds, on

FIGURE 11–2

Holding-Period Returns and Inflation, 1871 through December 2006

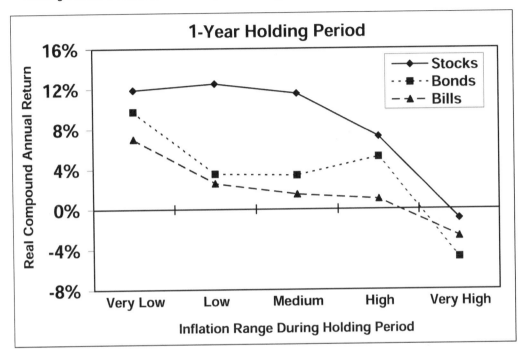

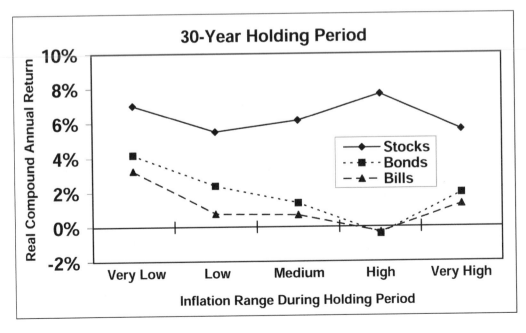

the other hand, have not matched the returns on stocks over any holding period.

This was the principal conclusion of Edgar L. Smith's 1924 book *Common Stocks as Long Term Investments*. He showed that stocks outperform bonds in times of falling as well as rising prices, taking the period after the Civil War up to just before the turn of the century as his test case. Smith's results are robust and have held up to more than 80 years of subsequent data.

WHY STOCKS FAIL AS A SHORT-TERM INFLATION HEDGE

Higher Interest Rates

If stocks represent real assets, why do they fail as a short-term inflation hedge? A popular explanation is that inflation increases interest rates on bonds, and higher interest rates on bonds depress stock prices. In other words, inflation must send stock prices down sufficiently to increase their dividends or earnings yields to match the higher rates available on bonds. Indeed, this is the rationale of the "Fed model" described in Chapter 7.

However, this explanation is incorrect. Certainly, expectations of rising prices do increase interest rates. Irving Fisher, the famous early-twentieth-century American economist, noted that lenders seek to protect themselves against inflation by adding the expected inflation to the real interest rate that they demand from borrowers. This proposition has been called the *Fisher equation*, after its discoverer.[10]

But higher expected inflation also raises the expected future cash flows available to stockholders. Stocks are claims on the earnings of real assets, whether these assets are the products of machines, labor, land, or ideas. Inflation raises the costs of inputs and consequently the prices of outputs (and those prices are in fact the measure of inflation). Therefore, future cash flows will also rise with the rise in price levels.

It can be shown that when inflation impacts input and output prices equally, the present value of the future cash flows from stocks is not adversely affected by inflation even though interest rates rise. Higher future cash flows will offset higher interest rates so that, over time, the price of stocks—as well as earnings and dividends—will rise at

---

[10] See Irving Fisher, *The Rate of Interest*, New York: Macmillan, 1907. The exact Fisher equation for the nominal rate of interest is the sum of the real rate plus the expected rate of inflation plus the cross product of the real rate and the expected rate of inflation. If inflation is not too high, this last term can often be ignored.

the rate of inflation. In theory the returns from stocks will keep up with rising prices and stocks will be a complete inflation hedge.

Nonneutral Inflation: Supply-Side Effects

The invariance of stock prices to the inflation rate holds when inflation is purely monetary in nature, influencing costs and profits equally. But there are many circumstances in which earnings cannot keep up with inflation. Stocks declined during the 1970s because the restriction in OPEC oil supplies dramatically increased energy costs. Firms were not able to raise the prices of their output by as much as the soaring cost of their energy inputs.

Earlier in the chapter it was noted that the inflation of the 1970s was the result of bad monetary policy trying to offset the contractionary effect of OPEC's oil price hikes. Yet one should not minimize the harm done by OPEC's policies on U.S. corporate profits. U.S. manufacturers, who for years had thrived on low energy prices, were totally unprepared to deal with surging energy costs. The recession that followed the first OPEC oil squeeze pummeled the stock market. Productivity plummeted, and by the end of 1974 real stock prices, measured by the Dow Jones averages, had fallen 65 percent from the January 1966 high—the largest decline since the crash of 1929. Pessimism ran so deep that nearly half of all Americans in August 1974 believed the economy was heading toward a depression such as the one the nation had experienced in the 1930s.[11]

Inflation can also harm stock prices since it increases investors' fears that the central bank will take restrictive action by raising short-term real interest rates. Such restrictive policies are often followed by an economic slowdown, which also depresses stock prices. This is another good rationale for investors to take stock prices down when inflation rises.

Looking at international markets, inflation, especially in less-developed countries, is also closely linked with large government budget deficits and excessive government spending. Inflation therefore often signals that the government is taking too large a role in the economy, which leads to lower growth, lower corporate profits, and lower stock prices. In short, there are many good economic reasons why stock prices should fall in response to increased inflation.

Taxes on Corporate Earnings

Another very important reason why stocks are poor short-term hedges against inflation is the tax code. There are two significant areas in which

---

[11] Gallup poll taken August 2 to 5, 1974.

the U.S. tax code works to the detriment of shareholders during inflationary times: corporate profits and capital gains.

Earnings are distorted by standard and accepted accounting practices that do not properly take into account the effects of inflation on corporate profits. This distortion shows up primarily in the treatment of depreciation, inventory valuation, and interest costs.

Depreciation of plant, equipment, and other capital investments is based on *historical* costs. These depreciation schedules are not adjusted for any change in the price of capital that might occur during the life of the asset. During inflation, the cost of replacing capital rises, but reported depreciation does not make any adjustment for this. Therefore, depreciation allowances are understated since adequate allowances for the rising cost of replacing capital are not reported. As a result, reported depreciation is understated, and reported and taxable earnings are overstated.

But depreciation is not the only source of bias in reported earnings. In calculating the cost of goods sold, firms must use the historical cost, with either "first-in-first-out" or "last-in-first-out" methods of inventory accounting. In an inflationary environment, the gap between historical costs and selling prices widens, producing inflationary profits for the firm. These "profits" do not represent an increase in the real earning power of the firm; instead, they represent just that part of the firm's capital—namely, the inventory—that turns over and is realized as a monetary profit. The accounting for inventories differs from the firm's other capital, such as plant and equipment, which are not revalued on an ongoing basis for the purpose of calculating earnings.

The Department of Commerce, the government agency responsible for gathering economic statistics, is well aware of these distortions and has computed both a depreciation adjustment and an inventory valuation adjustment in the National Income and Product Accounts going back to 1929. But the Internal Revenue Service does not recognize any of these adjustments for tax purposes. Firms are required to pay taxes on reported profits, even when these profits are biased upward by inflation. These biases reduce the quality of the earnings that firms report to stockholders.

Inflationary Biases in Interest Costs

There is another inflationary distortion to corporate profits that is not reported in government statistics. This distortion is based on the inflationary component of interest costs, and, in contrast to depreciation and

inventory profits, it leads to a *downward bias* in reported corporate earnings during periods of inflation.

Most firms raise some of their capital by issuing fixed-income assets such as bonds and bank loans. This borrowing leverages the firm's assets since any profits above and beyond the debt service go to the stockholders. In an inflationary environment, nominal interest costs rise, even if real interest costs remain unchanged. But corporate profits are calculated by deducting *nominal* interest costs, which overstates the real interest costs to the firm. Hence, reported corporate profits are depressed compared to true economic profits.

In fact, the firm is paying back debt with depreciated dollars, so the higher nominal interest expense is exactly offset by the reduction in the real value of the bonds and loans owed by the firm. But this reduction in the real indebtedness is not reported in any of the earnings reports released by the firm. Unfortunately, it is not easy to quantify this earnings bias because it is not easy to separate the share of interest cost due to inflation from that due to real interest rates.

Capital Gains Taxes

In the United States, capital gains taxes are paid on the difference between the cost of an asset and the sale price, with no adjustment made for the impact of inflation on the amount of the real gain. Thus, if asset values rise with inflation, the investor accrues a tax liability that must be paid when the asset is sold, whether or not the investor has realized a real gain. This means that an asset that appreciates by less than the rate of inflation—meaning the investor is worse off in real terms—will still be taxed upon sale.

Chapter 5 showed that the tax code has a dramatic impact on investors' realized after-tax real returns. For even a moderate inflation rate of 3 percent, an investor with a five-year average holding period suffers a 31-basis-point (hundredths of a percentage point) reduction in average after-tax real returns compared with the after-tax returns that he or she would have realized if the rate of inflation had been zero. If the rate of inflation rises to 6 percent, the loss of returns is more than 65 basis points.

The inflation tax has a far more severe effect on realized after-tax real returns when the holding period is short than when it is long. This is because the more frequently an investor buys and sells assets, the more the government can capture the tax on nominal capital gains. Nevertheless, even for long-term investors, the capital gains tax reduces real returns in inflationary times.

CONCLUSION

This chapter documents the role of money supply in the economy and financial markets. Before World War II, persistent inflation in the United States and in most industrialized countries was nonexistent. But when during the Great Depression the gold standard was dethroned, the control of the money supply passed directly to the central banks. And with the dollar or other major currencies no longer being pegged to gold, it was inflation, and not deflation, that proved to be the evil that central banks sought to control.

The message of this chapter is that stocks are not good hedges against increased inflation in the short run. However, no financial asset is. In the long run, stocks are extremely good hedges against inflation, while bonds are not. Stocks are also the best financial asset if you fear rapid inflation since many countries with high inflation can still have quite viable, if not booming, stock markets. Fixed-income assets, on the other hand, cannot protect investors from excessive government issuance of money.

Inflation, although kinder to stocks than bonds, is still not good for equity holders. Fear that the Fed will fight inflation by tightening credit and raising real interest rates causes traders to sell stocks. Inflation also overstates corporate profits and increases the taxes firms have to pay. Furthermore, because the U.S. capital gains tax is not indexed, inflation causes investors to pay higher taxes than they would pay in a noninflationary environment.

Fortunately for shareholders, central bankers around the world are committed to keeping inflation low, and they have largely succeeded. But if inflation again rears its head, investors will do much better in stocks than in bonds.

CHAPTER 12

STOCKS AND THE BUSINESS CYCLE

The stock market has predicted nine out of the last five recessions!

PAUL SAMUELSON, 1966[1]

I'd love to be able to predict markets and anticipate recessions, but since that's impossible, I'm as satisfied to search out profitable companies as Buffett is.

PETER LYNCH, 1989[2]

A well-respected economist is about to address a large group of financial analysts, investment advisors, and stockbrokers. There is obvious concern in the audience. The stock market has been surging to new all-time highs almost daily, driving down dividend yields to record lows and sending price-to-earnings ratios skyward. Is this bullishness justified? The audience wants to know if the economy is really going to do well enough to support these high stock prices.

This chapter is an adaptation of my paper "Does It Pay Stock Investors to Forecast the Business Cycle?" in *Journal of Portfolio Management*, vol. 18 (Fall 1991), pp. 27–34. The material benefited significantly from discussions with Professor Paul Samuelson.

[1] "Science and Stocks," *Newsweek*, September 19, 1966, p. 92.

[2] Peter Lynch, *One Up on Wall Street*, New York: Penguin Books, 1989, p. 14.

The economist's address is highly optimistic. He predicts that the real gross domestic product of the United States will increase over 4 percent during the next four quarters, a very healthy growth rate. There will be no recession for at least three years, and even if one occurs after that, it will be very brief. Corporate profits, one of the major factors driving stock prices, will increase at double-digit annual rates for at least the next three years. To boot, he predicts that a Republican will easily win the White House in next year's presidential elections, a situation obviously comforting to the overwhelmingly conservative audience. The crowd obviously likes what it hears. Their anxiety is quieted, and many are ready to recommend that their clients increase their stake in stocks.

The time of this address is the summer of 1987, with the stock market poised to take one of its sharpest falls in history, including the record-breaking 23 percent decline on October 19, 1987. In just a few weeks, most stocks can be bought for about half the price paid at the time of the address. But the biggest irony of all is that the economist is dead right in each and every one of his bullish economic predictions.

The lesson is that the markets and the economy are often out of sync. It is not surprising that many investors dismiss economic forecasts when planning their market strategy. The substance of Paul Samuelson's famous words, cited at the beginning of this chapter, still remains true more than 40 years after they were first uttered.

But do not dismiss the business cycle too quickly when examining your portfolio. The stock market still responds quite powerfully to changes in economic activity. The reaction of the S&P 500 Index to the business cycle is displayed in Figure 12-1. Although there were many "false alarms" when a substantial market decline was not followed by a recession, stocks almost always fell prior to a recession and rallied rigorously at signs of an impending recovery. If you can predict the business cycle, you can beat the buy-and-hold strategy that has been advocated throughout this book.

But this is no easy task. To make money by predicting the business cycle, one must be able to identify peaks and troughs of economic activity *before* they actually occur, a skill very few if any economists possess. Yet business cycle forecasting is a popular Wall Street endeavor not because it is successful—most of the time it is not—but because the potential gains are so large.

WHO CALLS THE BUSINESS CYCLE?

It is surprising to many that the dating of business cycles is not determined by any of the myriad government agencies that collect data on

FIGURE 12-1

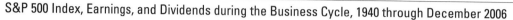

S&P 500 Index, Earnings, and Dividends during the Business Cycle, 1940 through December 2006

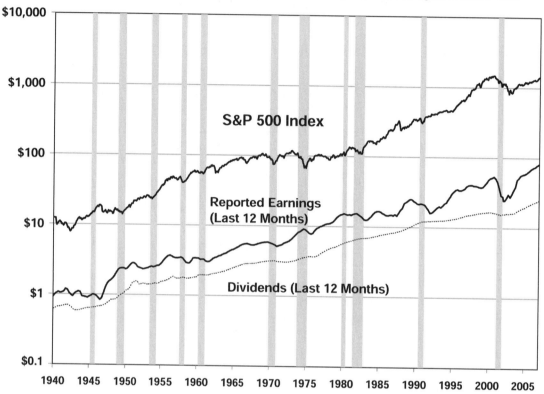

the economy. Instead, the task falls to the National Bureau of Economic Research (the NBER), a private research organization founded in 1920 for the purpose of documenting business cycles and developing a series of national income accounts. In the early years of its existence, the bureau's staff compiled comprehensive chronological records of the changes in economic conditions in many of the industrialized economies. In particular, the bureau developed monthly series on business activity for the United States and Great Britain back to 1854.

In a 1946 volume entitled *Measuring Business Cycles*, Wesley C. Mitchell, one of the founders of the bureau, and Arthur Burns, a renowned business cycle expert who later headed the Federal Reserve Board, gave the following definition of a *business cycle*:

> Business cycles are a type of fluctuation found in the aggregate economic activity of nations that organize their work mainly in business enterprises:

a cycle consists of expansion occurring at about the same time in many economic activities, followed by similarly general recessions, or contractions, and revivals that merge into the expansion phase of the next cycle; this sequence of changes is recurrent but not periodic; in duration business cycles vary from more than one year to ten or twelve years and they are not divisible into shorter cycles of similar character.[3]

It is commonly assumed that a recession occurs when real gross domestic product (GDP), the most inclusive measure of economic output, declines for two consecutive quarters. But this is not necessarily so. Although this criterion is a reasonable rule of thumb for indicating a recession, there is no single rule or measure used by the NBER. Rather the bureau focuses on four different series to determine the turning points in the economy: employment, industrial production, real personal income, and real manufacturing and trade sales.

The Business Cycle Dating Committee of the National Bureau of Economic Research confirms the business cycle dates. This committee consists of academic economists who are associated with the bureau and who meet to examine economic data whenever conditions warrant. Over the entire period from 1802 through 2006, the United States has experienced 46 recessions, and these recessions have averaged nearly 19 months in length, while expansions have averaged 34 months.[4] This means that, over these 205 years, almost slightly over one-third of the time the economy has been in a recession. However, since World War II, there have been 10 recessions, averaging 10 months in length, while the expansions have averaged 66 months. So in the postwar period, the economy has been in a recession less than one-seventh of the time, far less than the prewar average.

The dating of the business cycle is of great importance. The designation that the economy is in a recession or an expansion has political as well as economic implications. For example, when the bureau called the onset of the 1990 recession in July rather than August, it raised quite a few eyebrows in Washington. This was so because the Bush administration had told the public that the Iraqi invasion of Kuwait and the surge in oil prices were responsible for the economic recession. This explanation was undermined when the bureau actually dated the onset of the re-

---

[3] Wesley C. Mitchell and Arthur Burns, "Measuring Business Cycles," *NBER Reporter*, 1946, p. 3.

[4] The data from 1802 through 1854 are taken from Wesley C. Mitchell, *Business Cycles: The Problem and Its Setting*, Studies in Business Cycles No. 1, Cambridge, Mass.: National Bureau of Economic Research (NBER), 1927, p. 444. The data on U.S. recessions are taken from the NBER's Web site (www.nber.org), which lists business cycles from 1854 onward.

cession a month earlier. Similarly the 2001 recession began in March when technology spending dropped sharply and well before the 9/11 terrorist attacks.

The Business Cycle Dating Committee is in no rush to call the turning points in the cycle. Never has a call been reversed because of new or revised data that have become available—and the NBER wants to keep it that way. As Robert E. Hall, current chair of the seven-member Business Cycle Dating Committee indicated, "The NBER has not made an announcement on a business cycle peak or trough until there was almost no doubt that the data would not be revised in light of subsequent availability of data."[5]

Recent examples of the NBER's dating make the point: The July 1981 peak was not called until early January 1982, while the November trough was not dated until July 1983. The July 1990 peak of the expansion was not officially called until 9 months later. The March 1991 trough was not designated until December 1992, 21 months later, and the March 2001 peak was not called until late in November. And the trough of that recession in November 2001 was not called until July 2003. Clearly, waiting for the bureau to designate business cycles is far too late to be of any use in timing the market.

STOCK RETURNS AROUND BUSINESS CYCLE TURNING POINTS

Almost without exception, the stock market turns down prior to recessions and rises before economic recoveries. In fact, out of the 46 recessions from 1802, 42 of them, or more than 9 out of 10, have been preceded (or accompanied) by declines of 8 percent or more in the total stock returns index. Two exceptions followed World War II: the 1948 to 1949 recession that immediately followed the war and the 1953 recession, when stocks fell just shy of the 8 percent criterion.

The return behaviors for the 10 post–World War II recessions are summarized in Table 12-1. You can see that the stock return index peaked anywhere from 0 to 13 months before the beginning of a recession. The recessions that began in January 1980 and July 1990 are among the very few in U.S. history for which the stock market gave no advance warning of the economic downturn.

As the Samuelson quote at the beginning of this chapter indicates, the stock market is also prone to false alarms, and these have increased in the postwar period. Excluding the war years, when declining stock

---

[5] Robert Hall, "Economic Fluctuations," *NBER Reporter*, Summer 1991, p. 1.

T A B L E   12–1

Recessions and Stock Returns

Recession	Peak of Stock Index (1)	Peak of Business Cycle (2)	Lead Time Between Peaks (3)	Decline in Stock Index from (1) to (2) (4)	Maximum 12 Month Decline in Stock Index (6)
1948-1949	May 1948	Nov 1948	6	-8.91%	-9.76%
1953-1954	Dec 1952	Jul 1953	7	-4.26%	-9.04%
1957-1958	Jul 1957	Aug 1957	1	-4.86%	-15.32%
1960-1961	Dec 1959	Apr 1960	4	-8.65%	-8.65%
1970	Nov 1968	Dec 1969	13	-12.08%	-29.16%
1973-1975	Dec 1972	Nov 1973	11	-16.29%	-38.80%
1980	Jan 1980	Jan 1980	0	0.00%	-9.55%
1981-1982	Nov 1980	Jul 1981	8	-4.08%	-13.99%
1990-1991	Jul 1990	Jul 1990	0	0.00%	-13.84%
2001	Aug 2000	Mar 2001	7	-22.94%	-26.55%
		Average	5.7	-8.21%	-17.47%

markets coincided with expanding war economies, there have been 12 episodes since 1802 when the cumulative returns index for stocks fell by 8 percent or more, but the drop was not then followed by a recession within the next 12 months. This happened five times in the nineteenth century and seven times in the twentieth century. All the occasions in this century have occurred since World War II.

Declines greater than 10 percent in the Dow Jones Industrial Average during the postwar period that were not followed by recessions are listed in Table 12-2. The 1987 decline of 35.1 percent from August through early December is the largest decline in the near-200-year history of stock returns data after which the economy did not fall into a recession. Chapter 16 will discuss the 1987 stock crash and explain why it did not lead to an economic downturn.

The trough in the stock return index and the trough in the NBER business cycle are compared in Table 12-3. The average lead time between a market upturn and an economic recovery has been 4.8 months, and in 8 of the 10 recessions, the lead time has been in an extremely narrow range of 4 to 6 months. This compares to an average of 5.7 months that the peak in the market precedes the peak in the business cycle; this peak market to peak economy lead time also has shown much greater

TABLE 12–2

False Alarms by Stock Market (Postwar Declines of 10 Percent or More in the Dow Jones Industrial Average When No Recession Followed within 12 Months)

Peak of Stock Index	Trough of Stock Index	% Decline
May 29, 1946	May 17, 1947	-23.2%
Dec 13, 1961	Jun 26, 1962	-27.1%
Jan 18, 1966	Sept 29, 1966	-22.3%
Sept 25, 1967	Mar 21, 1968	-12.5%
Apr 28, 1971	Nov 23, 1971	-16.1%
Aug 17,1978	Oct 27, 1978	-12.8%
Nov 29, 1983	Jul 24, 1984	-15.6%
Aug 25, 1987	Dec 4, 1987	-35.1%
Aug 6, 1997	Oct 27, 1997	-13.3%
Jul 17, 1998	Aug 31, 1998	-19.3%
Mar 19, 2002	Oct 9, 2002	-31.5%

variability and less predictability than the market trough to economy trough lead time.

There are two ways to treat the 2000 to 2002 bear market. The first interpretation is that there was one bear market that peaked on a total return basis on September 1, 2000, and bottomed on October 9, 2002, for a loss of 47.4 percent, or there were two bear markets: a drop of 35.7 percent from September 1, 2000, through September 21, 2001, 10 days after the 9/11 terrorist attacks, then a subsequent rally of 22.1 percent to March 19, 2002, and finally another bear market of 33.0 percent, ending in October.

The second interpretation is more in line with the economic data, which show that the 2001 recession that began in March ended in November, two months after the stock market began its rebound. Under this interpretation, however, the second leg of the bear market was the second largest decline in U.S. history (after the 35.1 percent drop that accompanied the stock crash of 1987), which did not end in a recession.[6]

---

[6] To be sure, there was some controversy about the NBER timing of the 2001 recession. The economy did bounce back from the September 2001 terrorist attacks by year-end, but in the ensuing months the recovery was very weak by historical norms and GDP growth in the fourth quarter of 2002 was essentially zero. As noted earlier in this chapter, the NBER did not indicate that November 2001 ended the 2001 recession until July 2003, when the economy had noticeably picked up. The stock market rally that began in October 2002 did precede the subsequent acceleration of economic growth, but it did not signal the end of the NBER-dated recession.

T A B L E   12–3

Expansion and Stock Returns, 1948 through December 2001

Recession	Trough of Stock Index (1)	Trough of Business Cycle (2)	Lead Time between Troughs (3)	Rise in Stock Index from (1) to (2) (4)
1948-1949	May 1949	Oct 1949	5	15.59%
1953-1954	Aug 1953	May 1954	9	29.13%
1957-1958	Dec 1957	April 1958	4	10.27%
1960-1961	Oct 1960	Feb 1961	4	21.25%
1970	Jun 1970	Nov 1970	5	21.86%
1973-1975	Sep 1974	Mar 1975	6	35.60%
1980	Mar 1980	Jul 1980	4	22.60%
1981-1982	Jul 1982	Nov 1982	4	33.13%
1990-1991	Oct 1990	Mar 1991	5	25.28%
2001	Sep 2001	Nov 2001	2	9.72%
		Average	**4.8**	**22.44%**
		Std. Dev.	1.81	8.81%

It is important to note that by the time the economy has reached the end of the recession, the stock market has risen 22.4 percent on average. Therefore, an investor waiting for tangible evidence that the business cycle has hit bottom has already missed a very substantial rise in the market.

GAINS THROUGH TIMING THE BUSINESS CYCLE

The excess returns of investors who can time their investment strategy in relation to the peaks and troughs in economic activity are displayed in Table 12-4. Since stocks fall prior to a recession, investors want to switch out of stocks and into Treasury bills before the business downturn begins—if they can identify the turning point—and return to stocks when prospects for economic recovery look good. *Switching returns* are defined as the returns to an investor who switches from stocks to bills a given number of months before (or after, if his or her predictions are not accurate) a business cycle peak and switches back to stocks a given num-

ber of months before (or after) a business cycle trough. *Buy-and-hold returns* are defined as the returns from holding the market through the entire business cycle. *Excess returns* are defined as switching returns minus the returns from the buy-and-hold strategy.[7]

Over the entire period from 1802 through 2006, the excess returns are minimal over a buy-and-hold strategy if investors switch into bills exactly at the business cycle peak and into stocks exactly at the business cycle trough. In fact, investors switching into bills just one month after the business cycle peak and back into stocks just one month after the business cycle trough would have lost 0.6 percent per year compared to the benchmark buy-and-hold strategy.

Interestingly, it is more important to be able to forecast troughs of the business cycle than it is peaks. An investor who buys stocks before the trough of the business cycle gains more than an investor who sells stocks an equal number of months before the business cycle peak.

The maximum excess return of 4.8 percent per year is obtained by investing in bills four months before the business cycle peaks and in stocks four months before the business cycle troughs. The strategy of switching between bills and stocks gains almost 30 basis points ($^{30}/_{100}$ of a

---

[7] The returns of the buy-and-hold strategy are adjusted to reflect the same level of market risk as the buy-and-hold strategy.

T A B L E 12–4

Switching Returns (Percent) Minus Buy-and-Hold Returns (Percent) around Business Cycle Turning Points, 1802 through December 2006

		Switching from Stocks to Bills before Peaks				At Peak	Switching from Stocks to Bills after Peaks			
		4 month	3 month	2 month	1 month		1 month	2 month	3 month	4 month
Switching from Bills to Stocks before Trough	4 month	**4.8**	4.0	4.2	4.1	3.3	2.7	2.1	2.2	1.9
	3 month	4.0	**3.3**	3.5	3.3	2.6	1.9	1.4	1.5	1.3
	2 month	3.3	2.6	**2.8**	2.6	1.9	1.2	0.7	0.8	0.7
	1 month	2.5	1.8	2.0	**1.8**	1.1	0.5	0.0	0.1	0.0
At Trough		1.9	1.2	1.4	1.2	**0.5**	-0.2	-0.7	-0.6	-0.7
Switching from Bills to Stocks after Trough	1 month	1.5	0.8	1.0	0.8	0.1	**-0.6**	-1.1	-1.0	-1.1
	2 month	0.9	0.2	0.4	0.2	-0.5	-1.1	**-1.7**	-1.6	-1.7
	3 month	0.5	-0.2	0.0	-0.2	-0.9	-1.5	-2.1	**-2.0**	-2.1
	4 month	0.3	-0.4	-0.2	-0.3	-1.1	-1.7	-2.2	-2.1	**-2.2**

percentage point) in average annual returns for each week during the four-month period in which investors can predict the business cycle turning point.

The extra returns from successfully forecasting the business cycle are impressive. An increase of 1.8 percent per year in returns, achieved by predicting the business cycle peaks and troughs only one month before they occur, will increase your wealth by over 60 percent over any buy-and-hold strategy over 30 years. If you can predict four months in advance, the annual increase of 4.8 percent in your returns will more than triple your wealth over the same time period compared to a buy-and-hold strategy.

HOW HARD IS IT TO PREDICT THE BUSINESS CYCLE?

Billions of dollars of resources are spent trying to forecast the business cycle. The previous section showed that it is not surprising that Wall Street economists desperately try to predict the next recession or upturn since doing so dramatically increases returns. But the record of predicting exact business cycle turning points is extremely poor.

Stephen McNees, vice president of the Federal Reserve Bank of Boston, has done extensive research into the accuracy of economic forecasters' predictions. He claims that a major factor in forecast accuracy is the time period over which the forecast was made. He concludes, "Errors were enormous in the severe 1973–1975 and 1981–1982 recessions, much smaller in the 1980 and 1990 recessions, and generally quite minimal apart from business cycle turning points."[8] But it is precisely these business cycle turning points that turn a forecaster into a successful market timer.

The 1974 to 1975 recession was particularly tough for economists. Almost every one of the nearly two dozen of the nation's top economists invited to President Ford's anti-inflation conference in Washington in September 1974 was unaware that the U.S. economy was in the midst of its most severe postwar recession to date. McNees, studying the forecasts issued by five prominent forecasters in 1974, found that the median forecast overestimated GNP growth by 6 percentage points and underestimated inflation by 4 percentage points. Early recognition of the 1974 recession was so poor that many economists "jumped the gun" on the

---

[8] Stephen K. McNees, "How Large Are Economic Forecast Errors?" *New England Economic Review*, July/August 1992, p. 33.

next recession, which didn't strike until 1980 while most economists thought it had begun early in 1979.

From 1976 to 1995, Robert J. Eggert and subsequently Randell Moore have documented and summarized the economic forecasts of a noted panel of economic and business experts. These forecasts are compiled and published in a monthly publication entitled *Blue Chip Economic Indicators*.

In July 1979, the *Blue Chip Economic Indicators* report said that a strong majority of forecasters believed that a recession had already started—forecasting negative GNP growth in the second, third, and fourth quarters of 1979. However, the NBER declared that the peak of the business cycle did not occur until January 1980 and that the economy expanded throughout 1979.

By the middle of the next year, forecasters were convinced that a recession had begun. But as late as June 1980 the forecasters believed that the recession had started in February or March and would last about a year, or about one month longer than the average recession. This prediction was reaffirmed in August, when the forecasters indicated that the U.S. economy was about halfway through the recession. In fact, the recession had ended the month before, in July, and the 1980 recession turned out to be the shortest in the postwar period.

Forecasters' ability to predict the severe 1981 to 1982 recession, when unemployment reached a postwar high of 10.8 percent, was no better. The headline of the July 1981 *Blue Chip Economic Indicators* report read, "Economic Exuberance Envisioned for 1982." Instead, 1982 was a disaster. By November 1981 the forecasters realized that the economy had faltered, and optimism turned to pessimism. Most thought that the economy had entered a recession (which it had done four months earlier), nearly 70 percent thought that it would end by the first quarter of 1982 (which it would not, instead tying the record for the longest postwar recession, ending in November), and 90 percent thought that it would be mild, like the 1971 recession, rather than severe—wrong again!

In April 1985, with the expansion well underway, forecasters were queried as to how long the economy would be in an expansion. The average response was for another 20 months, which would put the peak at December 1986, more than 3.5 years before the cycle actually ended. Even the most optimistic forecasters picked spring 1988 as the latest date for the next recession to begin. This question was asked repeatedly throughout 1985 and 1986, and no forecaster imagined that the 1980s expansion would last as long as it did.

Following the stock market crash of October 1987, forecasters reduced their GNP growth estimates of 1988 over 1987 from 2.8 percent to 1.9 percent, the largest drop in the 11-year history of the survey. Instead, economic growth in 1988 was nearly 4 percent, as the economy grew strongly despite the stock market collapse.

As the expansion continued, belief that a recession was imminent turned into the belief that prosperity was here to stay. The continuing expansion fostered a growing conviction that perhaps the business cycle had been conquered—by either government policy or the "recession-proof" nature of our service-oriented economy. Ed Yardeni, senior economist at Prudential-Bache Securities, wrote a "New Wave Manifesto" in late 1988, concluding that self-repairing, growing economies were likely through the rest of the decade.[9] On the eve of one of the worst worldwide recessions in the postwar era, Leonard Silk, senior economics editor of the *New York Times* stated in May 1990 in an article entitled "Is There Really a Business Cycle?":

> Most economists foresee no recession in 1990 or 1991, and 1992 will be another presidential year, when the odds tip strongly against recession. Japan, West Germany, and most of the other capitalist countries of Europe and Asia are also on a long upward roll, with no end in sight.[10]

By November 1990, *Blue Chip Economic Indicators* reported that the majority of the panel believed the U.S. economy had already slipped, or was about to slip, into a recession. But by then, not only had the economy been in recession for four months, but the stock market had already hit its bottom and was headed upward. Had investors given in to the prevailing pessimism at the time when the recession seemed confirmed, they would have sold after the low was reached and stocks were headed for a strong three-year rally.

The record 10-year expansion of the U.S. economy from March 1991 through March 2001 again spawned talk of "new era economics" and economies without recession.[11] Even in early 2001, the vast majority of forecasters did not see a recession. In fact, in September 2001, just before the terrorist attack, only 13 percent of the economists surveyed by *Blue Chip Economic Indicators* believed the United States was in a recession even though the NBER subsequently indicated that the United States recession had begun six months earlier in March.[12] And by February 2002,

---

[9] "New Wave Economist," *Los Angeles Times*, March 18, 1990, Business Section, p. 22.

[10] Leonard Silk, "Is There Really a Business Cycle?" *New York Times*, May 22, 1992, p. D2.

[11] See Steven Weber, "The End of the Business Cycle?" *Foreign Affairs*, July/August 1997.

[12] *Blue Chip Economic Indicators*, September 10, 2001, p. 14.

less than 20 percent thought the recession had ended in 2001 although the NBER eventually dated November 2001 as the end of the recession.[13] Once again, economists have been unable to call the turning point of the business cycle until well after the date has passed.

CONCLUSION

Stock values are based on corporate earnings, and the business cycle is a prime determinant of changes in these earnings. The gains of being able to predict the turning points of the economic cycle are enormous, yet doing so with any precision has eluded economists of all persuasions. Despite the growing body of economic statistics, predictions are not getting much better over time.

The worst course an investor can take is to follow the prevailing sentiment about economic activity. The reason is that it will lead the investor to buy at high prices when times are good and everyone is optimistic, and sell at the low when the recession nears its trough and pessimism prevails.

The lessons to investors are clear. Beating the stock market by analyzing real economic activity requires a degree of prescience that forecasters do not yet have. Turning points are rarely identified until several months after the peak or trough has been reached. By then, it is far too late to act in the market.

---

[13]   *Blue Chip Economic Indicators*, February 10, 2002, p. 16.

CHAPTER 13

WHEN WORLD EVENTS IMPACT FINANCIAL MARKETS

I can predict the motion of heavenly bodies, but not the madness of crowds.

ISAAC NEWTON

As the sun rose over New York City on a beautiful Tuesday morning, September 11, 2001, traders expected a dull day on Wall Street. There was no economic data coming out of Washington, nor any earnings releases scheduled. The previous Friday the markets had fallen on a horrible employment report, but on Monday the markets had bounced back slightly.

The U.S. equity markets had not yet opened, but contracts on the S&P 500 Index futures had been trading all night as usual on the electronic Globex exchange. The futures markets were up, indicating that Wall Street was expecting a firm opening. But then a report came at 8:48 a.m. on what was to be one of the most fateful days in world history: a plane crashed into the World Trade Center Towers. The pattern of trading over the next 27 minutes, before the market closed, is shown in Figure 13-1.

FIGURE 13–1

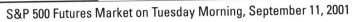

S&P 500 Futures Market on Tuesday Morning, September 11, 2001

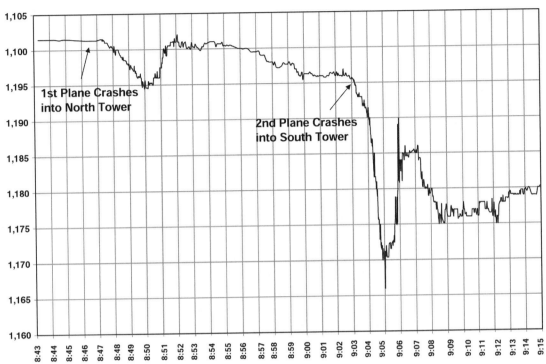

The news of the plane crash spread quickly, but few imagined what had really happened. Was it a large or small plane? Was it an accident? Or was there something more sinister going on? Although nobody knew the answers yet, immediately the stock index futures market traded down a few points, as it often does when uncertainty increases. Within a few minutes, however, buyers reappeared and the index returned to its previous level, as most traders concluded that nothing significant had happened.

Fifteen minutes later, at 9:03, with news cameras focused on the World Trade Center and millions around the world watching, a second plane crashed into the Towers. The entire world changed in that moment. Americans' worst fears had been realized. This was a terrorist attack. For the first time since World War II, America was under direct attack on its own soil.

By 9:05, two minutes after the second crash, the S&P futures plunged 30 points, about 3 percent, indicating that if the exchanges had

been open, nearly $300 billion would have been wiped off of U.S. stock values. But then, miraculously, buyers did appear. Despite the enormity of the events unfolding, some traders bet that the market overreacted to these attacks and decided that this was a good time to buy stocks. The futures firmed and ended the session at 9:15 down about 15 points, gaining back one-half of the earlier loss.

Despite this comeback, the gravity of this attack quickly sunk in. All the stock, bond, and commodity exchanges first delayed opening and then canceled trading for the day. In fact, stock exchanges in the United States would remain closed for the remainder of the week, the longest closing since FDR declared a "Bank Holiday" in March 1933 to try to restore America's collapsing banking system.

Foreign stock exchanges, however, remained open. It was 2 p.m. in London and 3 p.m. in Europe when the planes struck. The German DAX index immediately fell over 9 percent and ended the session around that level. London stocks suffered but not as much. There was a feeling that with the world's financial center, the United States, vulnerable to attack, some business might move to the United Kingdom. The British pound rallied, as did the euro against the dollar. Normally it is the U.S. dollar that gains in international crisis. But this time, with the attack centering on New York, foreign traders were unsure which direction to go.

When the New York Stock Exchange reopened the following Monday, September 17, the Dow Industrials fell 685 points, or 7.13 percent, the fourteenth-largest percentage drop in its history. The Dow continued to fall during the week and closed Friday, September 21, at 8,236—down more than 14 percent from its September 10 close and nearly 30 percent from its all-time high of 11,723 reached on January 14, 2000.

WHAT MOVES THE MARKET?

It was vividly clear why the markets fell after the terrorist attacks. But it might surprise investors that in the vast majority of cases, major market movements are *not* accompanied by any news that explains why prices change. Since 1885, when the Dow Jones averages were first formulated, there have been 126 days when the Dow Jones Industrial Average has changed by 5 percent or more. Of these, only 30 of these major moves can be identified with a specific world political or economic event, such as wars, political changes, or governmental policy shifts. That means that less than 1 in 4 major market moves can be clearly linked to a specific world event. A ranking of the 51 largest changes is shown in Table 13-1a, and market changes greater than 5 percent that are associated

TABLE 13–1a

Daily Changes over 5 Percent in the Dow Jones Industrial Average (Negative Changes Are Boldface, and Asterisks Denote Changes Associated with News Items; Excludes 15.34 Percent Change from March 3 to 15, 1933, for U.S. Bank Holiday)

Rank	Date	Change	Rank	Date	Change	Rank	Date	Change
1	Oct 19, 1987	-22.61%	18	Aug 12, 1932	-8.40%	35	Jan 8, 1988	-6.85%
2*	Oct 6, 1931	14.87%	19	Mar 14, 1907	-8.29%	36	Oct 14, 1932	6.83%
3	Oct 28, 1929	-12.82%	20	Oct 26, 1987	-8.04%	37	Nov 11, 1929	-6.82%
4	Oct 30, 1929	12.34%	21	Jun 10, 1932	7.99%	38*	May 14, 1940	-6.80%
5	Oct 29, 1929	-11.73%	22	Jul 21, 1933	-7.84%	39	Oct 5, 1931	-6.78%
6	Sep 21, 1932	11.36%	23	Oct 18, 1937	-7.75%	40*	May 21, 1940	-6.78%
7	Oct 21, 1987	10.15%	24*	Sep 5, 1939	7.26%	41	Mar 15, 1907	6.70%
8	Nov 6, 1929	-9.92%	25*	Feb 1, 1917	-7.24%	42*	Jun 20, 1931	6.64%
9	Aug 3, 1932	9.52%	26*	Oct 27, 1997	-7.18%	43	Jul 24, 1933	6.63%
10*	Feb 11, 1932	9.47%	27	Oct 5, 1932	-7.15%	44*	Jul 26, 1934	-6.62%
11*	Nov 14, 1929	9.36%	28*	Sep 17, 2001	-7.13%	45	Dec 20, 1895	-6.61%
12	Dec 18, 1931	9.35%	29	Jun 3, 1931	7.12%	46*	Sep 26, 1955	-6.54%
13	Feb 13, 1932	9.19%	30	Jan 6, 1932	7.12%	47	Jun 19, 1933	6.38%
14*	May 6, 1932	9.08%	31	Sep 24, 1931	-7.07%	48	May 10, 1901	6.36%
15*	Apr 19, 1933	9.03%	32	Jul 20, 1933	-7.07%	49	Oct 23, 1929	-6.33%
16	Dec 18, 1899	-8.72%	33*	Oct 13, 1989	-6.91%	50	Aug 6, 1932	6.33%
17	Oct 8, 1931	8.70%	34*	Jul 30, 1914	-6.90%	51*	Jul 26, 1893	-6.31%

with specific events are shown in Table 13-1b.[1] Monetary policy is the biggest single driver of these massive market outbreaks of euphoria or fear. Out of the 5 largest moves in the stock market over the past century for which there is a clearly identifiable cause, 4 have been directly associated with changes in monetary policy.

If you focus in on just the 10 largest daily market moves since 1885, only 2 can be attributed to a specific news event. The record 22.6 percent one-day fall in the stock market on October 19, 1987, is not associated with any one readily identifiable news event. In more recent years, since 1940, there have been only four days of big moves where the cause is identified: the 7.13 percent drop on September 17, 2001, when the markets reopened after the terrorist attacks; the 7.18 percent drop on October 27, 1997, when there was an attack on the Hong Kong dollar; the 6.91 percent drop on Friday, October 13, 1989, when the leveraged buyout of United Airlines collapsed; and the 6.54 percent drop on September 26, 1955, when President Eisenhower suffered a heart attack. The decline in October 1989, although often attributed to the collapse of the leveraged

---

[1] This expands the research originally published in David M. Cutler, James M. Poterba, and Lawrence H. Summers, "What Moves Stock Prices," *Journal of Portfolio Management*, Spring 1989, pp. 4–12.

T A B L E   13–1b

Largest News-Related Movements in the Down Jones Industrial Average (Negative Changes Are Boldface)

Rank	Date	Change	News Headline
2	Oct 6, 1931	14.87%	Hoover Urges $500M Pool to Help Banks
10	Feb 11, 1932	9.47%	Liberalization of Fed discount policy
11	Nov 14, 1929	9.36%	Fed Lowers Discount Rate/Tax Cut Proposed
14	May 6, 1932	9.08%	U.S. Steel Negotiates 15% Wage Cut
15	Apr 19, 1933	9.03%	U.S. Drops Gold Standard
24	Sep 5, 1939	7.26%	World War II Begins in Europe
25	**Feb 1, 1917**	**-7.24%**	**Germany announces unrestricted submarine warfare**
26	**Oct 27, 1997**	**-7.18%**	**Attack on Hong Kong Dollar**
28	**Sep 17, 2001**	**-7.13%**	**World Trade Center and Pentagon Terrorist Attacks**
33	**Oct 13, 1989**	**-6.91%**	**United Airline Buy-out Collapses**
34	**Jul 30, 1914**	**-6.90%**	**Outbreak of World War I**
38	**May 14, 1940**	**-6.80%**	**Germans Invade Holland**
40	**May 21, 1940**	**-6.78%**	**Allied Reverses in France**
42	Jun 20, 1931	6.64%	Hoover Advocates Foreign Debt Moratorium
44	**Jul 26, 1934**	**-6.62%**	**Fighting in Austria; Italy mobilizes**
46	**Sep 26, 1955**	**-6.54%**	**Eisenhower Suffers Heart Attack**
51	**Jul 26, 1893**	**-6.31%**	**Erie Railroad Bankrupt**
65	Oct 31, 1929	5.82%	Fed Lowers Discount Rate
66	**Jun 16, 1930**	**-5.81%**	**Hoover to Sign Tariff Bill**
67	Apr 20, 1933	5.80%	Continued Rally on Dropping of Gold Standard
73	May 2, 1898	5.64%	Dewey Defeats Spanish
76	Mar 28, 1898	5.56%	Dispatches of Armistice with Spain
85	Dec 22, 1916	5.47%	Lansing Denies U.S. Near War
88	**Dec 18, 1896**	**-5.42%**	**Senate votes for Free Cuba**
89	**Feb 25, 1933**	**-5.40%**	**Maryland Bank Holiday**
93	Oct 23, 1933	5.37%	Roosevelt Devalues Dollar
95	**Dec 21, 1916**	**-5.35%**	**Sec. of State Lansing implies U.S. Near War**
104	Apr 9, 1938	5.25%	Congress Passes Bill Taxing U.S. Government Bond Interest
125	Oct 20, 1931	5.03%	ICC Raises Rail Rates
126	**Mar 31, 1932**	**-5.02%**	**House Proposes Stock Sales Tax**

buyout, can be questioned since the market was already down substantially on very little news before the collapse was announced.

War is usually the biggest market mover. But the market drop on September 17, 2001, was more than twice the 3.5 percent drop that occurred on the day following the attack on Pearl Harbor, and it was more than that of any other one-day decline during a period when the United States was officially at war.

Even when news has occurred, there can be sharp disagreement over *what* news caused the market change. On November 15, 1991, when the Dow fell over 120 points or nearly 4 percent, *Investor's Business Daily* ran an article about the market entitled "Dow Plunges 120 in a Scary Stock Sell-off: Biotechs, Programs, Expiration and Congress Get the Blame."[2] In contrast, the London-based *Financial Times* published a front-page article written by a New York writer entitled "Wall Street Drops 120 Points on Concern at Russian Moves." What is interesting is that such news, specifically that the Russian government had suspended oil licenses and taken over the gold supplies, was not mentioned even once in the *Investor's Business Daily* article! That one major newspaper can highlight "reasons" that another does not even report illustrates the difficulty of finding fundamental explanations for the movements of markets.

UNCERTAINTY AND THE MARKET

The stock market hates uncertainty, which is why events that jar investors from their customary framework for analyzing the world can have devastating effects. September 11 serves as the perfect example. Americans were unsure what these terrorist attacks meant for the future. How severe would the drop in air travel—or any travel—be? How big a hit would the approximately $600 billion tourist industry take? Unanswered questions generate anxiety and declining prices.

Uncertainty about the presidency is another downer. The market almost always declines in reaction to sudden, unexpected changes related to the presidency. As noted previously, President Eisenhower's heart attack on September 26, 1955, caused a 6.54 percent decline in the Dow Industrials, the seventh largest in the postwar period. The drop was a clear sign of Eisenhower's popularity with investors. The assassination of President Kennedy on Friday, November 22, 1963, caused the Dow Industrials to drop 2.9 percent and persuaded the New York Stock Exchange to close two hours early to prevent panic selling. Trading remained suspended the following Monday, November 25, for Kennedy's funeral. Yet, the following Tuesday, by which time Lyndon Johnson had taken over the reins of government, the market soared 4.5 percent, representing one of the best days in the postwar period.

When William McKinley was shot on September 14, 1901, the market dropped by more than 4 percent. But stocks regained all of their losses

[2] Virginia Munger Kahn, *Investor's Business Daily*, November 16, 1991, p. 1.

on the following trading day. The death of Warren Harding in 1923 caused a milder setback, which was soon erased. Sell-offs such as these provide good opportunities for investors to buy stocks since the market usually reverses itself quickly following the change in leadership.[3]

DEMOCRATS AND REPUBLICANS

It is well known that the stock market prefers Republicans to Democrats. Most corporate executives and stock traders are Republicans, and many Republican policies are perceived to be favorable to stock prices and capital formation. Democrats are perceived to be less amenable to favorable tax treatment of capital gains and dividends and more in favor of regulation and income redistribution. Yet the stock market has actually done better under Democrats than Republicans.

The performance of the Dow Jones Industrials during every administration since Grover Cleveland was elected in 1888 is shown in Figure 13-2. The greatest bear market in history occurred during Herbert Hoover's Republican administration, while stocks did quite well under Franklin Roosevelt, despite the fact that the Democrat was frequently reviled in boardrooms and brokerage houses around the country. The immediate reaction of the market—the day before the election to the day after—does indeed conform to the fact that investors like Republicans better than Democrats. Since 1888, the market fell an average of 0.5 percent on the day following a Democratic victory, but it rose by 0.7 percent on the day following a Republican victory. But the market's reaction to the Republicans' success in presidential elections has been muted since World War II. There have been occasions, like Clinton's second-term election victory, when the market soared because the Republicans kept control of Congress, not because Clinton was reelected.

It is also instructive to examine the returns in the first, second, third, and fourth years of a presidential term, which are displayed in Table 13-2. The returns in the third year of a presidential term are clearly the best, especially since 1948. It is striking that this is true since the third year includes the disastrous 43.3 percent drop that occurred in 1931, during the third year of Hoover's ill-fated administration and the worst 1-year performance in more than 120 years.

Why the third year stands out is not clear. One would think that the fourth year of a presidential term, when the administration might in-

---

[3] But there are some whom the market never forgives. Stocks rallied over 4 percent in the week following the news of the death of Franklin Roosevelt, who was never a favorite on Wall Street.

F I G U R E   13–2

The Dow Jones Industrial Average and Presidential Terms (Vertical Lines Represent a Change of Administration, Dark Lines Represent a Change of Party, and Shaded Areas Represent a Democratic President in Office)

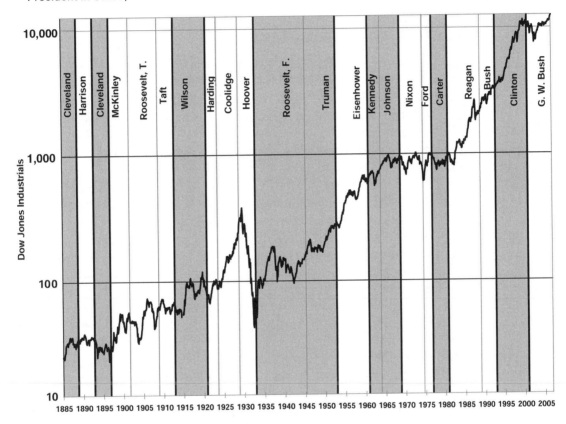

crease spending or put pressure on the Fed to stimulate the economy for the upcoming election, would be the best year for stocks. But the fourth year, although good, is clearly not the best. Perhaps the market anticipates favorable economic policies in the election year, causing stock prices to rise the year before.

The superior performance under the Democrats in recent years is documented in Table 13-3. This table records the total real and nominal returns in the stock market, as well as the rate of inflation, under Democratic and Republican administrations. Since 1888, the market has fared better in nominal terms under Democrats than under Republicans, but since inflation has been lower when the Republicans have held office, real stock returns have been slightly higher under Republicans than

T A B L E   13–2

Stock Returns during Presidential Administrations (Measured in Percent by S&P Total Returns Index; Italics Represent Democratic Administrations)

President's Name	Party	Election Date	From: 1 day before To: 1 day after	First Year of Term	Second Year of Term	Third Year of Term	Fourth Year of Term
Harrison	R	11/6/1888	0.4	6.9	-6.2	18.7	6.2
Cleveland	D	*11/8/1892*	*-0.5*	*-19.1*	*3.2*	*5.0*	*3.0*
McKinley	R	11/3/1896	2.7	20.2	29.1	3.8	21.2
McKinley	R	11/6/1900	3.3	19.7	8.3	-17.4	31.4
Roosevelt, T.	R	11/8/1904	1.3	21.3	0.8	-24.5	38.9
Taft	R	11/3/1908	2.4	16.4	-3.6	3.4	7.3
Wilson	D	*11/5/1912*	*1.8*	*-5.1*	*-5.9*	*31.1*	*8.7*
Wilson	D	*11/7/1916*	*-0.4*	*-18.5*	*17.1*	*19.6*	*-14.3*
Harding	R	11/2/1920	-0.6	9.2	29.6	5.1	26.6
Coolidge	R	11/4/1924	1.2	25.7	11.6	37.5	43.6
Hoover	R	11/6/1928	1.2	-8.4	-24.9	-43.3	-8.2
Roosevelt, F.	D	*11/8/1932*	*-4.5*	*54.0*	*-1.4*	*47.7*	*33.9*
Roosevelt, F.	D	*11/3/1936*	*2.3*	*-35.0*	*31.1*	*-0.4*	*-9.8*
Roosevelt, F.	D	*11/5/1940*	*-2.4*	*-11.6*	*20.3*	*25.9*	*19.8*
Roosevelt, F.	D	*11/7/1944*	*-0.3*	*36.4*	*-8.1*	*5.7*	*5.5*
Truman	D	*11/2/1948*	*-3.8*	*18.8*	*31.7*	*24.0*	*18.4*
Eisenhower	R	11/4/1952	0.4	-1.0	52.6	31.6	6.6
Eisenhower	R	11/6/1956	-0.9	-10.8	43.4	12.0	0.5
Kennedy	D	*11/8/1960*	*0.8*	*26.9*	*-8.7*	*22.8*	*16.5*
Johnson	D	*11/3/1964*	*-0.2*	*12.5*	*-10.1*	*24.0*	*11.1*
Nixon	R	11/5/1968	0.3	-8.5	4.0	14.3	19.0
Nixon	R	11/7/1972	-0.1	-14.7	-26.5	37.2	23.8
Carter	D	*11/2/1976*	*-1.0*	*-7.2*	*6.6*	*18.4*	*32.4*
Reagan	R	11/4/1980	1.7	-4.9	21.4	22.5	6.3
Reagan	R	11/6/1984	-0.9	32.2	18.5	5.2	16.8
Bush, G. H. W.	R	11/8/1988	-0.4	31.5	-3.2	30.5	7.7
Clinton	D	*11/3/1992*	*-0.9*	*10.0*	*1.3*	*37.6*	*23.0*
Clinton	D	*11/5/1996*	*2.6*	*33.4*	*28.6*	*21.0*	*-9.1*
Bush, G. W.	R	11/7/2000*	-1.6	-11.9	-21.9	28.7	12.8
Bush, G. W.	R	11/7/2004	1.1	8.4			

*Outcome of race was officially undetermined until December 13, 2000

Average from 1888 to 2006	Democratic	-0.5	7.3	8.1	21.7	10.7
	Republican	0.7	7.7	9.3	10.3	16.3
	Overall	0.2	7.6	8.5	15.4	13.8
Average from 1948 to 2006	Democratic	-0.4	15.7	8.2	24.6	15.4
	Republican	-0.0	2.3	13.0	22.8	11.7
	Overall	-0.2	7.6	10.2	23.6	13.3

T A B L E   13–3

Presidential Administrations and Stock Returns (Stock Returns Taken from Election Date or Date of Taking Office, Whichever Is Earlier; Italics Represent Democratic Administrations)

President's Name	Party	Date	Months in Office	Annualized Nominal Stock Return	Annualized Inflation	Annualized Real Return
Harrison	R	11/88 - 10/92	48	5.74	0.04	5.70
Cleveland	*D*	*11/92 - 10/96*	*48*	*-3.31*	*-1.91*	*-1.43*
McKinley	R	11/96 - 8/01	58	20.66	0.00	20.66
Roosevelt, T.	R	9/01 - 10/08	86	4.81	1.39	3.38
Taft	R	11/08 - 10/12	48	7.54	0.82	6.67
Wilson	*D*	*11/12 - 10/20*	*96*	*4.68*	*9.42*	*-4.33*
Harding	R	11/20 - 7/23	33	5.48	-4.05	9.93
Coolidge	R	8/23 - 10/28	63	28.04	0.12	27.88
Hoover	R	11/28 - 10/32	48	-20.42	-6.29	-15.08
Roosevelt, F.	*D*	*11/32 - 3/45*	*149*	*11.52*	*2.36*	*8.94*
Truman	*D*	*4/45 - 10/52*	*91*	*14.66*	*5.54*	*8.64*
Eisenhower	R	11/52 - 10/60	96	14.96	1.35	13.42
Kennedy	*D*	*11/60 - 10/63*	*36*	*15.15*	*1.11*	*13.88*
Johnson	*D*	*11/63 - 10/68*	*60*	*10.39*	*2.77*	*7.42*
Nixon	R	11/68 - 7/74	69	-1.32	6.03	-6.93
Ford	R	8/74 - 10/76	27	17.21	7.27	9.27
Carter	*D*	*11/76 - 10/80*	*48*	*11.04*	*10.02*	*0.93*
Reagan	R	11/80 - 10/88	96	15.18	4.46	10.26
Bush, G. H. W.	R	11/88 - 10/92	48	14.44	4.22	9.81
Clinton	*D*	*11/92 - 10/00*	*96*	*19.01*	*2.58*	*16.01*
Bush, G.W.	R	11/00 - 12/01	74	1.62	2.51	-0.87
Average from 1888 to October 2006	Democrat	44.0%	10.85	4.12	6.49
	Republican	56.0%	8.59	1.57	6.91
	Overall	100%	9.58	2.69	6.71
Average from 1948 to October 2006	Democrat	42.1%	15.26	3.64	11.27
	Republican	57.9%	9.71	3.78	5.71
	Overall	100%	12.01	3.72	7.99

under Democrats. But this has not been true over the past 60 years, when the market performed far better under the Democrats whether or not inflation is taken into account. Perhaps this is why the market's reaction to a Democratic presidential victory has not been as negative in recent years as it was in the past.

STOCKS AND WAR

Since 1885, the U.S. economy has been at war or on the sidelines of a world war about one-fifth of the time. The stock market does equally well in nominal returns whether there is war or peace. Inflation, however, has averaged nearly 6 percent during wartime and less than 2 percent during peacetime, so the real returns on stocks during peacetime greatly outstrip those during wars.

While returns are better during peacetime, the stock market has actually been more volatile during peacetime than during war, as measured by the monthly standard deviation of the Dow Industrials. The greatest volatility in U.S. markets occurred in the late 1920s and early 1930s, well before the United States was engaged in World War II. Only during World War I and the short Gulf War did stocks have higher volatility than the historical average.

In theory, war should have a profound negative influence on stock prices. Governments commandeer tremendous resources, while high taxes and huge government borrowings compete with investors' demand for stocks. Whole industries are nationalized to further the war effort. Moreover, if losing the war is deemed a possibility, stocks could well decline as the victors impose sanctions on the vanquished. However, the economies of Germany and Japan were quickly restored to health following World War II, and stocks subsequently boomed.

The World Wars

The market was far more volatile during World War I than during World War II. The market rose nearly 100 percent during the early stages of World War I, then fell 40 percent when the United States became involved in the hostilities, and finally rallied when the Great War ended. In contrast, during the six years of World War II, the market never deviated more than 32 percent from its prewar level.

The outbreak of World War I precipitated a panic, as European investors scrambled to get out of stocks and into gold and cash. After Austria-Hungary declared war on Serbia on July 28, 1914, all the major European stock exchanges closed. The European panic spread to New York, and the Dow Jones Industrials closed down nearly 7 percent on Thursday, July 30, the most since the 8.3 percent drop during the Panic of 1907. Minutes before the opening of the New York Stock Exchange on Friday, the exchange voted to close for an indefinite period.

The market did not reopen until December. Never before had the New York Stock Exchange been closed for such an extended period, nor has it since. Emergency trades were permitted, but only by approval of a special committee and only at prices at or above the last trade before the exchange closed. Even then, the trading prohibition was observed in the breach as illegal trades were made outside the exchange (on the curb) at prices that continued to decline through October. Unofficially, by autumn, prices were said to be 15 to 20 percent below the July closing.

It is ironic that the only extended period during which the New York Stock Exchange was closed occurred when the United States was not yet at war or in any degree of financial or economic distress. In fact, when the exchange was closed, traders realized that the United States would be a strong economic beneficiary of the European conflict. Once investors realized that America was going to make the munitions and provide raw materials to the belligerents, public interest in stocks soared.

By the time the exchange reopened on December 12, prices were rising rapidly. The Dow Industrials finished the historic Saturday session about 5 percent higher than the closing prices on the previous July. The rally continued, and 1915 records the best single-year increase in the history of the Dow Industrials, as stocks rose a record 82 percent. Stocks continued to rise in 1916 and hit their peak in November, with prices more than twice the level they were when the war had started more than two years earlier. But then stocks settled back about 10 percent when the United States formally entered the war on April 16, 1917, and fell another 10 percent through November 1918, when the Armistice was signed.

The message of the great boom of 1915 was not lost on traders a generation later. When World War II erupted, investors took their cue from what happened at the beginning of the previous world war. When Great Britain declared war on Germany on September 3, 1939, the rise was so explosive that the Tokyo Stock Exchange was forced to close early. When the market opened in New York, a buying panic erupted. The Dow Industrials gained over 7 percent, and even the European stock exchanges were firm when trading reopened.

The enthusiasm that followed the onset of World War II quickly faded. President Roosevelt was determined not to let corporations earn easy profits as they had in World War I. These profits had been a source of public criticism as Americans felt that the war costs were not being borne equally as its young men died overseas while corporations earned record income. An excess profits tax enacted by Congress during World War II removed the wartime premium that investors had expected from the conflict.

The day before the Japanese attacked Pearl Harbor, the Dow was down 25 percent from its 1939 high and still less than one-third its 1929 peak. Stocks fell 3.5 percent on the day following Pearl Harbor and continued to fall until they hit a low on April 28, 1942, when the United States suffered losses in the early months of the war in the Pacific.

But when the tide turned toward the Allies, the market began to climb. By the time Germany signed its unconditional surrender on May 7, 1945, the Dow Industrials were 20 percent above the prewar level. The detonation of the atomic bomb over Hiroshima, a pivotal event in the history of warfare, caused stocks to surge 1.7 percent as investors recognized the end of the war was near. But World War II did not prove as profitable for investors as World War I, as the Dow was up only 30 percent during the six years from the German invasion of Poland to V-J Day.

Post-1945 Conflicts

The Korean War took investors by surprise. When North Korea invaded its southern neighbor on June 25, 1950, the Dow fell 4.65 percent, greater than the day following Pearl Harbor. But the market reaction to the growing conflict was contained, and stocks never fell more than 12 percent below their prewar level.

The Vietnam War was the longest and one of the least popular of all U.S. wars. The starting point for U.S. involvement in the conflict can be placed at August 2, 1964, when two American destroyers were reportedly attacked in the Gulf of Tonkin.

One and a half years after the Gulf of Tonkin incident, the Dow reached an all-time high of 995, more than 18 percent higher than before the Tonkin attack. But it fell nearly 30 percent in the following months after the Fed tightened credit to curb inflation. By the time American troop strength reached its peak in early 1968, the market had recovered. Two years later, when Nixon sent troops into Cambodia and interest rates were soaring and a recession was looming, the market fell again, down nearly 25 percent from its prewar point.

The Peace Pact between the North Vietnamese and the Americans was signed in Paris on January 27, 1973. But the gains made by investors over the eight years of war were quite small, as the market was held back by rising inflation and interest rates as well as other problems not directly related to the Vietnam War.

If the war in Vietnam was the longest American war, the 1991 Gulf War against Iraq in the Middle East was the shortest. The trigger occurred on August 2, 1990, when Iraq invaded Kuwait, sending oil prices

skyward and sparking a U.S. military buildup in Saudi Arabia. The rise in oil prices combined with an already slowing U.S. economy to drive the United States deeper into a recession. The stock market fell precipitously, and on October 11, the Dow slumped over 18 percent from its prewar levels.

The United States began its offensive action on January 17, 1991. It was the first major war fought in a world where markets for oil, gold, and U.S. government bonds were traded around the clock in Tokyo, Singapore, London, and New York. The markets judged the victors in a matter of hours. Bonds sold off in Tokyo for a few minutes following the news of the U.S. bombing of Baghdad, but the stunning reports of the United States and its allies' successes sent bonds and Japanese stocks straight upward in the next few minutes. Oil prices traded in the Far East collapsed, as Brent crude fell from $29 a barrel before hostilities to $20.

On the following day, stock prices soared around the world. The Dow jumped 115 points, or 4.4 percent, and there were large gains throughout Europe and Asia. By the time the United States deployed ground troops to invade Kuwait, the market had known for two months that victory was at hand. The war ended on February 28, and by the first week in March, the Dow was more than 18 percent higher than when the war started.

As noted at the outset of this chapter, the War on Terrorism began with the terrorists' attacks on New York and the Pentagon on September 11, 2001. The Dow Industrials were down 16 percent from their close of 9,606 on September 10 to an intraday low of 8,062 reached on Friday, September 21. But the market rebounded sharply by the next week, and it had recovered to 9,120 by the time the United States began offensive action against the Taliban in Afghanistan on October 7.

Because of aggressive easing policies by the Federal Reserve and the successful execution of the Afghanistan war, the Dow surpassed its September 10 level on November 13 and continued rising to year-end. From its intraday low on September 21 to its intraday high of 10,184 on December 28, the Dow rose an astounding 26.3 percent in three months.

The market continued its rise to 10,673 on March 19, 2002, but the bear market, which had begun two years earlier, was far from over. A sluggish economy, combined with the accounting scandals of Enron, WorldCom, and others, sent stocks into another dive that didn't end until October 10, 2002, when the Dow hit an intraday low of 7,197. From the intraday high of 11,750 reached on January 14, 2000, through the October 10, 2002, low, the Dow Industrials fell nearly 39 percent, a

decline far less than the S&P 500 Index that was bloated by overpriced technology stocks.

The market subsequently rallied to over 9,000, but anxiety about a second U.S. operation in Iraq sent the stock back down to 7,524 five months later on March 11, 2003, just days before the invasion. But as it responded 12 years earlier when the Gulf War started, the market rallied on news of the invasion and continued to rise despite the growing insurgency in Iraq that made the war particularly unpopular.

Notwithstanding the Republican defeat in Congress in November 2006, stocks hit new all-time highs in the summer of 2007, more than recovering all the ground that had been lost during the 2000 to 2002 bear market. From the end of March 2003, the first month of the Iraq invasion, through June 2007, the annual return on the market was an extremely strong 17.5 percent per year.

CONCLUSION

When investigating the causes of major market movements, it is sobering to realize that less than one in four can be linked to a news event of major political or economic import. This confirms the unpredictability of the market and the difficulty in forecasting market moves. Those who sold in panic at the outbreak of World War I missed out on 1915, the best year ever in the stock market. But those who bought at the onset of World War II, believing there would be a replay of the World War I gains, were sorely disappointed because of the government's determination to cap wartime profits. World events may shock the market in the short run, but thankfully they have proven unable to dent the long-term returns that have become characteristic of stocks over the long run.

CHAPTER 14

STOCKS, BONDS, AND THE FLOW OF ECONOMIC DATA

The thing that most affects the stock market is everything.
JAMES PALYSTED WOOD, 1966

It's 8:28 a.m. eastern daylight time, Friday, July 5, 1996. Normally a trading day wedged between a major U.S. holiday and a weekend is slow, with little volume or price movement. But not today. Traders around the world are anxiously glued to their terminals, eyes riveted on the scrolling news that displays thousands of headlines every day. It is just two minutes before the most important announcement each month—the U.S. employment statistics.

All week, stock, bond, and currency traders have anticipated this day. The Dow has been trading within a few points of its all-time high, reached at the end of May. But interest rates have been rising, giving traders cause for concern. The seconds tick down. At 8:30 sharp, the words come across the screen:

PAYROLL UP 239,000, UNEMPLOYMENT AT SIX-YEAR LOW OF 5.3 PERCENT, WAGES UP 9 CENTS AN HOUR, BIGGEST INCREASE IN 30 YEARS.

President Clinton hailed the economic news, claiming, "We have the most solid American economy in a generation; wages for American workers are finally on the rise again."

But the financial markets were stunned. Long-term bond prices immediately collapsed on both domestic and foreign exchanges as traders expected higher interest rates. Interest rates on long- and short-term bonds climbed nearly a quarter point. Although the stock market would not open for an hour, the S&P 500 Index futures, which represent claims on this benchmark index and are described in detail in the next chapter, fell from 676 to 656, about 2 percent. European stock markets, which had been open for hours, sold off immediately. The benchmark DAX index in Germany, CAC in France, and FT-SE in Britain instantly fell almost 2 percent. Within seconds, world equity markets lost $200 billion, and world bond markets fell at least as much.

This episode demonstrates that what Main Street interprets as good news is often bad news on Wall Street. This is because it is more than mere profits that move stocks; interest rates, inflation, and the future direction of the Federal Reserve's monetary policy also have a major impact.

ECONOMIC DATA AND THE MARKET

News moves markets. The timing of much news is unpredictable—like war, political developments, and natural disasters. In contrast, news based on data about the economy comes at preannounced times that are set a year or more in advance. In the United States, there are hundreds of scheduled releases of economic data each year—mostly by government agencies, but increasingly by private firms. Virtually all of the announcements deal with the economy, particularly economic growth and inflation, and all have the potential to move the market significantly.

Economic data not only frame the way traders view the economy but also impact traders' expectations of how the central bank will implement its monetary policy. Stronger economic growth or higher inflation increases the probability that the central bank will either tighten or stop easing monetary policy. All these data influence traders' expectations about the future course of interest rates, the economy, and ultimately stock prices.

PRINCIPLES OF MARKET REACTION

Markets do not directly respond to what is announced; rather, they respond to the *difference* between what the traders *expect* to happen and

what *actually* happens. Whether the news is "good" or "bad" for the economy is of no importance. If the market expects that 200,000 jobs were lost last month but the report shows that only 100,000 jobs were lost, this will be considered "stronger-than-expected" economic news by the financial markets—having about the same effect on markets as a gain of 200,000 jobs would when the market expected a gain of only 100,000.

The reason why markets react only to the difference between expectations and what actually occurs is that the prices of securities already incorporate all the information that is expected. If a firm is expected to report bad earnings, the market has already priced this gloomy information into the stock price. If the earnings report is not as bad as anticipated, the price will rise on the announcement. The same principle applies to the reaction of bonds, stocks, and foreign exchanges to economic data.

Therefore, to understand why the market moves the way it does, you must identify the *market expectation* for the data released. The market expectation, often referred to as the *consensus estimate*, is gathered by news and research organizations. They poll economists, professional forecasters, traders, and other market participants for their predictions for an upcoming government or private release. The results of their surveys are sent to the financial press and widely reported online and in many other news outlets.[1]

INFORMATION CONTENT OF DATA RELEASES

The economic data are analyzed for their implications for future economic growth, inflation, and central bank policy. The following principle summarizes the reaction of the bond markets to the release of data relating to economic growth:

> Stronger-than-expected economic growth causes both long- and short-term interest rates to rise. Weaker-than-expected economic growth causes interest rates to fall.

Faster-than-expected economic growth raises interest rates for several reasons. First, stronger economic activity makes consumers feel more confident and more willing to borrow against future income, increasing loan demand. Faster economic growth also motivates firms to

---

[1] Usually both the median and range of estimates are reported. The consensus estimate does vary a bit from service to service, but the estimates are usually quite close.

expand production. As a result, both firms and consumers will likely increase their demand for credit and push interest rates higher.

A second reason why interest rates rise in tandem with a stronger-than-expected economic report is that such growth might be inflationary, especially if it is near the end of an economic expansion. Economic growth associated with increases in productivity, which often occur in the early and middle stages of a business expansion, is rarely inflationary.

Going back to the example above, inflationary fears were the principal reason why interest rates soared when the Labor Department released its report on July 5, 1996. Traders feared that the large increase in wages caused by the tight labor markets and falling unemployment would cause inflation, a nemesis to both the bond and the stock markets.

Reports on economic growth also have significant implications for the actions of central banks. The threat of inflation from an overly strong economy will make it likely that the central bank will tighten credit. If the aggregate demand is expanding too rapidly relative to the supply of goods and services, the monetary authority can raise interest rates to prevent the economy from overheating.

Of course, in the case of a weaker-than-expected employment report, the bond market will respond favorably as interest rates decline in response to weaker credit demand and lower inflationary pressures. Recall that the price of bonds moves in the opposite direction of interest rates.

An important principle to understand is that the market reacts more strongly after several similar reports move in the same direction. For example, if an inflation report is higher than expected, then the following month the market will react even more strongly to another higher-than-expected reading. The reason for this is that there is a lot of noise in the individual data report and a single month's observation may be reversed in subsequent data. But if the subsequent data confirm the original data, then it is more likely that a new trend has been established and the market will move accordingly.

ECONOMIC GROWTH AND STOCK PRICES

It surprises the general public and even the financial press when a strong economic report sends the stock market lower. But stronger-than-expected economic growth has two important implications for the stock market, and each tugs in the opposite direction. A strong economy increases future corporate earnings, which is bullish for stocks. But it also raises interest rates, which raises the discount rate at which these future profits are discounted. Similarly, a weak economic report may lower ex-

pected earnings; but if interest rates decline, stock prices could possibly move up because of the decline in the rate at which these profits are discounted. It is a struggle, in asset pricing terms, between the numerator, which contains future cash flows, and the denominator, which discounts those cash flows.

Which effect is stronger—the change in the interest rate or the change in corporate profits—depends often on where the economy is in the business cycle. Recent analysis shows that in a recession, a stronger-than-expected economic report increases stock prices since the implications for corporate profits are considered more important than the change in interest rates at this stage in the business cycle.[2] Inversely, a weaker-than-expected report depresses stock prices. During economic expansions, and particularly toward the end of an expansion, the interest rate effect is usually stronger since inflation is more of a threat.

Many stock traders look at the movements in the bond market to guide their trading. This is particularly true of portfolio managers who actively apportion their portfolio between stocks and bonds on the basis of changes in interest rates and expected stock returns. When interest rates fall after a weak economic report, these investors are immediately ready to increase the proportion of stocks that they hold since the relative returns on stocks or bonds have, at that moment, turned in favor of stocks. On the other hand, investors who recognize that the weak employment report means lower future earnings may sell stocks. The stock market often gyrates throughout the day as investors digest the implications of the data for stock earnings and interest rates.

THE EMPLOYMENT REPORT

The *employment report*, compiled by the Bureau of Labor Statistics (BLS), is the single most important data report released by the government each month. To measure employment, the BLS does two entirely different surveys, one that measures employment and the other that measures unemployment. The *payroll survey* counts the total number of *jobs* that companies have on their payrolls, while the *household survey* counts the number of *people* who are looking for jobs. The payroll survey, sometimes called the *establishment survey*, collects payroll data from nearly 400,000 business establishments, covering nearly 50 million workers,

---

[2] See John Boyd, Jian Hu, and Ravi Jagannathan, "The Stock Market's Reaction to Unemployment News: Why Bad News Is Usually Good for Stocks," National Bureau of Economic Research (NBER) Working Paper No. W8092, NBER, Cambridge, Mass., January 2001.

about 40 percent of the total workforce. It is this survey that most fore-casters use to judge the future course of the economy. Of the greatest im-portance to traders is the change in the *nonfarm payroll* (the number of farm workers is excluded since it is very volatile and not associated with cyclical economic trends).

The *unemployment rate* is determined from an entirely different sur-vey than the payroll survey. It is the unemployment rate, however, that often gets the top billing in the evening news. The unemployment rate is calculated from a "household survey" in which data from about 60,000 households are accumulated. It asks, among other questions, whether anyone in the household has "actively" sought work over the past four weeks. Those who answer yes are classified as unemployed. The result-ing number of unemployed people is divided by the number of people in the total labor force, which yields the unemployment rate. The labor force in the United States, defined as those employed plus those unem-ployed, comprises about two-thirds of the adult population. This ratio had risen steadily in the 1980s and 1990s as more women have success-fully sought work, but it has stabilized recently.

The BLS statistics can be very tricky to interpret. Because the pay-roll and household data are based on totally different surveys, it is not unusual for payroll employment to go up at the same time that the un-employment rate rises, and vice versa. One reason is because the payroll survey counts jobs, while the household survey counts people. So work-ers with two jobs are counted only once in the household survey but twice in the payroll survey. Furthermore, self-employed individuals are not counted in the payroll survey but are counted in the household sur-vey. Finally, increases in the number seeking work in the early stage of an economic recovery may increase the unemployment rate due to the influx of job seekers into an improved labor market.

For these reasons, economists and forecasters have downplayed the importance of the unemployment rate in forecasting the business cycle. But this does not diminish the political impact of this number. The un-employment rate is an easily understood figure that represents the frac-tion of the workforce looking for but not finding work. Much of the public looks more to this statistic than any other to judge the health of the economy. As a result, pressure to shift policy mounts on politicians and policymakers whenever the unemployment rate rises.

Since 2005, the Automatic Data Processing (ADP) corporation has released its own payroll data, called *The ADP National Employment Re-port*, two days before the BLS labor report. The ADP report is a measure of nonfarm private employment, based on approximately three-fourths

of ADP's 500,000 U.S. business clients and approximately 23 million employees. Because ADP processes the paychecks for 1 out of every 6 private sector employees in the United States every pay period across a broad range of industries, firm sizes, and geographies, ADP's numbers provide a good clue for the upcoming labor data. Early indications are that the ADP number may give a better estimate of payroll changes than the consensus forecast, although more data are needed to confirm this.

THE CYCLE OF ANNOUNCEMENTS

The employment report is just one of several dozen economic announcements that come out every month. The usual release dates for the various data reports that the BLS, the Conference Board, and other entities generate in a typical month is displayed in Table 14-1. The number of asterisks represents the importance of the report to the financial market.

The payroll report is the culmination of important data on economic growth that come out around the turn of the month. On the first business day of each month, a survey by the Institute for Supply Management (ISM, formerly the National Association of Purchasing Managers, the NAPM) called the *purchasing managers index* (PMI) is released.

The institute's report surveys 250 purchasing agents of manufacturing companies and inquires as to whether orders, production,

T A B L E   14–1

Monthly Economic Calendar

Monday	Tuesday	Wednesday	Thursday	Friday
1 10:00 Purchasing Mgrs. Index** (PMI)	2 8:30 Leading Economic Indicator* (2 months lag)	3 8:15 ADP Employment Est.** 10:00 Service PMI**	4 8:30 Jobless Claims**	5 8:30 Employment Report****
8	9	10	11 8:30 Jobless Claims**	12 8:30 Retail Sales** 8:30 Producer Prices****
15	16 8:30 Consumer Prices****	17 8:30 Housing Starts*** 9:15 Industrial Production*	18 8:30 Merchandise Trade* 8:30 Jobless Claims**	19 10:00 Cons. Sentiment (Univ. of Mich., Prelim.)** 12:00 Phila. Fed Rep*
22	23 8:30 Durable Goods Orders**	24	25 8:30 Jobless Claims**	26 8:30 Gross Dom. Prod.*** 8:30 PCE Deflator***
29	30 10:00 Cons. Confidence (Conference Board)***	31 10:00 Chicago Purchasing Managers**		

Stars Rank Importance to Market (**** = most important)

employment, or other indicators are rising or falling, and it forms an index from these data. A reading of 50 means that half the managers report rising activity and half report falling activity. A reading of 52 or 53 is the sign of a normally expanding economy. A reading of 60 represents a strong economy in which three-fifths of the managers report growth. A reading below 50 represents a contracting manufacturing sector, and a reading below 40 is almost always a sign of recession. Two days later, on the third business day of the month, the ISM publishes a similar index for the service sector of the economy.

There are other releases of very timely data reports on manufacturing activity. The Chicago Purchasing Managers report comes out on the last business day of the month, the day before the national PMI report. The Chicago area is well diversified in manufacturing, so about two-thirds of the time the Chicago index will move in the same direction as the national index.

And if you want an even earlier reading on the economy, there are the consumer sentiment indicators: one from the University of Michigan and another from the Conference Board, a business trade association. These surveys query consumers about their current financial situation and their expectations of the future. The Conference Board survey, released on the last Tuesday of the month, is considered a good early indicator of consumer spending. For many years, the University of Michigan monthly index was not published until after the Conference Board release, but pressure for early data reports has persuaded the university to release a preliminary report before the Conference Board.

INFLATION REPORTS

Although the employment report forms the capstone of the news about economic growth, the market knows that the Federal Reserve is equally if not more interested in the inflation data. That's because inflation is the primary variable that the central bank can control in the long run. Some of the earliest signals of inflationary pressures arrive with the midmonth inflation statistics.

The first monthly inflation release is the *producer price index* (PPI), which was known before 1978 as the "wholesale price index." The PPI, first published in 1902, is one of the oldest continuous series of statistical data published by the government.

The PPI measures the prices received by producers for goods sold at the wholesale level, the stage before the goods are resold to the public. About one-quarter of the PPI comes from the price of capital goods sold

to manufacturers, and about 15 percent of the PPI is energy related. There are no services in the producer price index. At the same time the PPI is announced, indexes for the prices of intermediate and crude goods are released, both of which track inflation at earlier stages of production.

The second monthly inflation announcement, which follows the PPI by a day or so, is the all-important *consumer price index* (CPI). The CPI does cover the prices of services as well as goods. Services, which include rent, housing, transportation, and medical services, now comprise over half the weight of the CPI.

The consumer price index is considered the benchmark measure of inflation. When price level comparisons are made, both on a historical and an international basis, the consumer price index is almost always the chosen index. The CPI is also the price index to which so many private and public contracts, as well as Social Security and government tax brackets, are linked.

The financial market probably gives a bit more weight to the consumer price index than to the producer price index because of the CPI's widespread use in indexing and political importance. But many economists regard the producer price index as more sensitive to early price trends as inflation often shows up at the wholesale level before it shows up on the retail level.

Core Inflation

Of importance to the market is not only the overall inflation rate but inflation that excludes the volatile food and energy sectors. Since weather has a great influence on food prices, a rise or fall in the price of food over a month does not have much meaning for the overall inflationary trend. Similarly, the fluctuations of oil and natural gas prices are due to weather conditions, temporary supply disruptions, and speculative trading that do not necessarily persist into future months. To obtain an index of inflation that measures the more persistent and long-term trends of inflation, the government also computes the *core* consumer and producer price indexes, which measure inflation excluding food and energy.

The core rate of inflation is more important to the central banks as it identifies underlying inflation better than changes in the overall index that include food and energy. Forecasters are usually able to predict the core rate of inflation better than the overall rate since the latter is influenced by the volatile food and energy sectors. An error of three-tenths of a percentage point in the consensus forecast for the month-to-month rate of inflation might not be that serious, but such an error would be con-

sidered quite large for the core rate of inflation and would significantly affect the financial markets.

Another inflation indicator that both Fed chairmen Alan Greenspan and Ben Bernanke have supported is the *personal consumption expenditure* (PCE) *deflator*, which is the price index calculated for the consumption component of the GDP accounts. The PCE deflator differs from the consumer price index in that the PCE deflator uses a more up to date weighting scheme and includes the cost of the employer-paid as well as the employee-paid medical insurance.

Employment Costs

Other important releases bearing on inflation relate to labor costs. The monthly employment report issued by the BLS contains data on the hourly wage rate. This report sheds light on cost pressures arising in the labor market. Since labor costs average nearly two-thirds of a firm's production costs, increases in the hourly wage not matched by increases in productivity increase labor costs and threaten to cause inflation.

Every calendar quarter, the government also releases the *employment cost index* (ECI). This index includes benefit costs as well as wages, and it is considered the most comprehensive report of labor costs. The Federal Reserve considers this a more important indicator of inflation than the hourly wage, so the financial markets closely scrutinize these data.

IMPACT ON FINANCIAL MARKETS

The following summarizes the impact of inflation on the financial markets:

> A lower-than-expected inflation report lowers interest rates and boosts bond and stock prices. Inflation worse than expected raises interest rates and depresses stock and bond prices.

That inflation is bad for bonds should come as no surprise. Bonds are fixed-income investments whose cash flows are not adjusted for inflation. Bondholders demand higher interest rates to protect their purchasing power when inflation increases.

Worse-than-expected inflation is also bad for the stock market. As I noted in Chapter 11, stocks have proven to be poor hedges against inflation in the short run. Stock investors know that worsening inflation increases the effective tax rate on both corporate earnings and capital gains and induces the central bank to tighten credit, raising real interest rates.

CENTRAL BANK POLICY

Central bank policy is of primary importance to financial markets. Martin Zweig, a noted money manager has described the relationship this way:

> In the stock market, as with horse racing, money makes the mare go. Monetary conditions exert an enormous influence on stock prices. Indeed, the monetary climate—primarily the trend in interest rates and Federal Reserve policy—is the dominant factor in determining the stock market's major direction.[3]

Chapter 13 showed that four of the top five largest one-day rallies in Wall Street history were involved with monetary policy. Lowering short-term interest rates and providing more credit to the banking system is almost always extremely welcome by stock investors. When the central bank eases credit, it lowers the rate at which stock future cash flows are discounted and stimulates demand, which increases future earnings.

Chapter 11 showed that over the past half century, tightening by the Fed was associated with poor returns over the next year while easing boosted the market. Although the impact of changes in the fed funds rate on 3- to 12-month returns has not been as reliable in recent years as in the past, surprise intermeeting moves by the central bank are as powerful as ever. The unexpected one-half-point cut in the funds rate from 6.5 to 6 percent that took place on January 3, 2001, sent the S&P 500 Index up 5 percent and the tech-heavy Nasdaq up an all-time record 14.2 percent. A smaller, but still substantial response met the Fed's decision to lower the discount rate on August 17, 2007, during the subprime mortgage crisis.

The only case in which stocks will react poorly is if the central bank eases excessively, so that the market fears an increase in inflation. But if the central bank eases excessively, an investor would prefer to be in stocks than bonds, as fixed-income assets are hurt more than stocks by unexpected inflation.

CONCLUSION

The reactions of financial markets to the release of economic data are not random but instead can be predicted by economic analysis. Strong economic growth invariably raises interest rates, but it has an ambiguous

---

[3] Martin Zweig, *Winning on Wall Street*, New York: Warner Books, 1986, p. 43.

effect on stock prices, as higher interest rates battle against stronger corporate profits. Higher inflation is bad for both the stock and bond markets. Central bank easing is very positive for stocks and has historically sparked some of the strongest stock rallies.

Although the most important monthly report for the markets is usually the employment data, the focus of traders constantly shifts. In the 1970s, inflation announcements took center stage, but after Fed chairman Paul Volcker shifted the focus to monetary aggregates, the Thursday afternoon money supply announcements captured the attention of traders. Later, in the 1980s when the dollar soared, trade statistics were given top billing. Employment and inflation reports are always important to the markets, and the central banks' reaction to these data is probably the most important factor that impacts markets.

In the end it should be noted that this chapter focuses on the short-run reaction of financial markets to economic data. Although it is fascinating to observe and understand the market's reaction, investing on the basis of these releases is a tricky game that is best left to speculators who can stomach the short-term volatility. Most investors will do well to watch from the sidelines and stick to an investment strategy for the long run.

PART 4

STOCK FLUCTUATIONS IN THE SHORT RUN

CHAPTER 15

THE RISE OF EXCHANGE-TRADED FUNDS, STOCK INDEX FUTURES, AND OPTIONS

When I was a kid—a runner for Merrill Lynch at 25 dollars a week—I'd heard an old timer say, "The greatest thing to trade would be stock futures—but you can't do that, it's gambling."

LEO MELAMED, 1988[1]

Warren Buffett thinks that stock futures and options ought to be outlawed, and I agree with him.

PETER LYNCH, 1989[2]

If someone were to ask what stock traded the largest dollar volume in the United States in 2006, what would you guess? General Electric, Exxon Mobil, Microsoft? The surprising answer is a stock that was not in

---

[1] Leo Melamed is the founder of the International Money Market, the home of the world's most successful stock index futures market. Quoted in Martin Mayer, *Markets*, New York: Norton, 1988, p. 111.

[2] Peter Lynch, *One Up on Wall Street*, New York: Penguin, 1989, p. 280.

existence before 1993 and does not even represent a company. The security with the highest dollar volume was *spiders*, the nickname given to the S&P 500 Depository Receipts (SPDRs), an exchange-traded fund that represents the value of the S&P 500 Index. In 2006, over 17.6 billion shares were traded, representing a value of over $2.3 trillion.

EXCHANGE-TRADED FUNDS

Exchange-traded funds (ETFs) are the most innovative and successful new financial instruments since stock index futures contracts debuted two decades earlier. ETFs are shares issued by an investment company that represent an underlying portfolio. They are traded throughout the day on an exchange where the prices are determined by supply and demand. Most ETFs issued in the 1990s tracked only well-known stock indexes, but more recently they have been tracking new customized indexes and even actively managed portfolios.

The growth of exchange-traded funds has been explosive. At the end of 2006, ETF assets totaled $422 billion, and although this is only a small fraction of the $10.4 trillion in standard mutual funds, ETFs have grown more than 300 percent since 2002.

Spiders were the first and most successful ETF, launched in 1993. But spiders were soon joined by others, with nicknames like *cubes*, a corruption of the QQQ ticker symbol given to the Nasdaq-100 Index, and *diamonds*, with the ticker DIA, which represents the Dow Jones Industrial Average.

These ETFs track their respective indexes extremely closely. That's because designated institutions, market makers, and large investors, called *authorized participants*, can buy the underlying shares of the stocks in the index and deliver them to the issuer in exchange for units of ETFs and deliver units of ETFs in exchange for the underlying shares. The minimum size for such an exchange, called a *creation unit*, is usually 50,000 shares. For example, an authorized participant who delivers 50,000 shares of spiders to State Street Bank & Trust will receive a prorated number of shares of each member of the S&P 500 Index. These authorized participants keep the prices of the ETFs extremely close to the value of the index. For the active ETFs, such a spiders and cubes, the bid-ask spread is as low as 1 cent.

There are several advantages of ETFs over mutual funds. ETFs, unlike mutual funds, can be bought or sold at any time during the day. Second, an investor can sell ETFs short, hoping to make a profit by buying

them back at a lower price.[3] This proves to be a very convenient way of hedging portfolio gains if an investor fears the market may fall. And finally, ETFs are extremely tax efficient since, unlike mutual funds, they generate almost no capital gains either from the sales of other investors or from portfolio changes to the index. This is because swaps between the ETFs and underlying shares are considered *exchanges in kind* and are not taxable events. Later in this chapter we will list the advantages and disadvantages of ETFs as compared to alternative forms of index investing.

STOCK INDEX FUTURES

ETFs are really the outgrowth of one of the most important trading innovations of the last 50 years—the development of stock index futures in the early 1980s. Despite the enormous popularity of these new exchange-traded funds, the total dollar volume in ETFs is still dwarfed by the dollar volume represented by trading in index futures, most of which began trading in Chicago but are mostly now traded on electronic exchanges. Shifts in overall market sentiment often impact the index futures market first and then are transmitted to stocks traded in New York.

To understand how important index futures were to stock prices in the 1980s and 1990s, one need only look at what happened on April 13, 1992. It began as an ordinary trading day, but at about 11:45 in the morning, the two big Chicago futures exchanges, the Board of Trade and the Mercantile Exchange, were closed when a massive leak from the Chicago River coursed through the tunnels under the financial district and triggered extensive power outages. The intraday movement of the Dow Industrials and the S&P futures is shown in Figure 15-1. As soon as the Chicago futures trading was halted, the volatility of the stock market declined significantly.

It almost looks as if the New York Stock Exchange went "brain dead" when there was no lead from Chicago. The volume in New York dropped by more than 25 percent on the day the Chicago futures market was closed; and some dealers claimed that if the futures exchange remained inoperative, it would cause liquidity problems and difficulty in executing some trades in New York.[4] Michael Metz, a market strategist at Oppenheimer & Co., declared: "It's been absolutely delightful; it

---

[3] ETFs are exempt from the uptick rule that until recently restricted shorting stock when the price is falling.

[4] Robert Steiner, "Industrials Gain 14.53 in Trading Muted by Futures Halt in Chicago," *Wall Street Journal*, April 14, 1992, p. C2.

F I G U R E   15–1

When Stock Index Futures Closed Down, April 13, 1992

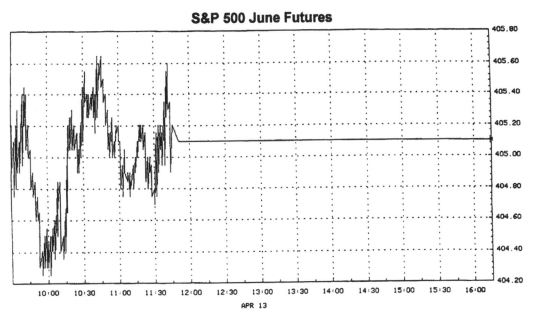

S&P 500 June Futures

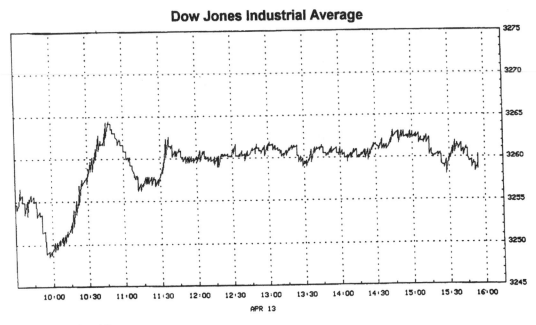

Dow Jones Industrial Average

SOURCE: Bloomberg L.P.

seems so sedate. It reminds me of the halcyon days on Wall Street before the program traders took hold."[5]

Who are these *program traders* that investors hear so much about, and what do they do? The floor of the New York Stock Exchange has always been alive with a constant din of people scurrying about delivering orders and making deals. But in the mid-1980s, just a few years after index futures were introduced, the background noise was punctuated every so often by the rat-tat-tat of dozens of automated machines printing hundreds of buy or sell tickets. These orders were almost always from stock index futures *arbitrageurs*—that is, program traders who rely on differences between the prices of stock index futures traded in Chicago and the prices of the component stocks traded in New York.

The noise signaled that the futures market was moving quickly in Chicago and stock prices would soon change accordingly in New York. It was an eerie warning, something akin to the buzz of locusts in biblical times, portending decimated crops and famine. And famine it might be, for during the 1980s and early 1990s some of the most vicious declines in stock prices have been preceded by computers tapping out orders emanating from the futures markets.

In those days, changes in the overall level of stocks did not originate on Wall Street but on Wacker Drive at the Chicago Mercantile Exchange. *Specialists* on the New York Stock Exchange, those dealers assigned to make and supervise markets in specific stocks, kept their eyes glued on the futures markets to find out where stocks would be heading. These dealers learned from experience not to stand in the way of index futures when they are moving quickly. If they did, they might get caught in an avalanche of trading such as the one that buried several specialists on October 19, 1987, that fateful day when the Dow crashed nearly 23 percent.

BASICS OF THE FUTURES MARKETS

Most investors regard index futures and exchange-traded funds as esoteric securities that have little to do with the market in which stocks are bought and sold. Many investors do very well trading stocks without any knowledge of these new instruments. But no one can comprehend the short-run market movements without an understanding of stock index futures and ETFs.

---

[5] "Flood in Chicago Waters Down Trading on Wall Street," *Wall Street Journal*, April 14, 1992, p. C1. Today the proliferation of electronic trading has made it impossible for an incident such as the one that crippled the Chicago exchange 15 years ago to happen again.

Futures trading goes back hundreds of years. The term *futures* was derived from the promise to buy or deliver a commodity at some future date at some specified price. Futures trading first flourished in agricultural crops, where farmers wanted to have a guaranteed price for the crops they would harvest at a later date. Markets developed where buyers and sellers who wanted to avoid uncertainty could come to an agreement on the price for future delivery. The commitments to honor these agreements, called *futures contracts*, were freely transferable, and markets developed where they were actively traded.

Stock index futures were launched in February 1982 by the Kansas City Board of Trade using the Value Line Index of about 1,700 stocks. But two months later, at the Mercantile Exchange in Chicago, the world's most successful stock index future, based on the S&P 500 Index, was introduced. By 1984, the value of the contracts traded on this index future surpassed the dollar volume on the New York Stock Exchange for all stocks. Today, the value of stocks represented by S&P 500 futures trading exceeds $100 billion *per day*.

All stock index futures are constructed similarly. In the case of the seller, the S&P Index future is a promise to deliver a fixed multiple of the value of the S&P 500 Index at some date in the future, called a *settlement date*. In the case of the buyer, the S&P Index future is a promise to receive a fixed multiple of the S&P 500 Index's value. The multiple for the S&P Index future is 250, so if the S&P 500 Index is 1,400, the value of one contract is $350,000. In 1998, a *mini* version of the contract (called an *e-mini*), with a multiple of 50 times the index, was offered, and it trades on the electronic markets. The dollar volume of these minis now far exceeds that of the standard-sized contracts.

There are four evenly spaced settlement dates each year. They fall on the third Friday of March, June, September, and December. Each settlement date corresponds to a contract. If you buy a futures contract, you are entitled to receive (if *positive*) or obligated to pay (if *negative*) 250 times the difference between the value of the S&P 500 Index on the settlement date and the price at which you purchased the contract.

For example, if you buy one September S&P futures contract at 1,400, and on that third Friday of September the S&P 500 Index is at 1,410, you have made 10 points, which translates into $2,500 profit ($250 times 10 points). Of course, if the index has fallen to 1,390 on the settlement date, you will lose $2,500. For every point the S&P 500 Index goes up or down, you make or lose $250 per contract.

On the other hand, the returns to the seller of an S&P 500 futures contract are the mirror image of the returns to the buyer. The seller

makes money when the index falls. In the previous example, the seller of the S&P 500 futures contract at 1,400 will lose $2,500 if the index at settlement date rises to 1,410, while he or she would make the same amount if the index fell to 1,390.

One source of the popularity of stock index futures is their unique settlement procedure. With a standard futures contract, if you bought it, you would be obligated at settlement to receive, or if you sold it, you would be obligated to deliver, a specified quantity of the good for which you have contracted. Many apocryphal stories abound about how traders, forgetting to close out their contract, find bushels of wheat, corn, or frozen pork bellies dumped on their lawn on settlement day.

If commodity delivery rules applied to the S&P 500 Index futures contracts, delivery would require a specified number of shares for each of the 500 firms in the index. Surely this would be extraordinarily cumbersome and costly. To avoid this problem, the designers of the stock index futures contract specified that settlement be made in cash, computed simply by taking the difference between the contract price at the time of the trade and the value of the index on the settlement date. No delivery of stock takes place. If a trader does not close a contract before settlement, his or her account would just be debited or credited on settlement date.

The creation of cash-settled futures contracts was no easy matter. In most states, particularly Illinois where the large futures exchanges are located, settling a futures contract in cash was considered a wager—and wagering, except in some special circumstances, was illegal. In 1974, however, the Commodity Futures Trading Commission, a federal agency, was established by Congress to regulate all futures trading. Since futures trading was now governed by this new federal agency and since there was no federal prohibition against wagering, the prohibitory state laws were superseded.

INDEX ARBITRAGE

The prices of commodities (or financial assets) in the futures market do not stand apart from the prices of the underlying commodity. If the value of a futures contract rises sufficiently above the price of the commodity that can be purchased for immediate delivery in the open market, often called the *cash* or *spot market*, traders can buy the commodity, store it, and then deliver it at a profit against the higher-priced futures contract on the settlement date. If the price of a futures contract falls too far below its current spot price, owners of the commodity can sell it

today, buy the futures contract, and take delivery of the commodity later at a lower price—in essence, earning a return on goods that would be in storage anyway.

Such a process of buying and selling commodities against their futures contracts is one type of arbitrage. Arbitrage involves traders who take advantage of temporary discrepancies in the prices of identical or nearly identical goods or assets. Those who reap profits from such trades are called *arbitrageurs*.

Arbitrage is very common in both the stock index futures market and the ETF market. If the price of futures contracts sufficiently exceeds that of the underlying S&P 500 Index, it pays for arbitrageurs to buy the underlying stocks and sell the futures contracts. If the futures price falls sufficiently below that of the index, arbitrageurs will sell the underlying stocks and buy the futures. On the settlement date, the futures price must equal the underlying index by the terms of the contract, so the difference between the futures price and the index—called a *premium* if it is positive and a *discount* if it is negative—is an opportunity for profit.

Arbitrage in the ETF market is similar, except here an arbitrageur must buy or sell all the stocks in the index and simultaneously make an offsetting transaction in the ETF in the open market. An arbitrageur in the ETF makes a profit when the prices of the stocks that she buys to create the ETF are less than the funds that she receives by selling, or *creating*, an ETF. Alternatively if the prices she receives from selling the stocks in the index exceed the cost of buying the ETF, the arbitrageur will buy the ETF, exchange it into its component stocks, and sell them in the open market.

Index arbitrage has become a finely tuned art. The prices of stock index futures and ETFs usually stay within very narrow bands of the index value based on the price of the underlying shares. When the buying or selling of stock index futures or ETFs drives the price outside this band, arbitrageurs step in, and a flood of orders to buy or sell are immediately transmitted to the exchanges that trade the underlying stocks in the index. These simultaneously placed orders are called *programmed trading*, and they consist of either *buy programs* or *sell programs*. When market commentators talk about "sell programs hitting the market," they mean that index arbitrageurs are selling stock and buying futures or ETFs that have fallen to a discount.

PREDICTING THE NEW YORK OPEN WITH GLOBEX TRADING

Although trading index futures closes at 4:15 p.m. Eastern time, 15 minutes after the close of the New York stock exchanges, trading reopens in

index futures at 4:30 in an electronic market called *Globex*. Globex has no centralized floor, and traders post their bids and offers on computer screens where all interested parties have instant access. Trading in Globex proceeds all night until 9:15 the next morning, 15 minutes before the start of stock trading in New York.[6]

Index futures trading can be active just after the close of regular trading on the NYSE and Nasdaq. This trading is especially popular in the weeks following the end of a quarter when many firms release their earnings reports and give guidance about future earnings and revenues. Unless there is important breaking news, trading is usually slow during the night hours, although activity can pick up if there is dramatic movement on the Tokyo or European stock exchanges. Trading again becomes very active around 8:30 a.m., when many of the government economic data, such as the employment report and the consumer price index, are announced.[7]

Market watchers can use the Globex futures in the S&P, Nasdaq, and the Dow to predict how the market will open in New York. The *fair market value* of these index futures are calculated based on the arbitrage conditions between the future and current prices of stocks.

The fair market value for the futures contract is determined on the basis of the current index value when markets are open and on the previous closing level when markets are closed. Because of the continuous stream of news, the futures price overnight will usually be either above or below the fair market value computed at the close. If, for instance, better-than-expected earnings reports came out after the market closed, then the futures price will trade above fair market value computed on the basis of previous closing prices. The amount by which the futures price trades above or below its fair market value will be the best estimate of where stocks will trade when the exchanges open. Many financial news channels post the overnight trading in the S&P 500, Dow, and Nasdaq futures to inform viewers of the likely opening of the market.

The formula to calculate the fair market value depends on two variables: the dividend yield on stocks and the interest rate. If an investor puts a sum of money today in risk-free bonds, that sum will earn interest at the ongoing interest rate. If instead the investor buys a portfolio of stocks and simultaneously sells a one-year futures contract that guarantees the price of those stocks one year from now, the investor will earn the

---

[6] In Chapter 13, we examined the reaction of S&P futures to the terrorist attacks on the morning of September 11, 2001.

[7] In Chapter 14 we noted the dramatic fall in the S&P futures traded on the Globex that occurred in response to the strong July 5, 1996, employment report.

dividend yield on stocks and be guaranteed a return on his or her stocks that is the difference between the futures price and the current price.

Since both these investments deliver a guaranteed, riskless sum, they must earn the same rate of return. That means that the futures price for stocks must be sufficiently above the current price to compensate the investor for the difference between the yield on stocks and the yield on bonds. In other words, the futures price must be above the current price (in percentage terms) by $i - d$, the interest rate minus the dividend yield.[8]

DOUBLE AND TRIPLE WITCHING

Index futures play some strange games with stock prices on the days when futures contracts expire. Recall that index arbitrage works through the simultaneous buying or selling of stocks against futures contracts. On the day that contracts expire, arbitrageurs unwind their stock positions at precisely the same time that the futures contracts expire.

Index futures contracts expire on the third Friday of the last month of each quarter: in March, June, September, and December. Index options and options on individual stocks, which are described later in the chapter, settle on the third Friday of every month. Hence four times a year, all three types of contracts expire at once. This expiration has in the past produced violent price movements in the market, and it is consequently termed a *triple witching hour*. The third Friday of a month when there are no futures contract settlements is called a *double witching*, and it displays less volatility than triple witching.

There is no mystery why the market is volatile during double or triple witching dates. On these days, the specialists on the New York Stock Exchange and the market makers on the Nasdaq are instructed to buy or sell large blocks of stock on the close, whatever the price, because institutional investors are closing out their arbitrage positions. If there is a huge imbalance of buy orders, prices will soar; if sell orders predominate, prices will plunge. These swings, however, do not matter to arbitrageurs since the profit on the future position will offset losses on the stock position, and vice versa.

In 1988, the New York Stock Exchange urged the Chicago Mercantile Exchange to change its procedures and stop futures trading at the close of Thursday's trading and settle the contracts at Friday opening prices rather than at Friday closing prices. This change gave specialists

---

[8] If the dividend yield is more than the interest rate, then the futures price will be below the current price.

more time to seek out balancing bids and offers, and it has greatly moderated the movements in stock prices on triple witching dates.

MARGIN AND LEVERAGE

One of the reasons for the popularity of futures contracts is that the cash needed to enter into the trade is a very small part of the value of the contract. Unlike stocks, there is no money that transfers between the buyer and seller when a futures contract is bought or sold. A small amount of good-faith collateral, or *margin*, is required by the broker from both the buyer and seller to ensure that both parties will honor the contract at settlement. For the S&P 500 Index, the current initial margin is about 5 percent of the value of the contract. This margin can be kept in Treasury bills with interest accruing to the investor, so trading a futures contract involves neither a transfer of cash nor a loss of interest income.

The *leverage*, or the amount of stock that you control relative to the amount of margin you have to put down with a futures contract, is enormous. For every dollar of cash (or Treasury bills) that you put in margin against an S&P futures contract, you command about $20 of stock. And for *day trading*, when you close your positions by the end of the day, the margin requirements are significantly less. These low margins contrast with the 50 percent margin requirement for the purchase of individual stocks that has prevailed since 1974.

This ability to control $20 or more of stock with $1 of cash is reminiscent of the rampant speculation that existed in the 1920s before the establishment of minimum stock margin requirements. In the 1920s, individual stocks were frequently purchased with a 10 percent margin. It was popular to speculate with such borrowed money, for as long as the market was rising, few investors lost money. But if the market dropped precipitously, margin buyers often found that not only did they lose their equity but they were also indebted to the brokerage firm. Buying futures contracts with low margins can result in similar repercussions today. The tendency of low margins to fuel market volatility is discussed in Chapter 16.

USING ETFs OR FUTURES

The use of ETFs or index futures greatly increases an investor's flexibility to manage portfolios. Suppose an investor has built up gains in individual stocks but is now getting nervous about the market. Selling one's individual stocks may trigger a large tax liability.

But by using ETFs (or futures), a good solution is available. The investor sells enough ETFs to cover the value of the portfolio that he seeks to hedge and continues to hold his individual stocks. If the market declines, the investor profits on his ETF position, offsetting the losses of the stock portfolio. If the market instead goes up, contrary to expectation, the loss on ETFs will be offset by the gains on the individual stock holdings. This is called *hedging stock market risk*. Since the investor never sells his individual stocks, he triggers no tax liability from these positions.

Another advantage of ETFs is that they can yield a profit from a decline in the market even if one does not own any stock. Selling ETFs substitutes for *shorting stock*, or selling stock you do not own in anticipation that the price will fall and you can buy it back at a lower price. Using ETFs to bet on a falling market is much more convenient than shorting a portfolio of stocks since regulations prohibit individual stocks from being shorted if their price is declining, but ETFs are exempt from this rule.

WHERE TO PUT YOUR INDEXED INVESTMENTS: ETFs, FUTURES, OR INDEX MUTUAL FUNDS?

With the development of index futures and ETFs, investors have three major choices to match the performance of one of many stock indexes: exchange-traded funds, index futures, and index mutual funds.[9] The important characteristics of each type of investment are given in Table 15-1.

As far as trading flexibility, ETFs and index futures far outshine mutual funds. ETFs and index futures can be bought or sold any time during the trading day and after hours on the Globex and other exchanges. In contrast, mutual funds can be bought or sold only at the market close, and the investor's order must often be in several hours earlier. ETFs and index futures can also be shorted to hedge one's portfolio or speculate on a market decline, which mutual funds cannot. And ETFs can be margined like any stock (with current Fed regulations at 50 percent), while index futures possess the highest degree of leverage, as investors can control stocks worth 20 or more times the value of cash.

The trading flexibility of ETFs or futures can be either a bane or a boon to investors. It is easy to overreact to the continuous stream of optimistic and pessimistic news, causing an investor to sell near the low or buy near the high. Furthermore, the ability to short stocks (except for hedging) or to leverage might tempt investors to play their short-term hunches on the market. This is a very dangerous game. For most in-

---

[9] Index mutual funds are described in detail in Chapter 20.

T A B L E   15–1

Comparison of Indexed Investments

	ETFs	Index Futures	Index Mutual Funds
Continuous Trading	Yes	Yes	No
Can Be Sold Short	Yes	Yes	No
Leverage	Can Borrow 50%	Can Borrow over 90%	None
Expense Ratio	Extremely Low	None	Very Low
Trading Costs	Stock Commission	Futures Commission	None
Dividend Reinvestment	Yes*	No†	Yes
Tax Efficiency	Extremely Good	Poor	Very Good

*Depends on policy of brokerage firm
†Dividends built into price

vestors, restricting the frequency of trades and reducing leverage is beneficial to their total returns.

On the cost side, all these vehicles are very efficient. Index mutual funds are available at an annual cost of 20 basis points or less a year, and most ETFs are even cheaper. But both ETFs and futures must be bought through a brokerage account, and this involves paying both a commission and a "bid-ask spread," although these are quite low for actively traded indexes. On the other hand, most index funds are *no-load funds*, meaning there is no commission when the fund is bought or sold. Furthermore, although index futures involve no annual costs, these contracts must be rolled over into new contracts at least once a year, entailing additional commissions.

It is on the tax side that ETFs really shine. Because of the structure of ETFs, these funds generate very few if any capital gains. Index mutual funds are also very tax efficient, but they do throw off capital gains. This means funds must sell individual shares from their portfolio if investors redeem their shares or if stocks are removed from the index. Although capital gains have been small for most index funds, they are larger than ETFs.[10] Futures are not tax efficient since any gains or losses must be realized at the end of the year whether the contracts are sold or not.

Of course, these tax differences between ETFs and index mutual funds do not matter if an investor holds these funds in a tax-sheltered account, such as an individual retirement account (IRA) or a Keogh plan (futures are not allowed in these accounts). However, if these funds are held in taxable accounts, the after-tax return on ETFs is apt to be higher than it would be for even the most efficient index fund.

---

[10] From 1997 through 2006, there was no capital gain distribution from spiders (S&P 500 ETFs), while the Vanguard 500 Index Fund has had several (although none since 2000).

The bottom line is that unless you like to speculate and leverage your cash, you will want to avoid index futures. However, if you want to speculate on the direction of the market, I recommend *index options*, which are described below and which limit an investor's loss.

Whether to hold ETFs or low-cost index mutual funds is a very close decision. If you like to move in and out of the market frequently (which I do not recommend), ETFs are for you. If you like to invest in the market on a monthly basis or automatically reinvest your dividends, then no-load index funds may be the better instrument. However, in recent years automatic reinvestment of dividends has become possible for stocks and ETFs if you specify that option to your brokerage firm. This development further tips the scale in favor of ETFs over index mutual funds.

INDEX OPTIONS

Although ETFs and index futures are very important to investment professionals and institutions, the options market has caught the fancy of many investors. And this is not surprising. The beauty of an option is embedded in its very name: you have the option, but not the obligation, to buy or sell stocks or indexes at a given price by a given time. For the option buyer, this option, in contrast to the futures, automatically limits your maximum liability to the amount you invested.

There are two major types of options: puts and calls. *Calls* give you the right to buy a stock (or stocks) at a fixed price within a given period of time. *Puts* give you the right to sell a stock. Puts and calls have existed on individual stocks for decades, but they were not bought and sold through an organized trading system until the establishment of the Chicago Board Options Exchange (CBOE) in 1974.

What attracts investors to puts and calls is that liability is strictly limited. If the market moves against options buyers, they can forfeit the purchase price, forgoing the option to buy or sell. This contrasts sharply with futures contracts with which, if the market goes against buyers, losses can mount quickly. In a volatile market, futures can be extremely risky, and it could be impossible for investors to exit a contract without substantial losses.

In 1978, the CBOE began trading options on the popular stock indexes, such as the S&P 500 Index.[11] The CBOE options trade in multiples

---

[11] In fact, the largest 100 stocks of the S&P 500 Index, called the "S&P 100," comprise the most popularly traded index options. Options based on the S&P 500 Index are more widely used by institutional investors.

of $100 per point of index value—cheaper than the $250-per-point multiple on the popular S&P 500 Index futures.

An index allows investors to buy the stock index at a set price within a given period of time. Assume that the S&P 500 Index is now selling for 1,400, but you believe that the market is going to rise. Let us assume you can purchase a call option at 1,450 for three months for 30 points, or $3,000. The purchase price of the option is called the *premium*, and the price at which the option has value when it expires—in this case 1,450—is called the *strike price*. At any time within the next three months you can, if you choose, exercise your option and receive $100 for every point that the S&P 500 Index is above 1,450.

You need not exercise your option to make a profit. There is an extremely active market for options, and you can always sell them before expiration to other investors. In this example, the S&P 500 Index will have to rise above 1,480 for you to show a profit if you hold until the expiration, since you paid $3,000 for the option. But the beauty of options is that, if you guessed wrong and the market falls, the most you can lose is the $3,000 premium you paid.

An index put works exactly the same way as a call, but in this case the buyer makes money if the market goes down. Assume you buy a put on the S&P 500 Index at 1,350, paying a $3,000 premium. Every point the S&P 500 Index is below 1,350 at expiration will recoup $100 of your initial premium. If the index falls to 1,320 by expiration, you have broken even. Every point below 1,320 gives you a profit on your option.

The price that you pay for an index option is determined by the market and depends on many factors, including interest rates and dividend yields. But the most important factor is the expected volatility of the market itself. Clearly, the more volatile the market, the more expensive it is to buy either puts or calls. In a dull market, it is unlikely that the market will move sufficiently high (in the case of a call) or low (in the case of a put) to give options buyers a profit. If this low volatility is expected to continue, the prices of options are low. In contrast, in volatile markets, the premiums on puts and calls are bid up as traders consider it more likely that the options will have value by the time of their expiration.[12]

The price of options depends on the judgments of traders as to the likelihood that the market will move sufficiently to make the rights to buy or sell stock at a fixed price valuable. But the theory of options pricing was given a big boost in the 1970s when two academic economists, Fischer Black and Myron Scholes, developed the first mathematical for-

---

[12] Chapter 16 will discuss a valuable index of option volatility called *VIX*.

mula to price options. The *Black-Scholes formula* was an instant success. It gave traders a benchmark for valuation where previously they used only their intuition. The formula was programmed on traders' handheld calculators and PCs around the world. Although there are conditions when the formula must be modified, empirical research has shown that the Black-Scholes formula closely approximates the price of traded options. Myron Scholes won the Nobel Prize in Economics in 1997 for his discovery.[13]

Buying Index Options

Options are actually more basic instruments than futures or ETFs. You can replicate any future or ETF with options, but the reverse is not true. Options offer the investor far more strategies than futures. Such strategies can range from the very speculative to the extremely conservative.

Suppose you want to be protected against a decline in the market. You can buy an index put, which increases in value as the market declines. Of course, you have to pay a premium for this option, very much like an insurance premium. If the market does not decline, you have forfeited your premium. But if it does decline, the increase in the value of your put has cushioned, if not completely offset, the decline in your stock portfolio.

Another advantage of puts is that you can buy just the amount of protection that you like. If you want to protect yourself against only a total collapse in the market, you can buy a put that is way *out-of-the-money*, in other words, a put whose strike price is far below that of the current level of the index. This option pays off only if the market declines precipitously. In addition, you can also buy puts with a strike price above the current market, so the option retains some value even if the market does not decline. Of course, these *in-the-money* puts are far more expensive.

There are many recorded examples of fantastic gains in puts and calls. But for every option that gains so spectacularly in value, there are thousands of options that expire worthless. Some market professionals estimate that 85 percent of individual investors who play the options market lose money. Not only do options buyers have to be right about

---

[13] The original article was published in 1973: Fischer Black and Myron Scholes, "The Pricing of Options and Corporate Liabilities," *Journal of Political Economy*, vol. 81, no. 3, pp. 637–654. Fischer Black was deceased when the Nobel Prize was awarded in 1997. Myron Scholes shared the Nobel Prize with William Sharpe and Bob Merton, the latter contributing to the discovery of the formula.

the direction of the market but also their timing must be nearly perfect, and their selection of the strike price must be appropriate.

Selling Index Options

Of course, for anyone who buys an option, someone must sell—or write—an options contract. The sellers, or writers, of call options believe that the market will not rise sufficiently to make a profit for options buyers. Sellers of call options usually make money when they sell options since the vast majority of options expire worthless. But should the market move sharply against the options sellers, their losses could be enormous.

For that reason, most sellers of call options are investors who already own stock. This strategy, called *buy and write*, is popular with many investors since it is seen as a win-win proposition. If stocks go down, they collect a premium from buyers of the call, and so they are better off than if they had not written the option. If stocks do nothing, they also collect the premium on the call, and they are still better off. If stocks go up, call writers still gain more on the stocks they own than they lose on the call they wrote, so they are still ahead. Of course, if stocks go up strongly, they miss some of the rally since they have promised to deliver stock at a fixed price. In that case, call writers certainly would have been better off if they had not sold the call. But they still make more money than if they had not owned the stocks at all.

The buyers of put options are insuring their stock against price declines. But who are the sellers of these options? They are primarily those who are willing to buy the stock, but only if the price declines. A seller of a put collects a premium, but he or she receives the stock only if it falls sufficiently to go below the strike price. Since put sellers are not as common as call sellers, premiums on puts that are out-of-the-money are frequently quite high.

THE IMPORTANCE OF INDEXED PRODUCTS

The development of stock index futures and options in the 1980s was a major development for investors and money managers. Heavily capitalized firms, such as those represented in the Dow Jones Industrial Average, have always attracted money because of their outstanding liquidity. But with stock index futures, investors were able to buy the whole market, such as represented by the popular indexes.

Ten years later, exchange-traded funds gave investors still another way to diversify across all markets at low cost. These ETFs had the fa-

miliarity of stocks but, like index futures, much higher liquidity and superior tax efficiency. Today when investors want to take a position in the market, it is most easily done with stock index futures or exchange-traded funds. Index options give investors the ability to insure the value of their portfolio at the lowest possible price and save on transaction costs and taxes.

Despite the opposition of such notable investors as Warren Buffett and Peter Lynch, there is no hard evidence that these index products have increased volatility or harmed investors. In fact, it is my belief that these index products have increased the liquidity of the world's stock markets, enabled better diversification, and led to higher stock prices than would be available without them.

CHAPTER 16

MARKET VOLATILITY

The word crisis in Chinese is composed of two characters: the first, the symbol of danger, . . . the second, of opportunity.

A comparison of the Dow Jones Industrial Average from 1922 through 1932 and 1980 through 1990 is shown in Figure 16-1. There is an uncanny similarity between these two bull markets. In October 1987, the editors of the *Wall Street Journal*, looking at the then-incomplete version of the chart shown in Figure 16-1b, felt the similarity was so portentous that they printed a similar comparison in the paper that hit the streets on Monday morning, October 19, 1987. Little did they know that that day would witness the greatest one-day drop in stock market history, exceeding the great crash of October 29, 1929. Ominously, the market continued to trade very much like 1929 for the remainder of the year. Many forecasters, citing the similarities between the two periods, were certain that disaster loomed and advised their clients to sell everything.

But the similarity between the 1929 and the 1987 episodes stopped at year's end. The stock market recovered from its October 1987 crash, and by August 1989, it hit new high ground. In contrast, two years after the October 1929 crash, the Dow, in the throes of the greatest bear market in U.S. history, had lost more than two-thirds of its value and was about to lose two-thirds more.

1929 and 1987 Stock Crashes

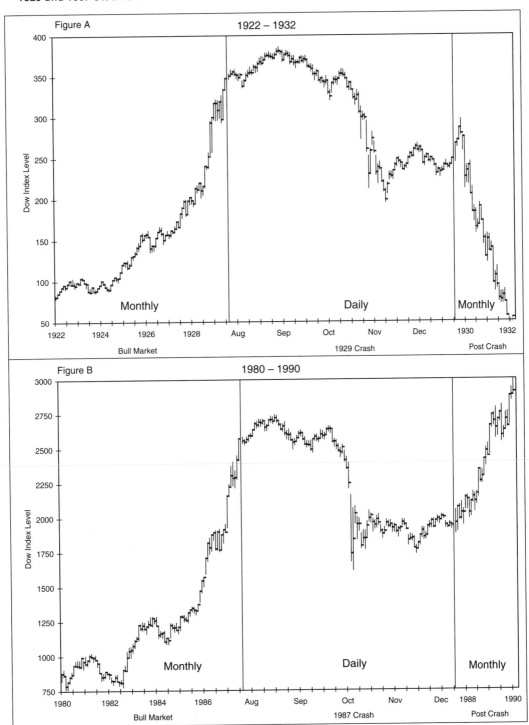

Figure A — 1922 – 1932

Figure B — 1980 – 1990

What was different? Why did the eerie similarities between these two events eventually diverge so dramatically? The simple answer is that in 1987 the central bank had the power to control the ultimate source of liquidity in the economy—the supply of money. And, in contrast to 1929, it did not hesitate to use it. Heeding the painful lessons of its mistakes in the early 1930s, the Fed temporarily flooded the economy with money and pledged to stand by all bank deposits to ensure that all aspects of the financial system would function properly.

The public was assured. There were no runs on banks, no contraction of the money supply, and no deflation in commodity and asset values. Indeed, the economy itself expanded despite the market collapse. The October 1987 stock market crash taught investors an important lesson—the world was indeed different from 1929 and a sharp sell-off can be an opportunity for profit, not a time to panic.

THE STOCK MARKET CRASH OF OCTOBER 1987

The stock crash of Monday, October 19, 1987, was one of the most dramatic financial events of the postwar era. The 508-point, or 22.6 percent, decline in the Dow Jones Industrials from 2,247 to 1,739 was by far the largest point drop up to that time and the largest one-day percentage drop in all history. Volume on the New York Stock Exchange soared to an all-time record, exceeding 600 million shares on both Monday and Tuesday, and for that fateful week the number of shares traded exceeded the volume for all of 1966.

The crash on Wall Street reverberated around the world. Tokyo, which two years later was going to enter its own massive bear market, fell the least, but it still experienced a record one-day drop of 15.6 percent. Stocks in New Zealand fell nearly 40 percent, and the Hong Kong market closed because collapsing prices brought massive defaults in their stock index futures market. In the United States alone, stock values on that infamous day dropped about $500 billion, and the total worldwide decline in stock values exceeded $1 trillion. A similar percentage decline in today's market would wipe out more than $7 trillion worldwide, a sum greater than the gross national product of every country but the United States.[1]

The stock market decline began in earnest the week prior to "Black Monday," as October 19 came to be called. At 8:30 a.m. on the preceding

---

[1] This is based on a $31.6 trillion worldwide total stock value in 2007, float adjusted. The sum would be much larger if we included the value of government-held shares in emerging markets.

Wednesday, the Department of Commerce reported that the United States suffered a $15.7 billion merchandise trade deficit, which at that time was one of the largest in U.S. history and far in excess of market expectations. The reaction in the financial markets was immediate. Yields on long government bonds rose to over 10 percent for the first time since November 1985, and the dollar declined sharply. The Dow Industrials fell 95 points on Wednesday, a record point drop at that time.

The situation continued to worsen on Thursday and Friday as the Dow fell 166 more points, to 2,246. Late Friday afternoon, about 15 minutes prior to close, heavy selling hit the stock index futures markets in Chicago. The indexes had fallen below crucial support levels, which led to the barrage of selling in Chicago by those wanting to get out of stocks at almost any price.

The December S&P 500 futures contract fell to an unprecedented 6 points (or almost 3 percent) below the spot index. The development of such a wide discount meant that money managers were willing to sell large orders at a significant concession in order to sell fast, rather than risk that their sell orders for individual stocks might sit in New York, unexecuted. At the close of trading on Friday, the stock market had experienced its worst week in nearly five decades.

Before New York opened the following Monday, there were ominous portents from the world markets. Overnight in Tokyo, the Nikkei average fell 2½ percent, and there were sharp declines in Sydney and Hong Kong. In London, prices had fallen by 10 percent as many money managers were trying to sell U.S. stocks trading there before the anticipated decline hit New York.

Trading on the New York Stock Exchange on Black Monday was chaotic. No Dow Jones Industrial stock traded near the 9:30 opening bell, and only 7 Dow stocks traded before 9:45. By 10:30, 11 Dow stocks still had not opened. "Portfolio insurers," described later in this chapter, heavily sold stock index futures, trying to insulate their clients' exposure to the plunging market. By late afternoon, the S&P 500 Index futures were selling at a 25-point, or 12 percent, discount to the spot market, a spread that was previously considered inconceivable. By the late afternoon, huge sell orders transmitted by program sellers cascaded onto the New York Exchange through the computerized system. The Dow Industrials collapsed almost 300 points in the final hour of trading, bringing the toll for the day to a record 508 points, or 22.6 percent.

Although October 19 is remembered in history as the day of the great stock crash, it was actually the next day—"Terrible Tuesday," as

it has become known—that the market almost failed. After opening up over 10 percent from Monday's low, the market began to plunge by midmorning, and shortly after noon it fell below its Monday close. The S&P 500 Index futures market collapsed to 181—an incredible 40 points, or 22 percent, under the reported index value. If index arbitrage had been possible, the futures prices would have dictated a Dow at 1,450. Stock prices in the world's largest market, on this calculation, were off nearly 50 percent from their high of 2,722 set just seven weeks earlier.

It was at this time that near meltdown hit the market. The NYSE did not close, but trading was halted in almost 200 stocks. For the first time, trading was also halted in the S&P 500 Index futures in Chicago.

The only futures market of any size that remained open was the Major Market Index that traded on the Chicago Board of Trade and represented blue-chip stocks similar to the Dow Industrials. These blue chips were selling at such deep discounts to the prices in New York that values proved irresistible to some speculators. And since it was the only market that remained open, buyers stepped in and futures shot up an equivalent of 120 Dow points, or almost 10 percent, in a matter of minutes. When traders and the exchange specialists saw the buying come back into the blue chips, prices rallied in New York and the worst of the market panic passed. A subsequent investigative report by the *Wall Street Journal* indicated that this futures market was a key to reversing the catastrophic market collapse.[2]

THE CAUSES OF THE OCTOBER 1987 CRASH

There was no single precipitating event—such as a declaration of war, a terrorist act, an assassination, or a bankruptcy—that caused Black Monday. However, worrying trends had threatened the rising stock market for some time: sharply higher long-term rates caused by a falling dollar and the rapid development of a new strategy, called *portfolio insurance*, that was designed to insulate portfolios from a decline in the overall market. The latter was born from the explosive growth of stock index futures markets detailed in the previous chapter, markets that did not even exist six years earlier.

---

[2] James Stewart and Daniel Hertzberg, "How the Stock Market Almost Disintegrated a Day after the Crash," *Wall Street Journal*, November 20, 1987, p. 1.

Exchange-Rate Policies

The roots of the surge in interest rates that preceded the October 1987 stock market crash are found in the futile attempts by the United States and other G7 countries (Japan, the United Kingdom, Germany, France, Italy, and Canada) to prevent the dollar from falling in the international exchange markets.

The dollar had bounded to unprecedented levels in the middle of the 1980s on the heels of huge Japanese and European purchases of dollar securities and a strong U.S. economy. Foreign investors were attracted to high dollar interest rates, in part driven by record U.S. budget deficits but also by a strengthening of the U.S. economy and the capital-friendly presidency of Ronald Reagan. By February 1985, the dollar became massively overvalued and U.S. exports became very uncompetitive, severely worsening the U.S. trade deficit. The dollar then reversed course and began a steep decline.

Central bankers initially cheered the fall of the overpriced dollar, but they grew concerned when the dollar continued to decline and the U.S. trade deficit, instead of improving, worsened. Finance ministers met in February 1987 in Paris with the goal of supporting the dollar. They worried that if the dollar became too cheap, their own exports to the United States, which had grown substantially when the dollar was high, would suffer.

The Federal Reserve reluctantly participated in the dollar stabilization program, whose success depended on either an improvement in the U.S. trade position or, absent that, a commitment by the Federal Reserve to raise interest rates to support the dollar.

But the trade deficit did not improve; in fact, it worsened after the initiation of the exchange stabilization policies. Traders, nervous about the deteriorating U.S. trade balance, demanded ever higher interest rates to hold U.S. assets. Leo Melamed, chairman of the Chicago Mercantile Exchange, was blunt when asked about the origins of Black Monday: "What caused the crash was all that f— around with the currencies of the world."[3]

The stock market initially ignored rising interest rates. The U.S. market, like most equity markets around the world, was booming. The Dow Jones Industrials, which started 1987 at 1,933, reached an all-time high of 2,725 on August 22—250 percent above the August 1982 low reached five years earlier. All world markets participated. Over the same

---

[3] Martin Mayer, *Markets*, New York: Norton, 1988, p. 62.

five-year period, the British stock market was up 164 percent; the Swiss, 209 percent; German, 217 percent; Japanese, 288 percent; and Italian, 421 percent.

But rising bond rates, coupled with higher stock prices, spelled trouble for the equity markets. The long-term government bond rate, which began the year at 7 percent, topped 9 percent in September and continued to rise. As stocks rose, the dividend and earnings yield fell, and the gap between the real yield on bonds and the earnings and dividend yields on stocks reached a postwar high. By the morning of October 19, the long-term bond yield had reached 10.47 percent despite the fact that inflation was well under control. The record gap between yields on stocks and the real yields on bonds set the stage for the stock market crash.

The Futures Market

The S&P 500 futures market also clearly contributed to the market crash. Since the introduction of the stock index futures market, a new trading technique, called *portfolio insurance*, had been introduced into portfolio management.

Portfolio insurance was, in concept, not much different than an oft-used technique called a *stop-loss order*. If an investor buys a stock and wants to protect herself from a loss (or if it has gone up, protect her profit), it is possible to place a sell order below the current price that will be triggered when and if the price falls to or below this specified level.

But stop-loss orders are not guarantees that you can get out of the market. If the stock falls below your specified price, your stop-loss order becomes a *market order* to be executed at the *next best* price. If the stock *gaps*, or declines dramatically, your order could be executed far below your hoped-for price. This means a panic might develop if many investors place stop-loss orders around the same price. A price decline could trigger a flood of sell orders, overwhelming the market.

Portfolio insurers, who sold the stock index futures against large portfolios to protect them against market decline, felt they were immune to such problems. It seemed extremely unlikely that the S&P 500 Index futures would ever decline dramatically in price and that the whole U.S. capital market, the world's largest, could fail to find buyers. This is one reason why the stock market continued to rise in the face of sharply higher long-term rates.

But the entire market did gap on October 19, 1987. During the week of October 12, the market declined by 10 percent and a large number of sell orders flooded the markets. So many traders and money managers

using portfolio insurance strategies tried to sell index futures to protect their clients' profits that the futures market collapsed. There were absolutely no buyers, and liquidity vanished.

What the overwhelming majority of stock traders once believed was inconceivable became a reality. Since the prices of index futures were so far below the prices of the stocks selling in New York, investors halted their buying of shares in New York altogether. The world's largest corporations failed to attract any buyers.

Portfolio insurance withered rapidly after the crash. It was dramatically demonstrated that it was not an insurance scheme at all because the continuity and liquidity of the market could not be assured. There was, however, an alternative form of portfolio protection: index options. With the introduction of these options markets in the 1980s, investors could explicitly purchase insurance against market declines by buying puts on a market index. Options buyers never needed to worry about price gaps or being able to get out of their position since the price of the insurance was specified at the time of purchase.

Certainly there were factors other than portfolio insurance contributing to Black Monday. But portfolio insurance and its ancestor, the stop-loss order, abetted the fall. All of these schemes are rooted in the basic trading philosophy of letting profits ride and cutting losses short. Whether implemented with stop-loss orders, index futures, or just a mental note to get out of a stock once it declines by a certain amount, this philosophy can set the stage for dramatic market moves.

CIRCUIT BREAKERS

As a result of the crash, the Chicago Mercantile Exchange, where the S&P 500 Index futures traded, and the New York Stock Exchange implemented rules that restricted or halted trading when certain price limits were triggered. To prevent destabilizing speculation when the Dow Jones Industrial Average changes by at least 2 percent, the New York Stock Exchange's Rule 80a placed "trading curbs" on index arbitrage between the futures market and the New York Stock Exchange.[4]

But of greater importance are measures that sharply restrict or stop trading on both the futures market and on the New York Stock Exchange when market moves are very large. When the S&P 500 Index futures fall by 5 percent, trading in futures is halted for 10 minutes. If the Dow In-

---

[4] The New York Stock Exchange Index replaced the Dow Jones Industrials to compute the 2 percent collar in 2005.

dustrials decline by 10 percent before 2 p.m., the New York Stock Exchange will declare a one-hour trading halt.[5] If the decline is 20 percent, a two-hour halt will be declared, and if the Dow declines by 30 percent, the NYSE will close for the day.[6] Futures trading will halt when the New York Stock Exchange is closed.[7]

The rationale behind these measures is that halting trading gives investors time to reassess the situation and formulate their strategy based on rapidly changing prices. This time-out could bring buyers into the market and help market makers maintain a liquid market.

The argument against halts is that they increase volatility by discouraging short-term traders from buying when prices fall sharply since they might be prevented from unwinding their position if trading is subsequently halted. This sometimes leads to an acceleration of price declines toward the price limits, thereby increasing short-term volatility, as occurred when prices fell to the limits on October 27, 1997.[8]

THE NATURE OF MARKET VOLATILITY

Although most investors express a strong distaste for market fluctuations, volatility must be accepted to reap the superior returns offered by stocks. For risk is the essence of above-average returns: investors cannot make any more than the risk-free rate of return unless there is some possibility that they can make less.

While the volatility of the stock market deters many investors, it fascinates others. The ability to monitor a position on a minute-by-minute basis fulfills the need of many to quickly validate their judgment. For many the stock market is truly the world's largest casino.

Yet this ability to know exactly how much one is worth at any given moment can also provoke anxiety. Many investors do not like the instantaneous verdict of the financial market. Some retreat into investments

---

[5] If the decline occurs between 2:00 and 2:30 p.m., the halt is one-half hour. After 2:30 p.m., there is no trading halt.

[6] These percentage changes are converted into points in the Dow Industrials and adjusted once each quarter. See www.nyse.com/press/circuit_breakers.html.

[7] These limits were established in 1998. Previously the New York Stock Exchange suspended trading for one-half hour when the Dow fell by 350 points and closed the exchange when the Dow fell by 550 points. Both of these halts were triggered on October 27, 1997, when the Dow Industrials fell by 554 points. Because of intense criticism of these closings, the NYSE sharply widened the limits to keep trading open. The new trading limits for closing the exchange have never yet been breached.

[8] When the markets reopened after the 350-point limit was reached, traders were so anxious to exit that the 550-point limit was reached in a matter of minutes.

such as real estate, for which daily quotations are not available. Others believe that not knowing the current price somehow makes an investment less risky. As Keynes stated nearly 60 years ago about the investing attitudes of the endowment committee at Cambridge University:

> Some Bursars will buy without a tremor unquoted and unmarketable investments in real estate which, if they had a selling quotation for immediate cash available at each audit, would turn their hair grey. The fact that you do not know how much its ready money quotation fluctuates does not, as is commonly supposed, make an investment a safe one.[9]

HISTORICAL TRENDS OF STOCK VOLATILITY

The annual variability, measured by the standard deviation of the monthly returns, from 1834 to 2006 is plotted in Figure 16-2. It is striking that there is so little overall trend of any sort in the volatility of the market. The period of greatest volatility was during the Great Depression, and the year of highest volatility was 1932. The annualized volatility of 1932 was over 65 percent, 17 times higher than 1964, which is the least volatile year on record. The volatility of 1987 was the highest since the Great Depression, but the volatility in the mid-1990s and 2006 fell to near record lows. Excluding the 1929 to 1939 period, when the volatility was 34 percent, the volatility of the market has remained remarkably stable at about 13 to 14 percent over the past 170 years.

These trends are confirmed by examining Figure 16-3a, which displays the average daily percentage change on the Dow Jones Industrial Average during each year since 1896. The downward trend in the Dow volatility in the early twentieth century is partially due to the increase in the number of stocks in the Dow Industrials from 12 to 20, and then to 30 in 1928. The average daily change in the Dow Industrials over the past 100 years is 0.73 percent, slightly less than three-quarters of 1 percent. Since the 1930s, there have been only three years—1974, 1987, and 2000—when the average daily change has exceeded 1 percent.[10]

The percentage of trading days when the Dow Industrials changed by more than 1 percent is shown in Figure 16-3b. It has averaged 23 percent over the period, or about once per week. But it has ranged from as low as 1.2 percent in 1964 to a high of 67.6 percent in 1932, when

---

[9] Charles D. Ellis, ed., "Memo for the Estates Committee, King's College, Cambridge, May 8, 1938," *Classics*, Homewood, Ill.: Dow Jones-Irwin, 1989, p. 79.

[10] The average percentage change in the Dow Industrials in 2001 was 0.9934 percent.

Annual Volatility of Stock Returns (Annualized Standard Deviation of Monthly Returns), 1834 through December 2006

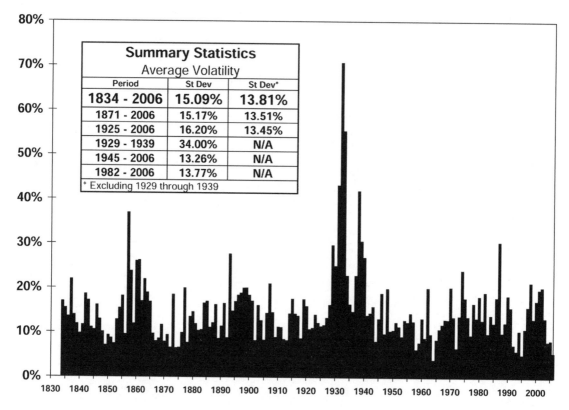

the Dow changed by more than 1 percent in two out of every three trading days.

Most of the periods of high volatility occur when the market has declined. The standard deviation of daily returns is about 25 percent higher in recessions than in expansions. There are two reasons why volatility increases in a recession. First, recessions are more unusual and entail greater economic uncertainty than expansions. The second is that, if earnings fall sharply, then the burden of fixed costs becomes higher and the volatility of profits greater. This leads to increased volatility in the equity value of firms.

If earnings turn into losses, then the equity value of the firms acts like an out-of-the-money option that pays off only if the firm eventually does well to cover its costs. Otherwise, it is worthless. It is not a puzzle why stock volatility was the greatest during the Great Depression when,

FIGURE 16–3

Daily Risk on the Dow Jones Industrial Average

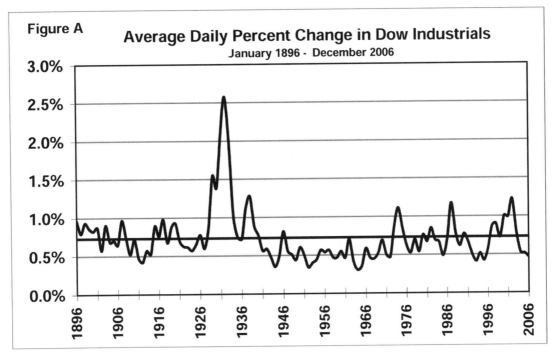

Figure A

Average Daily Percent Change in Dow Industrials
January 1896 - December 2006

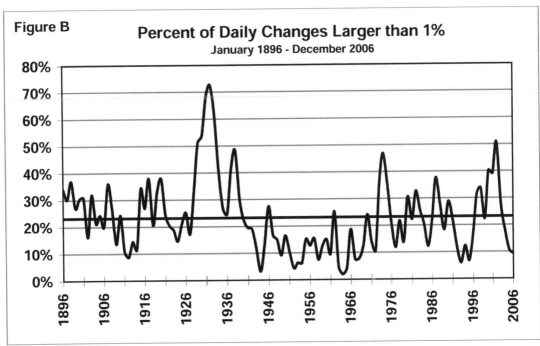

Figure B

Percent of Daily Changes Larger than 1%
January 1896 - December 2006

with aggregate profits negative, the equity market as a whole was trading like an out-of-money option.

THE VOLATILITY INDEX (VIX)

Measuring *historical* volatility is a simple matter, but it is far more important to measure the volatility that investors *expect* in the market. This is because expected volatility is a signal of the level of anxiety in the market, and periods of high anxiety have often marked turning points for stocks.

By examining the prices of put and call options on the major stock market indexes, one can determine the volatility that is built into the market, which is called the *implied volatility*.[11] In 1993, the Chicago Board Options Exchange (CBOE) introduced the *CBOE Volatility Index*, also called the *VIX Index* or the *VIX*, based on actual index options prices on the S&P 500 Index, and it calculated this index back to the mid-1980s.[12] A weekly plot of the VIX Index from 1986 appears in Figure 16-4.

In the short run, there is a strong negative correlation between the VIX and the *level* of the market. When the market is falling, investors are willing to pay more for downside protection and they purchase puts, causing the VIX to rise. When the market is rising, the VIX typically goes down as investors gain confidence and are less anxious to insure their portfolio against a loss.

This correlation may seem puzzling since one might expect investors to seek more protection when the market is high rather than low. One explanation of the behavior of the VIX Index is that historical volatility is higher in bear markets than bull markets, so falling markets should cause the VIX to rise. But a more persuasive argument is that changes in investor confidence change investors' willingness to hedge by buying puts. As put prices are driven up, arbitrageurs who sell puts sell stocks to hedge their position, thus sending stock prices down. The reverse occurs when investors feel more confident of stock returns.

It is easy to see in Figure 16-4 that the peaks in the VIX corresponded to periods of extreme uncertainty and sharply lower stock prices. The Volatility Index peaked at 172 on the Tuesday following the October 19, 1987, stock market crash, far eclipsing any other high.

---

[11] This is done by solving for the volatility using the Black-Scholes options pricing formula. See Chapter 15.

[12] Until 2003, the VIX Index was based on the S&P 100 (the largest 100 stocks in the S&P 500 Index). See the CBOE Web site (www.cboe.com) for more details on its calculation.

F I G U R E   16–4

The CBOE Volatility Index (VIX), 1986 to 2006

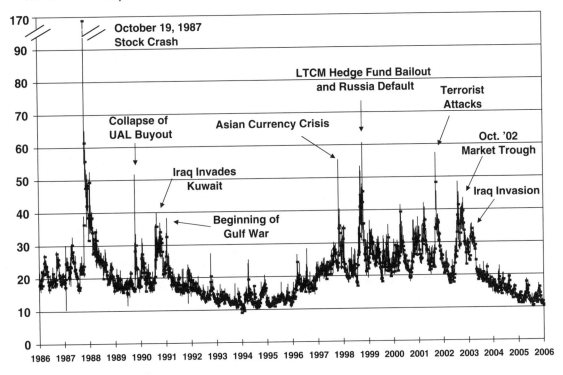

In the early and mid-1990s, the Volatility Index sank to between 10 and 20. But with the onset of the Asian crises in 1997, the VIX moved up to a 20 to 30 range. Spikes between 50 and 60 in the VIX occurred on three occasions: when the Dow fell 550 points during the attack on the Hong Kong dollar in October 1987; in August 1998 when Long-Term Capital Management (LTCM) was liquidated; and in the week following the terrorist attacks of September 11, 2001.

In recent years, buying when the VIX is high and selling when it is low has proved to be a profitable strategy for the short term. But so has buying during market spills and selling during market peaks. The real question is how high is high and how low is low. For instance, an investor might have been tempted to buy into the market on Friday, October 16, 1987, when the VIX reached 40. Yet such a purchase would have proved disastrous given the record one-day collapse that followed on Monday.

RECENT LOW VOLATILITY

As can be seen from Figures 16-3 and 16-4, volatility in 2005 and 2006 was among the lowest in history. There are goods reasons for this: (1) lower economic volatility as the business cycle is muted, (2) the globalization of financial markets that allows investors to diversify risks, and (3) the increased liquidity of markets that allows capital to be instantly allocated to take advantage of profitable opportunities.

But too much stability invites firms and investors to take increasing risk and leverage their positions with lower-cost debt. This means that investors should not become sanguine about recent low volatility. The interconnectedness of markets, for all its benefits, invites global volatility because bullish and bearish sentiment cannot be contained to one market.

THE DISTRIBUTION OF LARGE DAILY CHANGES

Chapter 13 noted that there were 126 days from 1885 through 2006 when the Dow Jones Industrials changed by 5 percent or more: 59 up and 67 down. Seventy-nine of these days, or nearly two-thirds of the total, occurred from 1929 through 1933. The most volatile year by far in terms of daily changes was 1932, which contained 35 days when the Dow moved by at least 5 percent. The longest period of time between two successive changes of at least 5 percent was the 17-year period that preceded the October 19, 1987, stock crash.

Some of the properties of large daily changes are displayed in Figure 16-5. Monday has seen only slightly more large changes than the rest of the week, and Tuesday has seen significantly fewer. Monday has the largest number of down days, but Wednesday has by far the highest number of up days.

Thirty of the large changes occurred in October, which has witnessed more than twice the large moves as any other month. October's reputation as a volatile month is fully justified. Not only has October witnessed nearly one-quarter of all big moves but it has also seen the two greatest stock crashes in history, in October 1929 and October 1987. It is interesting to note that nearly two-thirds of the large declines have occurred in the last four months of the year. Chapter 18 presents the seasonal aspects of stock price changes.

One of the most surprising bits of information about large market moves relates to the period of the greatest stock market collapse. From September 3, 1929, through July 8, 1932, the Dow Jones Industrials

FIGURE   16–5

Distribution of Dow Jones Industrial Average Changes over 5 Percent, 1885 through December 2006

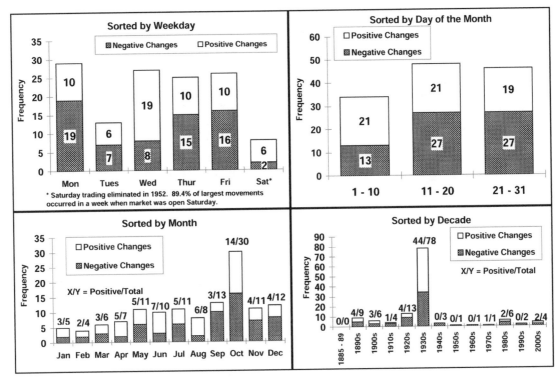

collapsed nearly 89 percent. During that period, there were 37 episodes when the Dow changed by 5 percent or more. Surprisingly, 21 of those episodes were increases! Many of these sharp rallies were the result of short-covering, which occurred as speculators who thought the market was on a one-way street rushed to sell stock they did not own and were then forced to buy it back, or cover their positions, once the market rallied.

It is not uncommon for markets that appear to be trending in one direction to experience occasional sharp moves in the other direction. In a bull market, the expression "up the staircase, down the elevator" is an apt description of market behavior. Ordinary investors must beware: it is not as easy to make money in trending markets as it looks, and investors who try to play these markets must be ready to bail out quickly when they see the market change direction.

THE ECONOMICS OF MARKET VOLATILITY

Many of the complaints about market volatility are grounded in the be-lief that the market reacts excessively to changes in news. But how news should impact the market is so difficult to determine that few can quan-tify the proper impact of an event on the price of a stock. As a result, traders often "follow the crowd" and try to predict how other traders will react when news happens.

Over half a century ago, Keynes illustrated the problem of in-vestors who try to value stock by economic fundamentals as opposed to following the crowd:

> Investment based on genuine long-term expectation is so difficult today as to be scarcely practicable. He who attempts it must surely lead much more laborious days and run greater risk than he who tries to guess better than the crowd how the crowd will behave; and, given equal intelligence, he may make more disastrous mistakes.[13]

In 1981, Robert Shiller of Yale University devised a method of de-termining whether stock investors tended to overreact to changes in div-idends and interest rates, the fundamental building blocks of stock values.[14] From the examination of historical data, he calculated what the value of the S&P 500 Index should have been given the subsequent real-ization of dividends and interest rates. We know what this value is be-cause, as shown in Chapter 7, stock prices are the present discounted value of future cash flows.

What he found was that stock prices were far too variable to be ex-plained merely by the subsequent behavior of dividends and interest rates. Stock prices appeared to overreact to changes in dividends, failing to take into account that most of the changes in dividend payouts were only temporary. For example, investors priced stocks in a recession as if they expected dividends to go much lower, completely contrary to his-torical experience.

The word *cycle* in *business cycle* implies that ups in economic activ-ity will be followed by downs, and vice versa. Since earnings and prof-its tend to follow the business cycle, they too should behave in a cyclical manner, returning to some average value over time. Under these cir-

---

[13] John Maynard Keynes, *The General Theory of Employment, Interest, and Money*, New York: Harcourt, Brace & World, 1965, First Harbinger Edition, p. 157. (This book was originally published in 1936 by Macmillan & Co.)

[14] Robert Shiller, *Market Volatility*, Cambridge, Mass.: MIT Press, 1989. The seminal article that spawned the excess volatility literature was "Do Stock Prices Move Too Much to Be Justified by Subsequent Changes in Dividends?" *American Economic Review*, vol. 71 (1981), pp. 421–435.

cumstances, a temporary drop in dividends (or earnings) during a recession should have a very minor effect on the price of a stock, which discounts dividends into the infinite future.

When stocks are collapsing, worst-case scenarios loom large in investors' minds. On May 6, 1932, after stocks had plummeted 85 percent from their 1929 high, Dean Witter issued the following memo to its clients:

> There are only two premises which are tenable as to the future. Either we are going to have chaos or else recovery. The former theory is foolish. If chaos ensues nothing will maintain value; neither bonds nor stocks nor bank deposits nor gold will remain valuable. Real estate will be a worthless asset because titles will be insecure. No policy can be based upon this impossible contingency. Policy must therefore be predicated upon the theory of recovery. The present is not the first depression; it may be the worst, but just as surely as conditions have righted themselves in the past and have gradually readjusted to normal, so this will again occur. The only uncertainty is when it will occur. . . . I wish to say emphatically that in a few years present prices will appear as ridiculously low as 1929 values appear fantastically high.[15]

Two months later the stock market hit its all-time low and rallied strongly. In retrospect, these words reflected great wisdom and sound judgment about the temporary dislocations of stock prices. Yet at the time they were uttered, investors were so disenchanted with stocks and so filled with doom and gloom that the message fell on deaf ears. Chapter 19 discusses why investors often overreact to short-term events and fail to take the long view of the market.

THE SIGNIFICANCE OF MARKET VOLATILITY

Despite the drama of the October 1987 market collapse, there was amazingly little lasting effect on the world economy or even the financial markets. Because the 1987 episode did not augur either a further collapse in stock prices or a decline in economic activity, it will never attain the notoriety of the crash of 1929. Yet its lesson is perhaps more important. Economic safeguards, such as prompt Federal Reserve action to provide liquidity to the economy and assure the proper functioning of the financial markets, can prevent an economic debacle of the kind that beset our economy during the Great Depression.

---

[15] Memorandum from Dean Witter, May 6, 1932.

This does not mean that the markets are exempt from violent fluc-tuations. Since the future will always be uncertain, psychology and sen-timent often dominate economic fundamentals. As Keynes perceptively stated more than 70 years ago in *The General Theory*, "The outstanding fact is the extreme precariousness of the basis of knowledge on which our estimates of prospective yield have to be made."[16] Precarious esti-mates are subject to sudden change, so prices in free markets will be volatile. But history has shown that investors who are willing to step into the market when others are running to the exits reap the benefits of market volatility.

---

[16] Keynes, *The General Theory*, p. 149.

CHAPTER

17

TECHNICAL ANALYSIS AND INVESTING WITH THE TREND

Many skeptics, it is true, are inclined to dismiss the whole procedure [chart reading] as akin to astrology or necromancy; but the sheer weight of its importance in Wall Street requires that its pretensions be examined with some degree of care.

BENJAMIN GRAHAM AND DAVID DODD, 1934[1]

THE NATURE OF TECHNICAL ANALYSIS

Flags, pennants, saucers, and head-and-shoulders formations. Stochastics, moving-average convergence-divergence indicators, and candlesticks. Such is the arcane language of the technical analyst, an investor who forecasts future returns by the use of past price trends. Few areas of investment analysis have attracted more critics, yet no other area has a core of such dedicated, ardent supporters. Technical analysis, often dismissed by academic economists as being as useful as astrology, is being given a new look, and some of the recent evidence is surprisingly positive.

---

[1] Benjamin Graham and David Dodd, *Security Analysis*, 1st ed., New York: McGraw-Hill, 1934, p. 618.

Technical analysts, or *chartists* as they are sometimes called, stand in sharp contrast to *fundamental analysts* who use such variables as dividends, earnings, and book values to forecast stock returns. Chartists ignore these fundamental variables, maintaining that useful information may be gleaned by analyzing past price patterns. These patterns tend to repeat themselves and are the result of market psychology or unusual price movements caused by informed traders. If these patterns are read properly, chartists maintain, investors can use them to outperform the market or share in the gains of those who are more knowledgeable about a stock's prospects.

CHARLES DOW, TECHNICAL ANALYST

The first well-publicized technical analyst was Charles Dow, the creator of the Dow Jones Industrial Average. But Charles Dow did not analyze only charts. In conjunction with his interest in market movements, Dow founded the *Wall Street Journal* and published his strategy in editorials in the early part of this century. Dow's successor, William Hamilton, extended Dow's technical approach and published the *Stock Market Barometer* in 1922. Ten years later, Charles Rhea formalized Dow's concepts in a book entitled *Dow Theory.*

Charles Dow likened the ebb and flow of stock prices to waves in an ocean. He claimed that there was a *primary wave,* which, like the tide, determined the overall trend. Upon this trend were superimposed secondary waves and minor ripples. He also claimed you could identify which trend the market was in by analyzing a chart of the Dow Jones Industrial Average, the volume in the market, and the Dow Jones Rail (now called the Transportation) Average.

Those that follow the Dow theory acknowledged that the strategy would have gotten an investor out of the stock market before the October 1929 stock crash. Martin J. Pring, a noted technical analyst, argues that, starting in 1897, investors who purchased stock in the Dow Jones Industrial Average and followed each Dow theory buy-and-sell signal would have seen an original investment of $100 reach $116,508 by January 1990, as opposed to $5,682 with a buy-and hold strategy (these calculations exclude reinvested dividends).[2] But confirming profits that come from trading based on the Dow theory is difficult because the buy-

[2] Martin Pring, *Technical Analysis Explained,* 3rd ed., New York: McGraw-Hill, 1991, p. 31. Also see David Glickstein and Rolf Wubbels, "Dow Theory Is Alive and Well!" *Journal of Portfolio Management,* April 1983, pp. 28–32.

and-sell signals are purely subjective and cannot be determined by precise numerical rules.

THE RANDOMNESS OF STOCK PRICES

Although the Dow theory might not be as popular as it once was, technical analysis is still alive and well. The idea that you can identify the major trends in the market, riding bull markets while avoiding bear markets, is still a fundamental pursuit of technical analysts.

Yet most economists still attack the fundamental tenet of the chartists—that stock prices follow predictable patterns. To these academic researchers, the movements of prices in the market more closely conform to a pattern called a *random walk* than to trends that forecast future returns.

The first to make this connection was Frederick MacCauley, an economist in the early part of this century. His comments at a 1925 dinner meeting of the American Statistical Association on the topic of "forecasting security prices" were reported in the association's official journal:

> MacCauley observed that there was a striking similarity between the fluctuations of the stock market and those of a chance curve which may be obtained by throwing dice. Everyone will admit that the course of such a purely chance curve cannot be predicted. If the stock market can be forecast from a graph of its movements, it must be because of its difference from the chance curve.[3]

More than 30 years later, Harry Roberts, a professor at the University of Chicago, simulated movements in the market by plotting price changes that resulted from completely random events, such as flips of a coin. These simulations looked like the charts of actual stock prices, forming shapes and following trends that are considered by chartists to be significant predictors of future returns. But since the next period's price change was, by construction, a completely random event, such patterns could not logically have any predictive content. This early research supported the belief that the apparent patterns in past stock prices were the result of completely random movements.

But does the randomness of stock prices make economic sense? Factors influencing supply and demand do not occur randomly and are

---

[3] *Journal of the American Statistical Association*, vol. 20 (June 1925), p. 248. Comments made at the Aldine Club in New York on April 17, 1925.

often quite predictable from one period to the next. Shouldn't these predictable factors make stock prices move in nonrandom patterns?

In 1965, Professor Paul Samuelson of MIT showed that the randomness in security prices did not contradict the laws of supply and demand.[4] In fact, such randomness was a result of a free and efficient market in which investors had already incorporated all the known factors influencing the price of the stock. This is the crux of the *efficient market hypothesis*.

If the market is efficient, prices will change only when new, unanticipated information is released to the market. Since unanticipated information is as likely to be good as it is to be bad, the resulting movement in stock prices is random. Price charts will look like a random walk since the probability that stocks go up or down is completely random and cannot be predicted.[5]

SIMULATIONS OF RANDOM STOCK PRICES

If stock prices are indeed random, their movements should not be distinguishable from counterfeits generated randomly by a computer. Figure 17-1 extends the experiment conceived by Professor Roberts 50 years ago. Instead of generating only closing prices, I programmed the computer to generate intraday prices, creating the popular high-low-close bar graphs that are found in most newspapers and chart publications.

There are eight charts in Figure 17-1. A computer, using a random-number generator, has simulated four of these charts. In these charts, there is absolutely no way to predict the future from the past because future movements are designed to be totally independent from the past. The other four charts were chosen from actual data of the Dow Jones Industrial Average over recent years. Before reading further, try to determine which are real historical prices and which are computer created.

Such a task is quite difficult. In fact, most of the top brokers at a leading Wall Street firm found it impossible to tell the difference between real and counterfeit data. Only two-thirds of brokers correctly identified Figure 17-1d, which depicts the period around the October 19, 1987, stock crash. With the remaining seven charts, the brokers showed

---

[4] Paul Samuelson, "Proof That Properly Anticipated Prices Fluctuate Randomly," *Industrial Management Review*, vol. 6 (1965), p. 49.

[5] More generally, the sum of the product of each possible price change times the probability of its occurrence is zero. This is called a *martingale*, of which a random walk (50 percent probability up, 50 percent probability down) is a special case.

F I G U R E 17–1

Real and Simulated Stock Indexes

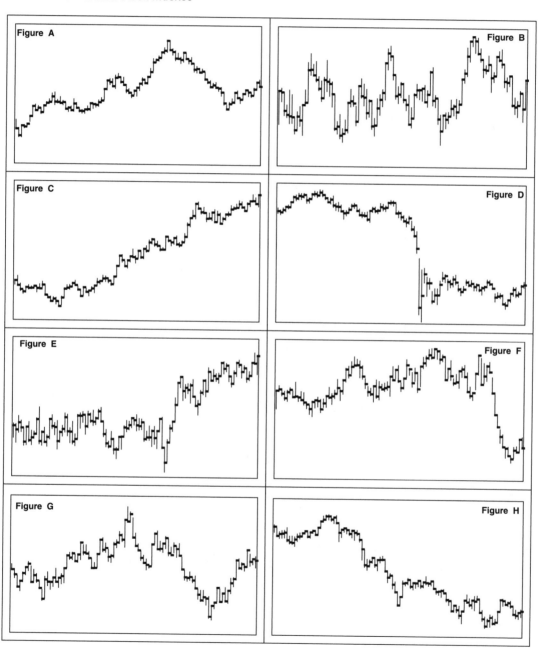

no ability to distinguish actual from counterfeit data. The true historical prices are represented by charts *b*, *d*, *e*, and *h*, while the computer-generated data are charts *a*, *c*, *f*, and *g*.[6]

TRENDING MARKETS AND PRICE REVERSALS

Despite the fact that many "trends" are in fact the result of the totally random movement of stock prices, many traders will not invest against a trend that they believe they have identified. Two of the most well-known sayings of market timers are "Make the trend your friend" and "Trust the thrust."

Martin Zweig, a well-known market timer who uses fundamental and technical variables to forecast market trends, has forcefully stated: "I can't overemphasize the importance of staying with the trend of the market, being in gear with the tape, and not fighting the major movements. Fighting the tape is an open invitation to disaster."[7]

When a trend appears established, technical analysts draw *channels* that enclose the path of stock prices. A channel encloses the upper and lower bounds within which the market has traded. The lower bound of a channel is frequently called a *support level*, and the upper bound a *resistance level*. When the market breaks the bounds of the channel, a large market move often follows.

The very fact that many traders believe in the importance of trends can induce behavior that makes trend following so popular. While the trend is intact, traders sell when prices reach the upper end of the channel and buy when they reach the lower end, attempting to take advantage of the apparent back-and-forth motion of stock prices. If the trend line is broken, many of these traders will reverse their positions: buying if the market penetrates the top of the trend line or selling if it falls through the bottom. This behavior often accelerates the movement of stock prices and reinforces the importance of the trend.

Options trading by trend followers reinforces the behavior of market timers. When the market is trading within a channel, traders will sell put and call options at strike prices that represent the lower and upper bounds of the channel. As long as the market remains within the channel, these speculators collect premiums as the options expire worthless.

---

[6] Figure 17-1b covers February 15 to July 1, 1991; Figure 17-1e covers January 15 to June 1, 1992; and Figure 17-1h from June 15 to November 1, 1990.

[7] Martin Zweig, *Winning on Wall Street*, New York: Warner Books, 1990, p. 121.

If the market penetrates the trading range, options sellers are exposed to great risks. Recall that sellers of options (as long as they do not own the underlying stock) face a huge potential liability, a liability that can be many times the premium that they collected upon sale of the option. When such unlimited losses loom, these option writers "run for cover," or buy back their options, accelerating the movement of prices.

MOVING AVERAGES

Successful technical trading requires not only identifying the trend but, more importantly, identifying when the trend is about to reverse. A popular tool for determining when the trend might change examines the relationship between the current price and a moving average of past price movements, a technique that goes back to at least the 1930s.[8]

A *moving average* is simply the arithmetic average of a given number of past closing prices of a stock or index. For example, a 200-day moving average is the average of the past 200 days' closing prices. For each new trading day, the oldest price is dropped and the most recent price is added to compute the average.

Moving averages fluctuate far less than daily prices. When prices are rising, the moving average trails the market and, technical analysts claim, forms a support level for stock prices. When prices are falling, the moving average is above current prices and forms a resistance level. Analysts claim that a moving average allows investors to identify the basic market trend without being distracted by the day-to-day volatility of the market. When prices penetrate the moving average, this indicates that powerful underlying forces are signaling a reversal of the basic trend.

The most popular moving average uses prices for the past 200 trading days, and it is therefore called the *200-day moving average*. It is frequently plotted in newspapers and investment letters as a key determinant of investment trends. One of the early supporters of this strategy was William Gordon, who indicated that, over the period from 1897 to 1967, buying stocks when the Dow broke above the moving average produced nearly seven times the return as buying when the Dow broke below the average.[9] Colby and Meyers claim that for the United

---

[8] See William Brock, Josef Lakonishok, and Blake LeBaron, "Simple Technical Trading Rules and the Stochastic Properties of Stock Returns," *Journal of Finance*, vol. 47, no. 5 (December 1992), pp. 1731–1764. The first definitive analysis of moving averages comes from a book by H. M. Gartley, *Profits in the Stock Market*, New York: H. M. Gartley, 1930.

[9] William Gordon, *The Stock Market Indicators*, Palisades, N.J.: Investors Press, 1968.

States the best time period for a moving average of weekly data is 45 weeks, just slightly longer than the 200-day moving average.[10]

Testing the Dow Jones Moving-Average Strategy

In order to test the 200-day moving-average strategy, I examined the daily record of the Dow Jones Industrial Average from 1885 to the present. In contrast to the previous studies on moving-average strategies, the holding-period returns include the reinvestment of dividends when the strategy suggests investing in the market and interest-bearing securities when one is not invested in the stock market. Annualized returns are examined over the entire period as well as the subperiods.

I adopted the following criteria to determine the buy-sell strategy: Whenever the Dow Jones Industrial Average closed by *at least* 1 percent above its 200-day moving average, stocks were purchased at these closing prices. Whenever the Dow Industrials closed by *at least* 1 percent below its 200-day moving average, stocks were sold. When sold, the portfolio was invested in Treasury bills and earned interest income.

There are two noteworthy aspects of this strategy. The 1 percent band around the 200-day moving average is used in order to reduce the number of times an investor would have to move in and out of the market. Without this band, investors using the 200-day moving-average strategy are often "whipsawed," a term used to describe the alternate buying and then selling of stocks in an attempt to beat the market. Such trades dramatically lower investor returns because of the large transactions costs incurred.

The second aspect of this strategy assumes that an investor buys or sells stocks at the closing price rather than at any time reached during the day. Only in recent years has the exact intraday level of the averages been computed. Using historical data, it is impossible to determine times when the market average penetrated the 200-day moving average during the day but closed at levels that did not trigger a signal. By specifying that the average must close above or below the signal, I present a theory that could have been implemented in practice.[11]

---

[10] Robert W. Colby and Thomas A. Meyers, *The Encyclopedia of Technical Market Indicators*, Homewood, Ill.: Dow Jones-Irwin, 1988.

[11] Historically, the daily high and low levels of stock averages were calculated on the basis of the highest or lowest price of each stock reached at any time during the day. This is called the *theoretical high* or *low*. The *actual high* is the highest level reached at any given time by the stocks in the average.

Back-Testing the 200-Day Moving Average

In Figure 17-2 are the daily and 200-day moving averages of the Dow Jones Industrial Average during two select periods: from 1924 to 1936 and 1999 to 2006. The time periods when investors are out of the stock market are shaded; otherwise, investors are fully invested in stocks.

Over the entire 120-year history of the Dow Jones average, the 200-day moving-average strategy had its greatest triumph during the boom and crash of the 1920s and early 1930s. Using the criteria outlined above, investors would have bought stocks on June 27, 1924, when the Dow was 95.33 and, with only two minor interruptions, ridden the bull market to the top at 381.17 on September 3, 1929. Investors would have exited the market on October 19, 1929, at 323.87, 10 days before the Great Crash. Except for a brief period in 1930, the strategy would have kept investors out of stocks through the worst bear market in history. They would have finally reentered the market on August 6, 1932, when the Dow was 66.56, just 25 points higher than its low.

Investors following the 200-day moving-average strategy would also have avoided the October 19, 1987, crash, selling out on the previous Friday, October 16. However, in contrast to the 1929 crash, stocks did not continue downward. Although the market fell 23 percent on October 19, investors would not have reentered the market until the following June when the Dow was only about 5 percent below the exit level of October 16. Nonetheless, following the 200-day moving-average strategy would have avoided October 19 and 20, traumatic days for many investors who held stocks.

The returns from the 200-day moving-average strategy and a buy-and-hold strategy of not timing the market are summarized in Table 17-1. From January 1886 through December 2006, the 10.21 percent annual return from the timing strategy beat the annual return on the holding strategy of 9.68 percent. As noted earlier, however, the timing strategy had its biggest success avoiding the 1929 to 1932 crash. If that period is excluded, the returns of the timing strategy are 43 basis points per year behind the holding strategy, although the timing strategy has lower risk.

Moreover, if the transactions costs of implementing the timing strategy are included in the calculations, the excess returns over the whole period, including the 1929 to 1932 Great Crash, more than vanish. Transactions costs include brokerage costs and bid-ask spreads, as well as the capital gains tax incurred when stocks are sold and are assumed to be on average half a percent when buying or selling the market. This number probably underestimates such costs, especially in the earlier

FIGURE 17–2

Dow Jones Industrials and the 200-Day Moving-Average Strategy (Shaded Areas
Are Out of the Market)

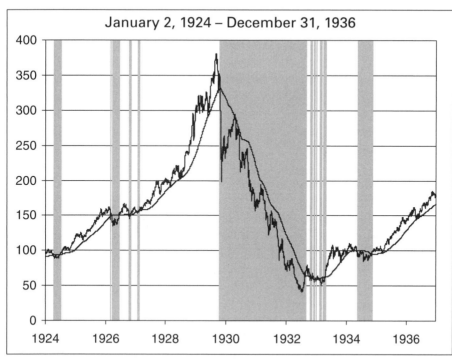

January 2, 1924 – December 31, 1936

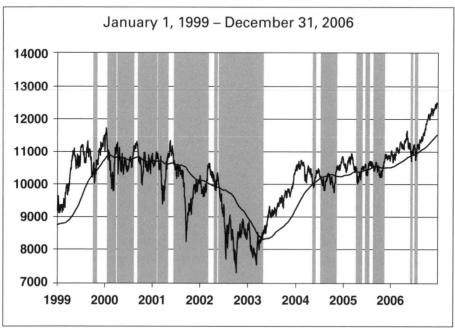

January 1, 1999 – December 31, 2006

TABLE 17–1

Annualized Returns of Timing and Holding Strategies, January 1886 through December 2006

Period	Holding Strategy		Timing Strategy					
	Return	Risk	No. Trans. Cost		Net Trans. Costs		% in Market	No. of Switches
			Return	Risk	Return	Risk		
1886 - 2006	**9.68%**	21.5%	**10.21%**	16.7%	**8.63%**	17.3%	**62.9%**	**350**
Subperiods								
1886 - 1925	**9.08%**	23.7%	**9.77%**	17.7%	**8.11%**	18.0%	**57.1%**	122
1926 - 1945	**6.25%**	31.0%	**11.10%**	21.8%	**9.44%**	22.7%	**62.7%**	60
1946 - 2006	**11.23%**	16.0%	**10.21%**	14.2%	**8.70%**	15.1%	**67.4%**	168
1990 - 2006	**11.76%**	14.7%	**6.60%**	16.9%	**4.30%**	18.3%	**73.7%**	74
Excl. 1929 - 1932 Crash								
1886 - 2006	**11.30%**	20.5%	**10.80%**	16.5%	**9.23%**	17.2%	**64.2%**	**334**
1926 - 1945	**17.72%**	25.9%	**15.75%**	21.3%	**14.24%**	22.1%	**71.2%**	44

years. In later years if this strategy is pursued with index futures or ETFs, the transactions costs would be lower. Each 0.1 percentage point increase of transactions costs lowers the compound annual returns by 29 basis points.

Although the excess returns from the timing strategy disappear when transactions costs are considered, the major gain from the timing strategy is a reduction in risk. Since the market timer is in the market less than two-thirds of the time, the standard deviation of returns is reduced by about one-quarter. This means that on a risk-adjusted basis, the return on the 200-day moving-average strategy is quite impressive, even when transactions costs are included.

Unfortunately, the timing strategy has broken down in the last 17 years. The year 2000 was particularly disastrous for the timing strategy. With the Dow Industrials meandering most of the year above and below the 200-day moving average, the investor pursuing the timing strategy was whipsawed in and out of the market, executing a record 16 switches in and out of stocks.

Each switch incurs transactions costs and must overcome the 1 percent pricing band. As a result, even ignoring transactions costs, the timing strategist lost over 28 percent in 2000 while the buy-and-hold strategist lost less than 5 percent. Since 1990, the buy-and-hold strategy

has returned 11.76 percent annually whereas the timing strategy has returned only 6.60 percent, even before transactions costs.[12]

The timing strategy did avoid some nasty bear markets over the past decade. A timing strategist would have exited the market on June 25, 2001, and avoided the entire drop associated with the terrorist attacks. But what looked like a big gain for the market timer was mostly eliminated by the sharp stock rally to close the year. The timing strategist would have reentered the market on January 3, 2002, at a price only 2.3 percent below the exit price six months earlier. But timing investors did miss the second leg of the bear market, exiting stocks on June 4, 2002, at 9,889 and not reentering until nearly a year later, on April 22, 2003, when the Dow was at 8,325, nearly 16 percent lower.

The Nasdaq Moving-Average Strategy

It is remarkable that during the 1990 to 2006 period when the moving-average strategy on the Dow Industrials failed to generate good returns, the exact same strategy proved very successful on the Nasdaq. In Table 17-2 it can be seen that the timing strategy outperformed the holding strategy by nearly 5 percent per year since 1972 and by nearly 4 percent per year since 1990. Again, the market timer achieved these superior returns with much lower risk.

What is most important about the moving-average strategy is that it keeps investors in major bull markets and out of major bear markets. The strategy worked beautifully during the technology bubble of 1999 to 2001. Using the timing strategy, an investor would have entered the Nas-

---

[12] Note that during the 1990 to 2006 period, the risk, measured in *annual* returns, is surprisingly higher for the timing strategy than for the holding strategy. This unusual reversal of risks is due to the extremely poor returns for the timing strategy in 2000. If *monthly* returns are considered, the timing strategy had lower risk than the holding strategy over the same period.

T A B L E   17–2

Annualized Returns of Nasdaq Timing and Holding Strategies, January 1972 through December 2006

Period	Holding Strategy		Timing Strategy					
	Return	Risk	No Trans. Costs		Net Trans. Costs		% in Market	Number of Switches
			Return	Risk	Return	Risk		
1972 - 2006	10.88%	27.09%	15.56%	19.81%	14.47%	20.21%	67.38%	93
1990 - 2006	11.04%	33.05%	14.99%	26.35%	13.27%	26.99%	69.18%	50

daq market at 1,801 on November 2, 1998, and rode the market to the peak of 5,049 on March 10, 2000. After moving in and out of the market several times, the market timer would have exited the Nasdaq market at 3,896 on September 11, 2000, and stayed out until December 5, 2001, when the Nasdaq was at 2,046, almost 50 percent lower. For those 15 months the timing strategist in Nasdaq would have avoided the most crushing bear market since the 1929 to 1932 stock market crash.

Distribution of Gains and Losses

There is no question that the 200-day moving-average strategy, even with transactions costs, avoids large losses, but it suffers many small defeats. In Figure 17-3 is shown the distribution of yearly gains and losses in the timing strategy after transactions costs and the holding strategy for the Dow Industrials from 1886 to 2006. As noted above, the timing strategist participates in most of the winning markets and avoids most of the losing markets but suffers many small losses. These losses occur when the market does not follow a definite trend. Despite the use of the 1 percent band to reduce whipsawing, investors in a trendless market

FIGURE 17–3

Distribution of Yearly Gains and Losses: Dow Jones Industrials Timing Strategy versus Holding Strategy

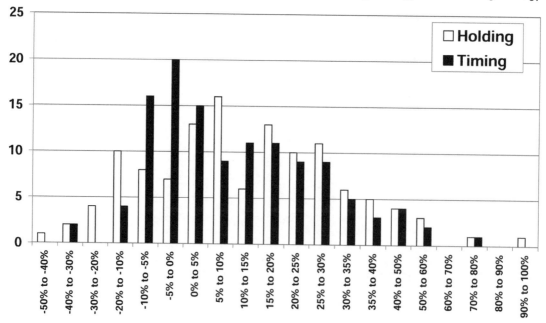

often find themselves moving in and out of the market frequently, sometimes incurring heavy transactions costs and trading losses as occurred in 2000.

The distribution in Figure 17-3 is quite similar to that of a buy-and-hold investor's purchasing index puts on the market. As noted in Chapter 15, purchasing index puts are equivalent to buying an insurance policy on the market, but the buyer must continually pay the premium. Similarly, the timing strategy involves a large number of small losses that come from moving in and out of the market, while avoiding most severe declines.

MOMENTUM INVESTING

Technical analysis can also be used to buy individual stocks. Academic economists call this *momentum investing*, and it has received increasing attention. Momentum strategies, unlike fundamental strategies, rely purely on past returns, regardless of earnings, dividends, or other valuation criteria. Momentum investors buy stocks that have recently risen in price and sell stocks that have recently fallen, expecting that the stock price will, for a time, continue to move in the same direction.

While this may seem at odds with the old maxim of "buy low, sell high," there is substantial research to support this "buy-high, sell-higher" strategy. In 1993, Narasimhan Jegadeesh and Sheridan Titman found that stocks with the highest 10 percent returns over the past six months outperformed stocks with the lowest 10 percent returns by about 1 percent per month over the next six months.[13,14] Other technical strategies, such as buying stocks priced near their 52-week high, have also been shown to be successful.[15]

It should be emphasized that these momentum strategies work only in the short term and should not be part of a long-term strategy. In the Jegadeesh and Titman study, over half of the excess returns generated in the first 12 months were lost over the following two years. Over the longer periods, the advantage of buying "winning" stocks is com-

---

[13] Narasimhan Jegadeesh and Sheridan Titman, "Returns to Buying Winners and Selling Losers: Implications for Stock Market Efficiency," *Journal of Finance*, vol. 48, no. 1 (March 1993), pp. 65–91.

[14] Moskowitz and Grinblatt have found that much of the success of these strategies is due to the price momentum in industries rather than of individual stocks. See Tobias Moskowitz and Mark Grinblatt, "Do Industries Explain Momentum?" *Journal of Finance*, vol. 54, no. 4 (August 1999), pp. 1249–1290.

[15] Thomas J. George and Chuan-Yang Hwang, "The 52-Week High and Momentum Investing," *Journal of Finance*, vol. 59, no. 5 (October 2004), pp. 2145–2176.

pletely eliminated. In fact, an earlier study by Werner De Bondt and Richard Thaler found that stocks that performed poorly over the previous three- to five-year period significantly *outperformed*, over the next three to five years, those stocks that had done well, implying a mean reversion of longer-run stock returns.[16]

The success of momentum investing cannot be explained within an efficient-market framework. It appears that investors underreact to short-term information, which causes the stock to continue to move in the same direction over time rather than adjusting instantaneously. Unfortunately momentum investing does not guarantee success: recent evidence suggests that while professional investors achieve excess returns with a momentum strategy, individual investors tend to underperform the market. This may be because individual investors often focus on the very best performing stocks, which tend to become overpriced quickly and suffer poor returns, while those well-performing stocks that do not make it to the very top of the list and are bought by professionals tend to have the best momentum returns.[17]

CONCLUSION

Proponents of technical analysis claim it helps investors identify the major trends of the market and when those trends might reverse. Yet there is considerable debate about whether such trends exist, or whether they are just runs of good and bad returns that are the result of random price movements.

Burton Malkiel has been quite clear in his denunciation of technical analysis. In his bestselling work *A Random Walk Down Wall Street*, he proclaims:

> Technical rules have been tested exhaustively by using stock price data on both major exchanges, going back as far as the beginning of the 20th century. The results reveal conclusively that past movements in stock prices cannot be used to foretell future movements. The stock market has no memory. The central proposition of charting is absolutely false, and investors who follow its precepts will accomplish nothing but increasing substantially the brokerage charges they pay.[18]

---

[16] Werner F. M. De Bondt and Richard Thaler, "Does the Stock Market Overreact?" *Journal of Finance*, vol. 40, no. 3 (July 1985), pp. 793–805.

[17] Glenn N. Pettengill, Susan M. Edwards, and Dennis E. Schmitt, "Is Momentum Investing a Viable Strategy for Individual Investors?" *Financial Services Review*, vol. 15, no. 3 (2006), pp. 181–197.

[18] Burton Malkiel, *A Random Walk Down Wall Street*, New York: Norton, 1990, p. 133.

Yet this contention, once supported nearly unanimously by academic economists, is cracking. Recent econometric research has shown that such simple trading rules as 200-day moving averages or short-term price momentum can be used to improve returns.[19]

Despite the ongoing academic debate, technical analysis and trend following draw huge numbers of adherents on Wall Street and among many savvy investors. The analysis in this chapter gives a cautious nod to these strategies, as long as transactions costs are not high. But trading on the basis of charts requires full-time attention. In October 1987, the Dow fell below its 200-day moving average on the Friday before the crash and gave a sell signal. But if you failed to sell your stocks that Friday afternoon, you would have been swept downward by the 22 percent nightmare decline of Black Monday.

Furthermore, as I have repeatedly noted throughout this book, actions by investors to take advantage of the past will change returns in the future. As Benjamin Graham stated so well nearly 70 years ago:

> A moment's thought will show that there can be no such thing as a scientific prediction of economic events under human control. The very "dependability" of such a prediction will cause human actions which will invalidate it. Hence thoughtful chartists admit that continued success is dependent upon keeping the successful method known to only a few people.[20]

---

[19] See William Brock, Josef Lakonishok, and Blake LeBaron, "Simple Technical Trading Rules and the Stochastic Properties of Stock Returns," *Journal of Finance*, vol. 47, no. 5 (December 1992), pp. 1731–1764, and Andrew Lo, Harry Mamaysky, and Jiang Wang, "Foundations of Technical Analysis: Computational Algorithms, Statistical Inference, and Empirical Implementation,"*Journal of Finance*, vol. 55 (2000), pp 1705–1765.

[20] Benjamin Graham and David Dodd, *Security Analysis*, 2d ed., New York: McGraw-Hill, 1940, pp. 715–716.

CHAPTER 18

CALENDAR ANOMALIES

October. This is one of the peculiarly dangerous months to speculate in stocks. The others are July, January, September, April, November, May, March, June, December, August, and February.

MARK TWAIN

The dictionary defines *anomaly* as something inconsistent with what is naturally expected. And what is more unnatural than to expect to beat the market by predicting stock prices based solely on the day or week or month of the year? Yet it appears that you can. Research has revealed that there are predictable times during which stocks as a whole, and certain stocks in particular, outperform the market.

The analysis in the first edition of *Stocks for the Long Run*, published in 1994, was based on long data series analyzed through the early 1990s. The calendar anomalies reported in that edition invited investors to try to outperform the market by adopting their strategies to these unusual calendar events. However, as more investors know of these anomalies, the prices of stocks may adjust so that much, if not all, of the anomaly is eliminated. That certainly would be the prediction of the efficient market hypothesis.

In this edition of *Stocks for the Long Run*, I shall look at the evidence over the past 14 years to determine whether the anomaly survived or

not. The results are surprising. Some anomalies have weakened and even reversed, while others remain as strong as they have always been. Here is a rundown.

SEASONAL ANOMALIES

The most important historical calendar anomaly is that small-capitalization stocks have far outperformed larger stocks in January. This effect is so strong that without January's return, small stocks would have a *lower* return than large stocks over the past 80 years![1]

This outperformance of small stocks in January has been dubbed the *January Effect*. It was discovered in the early 1980s by Donald Keim,[2] based on research he did as a graduate student at the University of Chicago. It was the first significant finding that flew in the face of the efficient market hypothesis that claimed there was no predictable pattern to stock prices.

The January Effect might be the granddaddy of all calendar anomalies, but it is not the only one. For inexplicable reasons, stocks generally do much better in the first half of the month than the second half, do well before holidays, and plunge in the month of September. Furthermore, they do exceptionally well between Christmas and New Year's Day, and until very recently, they have soared on the last trading day of December, which is actually the day that has launched the January Effect.

Why these anomalies occur is not well understood, and whether they will continue to be significant in the future is an open question. But their discovery has put economists on the spot. No longer can researchers be so certain that the stock market is thoroughly unpredictable and impossible to beat.

THE JANUARY EFFECT

Of all of the calendar-related anomalies, the January Effect has been the most publicized. From 1925 through 2006, the average arithmetic return on the S&P 500 Index in the month of January was 1.57 percent, while the average returns on the small stocks came to 6.07 percent. The 4.5 percentage point excess return of small stocks in January exceeds the entire

---

[1] This includes the dramatic 1975 to 1983 period during which small stocks returned over 30 percent per year.

[2] Donald Keim, "Size-Related Anomalies and Stock Return Seasonality: Further Empirical Evidence," *Journal of Financial Economics*, vol. 12 (1983), pp. 13–32.

1.9 percentage point difference in annual compound returns between large and small stocks. In other words, from February through December, the returns on small stocks are lower than the returns on large stocks. On the basis of history, the only advantageous time to hold small stocks is the month of January!

To see how important the January Effect is, look at Figure 18-1. It shows the total returns index on large and small stocks and on small stocks if the January return on small stocks is replaced with that of the S&P 500 Index in January. As shown in Chapter 9, a single dollar invested in small stocks in 1926 would grow to $11,250 by the end of 2006, while the same dollar would grow to only $2,736 in large stocks. Yet if the small stocks' return in January is eliminated, the total return to small stocks accumulates to only $394, merely 14 percent of the return on large stocks!

F I G U R E   18–1

Small and Large Stocks, with and without the January Effect, 1926 through December 2006

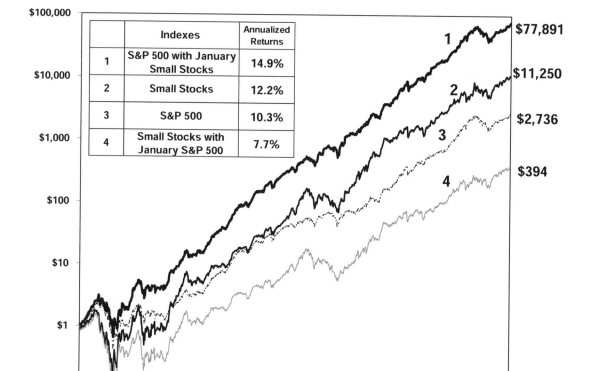

	Indexes	Annualized Returns
1	S&P 500 with January Small Stocks	14.9%
2	Small Stocks	12.2%
3	S&P 500	10.3%
4	Small Stocks with January S&P 500	7.7%

Also shown in Figure 18-1 is that if the large January small stock returns persist in the future, it could lead to some astounding investment results. By buying small stocks at the end of December and transferring them back to the S&P 500 Index at the end of January, a $1 investment in this strategy would have grown to $77,891 by the end of 2006 if begun in December 1925, or a 14.9 percent annual rate of return.

There have been only 16 years since 1925 when large stocks have outperformed small stocks in January. Furthermore, when small stocks underperform large stocks, it is usually not by much: the worst underperformance was 5.1 percent in January 1929. In contrast, since 1925, small-stock returns have exceeded large-stock returns in January by at least 5 percent for 28 years, by at least 10 percent for 13 years, and by over 20 percent for 2 years.

The January Effect also prevailed during the most powerful bear market in our history. From August 1929 through the summer of 1932, when small stocks lost over 90 percent of their value, small stocks posted consecutive January monthly returns of plus 13 percent, 21 percent, and 10 percent in 1930, 1931, and 1932. It is testimony to the power of the January Effect that investors could have increased their wealth by 50 percent during the greatest stock crash in history by buying small stocks at the end of December in those three years and selling them at the end of the following month, putting their money in cash for the rest of the year!

A fascinating feature of the January Effect is that you do not have to wait the entire month to see the big returns from small stocks roll in. Most of the buying in small stocks begins on the last trading day of December (often in the late afternoon), as some investors pick up the bargain stocks that are dumped by others on New Year's Eve. Strong gains in small stocks continue on the first trading day of January and with declining force through the first week of trading. On the basis of research published in 1989, on the first trading day of January alone, small stocks earn nearly 4 percentage points more than large stocks.[3] By the middle of the month, the January Effect is largely exhausted.

When any anomaly such as the January Effect is found, it is important to examine its international reach. When researchers turned to foreign markets, they found that the January Effect was not just a U.S. phenomenon. In Japan, the world's second-largest capital market, the excess returns on small stocks in January come to 7.2 percent per year,

---

[3] Robert Haugen and Josef Lakonishok, *The Incredible January Effect*, Homewood, Ill.: Dow Jones-Irwin, 1989, p. 47.

more than in the United States.[4] As you shall see later in the chapter, January is the best month for both large and small stocks in many other countries of the world.[5]

How could such a phenomenon go unnoticed for so long by investors, portfolio managers, and financial economists? Because in the United States, the returns in January are nothing special for large stocks that form the bulk of those indexes that are analyzed. That's not to say that January is not a good month for large stocks, as large stocks do quite well in January, particularly in foreign markets. But in the United States, January is by no means the best month for stocks of large firms.

Causes of the January Effect

Why do investors favor small stocks in January? No one knows for sure, but there are several hypotheses. In contrast to institutions, individual investors hold a disproportionate amount of small stocks, and they are more sensitive to the tax consequences of their trading. Small stocks, especially those that have declined in the preceding 11 months, are subject to tax-motivated selling in December. This selling depresses the price of individual issues. In January after the selling ends, these stocks bounce back in price.

There is some evidence to support this explanation. Stocks that have fallen throughout the year fall even more in December and then often rise dramatically in January. Furthermore, there is some evidence that before the introduction of the U.S. income tax in 1913, there was no January Effect. And in Australia, where the tax year runs from July 1 through June 30, there are abnormally large returns to small stocks in July.

If taxes are a factor, however, they cannot be the only one, for the January Effect holds in countries that do not have a capital gains tax. Japan did not tax capital gains for individual investors until 1989, but the January Effect existed before then. Furthermore, capital gains were not taxed in Canada before 1972, and yet there was a January Effect in that country as well. Finally, stocks that have risen throughout the pre-

[4] See Gabriel Hawawini and Donald Keim, "On the Predictability of Common Stock Returns: World-Wide Evidence," in Robert A. Yarrow, Vojislav Macsimovic, and William T. Ziemba, eds., *Handbooks in Operations Research and Management Science*, vol. 9, North Holland, 1995, Chap. 17, pp. 497–544.

[5] For an excellent summary of all this evidence, see Gabriel Hawawini and Donald Keim, "The Cross Section of Common Stock Returns: A Review of the Evidence and Some New Findings," in *Security Market Imperfections in Worldwide Equity Markets*, Donald B. Keim and William T. Ziemba, eds., Cambridge, England: Cambridge University Press, 2000.

vious year and should not be subject to tax-loss selling still rise in January, although not by as much as stocks that have fallen the previous year.

There are other potential explanations for the January Effect. Workers often receive extra income, such as from bonuses and other forms of compensation, at year-end. These individuals often invest their cash in stocks in the first week of January. Data show that there is a sharp increase in the ratio of public buy orders to public sell orders around the turn of the year. Since the public holds a large fraction of small stocks, this could be an important clue to understanding the January Effect.[6]

Although all these explanations appear quite reasonable, none jibes with what is called an "efficient capital market." If money managers know that small stocks will surge in January, these stocks should be bought well before New Year's Day to capture these spectacular returns. That would cause the price of small stocks to rise in December, which would prompt other managers to buy them in November, and so on. In the process of acting on the January Effect, the price of stocks would be smoothed out over the year and the phenomenon would disappear.

Of course, to eliminate the January Effect, money managers and investors with significant capital must know of the effect and feel comfortable about acting on it. Those in a fiduciary position might feel uneasy justifying what appears to be a very unusual investment strategy to their clients, especially if it does not work out. Others might be reluctant to take advantage of a phenomenon that seems to have no clear economic rationale.

The January Effect Weakened in Recent Years

Perhaps all the publicity about the January Effect has motivated traders to take advantage of this calendar anomaly since the effect has been far weaker since 1990 than before. From 1990 through January 2007, the average January return on the Russell 2000 Index has been 1.36 percent, only slightly more than the 0.70 percent return on the S&P 500 Index. Furthermore, the return on the Russell 2000 on the last trading day of December and the first trading day of January, which had previously been so high, has been no higher than the S&P 500 Index, and both have been approximately zero. Finally, the excess return on small stocks during the first seven trading days in January, which had been so large before 1990, has also vanished.

---

[6] Jay Ritter, "The Buying and Selling Behavior of Individual Investors at the End of the Year," *Journal of Finance*, vol. 43 (1988), pp. 701–717.

There has, however, been a bit of revival of the January Effect in recent years. Since 2000 the return on small stocks has risen to 1.68 versus 0.21 percent for large stocks. This is not as big as the historical advantage, but it is far larger than that in the 1990s. Perhaps the poor performance of the January Effect during that decade caused traders to ignore the phenomenon, and the anomaly has resurfaced. We all await further data.

LARGE MONTHLY RETURNS

There are other seasonal patterns to stock returns besides the January Effect. The monthly returns on the Dow Industrials and S&P 500 Index are displayed in Figure 18-2. December has been the best month since World War II for both indexes, but only the fifth-best month since 1885. In striking contrast, August, which was the best month for the past 116 years, is actually the second-to-worst month since World War II for the Dow and third-worst month for the S&P 500 Index. Since the end of World War II there has been really no evidence of the "summer rally" that used to be much trumpeted by brokers and investment advisors.

These monthly patterns of returns have a worldwide reach. Although January is a good month in the United States, it is an excellent month in most foreign countries. The January returns for the 20 countries covered by the Morgan Stanley Capital Market Index are shown in Figure 18-3. In every country, January returns are greater than average and constitute nearly one-quarter of the annual stock returns abroad. Investor enthusiasm in January also seems to infect the neighboring months of December and February. Well over one-half of all returns outside the United States occur in the three months of December through February.[7]

THE SEPTEMBER EFFECT

Summer months have good returns, but after the summer holidays, watch out! September is by far the worst month of the year, and in the United States, it is the only month to have a negative return including reinvested dividends. September is followed closely by October, which, as Chapter 16 indicated already, has a disproportionate percentage of crashes.

---

[7] The data presented in Figure 18-3 are from a value-weighted stock index calculated on large stocks. As noted previously, there is evidence that smaller stocks experience even higher January returns, so the January returns shown in Figure 18-3 are probably much lower than those that can be gained in the average stock.

Monthly Returns on the Dow Jones Industrials and the S&P 500

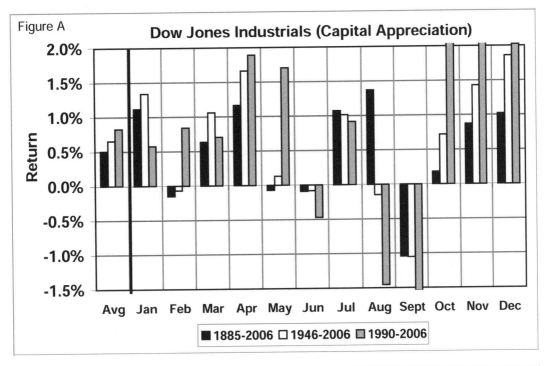

Figure A

Dow Jones Industrials (Capital Appreciation)

■ 1885-2006 □ 1946-2006 ▦ 1990-2006

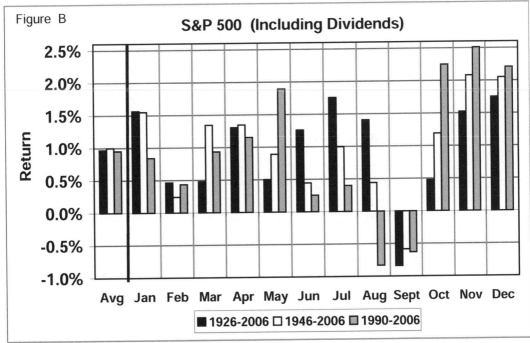

Figure B

S&P 500 (Including Dividends)

■ 1926-2006 □ 1946-2006 ▦ 1990-2006

FIGURE 18–3

International January and September Effects, 1970 through December 2006

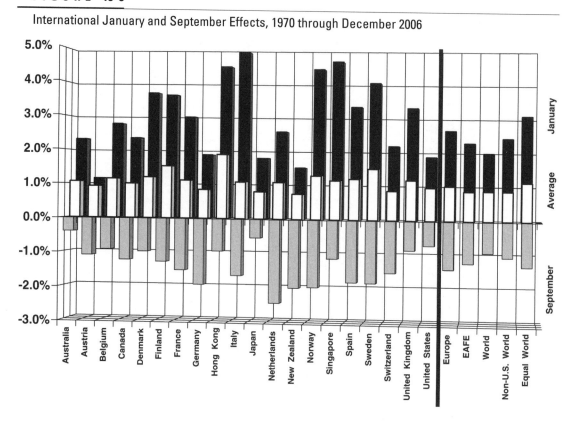

Shown in Figure 18-4 are the Dow Jones Industrial Averages from 1885 through 2006, both including and excluding the month of September. An investment of $1 in the Dow Jones Average in 1885 would be worth $490 by the end of 2006 (dividends excluded). In contrast, $1 invested in the Dow only in the month of September would be worth only 23 cents! On the other hand, if you put your money in the stock market every month except September, your dollar would have been worth $2,176 at the end of 2006.

The poor returns in September also prevail in the rest of the world. It is amazing that September is the only month of the year that has negative returns in a value-weighted index. September has been the worst month in 17 of the 20 countries analyzed and all the major world indexes, including the EAFE Index and the Morgan Stanley all-world index. In September investors would do better holding zero-interest currency than

FIGURE 18–4

The September Effect: Dow Jones Industrial Average, 1885 through December 2006

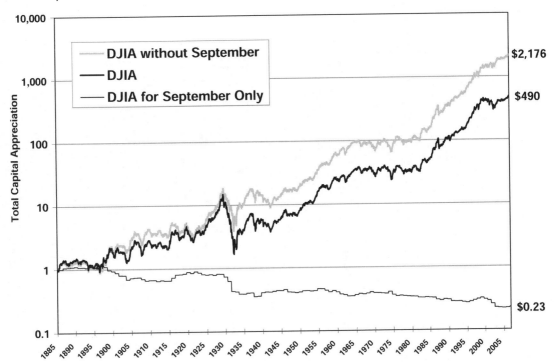

putting their assets in the stock market. Furthermore, in contrast to the January Effect, the September Effect has not only prevailed since 1990 but it has actually been stronger over the past 16 years. It is curious that the January Effect has received all the publicity while the September Effect remains strong with very little research to date.

We can only speculate on why returns are so poor in September. Maybe the poor returns have nothing directly to do with economics but are related to the approach of winter and the depressing effect of rapidly shortening daylight. Psychologists stress that sunlight is an essential ingredient to well-being: recent research has confirmed that the New York Stock Exchange does significantly worse on cloudy days than it does on sunny days.[8] But this explanation falters "down under" as September is

---

[8] Edward M. Saunders, Jr., "Stock Prices and Wall Street Weather," *American Economic Review*, vol. 83 (December 1993), pp. 1337–1345.

also a poor month in Australia and New Zealand, where the month marks the beginning of spring and longer days.[9]

Perhaps the poor returns in September are the result of investors' liquidating stocks (or holding off buying new stocks) to pay for their summer vacations. As discussed below, until recently Monday was by far the worst-performing day of the week. For many, September is the monthly version of Monday: the time you face work after a period of leisure.

OTHER SEASONAL RETURNS

Although psychologists say that many silently suffer depression around Christmas and New Year's, stock investors believe 'tis the season to be jolly. Over the past 120 years, daily price returns between Christmas and New Year's, as Table 18-1 indicates, have averaged 10 times the average.

_____
[9] Of course, many investors in the Australian and New Zealand market live north of the Equator.

T A B L E   18–1

Dow Jones Industrial Average Daily Price Returns, February 1885 through December 2006

	1885 - 2006	1885 - 1926	1926 - 1945	1946 - 1990	1990 - 2006
Overall Averages					
Whole Month	0.0238%	0.0192%	0.0147%	0.0273%	0.0400%
First Half of Month	0.0428%	0.0203%	0.0621%	0.0500%	0.0606%
Second Half of Month	0.0048%	0.0182%	-0.0316%	0.0040%	0.0199%
Last Day of Month	0.0998%	0.0875%	0.1633%	0.1460%	-0.0831%
Days of the Week					
Monday	-0.0946%	-0.0874%	-0.2106%	-0.1313%	0.1240%
Tuesday	0.0386%	0.0375%	0.0473%	0.0307%	0.0512%
Wednesday	0.0613%	0.0280%	0.0814%	0.0909%	0.0409%
Thursday	0.0246%	0.0012%	0.0627%	0.0398%	-0.0038%
Friday	0.0672%	0.0994%	0.0064%	0.0942%	-0.0077%
With Sat	0.0701%	0.0994%	0.0064%	0.0826%	0.0961%
Without Sat	0.0637%			0.0961%	-0.0077%
Saturday	0.0578%	0.0348%	0.0964%	0.0962%	
Holiday Returns					
Day before Holiday					
July 4th	0.3154%	0.2118%	0.8168%	0.2746%	0.0809%
Christmas	0.3510%	0.4523%	0.3634%	0.3110%	0.1959%
New Year's	0.3099%	0.5964%	0.3931%	0.2446%	-0.3101%
Holiday Avg	0.3254%	0.4201%	0.5244%	0.2767%	-0.0111%
Christmas Week	0.2412%	0.3242%	0.2875%	0.1828%	0.0746%

Even more striking is the difference between stock returns in the first and second half of the month.[10] Over the entire 122-year period studied, the percentage change in the Dow Jones Industrial Average during the first half of the month—which includes the last trading day of the previous month up to and including the fourteenth day of the current month—is almost nine times the gain that occurs during the second half.[11]

The average percentage changes in the Dow Jones Industrial Average over every calendar day of the month are shown in Figure 18-5. It is striking that the average percentage gain on the last trading day of the month (and the thirtieth calendar day, when that is not the last trading day) and the first six calendar days is more than equal to the entire return for the month. The net change in the Dow Industrials is negative for all the other days.

The strong gains at the turn of the month are probably related to the inflow of funds into the equity market from monthly pay cycles. Although this phenomenon has attenuated in recent years, the return in the first half of the month is still more than three times the return in the second half of the month since 1990.

DAY-OF-THE-WEEK EFFECTS

Many people hate Mondays. After two days of relaxing and doing pretty much what you like, having to face work on Monday is a drag. And stock investors apparently feel the same way. Monday has been by far the worst day of the week for the market. Over the past 121 years, the returns on Monday have been decisively negative—so negative that if Monday returns were instead like Tuesday through Friday, the Dow Industrial Average would have reached 68 million today!

Although investors hate Mondays, they have relished Fridays. Friday has been the best day of the week, yielding price returns about three times the daily average. Even when markets were open on Saturday (every month before 1946 and nonsummer months before 1953), Friday price returns were the best.

The Monday and Friday effects are not confined to U.S. equity markets. Studies by Keim and Hawawini have shown that throughout most

---

[10] R. A. Ariel, "A Monthly Effect in Stock Returns," *Journal of Financial Economics*, vol. 18 (1987), pp. 161–174.

[11] The difference in the returns to the Dow stocks between the first and second halves of the month is accentuated by the inclusion of dividends. Currently, about two-thirds of the Dow Industrial stocks pay dividends in the first half of the month, which means that the difference between the first and second half returns are accentuated even more.

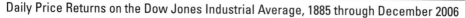

FIGURE 18–5

Daily Price Returns on the Dow Jones Industrial Average, 1885 through December 2006

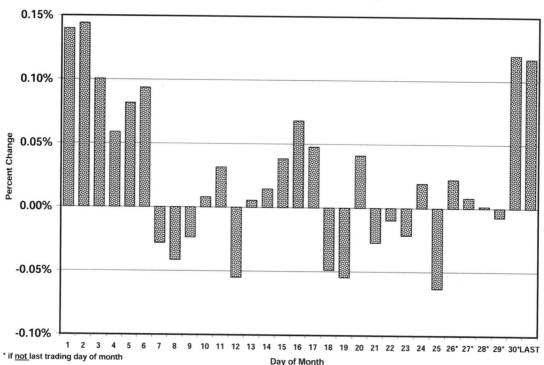

* if not last trading day of month

of the world, Monday is a poor day, garnering negative returns not only in the United States but also in Canada, the United Kingdom, Germany, France, Japan, Korea, and Singapore. On the other hand, none of the major countries have negative returns on Wednesday, Thursday, or Friday. Tuesday is also a poor day for the market, especially in Asia and Australia.[12] This might be due to the poor Monday just experienced in Western countries, since daily returns in the United States have been found to influence Asian markets the next day.

But the daily pattern of stock prices has changed dramatically. Since 1990 Monday has gone from the worst to the best and Friday from the best to the worst. This pattern might be an overreaction by traders to the widespread publication of the daily data during the 1990s. Knowing

---

[12] These results are taken from Hawawini and Keim, "On the Predictability of Common Stock Returns," pp. 497–544.

Monday is usually a bad day, traders sell the Friday before and buy back stock on Monday. Whatever the reason, it shows that, like the January Effect, well-publicized anomalies are often arbitraged out of the market.

Another calendar anomaly is that stocks do very well before major holidays, as shown in Table 18-1. Price returns before the Fourth of July, Christmas, and New Year's are, on average, almost 14 times the average daily price return. But this anomaly, like the day-of-the-week effect, has changed dramatically in recent years. Although stock returns on the day before July Fourth and Christmas have remained strong, returns on the last day of the trading year have switched from a strongly positive 0.31 percent to a decisively negative 0.31 percent since 1990. The negative returns on the last trading day in recent years are probably caused by a large number of "sell-on-close" orders that are automatically executed to offset a position in stock index futures. The downward movement of stock prices generally occurs in the last 30 minutes of trading. Of course, it is likely that once this pattern becomes widely known, it too will disappear.

Finally, there appears to be a diurnal pattern of stock returns. Evidence has shown that there is usually a sinking spell in the morning, especially on Monday. During lunch the market firms, then pauses or declines in the midafternoon before rising strongly in the last half hour of trading. This often leads the market to close at the highest levels of the day.

WHAT'S AN INVESTOR TO DO?

These anomalies are an extremely tempting guide to formulating an investing strategy. But these calendar-related returns do not always occur, and, as investors become more aware of them, some have moderated while others have disappeared altogether. Still others have completely switched, such as the behavior of stocks on the last trading day of the year.

Furthermore, investing in these anomalies requires the buying and selling of stock, which incurs transactions costs, and unless you are trading with tax-sheltered funds, you may realize gains that could be taxed. Nevertheless, investors who have already decided to buy or sell but have some latitude in choosing the timing of such a transaction, might wish to take these calendar anomalies into account before making their trades.

CHAPTER

19

BEHAVIORAL FINANCE AND THE PSYCHOLOGY OF INVESTING

The rational man—like the Loch Ness monster—is sighted often, but photographed rarely.

DAVID DREMAN, 1998[1]

The market is most dangerous when it looks best; it is most inviting when it looks worst.

FRANK J. WILLIAMS, 1930[2]

This book is filled with data, figures, and charts that support an internationally diversified, long-term strategy for stock investors. Yet advice is much easier to take in theory than to put in practice. The finance profession is increasingly aware that psychological factors can thwart rational analysis and prevent investors from achieving the best results for their portfolio. The study of these psychological factors has burgeoned into the field of *behavioral finance*.

---

[1] David Dreman, *Contrarian Investment Strategies: The Next Generation*, New York: Simon & Schuster, 1998.

[2] Frank J. Williams, *If You Must Speculate, Learn the Rules*, Burlington, Vt.: Freiser Press, 1930.

This chapter is written as a narrative to make it easier to understand the basic research and issues of behavioral finance. Dave is an investor who falls into psychological traps that prevent him from being effective. You may notice similarities between his behavior and your own. If so, the advice given in this chapter should help the reader become a more successful investor. Dave first talks to his wife Jennifer and then to an Investment Counselor who understands behavioral finance. The narrative begins in the fall of 1999, several months prior to the peak in the technology and Internet bubble that dominated markets at the turn of the century.

THE TECHNOLOGY BUBBLE, 1999 TO 2001

TIME: OCTOBER 1999

Dave: Jen, I've made some important investment decisions. Our portfolio contains nothing but these "old fogy" stocks like Philip Morris, Procter & Gamble, and Exxon. These stocks just aren't doing anything right now. My friends Bob and Paul at work have been making a fortune in Internet stocks. I talked with my broker, Allan, about the prospects of these stocks. He said the experts think the Internet is the wave of the future. I'm selling some of our stocks that just aren't moving and getting into the Internet stocks like Amazon, Yahoo!, and Inktomi.

Jennifer: I've heard that those stocks are very speculative. Are you sure you know what you're doing?

Dave: Allan says that we are entering a "New Economy," spurred by a communications revolution that is going to completely change the way we do business. Those stocks that we owned are Old Economy stocks. They had their time, but we should be investing for the future. I know these Internet stocks are volatile, and I'll watch them very carefully so we won't lose money. Trust me. I think we're finally on the right track.

TIME: MARCH 2000

Dave: Jen, have you seen our latest financial statements? We're up 60 percent since October. The Nasdaq crossed 5,000, and no one I've heard believes it will stop there. The excitement about the market is spreading, and it has become *the* topic of conversation around the office.

Jen: You seem to be trading in and out of stocks a lot more than you did before. I can't follow what we own!

Dave: Information is hitting the market faster and faster. I have to continuously adjust my portfolio. Commissions are so cheap now that it

pays to trade on any news affecting stocks. Trust me, look how well we're doing.

TIME: JULY 2000

Jen: Dave, I've looked at our broker's statement. We don't hold those Internet stocks anymore. Now we own (*she reads from the statement*) Cisco, EMC, Oracle, Sun Microsystems, Nortel Networks, JDS Uniphase. I don't know what any of these companies do. Do you?

Dave: When the Internet stocks crashed in April, I sold out right before we lost all our gains. Unfortunately, we didn't make much on those stocks, but we didn't lose either.

I think we're on the right track now. Those Internet companies weren't making any money. All the new firms we now own form the backbone of the Internet and all are profitable. Allan told me an important principle: Do you know who made the most money in the California Gold Rush of the 1850s? Not the gold miners. Oh, some of the early diggers found gold, but most found nothing. The real winners from the Gold Rush were those that sold supplies to the miners—pick axes, boots, pans, and hiking gear. The lesson is very clear, most of the Internet companies are going to fail, but those supplying the backbone of the Internet—the routers, software, and fiber optic cables—will be the big winners.

Jen: But I think I heard some economist say those companies are way overpriced now; they're selling for hundreds of times earnings.

Dave: Yes, but look at their growth over the last five years—no one has ever seen this before. The economy is changing, and many of the traditional yardsticks of valuation don't apply. Trust me; I'll monitor these stocks. I got us out of those Internet stocks in time, didn't I?

TIME: NOVEMBER 2000

Dave (to himself): What should I do? The last few months have been dreadful. I'm down about 20 percent. Just over two months ago, Nortel was over 80. Now it is around 40. Sun Microsystems was 65, and now it is around 40. These prices are so cheap. I think I'll use some of my remaining cash to buy more shares at these lower prices. Then, my stocks don't have to go up as much for me to get even.

TIME: AUGUST 2001

Jen: Dave. I've just looked at our brokerage statement. We've been devastated! Almost three-quarters of our retirement money is gone. I

thought you were going to monitor our investments closely. Our portfolio shows nothing but huge losses.

Dave: I know; I feel terrible. All the experts said these stocks would rebound, but they kept going down.

Jen: This has happened before. I don't understand why you do so badly. For years you watch the market closely, study all these financial reports, and seem to be very well informed, yet you seem to always make the wrong decisions. You buy near the highs and sell near the lows. You hold on to losers while selling your winners. You . . .

Dave: I know, I know. My stock investments always go wrong. I think I'm giving up on stocks and sticking with bonds.

Jen: Listen, Dave. I have talked to a few other people about your investing troubles, and I want you to go see an investment counselor. They use behavioral psychology to help investors understand why they do poorly. The investment counselor will help you correct this behavior. Dave, I made you an appointment already. Please go see him.

BEHAVIORAL FINANCE

TIME: NEXT WEEK

Dave was skeptical. He thought that understanding stocks required knowledge of economics, accounting, and mathematics. Dave never heard the word *psychology* used in any of those subjects. Yet he knew he needed help, and it couldn't hurt to check it out.

Investment Counselor (IC): I have read your profile and talked to your wife extensively. You are very typical of the investor that we counsel here. I adhere to a new branch of economics called *behavioral finance*. Many of the ideas my profession explores are based on psychological concepts that have rarely before been applied to the stock market and portfolio management.

Let me give you some background. Until recently, finance was dominated by theories that assumed investors maximized their expected *utility*, or well-being, and always acted rationally. This was an extension of the *rational theory of consumer choice* under certainty applied to uncertain outcomes.

In the 1970s two psychologists, Amos Tversky and Daniel Kahneman, noted that many individuals did not behave as this theory predicted. They developed a new model—called *prospect theory*—of how individuals actually behave and make decisions when faced with uncertainty.[3] Their

model established them as the pioneers of behavioral finance, and their research has been making much headway in the finance profession.

Fads, Social Dynamics, and Stock Bubbles

IC: Let us first discuss your decision to get into the Internet stocks. Think
back to October 1999. Do you remember why you decided to buy those
stocks?

Dave: Yes. My stocks were simply not going anywhere. My friends at
work were investing in the Internet and making a lot of money. There
was so much excitement about these stocks; everyone claimed that the
Internet was a communications revolution that would change business
forever.

IC: When everyone is excited about the market, you should be extremely
cautious. Stock prices are not based just on economic values but on psychological factors that influence the market. Yale economist Robert
Shiller, one of the leaders of the behavioral finance movement, has emphasized that fads and social dynamics play a large role in the determination of asset prices.[4] Shiller showed that stock prices have been far too
volatile to be explained by fluctuations in economic factors, such as dividends or earnings.[5] He has hypothesized that much of the extra volatility can be explained by fads and fashions that have a large impact on
investor decisions.

Dave: I did have my doubts about these Internet stocks, but everyone
else seemed so sure they were winners.

IC: Note how others influenced your decision against your better judgment. Psychologists have long known how hard it is to remain separate
from a crowd. This was confirmed by a social psychologist named
Solomon Asch. He conducted a famous experiment where subjects were
presented with four lines and asked to pick the two that were the same
length. The right answer was obvious, but when confederates of Dr. Asch
presented conflicting views, the subjects often gave the incorrect answer.[6]

---

[3] Daniel Kahneman and Amos Tversky, "Prospect Theory: An Analysis of Decision under Risk,"
Econometrica, vol. 47, no. 2 (March 1979).

[4] Robert Shiller, "Stock Prices and Social Dynamics," *Brookings Papers on Economic Activity*, Washington, D.C.: Brookings Institution, 1984.

[5] Robert Shiller, "Do Stock Prices Move Too Much to Be Justified by Subsequent Movements in Dividends?" *American Economic Review*, vol. 71, no. 3 (1981), pp. 421–436. See Chapter 16 for further discussion.

[6] Solomon Asch, *Social Psychology*, Englewood Cliffs, N.J.: Prentice Hall, 1952.

Follow-up experiments confirmed that it was not social pressure that led the subjects to act against their own best judgment but their disbelief that a large group of people could be wrong.[7]

Dave: Exactly, so many were hyping these stocks that I felt there had to be something there. If I didn't buy the Internet stocks, I thought that I was missing out.

IC: I know. The Internet and technology bubble is a perfect example of social pressures influencing stock prices. The conversations around the office, the newspaper headlines, and the analysts' predictions—they all fed the craze to invest in these stocks. Psychologists call this penchant to follow the crowd the *herding instinct*—the tendency of individuals to adapt their thinking to the prevailing opinion.

The Internet bubble has many precedents. In 1852, Charles Mackay wrote the classic *Extraordinary Delusions and the Madness of Crowds*, which chronicled a number of financial bubbles during which speculators were driven into a frenzy by the upward movement of prices: the South Sea bubble in England and the Mississippi bubble in France around 1720 and the tulip mania in Holland a century earlier.[8]

Let me read you my favorite passage from the book. See if you can relate with this:

> We find that whole communities suddenly fix their minds upon one subject, and go mad in its pursuit; that millions of people become simultaneously impressed with one delusion and run after it. . . . Sober nations have all at once become desperate gamblers, and risked most of their existence upon the turn of a piece of paper. . . . Men, it has been well said, think in herds. . . . They go mad in herds, while they only recover their senses slowly and one by one.

Dave (shaking his head): This happens again and again through history. Even though others were pointing to those very same excesses last year, I was convinced that "this time is different."

IC: As were many others. The propensity of investors to follow the crowd is a permanent fixture of financial history. There are many times when the "crowd" is right,[9] but often following the crowd can lead you astray.

---

[7] Morton Deutsch and Harold B. Gerard, "A Study of Normative and Informational Social Influences upon Individual Judgment," *Journal of Abnormal and Social Psychology*, vol. 51 (1955), pp. 629–636.

[8] Charles Mackay, *Memoirs of Extraordinary Popular Delusions and the Madness of Crowd*, London: Bentley, 1841.

[9] See James Surowiecki, *The Wisdom of Crowds*, New York: Anchor Books, 2005.

Dave, have you ever been in a new town and found yourself choosing between two restaurants? One perfectly rational way of deciding, if they are close in distance, is to see which restaurant is busier since there's a good chance that at least some of those patrons have tried both restaurants and have chosen to eat at the better one. But when you eat at the busier restaurant, you are increasing the chance that the next diner, using the same reasoning, will also eat there, and so on. Eventually, everybody will be eating at that one restaurant even though the other one could be much better.

Economists call this decision-making process an *information cascade*, and they believe that it happens often in financial markets.[10] For example, when one company bids for another, often other suitors will join in. When an IPO gets a strong following, other investors join in. Individuals have a feeling that "someone knows something" and that they shouldn't miss out. Sometimes that's right, but very often that is wrong.

Excessive Trading, Overconfidence, and the Representative Bias

IC: Dave, let me shift the subject. From examining your trading records, I see that you were an extremely active trader.

Dave: I had to be. Information was constantly bombarding the market; I felt I had to reposition my portfolio constantly to reflect the new information.

IC: Let me tell you something. Trading does nothing but cause extra anxiety and lower returns. A couple of economists published an article in 2000 called "Trading Is Hazardous to Your Wealth." (And, I may add, to your health also.) Examining the records of tens of thousands of traders, they showed that the returns of the heaviest traders were 7.1 percent below those who traded infrequently.[11]

Dave: You're right. I think trading has hurt my returns. I thought that I was one step ahead of the other guy, but I guess I wasn't.

IC: It is extraordinarily difficult to be a successful trader. Even bright people who devote their entire energies to trading stocks rarely make superior returns.

[10] Robert Shiller, "Conversation, Information, and Herd Behavior," *American Economic Review*, vol. 85, no. 2 (1995), pp. 181–185; S. D. Bikhchandani, David Hirshleifer, and Ivo Welch, "A Theory of Fashion, Social Custom and Cultural Change," *Journal of Political Economy*, vol. 81 (1992), pp. 637–654; and Abhijit V. Banerjee, "A Simple Model of Herd Behavior," *Quarterly Journal of Economics*, vol. 107, no. 3 (1992), pp. 797–817.

[11] Brad Barber and Terrance Odean, "Trading Is Hazardous to Your Wealth: The Common Stock Investment Performance of Individual Investors," *Journal of Finance*, vol. 55 (2000), pp. 773–806.

The problem is that most people are simply *overconfident* in their own abilities. To put it another way, the average individual—whether a student, a trader, a driver, or anything else—believes he or she is better than average, which of course is statistically impossible.[12]

Dave: What causes this overconfidence?

IC: Overconfidence comes from several sources. First, there is what we call a *self-attribution bias* that causes one to take credit for a favorable turn of events when credit is not due.[13] Remember in March 2000 bragging to your wife about how smart you were to have bought those Internet stocks?

Dave: Yes. And was I wrong!

IC: Your early success fed your overconfidence.[14] You and your friends attributed your stock gains to skillful investing, even though those outcomes were frequently the result of chance.

Another source of overconfidence comes from the tendency to see too many parallels between events that seem the same.[15] This is called the *representative bias*. This bias actually arises because of the human learning process. When we see something that looks familiar, we form a representative heuristic to help us learn. But the parallels we see are often not valid, and our conclusions are misguided.

Dave: The investment newsletters I get say that every time such-and-such event has occurred in the past, the market has moved in a certain direction, implying that it is bound to do so again. But when I try to use that advice, it never works.

IC: Conventional finance economists have been warning for years about finding patterns in the data when in fact there are none. Searching past data for patterns is called *data mining*, and it is easier than ever to do

[12] B. Fischhoff, P. Slovic, and S. Lichtenstein, "Knowing with Uncertainty: The Appropriateness of Extreme Confidence," *Journal of Experimental Psychology: Human Perception and Performance*, vol. 3 (1977), pp. 552–564.

[13] A. H. Hastorf, D. J. Schneider, and J. Polefka, *Person Perception*, Reading: Mass.: Addison-Wesley, 1970.

[14] For reference to a model that incorporates success as a source of overconfidence, see Simon Gervais and Terrance Odean, "Learning to Be Overconfident," *Review of Financial Studies*, vol. 14, no. 1 (2001), pp. 1–27.

[15] For references to models that incorporate the representative heuristic as a source of overconfidence, see either N. Barberis, A. Shleifer, and R. Vishny, "A Model of Investor Sentiment," National Bureau of Economic Research (NBER) Working Paper No. 5926, NBER, Cambridge, Mass., 1997, or Kent Daniel, David Hirshleifer, and Avandihar Subrahmanyam, "Investor Psychology and Security Market Under- and Overreactions," *Journal of Finance*, vol. 53 no. 6 (1998), pp. 1839–1886.

with computing power becoming so cheap.[16] Throw in a load of variables to explain stock price movements and you are sure to find some spectacular fits—like over the past 100 years stocks have risen on every third Thursday of the month when the moon is full!

The representative bias has been responsible for some spectacularly wrong moves in the stock market, even when the situations seem remarkably similar. When World War I broke out in July 1914, officials at the New York Stock Exchange thought it was such a calamity that the exchange closed down for five months. Wrong! The United States became the arms merchant for Europe; business boomed, and 1915 was one of the single best years in stock market history.

When Germany invaded Poland in September 1939, investors looked at the behavior of the market during World War I. Noting the fantastic returns, they bought stocks like mad and sent the market up by more than 7 percent on the next day's trading! But this was wrong again. FDR was determined not to let the corporations prosper from World War II as they had from World War I. After a few more up days, the stock market headed into a severe bear market, and it wasn't until nearly six years later that the market returned to its September 1939 level. Clearly, the representative bias was the culprit for this error, and the two events weren't as similar as people thought.

Psychologically, human beings are not designed to accept all the randomness that is out there. It is very discomforting for many to learn that most movements in the market are random and do not have any identifiable cause or reason. Individuals possess this deep psychological need to know why something happens. That is where the reporters and "experts" come in. They are more than happy to fill the holes in our knowledge with explanations that are wrong more often than not.

Dave: I can relate personally to this representative bias. I remember that before I bought the technology stocks in July 2000, my broker compared these companies to the suppliers providing the gear for the gold rushers of the 1850s. It seemed like an insightful comparison at the time, but in fact the situations were very different. It is interesting that my broker, who is supposed to be the expert, is subject to the same overconfidence that I am.

IC: There is actually evidence that experts are even more subject to overconfidence than the nonexperts. The so-called experts have been trained

---

[16] For a reference to data mining, see Andrew Lo and Craig MacKinlay, "Data-Snooping Biases in Tests of Financial Asset Pricing Models," *Review of Financial Studies*, vol. 3, no. 3 (Fall 1999), pp. 431–467.

to analyze the world in a particular way, and they sell their advice based on finding supporting—not contradictory—evidence.[17]

Recall the failure of analysts in 2000 to change their earnings forecasts for the technology sector despite the news that suggested that something was seriously wrong with their view of the whole industry. After being fed an upbeat outlook by corporations for many years, analysts had no idea how to interpret the downbeat news, so most just ignored it.

The propensity to shut out bad news was even more pronounced among analysts in the Internet sector. Many were so convinced that these stocks were the wave of the future that, despite the flood of ghastly news, many downgraded these stocks only *after* they had fallen 80 or 90 percent!

The predisposition to disregard news that does not correspond to one's worldview is called *cognitive dissonance*. Cognitive dissonance is the discomfort we encounter when we confront evidence that conflicts with our view or suggests that our abilities or actions are not as a good as we thought. We all display a natural tendency to minimize this discomfort, which makes it difficult for us to recognize our overconfidence.

Prospect Theory, Loss Aversion, and Holding On to Losing Trades

Dave: I see. Can we talk about individual stocks? Why do I end up holding so many losers in my portfolio?

IC: Remember I said before that Kahneman and Tversky had kicked off behavioral finance with prospect theory? A key point in their theory was that individuals form a *reference point* from which they judge their performance. They found that from that reference point individuals are much more upset about losing a given amount of money than they are from gaining the same amount. They called this behavior *loss aversion*, and they suggested that the decision to hold or sell an investment will be dramatically influenced by whether your stock has gone up or down—in other words, whether you have had a gain or loss.

Dave: One step at a time. What is this "reference point" you talk about?

IC: Let me ask you a question. When you buy a stock, how do you track its performance?

Dave: I calculate how much the stock has gone up or down since I bought it.

---

[17] David Dreman, *Contrarian Investment Strategies.*

IC: Exactly. Often the reference point is the purchase price that investors pay for the stock. Investors become fixated on this reference point to the exclusion of any other information. Richard Thaler from the University of Chicago, who has done seminal work in investor behavior, refers to this as *mental accounting*.[18]

When you buy a stock, you open a mental account with the purchase price as the reference point. Similarly, when you buy a group of stocks together, you will either think of the stocks individually or you may aggregate the accounts together.[19] Whether your stocks are showing a gain or loss will influence your decision to hold or sell the stock. Moreover, in accounts with multiple losses, you are likely to aggregate individual losses together because thinking about one big loss is an easier pill for you to swallow than thinking of many smaller losses. Avoiding the realization of losses becomes the primary goal of many investors.

Dave: You're right. The thought of realizing those losses on my technology stocks petrified me.

IC: That is a completely natural reaction. Your pride is one of the main reasons why you avoided selling at a loss. Every investment involves an emotional as well as financial commitment that makes it hard to evaluate objectively. You felt good that you sold out of your Internet stocks with a small gain, but the networking stocks you subsequently bought never showed a gain. Even as prospects dimmed, you not only hung on to those stocks but bought more, hoping against hope that they would recover.

Prospect theory predicts that many investors will do as you did—increase your position, and consequently your risk, in an attempt to get even.[20]

Dave: Yes. I thought that buying more stock would increase my chances of recouping my losses.

IC: You and millions of other investors. In 1982, Leroy Gross wrote a manual for stockbrokers in which he called this phenomenon the "get-even-itis disease."[21] He claimed get-even-itis has probably caused more destruction to portfolios than any other mistake.

---

[18] Richard Thaler, "Mental Accounting and Consumer Choice," *Marketing Science*, vol. 4, no. 3 (Summer 1985), pp. 199–214.

[19] Richard H Thaler, "Mental Accounting Matters," *Journal of Behavioral Decision Making*, vol. 12 (1999), pp. 183–206.

[20] Hersh Shefrin and Meir Statman, "The Disposition to Sell Winners Too Early and Ride Losers Too Long: Theory and Evidence," *Journal of Finance*, vol. 40, no. 3 (1985), pp. 777–792.

[21] Leroy Gross, *The Art of Selling Intangibles*, New York: New York Institute of Finance, 1982.

It is hard for us to admit we've made a bad investment, and it is even harder for us to admit that mistake to others. But to be a successful investor, you have no choice but to do so. Decisions on your portfolio must be made on a *forward-looking basis*. What has happened in the past cannot be changed. It is a "sunk cost," as economists say. When prospects don't look good, sell the stock whether or not you have a loss.

Dave: I thought the stocks were cheap when I bought more shares. Many were down 50 percent or more from their highs.

IC: Cheap relative to what? Cheap relative to their past price or their future prospects? You thought that a price of 40 for a stock that had been 80 made the stock cheap, yet you never considered the possibility that 40 was still too high. This demonstrates another one of Kahneman and Tversky's behavioral findings: *anchoring*, or the tendency of people facing complex decisions to use an "anchor" or a suggested number to form their judgment.[22] Figuring out the "correct" stock price is such a complex task that it is natural to use the recently remembered stock price as an anchor and then judge the current price a bargain.

Dave: If I follow your advice and sell my losers whenever prospects are dim, I'm going to register a lot more losses on my trades.

IC: Good! Most investors do exactly the opposite and realize poor returns. Research has shown that investors sell stocks for a gain 50 percent more frequently than they sell stocks for a loss.[23] This means that stocks that are above their purchase price are 50 percent more likely to be sold than stocks that show a loss. Traders do this even though it is a horrible strategy from a tax standpoint.

Let me tell you of one short-term trader I successfully counseled. He showed me that 80 percent of his trades made money, but he was down overall since he had lost so much money on his losing trades that they drowned out his winners.

After I counseled him, he became a successful trader. Now he says that only one-third of his trades make money, but overall he's way ahead. When things don't work out as he planned, he gets rid of losing trades quickly while holding on to his winners. There is an old adage on Wall Street that sums up successful trading: "Cut your losers short and let your winners ride."

---

[22] Amos Tversky and Daniel Kahneman, "Judgment under Uncertainty: Heuristics and Biases," *Science*, vol. 185 (1974), pp. 1124–1131.

[23] Terrance Odean, "Are Investors Reluctant to Realize Their Losses," *Journal of Finance*, vol. 53, no. 5 (October 1998), p. 1786.

Rules for Avoiding Behavioral Traps

Dave: I don't feel secure enough to trade again soon. I just want to learn the right longer-term strategy. How can I get over these behavioral traps and be a successful long-term investor?

IC: Dave, I'm glad you are not trading, since trading is right for only a very small fraction of my clients.

To be a successful long-term investor, you must set up rules and incentives to keep your investments on track—this is called *precommitment*.[24] Set an asset allocation rule and then stick to it. If you have enough knowledge, you can do this yourself or else with an investment advisor. Don't try to second-guess your rule. Remember that the basic factors generating returns change far less than we think as we watch the day-to-day ups and downs of the market. A disciplined investment strategy is almost always a winning strategy.

If you wish, you don't have to eliminate your trading altogether. If you do buy stocks for a short-term trade, set up a stop-loss order to minimize your losses. You don't want to let your losses mount, rationalizing that the stock will eventually come back. Also, don't tell your friends about your trades. Living up to their expectations will make you even more reluctant to take a loss and admit that you were wrong.

Dave: I'll have to admit that I sometimes enjoyed trading.

IC: If you really enjoy trading, set up a small trading account that is completely separate from the rest of your portfolio. All brokerage costs and all taxes must be paid from this account. Consider that the money you put into this trading account may be completely lost because it very well may be. And you should never consider exceeding the rigid limit you place on how much money you put into that account.

If that doesn't work, or if you feel nervous about the market or have a compulsion to trade, call me, I can help. And according to news reports, there are some reformed traders who are establishing Traders' Anonymous (TA) programs designed to help people who cannot resist the temptations of trading too frequently.[25] Maybe you should look into those.

---

[24] Hersh Shefrin and Richard Thaler, "An Economic Theory of Self-Control," *Journal of Political Economy*, vol. 89, no. 21 (1981), pp. 392–406.

[25] See Paul Sloan, "Can't Stop Checking Your Stock Quotes," *U.S. News & World Report*, July 10, 2000.

Myopic Loss Aversion, Portfolio Monitoring, and the Equity Risk Premium

Dave: Because of how badly I was doing in the market, I even considered giving up on stocks and sticking with bonds, although I know that in the long run that is a very bad idea. How often do you suggest that I monitor my stock portfolio?

IC: Important question. If you buy stocks, it is very likely that the value will drop below the price you paid, if but for a short time soon after your purchase. We have already spoken about how loss aversion makes this decline very disturbing. However, since the long-term trend in stocks is upward, if you wait some period of time before checking your portfolio, the probability that you will see a loss decreases.

Two economists tested whether the "monitoring interval" affected the choice between stocks and bonds.[26] They conducted a "learning experiment" in which they allowed individuals to see the returns on two unidentified asset classes. One group was shown the yearly returns on stocks and bonds, and other groups were shown the same returns, but instead of annually, the returns were aggregated over periods of 5, 10, and 20 years. The groups were then asked to pick an allocation between stocks and bonds.

The group that saw yearly returns invested a much smaller fraction in stocks than the groups that saw returns aggregated into longer intervals. This was because the short-term volatility of stocks dissuaded people from choosing that asset class, even though over longer periods it was clearly a better choice.

This tendency to base decisions on the short-term fluctuations in the market has been referred to as *myopic loss aversion*. Since over longer periods, the probability of stocks showing a loss is much smaller, investors influenced by loss aversion would be more likely to hold stocks if they monitored their performance less frequently.

Dave: That's so true. When I look at stocks in the very short run, they seem so risky that I wonder why anyone holds them. But over the long run, the superior performance of equities is so overwhelming, I wonder why anyone doesn't hold stocks!

IC: Exactly. Shlomo Bernartzi and Richard Thaler claim that myopic loss aversion is the key to solving the *equity premium puzzle*.[27] For years, econ-

---

[26] Shlomo Bernartzi and Richard Thaler, "Myopic Loss Aversion and the Equity Premium Puzzle," *Quarterly Journal of Economics*, 1995, pp. 73–91.

[27] See Chapter 8 for a further description of the equity premium puzzle.

omists have been trying to figure out why stocks have returned so much more than fixed-income investments. Studies show that over periods of 20 years or more, a diversified portfolio of equities not only offers higher after-inflation returns but is actually safer than government bonds. But because investors concentrate on an investment horizon that is too short, stocks seem very risky and investors must be enticed to hold stocks with a fat premium. If investors evaluated their portfolio less frequently, the equity premium might fall dramatically.

Bernartzi and Thaler have shown that the high equity premium is consistent with myopic loss aversion and yearly monitoring of returns. But they also showed that if investors had evaluated their portfolio allocation only once every 10 years, the equity premium needed to be only 2 percent to entice investors into stocks. With an evaluation period of 20 years, the premium fell to only 1.4 percent, and it would have been close to 1 percent if the evaluation period were 30 years. Stock prices would have had to rise dramatically to reduce the premium to these low levels.

Dave: Are you saying that perhaps I should not look at my stocks too frequently?

IC: You can look at them all you want, but don't alter your long-term strategy. Remember to set up rules and incentives. Commit to a long-run portfolio allocation, and do not alter it unless there is significant evidence that a certain sector is becoming greatly overpriced relative to its fundamentals, as the technology stocks did at the top of the bubble.

Contrarian Investing and Investor Sentiment: Strategies to Enhance Portfolio Returns

Dave: Is there a way for an investor to take advantage of others' behavioral weakness and earn superior returns from them?

IC: Standing apart from the crowd might be quite profitable. An investor who takes a different view is said to be a *contrarian*, one who dissents from the prevailing opinion. Contrarian strategy was first put forth by Humphrey B. Neill in a pamphlet called "It Pays to Be Contrary," first circulated in 1951 and later turned into a book entitled *The Art of Contrary Thinking*. In it Neill declared: "When everyone thinks alike, everyone is likely to be wrong."[28]

Some contrarian approaches are based on psychologically driven indicators such as investor "sentiment." The underlying idea is that most

---

[28] Humphrey B. Neill, *The Art of Contrary Thinking*, Caldwell, Idaho: Caxton Printers, 1954, p. 1.

investors are unduly optimistic when stock prices are high and unduly pessimistic when they are low.

This is not a new concept either. The great investor Benjamin Graham stated more than 70 years ago, "[T]he psychology of the speculator militates strongly against his success. For by relation of cause and effect, he is most optimistic when prices are high and most despondent when they are at bottom."[29]

Dave: But how do I know when the market is too pessimistic and too optimistic? Is that not subjective?

IC: Not entirely. Investors Intelligence, a firm based in New Rochelle, New York, publishes one of the long-standing indicators of investment sentiment. Over the past 40 years, the company has evaluated scores of market newsletters, determining whether each letter is bullish, bearish, or neutral about the future direction of stocks.

From Investors Intelligence data, I computed an index of investor sentiment by finding the ratio of bullish newsletters to bullish plus bearish newsletters (omitting the neutral category). I then measured the returns on stocks subsequent to these sentiment readings.

The results, shown in Table 19-1, indicate a strong predictive content to the sentiment index. Whenever the index of investor sentiment is high, subsequent returns on the market are poor, and when the index is low, subsequent returns are above average. The index is a particularly strong predictor of market return over the next 9 to 12 months.

The sentiment indicator since January 1986 is plotted in Figure 19-1. The crash of October 1987 was accompanied by investor pessimism. For the next few years, whenever the market went down, as it did in May and December 1988 and February 1990, investors feared another crash, and sentiment dropped sharply. Bullish sentiment also fell below 50 percent during the Iraqi invasion of Kuwait, the bond market collapse of 1994, the Asian crisis of October 1997, the LTCM bailout of the late summer of 1998, the terrorist attacks of September 2001, and the market bottom of October 2002. These have all been excellent times to invest.

It is of note that the VIX Index, the measure of implied market volatility computed from options prices, spikes upward at virtually the same time investor sentiment plunges.[30] Anxiety in the market, which can be measured from the premiums on put options, is strongly negatively correlated with investor sentiment.

---

[29] Benjamin Graham and David Dodd, *Security Analysis*, 1st ed., New York: McGraw-Hill, 1934, p. 12.

[30] A discussion of the VIX Index is found in Chapter 16.

TABLE 19–1

Investor Confidence and Subsequent Dow Price Returns: Sentiment = Bull/(Bull + Bear)
Bull and Bear from Investors Intelligence, New Rochelle, New York

1970 - 2006		Annualized Returns Subsequent to Sentiment Readings (January 2, 1970 - June 2, 2006)			
Sentiment	Frequency	Three Month	Six Month	Nine Month	Twelve Month
0.2 - 0.3	1.14%	18.52%	15.40%	22.79%	20.74%
0.3 - 0.4	8.34%	12.24%	13.79%	16.52%	15.82%
0.4 - 0.5	15.28%	20.30%	15.02%	13.06%	13.43%
0.5 - 0.6	27.29%	15.98%	13.61%	11.10%	10.21%
0.6 - 0.7	27.60%	8.61%	6.75%	6.66%	6.03%
0.7 - 0.8	15.95%	10.45%	7.17%	7.03%	6.74%
0.8 - 0.9	3.83%	-0.39%	0.23%	-3.32%	-1.79%
0.9 - 1.0	0.57%	0.35%	-3.87%	-9.17%	-10.18%
Overall	100.00%	12.72%	10.35%	9.45%	9.02%

1990 - 2006		Annualized Returns Subsequent to Sentiment Readings			
Sentiment	Frequency	Three Month	Six Month	Nine Month	Twelve Month
.30 - .35	1.28%	20.43%	15.83%	15.51%	20.66%
.35 - .40	3.27%	16.69%	18.19%	18.63%	20.85%
.40 - .45	4.78%	30.10%	22.52%	20.99%	21.24%
.45 - .50	7.12%	33.39%	18.61%	15.25%	15.24%
.50 - .55	15.17%	21.80%	17.98%	15.74%	14.81%
.55 - .60	17.97%	12.92%	11.61%	11.36%	11.05%
.60 - .65	24.85%	4.65%	5.67%	6.91%	6.25%
.65 - .70	14.35%	5.37%	5.34%	4.38%	5.35%
.70 - .75	8.63%	10.64%	7.04%	6.63%	6.43%
.75 - .80	2.57%	3.03%	6.86%	4.51%	5.02%
Overall	100.00%	13.19%	11.04%	10.38%	10.33%

Out-of-Favor Stocks and the Dow 10 Strategy

Dave: Can you use contrarian strategy to pick individual stocks?

IC: Yes. Contrarians believe that the swings of optimism and pessimism infect individual stocks as well as the overall markets. Therefore, buying out-of-favor stocks can be a winning strategy.

Werner De Bondt and Richard Thaler examined portfolios of both past stock winners and losers to see if investors became overly optimistic or pessimistic about future returns from studying the returns of the recent past.[31] Portfolios of winning and losing stocks were analyzed

---

[31] Werner F. M. De Bondt and Richard H. Thaler, "Does the Stock Market Overreact?" *Journal of Finance*, vol. 49, no. 3 (1985), pp. 793–805.

FIGURE 19–1

Investors Intelligence Sentiment Indicator, 1986 to 2007

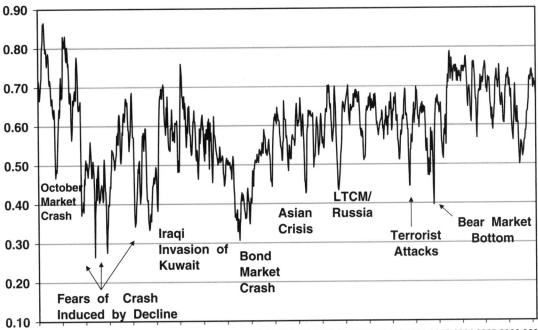

over five-year intervals. Portfolios that had been winners in the past five years subsequently lagged the market by 10 percent, while the subsequent returns on the loser portfolio beat the market by 30 percent.

One of the explanations for why this strategy works relates to the representativeness heuristic we talked about before. People extrapolate recent trends in stock prices too far in the future. Although there is some evidence that short-term momentum is positive in stock returns, over the longer term many stocks that have done poorly outperform, and stocks that have done well underperform. Another strategy based on out-of-favor stocks is called the *Dogs of the Dow* or the *Dow 10 strategy*.[32]

Dave: There has been so much to absorb from today's session. It seems like I fell into almost all of these behavioral traps. The comforting news is that I'm not alone and that your counseling has helped other investors.

---

[32] This strategy is discussed in great detail in Chapter 9.

IC: Not only have they been helped but they have also prospered. For many people, success in investing requires a much deeper knowledge of themselves than does success in their jobs or even in their personal relationships. There is much truth to an old Wall Street adage, "The stock market is a very expensive place to find out who you are."

BUILDING WEALTH
THROUGH STOCKS

CHAPTER

20

FUND PERFORMANCE, INDEXING, AND BEATING THE MARKET

I have little confidence even in the ability of analysts, let alone un-trained investors, to select common stocks that will give better than average results. Consequently, I feel that the standard portfolio should be to duplicate, more or less, the DJIA.

BENJAMIN GRAHAM[1]

How can institutional investors hope to outperform the market . . . when, in effect, they are the market?

CHARLES D. ELLIS, 1975[2]

There is an old story on Wall Street. Two managers of large equity funds go camping in a national park. After setting up camp, the first manager mentions to the other that he overheard the park ranger warning that black bears had been seen around this campsite. The second manager smiles and says, "I'm not worried; I'm a pretty fast runner." The first

---

[1] Benjamin Graham and Seymour Chatman (ed.), *Benjamin Graham: The Memoirs of the Dean of Wall Street*, New York: McGraw-Hill, 1996, p. 273.

[2] Charles D. Ellis, "The Loser's Game," *Financial Analysis Journal*, July/August 1975.

341

manager shakes his head and says, "You can't outrun black bears; they've been known to sprint over 25 miles an hour to capture their prey!" The second manager responds, "Of course I know that I can't outrun the bear. The only thing that's important is that I can outrun you!"

In the competitive world of money management, performance is measured not by absolute returns but the returns relative to some benchmark. These benchmarks include the S&P 500 Index, the Wilshire 5000, the Russell indexes, and the latest "style" of indexes popular on Wall Street. But there is a crucially important difference about investing compared to virtually any other competitive activity: Most of us have no chance of being as good as the average in a pursuit that others practice for hours to hone their skills. But anyone can be as good as the *average* investor in the stock market with no practice at all.

The reason for this surprising statement is based on a very simple fact: since the sum of each investor's holdings must be equal to the market, the performance of the whole market must, by definition, be the *average* dollar-weighted performance of each and every investor. Therefore, for each investor's dollar that outperforms the market, there must be another investor's dollar that underperforms the market. By just matching the performance of the overall market, you are guaranteed to do no worse than average.

But how do you match the performance of the whole market? Until 1975, this goal would have been virtually impossible for all but the most affluent investors. Who can hold shares in each of the thousands of firms listed on U.S. exchanges?

But since the mid-1970s, index mutual funds and then exchange-traded funds (ETFs) have been developed to match the performance of these broad stock indexes. Over the last several decades the average investor could match the performance of a wide variety of market indexes with very low costs and a very modest investment. And, over the last several years, new indexes have been developed, based on the research discussed in Chapter 9, that may allow investors to outperform the averages.

THE PERFORMANCE OF EQUITY MUTUAL FUNDS

Many claim that striving for average market performance is not the best strategy. If there are enough poorly informed traders who consistently underperform the market, then it might be possible for informed investors or professionals to outperform the market.

Unfortunately, the past record of the vast majority of such actively managed funds does not support this contention. There are two ways to

measure long-term fund returns. One is to compute the returns of all funds that have survived over the period examined. But the long-term returns on these funds suffer from *survivorship bias* that overestimates the returns available to investors. This survivorship bias exists because poorly performing funds are often terminated, leaving only the more successful ones with long-term track records to be included in the data. The second, and more accurate, method is to compute, year by year, the average performance of all equity mutual funds in existence.

Both of these computations are shown in Table 20-1. From January 1971 through December 2006, the average equity mutual fund returned 10.49 percent annually, 1.06 percentage points behind the Wilshire 5000 and 1.04 percentage points behind the S&P 500 Index. Indeed, the survivor funds returned 0.80 percentage points more per year but still lagged the averages. And all these fund returns exclude sales and redemption fees that would reduce their net returns to investors even more.[3]

The underperformance of mutual funds does not happen every year. Actively managed equity funds did on average outperform the Wilshire 5000 and the S&P 500 indexes during the period from 1975 through 1983 when small stocks returned a spectacular 35.32 percent per year. Equity mutual funds generally do well when small stocks outperform large stocks, as many money managers seek to boost performance by buying smaller-sized firms.

---

[3] Fund data provided by the Vanguard Group. See John C. Bogle, *Bogle on Mutual Funds*, Burr Ridge, Ill.: Irwin Professional Publishing, 1994, for a fuller description of these data.

T A B L E   20–1

Equity Mutual Funds and Benchmark Returns: Annual Compound Returns (Excluding Sales and Redemption Fees), January 1971 through December 2006 (Standard Deviations in Parentheses)

	All Funds	"Survivor" Funds	Wilshire 5000	S&P 500	Small Stocks	All Funds Minus Wilshire 5000	"Survivor" Funds Minus Wilshire 5000
1971-2006	10.49% (16.6%)	11.29% (16.4%)	11.55% (17.4%)	11.53% (17.0%)	13.47% (22.3%)	-1.06%	-0.26%
1975-1983	18.83% (12.9%)	20.13% (13.1%)	17.94% (15.0%)	15.74% (15.5%)	35.32% (14.3%)	0.89%	2.19%
1984-2006	10.80% (15.0%)	10.99% (14.7%)	12.26% (16.2%)	12.77% (16.1%)	10.15% (19.2%)	-1.46%	-1.27%

Since 1983, when the small stocks surge ended, the performance of the average mutual fund has been worse, falling nearly 1½ percentage points per year behind either the Wilshire 5000 or the S&P 500 Index.

The percentage of general equity funds that has outperformed the Wilshire 5000 and the S&P 500 Index each year from 1972 to 2006 is displayed in Figure 20-1. During this 35-year period, there were only 11 years when a majority of mutual funds beat the Wilshire 5000. All but 2 of these years occurred during a period when small stocks outperformed large stocks. In the last 25 years there have been only 5 years when the average equity mutual fund outperformed the broad market.

The underperformance of mutual funds did not begin in the 1970s. In 1970, Becker Securities Corporation startled Wall Street by compiling the track record of managers of corporate pension funds. Becker showed that the median performance of these managers lagged behind the S&P 500 by 1 percentage point and that only one-quarter of them were able to

F I G U R E   20-1

Yearly Percentage of General Equity Funds That Outperform the S&P 500 and the Wilshire 5000 (Excluding Sales and Redemption Fees), 1972 through December 2006

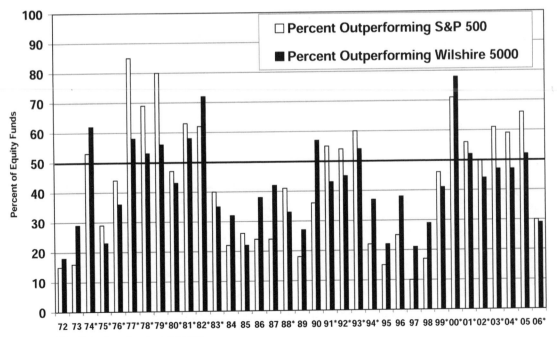

* Small stocks outperform S&P 500.

outperform the market.[4] This study followed on the heels of academic articles, particularly those by William Sharpe and Michael Jensen, that also confirmed the underperformance of equity mutual funds.

Figure 20-2 displays the distribution of the difference between the returns of 138 mutual funds that have survived since January 1972 and the Wilshire 5000.

Only 48, or less than 40 percent, of the 138 funds that have survived over the past 35 years have been able to outperform the Wilshire 5000. Only 30 have been able to outperform the market by more than 1 percent per year, while only 14 have bettered the market by at least 2 percent. On the other hand, over 65 percent of the surviving funds underperformed the market, and almost two-thirds of those underperformed by more than 1 percent per year. And, as noted above for Table 20-1, the actual returns on these funds are worse since these returns exclude sales and redemption fees.

Despite the generally poor performance of equity mutual funds, there are some winners. The best-performing mutual fund over the entire period is Fidelity's Magellan Fund, whose 16.07 percent annual

[4] Burton G. Malkiel, *A Random Walk Down Wall Street: The Time Tested Strategy for Successful Investing,* 5th ed., New York: Norton, 1990, p. 362.

F I G U R E   20–2

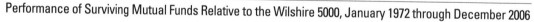

Performance of Surviving Mutual Funds Relative to the Wilshire 5000, January 1972 through December 2006

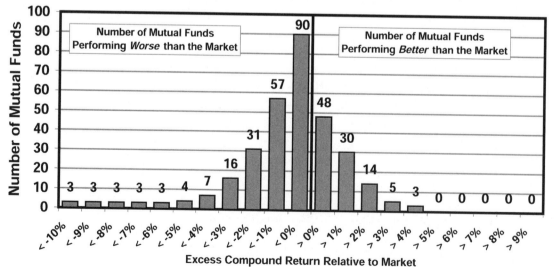

return from 1971 through December 2006 beat the market by over 4 per-
centage points per year. Close behind was Mutual Shares Z, run by
Franklin Templeton, with a return of 16.04 percent over the same pe-
riod. In a virtual tie in third and fourth places are the Columbia Acorn
Fund (previously known as the Liberty Acorn Fund), run by Charles
McQuaid and Robert Mohn, and the Sequoia Fund, run by the invest-
ment firm of Ruane, Cunniff, & Goldfarb that closely follows Warren
Buffett's philosophy and has a large portion of its holdings in Berkshire
Hathaway. These two have enjoyed annual returns of 15.57 and 15.54
percent, respectively.

Despite these sparkling returns, chance may have played a large
role in these outperformers. The probability that a fund would beat the
Wilshire 5000 by 4 percentage points or more over this period by chance
alone is 1 in 12. That means out of the 138 funds examined, one would
expect 11 to have done this well.

Yet luck could not explain Magellan's performance from 1977
through 1990. During that period, the legendary stock picker Peter
Lynch ran the Magellan Fund and outperformed the market by an incredible 13 percent per year. Magellan took somewhat greater risks in
achieving this return,[5] but the probability that Magellan would outperform the Wilshire 5000 by this margin over that 14-year period by luck
alone is only 1 in 500,000!

FINDING SKILLED MONEY MANAGERS

It is easy to determine that Magellan's performance during the Lynch
years was due to his skill in picking stocks. But for more mortal portfolio managers, it is extremely difficult to determine with any degree of
confidence whether the superior returns of money managers are due to
skill or luck. Table 20-2 computes the probability that managers with
better-than-average stock-picking ability will outperform the market.[6]

The results are surprising. Even if money managers choose stocks
that have an expected return of 1 percent per year better than the market, there is only a 61.9 percent probability that they will exceed the average market return after 10 years and only a 70.1 percent probability

---

[5] The standard deviation of the Magellan Fund over Lynch's period was 21.38 percent, compared to
13.88 percent for the Wilshire 5000, while its correlation coefficient with the Wilshire was 0.86.

[6] Money managers are assumed to expose their clients to the same risk as would the market, and the
money managers have a correlation coefficient of 0.88 with market returns, which has been typical
of equity mutual funds since 1971.

TABLE   20-2

Probability of Outperforming the Wilshire 5000, Based on Returns, Risk, and Correlations from 1972 through December 2006

Expected Excess Return	Holding Period (years)						
	1	2	3	5	10	20	30
1%	53.8%	55.4%	56.6%	58.5%	61.9%	66.6%	70.1%
2%	57.6%	60.7%	63.0%	66.6%	72.8%	80.4%	85.3%
3%	61.3%	65.7%	69.0%	73.9%	81.7%	90.0%	94.1%
4%	64.8%	70.4%	74.5%	80.2%	88.5%	95.5%	98.1%
5%	68.2%	74.8%	79.3%	85.5%	93.2%	98.3%	99.5%

that they will exceed the average market return after 30 years. If managers pick stocks that will outperform the market by 2 percent per year, there is still only a 72.8 percent chance that they will outperform the market after 10 years. This means there is a one-in-four chance that they will still fall short of the average market performance. The length of time needed to be reasonably certain that superior managers will outperform the market will most certainly outlive their trial period for determining their real worth.

Detecting a bad manager is an equally difficult task. In fact, a money manager would have to underperform the market by 4 percent a year for almost 15 years before you could be statistically certain (defined to mean being less than 1 chance in 20 of being wrong) that the manager is actually poor and not just having bad luck. By that time, your assets would have fallen to half of what you would have had by indexing to the market.

Even extreme cases are hard to identify. Surely you would think that a manager who picks stocks that are expected to outperform the market by an average of 5 percent per year, a feat achieved by no surviving mutual fund since 1970, would quickly stand out. But that is not necessarily so. After one year there is only a 7-in-10 chance that such a manager will outperform the market. And the probability rises to only 74.8 percent that the manager will outperform the market after two years.

Assume you gave a young, undiscovered Peter Lynch—someone who over the long run will outperform the market with a 5 percent per

year edge—an ultimatum: that he will be fired if he does not at least match the market after two years. Table 20-2 shows that the probability he will beat the market over two years is only 74.8 percent. This means there is almost a one-in-four chance that he will still underperform the market and you will fire Lynch, judging him incapable of picking winning stocks!

Persistence of Superior Returns

Do some money managers have "hot hands," meaning that if they outperformed the averages in the past, they are likely to do it again in the future? The conclusions of numerous studies are not clear-cut. There is some evidence that funds that outperform in one year are more likely to outperform the next.[7] This short-run persistence is probably due to the fact that managers follow a particular "style" of investing and styles often stay in favor over several years.

But over longer periods, the ability of fund managers to continue to outperform the market finds less support. Elton, Gruber, and Blake claim that outperformance persists over three-year periods,[8] but Burton Malkiel, Jack Bogle, and others disagree.[9,10] In any case, performance can change suddenly and unpredictably. Perhaps Magellan's underperformance after Peter Lynch left the fund did not surprise some investors. But Bill Miller's hot hand with Legg Mason's Value Trust, which recorded a record 15 consecutive years of beating the S&P 500 Index, suddenly and unexpectedly turned cold in 2006 and 2007.

REASONS FOR UNDERPERFORMANCE OF MANAGED MONEY

The generally poor performance of funds relative to the market is not due to the fact that managers of these funds pick losing stocks. Their performance lags the benchmarks largely because funds impose fees and trading costs that are often as high as 2 percent or more per year. First, in seeking superior returns, a manager buys and sells stocks, which involves brokerage commissions and paying the bid-ask spread, or the difference be-

---

[7] Darryll Hendricks, Jayendu Patel, and Richard Zeckhauser, "Hot Hands in Mutual Funds: Short-Run Persistence of Relative Performance, 1974–1988," *Journal of Finance*, vol. 48, no. 1 (March 1993), pp. 93–130.

[8] Edwin J. Elton, Martin J. Gruber, and Christopher R. Blake, "The Persistence of Risk-Adjusted Mutual Fund Performance," *Journal of Business*, vol. 69, no. 2 (April 1996), pp. 133–157.

[9] Burton G. Malkiel, *A Random Walk Down Wall Street*, 8th ed., New York: Norton, 2003, pp. 372–274.

[10] John C. Bogle, *The Little Book of Common Sense Investing*, Hoboken, N.J.: Wiley, 2007, Chap. 9.

tween the buying and the selling price of shares. Second, investors pay management fees (and possibly sales, or "load," fees) to the organizations and individuals that sell these funds. Finally, managers are often competing with other managers with equal or superior skills at choosing stocks. As noted earlier, it is a mathematical impossibility for everyone to do better than the market—for every dollar that outperforms the average, some other investor's dollar must underperform the average.

A LITTLE LEARNING IS A DANGEROUS THING

It is interesting that an investor who has some knowledge of the principles of equity valuations often performs worse than someone with no knowledge who decides to index his portfolio. For example, take the novice—an investor who is just learning about stock valuation. This is the investor to whom most of the books entitled *How to Beat the Market* are sold. A novice might note that the stock has just reported very good earnings but its price is not rising as much as he believes is justified by this good news and so he buys the stock.

Yet informed investors know that special circumstances caused the earnings to increase and that these circumstances will not likely be repeated in the future. Informed investors are therefore more than happy to sell the stock to novices, realizing that the rise in the price of the stock is not justified. Informed investors make a return on their special knowledge. They make their return from novices who believe they have found a bargain. Uninformed indexed investors, who do not even know what the earnings of the company are, often do better than the investor who is just beginning to learn about equities.

The saying "a little learning is a dangerous thing" proves itself to be quite apt in financial markets. Many seeming anomalies or discrepancies in the prices of stocks (or most other financial assets, for that matter) are due to the trading of informed investors with special information that is not easily processed by others. When a stock looks too cheap or too dear, the easy explanation—that emotional or ignorant traders have incorrectly priced the stock—is usually wrong. Most often there is a good reason why stocks are priced as they are. This is why beginners who buy individual stocks on the basis of their own research often do quite badly.

PROFITING FROM INFORMED TRADING

As novices become more informed, they will no doubt find some stocks that are genuinely undervalued or overvalued. Trading these stocks will

begin to offset their transactions costs and their poorly informed, losing trades. At some point, a trader might become well enough informed to overcome the transactions costs and match, or perhaps exceed, the market return. The key word here is *might* because the number of investors who have consistently been able to outperform the market is small indeed. And for individuals who do not devote much time to analyzing stocks, the possibility of consistently outperforming the averages is remote.

Yet the apparent simplicity of picking winners and avoiding losers lures many investors into active trading. We learned in Chapter 19 that there is an inherent tendency of individuals to view themselves and their performance as above average. The investment game draws some of the best minds in the world. Many investors are wrongly convinced that they are smarter than the next guy who is playing the same investing game. But even being just as smart as the next investor is not good enough. For being average at the game of finding market winners will result in underperforming the market as transactions costs diminish returns.

In 1975, Charles D. Ellis, a managing partner at Greenwood Associates, wrote an influential article called "The Loser's Game." In it he showed that, with transactions costs taken into account, average money managers must outperform the market by margins that are not possible given that they themselves are the major market players. Ellis concludes: "Contrary to their oft articulated goal of outperforming the market averages, investment managers are not beating the market; the market is beating them."[11]

HOW COSTS AFFECT RETURNS

Trading and managerial costs of 2 or 3 percent a year might seem small compared to the year-to-year volatility of the market and to investors who are gunning for 20 or 30 percent annual returns. But such costs are extremely detrimental to long-term wealth accumulation. Investing $1,000 at a compound return of 11 percent per year, the average nominal return on stocks since World War II, will accumulate $23,000 over 30 years. A 1 percent annual fee will reduce the final accumulation by almost a third. With a 3 percent annual fee, the accumulation amounts to just over $10,000, less than half the market return. Every extra percentage point of annual costs requires investors aged 25 to retire two years later than they would have in the absence of such costs.

---

[11] Charles D. Ellis, "The Loser's Game," *Financial Analysts Journal*, July/August 1975, p. 19.

THE INCREASED POPULARITY OF PASSIVE INVESTING

Many investors have realized that the poor performance of actively managed funds relative to benchmark indexes strongly implies that they would do very well to just *equal* the market return of one of the broad-based indexes. Thus, the 1990s witnessed an enormous increase in *passive investing*, the placement of funds whose sole purpose was to match the performance of an index.

The oldest and most popular of the index funds is the Vanguard 500 Index Fund.[12] The fund, started by visionary John Bogle, raised only $11.4 million when it debuted in 1976, and few thought the concept would survive. But slowly and surely indexing gathered momentum, and the fund's assets reached $17 billion at the end of 1995.

In the latter stages of the 1990s bull market, the popularity of indexing soared. By March 2000, when the S&P 500 Index reached its all-time high, the fund claimed the title of the world's largest equity fund with assets over $100 billion. Indexing became so popular that in the first six months of 1999 nearly 70 percent of the money that was invested went into index funds.[13] By 2007, all Vanguard 500 Index funds had attracted over $200 billion in assets, but the largest single equity mutual fund is the American Growth Fund with assets of $185 billion.[14]

One of the attractions of index funds is their extremely low cost. The total annual cost in the Vanguard 500 Index Fund is only 0.18 percent of market value (and as low as 2 basis points for large institutional investors). Because of proprietary trading techniques and interest income from loaning securities, Vanguard S&P 500 Index funds for individual investors have fallen only 9 basis points behind the index over the last 10 years, and its institutional index funds have actually outperformed the index.[15]

THE PITFALLS OF CAPITALIZATION-WEIGHTED INDEXING

Despite their past success, the popularity of indexing, especially those funds linked to the S&P 500 Index, may cause problems for index

---

[12] Five years before the Vanguard 500 Index Fund, Wells Fargo created an equally weighted index fund called "Samsonite," but its assets remained relatively small.

[13] Heather Bell, "Vanguard 500 Turns 25, Legacy in Passive Investing," *Journal of Index Issues*, Fourth Quarter 2001, pp. 8–10.

[14] Vanguard's number includes assets of its 500 Index Fund open to both individuals and institutions.

[15] The Vanguard Institutional Index Fund Plus shares, with a minimum investment of $200 million, have outperformed the S&P 500 Index by 7 basis points in the 10 years following the fund's inception on July 7, 1997.

investors in the future. The reason is simple. If a firm's mere entry into
the S&P 500 causes the price of its stock to rise, index investors will ultimately hold overpriced stocks that will depress future returns.

An extreme example of overpricing occurred when Yahoo!, the
well-known firm, was added to the S&P 500 Index in December 1999.
Yahoo!'s price during this period is graphically depicted in Figure 20-3.
Standard & Poor's announced after the close of trading on November 30
that Yahoo! would be added to the index on December 8. The next morning, Yahoo! opened up almost $9 per share at $115 and continued upward to close at $174 a share on December 7, when index funds had to
buy the shares in order to match the index. In just 5 trading days between the announcement of Yahoo!'s inclusion in the index until it formally became a member, the stock surged 64 percent. Volume during
those 5 days averaged 37 million shares, more than three times the average on the previous 30 days. On December 7, when index funds had to

FIGURE   20–3

Price of Yahoo! around Its Admission to the S&P 500

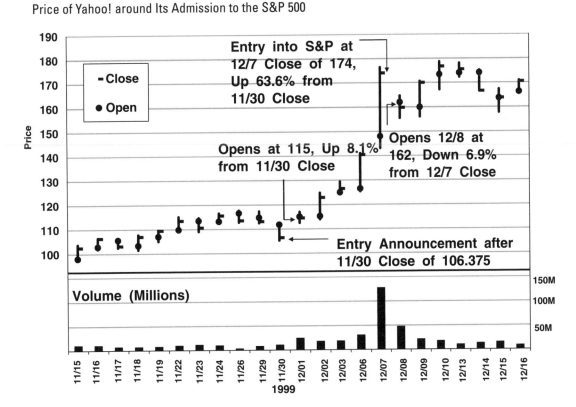

own the stock, volume hit 132 million shares, representing $22 billion of Yahoo! stock traded.

This story is repeated with virtually every stock added to the index, although the average size of the gain is considerably less than Yahoo!'s. Standard & Poor's published a study in September 2000 that had determined how adding a stock to an S&P index influenced the price. This study noted that from the announcement date to the effective date of admission in the S&P 500 Index, shares rose by an average of 8.49 percent.[16] During the next 10 days following their entrance, these stocks fell by an average of 3.23 percent, or about one-third of the preentry gain. Yet one year after the announcement, these postentry losses were wiped out, and the average gain of new entrants was 8.98 percent. All these percentages were corrected for movements in the overall market. A more recent study has shown that although the preentry gain has fallen in recent years, the price of stocks admitted to the S&P 500 still has jumped over 4 percent in response to the announcement.[17]

FUNDAMENTALLY WEIGHTED VERSUS CAPITALIZATION-WEIGHTED INDEXATION

Despite the overpricing of new entrants into the S&P 500 Index, virtually all indexes that have a significant investment following, such as those created by Standard & Poor's, the Russell Investment Group, or Wilshire Associates, are *capitalization weighted*. That means that each firm in the index is weighted by the *market value*, or the current price times the number of shares outstanding. More recently, most of these indexes adjust the quantity of shares by subtracting *insider holdings*, which include large positions held by insiders and governments from total shares outstanding. Government holdings can be especially large in the emerging economies. The number of shares after this adjustment is called *float-adjusted shares*, where "float" refers to the number of shares that are readily available to buy.[18]

Capitalization-weighted indexes have some very good properties. First, as noted earlier in the chapter, these indexes represent the *average*

---

[16] Roger J. Bos, *Event Study: Quantifying the Effect of Being Added to an S&P Index*, New York: McGraw-Hill, Standard & Poor's, September 2000.

[17] See David Blitzer and Srikant Dash, "Index Effect Revisited," *Standard & Poor's*, September 20, 2004.

[18] Practically there is no bright line between those shares "readily available" and those that are not. Holdings by index funds may actually be less available than those of close family members.

dollar-weighted performance of all investors, so that for anyone who does better than the index, someone else must do worse. Second, these portfolios, under certain assumptions, give investors the "best" trade-off between risk and return. This means that for any given risk level, these capitalization-weighted portfolios give the highest returns, and for any given return, these portfolios give the lowest risk. This property is called *mean-variance efficiency*.

But the assumptions under which this desirable property prevails are very stringent. Capitalization-weighted portfolios are optimal only if the market is *efficient* in the sense that the price of each stock is an unbiased estimate of the true underlying value of the enterprise. This does not mean that the price of each stock is always right; but it does mean that there is no other easily obtainable information that allows investors to make a better estimate of its true value. Under efficient markets, if a stock goes from $20 to $25 a share, the best estimate of the change in the underlying value of the enterprise is also 25 percent. There are *no* factors unrelated to fundamental value that could have changed the stock price.

But, as we learned in Chapter 9, there are many reasons why stock prices change that do not reflect changes in the underlying value of the firm. Transactions made for liquidity, fiduciary, or tax reasons can impact stock prices, as well as speculators acting on unfounded or exaggerated information. When stock price movements can be caused by factors unrelated to fundamental changes in firm value, market prices are "noisy" and are no longer unbiased estimates of true value. I call this way of looking at the market as the "noisy market hypothesis," and I find it an attractive alternative to the efficient market hypothesis that has dominated the finance profession over the last 40 years.

If the noisy market hypothesis is a better representation of how markets work, the capitalization-weighted indexes are no longer the best portfolios for investors. A better index is a *fundamentally weighted* index, in which each stock is weighted by some measure of a firm's fundamental financial data, such as dividends, earnings, cash flows, and book value, instead of the market capitalization of its stock.[19]

Fundamentally weighted indexes work in the following manner. Assume earnings are chosen as the measure of firm value. If E represents the total dollar earnings of the stocks chosen for the index, and E_j is the earnings from a particular firm j, then the weight given to firm j in the index is E_j/E, its percentage share of total earnings.

---

[19] As a matter of full disclosure, I am the senior investment strategy advisor at WisdomTree Investment, Inc., a company that issues fundamentally weighted ETFs.

For example, the total earnings of all stocks in the S&P 500 Index in 2006 were about $735 billion. Google's earnings came to about $3 billion, so in an earnings-weighted fundamental index, Google would have a weight of 0.41 percent. However, because Google has about twice the P-E ratio of the average firm in the S&P 500 Index, its weight in the market capitalization-weighted S&P 500 is 0.85 percent, about twice as high. Since Google does not yet pay any dividends, its weight in a dividend-weighted fundamental index would be zero.

In a capitalization-weighted index, stocks are never sold no matter what price they reach. This is because if markets are efficient, the price represents the fundamental value of the firm and no purchase or sale is warranted.

However, in a fundamentally weighted index, if a stock price rises but the fundamental, such as earnings, does not, then shares are sold until the value of the stock in the index is brought down to the original levels. The opposite happens when a stock falls for reasons not related to fundamentals—in this case shares are purchased at the lower price to bring the stock's value back to the original levels. Making these sales or purchases is called *rebalancing* the fundamentally weighted portfolio, and it usually takes place once per year.

One of the advantages of fundamentally weighted portfolios is that they avoid "bubbles," those meteoric increases in the prices of stocks that are not accompanied by increases in dividends, earnings, or other objective metrics of firm values. This was certainly the case in 1999 and early 2000 when the technology and Internet stocks jumped to extraordinary valuations based on the hope that their profits would eventually justify their price. Any fundamentally weighted portfolio would have sold these stocks as their prices rose, while capitalization-weighted indexes continued to hold them because the efficient market hypothesis assumes that all price increases are justified.

Note that fundamental indexation does not identify which stocks are over- or undervalued. It is a "passive" index, and the purchases and sales of individual stocks are made according to a predetermined formula. Certainly some overpriced stocks will be bought and some underpriced stocks sold. But it can be shown that if prices are determined by the noisy market hypothesis, then, on average, a portfolio that buys stocks that go down more than fundamentals and sells stocks that go up more than fundamentals will boost returns over a capitalization-weighted index and reduce risk.[20]

---

[20] Robert D. Arnott, Jason C. Hsu, and Philip Moore, "Fundamental Indexation," *Financial Analyst Journal* vol. 61, no. 2 (March/April 2005). Also Social Science Research Network (SSRN).

THE HISTORY OF FUNDAMENTALLY WEIGHTED INDEXATION

The motivation for fundamentally weighted indexation began in the international markets. In the 1980s, when Japan's stock market was in a bubble, many investors with internationally diversified portfolios were seeking a consistent way to reduce the weight of Japanese stocks. At that time Morgan Stanley Capital International (MSCI) formulated an international index that weighted each country by GDP rather than market capitalization and fortunately reduced the allocation to Japanese stocks.[21]

In 1987 Robert Jones of Goldman Sachs's quantitative asset management group developed and managed a U.S. stock index in which the weights of each firm in the index were corporate profits. Jones referred to his strategy as "economic investing" because the proportion of each firm in the index was related to its economic importance rather its market capitalization.[22] Later David Morris, founder and CEO of Global Wealth Allocation, devised a strategy that combined several fundamental factors into one "wealth" variable.[23]

In 2003, Paul Wood and Richard Evans published research on a fundamentally based approach that evaluated a profit-weighted index of the 100 largest companies.[24] In early 2005, Robert D. Arnott of Research Affiliates, along with Jason Hsu and Philip Moore, published a paper in the *Financial Analyst Journal* entitled "Fundamental Indexation" that exposed the flaws of capitalization-weighted indexes and laid the case for fundamentally based strategies.[25] In December 2005, the first fundamentally weighted ETF was launched by Powershares to track an index constructed by Research Affiliates based on sales, cash flows, book values, and dividends.[26] Six months later, WisdomTree Investments launched 20 ETFs based on dividends and followed up in 2007 with six more based on earnings.[27]

---

[21] Henry Fernandez, "Straight Talk," *Journal of Indexes*, July/August 2007.

[22] Robert Jones, "Earnings Basis for Weighting Stock Portfolios," *Pensions and Investments*, August 6, 1990.

[23] To see a complete set of the FTSE/GWA Index rules, go to www.ftse.com/Indices/FTSE_GWA_Index_Series/Downloads/FTSE_GWA_Index_Rules.pdf.

[24] Paul C. Wood and Richard E. Evans, "Fundamental Profit-Based Equity Indexation," *Journal of Indexes*, Second Quarter 2003.

[25] Arnott, Hsu, and Moore, "Fundamental Indexation."

[26] For a full description of the FTSE/RAFI Index methodology, visit www.ftse.com/Indices/FTSE_RAFI_Index_Series/2006Downloads/FTSE_RAFI_Indexrules.pdf.

[27] As a matter of full disclosure, I am the senior investment strategy advisor at WisdomTree Investment, Inc., a company that issues fundamentally weighted ETFs.

The historical evidence to support fundamentally weighted index-ation is impressive. From 1964 through 2005, the compound annual re-turn on a dividend-weighted index based on virtually all U.S. stocks was 11.88 percent per year, 123 basis points above a like capitalization-weighted portfolio based on the same stocks while the volatility and beta of the dividend-weighted portfolio was less than the capitalization-weighted portfolio. This return outperformance with lower volatility was reported across size sectors and internationally. Specifically, from 1996 through 2005, a dividend-weighted MSCI EAFE Index outper-formed an EAFE Index by nearly 5½ percentage points per year.[28]

The long-term outperformance of fundamentally weighted indexes principally relies on their emphasis of value-based strategies. Stocks with higher-than-average dividend yields or lower-than-average P-E ratios receive higher weights in fundamentally weighted indexes than capi-talization-weighted indexes. But fundamentally weighted indexes are better diversified than portfolios of only value stocks, and historically they have had better risk-returns trade-offs. In any case, fundamen-tally weighted indexes have very attractive characteristics that chal-lenge the supremacy of capitalization-weighted indexes for long-term investors.

CONCLUSION

The past performance of actively managed equity funds is not encour-aging. The fees that most funds charge do not provide investors with su-perior returns and can be a significant drag on wealth accumulation. Furthermore, a good money manager is extremely difficult to identify, for luck plays some role in all successful investment outcomes.

When costs are taken into account, most actively managed funds significantly lag the benchmark indexes. Index funds, be they capitaliza-tion weighted or fundamentally weighted, are an extremely attractive way to accumulate stocks for long-term investors.

But the past success of these capitalization-weighted indexes does not mean that they will always remain the best choice for investors. The enormous popularity of index funds, particularly those tied to the S&P 500 Index, cause prices of newly named stocks in the index to jump in price, a phenomenon that will likely reduce future returns.

The development of fundamentally indexed portfolios may offer an answer to some of the deficiencies of capitalization-weighted indexes.

---

[28] More data can be found on the Web site at www.wisdomtree.com.

This will be especially true if stock prices behave more like the noisy market hypothesis and less like the efficient market hypothesis. If some investors chronically chase the wrong type of stocks, it may indeed be possible to "beat the market."

CHAPTER 21

STRUCTURING A PORTFOLIO FOR LONG-TERM GROWTH

[The] long run is a misleading guide to current affairs. In the long run we are all dead. Economists set themselves too easy, too useless a task if in tempestuous seasons they can only tell us when the storm is long past, the ocean will be flat.

JOHN MAYNARD KEYNES, 1924[1]

My favorite holding period is forever.

WARREN BUFFETT, 1994[2]

No one can argue with Keynes's statement that in the long run we are all dead. But a vision of the long run must serve as a guide for action today. Those who keep their focus and perspective during trying times are far more likely to emerge as successful investors. Knowing that the sea will be flat after the storm passes is not useless, as Keynes asserted, but enormously comforting.

[1] John Maynard Keynes, *A Tract on Monetary Reform*, London: Macmillan, 1924, p. 80.
[2] Linda Grant, "Striking Out at Wall Street," *U.S. News & World Report*, June 20, 1994, p. 58.

PRACTICAL ASPECTS OF INVESTING

To be a successful long-term investor is easy in principle but difficult in practice. It is easy in principle because buying and holding a diversified portfolio of stocks, forgoing any forecasting ability, is available to all investors, no matter what their intelligence, judgment, or financial status. Yet it is difficult in practice because we are all vulnerable to emotional forces that can lead us astray. Tales of those who have quickly achieved great wealth in the market tempt us to play a game very different from that of the long-term investor.

Selective memory also pushes us in the wrong direction. Those who follow the market closely often exclaim: "I knew that stock (or the market) was going up! If I had only acted on my judgment, I would have made a mint!" But hindsight plays tricks on our minds. We forget the doubts we had when we made the decision not to buy. Hindsight can distort our past experiences and affect our judgment, encouraging us to play hunches and try to outsmart other investors, who in turn are playing the same game.

For most investors, going down this path leads to disastrous results. We take far too many risks, our transactions costs are high, and we often find ourselves giving into the emotions of the moment—pessimism when the market is down and optimism when the market is high. This leads to frustration as our misguided actions result in substantially lower returns than we could have achieved by just staying in the market.

GUIDES TO SUCCESSFUL INVESTING

Achieving good returns in stocks requires keeping a long-term focus and a disciplined investment strategy. The principles enumerated below are taken from the research described in this book and enable both new and seasoned investors to better achieve their investing goals.

1. Keep your expectations in line with history. Historically stocks have returned 6.8 percent after inflation over the last two centuries and have sold at an average P-E ratio of about 15.

A 6.8 percent annual real return, which includes reinvested dividends, will double the *purchasing power* of your stock portfolio on average every decade. If inflation stays within the 2 to 3 percent range, nominal stock returns will range between 9 and 10 percent per year, which doubles the money value of your stock portfolio every seven to eight years.

Despite this excellent long-run record, stock returns are not independent of the level of earnings. In Chapter 7 we learned that the long-term real return on the stock market is approximated by the earnings yield, which is the inverse of the price-to-earnings (or P-E) ratio. A 6.8 percent return is consistent with a market that sells at about 15 times estimated earnings.

But there is no reason why a 15 P-E ratio will always be the "right" ratio for stock prices. Chapter 8 maintains that there are good economic reasons why the stock market may rise to a higher P-E ratio in the future. The decrease in transactions costs, the ability to diversify internationally, and the greater stability of the macroeconomy may cause investors to bid the price of stocks higher and may lead to a higher justified level of prices, perhaps at 20 times earnings. If stocks do reach and stay at that level, forward-looking real returns will decline to the lower earnings yield of 5 percent per year after inflation, a return that is still considerably above the yields available on bonds.

2. Stock returns are much more stable in the long run than in the short run. Over time stocks, in contrast to bonds, compensate investors for higher inflation. Therefore, as an investor's horizon becomes longer, a larger fraction of one's assets should be in equities.

The percentage of your portfolio that you should hold in equities depends on individual circumstances. But based on historical data, an investor with a long-term horizon should keep an overwhelming portion of his or her financial assets in equities. Chapter 2 showed that over holding periods of 20 years or longer, stocks have both a higher return and lower risk than standard corporate or government bonds.

The only long-term risk-free assets are Treasury inflation-protected securities, or TIPS. In recent years the real yield on these bonds has ranged between 2 and 3 percent, which is about 4 percentage points a year below the historical returns on stocks. The difference between the returns on stocks and the returns on bonds is called the equity premium, and historically it has favored stocks in all countries where data are available.

3. Invest the largest percentage of your stock portfolio in low-cost stock index funds that span a global portfolio.

Chapter 20 showed that the broad-based indexes, such as the Wilshire 5000 and the S&P 500 Index, have outperformed nearly two out of three mutual funds since 1971. By matching the market year after year, an indexed investor is likely to be near the top of the pack when the long-term returns are tallied.

There are many ways in which to match the returns on major stock indexes. The last decade has witnessed the explosive growth of both exchange-traded funds (ETFs) and index mutual funds. Both investment vehicles closely track their respective indexes, have low turnover, and are very tax efficient. Investors in capitalization-weighted index funds should insist on a total annual expense ratio under 0.20 percent.

4. Invest at least one-third of your equity portfolio in international stocks, currently defined as those not headquartered in the United States. Stocks in high-growth countries often become overpriced and yield poor returns for investors.

Today the United States has less than one-half of the world's equity capital, and that fraction is declining rapidly. Owning foreign stocks is a must in today's global economy. In the future, the geographic location of the firm's headquarters will lose its importance as an investment factor. What, where, and to whom a firm sells its products will dominate a new classification system.

As Chapter 10 explains, traditional risk-return analysis on historical data indicates that more than one-third of dollar-based portfolios should be invested in stocks headquartered outside the United States. Despite the increase in the short-term correlation between country returns, the case for international investing is persuasive. In all countries studied, the return on stocks has handily beaten bonds and fixed-income assets over the last century. Do not overweight high-growth countries, as the data presented in Chapter 9 show that investors often overpay for growth.

5. Historically, value stocks—those with lower P-E ratios and higher dividend yields—have superior returns and lower risk than growth stocks. Tilt your portfolio toward value by buying passive indexed portfolios of value stocks or, more recently, fundamentally weighted index funds.

Chapter 9 demonstrated that stocks with low P-E ratios and high dividend yields have outperformed the market over the past 50 years and have done so with lower risk. One reason for this outperformance is that prices of stocks are often influenced by factors not related to their true value, such as liquidity and tax-motivated transactions, rumor-based speculation, and buying and selling by momentum traders. In these circumstances, stocks priced low relative to their fundamentals will likely offer investors a better risk and return profile.

Investors can take advantage of temporary mispricings by buying low-cost passively managed portfolios of value stocks or newly developed *fundamentally weighted indexes* that weight each stock by its share of

dividends or earnings rather than by its market value. Fundamentally weighted indexes have had higher returns and lower risks historically than capitalization-weighted indexes.

6. Finally, establish firm rules to keep your portfolio on track, especially if you find yourself giving in to the emotion of the moment. If you are particularly anxious about the market, sit down and reread the first two chapters of this book.

Swings in investor emotion almost always send stock prices beyond their fundamental values. The temptations to buy when everyone is bullish and sell when everyone is bearish are hard to resist. Since it is so difficult to stand apart from this market sentiment, most investors who trade frequently have poor returns. Chapter 19 shows how behavioral finance helps investors understand and avoid common psychological pitfalls that cause poor market performance. Chapters 1 and 2 keep investors focused on the big picture about risk and return.

IMPLEMENTING THE PLAN AND THE ROLE OF AN INVESTMENT ADVISOR

I wrote *Stocks for the Long Run* to spell out what returns could be expected on stocks and bonds and to analyze the major factors influencing those returns. Many investors will consider this book a "do-it-yourself guide" to choosing stocks and structuring a portfolio. But knowing the right investments is not the same as implementing the right investment strategy. As Peter Bernstein so aptly indicates in his foreword to this edition, there are many pitfalls on the path to successful investing that prevent investors from achieving their intended goals.

The first pitfall is trading frequently in an attempt to "beat the market." Many investors are not satisfied earning a 10 percent annual return on stocks when they know there are always stocks that will double or triple in price over the next 12 months. Finding such gems is extremely gratifying, and many dream of buying the next corporate giant in its infancy. But the evidence is overwhelming that such investors suffer poor returns as transactions costs and bad timing sink returns.

Investors who have been burned by picking individual stocks often turn to mutual funds in their search for higher returns. But choosing a mutual fund poses similar obstacles. "Hot managers" with superior past performance replace "hot stocks" as the new strategy to beat the market. As a result, many investors end up playing the same game as they had with individual stocks and also suffer below-average returns.

Those who finally abandon trying to pick the best funds are tempted to pursue an even more difficult strategy. They attempt to beat the market by timing market cycles. Surprisingly, it is often the best-informed investors who fall into this trap. With the abundance of financial news, information, and commentary at our beck and call, it is extraordinarily difficult to stay aloof from market opinion. As a result, one's impulse is to capitulate to fear when the market is plunging or to greed when stocks are soaring.

Many try to resist this impulse. The intellect may say "Stay the course!" but this is not easy to do when one hears so many others—including well-respected "experts"—advising investors to beat a hasty retreat. It is easier to follow what everyone else is doing rather than act independently. And as John Maynard Keynes aptly stated in *The General Theory*, "Worldly wisdom teaches that it is better for reputation to fail conventionally than to succeed unconventionally."[3] Standing against the crowd is hard because failing by following the advice of other "experts" is far more acceptable than failing by rejecting the investment consensus.

What does all this mean to the reader of this book? Proper investment strategy is as much of a psychological as an intellectual challenge. As with other challenges in life, it is often best to seek professional help to structure and maintain a well-diversified portfolio. If you should decide to seek help, be sure to select a professional investment advisor who agrees with the basic principles of diversification and long-term investing that I have espoused in these chapters. It is within the grasp of all to avoid investing pitfalls and reap the generous rewards that are available in equities.

CONCLUDING COMMENT

The stock market is exciting. Its daily movements dominate the financial press and mark the flows of billions of dollars of investment capital.

But stock markets are far more than the quintessential symbol of capitalism or repositories of wealth. Stock markets are now found in virtually every country in the world, be it communist or capitalist. They are the driving forces behind the allocation of the world's capital and the fundamental engines of economic growth. They are the key to enriching

---

[3] John Maynard Keynes, *The General Theory of Employment, Interest, and Money*, New York: Harcourt, Brace & World, 1965, First Harbinger Edition, p. 158. (The book was originally published in 1936 by Macmillan & Co.)

the lives of both workers and investors around the globe. The main thesis of this book, that stocks represent the best way to accumulate wealth in the long run, remains as true today as it was when I published the first edition of *Stocks for the Long Run* in 1994.

INDEX

Note: Page numbers followed by *i* refer to figures or tables; those followed by *n* refer to notes; those followed by *q* refer to quotations.

ABOUT THE AUTHOR

Jeremy J. Siegel is the Russell E. Palmer Professor of Finance at The Wharton School of the University of Pennsylvania, the academic director of the Securities Industry Institute, and a senior investment strategy advisor to WisdomTree Investments, which creates and markets exchange-traded funds.